OSPF Network Design Solutions

Thomas M. Thomas II

Macmillan Technical Publishing
201 West 103rd Street
Indianapolis, IN 46290 USA

OSPF Network Design Solutions

Thomas M. Thomas II

Copyright© 1998 Macmillan Technical Publishing

Cisco Press logo is a trademark of Cisco Systems, Inc.

Published by:
Macmillan Technical Publishing
201 West 103rd Street
Indianapolis, IN 46290 USA

Printed in the United States of America 2 3 4 5 6 7 8 9 0

Library of Congress Cataloging-in-Publication Number: 98-84225

ISBN: 1-57870-046-9

Warning and Disclaimer

Feedback Information

At Cisco Press, our goal is to create in-depth technical books of the highest quality and value. Each book is crafted with care and precision, undergoing rigorous development that involves the unique expertise of members from the professional technical community.

Readers' feedback is a natural continuation of this process. If you have any comments regarding how we could improve the quality of this book, or otherwise alter it to better suit your needs, you can contact us at cisco-press@mcp.com. Please make sure to include the book title and ISBN in your message.

We greatly appreciate your assistance.

Associate Publisher	Jim LeValley
Executive Editors	Julie Fairweather, John Kane
Cisco Systems Program Manager	H. Kim Lew
Managing Editor	Caroline Roop
Acquisitions Editors	Tracy Hughes, Brett Bartow
Development Editor	Christopher Cleveland
Project Editor	Tim Tate
Technical Editors	Matthew H. Birkner CCIE # 3719, Atif Kahn, Jim Thompson, Derek Yeung
Team Coordinator	Amy Lewis
Cover Designer	Karen Ruggles
Interior Layout and Design	Argosy
Cover Art	Provided by Cisco Systems
Indexer	Tim Wright

Trademark
Acknowledgments

All terms mentioned in this book that are known to be trademarks or service marks have been appropriately capitalized. Macmillan Technical Publishing or Cisco Systems, Inc. cannot attest to the accuracy of this information. Use of a term in this book should not be regarded as affecting the validity of any trademark or service mark.

Dedications

I want to dedicate this book to my family for their ever-faithful support and understanding during the many nights and weekends I spent writing. An extra special thank you goes to my wife, Rose, and daughter, Rebekah, who never voiced anything but encouragement and support. I certainly hope that the new tradition of girl's day out continues for them. To my new son, Daniel, who became a part of our family during this time and used his smile to brighten our lives. Without the support of my family I would never have been able to accomplish this book.

I want to say a few words of special meaning to my wife...

Always

    Forever

        Endlessly

            Until Eternity

Acknowledgments

I am very grateful to the group of talented people that were assembled to make this book a reality. Through their knowledge, dedication, and hard work, this book has become more than I ever thought possible.

The most important acknowledgement must go to my wife, Rose, who put up with me writing all night after working all day. Her unwavering support was the single greatest factor in my ability to complete the book you now hold in your hands. It is my hope she will no longer call herself a computer widow now that the book is finished.

Writing his book allowed me to assemble a team of technical professionals who have helped me make this book more than I thought possible. I had the privilege to be a part of an awesome team during this time. I had an excellent group of technical professionals who reviewed this text and in some cases contributed a great deal more. Foremost is Matthew H. Birkner, whose friendship and dedication helped more than I could ever express here. Jim Thompson for his support, constructive comments, and the time he spent with me regardless of the situation. Derek Yeung for always knowing that little bit extra. Atif Khan who came through when needed. Don Stoddard for his forward-looking contributions. Tom Kunath for his sense of dedication, experience, and the real world contributions he made to this book.

I have to recognize the extraordinary group of publishing professionals who helped guide me through the process. Kim Lew, the Cisco Press Program Manager, who saw something in me I never thought possible. Chris Cleveland, my developmental editor, whose hard work and instinctive corrections added value and polish. Brett Bartow, my acquisitions editor, who always had the time for my questions regardless of how many times I asked. Julie Fairweather, my executive editor, for knowing what my life was like during this time. Amy Lewis, for her generous and cheerful assistance, who helped me assemble a strong base of knowledge. John Kane for keeping me informed and laughing.

A portion of the proceeds from this book will be donated to the Hilltop Christian School Technology Program in Fuquay-Varina, North Carolina.

Contents

Foreword

Network routing protocols have emerged as key enabling technologies in a computing world now dominated by connectivity. From a very high-level perspective, these routing protocols can be split into interior gateway protocols (IGPs) and exterior gateway protocols (EGPs). In general, the routing techniques used by IGPs are based on either distance-vector or link-state algorithms.

The Open Shortest Path First (OSPF) routing protocol has evolved into the link-state protocol of choice for many IP networks. This has come about for a variety of converging reasons. Most importantly, OSPF has proved to be both reliable and scalable. In addition, its underlying protocol assumptions encourage a structured network design approach, while these same characteristics promote rapid route convergence during operation. The basic features and capabilities of OSPF are described together as a set of specifications under the Requests for Comment (RFCs) regulated by the OSPF Working Group of the Internet Engineering Task Force (IETF).

From OSPF's earliest days, Cisco has been closely involved with the evolution of related IETF standards. Throughout this process, Cisco's development engineering staff has worked carefully to ensure that the implementation of OSPF in Cisco routers is both robust and comprehensive. However, as with any complex network topology, uncontrolled growth without careful network design can lead to performance and convergence problems—even with OSPF. At its core, one of the key objectives of Tom Thomas' book, *OSPF Network Design Solutions,* is to help network engineers and architects avoid the pitfalls of unstructured network deployment.

This book aims to provide specific Cisco solutions for network engineers deploying OSPF in large-scale IP networks. In doing so, we hope that it contributes to your information toolkit in a substantive way and facilitates the creation of robust and reliable network infrastructures. While the emphasis here is on OSPF and Cisco's implementation, we also hope that the ideas presented will help anyone deploying large networks using link-state routing protocols—regardless of the specific underlying protocols or equipment.

Cisco's OSPF implementation was initially released in early 1992 with IOS software release 9.0 (1).

Since that time it has logged many operational years on large-scale production networks, incorporated countless improvements to add robustness, and added optimizations that allow Cisco's largest customers to succeed with globally dispersed networks. As always, Cisco continues to make enhancements based on lessons learned from customers and their implementations. This process of continuous improvement is at the very heart of Cisco's approach to supporting IP networks worldwide.

We at Cisco believe it is vitally important for information to be shared among networking professionals and we view this book as an important step in the process of disseminating practical hands-on knowledge—knowledge that is often locked up in the busy lives of networking gurus. Cisco will continue to support in its products many protocols for routing, transporting, protecting, and labeling networked data. As a mature, modern routing protocol, OSPF is an important member of that suite. We strongly support books like *OSPF Network Design Solutions* as being an important next step beyond basic product documentation for the people who actually plan and implement real IP networks.

Dave Rossetti

Vice President and General Manager

IP Internet Services Unit

Cisco Systems, Inc.

PART 1

Contemporary Intranets

The complexity of networks has been increasing steadily since the 1970s into the contemporary intranets we see in use today. In order to fully understand the information presented in this book, a firm foundation in network technologies must first be built.

Chapter 1, **"Foundations of Networking,"** provides an essential perspective on the historical foundations and issues facing networks and intranets.

Chapter 2, **"Network Routing Fundamentals,"** discusses the fundamentals of routing within a networked environment.

Chapter 3, **"Understanding & Selecting Network Protocols,"** discusses one of the most important subjects facing anyone involved in today's growing networks.

CHAPTER 1

Foundations of Networking

"Priorities: A hundred years from now it will not matter what my bank account was, the sort of car I drove . . . but the world may be a different because I was important in the life of a child."—Successories

The physical and logical structures of networks have become varied and diverse as the technologies they use have evolved. The "legacy networks" of years past have evolved into the complex architectures known as Enterprise Networks. In many cases, these intranets of today have also generated new networking challenges.

To understand the value of intranets and the challenges they create, it helps to remember how people traditionally have connected to corporate information. This chapter covers the following important topics and objectives:

- **Intranets—The Latest Stage in the Evolution of Networking.** What is an intranet? A brief history on network evolution and an overview of the issues facing today's corporate intranets.

- **Open Systems Interconnection (OSI) Reference Model.** An overview of the OSI reference model and description of the various layers to include how and where routers operate within the model.

- **Intranet Topologies.** Description, brief discussion, and examples of the most common Local Area Network (LAN) and Wide Area Network (WAN) topologies.

INTRANETS—THE LATEST STAGE IN THE EVOLUTION OF NETWORKING

One of the most important questions that must be answered is: "What is an intranet?" Although there are many definitions possible, for the purposes of this book, an intranet is an Internet Protocol (IP)-based network that can span various geographical regions or just connect several buildings in a campus environment. This is a somewhat simplistic definition, but you can ask 10 network engineers to define an intranet and get 10 different responses. The characteristics and their relationship to networking are shown in Table 1-1.

As demonstrated Table 1-1, the various networking archetypes have become very complex. How did they get way? The evolution of networking archetypes has generally moved towards shorter application development times, faster deployment of new technology, lower cost per user, greater scalability, and higher performance. As they have made this movement throughout the evolution of networking, vast improvements have been made. This evolution is discussed in the following sections.

Gordon Moore of Intel made an interesting observation in 1965, just six years after he invented the first planar transistor. His observation was that the "doubling of transistor density on a manufactured die every year" would occur. Now some 30 years later his statement has become known as "Moore's Law," and it has continued to hold true. According to Intel, "There are no theoretical or practical challenges that will prevent

Table 1-1   *Internet, intranet, and network characteristics.*

	Internet	Intranet	Network
Underlying Protocol	TCP/IP	TCP/IP	Multiple Proprietary Protocols
Capabilities of Network Management	Limited Management	Varied Management Capabilities	Closely Managed
Level of Security	Unsecured	Varied Levels of Security	Varied of Security
Network Routing	Dynamic	Dynamic	Static and Dynamic
Overall Network Architecture	Web-based	Similar to the Internet	Legacy

Moore's Law being true for another 20 years at least, this is another five generations of processors." Using Moore's Law to predict into the year 2012, Intel should have the capability to integrate one billion transistors on a production die that will be operating at 10GHz. This could result in a performance of 100,000 MIPS. This is the same increase over the Pentium II processor as the Pentium II processor was to the 386."

Mainframe/Host Network Model

The first "networks" can be traced back to the standard mainframe/host model, which was pioneered by IBM in the early 1960s. This centralized computing was the topology of choice during this era of networking. The protocol running in this environment was known as System Network Architecture (SNA). It is a time-sensitive broadcast intensive protocol that is based hierarchically. SNA required large, powerful mainframes to properly operate within its standards.

The mainframe/host type of topology provided mission-critical applications that stored data on the mainframe. Terminals, known as logical units or hosts, provided a common interface to the user for running the applications and accessing the data.

The terminals in this model were considered "dumb" in the sense that they had no capability to process data. Equipment known as the cluster controllers formatted the screens and collected data for the terminals. They were known as cluster controllers because each one had a "cluster" of terminals connected to it. These controllers were in turn connected to communication controllers that handled the input and output processing needed by the terminals. Then the communication controllers in turn were connected to the mainframe computer that housed the company's applications and processors. Figure 1-1 illustrates typical mainframe architecture.

On a logical level, the mainframe model has many drawbacks when compared to the networks and applications of today. Its application development was a slow and ponderous process and the cost of computing power was very high; however, the mainframe model did have some benefits as well:

- Mainframe components were networked together with a single protocol, typically SNA
- The largely text-based traffic consumed little bandwidth
- Tight security with a single point of control
- Hierarchical design had highly predictable traffic flows

Figure 1–1
*Mainframe-
centered
network with
remote
terminals.*

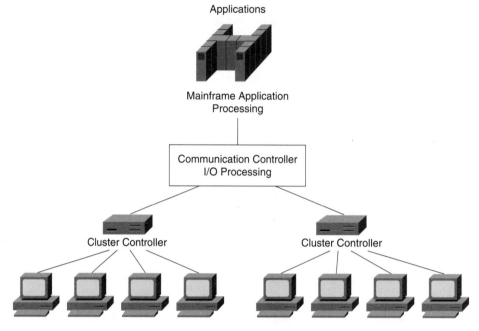

Figure 1–1 *Mainframe-centered network with remote terminals.*

Client/Server Model

During the 1980s, the computing world was rocked by the introduction of the personal computer (PC). This intelligent terminal or workstation drove an industry-wide move towards intelligent workstations. This move had wide ramifications that continue to be felt to this day.

The introduction of the PC propelled the evolution of the mainframe model toward LANs. There were already quite a few token-ring networks deployed in support of mainframes, but they did not yet have the large number of PCs attached to them as they have today. It was during this time that mainframes and client/servers melded together as the PC slowly replaced mainframe systems. The PC's capability to be both a terminal emulator and an intelligent workstation—client—blurred the lines between host-based systems and client servers, because applications and data were stored on a dedicated workstation that became known as a server. This melding also resulted in early routers known as gateways that provided the connectivity between various types of clusters and the evolving LANs back to the mainframes. Figure 1-2 shows a typical client/server-mainframe hybrid network.

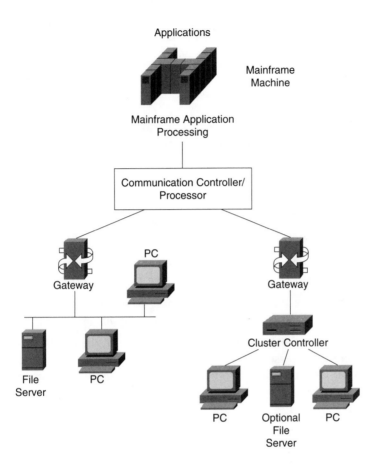

Applications

Mainframe
Machine

Mainframe Application
Processing

Communication Controller/
Processor

Gateway

PC

Gateway

File
Server

PC

Cluster Controller

PC

Optional
File
Server

PC

Figure 1–2
*Client/server-
mainframe
hybrid
network.*

The importance of digital-based WANs became more prevalent at this time. This was also assisted by the PC's capability to perform protocol-based calculations as required for different physical media types.

In the client/server model, computing power is less expensive and the application development cycles are shorter; however, this architecture results in multi-protocol traffic and unpredictable traffic flows. This is a drawback of the decentralized control of the client/server model with its dispersed architecture. Although the traffic can be uneven and bursty, it is still somewhat predictable due to the hierarchical structure that still exists, in which clients communicate primarily with the server.

As this model developed and evolved through the 1980s, it drove the development of technology in both the LAN and WAN arenas. This resulting evolution of networking models has resulted in the corporate intranets of today.

TYPICAL CORPORATE INTRANETS

The typical intranet model of today has toppled traditional hierarchies of previous network models. The rapid changes in networking during the 1990s are astounding and far-reaching, as indicated by the following factors:

- **Distributed processing** enables many different intelligent devices to work together so that they meet and, in many cases, exceed the computing power of mainframes.

- **Corporate legacy systems** are downsized as movement continues away from mainframe-based computing.

- **Increased demands for more bandwidth** have created many emerging technologies that have pushed networks to the limit.

- **Intelligent routing protocols and equipment** intelligently and dynamically build routing databases, reducing design and maintenance work.

- **Internetworking topologies** have evolved as routers and bridges are used to network more and more mini and personal computers.

- **Protocol interoperability** connecting different LAN and WAN architectures together has increased standards between protocols. Through the increasingly prevalent melding of the two network types, the applicable protocols become more and more intertwined.

- **The Telecommunications Act of 1996,** known as Public Law 104-104, provided opportunities for telecommunications suppliers to increase bandwidth and competition.

All of these factors have resulted in and raised many issues that must be considered by everyone involved in networking. Foremost is the issue of accelerated network growth. As sweeping changes have become standard, everyone must learn how to react and manage this growth.

Reacting to Accelerated Network Growth

In recent years, the growth of networks everywhere has accelerated as many organizations move into the international business arena and join the Internet. This expansion has continued to drive the development, refinement, and complexity of network equipment and software, consequently resulting in some unique issues and exciting advances.

Can you imagine modern business or life these days without computers, fax machines and services, e-mail, Internet commerce and access, automatic teller machines, remote banking, check cards, or video conferencing? Even more importantly, today's children will think that these tools are commonplace and that business cannot be done without them.

Nevertheless, many of these tools are used to track, process, and perform the day-to-day business of today's organizations in a variety of different ways. The need for the newest and best technology appears to be the solution to growing organizational requirements. As this newer technology becomes available, it must be implemented, immediately.

Perhaps the most frustrating issue in dealing with unrestrained network growth is the reactive management required as opposed to the more effective proactive style. This issue is further exasperated by the melding of many different technologies.

Managing Accelerated Network Growth

To properly manage the current and future needs of a rapidly growing network, you must have the necessary tools and techniques at your disposal.

Part IV, "Network Security & Future Expansion," discusses some of the emerging tools and technology in further detail. Some of the things you need to consider doing now in order to effectively manage your network's growth, include the following:

- **Reliability.** This can have a major impact on how expensive it is, in both time and money, to maintain your network. An unreliable network will consume vast amounts of technically skilled labor made up of people who must constantly configure and react to network problems. Chapter 10, "Securing Your OSPF Network," discusses the actual ways you go about increasing the reliability of your OSPF network.

- **Base Line Measurement.** This is an essential part of planning the expansion of and troubleshooting of your network. How can you accurately understand the impact of growth, changes, modifications, or possible future network changes? You can easily do so if you understand the utilization, error rates, and characteristics of your network from a point in time. Chapter 12, "Future Network Considerations," discusses some of the more useful tools and techniques used to address these types of issues.

- **Capacity Planning.** An integral part of determining when you should expand network capacity. Chapter 11, "The Continuing Evolution of OSPF," discusses the overhead OSPF demands of a network, enabling you to plan your network's needs accordingly.

- **Network Monitoring.** This is a fundamental toolset that should be used for managing the network's growth. Tracking and monitoring expansion and changes within the network is important to ensure that these changes are fulfilling their purpose. Of course, this also works in reverse; you can monitor your existing network to ensure legacy equipment is also performing. Chapter 9, "Managing Your OSPF Network," discusses managing your OSPF network in much greater detail.

Scaling Performance

Network growth can impose heavy new loads on your infrastructure. Financial data or inventory reports, for example, can be extremely popular when initially released, resulting in an increased network load. Within a week, network performance is back to "normal." It is during these surges that your planning is extremely important. Chapter 6, "Advanced OSPF Design Concepts," discusses methods to partition and load balance your network.

Extending Network Reach

Extending network reach seems like an issue that is never ending in intranets the world over. There are always new sites to add or another feature that needs to be implemented. Many networks have kept pace with the growth on their backbone but have sites located away from the backbone that must also be considered. Intranets require that users at one site have transparent access to resources located at any other site. In the yet to be discovered "perfect" network, local and remote connectivity and performance must be considered equally.

You can strive for equality in the network's performance, response time, and reliability, between local and remote users by following a few steps:

- Optimize your WAN bandwidth and its use throughout your network to keep bandwidth costs at a minimum. Chapter 5, "The Fundamentals of OSPF Routing & Design," covers the methods OSPF provides to assist you in optimizing network bandwidth.

- Properly secure the network in such a way that it does not exact performance penalties or place unneeded barriers. Chapter 10 covers the security features of OSPF in detail.

- Make your Enterprise network accessible throughout to provide yourself with a dynamic "end-to-end" infrastructure. Making the Enterprise network accessible provides you with several advantages, such as low bandwidth usage, scalability, and a widely supported underlying protocol. OSPF is an obvious choice for implementing an Enterprise network because OSPF is a supported protocol found in many Enterprise networks.

- An intranet can intensify the bandwidth crunch that rules most planning and strategy due to its distributed architecture and unpredictable traffic flows; however, effective allocation of bandwidth, security, and proper routing protocol implementation can provide the performance, security, and flexibility needed to extend intranet reach.

Controlling Your Intranet

It is essential that you keep control of your intranet. Without control, the dangers and issues can result in a loss of connectivity to a full network crash. This book covers some of the more common problems and issues relating to accelerated growth. The proposed solutions have been tested in network after network, and through the use of OSPF, you will be able to address the many different problems. First, you build the structure of a network.

To monitor and evaluate reliability, baseline measurements, capacity planning, and network monitoring ensure controlled network growth. This is much more desirable than allowing uncontrolled network growth to be the norm for your intranet.

UNDERSTANDING THE OSI REFERENCE MODEL

It is important for you to understand the basic concepts of the OSI reference model because it is the underpinning of every intranet and network. This section will introduce the reader to the OSI reference model's history, purpose, basic terminology, as well as concepts associated with the OSI reference model. A thorough discussion of the OSI reference model is outside the scope of this book. For complete and exhaustive coverage of the OSI reference model, the following important ISO standards and specifications for the OSI protocol are recommended:

- **Physical layer**
    - **CCITT X.21.** 15-pin physical connection specification
    - **CCITT X.21 BIS**-25 pin connection similar to EIA RS-232-C

- Data Link layer

  - ISO 4335/7809. High-level data link control specification (HDLC)
  - ISO 8802.2. Local area logical link control (LLC)
  - ISO 8802.3. (IEEE 802.3) Ethernet standard
  - ISO 8802.4. (IEEE 802.4) Token Bus standard
  - ISO 8802.5. (IEEE 802.5) Token Ring standard
  - ISO 802.3u. Fast Ethernet standard
  - ISO 802.3z. Gigabit Ethernet standard
  - ISO 802.10. VLAN standard

- Network layer

  - ISO 8473. Network layer protocol and addressing specification for connectionless network service
  - ISO 8208. Network layer protocol specification for connection-oriented service based on CCITT X.25
  - CCITT X.25. Specifications for connecting data terminal equipment to packet-switched networks
  - CCITT X.21. Specifications for accessing circuit-switched networks

- Transport layer

  - ISO 8072. OSI Transport layer service definitions
  - ISO 8073. OSI Transport layer protocol specifications

- Session layer

  - ISO 8326. OSI Session layer service definitions, including transport classes 0, 1, 2, 3, and 4
  - ISO 8327. OSI Session layer protocol specifications

- Presentation layer

  - ISO 8822/23/24. Presentation layer specification
  - ISO 8649/8650. Common application and service elements (CASE) specifications and protocols

- Application layer

  - X.400. OSI Application layer specification for electronic message handling (electronic mail)
  - FTAM. OSI Application layer specification for file transfer and access method
  - VTP. OSI Application layer specification for virtual terminal protocol, specifying common characteristics for terminals
  - JTM. Job transfer and manipulation standard

Some other good references include the ISO Web page (`http://www.iso.ch/cate/35.html`) and the Institute of Electrical and Electronics Engineers (IEEE) Web page (`http://www.ieee.com`)

NOTES —————————————————————————————————————

The Consultative Committee for International Telephone and Telegraph (CCITT) is responsible for wide-area aspects of national and international communications and publishing recommendations.

In addition, because the OSI reference model has become the standard upon which protocols and applications are based throughout the networking community, knowledge about its features and functionality will always be of use to you. The sections that follow will answer a few basic questions concerning the OSI reference model.

What Is the OSI Reference Model?

OSI stands for Open Systems Interconnection, where *"open systems"* refers to the specifications surrounding its structure as well as its non-proprietary public availability. Anyone can build the software and hardware needed to communicate within the OSI structure.

The work on OSI reference model was initiated in the late 1970s, and came to maturity in the late 1980s and early 1990s. The International Organization of Standardization (ISO) was the primary architect of the model in place today.

Why Was the OSI Reference Model Needed?

Before the development of the OSI reference model, the rapid growth of applications and hardware resulted in a multitude of vendor-specific models. In terms of future network growth and design, this rapid growth caused a great deal of concern among network engineers because they had to ensure the systems under their control could to interact with *every* standard. This concern encouraged the International Organization of Standardization (ISO) to initiate the development of the OSI reference model.

Characteristics of the OSI Layers

To provide the reader with some examples of how the layers are spanned by a routing protocol, please refer to Figure 1-3. You might also want to contact Network General, as their Protocol chart shows how almost every single protocol spans the seven layers of the OSI reference model (see below).

Figure 1-3 provides a very good illustration to help the reader understand how the seven layers are grouped together in the model, as previously discussed. For a larger picture of how protocols are laid in the OSI reference model, go to the following locations and request a copy of their applicable posters:

Wandell & Golterman offer free OSI, ATM, ISDN, and Fiber Optics posters at `http://www.wg.com`
Network Associates offers a Guide to Communications Protocols at `http://www.nai.com`

Figure 1-4 shows the division between the upper and lower OSI layers.

A cute little ditty to help you remember all seven OSI Layers and their order is as follows:

All	Application
People	Presentation
Seem	Session
To	Transport
Need	Network
Data	Data Link
Processing	Physical

UNDERSTANDING THE SEVEN LAYERS OF THE OSI REFERENCE MODEL

The seven layers of the OSI reference model can be divided into two categories: upper layers and lower layers. The upper layers of the model are typically concerned only with applications, and the lower layers primarily handle data transportation.

Upper Layers (Layers 5, 6, 7—Handle Application Issues)

The upper layers of the OSI referece model are concerned with application issues. They are generally implemented only in software. The Application layer is the highest layer and is closest to the end user. Both users and Application layer processes interact with software applications containing a communications component.

NOTES

The term *upper layer* is often used to refer to any higher layer, relative to a given layer.

Layer 7—Application

Essentially, the Application layer acts as the end-user interface. This is the layer where interaction between the mail application (cc:Mail, MS Outlook, and so forth) or communications package and the user occurs. For example, when a user desires to send an e-mail message or access a file on the server, this is where the process starts. Another example of the processes going on at this layer are things like Network File System (NFS) use and the mapping of drives through Windows NT.

Layer 6—Presentation

The Presentation layer is responsible for the agreement of the communication format (syntax) between applications. For example, the Presentation layer enables Microsoft Exchange to correctly interpret a message from Lotus Notes. Another example of the actions occurring in this layer is the encryption and decryption of data in PGP (Pretty Good Privacy).

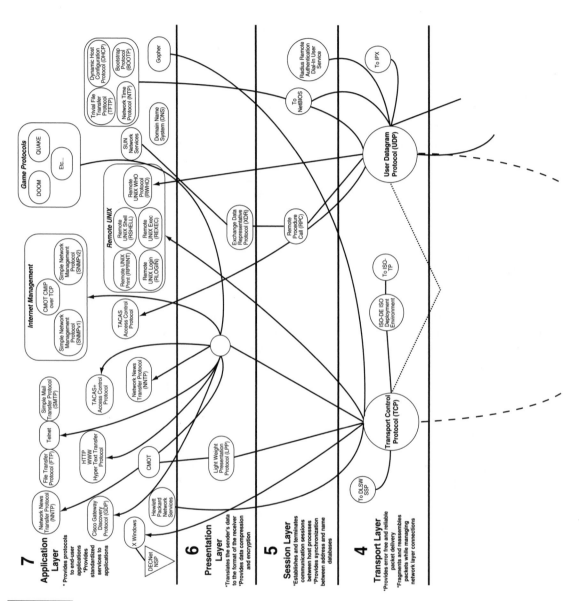

Figure 1–3
How a protocol spans the OSI reference model.

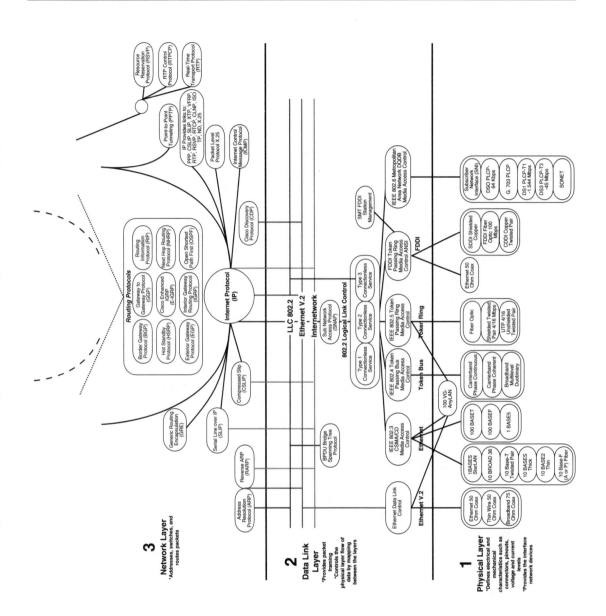

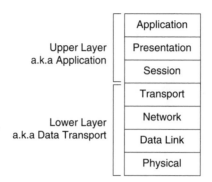

Figure 1–4
*OSI layer
groupings.*

Layer 5—Session

The Session layer is responsible for the Application Layer's management of information transfer, to the Data Transport portion of the OSI reference model. An example is Sun's or Novell's Remote Procedure Call (RPC), this functionality uses Layer 5.

Lower Layers (Layers 1, 2, 3, 4—Handle Data Transport Issues)

The lower layers of the OSI reference model handle data transport issues. The Physical and Data Link layers are implemented in hardware and software. The other lower layers are generally implemented only in software.

Layer 4—Transport

The Transport layer is responsible for the logical transport mechanism, which includes functions conforming to the mechanism's characteristics. For example, the Transmission Control Protocol (TCP), a logical transport mechanism, provides a level of error checking and reliability to the transmission of user data to the lower layers of the OSI reference model. This layer is the only layer that provides true source-to-destination end-to-end connectivity. This layer also supports multiple connections based upon port as found in TCP or UDP.

Layer 3—Network

The Network layer determines physical interface address locations. Routing decisions are made based upon the locations of the Internet Protocol (IP) address in question. For example, IP addresses establish logical topologies known as subnets. Applying this definition to a LAN workstation environment, the workstation determines the location of a particular IP address and where its associated subnet resides through the Network layer. Therefore, a packet sent to IP address A.B.C.D will be forwarded through the workstation's Ethernet card and out onto the network.

NOTES

At this time it would be beneficial to give a brief high-level overview of the ARP process. *Address Resolution Protocol (ARP)* picks up where the IP address and the routing table fall short. As data travels across a network, it must obey the Physical layer protocols that are in use; however, the Physical layer protocols do not understand IP addressing. The most common example of the Network layer translation function is the conversion from IP address to Ethernet address. The protocol responsible for this is ARP, which has been defined in RFC 826. ARP maintains a dynamic table of translations between IP addresses and Ethernet addresses. When ARP receives a request to translate an IP address it checks this table; if it is found, the Ethernet address is returned to the requestor. If it is not found, ARP broadcasts a packet to every host on the Ethernet segment. This packet contains the IP address in question. If the host is found, it responds back with its Ethernet address, which is entered into the ARP table.

The opposite of this is *Reverse Address Resolution Protocol (RARP). RARP* translates addresses in the opposite direction as defined in RFC 903. RARP is used to enable a diskless workstation to learn its IP address because it has no disk from which to read its TCP/IP configuration. Nevertheless, every system knows its Ethernet address because it is burned in on its Ethernet card. So the diskless workstation uses the Ethernet broadcast ability to request its IP address from a server that looks it up by comparing the Ethernet address to a table that can match it to the appropriate IP address. It is important to note that RARP has *nothing* to do with routing data from one system to another, and it is often confused with ARP.

Layer 2—Data Link

The Data Link layer provides framing, error, and flow control across the network media being used. An important characteristic of this layer is that the information that is applied to it is used by devices to determine if the packet needs to be acted upon by this layer (that is, proceed to Layer 3 or discard). The Data Link layer also assigns a Media Access Control (MAC) address to every LAN interface on a device. For example, on an Ethernet LAN segment, all packets are broadcast and received by every device on the segment. Only the device whose MAC address is contained within this layer's frame acts upon the packet; all others do not. It is important to note at this point that serial interfaces do not normally require MAC addresses unless it is necessary to identify the receiving end.

TIPS

It is important to note that MAC addresses are 48-bits in size, three of which are dedicated for vendor identification and another three of which are for unique identification. Additional information on this subject can be found at: `http://www.Cisco.com/warp/public/701/33.html`.

Layer 1—Physical

The Physical layer is the lowest layer and is closest to the physical network medium (the network cabling connecting various pieces of network equipment, for example). It is responsible for actually placing information on the physical media in the correct electrical format (that is, raw bits). For example, an RJ45 cable is wired very differently from an Attachment Unit Interface (AUI); this means that the Physical layer must place the information slightly differently for each media type. Figure 1-5 shows the actual relationship (peering) between the seven layers.

OSI REFERENCE MODEL LAYERS AND INFORMATION EXCHANGE

The seven OSI layers use various forms of control information to communicate with their peer layers in other computer systems. This control information consists of specific

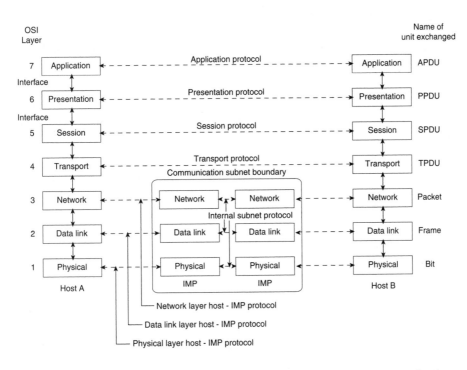

Figure 1–5
Detailed OSI layer relationships.

requests and instructions that are exchanged between peer OSI layers. Control information typically takes one of two forms:

- **Headers:** Appended to the front of data passed down from upper layers.
- **Trailers:** Appended to the back of data passed down from upper layers.

An OSI layer is not necessarily required to attach a header or trailer to upper layer data.

NOTES

Even though OSI is currently one of the most widely recognized frameworks, that was not always the case. Several other frameworks, such as the Digital Network Architecture (DNA), used to compete with ISO, but they did not stand the test of time.

Headers and Data

Headers (and trailers) and data are relative concepts, depending on the layer that is analyzing the information unit at the time.

For example, at the Network layer, an information unit consists of a Layer 3 header and data, known as the payload. At the Data Link layer (Layer 2), however, all of the information passed down by the Network layer (the Layer 3 header and the data) is treated simply as data.

In other words, the data portion of an information unit at a given OSI layer can potentially contain headers, trailers, and data from all of the higher layers. This is known as *encapsulation*. Figure 1-6 shows the header and data from one layer encapsulated in the header of the next lowest layer.

Figure 1–6
OSI packet encapsulation through the OSI layers.

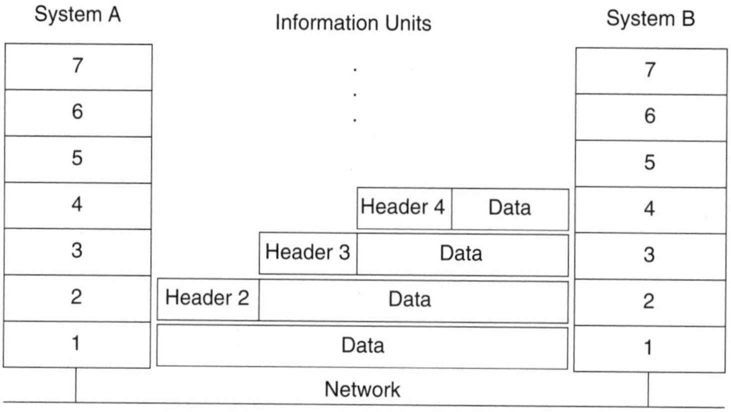

How Does the OSI Reference Model Process Work?

Every person who uses a computer residing upon a network is operating under the OSI reference model. The following real world example takes this statement a step further.

You have written an e-mail message and want to send it a coworker (Dan) who is in another state. The following sequence illustrates how this transaction operates under the OSI reference model. Figure 1-7 depicts the necessary sequence of events.

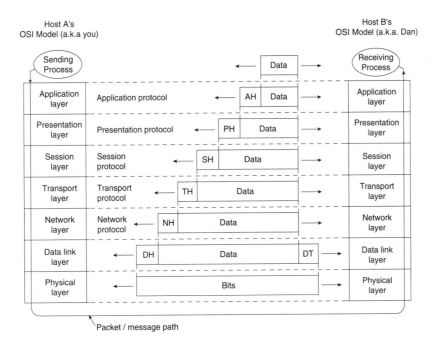

Host A's
OSI Model (a.k.a. you)

Host B's
OSI Model (a.k.a. Dan)

Figure 1–7
How the OSI reference model is used.

AH = Application Header
PH = Presentation Header, etc...

1. You finish writing your e-mail message and enter the send command.

2. The e-mail application determines how the workstation is configured to process this command. In this scenario, the workstation is connected via an Ethernet card to the LAN.

3. The e-mail application knows that the message needs to be formatted a certain way to be sent. The e-mail application knows how do this because its code is written to interpret the command and sends the data. The e-mail application begins the encapsulation process and sends the message through the first three top layers of the OSI reference model: Application, Presentation, and Session.

4. Within the workstation, the encapsulated e-mail message is sent to the Ethernet card. The e-mail message becomes encapsulated in whatever protocol stack happens to be configured on the PC. For purposes of this discussion you will assume TCP/IP is configured.

5. The Ethernet card receives the message and knows that all outgoing traffic must be TCP, so it encapsulates the message accordingly (that is, the packet now contains the destination IP address). The message has now passed through Layer 4, the Transportation layer.

6. Further encapsulation takes place at the Network layer (Layer 3), which is IP in this scenario. The message is now further encapsulated in IP. Here, between Layers 3 and 4, ARP is executed to find out the next hops IP address, and the information is added to the IP packet.

7. The message is now ready to leave the network card; however, the type of LAN on which the message is going to be traveling must be determined (Ethernet, token ring, FDDI, and so on). In this case, the LAN is Ethernet, so the Data Link layer (Layer 2) encapsulates the message to travel on an Ethernet segment.

8. Now the message needs to know the type of physical connection from which it has to enter the LAN segment. Let's say your workstation happens to use an RJ45 cable. Therefore, the very last encapsulation is done at the Physical layer (Layer 1). The message is now transitioned to use the RJ45 physical connection type.

9. POOF! In a zing of electrons, the ones and zeros in the message to Dan now become a series of voltages and electrical impulses out onto your LAN ready for transmission.

10. The message enters the Ethernet interface as a series of bits that the interface can interpret and process, based upon a set of standards that define the interface.

11. The information that has been received is error-checked using a Cycle Redundancy Check (CRC). If the frame is received intact, the interface continues to process the packet by looking for the destination address in the IP packet header. If the destination is not found, the frame is discarded and an error is registered on the interface. The end user will then need to resend the message.

12. At this point, the interface acts as an interpreter for the binary transmissions, and forwards the data based upon the logical destination address.

13. The device (router, bridge, hub, and so forth) continues to forward the message based upon the type of media (Frame Relay, ISDN, ATM, and so on) needed to connect to Dan's LAN.

14. After the message reaches the device that is physically connected to Dan's LAN, steps 11, 12, and 13 are repeated inversely until the message is sent onto the LAN to which Dan's workstation is connected.

15. Steps 1–9 are now repeated inversely as all of the information on how to send the data, how to route the data, and so forth that is needed to deliver the message is transferred to Dan's e-mail application.

16. TADA! "You've Got Mail."

17. Now Dan determines the importance of the message and whether to read it now or wait until his schedule permits.

Open Systems Interconnection (OSI) Protocols

The OSI protocols are a suite of protocols that encompass all seven layers of the OSI reference model. They are part of an international program to develop data networking protocols that are based upon the OSI model as a reference. It is important to mention these briefly, but they are truly beyond the scope of this book. If you desire to learn more about them, read the following books to achieve a solid understanding:

- *Internetworking Technologies Handbook,* published by Cisco Press.

- *Network Protocol Handbook,* published by McGraw-Hill and authored by Mathew Naugle.

INTRANET TOPOLOGIES

The preceding sections discussed the evolution of networks into today's intranets. The sections on the OSI reference model showed the essential means of how data is transported between the various layers running on all intranet devices. This section addresses the media operating on your Internet. Both local- and wide-area topologies will be discussed in the following sections.

Local Area Networks (LANs)

LANs connect workstations, servers, legacy systems, and miscellaneous network-accessible equipment, which are in turn interconnected to form your network. The most common types of LANs include the following:

- **Ethernet.** A communication system that has only one wire with multiple stations attached to the single wire and operates at a speed of 10Mbps.

- **Fast Ethernet.** An improved version of Ethernet that also operates with a single wire with multiple stations. However, the major improvement is in the area of speed as Fast Ethernet operates at a speed of 100Mbps.

- **Gigabit Ethernet.** Yet another version of Ethernet that allows for operational speeds of 1Gbps.

- **Token Ring.** Probably one of the oldest "ring" access techniques originally proposed in 1969. It has multiple wires that connect stations together forming a ring and operates at speeds of 4Mbps and 16Mbps.

- **Fiber Distributed Data Internetworking (FDDI).** A "dual" fiber optic ring that provides increased redundancy and reliability. FDDI operates at speeds of 100Mbps.

Ethernet

Ethernet technology adheres to IEEE Standard 802.3. The requirements of the standard are that the LAN supports 10Mbps over coaxial cabling. Ethernet was originally developed by Xerox in the early 1970s to serve networks with sporadic, and occasionally heavy, network traffic.

Ethernet Version 2.0 was jointly developed by Digital Equipment Corp., Intel Corp., and Xerox Corp. It is compatible with IEEE 802.3 Standards.

Ethernet technology is commonly referred to as Carrier Sense Multiple Access with Carrier Detect (CSMA/CD). What this means is that the Ethernet device will operate as long as it senses a carrier (or a signal) on the physical wire. When an Ethernet device wants to send a packet out of its interface, it will sense for traffic on the wire. If no other traffic is detected, the device will put its data onto the wire and send it to all other devices that are physically connected to the LAN segment.

From time to time, two devices will send data out at the same time. When this occurs, the two packets that are on the wire have what is known as a collision. Built into Ethernet is a retransmission timer known as a back-off algorithm. If an Ethernet device detects a collision, it will perform a random calculation based upon the back-off algorithm before it will send another packet (or resend the original) to prevent further collisions on the wire. Because each device that detects the original collision performs this random calculation, each derives a different value for the resend timer; therefore, the possibility of future collisions on the wire are reduced. Figure 1-8 illustrates a typical Ethernet LAN.

Figure 1–8
A typical Ethernet LAN.

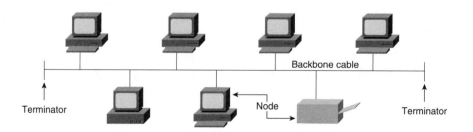

If you need further information on this subject, a very good reference can be found at: http://wwwhost.ots.utexas.edu/ethernet/ethernet-home.html.

Token Ring

Token Ring is defined in IEEE Standard 802.5, developed by IBM in the 1970s. It is known as Token Ring because of its built-in token passing capability. Token Ring runs at speeds of 4 and 16Mbps. It also passes a small packet, known as a token, around the network. Whenever a workstation desires to send information out on the wire (ring), it must first have possession of this token.

After the workstation has the token, it alters one bit (frame copied) within it and retransmits it back onto the network. It is retransmitted as a start of frame sequence and is immediately followed with the information it wants to transmit. This information will circle the ring until the destination is reached, at which time it retrieves the information off the wire. The start of frame packet is then released to flow back to the sending workstation, at which time it changes it back to the original format and releases the token back onto to the wire. Then, the process begins again.

Token Ring technology has two fault management techniques:

- Active monitoring in which a station acts as monitor for the ring and removes any frame that is continually flowing around the ring without being picked up.

- A beaconing algorithm that detects and attempts to repair certain network failures.

Whenever a serious ring problem is detected, a beacon frame is sent out. This beacon frame commands stations to reconfigure to repair the failure. Figure 1-9 illustrates a typical Token Ring LAN.

TIPS

If you need additional information on Ethernet or Token Ring operation and troubleshooting, refer to the following additional resources: Dan Nassar's book at http://www.lanscope.com or Wandell & Goltermann's Ethernet and Token Ring Troubleshooting Guides: http://www.wg.com.

Figure 1–9
*A typical Token
Ring LAN.*

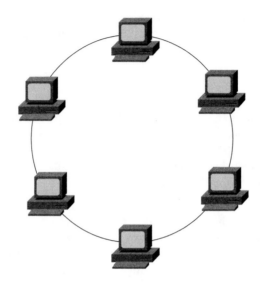

Fiber Distributed Data Internetworking (FDDI)

FDDI technology is an ANSI Standard, X3T9.5, developed in the mid-1980s in order to accommodate the need for more local-area bandwidth. The standard was submitted to ISO, which created an international version of FDDI that is completely compatible with the ANSI version.

FDDI operates at a speed of 100Mbps. The technology is a token passing, dual-ring LAN using fiber optic cable. The dual ring provides redundancy and reliability, with the increased operating speed over standard Ethernet, making FDDI desirable for LAN backbones and interoffice infrastructure. FDDI also uses a token passing technique in order to determine which station is allowed to insert information onto the network.

The function of the second ring is for redundancy, as previously mentioned. If one of the fiber wires is broken, the ring will mend itself by wrapping back toward the portion of the fiber wires that are intact. For this reason, FDDI is highly resilient. Figure 1-10 illustrates a typical FDDI LAN.

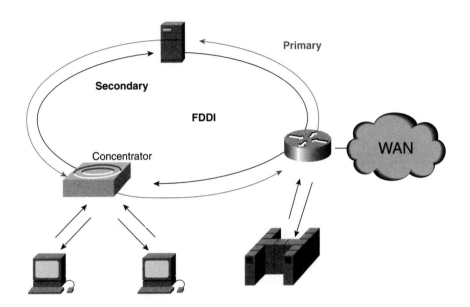

Figure 1–10
A typical FDDI LAN.

Wide Area Networks (WANs)

WANs are used to connect physically separated applications, data, and resources, thereby extending the reach of your network to form an intranet. The ideal result is seamless access to remote resources from geographically separated end users. The most common types of WAN connectivity technologies include the following:

- **Frame Relay.** A high-performance, connection-oriented, packet-switched protocol for connecting sites over a WAN.

- **Point-to-Point Protocol (PPP).** A protocol that uses various standards via encapsulation for IP traffic between serial links.

- **Asynchronous Transfer Mode (ATM).** A fixed packet or cell protocol that emulates LANs for ease of connectivity and transmission. This emulation is referred to LANE—LAN Emulation over ATM.

- **X.25.** A widely available transport that typically operates at T1 speeds. It has extensive error checking to ensure reliable delivery through its permanent and switched virtual circuits.

- **Integrated Systems Digital Network (ISDN).** Consists of digital telephony and data transport services using digitization over a specialized telephone network.

These WAN technologies are discussed in full detail in the sections that follow. Their connectivity and protocol characteristics are also compared and contrasted. The tree shown in Figure 1-11 shows some of the basic differences and choices regarded when switching is involved.

Figure 1–11
*Available WAN
technology
options.*

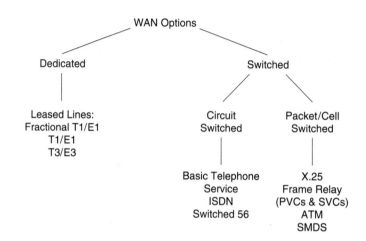

Frame Relay

Frame Relay is a high performance WAN protocol that operates at the Physical and Data Link layers of the OSI reference model. Frame Relay is an example of a packet-switched technology. Frame Relay was developed in 1990 when Cisco Systems, Digital Equipment, Northern Telecom, and StrataCom formed a consortium to focus on Frame Relay technology development. This was required because initial proposals submitted during the 1980s failed to provide a complete set of standards. Since that time, ANSI and CCITT have subsequently standardized their own variation, which is now more commonly used than the original version.

Packet-switched networks enable end stations to dynamically share the network media and its available bandwidth. For example, this means that two routers, a type of end station, can communicate in both directions along the circuit simultaneously. Variable length packets are used for more efficient and flexible data transfers. The advantage of this technique is that it accommodates more flexibility and a more efficient use of the available bandwidth.

Devices attached to a Frame Relay WAN fall into two general categories: DTE and DCE devices, which are logical entities. That is, DTE devices initiate a communications exchange, and DCE devices respond. Descriptions and examples of DTE and DCE devices follow.

- **Data terminal equipment (DTE):** Customer-owned end-node and internetworking devices. Examples of DTE devices are terminals, personal computers, routers, and bridges.

- **Data circuit-terminating equipment (DCE):** Carrier-owned internetworking devices. In most cases, these are packet switches (although routers or other devices can be configured as DCE as well). An important function of these devices is the capability to provide clocking, which is critical to Layer 1's sequencing.

TIPS

A good memory trick to remember which of the two types of equipment provides clocking is D-C-E (Data CLOCK Equipment)

Figure 1-12 illustrates the relationship between the two different types of devices (DTE and DCE).

Frame Relay provides connection-oriented Data Link layer communication. This connection is implemented using virtual circuits. Virtual circuits provide a bi-directional communications path from one DTE device to another. A Data Link Connection Identifier (DLCI) uniquely identifies them and they become locally significant. A Permanent Virtual Circuit (PVC) is one of two types of virtual circuits used in Frame Relay implementations. PVCs are permanently established connections that are used when there is frequent and consistent data transfer between DTE devices across the Frame Relay network. Switched Virtual Circuits (SVCs) are the other types of virtual circuits used in Frame Relay implementations. SVCs are temporary connections used in situations requiring only sporadic data transfer between devices. These circuits are very similar in operation and function to ISDN (discussed later in the chapter).

Figure 1–12
The relationship between DTE and DCE devices.

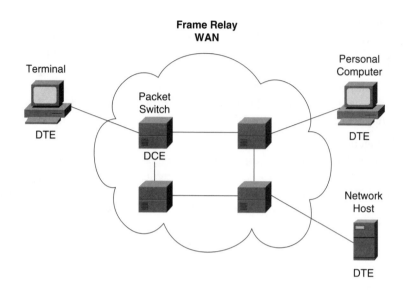

Frame Relay reduces network overhead by providing simple network congestion notification in the form of Forward Explicit Congestion Notification (FECN) and Backward Explicit Congestion Notification (BECN). Both types of congestion notification are controlled by a single bit within the Frame Relay packet header. This bit also contains a Discard Eligible (DE) bit that, if set, will identify less important traffic that can be discarded during periods of congestion.

TIPS

How are Discard Eligible (DE) packets determined?

If your contracted Committed Information Rate (CIR) is exceeded, the Frame Relay switch automatically marks the any frames above your CIR as Discard Eligible (DE). If the Frame Relay backbone is congested, then the switch will discard them; otherwise, they will be allowed through. When the router receives them it will note them on the interface statistics.

Frame Relay uses a common error checking mechanism known as the Cyclic Redundancy Check (CRC). The CRC compares two calculated values to determine whether errors occurred during the transmission from source to destination. Frame Relay reduces network overhead by implementing error checking rather than error correction. Because Frame Relay is typically implemented on reliable network media, data integrity is not sacrificed because error correction can be left to higher-layer protocols, such as OSPF, which runs on top of Frame Relay.

The Local Management Interface (LMI) is a set of enhancements to the basic Frame Relay specification. The LMI offers a number of features (called extensions) for managing complex internetworks. Some of the key Frame Relay LMI extensions include global addressing and virtual circuit status messages (see Figure 1-13).

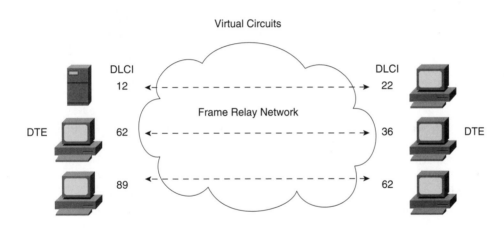

Figure 1–13
Typical Frame Relay connectivity.

Switched Virtual Circuits (SVCs)

SVC technology is the newest kid on the block, and MCI was the first carrier to offer SVCs to customers via their Hyperstream Frame Relay network. SVCs, unlike PVCs, are set up and torn down on-the-fly as needed. Through this capability, SVCs are able to save organizations thousands of dollars a month in service charges when compared to PVCs. When used as a true bandwidth on demand, service router capacity and management is conserved. This is done by putting one entry for each router in its routing table, which allows the SVC to do the rest. For additional information refer to http://www.mci.com.

Point-to-Point Protocol (PPP)

PPP is an encapsulation protocol for transporting IP traffic over point-to-point links. It provides a method for transmitting packets from serial interface to serial interface. PPP also established a series of standards dealing with IP address management, link management, and error checking techniques. PPP supports these many functions through the use of Link Control Protocol (LCP) and Network Control Protocols (NCP) to negotiate optional configuration parameters.

Asynchronous Transfer Mode (ATM)

ATM was originally developed to support video, voice, and data over WANs. ATM was developed by the International Telecommunications Union Telecommunication Standardization Sector (ITU-T). ATM has also been referred to as Broadband ISDN or B-ISDN.

ATM is a cell-switching and multiplexing technology that provides flexibility and efficiency for intermittent traffic, along with constant transmission delay and guaranteed capacity.

An ATM network consists of an ATM switch and endpoints that support the LAN Emulation (LANE) technology. LANE uses an ATM device to emulate a LAN topology by encapsulating the packet in an Ethernet or Token Ring frame when going from media to media. Essentially, LANE enables an ATM device to behave as if it were in a standard LAN environment. LANE supports all versions of Token Ring and Ethernet but currently is not compatible with FDDI. The support for these technologies is possible because these protocols use the same packet format regardless of link speed.

ATM can be configured to support either PVCs or SVCs. PVCs provide for a point-to point-dedicated circuit between end devices. PVCs do not require a call set up or guarantee the link will be available but are more manual in nature and require static addressing than SVCs. SVCs, however, are dynamically allocated and released. They remain in use only as long as data is being transferred. SVCs require a call set up for each instance of the circuit's connection. The switched circuits provide more flexibility and efficiency; however, they are burdened by the overhead associated with the call set up, in terms of the extra time and configuration. Figure 1-14 illustrates a typical ATM network.

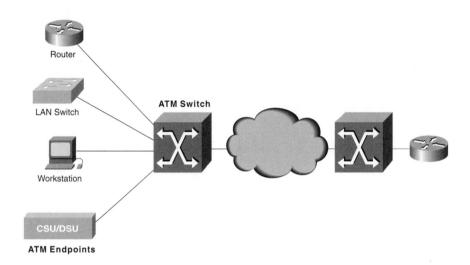

Figure 1-14
A typical ATM network.

Integrated Systems Digital Network (ISDN)

ISDN is defined by ITU-T Standards Q.921 and Q.931. The Q.921 specification requires the user to designate a network interface that is needed for digital connectivity. The Q.931 determines call setup and configuration. ISDN components include the following:

- Terminals
- Terminal adapters (TAs)
- Network termination devices
- Line termination equipment
- Exchange termination equipment

It is important to point out that there is specialized ISDN equipment known as terminal equipment type 1 (TE1). All other equipment that does not conform to ISDN Standards is known as terminal equipment type 2 (TE2). TE1s connect to the ISDN network through specialized cables. TE2s connect to the ISDN network through a terminal adapter.

Another ISDN device is the network connection type—network termination type 1 or 2 devices. These termination devices connect the specialized ISDN cables to normal two wire local wiring.

ISDN reference points define logical interfaces. Four reference points are defined:

- **R reference point.** Defines the reference point between non-ISDN equipment and a TA.

- *S* **reference point.** Defines the reference point between user terminals and an NT2.

- **T reference point.** Defines the reference point between NT1 and NT2 devices.

- *U* **reference point.** Defines the reference point between NT1 devices and line-termination equipment in a carrier network. (This is only in North America, where the NT1 function is not provided by the carrier network.)

Figure 1-15 illustrates the various devices and reference points found in ISDN implementations, as well as their relationship to the ISDN networks they support.

Figure 1–15
A typical ISDN configuration.

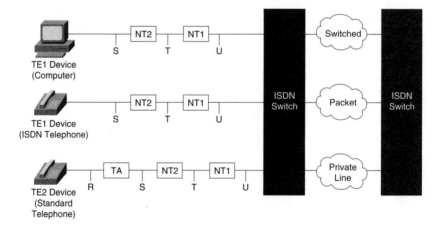

The ISDN Basic Rate Interface (BRI) service provides two B channels and one D channel. The BRI B-channel service operates at 64Kbps and carries data, while the BRI D-channel service operates at 16Kbps and usually carries control and signaling information.

The ISDN Primary Rate Interface (PRI) service delivers 23 B channels and one 64Kbps D channel in North America and Japan for a total bit rate of up to 1.544Mbps. PRI in Europe and Australia carry 30 B channels and 1 D channel for a total bit rate of up to 2.048Mbps.

The ISDN network layer operation involves a series of call stages that are characterized by specific message exchanges. In general, an ISDN call involves call establishment, call termination, information, and miscellaneous messages.

The call stage characteristics define the way an ISDN call is initiated, acknowledged, and completed. The specifics of ISDN call stages and their supported characteristics are defined in the OSI reference model Network layer definition of ISDN.

Formal call stage components include the following, in order:

- SETUP
- CONNECT
- RELEASE
- USER INFORMATION
- CANCEL
- STATUS
- DISCONNECT

The formal call components as presented in the preceding list can also be tracked through a typical ISDN call negotiation as shown in Figure 1-16.

SUMMARY

This chapter discussed how networks began and how they have been increasing in complexity ever since. You also learned about the physical layout of early networks as well as the issues surrounding the evolution of contemporary intranets and what the future holds for network engineers. This chapter also established the physical foundations and needs of past, current, and future networks.

You also explored the OSI reference model down to each individual layer and learned how a typical data packet flows up and down the OSI layers as well as the way it flows between geographically separated networks. At this point, you should understand the basic functions of the logical network through the discussion and demonstrations illustrated.

Figure 1–16
A typical ISDN Network layer call negotiation.

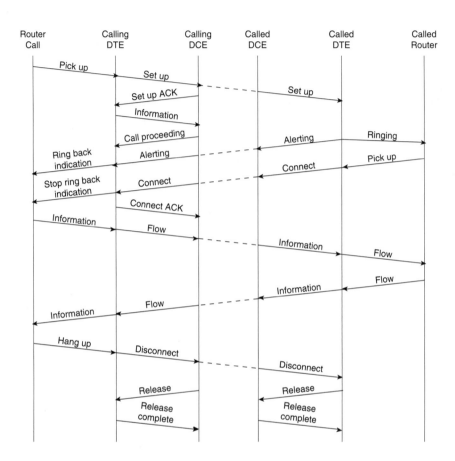

The chapter continued with coverage of the LAN and WAN intranet topologies. The section on LAN topologies included coverage of the three most widely deployed topologies: Ethernet, Token Ring, and FDDI, as well as the standards and basic characteristics of each. The section on WAN topologies included coverage of the three most widely deployed topologies: Frame Relay, PPP, ATM, and ISDN. Discussion of each topology included the standards applicable for each and some of the more important aspects of each.

In conclusion, the reader should now understand the evolution of networks, intranet evolution, current challenges, physical and logical network fundamentals, popular LAN and WAN topologies. Chapter 2, "Network Routing Fundamentals," will build further upon the foundations of networking covered in this chapter.

Networking Routing Fundamentals

"Achievement: Unless you try to do something beyond what you have already mastered, you will never grow."—Successories

Routing with a network, whether it is the Internet or an intranet, requires a certain amount of "common" information. This chapter provides a broad overview that covers some of the most essential points.

- **Internet Protocol (IP) addressing.** An overview of IP addressing methodology and understanding, subnetting, variable-length subnet masking, and classless interdomain routing is provided in this section. Why these techniques are needed will also be briefly discussed.

- **Internetwork components.** This section provides an examination of the actual physical components that make use of the theories previously discussed: OSI Model, IP addresses, subnet masks, and protocols.

- **Network protocols.** Basic theory on network protocols is discussed, with emphasis on understanding the difference between routed and routing protocols. Some of the fundamentals of protocol operation, with an emphasis on the evolution and operation of the Internet Protocol (IP), will be explained.

INTERNET PROTOCOL (IP) ADDRESSING

This section discusses IP addressing methodology and understanding, basic subnetting, variable length subnet masking (VLSM), and classless interdomain routing (CIDR).

In a properly designed and configured network, communication between hosts and servers is transparent. This is because each device using the TCP/IP protocol suite has a unique 32-bit Internet Protocol (IP) address. A device will "read" the destination IP address in the packet and make the appropriate routing decision based upon this information. In this case, a device could be either the host or server using a default gateway or a router using its routing table to forward the packet to its destination.

IP addresses can be represented as a group of four decimal numbers, each within the range of 0 to 255. Each of these four decimal numbers will be separated by a decimal point. This method of displaying these numbers is known as *dotted decimal notation.* It is important to note that these numbers can also be displayed in both the binary and hexadecimal numbering systems. Figure 2-1 illustrates the basic format of an IP address as determined by using dotted decimal notation.

Figure 2–1
An IP address format as determined by dotted decimal notation.

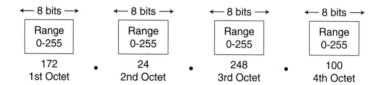

IP addresses have only two logical components, network and host addresses, the use of which is extremely important. A network address identifies the network and must be unique; if the network is to be a part of the Internet, then it must be assigned by the Internet Network Information Center (InterNIC). A host address, on the other hand, identifies a host (device) on a network and is assigned by a local administrator.

Suppose a network has been assigned an address of 172.24, for example. An administrator then assigns a host the address of 248.100. The complete address of this host is 172.24.248.100. This address is unique because only one network and one host can have this address.

NOTES

The network address component must be the same for all devices on that network, yet must be unique from all other networks. Additional information can be found in RFC 1600, which discusses reserved IP addresses.

Class A Addresses

In a class A address (also known as /8), the first octet contains the network address and the other three octets make up the node address. The first bit of a class A network address must be set to 0. Although mathematically it would appear that there are 128 possible class A network addresses (remember the first is set to zero), the address 00000000 is not available, so there are only 127 such addresses. This number is further reduced because network 127.0.0.0 is reserved for loopback addressing purposes. There are only 126 class A addresses available for use. Each class A address, however, can support 126 networks that correspond to 16,777, 214 node addresses per class A address.

NOTES

Please note that the node addresses 00000000.00000000.00000000.00000000 and 11111111.11111111.11111111.11111111 are not available in ANY address class, with the example shown being a class A address. These node addresses translate into 0.0.0.0 and 255.255.255.255, respectively. These are typically used for protocol advertisements, such as ARP, RIP, and broadcast packets. Also note that 127.x.x.x (where x is any number between 0 and 255) is referred to as the local loopback address. A packet's use of this address will immediately result in it being sent back to the application from which it was sent. This information can be used to assist you in troubleshooting network problems.

Class B Addresses

In a class B (also known as /16) address, the network component uses the first two octets for addressing purposes. The first two bits of a class B address are always 10; that is, one and zero, not ten. The address range would then be 128.1.0.0 to 191.254.0.0. This leaves you with the first six bits of the first octet and all eight bits of the second octet, thereby providing 16,384 possible class B network addresses. The remaining octets are used to provide you with over 65,534 hosts per class B address.

Class C Addresses

In a class C (also known as /24) address, the first three octets are devoted to the network component. The first three bits of a class C address must be 110. The address range would then be 192.0.1.0 to 223.255.254.0. This leaves you with five bits of the first octet and eight bits of the second and third octets, thereby providing you with 2,097,152 possible class C addresses. The node address is determined by the last octet, which provides 254 nodes per network.

Class D Addresses

Class D addresses are special addresses that do not refer to individual networks. The first four bits of these addresses begin with 1110. The address range would then be in the range of 224 to 239. Class D addresses are used for multicast packets, which are used by many different protocols to reach multiple groups of hosts (such as ICMP router discovery or Internet Group Membership Protocol (IGMP), which is gaining in popularity since its release in IOS 11.2).

Consider these addresses as "preprogrammed" within the logical structure of most network components in that when they see a destination address of this type within a packet, it triggers a response. For instance, if a host sends out the IP address 224.0.0.2, all routers (using OSPF) on its Ethernet segment respond.

Class E Addresses

Addresses in the range 240.0.0.0 to 254.255.255.255 are termed class E addresses. The first octet of these addresses begins with the bits 1111. These addresses are reserved for future additions to the IP addressing scheme. These future additions might or might not come to fruition with the advent of IPv6, which will be discussed in later chapters.

In most networks, the IP addresses assigned to each have been broken into parts that logically relate to different areas. For example, part of an IP address identifies a particular network, part identifies a subnet (that is, subnetwork), and part identifies a specific host within that subnetwork (that is, subnet).

The following three blocks of IP address space for private networks have been reserved according to RFC 1597: Address Allocation for Private Internets.

- 10.0.0.0-10.255.255.255. Single class A network numbers
- 172.16.0.0-172.31.255.255. Contiguous class B network numbers
- 192.168.0.0-192.168.255.255. Contiguous class C network numbers

How IP Addresses Are Used

Routers examine the most significant or left-most bit of the first octet when determining the class of a network address. This technique of reading IP addresses (also known as the first octet rule) is discussed further as the different classes of addresses are defined.

Table 2-1 provides a variety of quick reference information relating to the different IP address classes. Note that in the format column, N=Network number and H=Host number. Also, for Class A addresses, one address is reserved for the broadcast address, and one address is reserved for the network.

Table 2-1   *Quick IP Address Reference Information*

IP Address Class	Format	Purpose	High-Order Bit(s)	Address Range	No. Bits Network/ Host	Maximum Hosts
A	N.H.H.H	Few large organizations	0	`1.0.0.0-126.0.0.0`	7/24	16,777,2 14 ($2 [24]- 2$)
B	N.N.H.H	Medium-sized organizations	1,0	`128.1.0.0-191.254.0.0`	14/16	65,543 ($2[16] -2$)
C	N.N.N.H	Relatively small organizations	1,1,0	`192.0.1.0-223.255.254.0`	22/8	254 ($2[8]$ -2)
D	N/A	Multi-cast groups (RFC 1112)	1,1,1,0	`224.0.0.0-239.255.255.255`	N/A (not for commer-cial use)	N/A
E	N/A	Experimental	1,1,1,1	`240.0.0.0-254.255.255.255`	N/A	N/A

Tables 2-2 through 2-4 list the actual number of hosts and subnets for Class A, B, and C IP addresses. For the subnets and hosts, all zeroes and all ones are excluded.

Table 2-3 lists the actual number of hosts and subnets for Class B IP addresses.

Table 2-4 lists the actual number of hosts and subnets for Class C IP addresses.

Table 2-2   *Host/Subnet Quantities for Class A IP Addresses*

Number of bits	Mask	Effective Subnets	Effective Hosts
2	255.192.0.0	2	4,194,302
3	255.224.0.0	6	2,097,150
4	255.240.0.0	14	1,048,574
5	255.248.0.0	30	524,286
6	255.252.0.0	62	262,142
7	255.254.0.0	126	131,070
8	255.255.0.0	254	65,536
9	255.255.128.0	510	32,766
10	255.255.192.0	1,022	16,382
11	255.255.224.0	2,046	8,190
12	255.255.240.0	4,094	4,094
13	255.255.248.0	8,190	2,046
14	255.255.252.0	16,382	1,022
15	255.255.254.0	32,766	5,10
16	255.255.255.0	65,536	254
17	255.255.255.128	131,070	126
18	255.255.255.192	262,142	62
19	255.255.255.224	524,286	30
20	255.255.255.240	1,048,574	14
21	255.255.255.248	2,097,150	6
22	255.255.255.252	4,194,302	2

Table 2-3   *Host/Subnet Quantities for Class B IP Addresses*

Number of bits	Mask	Effective Subnets	Effective Hosts
2	255.255.192.0	2	16,382
3	255.255.224.0	6	8,190
4	255.255.240.0	14	4,094
5	255.255.248.0	30	2,046
6	255.255.252.0	62	1,022
7	255.255.254.0	126	510
8	255.255.255.0	254	254
9	255.255.255.128	510	126
10	255.255.255.192	1,022	62
11	255.255.255.224	2,046	30
12	255.255.255.240	4,094	14
13	255.255.255.248	8,190	6
14	255.255.255.252	16,382	2

Table 2-4   *Host/Subnet Quantities for Class C IP Addresses*

Number of bits	Mask	Effective Subnets	Effective Hosts
2	255.255.255.192	2	62
3	255.255.255.224	6	30
4	255.255.255.240	14	14
5	255.255.255.248	30	6
6	255.255.255.252	62	2

NOTES

You can derive the maximum number of hosts in each of the address classes by doing the following: N.H.H.H for H*H*H=total number of hosts, where 254*254*254=16 million, N is the network number, and H is the host.

Figure 2-2 lays out the various IP address classes by network and host components.

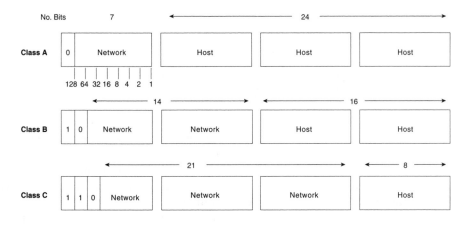

Figure 2–2
IP addresses by class.

In most networks, the IP addresses assigned to that network have been broken into parts that logically relate to its different areas. For example, part of an IP address identifies a particular network, part identifies a subnet (that is, subnetwork), and part identifies a specific host within that subnetwork (that is, host).

How IP Addresses Are Read

Routers examine the most significant or left-most bit of the first octet when determining the class of a network address. This technique of reading IP addresses (also known as the first octet rule) is discussed further as we define the different classes of addresses.

The Role of IP Addresses

IP uses a hierarchical addressing structure. A router simply sends the packet to the next hop in the route to reach its destination. For example, if a packet has a destination IP address of 172.24.50.10, the router will begin with the first octet (172) and search its routing tables for it. When a match is found, the router goes on to the next octet (24) until enough information is learned so that it can route the packet to its next destination. If the router does not have enough information to route the packet, then it will be dropped.

Routers make their hierarchical decisions based upon the network and host components of an IP address, as demonstrated in Figure 2-3.

Figure 2–3
A hierarchical IP address example.

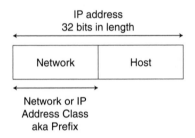

Class A address is 8 bits long and always starts with 0
Class B address is 16 bits long and always starts with 10
Class C address is 24 bits long and always starts with 110

Another very good example of the hierarchical addressing technique used by routers is your phone number. For example, if the phone number 919-779-xxxx is dialed, the phone system knows that 919 is located in North Carolina, 779 is in the Raleigh area, and the last four numbers are assigned to a residence. An interesting side note here is that the telephone system is also running out of numbers, hence the implementation of the new toll-free extension, 888. Even in the use of phone numbers, you can see how technology has depleted the "bank" of possible numbers as a result of the use of modems, pagers, cellular phones, personal 800 numbers, and multiple phone lines in a residence.

A router usually has an interface to which it connects. This interface will be assigned an IP address and subnet mask. Devices trying to reach a host within the network assigned to that interface will be routed through the interface. For example, a Token Ring interface has an IP address of 172.24.248.100. The router knows that packets going into or coming out of network 172.24.0.0 will need to interact with this interface.

IP Subnet Addressing

The need for subnetting has resulted in the massive growth of networks in the past decade. As the available address space rapidly continues to shrink, network managers needed to use the existing space more efficiently; hence, subnetting was born.

There are also some additional benefits to using subnetting have, such as:

- Efficient use of available network addresses (already mentioned)
- Flexibility in planning network growth and design
- Capability to contain broadcast traffic
- Subnets under local administrative control

NOTES

Broadcast traffic is defined as data packets that will be sent to all nodes on a network. Broadcasts are identified by a broadcast address.

To understand subnets better, just think of them as extensions of the network number. Essentially, you are reassigning part of what is "officially" the node address space to act as an additional network address.

There are essentially three steps in assigning addresses in a network that has been subnetted:

1. Define the subnet mask.
2. Assign an address to each subnet.
3. Assign IP addresses to each node.

In many organizations, subnets are used to divide one large network into a number of smaller networks. For example, the class B network used earlier (172.24.0.0) can be subdivided into 254 subnets:

```
172.24.1.0
172.24.2.0
172.24.3.0
172.24.4.0
172.24.5.0
etc. . .
```

This would provide 254 possible subnets, each having 254 hosts per subnet.

NOTES

According to RFC 1812, section 5.3.5.3, all-subnet broadcast is no longer supported, so all of 1's subnet is allowed.

Subnet Masking

Subnet masks use the same format and representation technique as regular IP addresses. The subnet mask, however, has binary 1s in all bits specifying the network field. Essentially, a subnet mask is a 32-bit number that is applied to an IP address to override the default network/node address convention. The subnet mask also tells the router which octets of an IP address to pay attention to when comparing the destination address of a packet to its routing table.

For example, for the subnet 172.24.1.0 you created to be properly configured, a mask must be applied of 255.255.255.0. This gives you a complete IP subnet address of 172.24.1.0 255.255.255.0. If you were to then apply this to an Ethernet interface of a router, and a packet came into the router with a destination address of 172.24.1.30, the router would be able to route the packet appropriately because it knows (via the assigned IP address and mask) that any packet destined for the network 172.24.1.0 is to be sent out the router's Ethernet interface.

All class addresses have default subnet masks because the subnet bits come from the high order bits of the host field. The following list provides the default subnet masks used for each class of IP address:

- **Class A:** `255.0.0.0` default mask
- **Class B:** `255.255.0.0` default mask
- **Class C:** `255.255.255.0` default mask

These default masks have a binary 1 in every position that corresponds to the default network address component of the appropriate IP address class.

Now that you are familiar with the complete technical explanation of subnet masking, let's discuss it in terms that might be a bit easier to understand. The most important thing to remember about subnet masks is that you cannot just assign IP addresses without any consideration. The question then becomes: Why should I use subnetting on my network? The simple answer is that you should do so in order to route across your network. Then we must ask: Why route? Complicated and convoluted, isn't it?

Assume for the purpose of this discussion that you have a large Ethernet segment that has gotten so full of users that the collisions occurring on it are negatively impacting the users' and the segments' performance. The quick and easy answer is to use a bridge that will enable you to split the network but retain connectivity. The problem here is that bridges use MAC addresses to make decisions on where to forward packets. The bad news is that if the bridge does not know where to send a packet, it resorts to broadcasting it to everyone. **The catch is that your slow, busy Ethernet segment will have been split into two segments; your network performance should increase as a result.** The problem is that as you begin to connect more and more segments, you end up with broadcasts flowing all across the network to the point that it could bring the whole intranet to a standstill. Typically, large amounts of broadcasts, such as those described here, are called broadcast storms, which are definitely a bad thing. What is needed is a piece of hardware with more intelligence—the router.

In general terms, the router connects multiple networks and makes decisions on where to and if it should forward packets based upon the packets' addresses. The router has been designed to drop all packets if it does not know where to forward them; hence, there are no more out-of-control broadcasts.

For example, let's say you have network `172.24.0.0` out interface #1 of your router and network `10.37.0.0` out interface #2. First, IP addresses must be assigned to each router interface—let's say `xxx.xxx.1.1`—and at least one PC would need to be on each network. Figure 2-4 demonstrates this scenario.

Figure 2–4
*Basic
subnetting
example.*

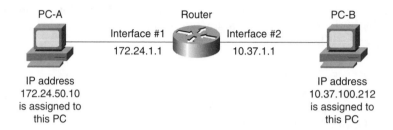

IP address
172.24.50.10
is assigned to
this PC

IP address
10.37.100.212
is assigned to
this PC

A router will not learn about every individual address out there. Instead, the router believes that if interface #1 has an IP address of 172.24.1.1 255.255.255.0, then all packets destined for the 172.24.0.0 network must be located out on that interface. To recap, if the router receives a packet that is not destined to either of the networks it knows about (in this case, 172.24.0.0 or 10.37.0.0), then that packet is dropped, or rather erased, from its memory.

If PC-A is trying to communicate with PC-B, then the packet's destination IP address will be 10.37.100.212. So how does the router actually know that this IP address is located in the same network as the IP address assigned to its interface (10.37.1.1)? Well, simply put, the subnet mask must be entered.

Thus, when you assign the IP address 10.37.1.1 to interface #2, you must also specify a subnet mask.

TIPS

Remember that every interface in a router must be assigned a local subnet mask! Fortunately, Cisco routers will not accept an IP address without a mask.

If you have assigned a subnet mask of 255.255.0.0 to interface #2, then you are telling the router when it needs to make a routing decision on a packet if the first two octets of the destination IP address match (10.37). The router then forwards the packet out interface #2.

This is because when designing a subnet mask (as previously discussed), 255 in a subnet mask means the router needs an exact match, whereas 0 means it doesn't matter what this octet's value is.

Let's look at this in another way. If you give that interface a subnet mask of 255.255.255.0, then you are telling the router to only look at the first three octets of the destination IP address when it needs to make a routing decision. Because, as previously discussed, the first three octets for a "natural" class C address define the network number.

You can even make subnet masks extremely explicit by applying a subnet mask of 255.255.255.255 to the interface. By doing this, you are telling the router to only look at the first four octets of the destination IP address when it needs to make a routine decision. Therefore, only packets destined to IP address 10.37.100.212 would be routed through that interface.

There are a variety of different ways that you use subnet masks to segment your network, and that really goes beyond the scope of this book. If you are interested in learning more about basic subnetting techniques, then refer to the RFCs mentioned at the end of this section. But before you move on, there are some restrictions you must be aware of when using subnets.

Subnetting Restrictions

In a traditional subnetted network, several restrictions apply that have been lifted if classless interdomain routing (CIDR) is being used along with a protocol that supports CIDR (such as OSPF or BGP). However, if older, non-CIDR routing protocols (such as RIPv1) are in use, these restrictions must still be observed.

For identical subnet masks, a router assumes that the subnet mask, which has been configured, is valid for all subnets. Therefore, a single mask must be used for all subnets with a network. Different masks can be used for different networks.

A subnetted network can't be split into isolated portions because all subnets must be contiguous. Within a network, all subnets must be able to reach all other subnets without passing traffic through other networks.

Further discussion or examples on this topic would fall outside the scope of this book; however, if you require further information, I would recommend the following sources:

- RFC 791: Subnet Addressing
- RFC 950: Subnet Specifications
- RFC 1219: Strategies for Assigning IP Addresses
- RFC 1597: Address Allocation for Private Internets
- RFC 1700: Assigned Numbers

EXPLAINING THE NEED FOR VLSM AND CIDR

VLSM (variable-length subnet mask) is defined as the capability to specify a different subnet mask for the same network number on different subnets. VLSM can help optimize available address space.

CIDR (classless interdomain routing) is a technique supported by BGP4 and based on route aggregation. CIDR enables routers to group routes to cut down on the quantity of routing information carried by the core routers. With CIDR, several IP networks appear to networks outside the group as a single, larger entity.

Why are VLSM and CIDR needed? This question can be answered in three words—IP address depletion. However, what does this mean? It means that the current IP address scheme, which is known as IPv4, is beginning to run out of IP addresses. This is an unacceptable situation that many network engineers have to deal with every day. However, relief for this problem is discussed in Chapter 12, "Future Network Considerations," later in the book. CDR and VLSM are just interim solutions but effective nonetheless.

NOTES

Not only is address depletion an issue, but many networks are also faced with very large routing tables that need to be reduced to enable smoother network and router operation.

I am certain that when this addressing scheme was first designed many years ago, the engineers at that time believed it would be more than enough. Nevertheless, the recent explosive growth of the Internet and corporate intranets has made it necessary for new technology and strategies to deal with this looming problem. The situation becomes even more critical when you consider that corporations of all sizes are beginning to use and look to the Internet as a means of revenue. It's a very exciting time for our field when you consider that less than fifteen years ago, computers and networks were things of ponderous size with only specific applications. This is a time of constant change and advancement, and it is interesting to consider what the world of technology will be like for the next generation.

One of the most interesting enhancements on the horizon is IP version 6 (IPv6), also known as IP next generation (IPng) during its developmental stage. This is a move to improve the existing IPv4 implementation, which is quickly reaching critical mass. The proposal was released in July 1992 at the Boston Internet Engineering Task Force (IETF) meeting. IPv6 tackles issues such as the IP address depletion problem, quality of service capabilities, address autoconfiguration, authentication, and security capabilities.

Because these issues are facing us in the here and now, it is in response to these concerns that the technologies of VLSM and CIDR were developed. Not only do these techniques enable us to better use the remaining IP addresses, but they have enabled large networks to continue growing without having the routers become saturated by the various routes within the network. A prime example of this is the Internet. This example will be discussed in further detail, but keep it in mind as you read through these sections.

There are several items that are used within the discussions of VLSM and CIDR that are important to discuss before proceeding any further.

Route Summarization (Aggregation or Supernetting)

What is route summarization? This technique is known by several names, but simply described, it is a method of representing a series of network numbers in a single summary address that is advertised to other routers. Assume, for instance, that a router knows about the following networks that are attached to it:

```
172.24.100.0
172.24.101.0
172.24.102.0
172.24.103.0
```

The router would summarize that information to other routers by saying I know how to get to these networks in this summarization 172.24.100.0/22. You can also say that subnetting extends the prefix to the right by making the router know a very specific IP addresses; summarization, on the other hand, reduces the prefix to the left, thereby enabling the router to only advertise the higher order bits. Figure 2-5 demonstrates how subnetting and route summarization differ.

TIPS

Refer to Cisco's document "Internetwork Design Guide," Chapter 3, "Designing Large Scale IP Internetworks," for a good overview that describes the best practices concerning summarization.

Figure 2–5
Comparison of subnetting and route summarization.

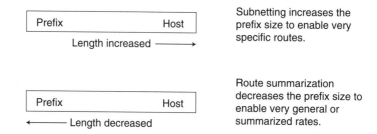

Subnetting increases the prefix size to enable very specific routes.

Route summarization decreases the prefix size to enable very general or summarized rates.

An example of this technique is classless interdomain routing (CIDR), which is discussed in detail in a later section of this chapter. There are a few requirements that you should keep in mind in order to have route summarization work properly:

• Multiple IP addresses must share the same high order bit in order to be properly summarized

• Routing tables and protocols must base their routing decisions on a normal 32-bit IP address and prefix length, which can also be up to 32 bits in size

• Routing protocols must carry this prefix (such as /16, which translates into a 255.255.0.0 mask) with the 32-bit IP address

Classful Routing

Classful routing always summarizes routes by the major network numbers. RIP and IGRP are protocols that use this type of routing. They are called classful because they always consider the network class. This is always done at network boundaries.

The Impact of Classful Routing

The use of classful routing has some considerable impact on a network. For one thing, subnets are not advertised to a different major network. In addition, noncontiguous subnets are not visible to each other. Figure 2-6 illustrates how classful routing and subnetting can affect your network.

There are certain techniques that have been developed to assist in overcoming this problem: IP unnumbered, secondary addressing, and using OSPF. Further discussion of classful routing and the issues surrounding its use (that is, discontiguous subnets) are beyond the scope of this book.

Figure 2–6
How classful routing and subnetting affect the network.

172.24.9.0
255.255.255.0

182.68.10.16
255.255.255.240

172.24.10.0
255.255.255.0

Each router has a subnet that it attaches to,
but in a classful environment, they cannot
and will not be advertised because the subnets
are not on a classful boundary

Classless Routing

Classless routing differs from classful routing in that the prefix length is transmitted. This prefix length is evaluated at each place it is encountered throughout your network. In other words, it can be changed to advertise routes differently at different locations within a network. This capability of classless routing enables more efficient use of IP address space and reduces routing traffic. A very good example of this type of routing is VLSM. Classless routing has the following characteristics:

- One routing entry might match a block of host, subnet, or network addresses

- Routing tables can be much shorter

- Switching performance can be faster

- Routing protocol traffic is reduced

VARIABLE-LENGTH SUBNET MASKS (VLSM)

The basic concept of variable-length subnet masks (VLSM) is to provide more flexibility by dividing a network into multiple subnets. The trick to using this technique is ensuring that you have an adequate number of hosts allocated per subnet.

NOTES

Note that not every protocol supports VLSM. If you decide to implement VLSM, make sure you are using a VLSM-capable routing protocol such as OSPF.

OSPF and static routes support variable-length subnet masks (VLSMs). With VLSMs, you can use different masks for the same network number on different interfaces, which enables you to conserve IP addresses for better efficiency. VLSMs do this by allowing both big subnets and small subnets. As mentioned previously, you need to ensure that the number of hosts is sufficient for your needs within each subnet.

In the following example, a 30-bit subnet mask is used, leaving two bits of address space reserved for serial line host addresses. There is sufficient host address space for two host endpoints on a point-to-point serial link.

```
interface ethernet 0
 ip address 131.107.1.1 255.255.255.0
! 8 bits of host address space reserved for Ethernet hosts
interface serial 0
 ip address 131.107.254.1 255.255.255.252
! 2 bits of address space reserved for serial lines
! System is configured for OSPF and assigned 107 as the process number
router ospf 107
! Specifies network directly connected to the system
network 131.107.0.0 0.0.255.255 area 0.0.0.0
```

As shown in the preceding example, VLSM is very efficient when used on serial lines because each line requires a distinct subnet number, even though they only have two host addresses. This requirement wastes subnet numbers. However, if you use VLSM to address serial links in a core router, then you can save space. In Figure 2-7, the regular subnet 172.24.10.0 is further subnetted with six additional bits. These additional subnets make 63 additional subnets available. VLSM also enables the routes within the core to be summarized as 172.24.10.0.

Most early networks never had their IP addresses assigned to them in a way that would enable network engineers to group them in blocks. Instead, they had been assigned as needed, so massive renumbering projects would need to be performed—not one of the most popular pastimes of anyone involved in networking. However, although hindsight is 20/20, remember the past when considering the future and newer technology, such as IPv6. Otherwise, you might end up doing quite a lot of static routing and odd configuring just to keep your network stable.

VLSM Design Guidelines & Techniques

To assist you when designing the use of VLSM within your network, please consider some of the following guidelines:

- Optimal summarization occurs with contiguous blocks of addresses

- If small subnets are grouped, routing information can be summarized

- Group VLSM subnets so that routing information can be consolidated

Figure 2–7
*VLSM
conserves
subnets.*

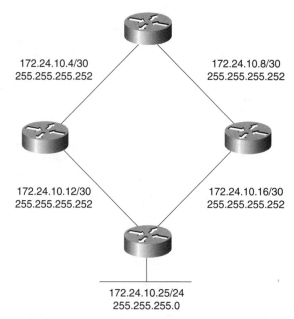

172.24.10.4/30
255.255.255.252

172.24.10.8/30
255.255.255.252

172.24.10.12/30
255.255.255.252

172.24.10.16/30
255.255.255.252

172.24.10.25/24
255.255.255.0

- Allocate VLSM by taking one regular subnet and subnetting it further

- Avoid using two different subnet masks inside a given network address

In conclusion, you might ask yourself why there are any questions about implementing VLSM. This is a good question with a few different answers available, depending upon the network in question. As mentioned previously, VLSM is not supported by every protocol, though it is supported by OSPF, EIGRP, ISIS, and RIPv2. So these newer protocols might have to co-exist with older protocols that do not support VLSM and would have trouble routing. In addition, the use of VLSM can be very difficult. If it is not properly designed, it can cause the network to not operate properly and it increases the complexity of troubleshooting any network.

CLASSLESS INTERDOMAIN ROUTING (CIDR)

VLSM was a step up from subnetting because it relayed subnet information through routing protocols. This idea leads us directly into this section on CIDR, which stands for classless interdomain routing. CIDR is documented in the following RFCs: 1517, 1518, 1519, and 1520. CIDR is an effective method to stem the tide of IP address allocation, as well as routing table overflow. Without the implementation of CIDR in 1994 and 1995, the Internet would not be functioning today because the routing tables would have been too great in magnitude for the routers to handle.

The primary requirement for CIDR is the use of routing protocols that support it, such as RIPv2, OSPFv2, and BGPv4. CIDR can be thought of as "advanced subnetting." The subnetting mask, previously a number with special significance, becomes an integral part of routing tables and protocols. A route is no longer just an IP address that has been interpreted according to its class with the corresponding network and host bits.

Validating a CIDRized Network

Let's use the routing tables in the Internet or any other large network as an example. The routing tables within the Internet have been growing as fast as the Internet itself. This growth has caused an overwhelming utilization of the Internet's routers' processing power and memory utilization, consequently resulting in saturation.

Between 1988 and 1991, the Internet's routing tables doubled in size every 10 months. This growth would have resulted in about 80,000 routes by 1995. Routers would have required approximately 25MB of dedicated RAM in order to keep track of them all, and this is just for a router with a single peer. Through the implementation of CIDR, the actual number of routes in 1996 was around 42,000.

The major benefit of CIDR is that it enables continuous, uninterrupted growth of large networks. CIDR enables routers to group routes to cut down on the quantity of routing information carried by a network's routers. With CIDR, several IP networks appear to networks outside the group as a single, larger entity. CIDR eliminates the concept of class A, B, and C networks and replaces this with a generalized "IP prefix."

Some of the benefits of using CIDR within your network are as follows:

- Reduces the local administrative burden of updating external route information
- Saves routing table space in routers by using route aggregation
- Reduces route flapping and convergence issues
- Reduces CPU and memory load on a router
- Enables the delegation of "network numbers" to customers or other portions of the network
- Increased efficiency in the use of available address space

What Do Those /16s and /24s Mean?

/16 and /24 refer to the number of bits of the network part of the IP address. A former class B address might appear as 172.24.0.0/16, which is the same as 256 class Cs, which can appear as `192.200.0.0/16`. A single class C appears as `192.201.1.0/24` when using CIDR. This new "look" to IP addresses consists of an IP address and a mask length. A mask length is often called an "IP prefix." The mask length specifies the number of left-most contiguous significant bits in the corresponding IP address.

For example, the CIDRized IP address of `172.24.0.0/16` indicates you are using `172.24.0.0 255.255.0.0`. The /16 is an indication that you are using 16 bits of the mask when counting from the far left. Figure 2-8 demonstrates an excellent example of how CIDR defines its mask.

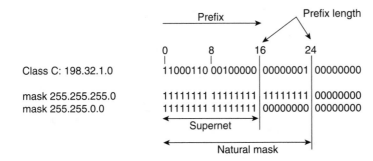

Figure 2–8
An example of CIDR addressing.

Important CIDR Terms

A network is called a *supernet* when the IP prefix contains fewer bits than the network's natural mask. For example, the class C address `200.34.5.0` has a *natural* mask of `255.255.255.0`. This address can also be represented in CIDR terms as `200.34.0.0/16`. Therefore, because the natural mask is 24 bits and the CIDR mask is 16 bits (16 < 24), this network is referred to as a *supernet*. Simply put, supernets have an IP prefix shorter than the natural mask.

This enables the more specific contiguous networks—such as `200.34.5.0`, `200.34.6.0`, and `200.34.7.0`—to be summarized into the one CIDR advertisement, which is referred to as an *aggregate*. Simply put, aggregates indicate any summary route. Figure 2-9 demonstrates how CIDR can be used to benefit your network by reducing routing tables.

Figure 2–9
*An example of
CIDR benefits
on routing
tables.*

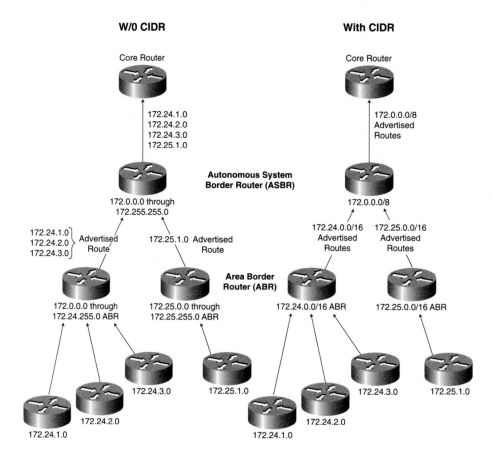

IP Classless

Use ip classless in your routers and use a default route inside your Autonomous System (AS). The ip classless command prevents the existence of a single "subnet" route from blocking access via the default route to other subnets.

CIDR Translation Table

Table 2-5 provides you with some basic CIDR information already laid out.

Table 2-5   *CIDR Translation Table*

CIDR Prefix	Dotted Decimal	Inverse Dotted Decimal
/1	128.0.0.0	127.255.255.255
/2	192.0.0.0	63.255.255.255
/3	224.0.0.0	31.255.255.255
/4	240.0.0.0	15.255.255.255
/5	248.0.0.0	7.255.255.255
/6	252.0.0.0	3.255.255.255
/7	254.0.0.0	1.255.255.255
/8	255.0.0.0	0.255.255.255
/9	255.128.0.0	0.127.255.255
/10	255.192.0.0	0.63.255.255
/11	255.224.0.0	0.31.255.255
/12	255.240.0.0	0.15.255.255
/13	255.248.0.0	0.7.255.255
/14	255.252.0.0	0.3.255.255
/15	255.254.0.0	0.1.255.255
/16	255.255.0.0	0.0.255.255
/17	255.255.128.0	0.0.127.255
/18	255.255.192.0	0.0.63.255
/19	255.255.224.0	0.0.31.255
/20	255.255.240.0	0.0.15.255
/21	255.255.248.0	0.0.7.255
/22	255.255.252.0	0.0.3.255
/23	255.255.254.0	0.0.1.255

Table 2-5   *CIDR Translation Table, continued.*

CIDR Prefix	Dotted Decimal	Inverse Dotted Decimal
/24	255.255.255.0	0.0.0.255
/25	255.255.255.128	0.0.0.127
/26	255.255.255.192	0.0.0.63
/27	255.255.255.224	0.0.0.31
/28	255.255.255.240	0.0.0.15
/29	255.255.255.248	0.0.0.7
/30	255.255.255.252	0.0.0.3
/31	255.255.255.254	0.0.0.1
/32	255.255.255.255	0.0.0.0

Manually Computing the Value of a CIDR IP Prefix

If you manually wanted to compute the CIDR IP prefix, then refer to the following (in which a subnet that is five bits long is used).

Example: `166.38.0.0/19`

1. The four octets represent 32 bits.

2. This example is using only 19 bits.

3. The first two octets use 16 bits. The third octet uses only three bits. There are five remaining bits that were not used:

128	64	32	16	8	4	2	1
x	x	x	1	1	1	1	1

4. Add the remaining five bits using the binary conversion. 16+8+4+2+1=31

5. Add 31 to the octet where the value was computed from (0+31=31)

6. The final output of this CIDR block is `166.38.0.0-166.38.31.0`.

INTERNETWORK COMPONENTS

This section discusses some of the actual physical components that make use of the theories previously discussed: OSI model, IP addresses, subnet masks, routing, and so forth. There will be a bit more theory as the basic assumptions or common definitions many people have for the following terms and conditions are discussed. These definitions are based upon Cisco's Internetworking Terms and Acronyms. In some cases, their definitions have been expanded to help readers of all knowledge levels better understand and grasp their place in a network.

Networks

A *network* is defined as a collection of computers, printers, routers, switches, and other devices that are able to communicate with each other over some transmission medium, such as Frame Relay, ISDN, or ATM.

Bridges

A *bridge* is a device that connects and passes packets between two network segments that use the same communications protocol. Bridges operate at the Data Link layer (Layer 2) of the OSI reference model. In general, a bridge will filter, forward, or flood an incoming frame based on the MAC address of that frame.

Gateways

In the IP community, a *gateway* was an older term used to refer to a routing device. Today, the term *router* is used to describe nodes that perform this function, and *gateway* refers to a special-purpose device that performs an Application layer conversion of information from one protocol stack to another.

Hubs

Hubs are devices that contain multiple independent, but connected, modules of network and internetwork equipment. Hubs can be active (where they repeat signals sent through them) or passive (where they do not repeat, but merely split, signals sent through them).

Switches

Switch is the general term applied to an electronic or mechanical device that enables a connection to be established as necessary and terminated when there is no longer a session to support. Switches are network devices that filter, forward, and flood frames based on the destination address of each frame. The switch operates at the Data Link layer of the OSI model.

LAN Switches

LAN switches are high-speed switches that forward packets between data-link segments. Most LAN switches forward traffic based on MAC addresses. This variety of LAN switch is sometimes called a frame switch. LAN switches are often categorized according to the method they use to forward traffic: cut-through packet switching or store-and-forward packet switching. Multilayer switches are an intelligent subset of LAN switches.

NOTES

One of the more interesting advances in switching technology has been the recent addition of OSPF to switches. Many of today's newer switches actually have the power of the OSPF protocol included within them. This makes for a very powerful combination and makes us wonder: What will happen to routers in the years to come?

Packet Switches

Packet switches are WAN devices that route packets along the most efficient path and enable a communications channel to be shared by multiple connections. Sometimes a packet switch is referred to as a packet switch node (PSN).

CSU

A *channel service unit* (CSU) is a digital interface device that connects end-user equipment to the local digital telephone loop. Often referred to with DSU as CSU/DSU. See also DSU.

DSU

A *data service unit* (DSU) is a device used in digital transmission that adapts the physical interface on a DTE device to a transmission facility such as T1 or E1. The DSU is also responsible for functions such as signal timing. Often referred to with CSU as CSU/DSU. See also CSU.

Router

A *router* is a network layer device that uses one or more metrics to determine the optimal path along which network traffic should be forwarded. Routers forward packets from one network to another based on network layer information. They are occasionally called gateways (although this definition of gateway is becoming increasingly outdated). Compare with gateway.

Routing

Routing is the process of finding a path to a destination host. Routing is very complex in large networks because of the many potential intermediate destinations a packet might traverse before reaching its destination host.

Component Interaction with the OSI Model

The only layers of the OSI model you are concerned with are Layers 1, 2, and 3.

Layer 1 (Physical layer) is the hardware layer that deals strictly with the electrical interfaces between devices, the format of the bit stream, and so forth.

Layer 2 (Data Link layer) interfaces between the hardware and the software and provides error correction. From a TCP/IP view, the Data Link layer is made up of the MAC (Media Access Control) layer.

Layer 3 (Network layer) and below are responsible for the establishment, maintenance, and termination of connections.

For purposes here, these are the only layers you are concerned with when discussing how the various network components interact with the OSI model. The other upper layers are only concerned with the payload that needs to be delivered. To put it another way, Layer 1 is the electrical interface, and Layer 2 is the layer in which software of the device talks to the next device on the LAN or WAN (not the hub which really is part of Layer 1). Layer 2 is also where bridges work. To a bridge, everything above Layer 2 is its payload, and it doesn't care about anything else—it just provides bridging to everything above Layer 2. Layer 3 is the Network layer. In this example, it is where routing of setting up sessions and connections occurs. However, this is not done by the routing protocol, which is independent of all this. The routing protocol really is more like an application whose data is used in the actual routing process.

The examples that follow assume a lot of things (protocol-wise) have already occurred with which the reader need not be concerned for the purposes of this discussion. Let's look at a connection end to end:

The scenario is Host A on LAN A wants to talk to Host B on LAN B.

Figure 2–10
OSI component interaction.

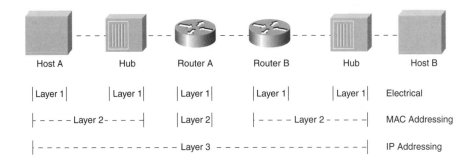

As you can see from Figure 2-10, the layers terminate in different places. The Layer 1 parts are not very important; you need only to note that they are there.

The Layer 2 and 3 parts concern you the most. When a host wants to talk to another host and they are not on the same logical IP network, the host establishes a Layer 2 session between its MAC address and the MAC address of the router. The host passes its Layer 3 packet to the router. The router looks at it, determines where it needs to send it next, and passes it on to the next device, establishing a Layer 2 session with it. This process continues until the packet is received by Host B, who sends back an acknowledgment. The process starts over, but in the reverse direction. These sessions stay up until the host ends the conversation or there is some kind of unrecoverable error.

To put it another way, at Layer 2, Host A only talks to Router A; but at Layer 3, Host A is talking to Host B. To understand what a bridge does, replace the hub (in the figure) with a bridge. The Layer 2 session terminates at the bridge, and there will be a lot more Layer 1 sessions.

The most interesting thing about the preceding scenario is that in establishing the various sessions, the routing protocol never came into play because the routing protocol has nothing to do with setting up a session. The routing protocol keeps tables of where to send the routed packet next, and it always hands the packet off to the next device to decide what to do with the packet next. OSPF might confuse this a little because it does interact with other layers, but it still hands the packet off to the next device to decide what to do next.

UNDERSTANDING ROUTER SUBINTERFACES

One of the most difficult concepts to understand is the difference between point-to-point and multipoint interfaces on a router. This section will briefly discuss the different scenarios regarding the use of each.

A router's two different types of subinterfaces provide a flexible solution for routing various protocols over partially meshed networks. A single, physical interface can be logically divided into multiple, virtual subinterfaces. The subinterface might be defined as either a point-to-point connection or a multipoint connection.

The concept of subinterfaces was originally created to better handle issues caused by split horizon over nonbroadcast multiaccess (NBMA) networks (such as Frame Relay and X.25) and distance-vector based routing protocols (such as IPX, RIP/SAP, and AppleTalk).

Split horizon dictates that a routing update received on an interface cannot be retransmitted out onto the same interface. This rule holds even if the routing update was received on one Frame Relay PVC and destined to retransmit out onto another Frame Relay PVC. Assuming a Frame Relay setup of sites A, B, and C, this would mean that sites B and C can exchange routing information with site A, but would not be able to exchange routing information with each other. Split horizon does not allow Site A to send routing updates received from Site B on to Site C, and vice versa.

TIPS

For TCP/IP, Cisco routers can disable split horizon limitations on all Frame Relay interfaces and multipoint subinterfaces and can do this by default. However, split horizon cannot be disabled for other protocols, such as IPX and AppleTalk. These other protocols must use subinterfaces if dynamic routing is desired.

Point-to-Point Subinterfaces

By dividing the partially meshed Frame Relay network into a number of virtual, point-to-point networks using subinterfaces, the split horizon problem can be overcome. Each new point-to-point subnetwork is assigned its own network number. To the routed protocol, each subnetwork now appears to be located on separate interfaces. Routing updates received from Site B on one logical point-to-point subinterface can be forwarded to site C on a separate logical interface without violating split horizon.

Multipoint Subinterfaces

Cisco serial interfaces are multipoint interfaces by default unless specified as a point-to-point subinterface. Though less common than point-to-point subinterfaces, it is possible to divide the interface into separate virtual multipoint subinterfaces.

Multipoint interfaces/subinterfaces are still subject to the split horizon limitations, as discussed previously. All nodes attached to a multipoint subinterface belong to the same network number. Typically, multipoint subinterfaces are used in conjunction with point-to-point interfaces in cases in which an existing multipoint Frame Relay cloud is migrating to a subinterfaced point-to-point network design. A multipoint subinterface is used to keep remote sites on a single network number while slowly migrating remote sites to their own point-to-point subinterface network. Eventually, all remote sites can be moved to their own point-to-point subinterface networks and the multipoint subinterface will not be necessary.

NETWORK PROTOCOLS

The OSI model as discussed in Chapter 1, "Foundations of Networking," was shown to be a framework for communication but was not to be itself a method of communication in the sense that the model could pass data. The actual communication between two devices, whether they are hosts or routers, is implemented by a protocol.

A protocol is a formal description (documented in RFCs) of a set of rules and conventions that govern how devices on a network exchange information. There are two basic types of protocols that will be discussed, and although there are others, they are beyond the scope of this book. If you are interested in reading on these other protocols, please refer to the bibliography, as many of the books referenced there cover multiple protocols in more depth. The two basic types of protocols that should concern you for the purposes of this chapter are as follows:

- **Rout*ed* Protocols:** Protocols that can be routed by a router. A router must be able to interpret the logical network as specified by the rout*ed* protocol for them to operate properly. Examples of rout*ed* protocols include AppleTalk, DECnet, and IP.

- **Rout*ing* Protocols:** Protocols that accomplish routing with a routing algorithm. A rout*ing* protocol supports a rout*ed* protocol and is used to maintain routing tables. Examples of rout*ing* protocols include OSPF, IGRP, and RIP.

You now know why a protocol is needed and what a protocol actually is. You have also determined the difference between the two main types of internetworking protocols, rout*ed* and rout*ing*.

TCP/IP Protocol Suite

Knowing that a protocol is a set of rules and conventions that govern how devices on a network exchange information, this section discusses one of the more commonly used protocol suites, TCP/IP. This discussion will not provide the reader with the amount of information he would need if doing an in-depth study of TCP/IP. Nevertheless, TCP/IP needs to be covered to some degree for the reader to better understand the overall operation of network protocols as the discussions expand in later chapters concerning OSPF.

The TCP/IP protocol suite is also referred to as a stack, and it is one of the most widely implemented internetworking standards in use today. The term *TCP/IP* literally means Transmission Control Protocol/Internet Protocol. TCP and IP are the two core protocols found within the TCP/IP protocol suite, and their place in the IP protocol stack is clarified in the following paragraphs.

TCP/IP was originally developed for ARPANET, a U.S. Government packet switched WAN, over twenty-five years ago. Although at the time this was a private network and a protocol was designed specifically for use within it, TCP/IP has since grown in popularity and is one of the most open protocols available for use in networks today. This growth and popularity is primarily due to TCP/IP's capability to connect different networks regardless of their physical environments. This has made TCP/IP today's de facto standard.

Because TCP/IP was developed long before the OSI model, it is not 100 percent compatible with the OSI model. However, TCP/IP can run over OSI-compliant lower layers, such as the Data Link and Physical layers of the OSI model. TCP/IP can communicate at the Network layer as well using IP.

TCP is the main transport layer protocol that offers connection-oriented transport services. TCP accepts messages from upper-layer protocols and provides the messages with an acknowledged reliable connection-oriented transport service to the TCP layer of a remote device. TCP provides five important functions within the TCP/IP protocol suite:

- Provides format of the data and acknowledgements that two computers exchange to achieve a reliable transfer

- Ensures that data arrives correctly

- Distinguishes between multiple destinations on a given machine

- Explains how to recover from errors

- Explains how a data stream transfer is initiated and when it is complete

IP is the main network layer protocol that offers unreliable connectionless service because it depends on TCP to detect and recover from lost packets. IP provides three important functions within the TCP/IP protocol suite:

- IP defines the basic format and specifications of all data transfer used throughout the protocol suite

- IP performs the routing function by choosing a path to the required destination over which data will be sent

- IP includes the rules mentioned previously, as well as those covering unreliable packet delivery. Essentially, these rules cover how packets should be processed, what error message parameters are, and when a packet should be discarded

TCP/IP Packets

The term *datagram* describes a unit of data at the TCP layer. At the IP layer, it is called a *packet*, and at the lower layers, it is called a *frame*.

If a message is too large for the underlying network, it is up to the IP layer to fragment the datagram into smaller parts.

Different paths might be available through the Internet, between a source and a destination station. Fragments of a datagram might take different paths through a network.

So, when messages arrive at the destination station, the IP protocol stack must sequence them and reassemble them into their original datagram.

Each datagram or fragment is given an IP header and is transmitted as a frame by the lower layers.

NOTES

In addition to the two IP layer protocols (IP and ICMP) and the two TCP layer protocols (TCP and UDP), the TCP/IP suite includes a cluster of protocols that operate at the upper layers, such as FTP, Telnet, and so forth.

Some of these are TCP/IP-specific, and some are protocols that can run with TCP/IP but originated elsewhere. However, any discussion on them is beyond the scope and purpose of this book.

Common TCP/IP Routing Protocol Characteristics

This section will briefly describe the two most common and relevant—to this book—routing protocols that TCP/IP has available for use—RIP and OSPF. A more thorough discussion of these routing protocols will be provided in Chapter 3, "Understanding & Selecting Networking Protocols," and throughout other parts of this book.

RIP (Routing Information Protocol) Characteristics

RIP is a distance vector protocol designed at Berkeley in the late 1960s that is still widely deployed today, in which the router only exchanges routing information from the connected neighbors.

- RIP broadcasts every 30 seconds to maintain network integrity

- RIP maintains routing tables, showing the number of hops between routers

- A router using RIP passes its entire routing table to each router it knows of

OSPF (Open Shortest Path First) Characteristics

OSPF is a link state protocol in which all routers in the routing domain exchange information and thus know about the complete topology of the network. Because each router knows the complete topology of the network, the use of the shortest path first algorithm creates an extremely fast convergence.

- Provides routing information to the IP section of the TCP/IP protocol suite. The most commonly used alternative to RIP.

- If this routing protocol is in use, updates to tables only, instead of whole tables, are sent to routers.

- Because it involves less network traffic, OSPF is a more economical routing protocol than RIP.

Basic Protocol Operations

A routed protocol such as IP is used as the method of communication between devices on a network. Using a selected routing protocol, such as OSPF, which is supported by the routed protocol, such as IP, you can build the network so that every device can communicate. For example, as mentioned previously, IP is a routed protocol that can use either OSPF or RIP as its routing protocol.

The routing protocol used builds routing tables that tell the router the optimal path to a destination. Routers compare metrics (measurements based upon path characteristics) to determine the optimal path, which is then stored in a routing table. Each routing protocol has an algorithm that it uses as a basis for its calculations, which might lead you to ask: Why is an algorithm needed?

Consider an example of a router that is initially configured with two networks to which it is directly connected. The router will have only these two networks in its routing tables. However, because there are other networks beyond the initial two, they are not entered into the routing table because they are not directly connected to the router. Then how are these other networks recognized by the router? Simply put, there are three ways in which this can be accomplished:

- **Static routing.** Manually defined within the router as the only path to a given destination. This type of routing forces the destination within routing tables. This type of routing also take precedence over routes chosen by dynamic routing protocols.

- **Default routing.** Manually defined within the router as the path to take when no route to the destination needed is known. The router to which this information is sent is also known as the router of last resort.

- **Dynamic routing.** Uses routing algorithms that analyze incoming routing update messages from one or more routing protocols to determine the optimal path to a destination. This type of routing has the greatest advantage in that routing automatically adapts to a change in the network's topology.

TIPS

Static routes are generally unsuitable for today's large, constantly changing networks and should be limited to routers that can only be reached through one link.

Overall, dynamic routing is the most commonly used method of routing. Associated with this type of routing are several terms and characteristics that assist in defining how it is to operate.

It is fundamental to dynamic routing that the routing table consistently reflects accurate and up-to-date information concerning the network topology. The amount of time it takes for changes to be reflected in every network router's routing table is known as *convergence*.

Convergence is defined as the speed and capability of a group of internetworking devices (such as routers) running a routing protocol to agree on the new topology of an internetwork after a change occurs in the existing topology.

Having a routing protocol with a fast convergence time is very desirable because disruption of routing can occur during the time a router spends calculating the new optimal path.

CHAPTER SUMMARY

This chapter discussed routing fundamentals within a network, whether to the Internet or an intranet. All networks require a certain amount of "common" information with which to operate. Chapter 1 discussed many of the more common physical topologies and how the OSI model was used as a template for network communications. This chapter built on that overlay through the discussion of IP addressing, network protocols, and routing components. These three topics have built a foundation of basic networking and routing fundamentals.

The section "IP Addressing" provided an overview of how addresses are classified. You were also familiarized with several commonly used techniques to help better manage your IP addresses: subnet masking, variable length subnet masking (VLSM), and classless interdomain routing (CIDR).

The section "Routing Components" defined and listed the use, function, and purpose of the actual equipment needed to make a network operate. You also learned about some of the more commonly used terms within this environment.

The final section of this chapter, "Network Protocols," emphasized the difference between routed and routing protocols. This section also briefly discussed some of the more important characteristics and background of the TCP/IP protocol stack.

With this information and understanding, Chapter 3 will move on to cover how to understand and select a network protocol, with an emphasis on OSPF.

CASE STUDY: WHERE IS THE NETWORK BROKEN?

You can acquire a variety of useful information when designing a good network. When implementing or troubleshooting, there are many factors that can affect the network. This case study will briefly discuss some of the techniques that you can use to ensure that during the many phases of network development, you have the tools necessary to troubleshoot any problems in a network, such as that illustrated in Figure 2-11.

Figure 2–11
Where is the network broken?

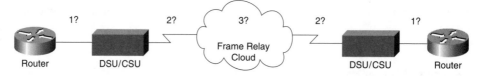

Where is the network broken?

After a Frame Relay line has been properly provisioned by the provider, the installation of a Frame Relay network using Cisco routers is usually a trouble-free task involving minimal configuration. However, if problems arise in a Frame Relay network, proven techniques can be applied to help isolate and solve them. Troubleshooting a Frame Relay network problem can be broken down into four easy steps:

1. Verify the physical connection exists between the DSU/CSU and the router.

2. Verify that the router and Frame Relay provider are properly exchanging LMI.

3. Verify that the PVC status is active.

4. Verify that the Frame Relay encapsulation matches on both routers.

Cisco routers offer extensive diagnostic tools to assist in the previous tasks. However, most Frame Relay problems can be diagnosed by using the following simple commands:

- `show interface`
- `show frame-relay lmi`
- `show frame-relay pvc`

Verifying the Physical Connection
Between the DSU/CSU and the Router

Above all else, a good physical connection must exist between the router and the local DSU/CSU. You can use the show interface command to determine the status of the physical connection. Figure 2-12 is a sample output of a show interface serial1 command.

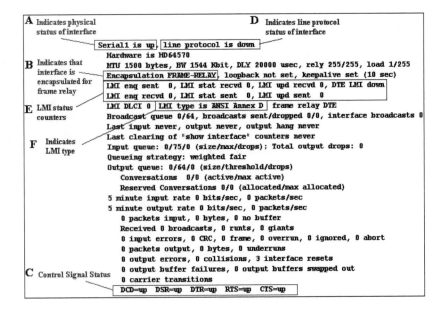

A Indicates physical status of interface

D Indicates line protocol status of interface

B Indicates that interface is encapsulated for frame relay

E LMI status counters

F Indicates LMI type

C Control Signal Status

```
Serial1 is up, line protocol is down
Hardware is HD64570
MTU 1500 bytes, BW 1544 Kbit, DLY 20000 usec, rely 255/255, load 1/255
Encapsulation FRAME-RELAY, loopback not set, keepalive set (10 sec)
LMI enq sent  0, LMI stat recvd 0, LMI upd recvd 0, DTE LMI down
LMI enq recvd 0, LMI stat sent  0, LMI upd sent  0
LMI DLCI 0  LMI type is ANSI Annex D  frame relay DTE
Broadcast queue 0/64, broadcasts sent/dropped 0/0, interface broadcasts 0
Last input never, output never, output hang never
Last clearing of "show interface" counters never
Input queue: 0/75/0 (size/max/drops); Total output drops: 0
Queueing strategy: weighted fair
Output queue: 0/64/0 (size/threshold/drops)
    Conversations  0/0 (active/max active)
    Reserved Conversations 0/0 (allocated/max allocated)
5 minute input rate 0 bits/sec, 0 packets/sec
5 minute output rate 0 bits/sec, 0 packets/sec
    0 packets input, 0 bytes, 0 no buffer
    Received 0 broadcasts, 0 runts, 0 giants
    0 input errors, 0 CRC, 0 frame, 0 overrun, 0 ignored, 0 abort
    0 packets output, 0 bytes, 0 underruns
    0 output errors, 0 collisions, 3 interface resets
    0 output buffer failures, 0 output buffers swapped out
    0 carrier transitions
DCD=up  DSR=up  DTR=up  RTS=up  CTS=up
```

Figure 2–12
Show interface serial1 output.

Referring to Figure 2-12, the field marked with an "A" indicates the physical status of the interface. An interface can be in one of three possible states: up, down, or administratively down. The following sections outline the possible states and offer some suggested actions to correct physical connection problems.

Interface State: Serial x Is Up

If serial x is up, this is an indication that the interface has a good connection to the DSU/CSU. Proceed to Step 2 and verify that the router and Frame Relay provider are properly exchanging LMI.

Interface State: Serial x Is Administratively Down

If serial x is administratively down, this is an indication that the interface is in shutdown mode. The following commands are used to take an interface out of shutdown:

- `Router# config term`
- `Router(config)# interface serial x`
- `Router(config-if)# no shutdown`
- `Router(config-if)# exit`

Interface State: Serial x Is Down

If serial x is down, this is an indication of a poor physical connection to the DSU/CSU. The router is not receiving all of the control signals from the DSU/CSU. The `show interface` command will display which control signals are missing (see field C in Figure 3-7). A missing signal will be indicated with a "down" state (such as `DCD=down`).

To correct this problem, you can take the following actions:

- Verify that the cable is securely inserted into the serial interface on the router.
- Verify that the cable is securely inserted into the DSU/CSU DTE port.
- The DSU/CSU might need to be configured to properly assert the control signals (DSR, RTS, and DCD). With some DSU/CSUs, DSR needs to be set to properly reflect DCD. This will vary, depending on DSU/CSU manufacturers. Check the DSU/CSU documentation.
- The cable's, router's, or DSU/CSU's serial port might not be functional. If possible, first try moving the cable and configuration to an unused serial port on the router. This will isolate the problem to or away from a faulty router port. Next, try swapping the serial cable. This will isolate the problem to or away from a cable issue. Finally, try swapping out the DSU/CSU.

Verifying That the Router and Frame Relay Provider Are Properly Exchanging LMI

After a good physical connection has been established between the router and the local DSU/CSU, the next goal is to verify that the line protocol is up between the router and the Frame Relay provider. For a Frame Relay network, the line protocol is the periodic exchange of local management interface (LMI) packets between the router and the

Frame Relay provider. The first line of the show interface command will indicate if line protocol is up or down (see field D in Figure 3-7), indicating whether LMI is properly exchanging or not. The following sections outline the possible line protocol states and offer some suggestions to correct line protocol problems.

Line Protocol State: Line Protocol Is Up

If the line protocol is up, this is an indication that Frame Relay LMI is properly exchanging between the router and the Frame Relay provider. At this point, you should proceed to Step 3 and verify that the PVC status is active.

Line Protocol State: Line Protocol Is Down

If the line protocol is down, this is an indication that LMI is not properly exchanging between the router and the Frame Relay provider. To correct this problem, you can take the following actions:

- Verify that the router's LMI type matches the LMI type used by the Frame Relay provider
- Verify that the router is sending LMI packets to the Frame Relay provider
- Verify that DSU/CSU parameters are properly configured
- Verify that the Frame Relay provider has turned on the circuit

These solutions are covered in greater depth in the sections that follow.

Verifying That the Router's LMI Type
Matches the LMI Type Used by the Frame Relay Provider

The only parameter that can be configured on the router that relates to the line protocol is the LMI type. After the router is configured with the proper LMI type, all other line protocol problems depend on the DSU/CSU settings or carrier provisioning. The router's LMI type can be verified with either the show interface command (see the field marked F in Figure 2-12) or the show frame-relay lmi command (see the field marked A in Figure 2-13).

If the Frame Relay provider is using "ANSI Annex-D" LMI, configure the router to use frame-relay lmi-type ansi. Also, be aware that Frame Relay providers often generically refer to lmi-type cisco as simply LMI. If the frame provider states that it is using LMI type LMI, make sure the router is configured to use frame-relay lmi-type cisco.

Verifying That the Router Is Sending
LMI Packets to the Frame Relay Provider

This procedure is a sanity check to make sure the router is doing its half of the LMI exchange. Use either the show interface command (see field E in Figure 3-7) or the show frame-relay lmi (see fields B and C in Figure 2-13) repetitively to determine whether the router is sending LMI packets to the Frame Relay switch.

Figure 2–13
The show
frame-relay
lmi output.

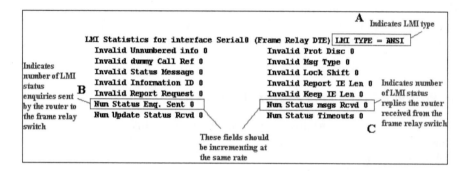

The "Num Status Enq. sent" counter will increment every ten seconds if the router is attempting to send LMI packets. If this counter is not incrementing, re-verify physical connections and make sure the interface is not in shutdown. Alternatively, the debug frame-relay lmi command can be used to actively monitor the exchange of LMI packets.

The Num Status Enq. sent counter will increment at the same rate as the Num Status msgs. Rcvd counter if the router is successfully exchanging LMI with the Frame Relay switch.

Verifying That DSU/CSU Parameters Are Properly Configured

The successful exchange of LMI packets between the Frame Relay switch and the router relies upon the successful delivery of frames by the DSU/CSU. The router might be sending LMI packets (in which case you should refer to the operations outlined in the two preceding sections), but this is meaningless if the DSU/CSU is not correctly forwarding these frames onto the Frame Relay switch. There are three main parameters that MUST be correctly configured on the DSU/CSU: clocking, framing, and line encoding. The Frame Relay provider supplies the following information:

- **Clocking.** The clock source can either be internally generated by the DSU/CSU or supplied by the Frame Relay provider. For Frame Relay networks, the DSU/CSU normally gets its clocking from the network (that is, frame provider). Check with the Frame Relay provider about the clock source and configure the DSU/CSU accordingly.

- **Framing.** A DSU/CSU can be configured to frame data either in extended super frame (ESF) format or super frame (D4 framing) format. Ask the Frame Relay provider which data framing they are using and configure the DSU/CSU accordingly.

- **Line encoding.** A DSU/CSU can be configured to use alternate mark inversion (AMI), encoding, or binary eight zero substitution (B8ZS) encoding. Usually, AMI is associated with D4 framing, and B8ZS is associated with ESF framing. Check which type of line is used for encoding the Frame Relay provider is using and configure the DSU/CSU accordingly.

Verifying That the Frame Relay Provider Has Turned the Circuit On

If none of the three preceding troubleshooting operations work, it could be that the telco has yet to turn on the Frame Relay circuit. Use the `debug frame-relay lmi` command to display whether the router is receiving LMI responses from the Frame Relay switch or not. Double-check with the Frame Relay provider to make sure that the circuit has been activated.

Verifying That the PVC Status Is Active

After the interface is up and the line protocol is up, the next step is to verify that the PVC status is active. To view the status of PVCs on the router, use the `show frame-relay pvc` command. Figure 2-14 displays a sample output of the `show frame-relay pvc` command.

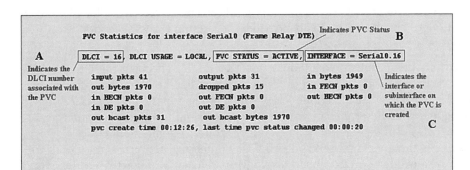

Figure 2–14
The show
frame-relay
pvc output.

The show `frame-relay pvc` command indicates that the PVC is in one of three different states (see field "B" in Figure 3-9). The sections that follow outline the possible PVC states and offer some suggested actions to correct PVC problems.

PVC Status: Active

If the PVC status is active, a permanent virtual circuit (PVC) has been created. The Frame Relay link between the two sites is up. You can proceed to Step 4 and verify that the Frame Relay encapsulation matches on both routers.

PVC Status: Inactive

If the PVC status is inactive, the PVC associated with the corresponding DLCI number (see Field A in Figure 2-14) is being offered by the Frame Relay provider but not being used by the router.

To correct this problem, you should begin by verifying DLCI numbering. Double-check the DLCI numbering with the Frame Relay provider and make certain that the router is configured with the DLCI numbering that the Frame Relay provider has supplied. The DLCI numbers are configured with either the `frame-relay map` command for multipoint interfaces or the `frame-relay interface-dlci` command for point-to-point subinterfaces. A common mistake is the accidental reversal of DLCI numbering between sites. For instance, if the DLCI number that is supposedly assigned to the remote site shows up as "inactive" at the local site, there is a good chance that the DLCI numbers are reversed.

PVC Status: Deleted

If the PVC status is "deleted," the router has been configured with a DLCI number that is not offered by the Frame Relay provider. As a result, the PVC cannot be created and therefore is "deleted."

To correct this problem, you should begin by double-checking the DLCI numbering with the Frame Relay provider and making certain that the router is configured with the DLCI numbering that the Frame Relay provider has supplied. The DLCI numbers are configured with either the `frame-relay map` command for multipoint interfaces or the `frame-relay interface-dlci` command for point-to-point subinterfaces. A common mistake is the accidental reversal of DLCI numbering between sites. Check to see if there are any other DLCI numbers showing up as inactive. If inactive entries exist, there is a good chance that the correct DLCI number should be the DLCI number that is showing up as inactive. Check with the Frame Relay provider to be certain!

Another tactic to employ is to verify that the Frame Relay provider has activated the PVC. There is a possibility that the Frame Relay provider has not yet activated the PVC. Check with the Frame Relay provider to verify that the PVC has been activated.

Verifying That the Frame Relay Encapsulation Matches on Both Routers

Finally, if all three of the previous steps have not solved the Frame Relay problem, the problem might be related to Frame Relay encapsulation. Cisco routers default to "cisco" Frame Relay encapsulation. "cisco" Frame Relay encapsulation is only valid between other Cisco routers that are using "cisco" Frame Relay encapsulation. If connecting to a third-party router, the Frame Relay encapsulation must be changed from "cisco" to "IETF". To configure IETF Frame Relay encapsulation, replace the "encapsulation frame-relay" command with "encapsulation frame-relay IETF". Most Frame Relay problems can be solved by following the steps outlined in this case study.

FREQUENTLY ASKED QUESTIONS (FAQS)

Q— *What is the difference between classful and classless routing protocols?*

A— Classful protocols, such as RIP and IGRP, consider the IP network class (A, B, C . . . and their default masks) when doing route summarization. Whereas, with classless protocols, such as OSPF, several networks can appear as a single larger network to those outside the network in question when using aggregation.

Q— *Are routing updates sent out on links that are defined only by static routes?*

A— No routing updates are sent. The thought behind this routing characteristic is as follows: Because this route has been manually configured by the user, updates are not needed, so you can conserve bandwidth by not sending updates out the link. Dynamic and static routing can be used together; they are mutually exclusive.

For example, with OSPF, you can learn the route:

```
O 171.69.0.0/16 interface e 0 via 1.1.1.1
```

You can also add a static route with various administrative distances applied to them—for example:

```
ip route 123.0.0.0 255.0.0.0 e 0 1.1.1.1
ip route 171.69.0.0 255.255.0.0 bri 0 200
```

Then you will have the following entries in your routing table:

```
O 171.69.0.0/16 interface e 0 via 1.1.1.1
S 123.0.0.0/8 interface e 0 via 1.1.1.1
```

In this case, you will still have an OSPF update going out interface e 0, which is not affected by the static route configured. However, if then you lose the OSPF route for 171.69.0.0, the static route will come into play:

```
S 171.69.0.0/16 interface bri 0
S 123.0.0.0/8 interface e 0 via 1.1.1.1
```

And so you and have bri 0 as our backup to 171.69.0.0.

Q— *Will static routes be sent out to other routers?*

A— No, they are considered local routes only and are sent out to other routers only if you specifically tell the router to do so through the use of a redistribute static command.

3

Understanding & Selecting Network Protocols

This chapter helps you understand the basic types of protocols and uses that information to build a deeper understanding of how to implement them in your network. The main objectives in this chapter are to understand the difference between distance vector and link state protocols and to provide you with information that will assist you in selecting the correct routing protocol for your network. This chapter covers the following important objectives:

- **Routing protocols.** Fundamental portions of understanding routing protocols are discussed. All types of routing table associations are provided and discussed, as well how a protocol algorithm is designed and what determines proper operation.

- **Distance vector protocols.** What distance vector protocols are and how they operate are discussed. This information is provided in theory and then again through a practical discussion of a distance vector protocol, such as RIP.

- **Link state protocols.** The fundamentals of link state protocols are extensively discussed. A practical example is provided through the discussion of Intermediate System-Intermediate System (IS-IS), one of the more intriguing link state protocols.

- **Selecting a network protocol.** One of the most practical objectives required by all network designers is the ability to understand the importance of how to select a network protocol. This information is presented, comparing and contrasting three different routing protocols using real-world concerns.

ROUTING PROTOCOLS

Routing network traffic through the use of routing protocols within any network involves two basic activities: determining optimal routing paths and transporting data packets through your network

In this chapter, the transportation of data packets will be referred to as "switching." Switching is relatively straightforward. Routing path determination, on the other hand, can be very complex.

Routing Concepts

Routing path determination may be based on a variety of metrics or a combination of different metrics. Software implementations of routing algorithms calculate route metrics to determine the optimal routes to a destination.

To aid in the process of path determination, routing algorithms initialize and maintain routing tables, which contain route information. Route information varies, depending on the routing algorithm used. There are three primary ways of building these routing tables, which are referred to as associations: destination/next hop associations, destination/metric associations, and destination/path associations.

Destination/Next Hop Associations

Some routing algorithms fill routing tables with destination/next hop associations. These associations tell a router that a particular "destination" can be gained optimally by sending the packet to the node identified in "next hop." For example, Router A knows that to get to Router C, the destination, the next hop is through Router B.

Destination/Metric Associations

Other algorithms provide destination/metric associations. These associations tell a router that a particular "destination" is some "metric" (sometimes referred to as "distance") away. The router compares metrics to determine optimal routes. Metrics differ depending on the design of the routing algorithm that is being used. The routing algorithm being used is a function of the routing protocol. For example, Router A knows that to get to Router C, the destination, the next hop is through Router B. However, the route is down, which results in an infinite metric, so the next optimal route is through the ISDN backup. This backup obviously has a lower cost than infinity, so routing is preserved.

Destination/Path Associations

Still other routing algorithms provide destination/path associations. These associations relate destinations to the path to be taken to reach a certain destination. Routers simply forward packets along this path until they reach the appropriate destination.

Routing Updates

Routers communicate with one another (and maintain their routing tables) through the transmission of a variety of messages. The routing update message is one such message. Routing updates generally consist of all or a portion of a routing table. Routing updates are the means by which routers communicate path (routes) information between each other. By using this path information from other routers, routers can determine optimal routes to various network destinations. Routing updates may be sent on a regular basis, when a network topology change affects route paths, or in both cases.

Switching Algorithms

Switching algorithms are relatively simple, and they are basically the same for many routing protocols. In most cases, switching algorithms operate as follows. A host determines that it must send a packet to another host. Having acquired a router's address, the source host sends a packet addressed specifically to a router's physical (MAC layer) address—but with the protocol (network layer/IP address) address of the destination host—via the default gateway.

Upon examining the packet's destination protocol (network layer/IP address) address, the router determines that it either knows or does not know how to forward the packet to the "next hop" or link to reach the required destination. When the router does not know where to forward the packet, the packet is dropped. When the router knows what the "next hop" is to the destination, it sends the packet to that hop. This is accomplished by changing the destination physical address (MAC layer) to that of the next hop and transmitting the packet out the appropriate interface.

The next hop might or might not be the destination host address. If it's not, the next hop is usually to another router, which executes the same switching decision process as previously described. As the packet moves through the network, its physical address changes, but its destination protocol address (IP address) remains constant.

Routing Algorithm Design Goals

Routing protocols are written and proposed in *draft* Request for Comments (RFCs). The person (or persons) writing them typically tries to maintain a clear set of goals for the new or updated protocol. Routing algorithms often have one or more of the following design goals:

- Accuracy

- Simplicity/low CPU and memory overhead

- Robustness/stability

- Rapid convergence

- Flexibility

Accuracy

Accuracy is perhaps the most general design goal, which refers to the capability of the routing algorithm to select the "best" route. The best route depends upon the metric(s) and metric weightings used to make the calculation. These metrics differ for each protocol and, as such, must be clearly defined and understood to assist in their proper deployment.

For example, one routing algorithm might use a number of hops and network delay as its metrics but might place more weight or consideration on delay during route calculation. Naturally, routing protocols must strictly define their metric calculation algorithms. In addition, these parameters must be clearly documented as they are implemented or modified. This is of course basic common sense, but this does not seem to be in common practice. The best bedtime reading for those suffering from insomnia is RFCs that cover this in great detail for every routing protocol.

Simplicity/Low Overhead

Routing algorithms are usually designed to be as simple as possible. This means that routing algorithms should offer their functionality efficiently, with a minimum of software, CPU, and memory utilization. Efficiency is particularly important when the software implementing the routing algorithm must run on a router or other device that has limited physical resources. Although some people might disagree, the fact remains that not every company can afford, or is willing to buy, the latest and greatest technology available. Nor is it always advisable to do so from a technical perspective. Routing algorithms constantly perform routing calculations and exchange routing information with other network devices. These actions, if done inefficiently, can add significant traffic to a network.

Robustness/Stability

Routing algorithms must be robust in their operation and route calculations. In other words, they must not malfunction by giving erroneous routes to a destination. The goal, of course, is to make this happen as infrequently as possible. Because routers are located at network junction points, they can cause considerable problems when they fail. The best routing algorithms are often those that have withstood the test of time and proven stable under a variety of network conditions.

Rapid Convergence

Routing algorithms must be able to converge rapidly. Convergence is the process of agreement/notification, by or to all routers, on optimal or changed routes. When a network event causes routes to either go up or down or discovers new ones, routers will distribute routing update messages. Routing update messages permeate networks, consequently stimulating recalculation by the routing algorithm of optimal routes and eventually causing all routers to agree on these routes (convergence). Routing algorithms that converge slowly can cause routing loops.

An example of a routing loop is as follows: A packet arrives at Router A at time t1. Router A has already been updated and knows that the optimal route to the destination calls for Router B to be the next hop. Router A therefore forwards the packet to Router B. Router B has not yet been updated and so believes that the optimal next hop is Router A. Router B therefore forwards the packet back to Router A. The packet will continue to bounce back and forth between the two until Router B receives its routing update or the packet is discarded because it is too old.

> **NOTES**
>
> It might help you to understand the importance of convergence if you realize that convergence is the time it takes for a change in the routing topology to be sent across the network. This can be expressed in the following formula:
>
> Total Convergence=Time to detect change+Time to propagate change to all routers+Time to calculate the new route using the change after it is received

Flexibility

Routing algorithms should also be flexible in their operation. In other words, routing algorithms need to adapt quickly and accurately to a variety of network circumstances. These circumstances can be any condition you would expect to find within a network, such as changes in routing tables, topology, connectivity, and so forth.

Suppose, for example, that a network link (circuit) such as a T1 has gone down. Many routing algorithms, upon becoming aware of this situation, will quickly select the next-best path for all routes normally using that link (circuit). Well-designed, flexible routing algorithms can be programmed to adapt to changes in network bandwidth, router buffer size, network delay, and other variables.

Routing Algorithm Types

Routing algorithms might be classified according to type. For example, algorithms might be:

- Static or dynamic
- Centralized or distributed
- Multi-path or single-path
- Flat or hierarchical
- Host-intelligent or router-intelligent
- Intradomain or interdomain
- Link state or distance vector

Static Routing Algorithms(?)

Static routing algorithms are hardly algorithms at all. Static routing table mappings are established by the network administrator before the beginning of routing. They do not change unless the network administrator changes them. Algorithms that use static routes are simple to design and work well in environments in which network traffic is relatively predictable and network design is relatively simple. However, when the network grows in complexity or its needs change, the true drawbacks of this method are seen.

Because static routing systems cannot react to network changes, they are generally considered unsuitable for today's large, constantly changing networks. Most of the dominant routing algorithms in the 1990s are dynamic.

Dynamic Routing Algorithms

Dynamic routing algorithms adjust to changing network circumstances by analyzing incoming routing update messages. If the routing update message indicates that a network change has occurred, the routing software recalculates routes and sends out new routing update messages. These messages permeate the network, stimulating routers to rerun their routing algorithms and change their routing tables to reflect information contained in the update message.

NOTES

Dynamic routing algorithms may be supplemented with static routes where appropriate. For example, a *router of last resort* (a router to which all unroutable packets are sent) may be designated by using static routes; therefore, all unknown packets would have a default next hop. This router acts as a clearinghouse for all packets with unknown destination addresses, ensuring that all packets are at least handled in some way.

Centralized and Distributed Routing Algorithms

Routing algorithms may be *centralized* or *distributed*. Centralized algorithms calculate all routing paths at one central device. This device is often called a *Routing Control Center* (RCC). The RCC periodically collects routing information from all routers and distributes optimal routing tables to them.

Centralized routing has several advantages. First, it relieves individual routers of the burden of route calculation. Second, it virtually ensures that all routing tables are the same.

Unfortunately, centralized routing also suffers from several serious flaws that have severely restricted its use. If any RCC should go down, the entire network is helpless or must, at best, rely on old routing tables. Lines leading to the RCC must have exceptionally high bandwidth because they will experience heavy utilization. Finally, depending on the size and hierarchical organization of the internetwork, routers close to the RCC may receive updated information well in advance of distant routers, creating routing loops.

Distributed algorithms calculate routing paths at each individual router. Each router periodically exchanges route information with (at a minimum) each of its neighbors. Distributed algorithms are more fault-tolerant than centralized algorithms. They also distribute update traffic over the entire network, so traffic bottlenecks are not such a serious problem. Like centralized routing, they might still generate routing loops. Overall, distributed routing algorithms are much more common than centralized routing algorithms.

Multi-Path and Single-Path Routing Algorithms

Some sophisticated routing protocols support multiple paths to the same destination. These multi-path algorithms permit traffic multiplexing over multiple lines; single-path algorithms do not. The advantages of multi-path algorithms are obvious; they can provide substantially better throughput and redundancy.

Flat and Hierarchical Routing Algorithms

Some routing algorithms operate in a flat space, and others use routing hierarchies. In a flat routing system, all routers are peers of all others. In a hierarchical routing system, some routers form what amounts to a routing backbone. Packets from non-backbone routers travel to the backbone routers, where they are sent through the backbone until they reach the general area of the destination. At this point, they travel from the last backbone router through zero or more non-backbone router(s) to the final destination.

Routing systems often designate logical groups of nodes called domains, autonomous systems, or areas. In hierarchical systems, some routers in a domain can communicate with routers in other domains; others can only communicate with routers within their domain. In very large networks, additional hierarchical levels might exist. Routers at the highest hierarchical level form the routing backbone.

TIPS

Areas are found in protocols that have a hierarchy, such as OSPF or ISIS. A (Routing) Domain is a group of routers running the same instance of Internal Gateway Protocol (IGP). Depending on the protocol, a domain may consist of one or more areas. In addition, Autonomous Systems (AS) may contain multiple domains.

The primary advantage of hierarchical routing is its capability to limit the pervasiveness of routing exchanges. Hierarchical routing limits routing exchanges because it mimics the organization of most companies and therefore supports their traffic patterns very well. Most network communication occurs within small company groups (domains).

Host-Intelligent or Router-Intelligent Routing Algorithms

Some routing algorithms assume that the source end-node will determine the entire route. This is usually referred to as *source routing*. In source routing systems, routers merely act as store-and-forward devices, mindlessly sending the packet to the next stop.

Other algorithms assume that the hosts know nothing about routes. In these algorithms, routers determine the path through the internetwork based on their own calculations.

In the first system, the hosts have the routing intelligence. In the latter system, routers have the routing intelligence.

The tradeoff between host-intelligent and router-intelligent routing is one of path optimality versus traffic overhead. Host-intelligent systems choose the better routes more often, because they typically "discover" all possible routes to the destination before the packet is actually sent. They then choose the best path based on that particular system's definition of "optimal." The act of determining all routes, however, often requires substantial "discovery" traffic and a significant amount of time.

TIPS

Source routing is not always supported due to security reasons and can impact firewall security. See the case study entitled "Increasing Security on IP Networks" which states: "If an address uses source routing, it can send and receive traffic through the firewall router. For this reason, you should always disable source routing on the firewall router with the no ip source-route command." You'll find this case study in Cisco's Documentation section on the Software and Support portion of their Web site (www.cisco.com) under Technology Information; Internetworking Case Studies.

Intradomain and Interdomain Routing Algorithms

As discussed previously, some routing algorithms work only within domains; others work within and between domains. The nature of these two algorithm types is different. It stands to reason, therefore, that an optimal *intradomain* routing algorithm would not necessarily be an optimal *interdomain* routing algorithm.

Link State and Distance Vector Routing Algorithms

Finally, much controversy surrounds the debate over link state versus distance vector routing algorithms. Link state algorithms (also known as "shortest path first" algorithms) flood routing information to all nodes in the internetwork. However, each router sends only that portion of the routing table that describes the state of its own links, as opposed to its entire routing table.

Distance vector algorithms (also known as "Bellman-Ford" algorithms) call for each router to send its entire routing table, but only to its neighbors.

In essence, link state algorithms send small updates everywhere; distance vector algorithms send large updates only to neighboring routers.

Because they create a consistent view of the internetwork, link state algorithms are somewhat less prone to routing loops than are distance vector algorithms. On the down side, link state algorithms can cause significant, widespread control traffic. They are also computationally difficult compared to distance vector algorithms, requiring more CPU power and memory than distance vector algorithms. Link state algorithms can therefore be more expensive to implement and support. Despite their differences, both algorithm types perform well in most circumstances.

Algorithm Metrics

As alluded to previously, routing tables contain information used (by switching software) to select the best route. How, specifically, are routing tables built? What is the specific nature of the information they contain? This section on algorithm metrics attempts to answer the following question: *"How do routing algorithms determine that one route is preferable to others?"*

Many different metrics have been used in routing algorithms. Sophisticated routing algorithms can base route selection on multiple metrics, combining them in a manner resulting in a single (hybrid) metric. All of the following metrics have been used:

- Reliability
- Delay
- Bandwidth
- Load
- Maximum Transfer Unit (MTU)
- Communication cost

Reliability

Reliability, in the context of routing algorithms, refers to the reliability of each network link. Some network links might go down more often than others.

After they go down, some network links can be repaired more easily or more quickly than other links. Any reliability factors can be taken into account in the assignment of reliability ratings. Reliability ratings are usually assigned to network links by network administrators. They are typically arbitrary numeric values based on factors such as circuit speed, traffic patterns, and overall network design considerations.

Delay

Routing delay refers to the length of time required to move a packet from source to destination through the internetwork. Delay depends on many factors, including the bandwidth of intermediate network links, the port queues at each router along the way, network congestion on all intermediate network links, and the physical distance to be traveled. Because it is a conglomeration of several important variables, delay is a common metric.

Bandwidth

Bandwidth refers to the available traffic capacity of a link. A 10Mbps Ethernet link, for instance, would be preferable to a 64Kbps leased line. Although bandwidth is a rating of the maximum attainable throughput on a link, routes through links with greater bandwidth do not necessarily provide better routes than routes through slower links. If, for example, a faster link is much busier, the actual time required to send a packet to the destination could be greater through the fast link.

Load

Load refers to the degree to which a network resource (such as a router interface or circuit) is busy. Load can be calculated in a variety of ways, including CPU utilization, actual/available, and packets processed per second. Monitoring these parameters on a continual basis can itself be resource intensive.

Maximum Transfer Unit (MTU)

MTU (Maximum Transfer Unit) refers to the maximum size of a packet that can traverse a particular network link. For example, an Ethernet network can handle frames as large as roughly 1.5 Kilobytes (KB). FDDI can handle frame sizes up to roughly 4KB. Token Ring networks do not specify frame size limits (practical Token Ring limits are introduced by the maximum token-hold time).

Communication Cost

Communication cost is another important metric. Some companies might not care about performance as much as they care about operating expenditures. Although line delay might be longer, they will send packets over their own lines rather than through public lines that will cost money for usage time.

DISTANCE VECTOR PROTOCOLS

This section details the type of routing protocols known as distance vector protocols. The basic characteristics that each must have to classify as a distance vector and what these mean to you and your network operations will be discussed.

Distance vector protocols have often been referred to as "Bellman-Ford" because they are based on a shortest path first computation algorithm described by R.E. Bellman, and the first description of the distributed algorithm is attributed to Ford and Fulkerson.

Distance vector means that information sent from router to router is based upon an entry in a routing table consisting of the distance and vector to destination—distance being what it "costs" to get there and vector being the path.

Distance vector protocols have been used in several networks, such as the early ARPA-NET. This and other early implementations were the basis for the development of RIP.

Distance vector algorithms are a class of routing algorithms that iterate on the number of hops in a route to find the shortest path. Distance vector routing algorithms call for each router to send its entire routing table in each update, but only to its neighbors. Distance vector routing algorithms can be prone to routing loops, but are computationally simpler than link state routing algorithms.

This chapter concentrates on the RIP distance vector protocol to demonstrate and correlate how OSPF has improved on RIP. This will help introduce some of the fundamental characteristics of these types of protocols.

ROUTING INFORMATION PROTOCOL (RIP)

The Routing Information Protocol (RIP) is a distance vector protocol that practices classful routing. The original incarnation of RIP was the Xerox protocol, GWINFO. A later version shipped with Berkeley Standard Distribution (BSD) UNIX in 1982.

RIP evolved as an Internet routing protocol. Other protocol suites use modified versions of RIP. For example, the AppleTalk Routing Table Maintenance Protocol (RTMP) and the Banyan VINES Routing Table Protocol (RTP) are both based on the Internet Protocol (IP) version of RIP.

The latest enhancement to RIP is the RIPv2 specification, which enables more information to be included in RIP packets and provides a simple authentication mechanism. The Routing Information Protocol (RIP) is a relatively old, but still commonly used, Interior Gateway Protocol (IGP) created to perform routing within a single autonomous system.

RIP Specifications

RIP is a classical distance vector routing protocol. RIP is primarily documented in RFC 1058. RIP uses broadcast User Datagram Protocol (UDP) data packets to exchange routing information. RIP is specified in the following Requests for Comments (RFCs): RFC 1058 and RFC 1723.

Key Characteristics of RIP

Some of the notable characteristics of RIP include the following:

- Distance vector routing protocol
- Hop count is the only metric used for path selection
- Maximum allowable hop count is 15
- Routing updates are broadcast every 30 seconds by default

Routing with RIP

RIP stores information on routes in routing tables. These routing tables consist of the ultimate destination and the distance in hops (metric). RIP table entries frequently include timers associated with the route in question and a route change flag, which indicates whether information about the route has already changed.

RIP maintains routing tables in internetwork nodes. Routing tables provide the following information about each destination network the protocol knows about:

- **Destination.** The destination indicates the Internet Protocol (IP) address of the destination network.
- **Metric.** The method by which a routing algorithm determines that one route is better than another. This information is stored in routing tables. The metric value indicates the total cost of the path to the destination, in hops.

- **Next hop.** The next hop indicates the IP address of the next router in the path to the packets destination IP address.

- **Route change flag.** The route change flag indicates whether information about the route has changed recently.

- **Timers.** The timers values provide information about various timers associated with the path.

The following example shows part of a typical RIP routing table that does not have many of the optional RIP features activated (such as timers):

```
#sho ip route rip
166.34.42.0 is variably subnetted, 42 subnets, 2 masks
R        166.34.42.168 255.255.255.255
  [120/1] via 166.34.42.3, 00:00:10, Ethernet0
R        166.34.42.169 255.255.255.255
  [120/1] via 166.34.42.3, 00:00:10, Ethernet0
```

RIP routing tables contain only the best route to a destination. They do not maintain information about multiple paths to a single destination. If a routing update provides a route with a lower metric value—that is, better—the old route is replaced.

TIPS

It is true that RIP can support parallel paths, though detailed discussion about that aspect of its operation is beyond the scope of this book.

RIP Routing Updates

RIP sends routing update messages at regular intervals and when the network topology changes. The Cisco IOS software sends routing information updates every 30 seconds—this process is called *advertising*. If a router does not receive an update from another router for 180 seconds or more, it marks the routes served by the non-updating router as being unusable. This waiting time is referred to as the hold down state. If there is still no update after 240 seconds, the router removes all routing table entries for the non-updating router.

TIPS

It should be noted that these timers are configurable, which enables a greater customization of the protocols operation within a network.

When a router receives a routing update that includes changes to an entry, it updates its routing table to reflect the new route. The metric value for the path is increased by one, and the sender is indicated as the next hop. RIP routers maintain only the best route (the route with the lowest metric value) to a destination.

After updating its routing table, the router immediately begins transmitting routing updates to inform other network routers of the change. These updates are sent independently of the regularly scheduled updates that RIP routers send.

RIP Routing Metric

RIP uses a single routing metric, hop count, to measure the distance between the source and a destination network. Each hop in a path from source to destination is assigned a hop count value (typically one).

When a router receives a routing update that contains a new or changed destination network entry, the router adds one to the metric value indicated in the update and enters the network in the routing table. The IP address of the sender is used as the next hop.

Hop Count Limit

RIP prevents routing loops from continuing indefinitely by implementing a limit on the number of hops allowed in a path from the source to a destination. The maximum number of hops in a path is 15.

The metric that RIP uses to rate the value of different routes is hop count. The hop count is the number of routers that can be traversed in a route. A directly connected network has a metric of zero; an unreachable network has a metric of 16. This small range of metrics makes RIP an unsuitable routing protocol for large networks.

If a router receives a routing update that contains a new or changed entry, and increasing the metric value by one causes the metric to be infinity (that is, more than 16 hops away), the network destination is considered unreachable.

RIP Timers

RIP has a number of configurable timers that enable the network engineer an added amount of flexibility when implementing RIP. These timers are also very good tools with which to monitor and regulate RIP performance. These timers are as follows:

- **Routing update timer.** Sets the interval between periodic routing updates—when the router sends a complete copy of its routing table to all neighbors. The default value for this timer is 30 seconds.

- **Route invalid timer.** If a router has not received an update about a particular route, the route might have become invalid. The route invalid timer determines the length of time that must expire before the indication "not heard" or the route is deemed invalid. After this occurs, the router's neighbors are notified of the fact. The Cisco default value for this timer is 180 seconds.

- **Route flush timer.** This timer sets the interval between a route becoming invalid and its removal from the routing table. But before the router removes the invalid route's entry from its table, the router must notify its neighbors. The default value for this timer is 240 seconds.

Increasing RIP Stability

RIP specifies a number of stability features to adjust for rapid network topology changes. These features are common to many routing protocols.

For example, RIP implements the split horizon and hold-down mechanisms to prevent incorrect routing information from being propagated. In addition, the RIP hop count limit prevents routing loops from continuing indefinitely.

Split Horizon

The split horizon rule states that it is never useful for a routing protocol to send information about a route back to the router from which it was learned. Split horizon helps prevent two-node routing loops. The split horizon rule takes two forms: simple split horizon and split horizon with poison reverse.

Simple Split Horizon

The simple form of the split horizon rule simply states that routing updates sent to a particular neighbor router should not contain information about routes that were learned from that neighbor.

An example of how RIP operates with simple split horizon implemented is as follows:

1. Router 1 advertises that it has a route to Network A.

2. Router 2 receives the update from Router 1 and inserts the information about how to reach Network A in its routing table.

3. When Router 2 sends a regular routing update, it does not include the entry for Network A in the update sent to Router 1 because that route was learned from Router 1 in the first place. This procedure prevents a two-node routing loop, also known as split horizon.

Split Horizon with Poison Reverse

The poison reverse form of the split horizon rule allows routing updates sent to a particular neighbor router to include information about routes learned from that neighbor. However, the metric for these routes is set to infinity.

An example of how RIP operates with split horizon with poisoned reverse implemented is as follows:

1. Router 1 advertises that it has a route to Network A.

2. Router 2 receives the update from Router 1 and inserts the information about how to reach Network A in its routing table.

3. Router 2 includes the entry for Network A in the update sent to Router 1, but the metric value is set to infinity, indicating that Network A is unreachable through Router 2 from Router 1.

Split horizon with poisoned reverse is usually preferred to simple split horizon. A routing loop is broken immediately if a router receives an update that sets the metric of a route to infinity. With simple split horizon, the routing loop will not be broken until a boundary is imposed, such as a hop count limit or a timer expiration.

The disadvantage of poisoned reverse is that it can greatly increase the size of routing messages, often simply to advertise multiple unreachable networks.

Hold-Down Mechanism

The hold-down mechanism prevents regular routing updates from inappropriately reinstating incorrect routing information. When a router receives an update that contains a topology change (that is, invalid), it starts the hold-down timer.

The hold-down timer prevents a router from implementing any change to its routing table until the timer expires. Any update received during this period is discarded. The hold-down period is usually slightly longer than the time necessary for the entire network to converge on a topology change.

In the following scenario, incorrect routing information is advertised because the hold-down mechanism is not implemented:

1. A route goes down, and neighboring routers detect the failure.

2. These routers calculate new routes and send out routing update messages to inform neighbors of the route change.

3. A device that has yet to be informed of a network failure sends a regular update message indicating that the failed route is good.

4. This update reaches a device that has just been notified of the failure. That device now contains incorrect routing information, which it advertises in the routing updates it sends to its neighbors.

The hold-down mechanism solves this problem by forcing every router to retain routing information changes for as long as it takes for all routers in the internetwork to converge on the change.

Hop Count Limit

RIP prevents routing loops from continuing indefinitely by implementing a limit on the number of hops allowed in a path from the source to a destination. The maximum number of hops in a path is 15.

If a router receives a routing update that contains a new or changed entry, and increasing the metric value by one causes the metric to be infinity (that is, 16), the network destination is considered unreachable.

RIP Packet Format

The RIPv2 specification (described in RFC 1723) enables more information to be included in RIP packets and provides a simple authentication mechanism. Figure 3-1 shows the IP RIP 2 packet format:

Figure 3–1
RIP packet format.

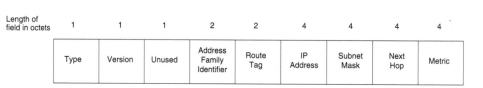

Length of field in octets	1	1	1	2	2	4	4	4	4
	Type	Version	Unused	Address Family Identifier	Route Tag	IP Address	Subnet Mask	Next Hop	Metric

The field definitions for a RIP packet are as follows:

- **Type.** Includes the following:

  - **Command.** Indicates whether the packet is a request or a response.
  - **Request.** Asks that a router send all or part of its routing table.
  - **Response.** Can be an unsolicited regular routing update or a reply to a request. Responses contain routing table entries. Multiple RIP packets are used to convey information from large routing tables.

- **Version.** Specifies the RIP version being used. In a RIP packet implementing any of the RIP fields or using authentication, this value is set to 2.

- **Zero.** Unused (2 byte).

- **Address Family Identifier (AFI).** Specifies the address family being used. RIP is designed to carry routing information for several different protocols. Each entry has an address family identifier to indicate the type of address being specified. The address family identifier for IP is 2.

- If the Address Family Identifier for the first entry in the message is 0xFFFF, the remainder of the entry contains authentication information. Currently, the only Authentication Type is simple password.

- **Route tag.** Provides a method for distinguishing between internal routes (learned by RIP) and external routes (learned from other protocols).

- **IP address.** Specifies the IP address for the entry.

- **Subnet mask.** Contains the subnet mask for the entry. If this field is zero, no subnet mask has been specified for the entry.

- **Next hop.** The IP address of the next hop to which packets for the entry should be forwarded.

- **Metric.** Indicates how many internetwork hops (routers) have been traversed in the trip to the destination. This value is between 1 and 15 for a valid route or 16 for an unreachable route.

Up to 25 occurrences of the Address Family Indicator, Address, and Metric fields are permitted in a single IP RIP packet. (That is, up to 25 routing table entries can be listed in a single RIP packet.)

If the address family indicator specifies an authenticated message, only 24 routing table entries can be specified.

Configuring RIP

If the router has a default network path, RIP advertises a route that links the router to the pseudo network 0.0.0.0. The network 0.0.0.0 does not exist; RIP treats 0.0.0.0 as a network to implement the default routing feature. The Cisco IOS software will advertise the default network if a default was learned by RIP, or if the router has a gateway of last resort and RIP is configured with a default metric.

RIP sends updates to the interfaces in the specified networks. If an interface's network is not specified, it will not be advertised in any RIP update.

Cisco's implementation of RIP Version 2 supports plain text and MD5 authentication, route summarization, classless interdomain routing (CIDR), and variable-length subnet masks (VLSMs).

RIP Configuration Task List

To configure RIP, complete the tasks in the following sequence. You must enable RIP. The remaining tasks are optional.

- Enable RIP
- Allow unicast updates for RIP
- Specify a RIP version
- Enable RIP authentication
- Disable route summarization

- Run IGRP and RIP concurrently to ensure that traffic is flowing properly across the network

- Disable the validation of source IP addresses

- Configure interpacket delay

LINK STATE PROTOCOLS

Link state routing protocols require routers to periodically send routing updates to all other routers in the internetwork. However, each router sends only that portion of the routing table that describes the state of its own links. Link state routing protocols are fast to converge their routing updates across the network in comparison to distance vector protocols.

Their fast convergence makes link state protocols less prone to routing loops than distance vector protocols. However, they also require more CPU power and system memory. One of the primary reasons additional CPU power and memory are needed is that link state protocols are based on the distributed map concept, which means every router has a copy of the network map that is regularly updated.

Link state protocols are based on link state algorithms, which are also called shortest path first (SPF) algorithms or Dijkstra algorithms.

A simple way to think about how link state technology operates is to picture the network as a large jigsaw puzzle; the number of pieces in your puzzle is dependent upon the size of your network. Each piece of the puzzle holds only one router or one LAN. Each router "draws" itself on that jigsaw piece, including little arrows to other routers and LANs. Those pieces are then replicated and sent throughout the network from router to router, until each router has a complete and accurate copy of each and every piece of the puzzle. Each router then assembles these pieces by using the shortest path first (SPF) algorithm. The SPF algorithm determines how the various pieces of the puzzle fit together.

The Link-State Database

As mentioned, the principle of link-state routing is that all the routers within a network maintain an identical copy of the network topology. From this map, each router will perform a series of calculations that will determine the best routes. This network topology is contained within a database, where each record represents the links to a particular node in the network.

Each record contains several pieces of information: an interface identifier, a link number, and metric information regarding the state of the link. With that information, each router can quickly compute the shortest path from itself to all other routers.

Integrated Intermediate System-to-Intermediate System (IS-IS)

IS-IS is an OSI link-state hierarchical routing protocol based on work originally done at Digital Equipment Corporation (Digital) for DECnet/OSI (DECnet Phase V). This protocol floods the network with link state information to build a complete, consistent picture of network topology.

The International Organization for Standardization (ISO) has developed the following routing protocols for use in the Open Systems Interconnection (OSI) protocol suite:

- Intermediate System-to-Intermediate System (IS-IS)

- End System-to-Intermediate System (ES-IS)

- Interdomain Routing Protocol (IDRP)

Because none of the OSI-based protocols have been covered, it is important to mention them so that you know they exist. For more information on IDRP or ES-IS, I would recommend starting with the RFCs, which can be found at `http://www.internic.net`.

The American National Standards Institute (ANSI) X3S3.3 (network and transport layers) committee was the motivating force behind ISO standardization of IS-IS, which was originally developed to route in ISO Connectionless Network Protocol (CLNP) networks. A version has since been created that supports both CLNP and Internet Protocol (IP) networks. It is usually referred to as Integrated IS-IS; this is the version we will be discussing.

OSI routing protocols are summarized in several ISO documents; those dealing with IS-IS are as follows:

> ISO 10589: Standards definition for IS-IS
> RFC 1195: Intermediate IS-IS

Both are available via the Internet at the appropriate standards home page or at Cisco Systems' home page:

```
ftp://ftp-eng.cisco.com/RFC/ISO/iso10589.ps
ftp://ftp-eng.cisco.com/RFC/rfc/rfc1195.ps
```

IS-IS Specific Terminology

Integrated IS-IS uses some interesting terminology; the following briefly defines some useful terms:

- **End System (ES).** An ES refers to any non-routing network component, such as a workstation.

- **Intermediate System (IS).** Refers to a router.

- **Area.** A specified group of contiguous networks and hosts.

- **Domain.** A group of connected areas.

- **Level 1 routing.** Refers to routing within an area (level 1).

- **Level 2 routing.** Refers to routing between level 1 areas.

To simplify router design and operation, IS-IS distinguishes between Level 1 and Level 2 Intermediate Systems (IS):

- **Level 1 ISs.** Level 1 Intermediate Systems (IS) communicate with other Level 1 ISs in the same area.

- **Level 2 ISs.** Level 2 ISs route between Level 1 areas and form an intradomain routing backbone.

Hierarchical routing simplifies backbone design because Level 1 ISs only need to know how to get to the nearest Level 2 IS. The backbone routing protocol can also change without affecting the level 2 IS routing protocol. Figure 3-2 demonstrates the relationship between areas and the different levels of routing.

Integrated IS-IS Overview

Integrated IS-IS is a version of the OSI IS-IS routing protocol that uses a single routing algorithm to support more network layer protocols than just CLNP. Integrated IS-IS is sometimes called Dual IS-IS, named after a version designed for IP and CLNP networks.

Several fields are added to IS-IS packets to enable IS-IS to support additional network layers. These fields inform routers about the following:

- The accessibility of network addresses from other protocol suites

- Which protocols are supported by which routers.

- Other information required by a specific protocol suite

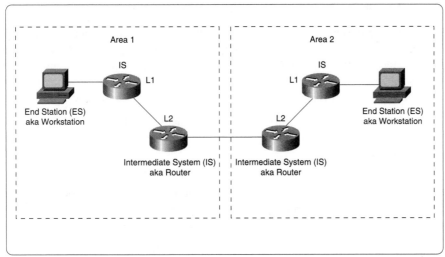

Figure 3–2
*IS-IS area and
domain
routing.*

Integrated IS-IS implementations send only one set of routing updates, making it more efficient than two separate implementations.

IS-IS Protocols

As in other powerful protocols, such as OSPF, the IS-IS protocol contains subprotocols. The two most important are the Hello protocol and the Flooding protocol. The Hello protocol is used to discover and to elect a Designated Router on broadcast links. The Flooding protocol is used to propagate the link state records within the areas. Each subprotocol has a very important function within the IS-IS protocol. These functions are detailed as follows:

- **Hello protocol.** This protocol carries the identification information, which characterizes a router as a Level 1, Level 2, or both.

- **Flooding protocol.** This protocol is used to propagate the link state records within the areas to ensure that proper routing updates take place.

Integrated Versus "Ships-in-the-Night" Routing

Integrated IS-IS represents one of the two ways to support multiple network layer protocols in a network, the other being the "ships-in-the-night" approach. In other words, using integrated routing with IS-IS will enable you to support the use of multiple protocols only through the use of IS-IS. The alternative ships-in-the-night routing technique requires configuring multiple protocols on your network to achieve the same results.

Integrated routing has the capability to route multiple network layer protocols through tables calculated by a single routing protocol, thus saving some router resources. Integrated IS-IS uses this approach.

Ships-in-the-night routing advocates the use of a completely separate and distinct routing protocol for each network protocol so that the multiple routing protocols essentially exist independently (with different types of routing information passing like ships in the night).

The very idea of "integrated" routing appears on the surface to be very seductive. Imagine the possibilities and ease of managing or designing a network that only had one routing protocol because that was all it ever needed—a very seductive thought for those of us who prefer working smarter instead of working harder.

The fact though is that integrated routing is not as seductive as it might first appear. The truth of the matter is that corporate networks often carry multiple protocols. This is done because different services are expected from the different protocols and, as is expected, each of these protocols has a slightly different routing algorithm. The drawback is that network engineers will have to find the one common denominator in order for the network to operate smoothly.

There is no real evidence that proves that integrated routing leads to a more efficient network management or design than "Ships In The Night," in which each protocol is routed based upon its own capabilities. Because there is more than one, the "ships" end up passing in the night like ships on the same ocean without ever interacting, each left to its own devices.

IS-IS Routing

The steps for IS-IS routing are as follows:

    1. Each End System (ES or host) belongs within a particular logical area. An end station discovers the nearest Intermediate System (IS or router) by listening for IS hello packets.

2. When an End System wants to send a packet to another End System, it sends the packet to one of the Intermediate Systems on its directly attached network.

3. The Intermediate System (router) looks up the destination address and forwards the packet along the best route.

4. If the destination end station is on the same subnetwork, the local Intermediate System will know this from listening to the End Station hellos and will forward the packet appropriately.

5. The IS might also provide a redirect (RD) message back to the source to tell it that a more direct route is available.

6. If the destination address is an ES on another subnetwork in the same area, the IS will know the correct route and will forward the packet appropriately.

7. If the destination address is an ES in another area, the Level 1 IS sends the packet to the nearest Level 2 IS.

8. Forwarding through Level 2 ISs continues until the packet reaches a Level 2 IS in the destination area.

9. Within the destination area, ISs forward the packet along the best path until the destination ES is reached.

IS-IS Timers

IS-IS has an impressive number of timers that can be configured when compared to other protocols. It is beyond the scope of this book to detail in depth each and every one. Basically, they are very extensive and not relevant.

Building the Topology Database

Link state update messages help ISs learn about the network topology through the following steps:

1. Each IS generates an update with IP addresses specifying the ESs and ISs to which it is connected, as well as the associated metrics.

2. This update is then sent to all neighboring ISs, which forward (flood) it to their neighbors, and so on.

3. Using these updates, each IS can build a complete topology of the network. Each update has a sequence number that is used to distinguish old updates from new ones.

4. When the network topology changes, new updates are sent as the process begins again.

IS-IS Metrics

IS-IS uses a single required default metric with a maximum path value of 1,023, with 1,024 being infinity. The metric number assigned is arbitrary and is typically assigned by a network administrator based upon the network architecture. Maximum metric values are set at this level to provide the granularity needed to support various link types, while at the same time ensuring that the shortest path algorithm used for route computation will be reasonably efficient.

Any single link can have a maximum value of 63. IS-IS also calculates the metric along the path to a destination by summing the single link values.

IS-IS also defines three optional metrics (costs) to further assist in defining the optimal routes:

- **Delay.** The delay cost metric reflects the amount of delay on the link.

- **Expense.** The expense cost metric reflects the communications cost associated with using the link.

- **Error.** The error cost metric reflects the error rate of the link.

IS-IS maintains a mapping of the default metric and three optional metrics to the quality of service (QoS) option in the CLNP packet header. IS-IS uses these mappings to compute routes through the internetwork.

IS-IS Packet Formats

IS-IS uses three basic packet formats:

- IS-IS hello packets (ISHs)

- Link-state packets (LSPs)

- Sequence numbers packets (SNPs)

IS-IS Logical Packet Format

Each of the three IS-IS packet types has a complex format with the following three different logical parts:

- **Common header.** An 8-byte fixed header shared by all three-packet types.

- **Fixed length packet specific header.** Packet-type-specific portion with a fixed format.

- **Variable length packet specific header.** Also packet–type-specific, but of variable length.

Figure 3-3 shows the logical format of IS-IS packets:

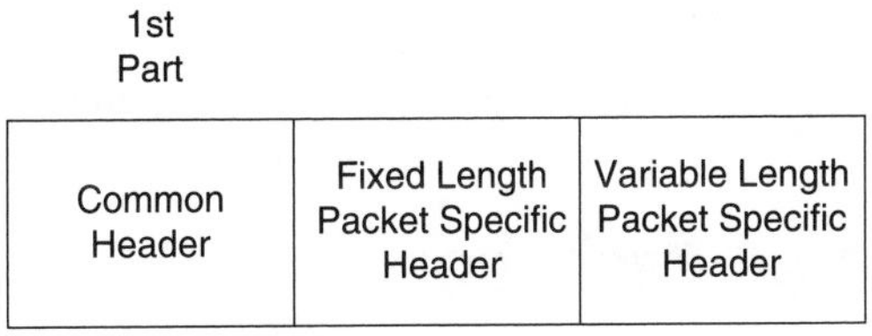

1st
Part

Common Header	Fixed Length Packet Specific Header	Variable Length Packet Specific Header

Figure 3–3
IS-IS logical packet format.

IS-IS Common Header Fields

Figure 3-4 shows the common header fields of the IS-IS packets:

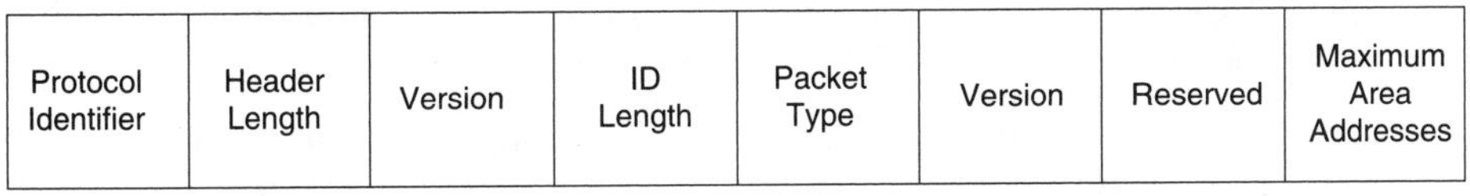

Protocol Identifier	Header Length	Version	ID Length	Packet Type	Version	Reserved	Maximum Area Addresses

Figure 3–4
IS-IS common header fields.

The following list defines the common header fields of IS-IS packets as depicted in Figure 3-4.

- **Protocol identifier.** Identifies the IS-IS protocol, contains a constant (131).

- **Header length.** Contains the fixed header length. (The length is always equal to eight bytes, but is included so that IS-IS packets do not differ significantly from CLNP packets.)

- **Version.** Contains a value of 1 in the current IS-IS specification.

- **ID length.** Specifies the size of the ID portion of an NSAP address. If the field contains a value between 1 and 8 inclusive, the ID portion of an NSAP address is that number of bytes. If the field contains a value of zero, the ID portion of an NSAP address is 6 bytes. If the field contains a value of 255 (all ones), the ID portion of an NSAP address is zero bytes.

- **Packet type.** Specifies the type of IS-IS packet (hello, LSP, or SNP).

- **Version.** Repeated after the Packet Type field. I do not know anyone who knows why, but it is better than just a spacer field.

- **Reserved.** Ignored by the receiver, and is equal to 0.

- **Maximum area addresses.** Specifies the number of addresses permitted in this area.

Following the common header, each packet type has a different additional fixed portion.

SELECTING A ROUTING PROTOCOL

One of the most frequent questions that network designers and engineers ask about routing protocols is "Which routing protocol should I use?" This section will compare and contrast the three protocols discussed in the chapter: RIP, IS-IS, and OSPF; however, you need to consider three important issues before selecting a routing protocol:

- **Operational considerations.** Determine how easy it is to manage a network over time. These considerations include a protocol's capability to adapt to changes, how to minimize disruptions to the network, and how easy is it to troubleshoot problems.

- **Technical considerations.** Assist in determining whether or not a given protocol is capable of supporting a particular set of network requirements.

- **Business considerations.** Defined as business priorities and policies that influence network design decisions. These types of considerations can originate from any area within a company and are sometimes the keystones to the success of the network.

Operational Considerations

The matrix shown in Table 3-1 provides a list of the more important features to consider when weighing the operational issues concerning the selection of a routing protocol.

Table 3-1 *Important operation considerations*

	RIP	OSPF	IS-IS
Protocols Supported	IP	IP	IP, OS, CLNP
Routing Hierarchies	None	Supported	Supported
IP Address Management	Optional	Required	Required

Protocols Supported

Historically, all routed protocols have had their own independent routing protocols: AppleTalk uses RTMP; Novell uses IPX RIP; and IP uses RIP, IGRP, or OSPF. This is conceptually simple to understand, but it is often difficult to implement. Yet, it is necessary for network engineers to design and operate networks that support multi-protocol environments. Hence, they need to be able to manage a mix of routing protocols.

Both RIP and OSPF support only the TCP/IP protocol suite. Although TCP/IP is the most popular suite in use today, it is not the only one being used. The inability of a routing protocol to support other protocols can be a detriment to legacy networks or networks with unique routing needs.

When IS-IS was created, the protocol designers asked a significant question: why can't one routing protocol handle multiple routed protocols? Consequently, Integrated IS-IS was enhanced to support both OSI CLNP and TCP/IP networks. In addition, Integrated IS-IS has the hooks in it to permit it to support other network protocols.

Using a single routing protocol simplifies the job of a network administrator considerably because she will need to learn the intricacies of only one protocol.

Logical Hierarchies

The key to building large networks is to introduce a logical hierarchy. Many problems of complexity and scale can be addressed with the proper use of hierarchy.

RIP does not support any type of logical hierarchy. This is a major drawback and makes it very unsuitable for today's growing networks.

OSPF was the first major routing protocol to support hierarchical networking within a single routing domain. OSPF supports two levels of hierarchy: a backbone area and other connected areas. OSPF routers carry full topology information about the backbone and connectivity information about all of the areas. Within each area, OSPF routers exchange full topology information about that area.

Integrated IS-IS uses the same two levels of hierarchy as OSPF; however, the two protocols differ in the quantity of information that is carried inside each area. Within an area, Integrated IS-IS routers send all traffic that needs to go out of the area to the nearest area border router (ABR). OSPF, on the other hand, injects all of the connectivity information about the other areas into each area. This enables every router in an OSPF area to choose the optimal ABR for traffic that needs to go out of their area.

IP Address Management

The key to a successful hierarchical network structure is proper IP address management. If addresses are assigned appropriately, it is possible to summarize routing information. There are two significant reasons to summarize routes. Summarization localizes the effects of topology changes and thus contributes to network stability, and summarization cuts down on the amount of routing information that is carried by all routers. This simplifies network administration and troubleshooting, in addition to cutting down the resources consumed by the routing protocol.

Proper IP address management in RIP depends upon which version you are running. The optimal RIP solution in this area is version 2, which will allow for the use of various IP address management tools, such as VLSM and CIDR.

Each area used by OSPF and Integrated IS-IS should have a contiguous set of maskable network or subnet numbers assigned to it. The area border routers should summarize that set of addresses with an address mask.

Technical Considerations

The matrix as shown in Table 3-2 provides a list of the more important features to consider when weighing the technical issues concerning the selection of a routing protocol.

Table 3-2   *Important technical considerations*

	RIP	IS-IS	OSPF
Fast convergence	Yes	Yes	Yes
Routing updates	Fast, whole table	Fast, change only	Fast, change only
VLSM support and CIDR	Yes (v2)	Yes	Yes
Load sharing	No	Yes, equal cost	Yes, equal cost
Metric range	0–15	0–65,535	0–65,535
Static metric pieces	Number of hops	Sum of bandwidth	Sum of bandwidth
Dynamic metric pieces	None	None	None

Fast Convergence

All routing protocols have three important characteristics when dealing with the issue of convergence:

1. Detecting that a change has occurred

2. Adapting to that change

3. Updating the network topology to reflect the change

RIP, IS-IS, and OSPF detect certain types of changes instantly. In general, any change that can be detected by a physical change (such as loss of carrier) will be detected immediately by any routing protocol.

In addition, all three routing protocols have mechanisms to detect other failures (such as the loss of an adjacent router or the degradation of an interface to the point where it should no longer be used). All three protocols cause adjacent routers to exchange information periodically.

After the routing protocol has detected the topology change, it needs to adjust the routing tables to accommodate the new topology. RIP generally updates its routing tables every 30 seconds (this is the default time), although during the normal update process, RIP sends out its entire routing table. OSPF and Integrated IS-IS have two mechanisms for updating routing tables. If the topology change were within the area, all of the existing routes affected by the change would be discarded and a new routing table would be generated. In general, OSPF and Integrated IS-IS converge in less than two seconds. The amount of CPU required to do the recompilation is strongly affected by the number of routes and the amount of redundancy in the network.

Routing Updates

All routing protocols exchange routing information dynamically. The three most important and interesting questions concerning the operation of routing updates are as follows:

- **When are they sent?** All three routing protocols exchange periodic hellos and full topology information when a router starts up and periodically thereafter, depending how they are configured. RIP will flood the full topology table every 30 seconds. OSPF will flood the full topology table every 1,800 seconds. Integrated IS-IS will flood the full topology table every 15 minutes

- **What is in them?** Within an area, OSPF and Integrated IS-IS exchange changed link state information. Between areas, OSPF and Integrated IS-IS exchange changed routes.

- **Where are they sent?** Changed information in a RIP network is broadcast out to all of its neighbors after it has finished updating its topology. Changed information in OSPF and Integrated IS-IS propagates throughout the area in which the change occurred. If route summarization is not done, change information might also propagate to the backbone and into other areas.

Variable-Length Subnet Masks

RIPv2, OSPF, and Integrated IS-IS all include support for variable-length subnet masks (VLSM). VLSM is required to support route summarization. In addition, VLSM also enables network administrators to use their address space more effectively.

Load Sharing

Today's networks are commonly designed with redundant paths. This has two positive benefits: re-routing in case of failure and load sharing. All routing protocols supported by Cisco provide load sharing across up to four equal-cost paths.

Metrics

The quality of route selection is essentially controlled by the value of the metrics placed upon the various routes. There are two components of importance in how a routing protocol uses metrics: the range of the values the metric can express and how the metric is computed.

RIP uses a very simple hop count metric that can be expressed with values between 0 and 16. The computation is also very straightforward in that the cost determined for the metric is a matter of how many hops the destination is from the source router.

OSPF uses a flat metric with a range of 16 bits. This results in OSPF having a metric range that is from zero to 65,535. By default, OSPF metrics are assigned as an inverse of the bandwidth available on an interface—normalized to give FDDI a metric of 1. OSPF computes the cost of a path by summing the metrics for each hop on that path.

Integrated IS-IS uses a flat metric. The metric range is 0–1,023. By default, all Integrated IS-IS metrics are 10. Network administrators need to configure non-default values. Integrated IS-IS computes the cost of a path by summing the metrics for each hop on that path.

Scaling

RIP has many problems associated with scaling into the larger network sizes. For example, if a network has more than 15 hops, RIP will run into problems due to its design limitations.

As for IS-IS, ISO 10589 states that 100 routers per area and 400 L2 routers should be possible. The biggest scaling issue now seems to be the overhead of the flooding in large meshed networks—for example, flat ATM clouds with many routers attached that form a full mesh.

OSPF, on the other hand, scales very well no matter how large the network is. In order to make the network operate optimally, however, you should implement physical and logical areas, as needed.

Business Considerations

Table 3-3 documents some of the more important features to consider when weighing the business issues concerning the selection of a routing protocol.

Table 3-3   *Important business considerations for routing protocol selection*

	RIP	Integrated IS-IS	OSPF
Standard-based	Yes	Yes	Yes
Multi-vendor environments	Yes	Yes	Yes
Proven technology	Yes	Yes	Yes

Standards

Many companies prefer to use protocols based upon standards whenever possible, which is strongly recommended in every network. Networks that are running today without the protocols in use having a proper standard will eventually cause problems. Either this could be network meltdown for no apparent reason, or you could become stranded on a technological desert island—just you and your protocol.

OSPF is a standard protocol developed by a committee of the Internet Engineering Task Force (IETF) as an alternative to the RIP protocol. OSPF is defined in RFC 1583.

IS-IS is a standard protocol developed by the International Standards Organization (ISO OSI). IS-IS is defined in International Standard 10589. Integrated IS-IS is a standard extension to IS-IS developed by the Internet Engineering Task Force. Integrated IS-IS is defined in an Internet Draft.

Multi-Vendor Environments

Large networks being designed today do not have the luxury of assuming a single vendor environment. It is very common to have portions of a network that are provided by one vendor and other portions that are provided by another. In a perfect world, all network components would be supplied by one vendor.

You can use several techniques to permit multi-vendor environments. The most common technique is to use the same routing protocol on all of the routers.

RIP and OSPF are implemented by every major routing vendor.

Integrated IS-IS is implemented by most of the major router vendors.

Another common technique to permit multi-vendor environments is to use different routing protocols in different parts of the network and set up communication paths between the routing protocols. This technique enables a network designer to optimize each portion of the network for the characteristics that it requires. This technique also allows for the gradual migration of a network from one protocol to another and for the inclusion of equipment, which is not capable of supporting today's advanced protocols.

Cisco supports two techniques to enable communication between different routing protocols, redistribution and external routing protocols, as documented in the list that follows.

- **Redistribution.** All Cisco routers can run more than one routing protocol at the same time and allow those routing protocols to exchange routing information. This technique is commonly used to permit communication with equipment that supports only RIP, for example. Cisco routers support redistribution between any set of routing protocols that are in the same family, such as those documented in the following points:

  - **IP.** RIP, OSPF, Integrated IS-IS (IP), EGP, BGP, IGRP, and Enhanced IGRP.
  - **Novell IPX.** IPX RIP, Enhanced IGRP, and NLSP.
  - **AppleTalk.** RTMP and Enhanced IGRP.

- **External routing protocols.** All Cisco routers support external routing protocols, which are designed to permit the exchange of routing information between different autonomous systems. Today's external routing protocols are defined only for IP. Cisco is involved in extending external routing protocols to include support for other network protocols as well.

Proven Technology

RIP has withstood the test of time. The future of RIP does not look that bright when compared to other solutions, but it is one of the most proven protocols available.

Integrated IS-IS has been available from Cisco for several years and is being deployed in a number of significant networks. IS-IS is the routing protocol of choice for networks that need to support both OSI and IP. Integrated IS-IS is the standard routing protocol for DECnet Phase V networks.

OSPF has been available for several years from all the major routing vendors and is being deployed in an increasing number of networks ranging from very simple to very complex.

CHAPTER SUMMARY

This chapter discussed fundamental concepts of how to understand routing protocols. It has provided all types of routing table associations and discussed as well how a protocol algorithm is designed and what determines proper operation.

This chapter has also analyzed the differences between the two most important classes of protocols: distance vector and link state. Distance vector protocols use the distance (hops) to a destination as their metric, as demonstrated in RIP. A broad overview of RIP was provided on its operation and communication methods as a routing protocol. Link state protocols are a slightly more complex subject to understand. In order to assist in this understanding, the information provided was a bit more in-depth, and one of the more popular Internet routing protocols was used to demonstrate this routing protocol. IS-IS was used to provide the level of sophistication necessary.

Instead of debating the merits and lack thereof for each protocol, an entire section was dedicated to objectively analyzing and supporting the choice of a network protocol. It is also important to understand that sometimes being able to make a business successful is almost as important as being able to implement and design a network.

CASE STUDY: CONFIGURING A RIP NETWORK

This case study has been taken from the Cisco internetworking case studies book as a simple example of how to configure a RIP network. Contained within this case study is a variety of useful information concerning the proper configuration of RIP with a Cisco router.

Figure 3-5 illustrates a RIP network. Three sites are connected with serial lines. The RIP network uses a Class B address and an 8-bit subnet mask. Each site has a contiguous set of network numbers.

Table 3-4 lists the network address assignments for the RIP network, including the network number, subnet range, and subnet masks. All interfaces indicate network 130.10.0.0; however, the specific address includes the subnet and subnet mask. For example, serial interface 0 on Router C has an IP address of 130.10.63.3 with a subnet mask of 255.255.255.0.

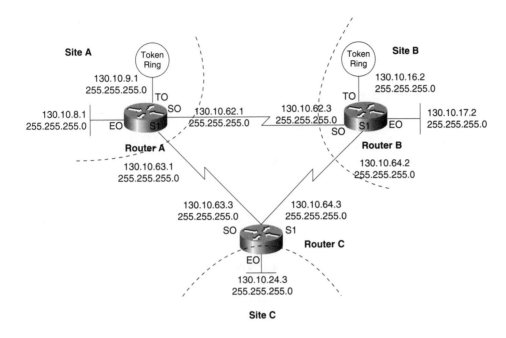

Figure 3–5
RIP network case study: configuring RIP.

Table 3-4 *RIP network address assignments*

Network Number	Subnets	Subnet Masks
130.10.0.0	Site A: 8–15	255.255.255.0
130.10.0.0	Site B: 16–23	255.255.255.0
130.10.0.0	Site C: 24–31	255.255.255.0
130.10.0.0	Serial Backbone: 62–64	255.255.255.0

The following commands in the configuration file for Router A determine the IP address for each interface and enable RIP on those interfaces:

```
interface serial 0
ip address 130.10.62.1 255.255.255.0
interface serial 1
ip address 130.10.63.1 255.255.255.0
interface ethernet 0
ip address 130.10.8.1 255.255.255.0
interface tokenring 0
ip address 130.10.9.1 255.255.255.0
router rip
network 130.10.0.0
```

The following commands in the configuration file for Router B determine the IP address for each interface and enable RIP on those interfaces:

```
interface serial 0
ip address 130.10.62.2 255.255.255.0
interface serial 1
ip address 130.10.64.2 255.255.255.0
interface ethernet 0
ip address 130.10.17.2 255.255.255.0
interface tokenring 0
ip address 130.10.16.2 255.255.255.0
router rip
network 130.10.0.0
```

The following commands in the configuration file for Router C determine the IP address for each interface and enable RIP on those interfaces:

```
interface serial 0
ip address 130.10.63.3 255.255.255.0
interface serial 1
ip address 130.10.64.3 255.255.255.0
interface ethernet 0
ip address 130.10.24.3 255.255.255.0
router rip
network 130.10.0.0
```

FREQUENTLY ASKED QUESTIONS

Q— *What are the advantages and disadvantages of OSPF and EIGRP?*

A— OSPF is an industry standard, and EIGRP is Cisco-specific. OSPF has had more time to evolve than EIGRP. EIGRP can be used for multiple protocols besides IP (AppleTalk and Novell, for example).

Q— *Does Cisco support RIP to OSPF redistribution over X.25 IP unnumbered?*

A— Yes.

Q— *Why does RIP only maintain a single table entry for any specific destination?*

A— Because it uses hop count as its sole metric, and for any specific destination it maintains information on the optimal route only.

Q— *Why must the RIP route invalid timer be less than the route flush timer?*

A— This is so that the router has time to update its neighbors before the invalid routes are deleted from its routing tables.

Q— *How many areas can a single ISIS process support?*

A— Trick question. There are two answers. A Level-1 process can support only one area. You can configure up to three areas (by configuring three NETs on the process), but by definition the areas are merged into one (the Level-1 LSPs are all merged together). A Level-2 process can support many areas, because each area at Level 2 is simply a route. I would imagine that many hundreds could be supported these days.

Q— *How does a router that is running IS-IS know it is a L1 or L2 router?*

A— You must configure the router despite what is documented in the manuals. The default is both L1 and L2. When two neighboring routers discover they are in different areas, they could stop sending L1 hellos. Cisco routers won't stop sending L1 hellos, because the neighbor's level might change. When two neighboring routers are in the same area, they know they need a L1 adjacency, but there is no way for them to tell whether they should be L2 routers as well. So a person who knows the design of the network needs to configure those interfaces to be L1 only for efficiency reasons if there is no need for L2 routing.

Q— *Should I specify the type of my router? (Level-1, Level-2, or Level-1-2)*

A— Yes. The manual says that you don't need to worry about this, but that is not true. In the default situation, each router will establish L2 adjacencies with all routers that have different area IDs, but L1 AND L2 adjacencies with all routers that have the same area ID. This is because a router cannot know whether its area is a transit area or not.

Not configuring the type of the router will result in each router having two databases (L1 and L2), all LSPs from both databases being flooded, and the SPF algorithm being run twice. So, configuring the type of route will save memory, CPU power, and bandwidth. When using ISIS for IP routing, not configuring L1 routers as L1 routers is even worse because each L2 router will report all IP prefixes reachable via L1 routing.

Q— *How do I configure ISIS for CLNS ?*

A— Talk to the network administrator to get an NSAP (prefix). If this is a new network, design an area and backbone layout. If this is a small network (less than 30 routers), use only one area, and use Level-1 routing only. This means that all routers have an NSAP with the same prefix, and only the last 7 bytes (systemID plus n-selector) are different. Configure the router isis process. Preferably, do this for L1 only. Configure ISIS for each interface that needs to forward CLNS traffic.

Q— *How do I configure the IS-IS router process.*

A— In the router's configuration mode, type:

```
router isis
net <my.variable.length.areaID>.<my.6.byte.systemID>.00
is-type level-1
```

Q— *How do I configure IS-IS for CLNS on an interface.*

A— As an interface subcommand, configure clns router isis. That's it!

```
interface ethernet 0
clns router isis
```

Q— *How do I configure IS-IS for IP ?*

A— Do the same as you do for IS-IS for CLNS. Get an NSAP and configure the router process. Now on each interface where you want to establish ISIS adjacencies, configure ip router isis:

```
interface ethernet 0
ip router isis
```

PART 2

OSPF Routing & Network Design

This section prepares you for designing and implementing an OSPF network by providing in-depth, practical coverage of introductory, fundamental, and advanced OSPF topics. This information is conveyed in the following three chapters of the book:

Chapter 4, **"Introduction to OSPF,"** covers the background and evolution of the OSPF protocol by tracing the RFCs relating to OSPF. Understanding the functional environment of OSPF is of great importance in order to work within the mechanics of the protocol and design a network in which it will operate properly.

Chapter 5, **"The Fundamentals of OSPF Routing & Design,"** covers the fundamentals of OSPF routing and design, including attention to the following topics: OSPF algorithms, OSPF convergence, OSPF design guidelines, area design considerations, OSPF route selection, and OSPF IP addressing and route summarization.

Chapter 6, **"Advanced OSPF Design Concepts,"** provides documentation to experienced OSPF network designers on sought-after information, including OSPF redistribution, OSPF on-demand circuit design, OSPF configuration commands, and OSPF error messages.

CHAPTER 4

Introduction to OSPF

"Teamwork: If everyone is moving forward together, then the success takes care of itself."—Successories

This chapter discusses in detail the background and evolution of the OSPF protocol by tracing the RFCs relating to OSPF. The functional environment of OSPF is of great importance in order to understand the workings of the protocol and design a network in which it will operate properly. As a hierarchical routing protocol, OSPF allows for a variety of different configurations and implementations. This hierarchical ability requires many different levels or areas and they are fully discussed. This chapter covers the following important objectives:

- **OSPF Overview.** This section discusses the earliest appearance and creation of the shortest path first algorithm. From the established beginnings of OSPF, the evolution and modifications applied to it will be traced through the RFCs. Each RFC relating directly and indirectly to the protocol will be summarized and discussed as needed.

- **OSPF Functional Environment.** The functional environment is a key element in understanding OSPF. This section discusses and explores several basics to the protocol: network types, router identification, adjacencies, designated routers, protocols within OSPF, and link-state advertisements.

- **OSPF Routing Hierarchy.** OSPF's capability to perform as a hierarchical routing protocol makes it a good candidate in many large networks. As a result of this capability, OSPF supports a variety of techniques and designations that make operation much smoother. This section discusses the types of OSPF routers and hierarchical design techniques, including how OSPF separates the hierarchy through the use of areas and autonomous systems.

OSPF Overview

OSPF is a link-state routing protocol. Such protocols are also referred to in literature and technical documents as shortest path first (SPF)-based or distributed database protocols. This section gives a brief description of the developments in link-state technologies that have influenced the evolution of the OSPF protocol.

NOTES

What is a link state protocol?
OSPF is a link state protocol. You can, for example, think of a link as being an interface on the router. The state of the link is a description of that interface. This description would include its IP address, mask, and the type of network to which it is connected. When you take this information for all the routers in your network, the information is compiled into a link-state database and the SPF algorithm is run against that data. *Link state* derives from the indication you would receive regarding whether or not the link is up or down.

The first link-state routing protocol was developed for use in the ARPANET packet switching network. This protocol formed the starting point for all other link state protocols. The homogeneous ARPANET environment (that is, single-vendor packet switches connected by synchronous serial lines) simplified the design and implementation of the original protocol.

The Development and Evolution of OSPF

The ARPANET used one of the first distance vector routing protocols, which evolved into RIP, which is still in use today. Serious limitations and problems were encountered with RIP as networks grew. This caused a demand for a new protocol that could run within an autonomous system (AS) and had the capability to grow (scale) to a large-sized network comprised of many routers and network links.

Into this gap stepped OSPF version 1, published as Request for Comments (RFC) 1131 in October 1989 by John T. Moy and the OSPF Working Group. OSPF made use of the famous Dijkstra Algorithm. This algorithm was not new and had not been created specifically to fill the demand of the networking community. In reality, this mathematical formula was initially created to demonstrate the ARMAC computer in 1956, over 30 years before OSPF was ever considered!

Edsger W. Dijkstra was born in 1930 in the city of Rotterdam in the Netherlands. Born into a scientifically oriented family, he quickly excelled and achieved his Ph.D. in Computer Science in 1959 from the University of Amsterdam, Holland. By the time he was 32, he had achieved a full professorship in mathematics at the Eindhoren University. His achievement remains extremely impressive to this day.

His most remembered contribution to the computer world is his algorithms, specifically the shortest path algorithm. Dijkstra did not consider his algorithm very remarkable at the time, and many years passed before he published it. Today, his algorithm is being applied to road building, routing of communications, and the airline industry. His algorithm was even altered slightly to determine the most inexpensive way to wire a computer. The goal of what has commonly become known as the Dijkstra algorithm is to find the shortest route between two points.

There are quite a few more resources available to you on this subject. If you require further information, I suggest you reference the following Web sites:

```
http://students.ceid.upatras.gr/~papagel/project/kef5_7_1.htm
http://cda.mrs.umn.edu/~englinjm/EWD.html
http://www.ctc.dcu.ie/ctcweb/courses/heuristics/course/dij.html
http://www.geekchic.com/repliq5.htm
http://www.cbi.umn.edu/inv/burros/ewddocs.htm
```

The goal of Edsger Dijkstra's shortest path algorithm is to find the shortest route between two points through a series. To describe the operation of his algorithm in layman's terms, look at the following example. Suppose you are trying to find the shortest path between two cities: Atlanta and Boston (a core set of routers). The purpose in this example is to determine the minimum time needed to drive to every city (routers) in an ever-expanding core of cities (network). The sequence to find this minimum time value is as follows:

1. Begin in the city of origin (router). The time (distance) needed to reach this city is, of course, zero because it is your origin.

2. Then you discover a new city, which you will call city X (router), that you wish to reach.

If the time to drive (distance) to city X is shorter than the time to drive to any other city outside the core set.

If the time to drive to city X is the minimum time to drive to city Y in the core set from Atlanta, plus the time to drive from Y to X.

3. Then add city X to the core set (network), and record the time (distance) computed.

4. If it is a city named Boston then you are done, if not, repeat.

This example helps demonstrate the reason behind the algorithm's name. Another important factor in its operation is how SPF converges. Essentially, it will converge in $0(M.\log M)$ iterations, where M is the number of links. This is far superior to the Bellman-Ford algorithm, which converges in $0(N.M)$ iterations where N, is the number of nodes.

These characteristics and because the specification was developed in an open fashion by the IETF explains the name of the OSPF protocol—"Open Shortest Path First." Also, the OSPF protocol is an open standard that allows the publication of all data relating to its design and function. This information has been published in a series of RFCs.

OSPF RFCs

To properly reference the technical documents used in the design and evolution of OSPF, each of them will be briefly discussed in chronological order. The following is a list of the Request for Comments (RFCs) that have been published by the IETF relating to the OSPF protocol. Each RFC will contain a brief summary of its contents and purpose. Furthermore, the tracking of the RFC evolution will include information on which are current and which have been made obsolete. This will enable the reader to understand where they should go for additional reading, as further discussion is beyond the scope of this book. Figure 4-1 provides a timeline of the development and evolution of OSPF.

- RFC 1131: OSPF Specification Version 1 (J. Moy, Oct. 1989)

- RFC 1245: OSPF Protocol Analysis (J. Moy, July 1991)

- RFC 1246: Experience with the OSPF Protocol (J. Moy, July 1991)

- RFC 1247: OSPF Version 2 [obsoletes 1131] (J. Moy, July 1991)

- RFC 1248: OSPF Version 2 Management Information Base (F. Baker & R. Coltun, July 1991)

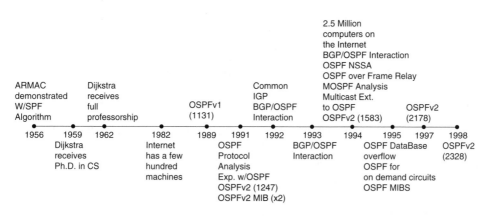

Figure 4–1
OSPF evolution timeline.

- RFC 1252: OSPF Version 2 Management Information Base [obsoletes 1248] (F. Baker & R. Coltun, July 1991)

- RFC 1253: OSPF Version 2 Management Information Base [obsoletes 1252] (F. Baker & R. Coltun, Aug. 1991)

- RFC 1364: BGP OSPF Interaction [obsoletes 1247 & 1267] (K. Varadhan, Sept. 1992; IAB; L. Chapin, Oct. 1992)

- RFC 1371: Choosing a "Common IGP" for the IP Internet (IESG; P. Gross, Oct. 1992)

- RFC 1403: BGP OSPF Interaction [obsoletes 1364] (K. Varadhan, Jan. 1993)

- RFC 1583: OSPF Version 2 [obsoletes RFC1247] (J. Moy, March 1994)

- RFC 1584: Multicast Extensions to OSPF (J. Moy, March 1994)

- RFC 1585: MOSPF: Analysis and Experience (J. Moy, March 1994)

- RFC 1586: Guidelines For Running OSPF Over Frame Relay Networks (O. deSouza & M. Rodriguez, March 1994)

- RFC 1587: The OSPF NSSA Option (V. Fuller & R. Coltun, March 1994)

- RFC 1745: BGP4/IDRP for IP-OSPF Interaction (K. Varadhan, S. Hares, Y. Rekhter, Dec 94)

- RFC 1765: OSPF Database Overflow (J. Moy, March 1995)

- RFC 1793: Extending OSPF to Support Demand Circuits (J. Moy, April 1995)

- RFC 1850: OSPF Version 2 Management Information Base [obsoletes 1253] (F. Baker & R. Coltun, Nov. 1995)

- RFC 2178: OSPF Version 2 [obsoletes 1583] (J. Moy, July 1997)

- RFC 2328: OSPF Version 2 [obsoletes 2178] (J. Moy, April 1998)

Before discussing the origins of the OSPF protocol, you should review some of its key characteristics. These characteristics and the protocol's many labels will be the focus while reviewing the RFCs.

The Open Shortest Path First protocol is also known by the following various definitions:

- Link-state routing protocol

- Shortest path first (SPF) protocol

- Interior gateway protocol

- Distributed routing protocol

OSPF also has the following characteristics:

- Open architecture

- Dynamically adjusts to changes in network topology

- Adjustable distance metrics

- Type of service (TOS) routing

- Support for hierarchical systems

- Load balancing

- Security features

- Supports three kinds of connections/networks

- Point to point

- Multiaccess networks with broadcasting

- Multiaccess networks without broadcasting

- Routing determined by computing a graph abstracting the topology of the network by using the shortest path algorithm

- Segmentation of the network through the use of Autonomous Systems and Areas for ease of management and traffic

- Multicasts rather than broadcasts

- Allows the use of virtual links

- Supports Variable Length Subnet Masking (VLSM) and Classless Interdomain Routing (CIDR)

The discussion of the RFCs will be somewhat brief and limited where the information will be repeated later in the text. If you require further information, refer to the following World Wide Web locations for the Internic and Cisco Systems:

```
http://www.internic.net
http://www.cisco.com
```

If you are not interested in the evolution of the RFCs and how they relate to each other, you can skip to the next section, "OSPF Functional Environment."

RFC 1131: OSPF Specification

RFC 1131 is the very first RFC that introduced OSPF version 1 to the networking community. There is not a lot to gain by discussing this RFC because it has been rendered obsolete several times over. This chapter will discuss the newer RFCs in more detail later.

RFC 1245: OSPF Protocol Analysis

OSPF version 1 was published in RFC 1131 on October 1, 1989. Between that time and the release of this RFC in July of 1991, OSPF version 2 was developed but had not yet become a standard. The Internet Architecture Board (IAB) and the Internet Engineering Steering Group (IESG) required two reports in order for OSPF version 2 to advance to Draft Standard Status. This RFC and the next one (RFC 1246) summarize the key features of OSPF version 2. In addition, it analyzes how the protocol will perform and scale in the Internet.

The requirements of this RFC are briefly summarized in the following list. The remaining sections of the RFC document how OSPF version 2 satisfies these requirements.

- What are the key features and algorithms of the protocol?

- How much link bandwidth, router memory, and router CPU cycles does the protocol consume under normal conditions?

- For these metrics, how does the usage scale as the routing environment grows? This should include topologies at least an order of magnitude larger than the current environment.

- What are the limits of the protocol for these metrics (that is, when will the routing protocol break)?

- For which networking environments is the protocol well-suited, and for which is it not suitable?

These requirements are actually exceptional questions that help determine the operating specifications of the protocol within a production environment. To discuss them at this point would be premature; please consult the RFC if further information is required.

RFC 1246: Experience with the OSPF Protocol

This RFC is the second of two reports on the OSPF protocol version 2. These reports are required by the IAB/IESG for an Internet routing protocol to advance to Draft Standard.

The requirements of this RFC are briefly summarized in the following list. The remaining sections of the RFC document how OSPF version 2 satisfies these requirements.

- The specification for the routing protocol must be well-written such that independent, interoperable implementations can be developed solely based on the specification. For example, it should be possible to develop an interoperable implementation without consulting the original developers of the routing protocol.

- A Management Information Base (MIB) must be written for the protocol. The MIB must be in the standardization process, but does not need to be at the same level of standardization as the routing protocol.

- The security architecture of the protocol must be set forth explicitly. The security architecture must include mechanisms for authenticating routing messages and may include other forms of protection.

- Two or more interoperable implementations must exist. At least two must be written independently.

- There must be evidence that all features of the protocol have been tested, running between at least two implementations. This must include that all of the security features have been demonstrated to operate, and that the mechanisms defined in the protocol actually provide the intended protection.

- There must be significant operational experience. This must include running in a moderate number routers configured in a moderately complex topology, and must be part of the operational Internet. All significant features of the protocol must be exercised. In the case of an Interior Gateway Protocol (IGP), both interior and exterior routes must be carried (unless another mechanism is provided for the exterior routes). In the case of an Exterior Gateway Protocol (EGP), it must carry the full complement of exterior routes.

The information presented in this RFC was compiled through a variety of sources. Because many of the goals and examples of the RFC require direct knowledge of the protocols operation, if you require further information, you should refer to the complete document.

RFC 1247: OSPF Version 2

The first three sections of this specification give a general overview of the protocol's capabilities and functions. Sections 4–16 explain the protocol's mechanisms in detail. Packet formats, protocol constants, configuration items, and required management statistics are specified in the appendices. The following list runs through the sections of the RFC.

- **Section 1: Introduction.** This section of the RFC briefly explains the history and background of the OSPF. It also includes a brief description of some of the more important design goals surrounding its use and operation.

- **Section 2: Topological Database.** This section of the RFC goes into great detail regarding the layout and operation of OSPF's database. It includes information regarding its functionality and usage.

- **Section 3: Splitting the AS into Areas.** This section of the RFC details the methods and procedures regarding the segmentation of Autonomous Systems (AS) into various OSPF areas. It also discusses some of the unique characteristics the routers within an area will have regarding the OSPF protocol.

- **Section 4: Functional Summary.** This section of the RFC contains information regarding the overall functionality of the protocol and includes the operation of the shortest path algorithm.

- **Section 5: Protocol Data Structures.** This section of the RFC describes in detail the terms of its operation on various protocol data structures. Discussion and a list is provided that comprises the top-level OSPF data structures. Areas, OSPF interfaces, and neighbors also have associated data structures that are described later in this specification.

- **Section 6: The Area Data Structure.** This section of the RFC discusses the characteristics of areas and how the protocol operates within that structure.

- **Section 7: Bringing Up Adjacencies.** This section of the RFC discusses, in general terms, the purpose and function of how OSPF forms adjacencies with the majority of routers that are neighbors.

- **Section 8: Protocol Packet Processing.** This section of the RFC discusses the general processing of routing protocol packets and their importance. The packet header of these routing protocol packets is also broken down for the reader.

- **Section 9: The Interface Data Structure.** This section of the RFC details their purpose and place within the operation of the protocol of an interface.

- **Section 10: The Neighbor Data Structure.** This section of the RFC covers the protocol's ability to converse with other routers that are considered its neighbors. This discussion includes additional information on adjacencies and how they are part of this structure.

- **Section 11: The Routing Table Structure.** This section of the RFC details the structure of the routing table and how the information provided within it can be used to forward packets correctly.

- **Section 12: Link-state Advertisements.** This section of the RFC discusses the functions of the five distinct types of link-state advertisements and how they form into the link-state database. Additional information regarding the link-state header structure is provided.

- **Section 13: The Flooding Procedure.** This section of the RFC provides an overview of how link-state update messages provide the mechanism for flooding advertisements throughout an area.

- **Section 14: Aging The Link-state Database.** This section of the RFC describes in detail the process of how a link-state advertisement uses its age field after it is placed in the database to determine which advertisement is most current.

- **Section 15: Virtual Links.** This section of the RFC provides information on the purpose and operation of virtual links and the part they play in ensuring the connectivity of different areas through the backbone.

- **Section 16: Calculation Of The Routing Table.** This section of the RFC details the OSPF routing table calculation.

RFC 1248: OSPF Version 2 Management Information Base

This RFC defines the experimental portion of the Management Information Base (MIB). Specifically, it defines objects for managing OSPF version 2. Additional information regarding the content of this RFC will not be provided, as it quickly became obsolete twice over through the publication of RFCs 1252 and 1253.

RFC 1252: OSPF Version 2 Management Information Base

This RFC defines the experimental portion of the Management Information Base (MIB). Specifically, it defines objects for managing OSPF version 2. This RFC replaced RFC 1248, which contained some minor errors in referring to "experimental" and "standard-mib." Additional information regarding the content of this RFC will not be provided, as it too quickly became obsolete.

RFC 1253: OSPF Version 2 Management Information Base

This RFC defines the experimental portion of the Management Information Base (MIB). Specifically, it defines objects for managing OSPF version 2. This memo replaces RFC 1252, which contained an error in the "standard-mib" number assignment in Section 5.

This RFC discusses network management and which RFCs were used as the basis for defining the new MIB objects associated with OSPF. A thorough discussion is then presented so that the reader has the ability to fully comprehend the standards of the MIBs implemented with OSPF.

RFC 1364: BGP OSPF Interaction

This RFC defines the various network design specifications and considerations to keep in mind when designing Autonomous System Border Routers (ASBR) that will run BGP with other ASBRs external to the Autonomous System (AS) and OSPF as its Interior Gateway Protocol (IGP).

RFC 1370: Applicability Statement for OSPF

This is probably one of the few RFCs that actually seems to encourage comments and suggestions. The purpose of this RFC was driven by the requests of users and vendors who wanted IP routers to have the ability to "interoperate" through the use of an Interior Gateway Protocol (IGP). Because OSPF was designed as an "open" standard, the protocol was recommended as follows:

"An IP router that implements any routing protocol (other than static routes) is required to implement OSPF [1] and the OSPF MIB [2]. Within OSPF, implementation of all features except TOS (Type-of-Service) routing is required; implementation of TOS routing is recommended." [direct quote rfc 1370]

RFC 1371: Choosing a "Common IGP" for the IP Internet

The authors of this RFC did an excellent job in providing a summary. Here you find a direct quote of selected sections taken directly from the RFC (entire section a direct quote from RFC 1371).

This document was originally prepared as an Internet Engineering Steering Group (IESG) recommendation to the Internet Architecture Board (IAB) in mid-summer 1991, reaching the current version by the date shown above. Although the document is now somewhat dated (CIDR and RIP II are not mentioned, for example), the IESG felt it was important to publish this along with the recent OSPF Applicability Statement [11] to help establish context and motivation.

This memo presents motivation, rationale and other surrounding background information leading to the IESG's recommendation to the IAB for a single "common IGP" for the IP portions of the Internet.

In this memo, the term "common IGP" is defined, the need for a common IGP is explained, the relation of this issue to other ongoing Internet Engineering Task Force (IETF) routing protocol development is provided, and the relation of this issue to the goal for multi-protocol integration in the Internet is explored.

Finally, a specific IGP is recommended as the "common IGP" for IP portions of the Internet—the Open Shortest Path First (OSPF) routing protocol.

The goal of this recommendation is for all vendors of Internet IP routers to make OSPF available as one of the IGP's provided with their routers.

There is a pressing need for a high functionality non-proprietary "common" Interior Gateway Protocol (IGP) for the TCP/IP protocol family. An IGP is the routing protocol used within a single administrative domain (commonly referred to as an "Autonomous System" (AS).

By "common", we simply mean a protocol that is ubiquitously available from all router vendors (as in "in common"). Users and network operators have expressed a strong need for routers from different vendors to have the capability to interoperate within an AS through use of a common IGP.

NOTES

Routing between Autonomous Systems is handled by a different type of routing protocol, called an "Exterior Gateway Protocol" ("an EGP," of which the Border Gateway Protocol [2] and

"The Exterior Gateway Protocol" [3] are examples). The issues of routing between Autonomous Systems by using "an" EGP is not considered in this memo.

There are two IGPs in the Internet standards track capable of routing IP traffic—Open Shortest Path First (OSPF) [4] and Integrated IS-IS [5] (based on the OSI IS-IS). These two protocols are both modern "link-state" routing protocols, based on the Dijkstra algorithm.

There has been substantial interaction and cooperation among the engineers involved in each effort, and the protocols share some similar features.

However, there are a number of technical design differences. Most notably, OSPF has been designed solely for support of the Internet Protocol (IP), while Integrated IS-IS has been designed to support both IP and the OSI Connectionless Network Layer Protocol (CLNP) simultaneously.

RFC 1403: BGP OSPF Interaction

This RFC is a republication of RFC 1364 to correct some editorial problems. This RFC defines the various network design specifications and considerations to keep in mind when designing Autonomous System Border Routers (ASBR) that will run BGP with other ASBRs external to the Autonomous System (AS) and OSPF as its Interior Gateway Protocol (IGP).

RFC 1583: OSPF Version 2

This RFC is very similar to RFC 1247, which it obsoletes. In fact, they are backward compatible and will interoperate with each other. The differences between them involve OSPF virtual links and some enhancements and clarifications, both minor in nature.

RFC 1247 has already been discussed in depth, and because of the rather lengthy overview given to it, this section will only discuss the differences as detailed in RFC 1583. They have been condensed for readability and the reader is referred to the RFC for more in depth information.

In RFC 1247, certain configurations of the OSPF virtual links could cause routing loops. To correct this problem, a new bit has been added, called bit "V," to the routers' links advertisement. A new algorithm parameter has been added to the OSPF area structure, which indicates if the area supports virtual links. New calculations are only to be performed by the area border routers, which examine all the summary links.

In RFC 1247, an OSPF router cannot originate separate Autonomous System (AS) external link advertisements for two networks that have the same IP address but different subnet masks. The link-state ID settings have been altered to allow the host bit portion of the network address to also be set.

The metric, LSInfinity, can no longer be used in router link advertisements to indicate unusable links. By doing this, it removes any possible confusion within an OSPF area about which links are reachable. In addition, it also assists MOSPF.

Some of the more general changes that were not discussed in detail but are mentioned and discussed in the RFC are: TOS encoding updated, flushing anomalous network links advertisements, summarizing routes into stub areas, summarizing routes into transit areas, and a variety of small changes.

RFC 1584: Multicast Extensions to OSPF

Implementations of OSPF up until this RFC only supported unicast, a message sent to a single network destination, as opposed to multicast, a message sent to a section of network addresses. It is my opinion that during the time of the writing of this RFC (1993-1994, which coincided with the network growth boom), that a need to be able to broadcast packets using the multicast technique was required, hence this RFC was developed. This RFC is extremely detailed and is over 100 pages long, allowing the complete detailing of the features and modification necessary for the deployment of the multicast feature. It is also within this RFC that a new acronym was developed—MOSPF. This new acronym stands for Multicast Open Shortest Path First (MOSPF), which allowed engineers to intelligently reference the difference between routers running OSPF using unicast and those running the new multicast implementation.

By implementing this new standard, OSPF gained the ability to forward multicast packets from one IP network to another. A new link-state Advertisement (LSA) is used to determine the exact location of all the Autonomous System's members. This RFC provides the information necessary to understand the operation of this new feature and its specific LSA, the group-membership-LSA. Also presented is how the link-state database operates to include the building, pruning, and caching of routes.

A potential area of concern was seen as a result of this new feature. When OSPF forwards multicasts between areas, incomplete routes are built; this may lead to routing inefficiency. To correct that problem, OSPF summary link advertisements or OSPF AS external link advertisements are used to approximate the neighbors needed for routing. The RFC provides a very good description of this issue and the resulting methodology needed to compensate.

Discussion is provided on the compatibility between network devices running MOSPF and non-multicast OSPF. To include some of the issues surrounding the networks operation if this topology will be in place.

Additional practical information on this subject can be found in RFC 1585, MOSPF: Analysis and Experience.

RFC 1585: MOSPF: Analysis and Experience

This RFC immediately followed the 100+ page RFC 1584 that fully detailed all relevant information regarding the ability of allowing OSPF to perform multicasting. This RFC is rather short and was written to fulfill the requirements imposed by the Internet Engineering Task Force (IETF) Internet Routing Protocol Standardization Criteria as detailed in RFC 1264.

A brief discussion surrounding the basic operation of the MOSPF and how it uses the Internet Group Management Protocol (IGMP) to monitor multicast group membership. This information is retrieved from the LAN and then forwarded out by the router by the OSPF flooding protocol through the use of the new group-membership-LSA. The specific benefits that result from this process and detailed operation is provided.

The six primary characteristics of the multicast datagram's path are also provided as well as some of the more interesting miscellaneous features.

The RFC further details the testing the author conducted and how MOSPF was implemented during these tests. Further discussion is provided on the scaling characteristics of MOSPF and some of the known difficulties surrounding it.

NOTES

Please note that Cisco routers do not currently support MOSPF because of scaling issues. The reasons for this will be discussed in later chapters.

RFC 1586: Guidelines for Running OSPF over Frame Relay Networks

This RFC specifies a set of guidelines for implementing the Open Shortest Path First (OSPF) routing protocol to bring about improvements in how the protocol runs over Frame Relay networks. The authors show the techniques that can be used to prevent the "fully meshed" connectivity that had been required by OSPF until the publication of this RFC. The benefits of following the guidelines detailed in this RFC allow for more straightforward and economic OSPF network designs. This RFC differs from many of the others in that it does not require changes to be made to the protocol itself but rather better ways to configure it.

The reason behind this RFC is that OSPF considers Frame Relay networks as non-broadcast multiple access (NBMA). OSPF does this because Frame Relay (FR) can support more than two connected routers but Frame Relay does not offer any broadcast capabilities. The following quote from the RFC addresses this issue.

OSPF characterizes FR networks as non-broadcast multiple access (NBMA) because they can support more than two attached routers, but do not have a broadcast capability [2]. Under the NBMA model, the physical FR interface on a router corresponds to a single OSPF interface through which the router is connected to one or more neighbors on the FR network; all the neighboring routers must also be directly connected to each other over the FR network. Hence OSPF implementations that use the NBMA model for FR do not work when the routers are partially interconnected. Further, the topological representation of a multiple access network has each attached router bi-directionally connected to the network vertex with a single link metric assigned to the edge directed into the vertex.

We see that the NBMA model becomes more restrictive as the number of routers connected to the network increases. First, the number of VCs required for full-mesh connectivity increases quadratically with the number of routers. Public FR services typically offer performance guarantees for each VC provisioned by the service. This means that real physical resources in the FR network are devoted to each VC, and for this the customer eventually pays. The expense for full-mesh connectivity thus grows quadratically with the number of interconnected routers. We need to build OSPF implementations that allow for partial connectivity over FR. Second, using a single link metric (per TOS) for the FR interface does not allow OSPF to weigh some VCs more heavily than others according to the performance characteristics of each connection. To make efficient use of the FR network resources, it should be possible to assign different link metrics to different VCs."

These rather expensive limitations can result in reducing the value and cost effectiveness of Frame Relay as network size increases. The RFC proposes a set of solutions that do not greatly increase the complexity of OSPF's configuration. A brief list of their recommendations is provided, though I recommend further reading in the actual RFC if more in depth information is required.

One of the recommendations is to expand the operation of an OSPF interface to allow the protocol to understand its function (point-to-point, broadcast, NBMA). In other words, allow OSPF to support both logical and physical interfaces.

The other recommendation proposed by the RFC is to use the NBMA model as OSPFs mode of operation for small homogenous networks.

NOTES

Cisco's recommendations for how to use the NBMA model can be found at: http://www.cisco.com/warp/public/104/3.html#11.0. In a nutshell, they consider point-to-point a good option because of the reduced OSPF operations required (that is, there are no DR or neighbor statements).

RFC 1587: The OSPF NSSA Option

This RFC provides a description of a new type of optional OSPF area, the "not-so-stubby" area or NSSA. This optional stubby area is very similar in operation to the existing stubby areas, but it has the additional ability to import external OSPF routes from the Autonomous System to which it belongs.

NOTES

Importing external OSPF routes will be covered later in this section.

This RFC is very good reading and its authors should be commended for bringing some of the real world into their discussion on the "not-so-stubby" area discussion. This RFC details a problem seen with the implementation of OSPF at the time of its writing. They provide a very good scenario and supporting documentation about the issue this RFC addresses.

Within this RFC, the authors propose adding a new option bit, referred to as the "N" bit and a new type of LSA area definition. This new "N" bit would assist in identifying routers that belong to a NSSA and allow them to agree upon the area's topology. The new LSA would allow for external route information to be exchanged within the area.

Discussion is provided on the new LSA and how it compares to existing LSAs and how the new LSA will operate. The need for NSSA area border routers to have a default route is also discussed and justified.

I would recommend reading more about this RFC because it provides a very good insight into how the OSPF protocol has matured and responded to the needs of its users. To assist the reader in clarifying that point, the following excerpt is provided from the RFC itself.

Why Was a "Not-So-Stubby" Area Needed?

"Wide-area transit networks (such as the NSFNET regionals) often have connections to moderately-complex "leaf" sites. A leaf site may have multiple IP network numbers assigned to it.

Typically, one of the leaf site's networks is directly connected to a router provided and administered by the transit network while the others are distributed throughout and administered by the site. From the transit network's perspective, all of the network numbers associated with the site make up a single "stub" entity. For example, BARRNet has one site composed of a class-B network, 130.57.0.0, and a class-C network, 192.31.114.0. From BARRNet's perspective, this configuration looks something like Figure 4-2

Figure 4–2
The BARRNet wide-area transit network.

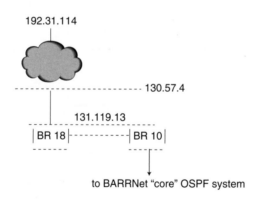

to BARRNet "core" OSPF system

The "cloud" consists of the subnets of *130.57* and network *192.31.114*, all of which are learned by RIP on router BR18. Topologically, this cloud looks very much like an OSPF stub area. The advantages of running the cloud as an OSPF stub area are:

1. Type-5 routes (OSPF external link-state advertisements (LSAs)) are not advertised beyond the router labeled "BR10". This is advantageous because the link between BR10 and BR18 may be a low-speed link or the router BR18 may have limited resources.

2. The transit network is abstracted to the "leaf" router BR18 by advertising only a default route across the link between BR10 and BR18.

3. The cloud becomes a single, manageable "leaf" with respect to the transit network.

4. The cloud can become, logically, a part of the transit network's OSPF routing system.

5. Translated type-5 LSAs that are sent into the backbone from the cloud (which is a separate stub area) may be considered "leaf" nodes when performing the Dijkstra calculation.

However, the current definition of the OSPF protocol [1] imposes topological limitations which restrict simple cloud topologies from becoming OSPF stub areas. In particular, it is illegal for a stub area to import routes external to OSPF; it is not possible for routers BR18 and BR10 to both be members of the stub area and to import the routes learned from RIP or other IP routing protocols as type-5 (OSPF external LSAs) into the OSPF system. In order to run OSPF out to BR18, BR18 must be a member of a non-stub area or the OSPF backbone to import routes other than its directly-connected network(s). Since it is not acceptable for BR18 to maintain all of BARRNet's external (type-5) routes, BARRNet is forced by OSPF's topological limitations to run OSPF out to BR10 and to run RIP between BR18 and BR10."

RFC 1745: BGP4/IDRP for IP-OSPF Interaction

This RFC has been included in this list in order to be as complete as possible, thereby helping the reader understand and be able to reference all the many sources of information available to them on OSPF.

This RFC provides the technical information necessary to design and deploy a network or implement an Autonomous System Border Router (ASBR) that will be running Border Gateway Protocol (BGP4) or Inter-Domain Routing Protocol (IDRP) for IP as your Exterior Gateway Protocol (EGP) with OSPF as your Interior Gateway Protocol (IGP). This document details the settings necessary between the fields and attributes of OSPF and the other protocols. BGP4 is referenced in RFC 1654.

RFC 1765: OSPF Database Overflow

This RFC deals with an undesirable occurrence known as OSPF Database Overflow. For OSPF to operate properly, a complete link-state database must be within each OSPF router in an area. The condition known as "database overflow" occurs when this link-state database becomes too large for the router to handle. This RFC allows for the handling on unanticipated overflows and gives some recommendations on how to configure your network if you are anticipating database overflow.

One way of handling database overflow is to encase routers having limited resources within OSPF stub areas or NSSAs. AS-external-LSAs are omitted from these areas' link-state databases, thereby controlling database size.

However, unexpected database overflows cannot be handled in the above manner. This RFC describes a way of dynamically limiting database size under overflow conditions.

The method used to recover from unexpected database overflow is discussed in great detail and if you are interested or believe you are experiencing this condition, then consult the RFC.

RFC 1793: Extending OSPF to Support Demand Circuits

The author of this RFC did an excellent job in summarizing its contents. A direct quote of selected sections taken from the RFC provides you with an excellent overview of this RFC and its contents. The following section comes directly from RFC 1371.

"This memo defines enhancements to the OSPF protocol that allow efficient operation over "demand circuits". Demand circuits are network segments whose costs vary with usage; charges can be based both on connect time and on bytes/packets transmitted. Examples of demand circuits include ISDN circuits, X.25 SVCs, and dial-up lines.

The periodic nature of OSPF routing traffic has until now required a demand circuit's underlying data-link connection to be constantly open, resulting in unwanted usage charges. With the modifications described herein, OSPF Hellos and the refresh of OSPF routing information are suppressed on demand circuits, allowing the underlying data-link connections to be closed when not carrying application traffic.

Demand circuits and regular network segments (e.g., leased lines) are allowed to be combined in any manner. In other words, there are no topological restrictions on the demand circuit support. However, while any OSPF network segment can be defined as a demand circuit, only point-to-point networks receive the full benefit. When broadcast and NBMA networks are declared demand circuits, routing update traffic is reduced but the periodic sending of Hellos is not, which in effect still requires that the data-link connections remain constantly open.

While mainly intended for use with cost-conscious network links such as ISDN, X.25 and dial-up, the modifications in this memo may also prove useful over bandwidth-limited network links such as slow-speed leased lines and packet radio.

The enhancements defined in this memo are backward-compatible with the OSPF specification defined in [1], and with the OSPF extensions defined in [3] (OSPF NSSA areas), [4] (MOSPF) and [8] (OSPF Point-to-MultiPoint Interface).

This memo provides functionality similar to that specified for RIP in [2], with the main difference being the way the two proposals handle oversubscription. However, because OSPF employs link-state routing technology as opposed to RIP's Distance Vector base, the mechanisms used to achieve the demand circuit functionality are quite different."

RFC 1850: OSPF Version 2 Management Information Base

This RFC defines a portion of the Management Information Base (MIB) for managing the Open Shortest Path First routing protocol. It had been over four years and twelve additional RFCs detailing many features of OSPF to include a new version. This RFC was needed to handle the many new enhancements to the protocol and includes over 20 new features or changes. Some of these are rather minor like name changes or clarifications and the reader is referred to the RFC for specific details. A brief list is provided of the more important modifications.

- Support for status entries were added.
- Range of the link-state database MIB was extended to include the multicast (group-membership-LSA) and NSSA (NSSA-LSA).
- The OSPF external link-state database was added.

RFC 2178: OSPF Version 2

At over 211 pages, it is a document that explains the smallest internal workings of the OSPF protocol. Armed with this document, you would be able to program the code necessary for OSPF to operate on any type of network equipment it supports. The RFC will also be able to take you through every step of its operation to include those that are not apparent to the user.

RFC 2328: OSPF Version 2

This RFC is almost a book itself and having been recently released, it is the most current RFC concerning OSPF. It surpasses the previous OSPF RFC by weighing in at 244 pages, all about OSPF. The differences between this RFC and the previous are detailed in Appendix G of the document.

Any Chief Information Officer (CIO) who is considering an OSPF network should have this document available for their design engineers. This RFC is definitely written for a very advanced and specific target audience within the networking arena.

The differences between RFC 2178 and RFC 1583 are explained in Appendix G of the RFC. All differences are backward-compatible in nature. Implementations following this RFC and of those following RFC 1583 will be able to interoperate.

RFC Conclusions

This section discussed the specific evolution of the OSPF protocol by tracing its path through the RFCs. Each RFC was examined and briefly discussed to include whether or not it is still relevant in today's networks. RFC 238 is the most current OSPF RFC, however, not every vendor's implementation supports it, so check to be sure.

Now that you have a complete picture concerning the technical resources and documentation surrounding OSPF, you should familiarize yourself with the functional environment and hierarchy used by OSPF, as discussed in the next sections.

OSPF FUNCTIONAL ENVIRONMENT

This section describes the basic characteristics and features of the OSPF functional environment. The environment in which OSPF operates is defined by the features and characteristics of its operation and design. Simply put, the functional environment of OSPF is defined as the network architecture in which the protocol will function correctly.

RFC 1793 provides an example that concerns adding to OSPF the capability to operate in demand-based circuits. Until this RFC was published and implemented, OSPF did not properly function when dealing with such circuits like ISDN. Now that the protocol has been adjusted to operate properly when dealing with demand-based circuits, you can say that the functional environment of the protocol has expanded.

With that example in mind, turn your attention to the three network types that OSPF recognizes.

OSPF Network Types

Figure 4-3 illustrates the three different network types within which OSPF operates.

The following list explains the physical characteristics of the OSPF network types illustrated in Figure 4-1:

- **Point-to-Point.** A single circuit that connects two OSPF routers, which will allow a single neighbor relationship to be built.

- **Multiaccess.** A circuit that has at least two OSPF routers connected to it and enables them to communicate with each other. This provides the potential for multiple neighbor relationships and adjacencies to be formed, but to prevent this, a Designated Router (DR) builds all the adjacencies and distributes them out to all connected routers.

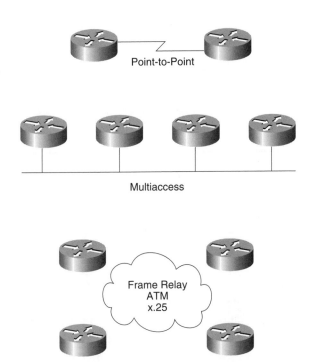

Figure 4–3
OSPF Network types.

Point-to-Point

Multiaccess

Frame Relay
ATM
x.25

Non-Broadcast Multi-Access (NBMA)

NOTES

OSPF Designated Routers (DR) will be fully explained in the next couple of chapters.

- **Nonbroadcast Multiaccess (NBMA).** NBMA networks are very similar to multiaccess networks, with the exception being that they do not allow for broadcast traffic (X.25, for example). NBMA networks also have the potential for multiple adjacencies, but the virtual circuits may not connect all routers. In some cases, this would require the adjacencies to be manually configured.

TIPS

ITU-T standard defines how connections between DTE and DCE are maintained for remote terminal access and computer communications in PDNs. X.25 specifies LAPB, a data link layer protocol, and PLP, a network layer protocol. Frame Relay has to some degree superseded X.25.

NOTES

You might ask what about point-to-multipoint? The RFC explains it best: "OSPF runs in one of two modes over non-broadcast networks. The first mode, called nonbroadcast multi-access or NBMA, simulates the operation of OSPF on a broadcast network. The second mode, called point-to-multipoint, treats the nonbroadcast network as a collection of point-to-point links. Nonbroadcast networks are referred to as NBMA networks or point-to-multipoint networks, depending on OSPF's mode of operation over the network." [RFC 2328]

Router Identification

Every router running OSPF within a network must have a unique router ID. This identification number is a 32-bit number that identifies one router to another router within an Autonomous System (AS). The router ID is used by the OSPF link-state database (LSDB) as a method of tracking each router within the AS and the links associated with it.

This identification number is unique to each OSPF router. You can employ a couple different methods to determine how your network decides upon the OSPF router ID.

To assign the router ID, OSPF uses the default method of determining the highest IP address on one of the router's active interfaces.

The other method involves manually assigning the router ID number by configuring a loopback address on the Cisco router in question. This method has the added benefit of being much more stable than the default method because a loopback address cannot go down or lose connectivity, which would result in the need to update routing tables. Chapter 7, "Designing & Implementing an OSPF Network," discusses loopback addresses in greater detail.

TIPS

Cisco is currently working on a new command to explicitly allow the setting of the router ID. It will be available in future IOS releases. The OSPF RFC does not specify how to determine the router ID; it suggests using the lowest IP address.

Configuring a loopback address as the OSPF router ID has a very significant benefit in its stability. The interface is essentially a software-based interface that can be used for many additional purposes such as summarizing IP address ranges or troubleshooting. They are reachable, provided they fall within the advertised IP address category.

TIPS

When configuring the IP address for your loopback interface, keep in mind that a "real" IP address uses valuable address space. The alternative is to use a "fake" or "bogus" IP address, which is essentially a made-up IP address that is not part of your network's normal IP address range. RFC 1597 might be a good place to start if you decide to use this method or make the first octet the last.

Neighbors

OSPF considers two routers that have an interface located on a common network as neighbors. When OSPF discovers its neighbors, this is the first step of discovering the network and building a routing table. This process begins by the router learning the router identification numbers. On multiaccess networks, these neighbors are dynamically discovered by the OSPF Hello protocol, which will be discussed in later chapters.

TIPS

To build stable OSPF neighbor relationships, ensure that the number of routers per LAN is small. Use the `priority` command to organize which is the DR and avoid having the same router as the DR for more than one link through the use of the `ip ospf priority` command.

Adjacencies

For adjacencies to form, OSPF must first have discovered its neighbors. Adjacencies are formed for the purpose of exchanging routing information. Not every neighboring router will form an adjacency. The six conditions under which OSPF will form adjacencies are as follows:

- Network connectivity is point-to-point
- Network connectivity is achieved through a virtual link
- The router is the Designated Router (DR)
- The neighboring router is the DR
- The router is the backup DR
- The neighboring router is the backup DR

Adjacencies control the distribution of routing updates in the sense that only routers adjacent to the one sending an update will process it.

Designated Routers (DRs)

OSPF builds adjacencies between routers for purposes of exchanging routing information. When OSPF has to deal with non-broadcast multiaccess (NBMA) or broadcast networks, however, a problem presents itself. In these types of networks, there are multiple routers, which would result in entirely too many adjacencies. To combat superfluous adjacencies, the Designated Router is introduced.

OSPF will designate a single router per multiaccess network to build adjacencies among all other routers. A DR is elected by OSPF's Hello protocol (which is discussed later). The presence of a DR will reduce the number of adjacencies that are formed, which in turn reduces the amount of routing protocol traffic, router overhead, and the size of the OSPF link-state database.

Designated Routers are very beneficial, but how does OSPF figure out which router on a network will be the DR? The following sequence describes how OSPF determines which router will be the DR:

NOTES

The steps described in how a DR is elected assumes that none exists on that network. If this is not the case, the process alters slightly and you should refer to the RFC 2328 for additional information.

1. OSPF selects a router at random and examines its list of neighbors; call this Router T. This list of router neighbors consists of all the routers that have begun bi-directional communication among themselves. This communication is referred to as "2-way" and is the most advanced state of communication neighboring routers can achieve without actually forming an adjacency.

2. Router T removes from that list all routers that are ineligible to become the DR. This would consist of routers that have an OSPF-assigned routing priority of 0. Proceed to the next step with the remaining routers on the list.

3. The backup DR is actually chosen first and is determined through calculations on which router has the highest priority. If more than one router has the same priority value, in essence they have become tied. Priority values can be defined

or allowed to default. OSPF will take the router with the highest router ID in order to break the tie. If there is already a DR in existence, then any router is ineligible for election at this point.

4. If no other router has declared itself to be the DR, then assign the newly commissioned backup DR to become the DR.

5. If Router T is now the new DR, then repeat Steps 3 and 4 to get a backup DR assigned and proceed to Step 6. For example, if Router T is the DR, it will not be eligible for election when Step 3 is repeated. This ensures that no router will declare itself both the DR and backup DR.

6. As a result of these calculations, Router T has become the DR and the router's OSPF interface state is set accordingly. For example, the DR has a new interface state of *DR* and the backup DR has an interface state of *DR Other*.

7. The DR will now begin sending hello packets to begin the process of building the necessary adjacencies with the remainder of the network's routers.

Protocols Within OSPF

OSPF routers communicate with each by using the OSPF protocol. OSPF runs on top of IP, though OSPF is composed of three subprotocols: Hello, Exchange, and Flooding. The following sections discuss these three subprotocols in greater detail. All OSPF packets start with a common header. Figure 4-4 illustrates a breakdown (by field) of the common header found at the beginning of each packet issued by an OSPF subprotocol.

Figure 4–4
Common OSPF subprotocol header.

Version #	Type	Packet length
Router ID		
Area ID		
Checksum		AuType
Authentication		
Authentication		

The Hello Protocol

The OSPF Hello protocol is used for three main purposes:

- To verify that links are operational

- To elect the DR and backup DR on broadcast and non-broadcast networks
- To discover, establish, and maintain neighbor relationships

In addition, the Hello protocol is responsible for ensuring that communication between OSPF neighbors is bi-directional (two-way). This type of communication is established when the router sees itself listed in its neighbor's hello packet. Figure 4-5 demonstrates how OSPF routers issue hello packets into the network in order to discover their neighbors.

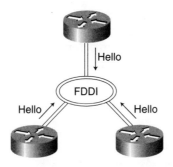

Figure 4–5
*Hello protocol
operation.*

The basic operation of the Hello protocol can be briefly listed as follows:

1. OSPF router sends out hello packet as a multicast.

2. The hello packet is received by the new OSPF router.

3. New router replies back with its own hello packet.

Hello Protocol Operation Variation in OSPF Network Types

The Hello protocol works differently on the point-to-point, multiaccess, and NBMA OSPF network types.

In broadcast networks, each router will advertise itself by periodically sending out multicasted hello packets, which allows neighbors to be discovered dynamically.

In NBMA networks, the OSPF router might require some configuration information in order for the Hello protocol to operate correctly. This configuration is actually the protocol going out onto the network to find or elect the designated router, as previously discussed in the section, "OSPF Network Types."

TIPS

Unless otherwise configured, Hello packets will default to a transmission time of once every 10 seconds or 30 seconds for NBMA. Alternatively, this can be set with the command: `ip ospf hello-interval`, which will be discussed in Chapter 6, "Advanced OSPF Design Concepts."

In point-to-point or point-to-multipoint networks, the OSPF router will send out hello packets to every neighbor with which it can communicate directly.

TIPS

In point-to-point networks, an OSPF hello packet is sent as a multicast packet. In point-to-multipoint networks, it could be sent as multicast if the data link layer replicated the packet. Or neighbor information could be configured to indicate who to send the hello to if the data link replication does not work, such as the ATM ARP server model.

Hello Protocol Packet Format

The OSPF Hello protocol packets are formatted in only one way. All OSPF packets start with a standardized 24-byte header which contains information that determines whether processing will take place on the rest of the packet. The packets contain the fields shown in Figure 4-6, always in the same order. All the fields in this format are 32 bits, except for the following fields: HelloInterval, which is 16 bits; Options, which is 8 bits; and Priority, which is 8 bits.

```
0                   1                   2                   3
0 1 2 3 4 5 6 7 8 9 0 1 2 3 4 5 6 7 8 9 0 1 2 3 4 5 6 7 8 9 0 1
```

Version #	3	Packet length	
Router ID			
Area ID			
Checksum		AuType	
Authentication			
Authentication			
Network Mask			
HelloInterval		Options	Rtr Pri
RouterDeadInterval			
Designated Router			
Backup Designated Router			
Neighbor			

Figure 4–6
Hello packet detail.

The following list describes what each of the packet fields represents.

- **Version #.** Identifies the OSPF version running on the router originating the hello packet

- **Packet length.** Provides the total length of the hello packet

- **Router ID.** Contains the originating router identification number of the appropriate interface

- **Area ID.** Contains the area number to which the originating router belongs

- **Checksum.** This section is, of course, used to ensure the packets integrity has not been comprised during transmission.

- **Network Mask.** The subnet mask associated with the interface. If subnetting is not used, it will be set to the appropriate hexadecimal value for each class of IP address.

- **HelloInterval.** The number of seconds between when the router transmits hello packets

- **Rtr Pri.** This is the where the router's priority would be annotated if this feature is used, otherwise the default is 1.

- **RouterDeadInterval.** Number of seconds since the last hello packet was received before declaring a silent router as no longer reachable

- **Designated Router.** The network's designated router (if present) IP address. This field defaults to 0.0.0.0 when a designated router is not present, like on point-to-point circuits.

- **Backup Designated Router.** The network's backup designated router (if present) IP address. This field defaults to 0.0.0.0 when a designated router is not present, like on-demand circuits.

- **Neighbor.** Contains the router IDs of each router that has sent a valid hello packet. This field can have multiple entries.

The Exchange Protocol

When two OSPF routers have established bi-directional communication, or two-way communication, they will synchronize their routing (link-state) databases. For point-to-point links, the two routers will communicate this information directly between themselves. On network links (that is, multiaccess network, either broadcast or nonbroadcast) this synchronization will take place between the new OSPF router and the DR. The Exchange protocol is first used to synchronize the routing (link-state) databases. After synchronization, any changes in the router's links will use the Flooding protocol to update all the OSPF routers.

An interesting note about the operation of this protocol is that it is asymmetric. The first step in the exchange process is to determine who is the master and who is the slave. After agreeing on these roles, the two routers will begin to exchange the description of their respective link-state databases. This information is passed between the two routers via the Exchange protocol packet layout as shown in Figure 4-7.

As they receive and process these database description packets, the routers will make a separate list that contains the records they will need to exchange later. When the comparisons are complete, the routers will then exchange the necessary updates that were put into the list so that their databases can be kept up to date.

OSPF packet header, type = 2 (dd)			
0	0	options	0 IMMs
DD sequence number			
Link State type			
Link State ID			
Advertising router			
Link State sequence number			
Link State checksum		Link State age	
- - -			

Figure 4–7
Exchange Protocol packet layout.

The Flooding Protocol

OSPF's Flooding subprotocol is responsible for distributing and synchronizing the link-state database whenever a change occurs to a link. When a link changes state (from up to down), the router that experienced the change will issue a Flooding packet which contains the state change. This update is flooded out to all of the routers' interfaces. In an attempt to ensure that the flooded packet has been received by all of its neighbors, the router will continue to retransmit the update until it receives an acknowledgement from its neighbors.

NOTES

A link is any type of connection (Frame Relay, Ethernet, and so forth) between OSPF routers.

There are two ways in which OSPF can acknowledge an update. The first is when the destination router sends an acknowledgement directly to the source router. In this case, there is no DR in use by OSPF if this is occurring. The second way is when a DR is in use and it receives the update; it will immediately retransmit this update to all other routers. Therefore, when the sending router hears this retransmission, it is considered an acknowledgement, and no further action will be taken. Figure 4-8 shows the field names and layout of the packet for the Flooding subprotocol.

Figure 4–8
*Flooding
protocol packet
layout.*

OSPF packet header, type = 4 (upd.)
Number of advertisements
Link State advertisements - - -

Link-State Advertisement (LSA)

A link is any type of connection between OSPF routers, like a frame-relay line. The state is the condition of the link, whether it is up or down. An advertisement is the method OSPF uses to provide information to other OSPF routers. You could say that link-state advertisements are packets that OSPF uses to advertise changes in the condition of a specific link to other OSPF routers.

There are six different and distinct link-state packet formats in use by OSPF, each of which is generated for a different purpose that helps keep the OSPF network routing table intact and accurate. Although there are six different packet types, these are shown later in this section. When a router receives an LSA, it checks its link-state database. If the LSA is new, the router floods the LSA out to its neighbors. After the new LSA is added to the LSA database, the router will rerun the SPF algorithm. This recalculation by the SPF algorithm is absolutely essential to preserving accurate routing tables. The SPF algorithm is responsible for calculating the routing table and any LSA change might also cause a change in the routing table. Figure 4-9 demonstrates this transaction where Router A loses a link and recalculates the shortest path first algorithm and then floods the LSA change out to the remaining interfaces. This new LSA is then analyzed by routers B and C, which recalculate and continue to flood the LSA out the other interfaces to Router D.

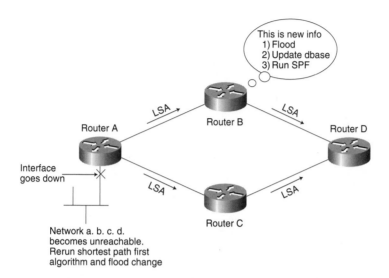

Figure 4–9
*Example of a
router sending
a new LSA and
flooding.*

NOTES

If there are no link-state changes, then every 30 minutes LSAs are sent to all neighboring routers to ensure that routers have the same link-state database.

Link-State Database Synchronization

Figure 4-10 illustrates the initial synchronization of the link-state database, which occurs in five steps as detailed in the numbered sequence following the figure.

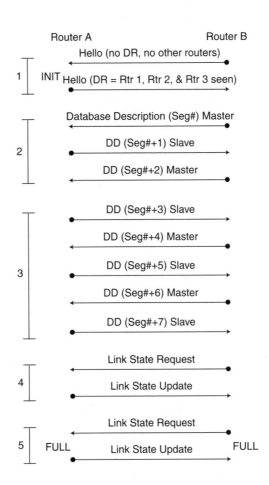

Figure 4–10
*Link-state
database
synchronization.*

The states for link-state database synchronization as illustrated in Figure 4-10 are as follows:

1. **Establish bi-directional (2-way) communication.** Accomplished by the discovery of the Hello protocol routers and the election of a DR.

2. **Exstart state.** Two neighbor routers form a master/slave relationship and agree upon a starting sequence that will be incremented to ensure LSAs are acknowledged properly and no duplication occurs. Database Description (DD) packets begin.

3. **Exchange state.** Database Description (DD) packets continue to flow as the slave router acknowledges the master's packets. At this step, OSPF (the adjacency) is considered operational because the routers can send and receive LSAs.

4. **Loading state.** Link-state requests are sent to neighbors asking for recent advertisements that have not yet been discovered. At this stage, the router builds several lists to ensure all links are up-to-date and have been acknowledged properly in the LSAs. Figure 4-11 shows the fields and information contained within the link-state request packet format.

5. **Full state.** Neighbor routers are fully adjacent because their link-state databases are fully synchronized.

During the five steps of link-state database synchronization, normal LSAs are not sent. Instead, the routers exchange packets known as Database Description (DD) packets, which are type 2 packets that are used when an adjacency is being initialized and the two routers in question are exchanging and synchronizing their link-state databases. These DD packets contain the contents of the link-state database. Figure 4-12 shows the fields and information contained within each DD packet.

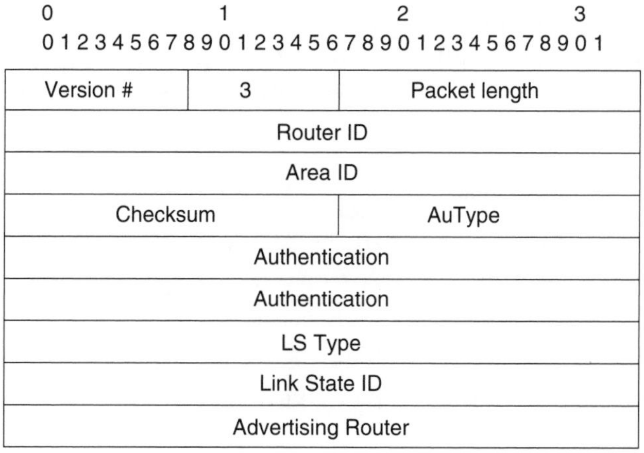

```
  0                   1                   2                   3
  0 1 2 3 4 5 6 7 8 9 0 1 2 3 4 5 6 7 8 9 0 1 2 3 4 5 6 7 8 9 0 1
 +-----------------+-----------+-----------------------------+
 |    Version #    |     3     |        Packet length        |
 +-----------------+-----------+-----------------------------+
 |                         Router ID                         |
 +-----------------------------------------------------------+
 |                          Area ID                          |
 +---------------------------+-------------------------------+
 |         Checksum          |            AuType             |
 +---------------------------+-------------------------------+
 |                       Authentication                      |
 +-----------------------------------------------------------+
 |                       Authentication                      |
 +-----------------------------------------------------------+
 |                          LS Type                          |
 +-----------------------------------------------------------+
 |                       Link State ID                       |
 +-----------------------------------------------------------+
 |                     Advertising Router                    |
 +-----------------------------------------------------------+
```

Figure 4–11
Link-state request packet format.

Of course, multiple packets might be needed to complete the synchronization and in that case a poll-response procedure is used with one router becoming the master and the other the slave.

Figure 4–12
Database
Description
packet format.

0	1	2	3
0 1 2 3 4 5 6 7 8 9	0 1 2 3 4 5 6 7 8 9	0 1 2 3 4 5 6 7 8 9	0 1

Version #	2	Packet length	
Router ID			
Area ID			
Checksum		AuType	
Authentication			
Authentication			
Interface MTU		Options 1010101010111M 1MS	
DD sequence number			
An LSA Header			

LSA Packet Types

Unlike distance vector protocols (RIP or IGRP), OSPF does not actually send its routing table to other routers. Instead, routing tables are derived from the LSA database. Table 4-1 lists and describes the six different types of LSA packets that can be generated by the source router and entered into the destination router's LSA database.

Table 4-1   *LSA packet types.*

LSA packet type	Description
1	Router Link Advertisements
2	Network Link Advertisements
3	Summary Link Advertisements (ABRs)
4	Summary Link Advertisements (ASBRs)
5	Autonomous System (AS) External Link Advertisements
7	Not-So-Stubby Areas (NSSA)

Although there are several different types of LSAs and each has a unique packet structure to reflect the information it contains, they all share a common header as shown in Figure 4-13.

LS age	options	LS type
Link State ID		
Advertising router		
LS sequence number		
LS checksum	length	

Figure 4–13
Link-state advertisement common header.

The sections that follow provide general descriptions of the six different LSA packet types.

Type 1: Router LSAs

Router LSAs are generated by each router for each area to which it belongs. These packets describe the states of the router's links to the area and are only flooded within a particular area. The link-state ID is the originating router's ID. Figure 4-14 shows the layout of each Router LSA packet.

- - 0 - - - EB	- - - 0 - - - -	number of links
Link ID		
Link data		
Type	#TOS	TOS 0 metric
TOS=x	0	TOS x metric
TOS=y	0	TOS y metric
- - -	- - -	- - -
TOS=z	0	TOS z metric

Figure 4–14
Router LSA packet layout.

Type 2: Network LSAs

Network LSAs are generated by Designated Routers (DR) and describe the set of routers attached to a particular network. They are flooded in the area that contains the network. The link-state ID is the IP interface address of the DR. Figure 4-15 shows the layout of each Network LSA packet.

Network mask		
E, TOS=0	0	TOS 0 metric
External route tag (0)		
E, TOS=x	0	TOS x metric
External route tag (x)		
- - -	- - -	- - -
E, TOS=z	0	TOS z metric
External route tag (z)		

NOTES

TOS has been removed from OSPF's specifications; however, most implementations in the field have yet to see this, so TOS fields will remain for clarity.

Type 3: Summary LSAs for ABRs (networks)

Summary LSAs are generated by Area Border Routers (ABRs) and describe inter-area routes to various networks. They can also be used for aggregating routes. The link-state ID is the destination network number. Figure 4-16 shows the layout of each Summary LSA packet.

Network mask		
TOS=0	0	TOS 0 metric
TOS=x	0	TOS x metric
- - -	- - -	- - -
TOS=z	0	TOS z metric

Type 4: Summary LSAs for ASBRs (networks)

Summary LSAs describe links to Autonomous System Border Routers (ASBRs) and are also generated by Area Border Routers (ABRs). The link-state ID is the router ID of the described ASBR. Figure 4-16 (shown previously) illustrates the layout of each packet.

Type 5: Autonomous System External LSAs

Type 5 LSAs are generated by the Autonomous System Border Routers (ASBRs). They describe routes to destinations external to the Autonomous System. They will be flooded everywhere with the exception of stub areas. The link-state ID is the external network number.

Type 7: Not-So-Stubby Area (NSSA)

Type 7 LSAs are generated by Area Border Routers (ABRs). They describe routes within the NSSA. They can be summarized and converted into Type 5 LSAs by the ABRs. After they are converted to Type 5 LSAs, they will be distributed to areas that can support Type 5 LSAs. Refer to RFC 1587 for further details on how this conversion is done.

Link-State Advertisement Operation Example

Now that all six LSAs have been discussed and you understand how they operate within the OSPF functional environment, refer to Figure 4-17 for a visual representation for the operation and interaction between the various types of LSAs within an OSPF network.

Link-State Database

OSPF routers in the same area will all have the same link-state database and run the same SPF algorithm with themselves as the root. The records in this database are used by the SPF algorithm to determine the network topology and to compute the shortest path to a destination. The characteristics of the link-state database are as follows:

- All routers belonging to the same area have the identical link-state database

- Calculating routes by using the SPF is performed separately for each area

- LSA flooding is contained within the area that experienced the change

- The link-state database is composed of the six different LSA types

- A router has a separate link-state database for each area to which it belongs

Figure 4–17
*Link-state
advertisement
operation.*

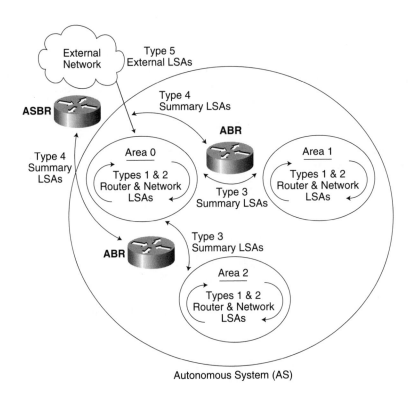

The link-state database is the data source to compute the network routes, which must be computed again after any change or potential change in the network's topology as this might have caused the routes to change. Each OSPF router will construct a routing table with itself as the center of the network. A topology that represents the network is extracted from the records contained within the link-state database.

The SPF algorithm is then used to compute the shortest path from the local OSPF router to each destination within the network. As these computations are run and the shortest path determined, this information is put into a routing table. From these computations the router derives the next router (hop) that must be used in order to reach the destination. This information is used by the router in order to route packets on to their destination.

There are many factors that can effect the results of these calculations such as, Type of Service (TOS) and externally derived routes.

OSPF ROUTING HIERARCHY

One of most important features within the OSPF protocol is its capability to use a hierarchical routing structure. There are two characteristics that you must keep in mind when considering how OSPF operates within this type of hierarchical structure.

- Structure must exist or be created in order for OSPF to operate properly
- Explicit topology has precedence over addressing

The following sections discuss types of OSPF routers, hierarchical network design techniques, Autonomous System, areas, and routing within a hierarchical structure. This information will be presented in how they all interact to bring an OSPF network together.

Types of OSPF Routers

The hierarchical routing structure used by OSPF is designated by four different types of routers. Each has a unique role and set of defining characteristics within the hierarchy. Figure 4-18 shows a typical OSPF network with multiple areas containing the different types of OSPF routers.

The sections that follow provide the general descriptions for the four different types of OSPF routers.

Internal Routers (IRs)

Internal Routers (IRs) are routers whose directly connected networks all belong to the same OSPF area. These types of routers will have a single link-state database because they only belong to one area.

Area Border Routers (ABRs)

ABRs are attached to multiple OSPF areas, so there can be multiple ABRs within a network. ABRs will have multiple instances of the link-state database because of this. The router will run one database for each area that will be summarized, and then it will be presented to the backbone for distribution to other areas. Routers located on the border of one or more OSPF areas and connects those areas to the backbone network are known as ABRs. ABRs are considered members of both the OSPF backbone and the attached areas. The ABRs therefore maintain routing tables describing both the back-bone topology and the topology of the other areas. Remember that an ABR only sends summarized information to the backbone area, and in order to be considered an ABR the router must be connected to the backbone.

Figure 4–18
*Types of OSPF
routers.*

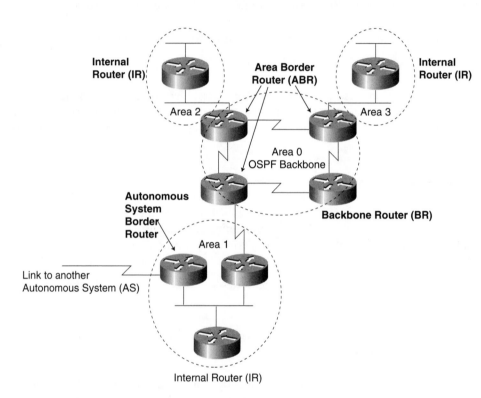

Autonomous System Border Routers (ASBRs)

ASBRs are connected to more than one Autonomous System and exchange routing information with routers in another autonomous system. ASBRs advertise the exchanged external routing information throughout their autonomous system. Every router within an autonomous system will know how to get to each ASBR with its AS. ASBRs run both OSPF and another routing protocol, such as RIP or BGP. ASBRs must reside in a non-stub OSPF area.

TIPS

When using Cisco routers, the `redistribution` command is often used to bring two routing protocols together. The Border Gateway Protocol (BGP) can also be used to bring multiple Autonomous Systems together. For additional information on this protocol and its use, please see *Internet Routing Architectures* by Bassam Halabi.

Backbone Routers (BRs)

BRs typically have an interface to the backbone area and several other OSPF areas. Backbone Routers do not have to be ABRs. Routers that only have interfaces connecting them to the backbone are also considered BRs.

Hierarchical Network Design Techniques

When considering how to design your OSPF network, remember the following factors that are supported by OSPF and currently accepted network design theories:

- A three-tiered backbone approach that will allow for fast convergence and economy of scale

- Never more than six router hops from source to destination

- 30 to 100 routers per area

- IP address space must be contiguous

- All areas connect to area 0

- Keep the backbone/area 0 simple, symmetrical, and restrict access by end users

- Do not allow more than two areas per ABR, in addition to its connection to area 0. Otherwise, it will have to keep track of to many link-state databases.

Understanding Autonomous Systems

An Autonomous System (AS) is a group of areas sharing a common routing strategy.

NOTES

The Internet Assigned Numbers Authority (IANA) is an organization operated under the auspices of the ISOC as a part of the IAB. IANA delegates authority for IP address-space allocation and domain-name assignment to the NIC and other organizations. IANA also maintains a database of assigned protocol identifiers used in the TCP/IP stack, including autonomous system numbers.

OSPF does not exchange AS numbers like B6P, so there is no need to register them with IANA.

The actual routing of information within an Autonomous System takes place in one of three ways:

- If the source and destination addresses of a packet reside within the same area, then intra-area routing is used.

- If the source and destination addresses of a packet reside within different areas but still within the AS, then inter-area routing is used.

- If the source and destination addresses of a packet reside outside the AS, then external routing is used.

These different types of routing will be discussed later under the section, "Routing Within a Hierarchical Structure."

Understanding Areas

A typical scenario for many networks as they grow and more sites are added is that the benefits of OSPF begin to degrade. For example, the link-state database will continue to grow in size as the number of routers grows. At some point it will become inefficient. The flooding LSAs from a large number of routers can also cause congestion problems. To solve these problems, you begin by segmenting your Autonomous System (AS) into multiple areas. As you group routers into areas, consider limiting the number of routers per area. Each router will then have a link-state database with entries for each router in its area.

Areas are similar to the idea of a subnet in that the routes and networks contained within can be easily summarized. In other words, areas are contiguous logical segments of the network that have been grouped together. Through the use of areas within OSPF, the network will be easier to manage and will provide a marked reduction in routing traffic. These benefits are gained because the actual topology of an area is invisible to other routers outside of the area.

Areas also allow the routers contained within them to run their own link-state database and SPF algorithm. In truth, a router will run one copy of the link-state database for each area to which it is connected.

Characteristics of an OSPF Area

The following list provides some general characteristics of an OSPF area.

- Areas contain a group of contiguous hosts and networks
- Routers have a per area topological database and run the same SPF algorithm
- Each area is connected to the backbone area known as area 0
- Virtual links can be used
- Allows for inter-area routing

The characteristics outlined in the preceding list need to be considered when working within an OSPF network.

Area Design Rules

When designing an OSPF area, you should keep some of the following requirements in mind:

- A backbone area must be present
- All areas must have a connection to backbone, even stub areas
- The backbone area must be contiguous

The Backbone Area

A backbone area is the logical and physical structure for the Autonomous System and is attached to multiple areas. The backbone area is responsible for distributing routing information between non-backbone areas. The backbone must be contiguous, but it need not be physically contiguous; backbone connectivity can be established and maintained through the configuration of virtual links, which will be discussed in Chapter 5, "The Fundamentals of OSPF Routing & Design."

Stub Areas

An area could be referred to as a stub area when there is a single exit point from that area, or if external routing to outside of the area does not have to take an optimal path. A stub is just what it sounds like, a dead end within the network. Packets can only enter and leave through the Area Border Router. A rather unique occurrence I will grant you, so why would you ever need such an area? The reason is that same old nuisance that keeps coming around—network size. By building stub areas, you can reduce the overall size of the tables within the routers that are inside the stub area.

- External networks, such as those redistributed from other protocols into OSPF, are not allowed to be flooded into a stub area.

- Configuring a stub area reduces the link-state database size inside an area and reduces the memory requirements of routers inside that area.

- Routing from these areas to the outside world is based on a default route. They do contain inter-area and intra-area routes.

- Stub areas should have one Area Border router.

All OSPF routers inside a stub area have to be configured as stub routers because whenever an area is configured as stub, all interfaces that belong to that area will start exchanging hello packets with a flag that indicates that the interface is stub. Actually this is just a bit in the hello packet ("E" bit) that gets set to 0. All routers that have a common segment have to agree on that flag. If the routers don't agree, then they will not become neighbors and routing will not take effect.

Stub Area Restrictions

Stub areas have certain restrictions applied to their operation. This is because they have been designed not to carry external routes and any of the situations in the following list could cause external links to be injected into the stub area.

- Stub areas cannot be used as a transit area for virtual links.

- An ASBR cannot be internal to a stub area.

- OSPF allows certain areas to be configured as stub areas.

TIPS

An extension to stub areas is what is called a *totally stubby area*. Cisco Systems indicates this type of stub area by adding a `no-summary` keyword to the stub area configuration within the router. A totally stubby area is one that blocks external routes and summary routes (inter-area routes) from going into the area. This way, only intra-area routes and the default route of `0.0.0.0` are injected into the area.

Routing Within a Hierarchical Structure

There are three types of routes that may be used by OSPF: intra-area, inter-area, and external routes. The sections that follow provide general descriptions of these route types.

Intra-Area Routing

Intra-area routing is the name used to describe routing within a logical area. These types of routes are described by Router LSAs (Type 1). In order for packets to be routed within a single area, intra-area routing is used. When displayed in the OSPF routing table, these types of links are designated with an "O."

Inter-Area Routing

Inter-area routing is the name used to describe routing between two or more logical areas that still fall within the source Autonomous System. These types of routes are described by Summary LSAs. When routing packets between two non-backbone areas, the backbone will be used. This means that inter-area routing has pieces of intra-area routing along its path, for example:

1. An intra-area path is used from the source router to the area border router.

2. The backbone is then used from the source area to the destination area.

3. An intra-area path is used from the destination area's area border router to the destination.

Put these three routes together and you will have an inter-area route. Of course, the SPF algorithm will calculate the lowest cost between these two points. When these types of routes are displayed in the OSPF routing table, these types of routes are indicated with an IA.

AS (Autonomous System) External Routes

External routing information can be gained by OSPF through a number of means as discussed. This information must then be made available throughout the Autonomous System in order for it to be of use. The ASBR routers will summarize the information and flood this information throughout the AS. Every router will receive this information with the exception of stub areas.

There are two specific types of external routes, which are as follows:

- **E1 routes.** E1 routes are the sum of internal and external OSPF metrics. They are identified by the E1 designation within the OSPF routing table. For example, if a packet is destined for another autonomous system, then E1 routes add all the metrics in both Autonomous Systems associated with reaching the destination.

- **E2 routes.** E2 routes are the default for OSPF. They do not add the internal OSPF metrics. For example, if a packet is destined for another autonomous system, then E2 routes only add the metrics from the destination AS associated with reaching the destination.

TIPS

Multiple routes to the same destination will use the following order of preference in order to route: intra-area, inter-area, E1, and E2.

CHAPTER SUMMARY

This chapter discussed in detail the background and evolution of the OSPF protocol by tracing the RFCs relating to OSPF. The "OSPF Overview" section of this chapter discussed the earliest appearance and creation of the shortest path first algorithm. From the established beginnings of OSPF, the evolution and modifications applied to it will be traced through the RFCs. Each RFC relating directly and indirectly to the protocol is summarized and discussed as needed.

The "OSPF Functional Environment" section of this chapter helped you understand the internetworking environment of the protocol so as to design a network in which it will operate properly. The functional environment is a key element in understanding OSPF. Within this section are several basics to the protocol that are discussed and explored: network types, router identification, adjacencies, Designated Routers, protocols within OSPF, and LSAs.

The "OSPF Routing Hierarchy" section demonstrated how the protocol allows for a variety of different configurations and implementations. This capability requires many different levels or areas. OSPF's capability to perform as a hierarchical routing protocol allows it to be considered in networks of varying sizes. As a result of this, OSPF supports a variety of techniques and designations that make operation and design much smoother. Within this section, you learned about the types of OSPF routers and hierarchical design techniques. The latter of which included how OSPF separates the hierarchy through the use of areas and Autonomous Systems.

CASE STUDY: ADDING A NEW OSPF ROUTER TO A NETWORK

This case study attempts to provide a scenario that will cover most of the information presented in this chapter. Suppose that a new OSPF router is added to a network. With this scenario in hand, follow along with the case study to understand the ramifications of how adding a new OSPF router would affect an operating network. Refer to Figures 4.19a–4.19d, which detail each step of the process as it occurs in the following sequence:.

1. A new OSPF router is added to the network.

2. This new router immediately transmits a multicast hello packet by using the all OSPF routers multicast address of 224.0.0.5. At this point, the router doesn't know who or if there is a designated router (see Figure 4-19a).

Figure 4–19a
Adding a new
router.

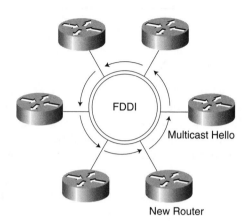

TIPS

If a Designated Router (DR) already exists on a network, a new router, even one with a better priority, will not take over as DR.

3. The DR and BDR will respond back to the new router with a unicast hello packet specifically addressed to it. This begins the process of building an adjacency (see Figure 4-19b).

4. After the adjacency has been established with the DR, the new router will send a Router LSA to the DR describing the specific links it has available and their status. During this time, the BDR is also listening to see if the DR responds, thus proving it is up and operational (see Figure 4-19c).

Designated Router   Backup Designated Router

DR   BDR

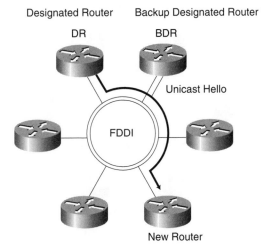

Unicast Hello

FDDI

New Router

Figure 4–19b
*DR and BDR
respond.*

DR   Router   BDR
            LSA

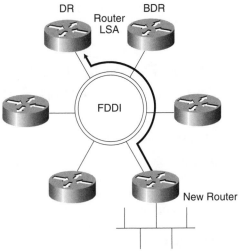

FDDI

New Router

Figure 4–19c
*Router LSA is
sent.*

5. The BDR continues to listen, thereby ensuring the DR is operating. The DR will send out a multicast (224.0.0.5) network LSA to the entire network informing them of the new routes available, as a result of the new router. All routers must then respond with an acknowledgement so the DR knows they have received the new information (see Figure 4-19d).

Figure 4–19d
Network LSA is sent.

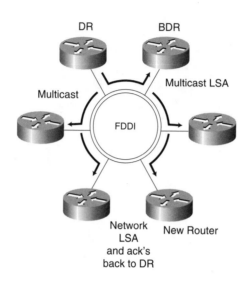

6. At this point, the new router has been fully identified to all other routers within the network. This information also includes any networks it can reach.

CASE STUDY: DYNAMIC IP ROUTING (OSPF) USING IP UNNUMBERED POINT-TO-POINT SUBINTERFACES

The sample configuration in Figure 4-20 routes TCP/IP over a partially-meshed Frame Relay network by using point-to-point subinterfaces.

IP routes are dynamically resolved by using Open Shortest Path First (OSPF) as the routing protocol. Special care is needed when configuring OSPF over partially-meshed Frame Relay. OSPF requires direct connections to each of its neighbors in order to elect a Designated Router (DR) and form adjacencies with neighboring OSPF routers. However, on a partially-meshed Frame Relay network, the physical topology does not provide the direct access that OSPF requires.

The solution to the adjacency problem is to use subinterfaces. In general, it is good practice to use subinterfaces for partially-meshed Frame Relay networks. A Frame Relay network designed by using subinterfaces scales much easier to future expansion. New sites and other protocols (e.g. AppleTalk and IPX) can be added much easier in the future if subinterfaces are used. Moreover, subinterfacing is the preferred method of implementing an OSPF network over Frame Relay.

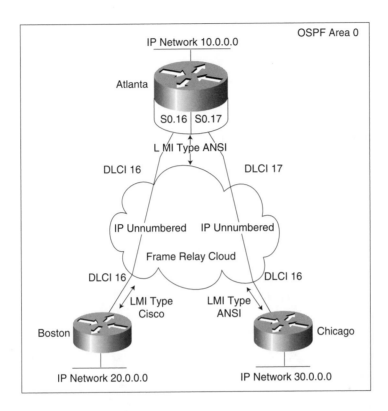

Figure 4–20
Hub-And-Spoke Frame Relay.

Subinterfaces can be used to split a single, physical interface into separate, virtual point-to-point interfaces. Each subinterface is now treated as its own point-to-point network segment and will require its own IP subnet. Fortunately, IP unnumbered can be used to alleviate the burden of designing the additional subnets as illustrated in the diagram above. With the Frame Relay network broken out into subinterfaces, OSPF will now consider the cloud as a set of point-to-point links rather than one multi-access network. The point-to-point connections will allow the routers to form OSPF adjacencies without DR election.

The central router (Atlanta) configuration for the network setup in Figure 4-20 is as follows:

```
version 11.2 <*>
service udp-small-servers <*>
service tcp-small-servers <*>
!
hostname Atlanta
```

```
!
enable secret cisco
!
ip subnet-zero
no ip domain-lookup
!
interface Ethernet0
 ip address 10.1.1.1 255.0.0.0
!
interface Serial0
 no ip address <*>
 encapsulation frame-relay
 frame-relay lmi-type ansi
!
interface Serial0.16 point-to-point
 description Frame Relay to Boston
 ip unnumbered Ethernet0
 frame-relay interface-dlci 16 broadcast
!
interface Serial0.17 point-to-point
 description Frame Relay to Chicago
 ip unnumbered Ethernet0
 frame-relay interface-dlci 17 broadcast
!
router ospf 1
 network 10.0.0.0 0.255.255.255 area 0
!
ip http server
ip classless
!
line con 0
 password console
 login
line aux 0 <*>
line vty 0 4
 password telnet
 login <*>
!
end <*>
```

The remote router (Boston) configuration for the network setup in Figure 4-20 is as follows:

```
version 11.2 <*>
service udp-small-servers <*>
service tcp-small-servers <*>
!
hostname Boston
!
enable secret cisco
!
ip subnet-zero
no ip domain-lookup
!
interface Ethernet0
 ip address 20.1.1.1 255.0.0.0
!
interface Serial0
 no ip address <*>
 encapsulation frame-relay
!
interface Serial0.16 point-to-point
 description Frame Relay to Atlanta
 ip unnumbered Ethernet0
 frame-relay interface-dlci 16 broadcast
!
router ospf 2
 network 20.0.0.0 0.255.255.255 area 0
!
ip http server
ip classless
!
line con 0
 password console
 login
line aux 0 <*>
line vty 0 4
 password telnet
 login <*>
!
end <*>
```

The remote router (Chicago) configuration for the network setup in Figure 4-20 is as follows:

```
version 11.2 <*>
service udp-small-servers <*>
service tcp-small-servers <*>
!
hostname Chicago
!
enable secret cisco
!
ip subnet-zero
no ip domain-lookup
!
interface Ethernet0
 ip address 30.1.1.1 255.0.0.0
!
interface Serial0
 no ip address <*>
 encapsulation frame-relay
 frame-relay lmi-type ansi
!
interface Serial0.16 point-to-point
 description Frame Relay to Atlanta
 ip unnumbered Ethernet0
 frame-relay interface-dlci 16 broadcast
!
router ospf 3
 network 30.0.0.0 0.255.255.255 area 0
!
ip http server
ip classless
!
line con 0
 password console
 login
line aux 0 <*>
line vty 0 4
 password telnet
 login <*>
!
end <*>
```

FREQUENTLY ASKED QUESTIONS

Q— *What type of "bogus" IP address should I use on my router's loopback interface?*

A— There are several techniques that would work just fine. Consider taking the IP address from the serial interface and transposing the first and last octets. For example, a serial address of 156.245.75.23 would become a loopback address of 23.245.75.156. Any combination of swapping octets around would work or you can make up a scheme that reflects the logic of your network.

Q— *How do I configure a loopback interface on my Cisco router?*

A— Enter the router's enable mode and then go into global configuration. Determine what number loopback address you want to access and type that into the router, then assign it an IP address and mask. Exit out of configuration mode and do a show interface on that loopback interface and it should be there for you. Examples to do this are provided in Chapter 7.

Q— *How do I decide which router I want to be the Designated Router and Backup Designated Router?*

A— Cisco routers by default do not have the ip OSPF priority ## command turned on. This means that OSPF will default to using the highest IP address on the router as the OSPF router ID. In order for the DR election process to be configured according to your needs, you must do the following:

1. Assign the router you desire to be the DR a high priority number by using the command: ip OSPF priority 10, for example.

2. Then, using the same command for the BDR, just use a smaller number in the command.

No other router needs to be configured with the OSPF priority command.

Q— *What is the multicast address for all OSPF routers?*
A— 224.0.0.5

Q— *What is the multicast address for all Designated Routers?*
A— 224.0.0.6

Q— *What is an area?*

A— An area is a collection of networks together with routers having interfaces to any of the included networks.

Q— *What technique should I use to number areas? The RFC says to number them like IP addresses.*

A— It is not required nor necessary to number your areas like IP addresses; either way, OSPF will operate just fine. You can use the normal decimal number technique (1, 2, 3, 4, for example) or the method that follows an IP address format. In my opinion, there is an added benefit of being able to make your areas very logical in their naming if you follow the IP address technique.

Q— *What is a stub area?*

A— A stub area is an area in which you don't allow advertisements of external routes.

Q— *When you define an area to be a stub area by the command* `area xx stub` *in every router in the stub area, do you need the* `area` xx `default- cost` yy *command in every router too?*

A— No, `area-default-cost` yy is only required in area border routers.

Q— *If your network has no externals, is there any benefit to using stub areas?*

A— No, you don't need the `stub area` command in the router if your network has no externals.

Q— *When OSPF is configured, does area 0 have to be there?*

A— There is no need to have area 0 if you have only one area in your network. You can use any number as the area ID. You only need area 0 to connect multiple areas if you have more than one area. But, when the Autonomous System is divided into areas, there has to be an area 0 which is the backbone area. The backbone must be contiguous. If the backbone is partitioned, then parts of the Autonomous System will become unreachable. Virtual links can be configured to repair the partition.

Q— *Could you configure an Autonomous System that contained one class B network and used multiple areas with backbone area 0?*

A— Yes.

Q— *Can you use an area ID based on IP addresses?*

A— Yes, Cisco's implementation takes area ID both in IP address format and decimal number.

Q— *There is a command to set the link-state Retransmit Interval. What is this?*

A— The command *ip ospf retransmit <interval>* will do this. Each newly received link-state advertisement must be acknowledged. This is done by sending LSA packets. LSAs are retransmitted until they are acknowledged. Link-state Retransmit Interval defines the time between retransmissions. The actual operation of this command is shown in Chapter 6.

Q— *What is a virtual link? When and how is it used?*

A— The backbone area must be contiguous; otherwise some areas of the Autonomous System will become unreachable. Virtual links establish connectivity to the backbone. The two end points of the virtual link are area border routers that both have virtual link configured. Whenever there is an area that does not have a connection to the backbone, the virtual link provides that connectivity. OSPF treats two routers joined by a virtual link as if they were connected by an unnumbered point-to-point network. Virtual links cannot be configured on unnumbered links or through stub areas.

Q— *A great deal of literature suggests that OSPF is a complete solution to the problems of discontiguous addressing in IP nets. However, many people were under the impression that only the static option of the virtual link in OSPF allowed discontiguous nets regardless of the mask propagation properties of OSPF. Is this an accurate statement?*

A— No. Virtual links in OSPF maintain connectivity to the backbone from non-backbone areas, but they are unnecessary for discontiguous addressing. OSPF provides support for discontiguous networks, because every area has a collection of networks and OSPF attaches a mask to each advertisement. However, it is not the panacea for poor network design.

Q— *Is there a limitation on the number of routers in an area?*

A— No, but this all depends on your network, available memory, processing, and so forth. In general, in order for OSPF to scale well, you should have less than 40 routers in an area. Though the factors regarding OSPF's operation can really make this figure vary, so go slowly.

Q— *All advertisements are sent by using multicast addressing. Are the multicast IP addresses mapped to MAC-level multicast addresses?*

A— Except for Token Ring, the multicast IP addresses are mapped to MAC-level multicast addresses. Cisco maps Token Ring to MAC-level broadcast and functional addresses.

Q— *What is the OSPF MAC Address for multicasting?*

A— `01-00-5E-00-00-00`

Q— *Does Cisco support the OSPF MIB definitions defined in RFC 1253?*

A— Release 11.0 supports the OSPF MIB as read only and with no trap.

Q— *Does Cisco's software comply with RFC 1364, "BGP OSPF Interaction?"*

A— Yes.

Q— *Do you have to manually set up adjacencies for routers on the SMDS cloud with the OSPF neighbor subcommand?*

A— In Cisco IOS 9.1, you need the OSPF `neighbor` command to make OSPF work on SMDS. As of 10.0, you need the `ip ospf network broadcast` command on the designated router.

Q— *Why must the* `neighbor` *command be used when running OSPF over NBMA (Frame Relay, X.25, etc.)?*

A— You need the `neighbor` command to make OSPF work on NBMA in Cisco IOS 9.1. As of 10.0, at the OSPF level, an NBMA network can be configured as a broadcast network, and OSPF would treat NBMA as a broadcast network only. You would need X.25 maps with BROADCAST keyword to make it work.

Q— *Can I assume that when routes are redistributed between OSPF processes, all SPF metrics are preserved and the default metric value is not used?*

A— Metrics are not preserved. The redistribution between them is like redistribution between any two IP routing processes.

Q— *What do the states DR/OTHER, DR, and BDR mean in* `sh IP OSPF int` *output?*

A— DR means Designated Router, BDR means Backup Designated Router, and DR/OTHER means a router that is neither the DR nor the BDR. DR will generated a Network LSA representing that network, listing all the routers on that network.

I have the following setup:

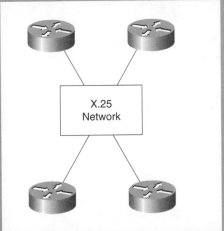

Figure 4–19d
X.25 network setup.

X.25 Network

Q— *R1 through R4 are running OSPF, and each router is declared as neighbor in the other three. I want to connect R5, a fifth router, to that network. Can I declare R5 as neighbor of the Designated Router only, and still get the whole routing table?*

A— You need to list all the routers only in the routers eligible for DR/BDR. If you list R5 only in the present DR, you might have some problems when that DR goes down and routers are trying to become DR/BDR. If you think a router should not be allowed to become DR or BDR (its priority is set to

0), there is no need to list any routers in that router. As of Cisco IOS 10.0, Cisco routers allow these nonbroadcast networks to be configured as broadcast so as to avoid all this neighbor configuration.

Q— *How does Cisco accommodate OSPF routing on partial-mesh Frame Relay networks? What about other routing protocols, like RIP and IGRP?*

A— You can configure OSPF to understand whether or not it should attempt to use multicast facilities on a multi-access interface. Also, if multicast is available, OSPF will use it for its normal multicasts.

Cisco IOS 10.0 includes a feature called "subinterfaces." This feature can be used with Frame Relay and similar interfaces to tie a set of VCs together to form a virtual interface, which acts as a single IP subnet. All systems within the subnet are expected to be fully meshed. This feature is routing protocol independent. As of 10.3 and 11.0, point-to-multipoint is also available.

RIP and IGRP have had other enhancements to deal with this same situation since Cisco IOS 8.3(3).

Q— *The* `ip ospf network` *subcommand associates router interfaces with OSPF areas, and it requires an address-wildmask pair. Which address-wildmask pair should be used for assigning an unnumbered interface to an area?*

A— Use the address-wildmask pair of the interface to which the unnumbered interface is pointing.

Q— *Does Cisco support RIP to OSPF redistribution over X.25 IP unnumbered?*
A— Yes.

Q— *In Cisco IOS 9.1, is the* `neighbor` *command required when running OSPF over X.25 networks?*

A— You need the `neighbor` command to make OSPF work on X.25 in Cisco IOS 9.1. In 9.21 and later, at OSPF level, an X.25 network can be configured to be a broadcast network, and OSPF treats X.25 as a broadcast network only. X.25 maps with the "broadcast" keyword are be needed to make it work.

Q— *In Cisco IOS 9.1, is the* `neighbor` *command required when running OSPF over X.25 networks?*

A— You need the `neighbor` command to make OSPF work on X.25 in Cisco IOS 9.1. In 9.21 and later, at OSPF level, an X.25 network can be configured to be a broadcast network, and OSPF treats X.25 as a broadcast network only. X.25 maps with the "broadcast" keyword are be needed to make it work.

SOLUTIONS TO COMMON OSPF PROBLEMS

OSPF Routers Not Establishing Neighbors

Symptom: OSPF routers are not establishing neighbor relationships properly. The result is that routing information is not properly exchanged between routers.

Possible Problem: Misconfigured or missing network router configuration command.

Solution: Perform the following procedure:

1. Use the `show ip ospf interfaces` EXEC command to see in which interfaces OSPF is enabled.

2. If the output indicates that an interface that should be running OSPF is not doing so, use the `show running-config` privileged EXEC command to view the router configuration.

3. Make sure that network router configuration commands are specified for each interface on which OSPF should run.

   For example, if the IP address of Ethernet interface 0 is 192.168.52.42 with a subnet mask of 255.255.255.0, enter the following commands to enable OSPF on the interface:

   ```
   c4500(config)# router ospf 100

   c4500(config-router)# network 192.168.52.0 0.0.0.255 area 0
   ```

   Make sure the proper process IDs, addresses, wildcard masks, and other variables are properly specified.

Take note that there is no correlation between OSPF wildcard masks (used in OSPF network commands) and the subnet mask configured as part of an interface IP address.

4. Check other OSPF routers on the network by using the preceding steps. Make sure that OSPF is configured properly on all neighboring routers so that neighbor relationships can be established.

Possible Problem: Mismatched Hello or dead timers, E-bits (set for stub areas), area IDs, authentication types, or network masks.

Solution: The values set for the Hello timer and dead timer intervals, E-bits (this bit is set if the router is configured in a stub area), area IDs, authentication types, and network masks should all be the same throughout an OSPF area and in some cases the entire OSPF network. Use the following procedure:

1. Use the `show ip ospf neighbor` privileged EXEC command to identify the OSPF neighbors of each router.

2. If the output does not list an expected neighbor, use the `show ip ospf interface` privileged EXEC command on the router and its expected neighbor. Examine the Hello and dead timer interval values configured on OSPF interfaces.

   ```
   C7010# show ip ospf interface
   [...]
   ```
   Timer intervals configured, Hello 12, Dead 48, Wait 40, Retransmit 5

3. Compare the values configured for the timers on each router. If there is a mismatch, reconfigure the timer values so that they are the same on the router and its neighbor.

   For example, to change the Hello timer interval to 10 on Ethernet interface 0/1, enter the following commands:

   ```
   C7010(config)# interface e0/1
   C7010(config-if)# ip ospf hello-interval 10
   ```

4. Use the `debug ip ospf adj` privileged EXEC command. Check the output for mismatched values.

   In the following example, there is a network mask mismatch. The mask received from router `141.108.10.3` is `255.255.255.0`, and the mask configured on the router C4500 is `255.255.255.252`:

```
C4500#  debug ip ospf adj
OSPF: Mismatched hello parameters from 141.108.10.3
Dead R 40 C 40, Hello R 10 C 10 Mask R 255.255.255.0 C 255.255.255.252
```

TIPS

You might need to use the `term monitor` command if you are not on the console port. A virtual terminal port (vty) does not monitor without this command.

5. If mismatches are indicated in the debug output, try to resolve the mismatch. For detailed information about configuring OSPF, see the Cisco *IOS Network Protocols Configuration Guide, Part 1*.

6. Perform the same types of steps for all of these parameters. Check that all routers in an area have the same area ID, whether all routers in the area are configured as stub routers, whether the same authentication type is configured for all routers, and so forth. For information on configuring these parameters, consult the Cisco IOS Network Protocols Configuration Guide, Part 1. Take note that the timer values are extremely important when Cisco routers interoperate with routers from other vendors.

Possible Problem: Access list is misconfigured

Solution: Perform the following procedure:

1. Use the `show access-list` privileged EXEC command on suspect routers to see if there are IP access lists configured on the router.

2. If there are IP access lists enabled on the router, disable them using the appropriate commands. For example, to disable input access list 10, use the following commands:

```
ROUTER_A# conf t
ROUTER_A(conf)# int s0
ROUTER_A(config-if)# no ip access-group 10 in
```

3. After disabling all access lists on the router, determine if the router is able to establish neighbor relationships normally. Use the show ip ospf neighbor privileged EXEC command. If the proper neighbor relationships have been established, an access list is probably filtering OSPF hello packets.

4. To isolate the problem access list, enable access lists one at a time until the router cannot establish neighbors (use the clear ip ospf neighbors privileged EXEC command to force the router to clear the neighbor table).

5. Check the access list to see if it is filtering traffic from port 89, the port used by OSPF. Remember that every access list ends with an implicit deny any statement. If an access list denies OSPF traffic, enter an explicit permit statement for port 89 to ensure that neighbor relationships can be established properly. (You can also use the ospf keyword when configuring the access list.)

For example, to configure input access list 101 to allow OSPF traffic to pass, enter the following command on the router:

ROUTER_A(config)# *access-list 101 permit ospf any any*

6. If you altered an access list, enable the list. Then enter the show ip ospf neighbor command to see if neighbor relationships are established normally.

7. If the router is establishing neighbors, perform the preceding steps for other routers in the path until all access lists are enabled and the router can still establish neighbors normally.

For more information on configuring access lists, see the Cisco IOS configuration guides.

Possible Problem: Virtual link and stub area configurations are mismatched.

Solution: Perform the following procedure:

NOTES

This section might not be applicable to you because this has been fixed in 11.2(11.1) and 11.3(1.1). Virtual links are no longer allowed if area is stub.

1. A virtual link cannot be configured across a stub area. Check router configurations for routers configured both as part of a stub area and as an ABR1 that is part of a virtual link. Use the `show running-config` privileged EXEC command and look for command entries that are similar to the following:

```
area 2 stub
area 2 virtual-link 192.169.100.10
```

2. If both of these commands are present, there is a misconfiguration. Remove one of the commands (using the no form of the command) to resolve the misconfiguration.

OSPF Routes Missing from Routing Table

Symptom: OSPF routes and networks are not being advertised to other routers. Routers in one area are not receiving routing information for other areas. Some hosts cannot communicate with hosts in other areas, and routing table information is incomplete.

Possible Problem: OSPF routers are not establishing neighbors.

Solution: Follow the procedures outlined in the section "OSPF: Routers Not Establishing Neighbors" earlier in this chapter.

Possible Problem: Routing information from IGRP or RIP is not redistributed correctly into OSPF

Solution: Perform the following procedure:

1. Check the router configuration by using the `show running-config` privileged EXEC command.

2. Look for a `redistribute router configuration` command entry. Make sure that redistribution is configured and that the `subnets` keyword is used with the command.

   The `subnets` keyword must be included when IGRP or RIP is redistributed into OSPF; otherwise, only major routes (not subnet routes) are redistributed.

3. If the `redistribute` command is not present, or if the `subnets` keyword is not specified, add or change the configuration by using the following commands:

```
GARNER_NC(config)# router ospf 100
GARNER_NC(config)# redistribute igrp subnets
GARNER_NC(config)# redistribute rip subnets
```

Possible Problem: There is no ABR configured in an area, which isolates that area from the OSPF backbone.

Solution: Perform the following procedure:

1. Use the show running-config privileged EXEC command on OSPF routers to verify that at least one ABR exists for the area. ABRs must belong to area 0, the OSPF backbone, as well as to another area. Look for network statements that indicate that the router is part of area 0.

2. If no ABR exists in an area, configure one where appropriate. Use the network router configuration command.

3. For example, to configure OSPF process 100 to participate in the OSPF backbone area, enter the following commands:

```
C4500(config)# router ospf 100
C4500(config-router)# network 192.21.3.7 0.0.0.255 area 0
```

Possible Problem: There is an interface network type mismatch on Frame Relay WAN.

Solution: In an OSPF Frame Relay environment, if one end of the link is a multipoint interface and the other end is a point-to-point interface, by default the multipoint interface will advertise the link as a non-broadcast network and the point-to-point interface will advertise the link as a point-to-point network. This creates a conflict in the link-state database and can prevent routing information from being learned properly.

1. Check each router interface on each side of the link to see if the network types are mismatched. Use the show ip ospf interface privileged EXEC command to check the network type configured for the interface. The following is an example of the output from the show ip ospf interface command:

```
Ethernet0 is up, line protocol is up
Internet Address 192.168.52.14 255.255.255.0, Area 0
Process ID 1, Router ID 192.168.52.14, Network Type BROADCAST, Cost: 10
[...]
```
In this example, the network type is broadcast.

2. Change the point-to-point interface to a multipoint interface by configuring subinterfaces, or change the network type of the point-to-point interface to broadcast by using the ip ospf network broadcast interface configuration command.

3. At this point, your changes will not take affect until you reload the router.

For information on configuring subinterfaces, see the Cisco IOS configuration guides.

Possible Problem: The area is configured as a stub area.

Solution: Route redistribution is not possible in OSPF stub areas. No external routes are advertised into a stub area, and if the `area area-id stub no-summary` router configuration command is used, no summary routes (inter-area routes) will be advertised into the stub area. Perform the following procedure:

1. If you want summary routes to be advertised into the stub area, but you do not see them in the routing table, use the `show running-config` privileged EXEC command to view the router configuration.

2. Look for an area area-id stub no-summary command entry. If this command is present, disable it by entering the following commands:

```
OSPF_STUB_RTR(config)# router ospf 100
OSPF_STUB_RTR(config-router)# no area 1 stub no-summary
```

   This disables the no-summary keyword and keeps the router configured as a stub.

3. To advertise external routes into the area, you must configure the area as a non-stub. Make certain that all routers in the area are reconfigured as non-stub routers.

Possible Problem: A misconfigured route is filtering.

Solution: Perform the following procedure:

1. Use the `show running-config` command to check suspect routers.

2. See if there are any `distribute-list in` or `distribute-list out` router configuration commands configured on the router.

   The `distribute-list in` command prevents specific information learned in LSAs1 from being included in the OSPF routing table. The `distribute-list out` command prevents a router from including specific information in routing updates that it transmits. However, in OSPF, `distribute-list out` can be configured only on an ASBR2 to filter external routes.

   Note that although `distribute-list` commands prevent specific information from being included in the OSPF routing table, information about those networks is contained in the link-state database and is flooded through the network in LSAs. This means that downstream routers will include that information in their routing tables unless they too filter those routes from the routing table.

3. If `distribute-list` commands are configured on the router, disable them by using the no version of the command.

For example, to disable an incoming filter that references access list 10, enter the following command:

`C7500(config)#` *no distribute-list 10 in*

4. After disabling all distribution lists, use the `clear ip route` privileged EXEC command to clear the routing table.

5. Determine if the routes appear in the routing table by using the `show ip route` privileged EXEC command. If routes appear properly in the routing table, the access list referenced by the distribute-list command is probably configured to deny certain updates.

6. To isolate the problem list, enable distribution lists one at a time until the routes no longer appear in the table.

7. Use the `show running-config` command and check the access list to make sure it does not deny updates inappropriately. If the access list denies updates from specific addresses, make sure that it does not deny the address of a router from which routing updates should be received. Change the access list to allow the router to receive updates from the proper addresses. Remember that an implicit deny any ends every access list.

Configure explicit permit statements for those addresses from which the router should receive updates.

8. If you altered an access list, enable the distribution list by using the `distribute-list` command. Use the `clear ip route` command and check to see if the missing routing information appears in the routing table.

9. If the routes appear in the routing table, perform the preceding steps on every router in the path until all distribution lists are enabled and routing information appears properly in the routing table.

For more information on configuring access lists, see the Cisco IOS configuration guides.

Possible Problem: The virtual link is misconfigured.

Solution: Perform the following procedure:

1. Check the configuration of the routers at each end of the virtual link by using the `show running-config` privileged EXEC command.

Look for area `area-id` `virtual-link` `router-id` router configuration command entries. These commands are used to configure the virtual link.

2. Use the `show` `ip` `ospf` EXEC command to find the router ID (IP address) of the routers.

3. Add the area `area-id` `virtual-link` `router-id` command if it is missing, or modify it if it is incorrect. Make sure that the proper area ID and router ID (IP address) are specified. The routers at each end of the virtual link must point to one another across the transit area.

For example, a virtual link from Router B to Router A is created across the transit area, Area 1.

The following commands are entered on Router A:

ROUTER_A(config)# *router ospf 250*

ROUTER_A(config-router)# *network 121.10.0.0 0.0.255.255 area 0*

ROUTER_A(config-router)# *network 169.192.56.0 0.0.0.255 area 0*

ROUTER_A(config-router)# *area 1 virtual-link 121.10.100.46*

On Router B, the following commands are used:

ROUTER_B(config)# *router ospf 250*

ROUTER_B(config-router)# *network 121.10.0.0 0.0.255.255 area 0*

ROUTER_B(config-router)# *network 108.31.0.0 0.0.255.255 area 2*

ROUTER_B(config-router)# area 1 virtual-link 121.10.1.1

CHAPTER 5

The Fundamentals of OSPF Routing & Design

The Art of Strategy: "Those who are victorious plan effectively and change decisively. They are like a great river that maintains its course but adjusts its flow . . . they have form but are formless. They are skilled in both planning and adapting and need not fear the result of a thousand battles; for they win in advance, defeating those that have already lost."—Sun Tzu, Chinese Warrior and Philosopher, 100 B.C.

This chapter covers a variety of subjects all relating to routing and designing OSPF networks. The foundation laid in the previous chapters is further expanded as the discussion of OSPF performance and design issues is expanded. Within each of the design sections, a series of "golden design rules" is presented. These rules will help the reader understand the constraints and recommendations of properly designing each section of an overall OSPF network. In many cases, examples that draw upon the material are presented to further reinforce key topics and ideas. The author would like to recognize the previous works presented on OSPF routing and design done by Dennis Black and Bassam Halabi. Both gentlemen penned internal Cisco documents and have done a commendable job of presenting the OSPF-related material in an easy-to-understand format. This chapter is built from that framework. In some cases, the material is presented directly from the original text, but the majority of the information has been expanded upon. For additional information on the two sources used in this chapter, please see the bibliography.

- **OSPF Algorithms**. The OSPF algorithm will be discussed in greater detail with the introduction of costs. With the addition of costs, the routing tables of OSPF become altered, and this section explains how and why.

- **OSPF Convergence**. This section covers the issues surrounding convergence with the protocol, including the benefits of OSPF and its ability to converge very quickly.

- **OSPF Design Guidelines**. This section begins the introduction to design OSPF networks and concentrates on two main points: network topology and scalability. This section begins to examine the physical requirements and layout needed before the actual work begins.

- **Area Design Considerations**. The true fundamentals of any OSPF network are its areas. The proper design of these areas is absolutely essential and the many different areas are discussed: backbone, non-stub, and all the variations of the stub area.

- **OSPF Route Selection**. Routing is the essence of every protocol, and how the protocol determines its routes is the primary area of focus in this section. Included within this chapter is OSPF's inherent capability to conduct load balancing. The derivation of external routes is also discussed at length.

- **OSPF IP Addressing & Route Summarization**. General route summarization techniques and procedures used by OSPF are examined and demonstrated through several different scenarios that a network engineer may come into contact with. This section concludes with an in-depth discussion of VLSM and the benefits of its use in your OSPF network.

OSPF ALGORITHMS

OSPF is a link-state protocol that uses a link-state database (LSDB) in order to build and calculate the shortest path to all known destinations. It is through the use of the SPF algorithm that the information contained within the LSDB is calculated into routes.

The shortest path algorithm by itself is quite complicated, and its inner workings are really beyond the scope of this book. But understanding its place and operation is essential to achieving a full understanding of OSPF. The text that follows reviews the operation of calculating the shortest path and then applies that to an example.

The following is a very high level, simplified way of looking at the various steps used by the algorithm:

1. Upon initialization or due to any change in routing information, a router will generate a link-state advertisement (LSA). This advertisement will represent the collection of all link-states on that router.

2. All routers will exchange LSAs by means of the OSPF Flooding protocol. Each router that receives a link-state update will store it in its LSDB and then flood the update to other routers.

3. After the database of each router is updated, each router will recalculate a shortest path tree to all destinations. The router uses the Shortest Path First (Dijkstra) algorithm to calculate the shortest path tree based on the LSDB. The destinations, their associated costs, and the next hop to reach those destinations will form the IP routing table.

The shortest path is calculated using the Dijkstra algorithm. The algorithm places each router at the root of a tree and calculates the shortest path to each destination based on the cumulative cost required to reach that destination. Each router will have its own view of the network's topology even though all the routers will build a shortest path tree using the same LSDB. This view consists of what paths and their associated costs are available to reach destinations throughout the network. In Figure 5-1, the Headquarters router is at the base of the tree (turn figure upside down). The following sections indicate what is involved in building a shortest path tree.

OSPF Cost

The cost or metric associated with an interface in OSPF is an indication of the overhead required to send packets across that interface. For example, in Figure 5-1, for Headquarters to reach network 192.213.11.0, a cost of 15 (10+5) is associated with the shortest path.

The cost of an interface is inversely proportional to the bandwidth of that interface. A higher bandwidth indicates a lower cost. There is more overhead (higher cost) and time delays involved in crossing a 56K serial line than crossing a 10M Ethernet line. The formula used by OSPF to calculate the cost is

Cost=100,000,000/bandwith in bps

Figure 5–1
*Shortest path
cost
calculation:
How the
network looks
from the HQ
router
perspective.*

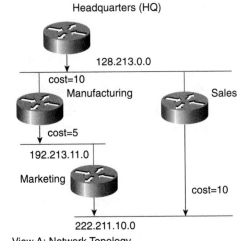

View A: Network Topology

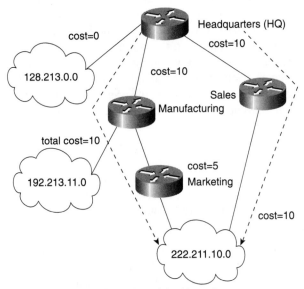

View B: SPF Tree View of the Network

For example, it will cost 10 EXP8/10 EXP7=10 to cross a 10M Ethernet line and will cost 10 EXP8/1544000=64 to cross a T1 line. By default, the cost of an interface is calculated based on the bandwidth, but you can place a cost on an interface through the use of the `ip ospf cost [value]` interface command.

In Cisco IOS release 10.2 and earlier, OSPF assigned default metrics to a router's interface, regardless of the bandwidth actually attached to the interface. For example, it would give a 64K and a T1 link the same metric. This required the user to override the default value in order to take advantage of the faster link. This overriding was accomplished through the use of the `ip ospf cost [value]` command, which would be placed on each interface as desired.

In Cisco IOS 10.3 and later, OSPF by default now calculates the cost (metric) for an interface according to the bandwidth of the interface. If needed, this feature can also be disabled through the use of the `no ospf auto-cost-determination` router command. You will then be able to customize the routing costs as needed.

Shortest Path Tree

Assume you have the network diagram as shown in Figure 5-1 with the indicated interface costs. To build the shortest path tree for the Headquarters router, you would have to make it the root of the tree and calculate the smallest cost for each destination.

The directions of the arrows in this figure are used to calculate the route's cost. For example, the cost of the Manufacturing router's interface to network 128.213.0.0 is not relevant when calculating the cost to 192.213.11.0.

Headquarters can reach 192.213.11.0 via the Manufacturing router with a cost of 20 (10+10). Headquarters can also reach 222.211.10.0 via the Sales router with a cost of 15 (10+5) or via the manufacturing router with a cost of 15 (10+5).

TIPS

In case equal cost paths to the same destination exist, Cisco's implementation of OSPF will keep track of up to six next hops to the same destination, not the OSPF standard.

To build the shortest path tree for Headquarters, you would have to make Headquarters the root of the tree and calculate the smallest cost for each destination. After the router builds the shortest path tree, it will start building the routing table accordingly. Directly connected networks will be reached via a metric (cost) of 0 and other networks will be reached according to the cost as calculated in the tree.

OSPF CONVERGENCE

One of the most attractive features about OSPF is its capability to quickly adapt to topology changes. The two essential components to routing convergence are

- Detecting changes to the network topology

- Rapid recalculation of routes

Detecting Changes to the Network Topology

OSPF uses two mechanisms to detect topology changes. Interface status changes (such as carrier failure on a serial link) is the first mechanism. The second mechanism is the failure of OSPF to receive a hello packet from its neighbor within a timing window called a dead timer. After this timer expires, the router assumes the neighbor is down. The dead timer is configured using the `ip ospf dead-interval` interface configuration command. The default value of the dead timer is four times the value of the hello interval, which results in a dead timer default of 40 seconds for broadcast networks and 2 minutes for nonbroadcast networks.

To summarize, fault detection by OSPF can differ slightly depending upon the media type. In general, the failure of a hello packet can supersede the failure of keepalive packets. The media type will affect how OSPF detects a failure as shown in the following list:

- Serial interface faults are detected in one of two ways:
  - Immediate detection of carrier (lmi) loss
  - Two to three times the time of the keepalive packet (default 10 seconds)
- Token Ring and FDDI are detected immediately.
- Ethernet is detected after the keepalive packet fails two to three times.

Rapid Recalculation of Routes

After a failure has been detected, the router that detected the failure floods an LSA packet with the change information to all routers to which it is directly connected. The detecting router will continue to flood this information until each router to which it is directly connected acknowledges its receipt.

All of the routers will recalculate their routes using the Dijkstra (or SPF) algorithm. Remember that each router builds its routing table based upon the LSDB, and this change alters the contents of that database. Therefore, the router will rebuild its routing tables with it as the base of the route tree. The time required to run the algorithm depends on a combination of the size of the area and the number of routes in the database.

TIPS

OSPF load balances along equal cost paths, this in turn allows for almost immediate convergence. OSPF can also load share across four equal cost paths.

OSPF DESIGN GUIDELINES

The OSPF protocol, as defined in RFC 1583 and RFC 2178, provides a high functionality open protocol that enables multiple vendor networks to communicate using the TCP/IP protocol family. Some of the benefits of OSPF are: fast convergence, VLSM, authentication, hierarchical segmentation, route summarization, and aggregation, all of which are needed to handle large and complicated networks.

Whether you are building an OSPF internetwork from the ground up or converting your internetwork to OSPF, the design guidelines highlighted in the following sections provide a foundation from which you can construct a reliable, scalable OSPF-based environment.

Different people have different approaches to designing OSPF networks. The important thing to remember is that any protocol can fail under pressure. The idea is not to challenge the protocol but rather to work with it in order to get the best performance possible from your network.

The OSPF RFCs 1583 and 2178 do not specify several very important considerations that are essential to a properly designed OSPF network. But RFC 2178 is a very good resource to consult when laying out the design of your OSPF network. It is also backward compatible with RFC 1583.

The two design activities that are critically important to a successful OSPF implementation are defining area boundaries and assigning addresses. Ensuring that these activities are properly planned and executed will make all the difference in your OSPF implementation.

OSPF Network Topology

OSPF works best in a hierarchical routing environment. The first and most important decision when designing an OSPF network is to determine which routers and links are to be included in the backbone (area 0) and which are to be included in each area. The following are three important characteristics to OSPF and its need for a hierarchical routing structure:

- The hierarchical routing structure must exist or be created.

- A contiguous backbone area must be present and all areas must have a connection to the backbone.

- Explicit topology has precedence whatever IP addressing schemes might have been applied.

Several important items to consider when designing the topology for an OSPF network (discussed at length in the sections that follow) are as follows:

- The number of routers in an area

- The number of areas connected to an area border router (ABR)

- The number of neighbors for any one router

- The number of areas supported by any one router

- Selecting the Designated Router (DR)

- The LSDB

The Number of Routers in an Area

OSPF uses the CPU-intensive SPF algorithm. Experience has shown that 40 to 50 routers per area is the optimal upper limit for OSPF. The number of calculations that must be performed by the router given n link-state packets (LSPs) is proportional to $n \log n$. As a result, the larger and more unstable the area, the greater the likelihood for performance problems associated with OSPF routing recalculation.

Generally, an area should have no more than 50 routers. That does not mean that networks with 60 or 70 routers in an area won't function, but why experiment with stability if you don't need to? Areas with unstable links should be smaller.

One of the main problems with areas is that network administrators let their backbone area grow too large. Try to outline the logical view of the network from the start, and remember that it doesn't hurt to start creating that other area before it is needed. A good rule of thumb is to plan for maximum growth coupled with long term planning. This has the added benefit of ensuring your network can handle rapid growth. In this case, planning for too much is never a bad thing to do.

However, those recommendations are made in accordance with "official" Cisco recommendations regarding OSPF networks. Studies and real world implementations have gone further. For example, the statistics in Table 5-1 came from the "IETF OSPF Standard Report."

Table 5-1   *OSPF network size recommendations*

Parameter	Minimum	Mean	Maximum
Routers in a domain	20	510	1000
Routers per single area	20	160	350
Areas per domain	1	23	60

It is good to know that OSPF has been thoroughly tested and can withstand scaling to a phenomenal size.

The Number of Areas Connected to an Area Border Router

ABRs will keep a copy of the database for all areas they service. If a router is connected to five areas, for example, it will have to keep a list of five different databases. It is better not to overload an ABR; you should try to spread the areas over other routers. The ideal design is to have each ABR connected to two areas only, the backbone, and another area, with three areas being the upper limit. Figure 5-2 shows the difference between one ABR holding five different databases, including area 0 (part a) and two ABRs holding three databases each (part b).

Figure 5–2
How many areas should be connected per ABR?

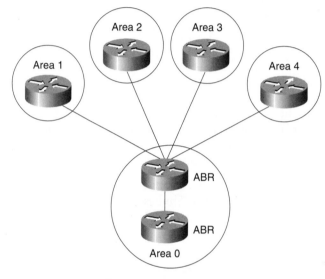

Too Many Areas per ABR
(a)

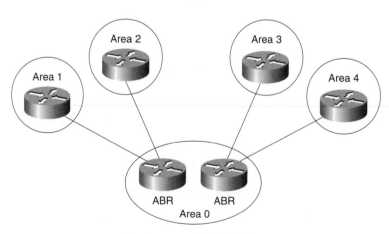

Two Areas per ABR Is Optimal
(b)

These are just guidelines; the more areas you attach per ABR, the lower the performance you get from that router. In some cases, the lower performance can be tolerated, but end users probably won't see it that way.

The Number of Neighbors for Any One Router

OSPF floods all link-state changes to all routers in an area. Routers with many neighbors have the most work to do when link-state changes occur. In general, any one router should have no more than 60 neighbors.

The number of routers connected to the same LAN is also important. Each LAN has a DR and BDR that build adjacencies with all other routers. The fewer neighbors that exist on the LAN, the smaller the number of adjacencies a DR or BDR have to build. You can see in Figure 5-3 that the more neighbors the DR or BDR has, the more work they must do.

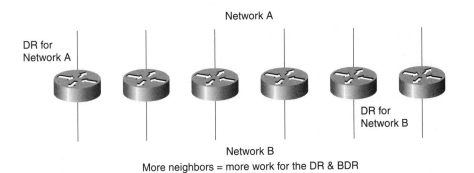

Network A

DR for
Network A

DR for
Network B

Network B
More neighbors = more work for the DR & BDR

Figure 5–3
*More
neighbors
equal more
work for the DR
and BDR.*

This, of course, depends on how much processing power your router has. You could always change the OSPF priority to select your DR. Also, if possible, try to avoid having the same router be the DR on more than one segment. If DR selection is based on the highest RID, then one router could accidentally become a DR over all segments to which it is connected. This router would be doing extra effort while other routers are idle.

The Number of Areas Supported by Any One Router

A router must run the link-state algorithm for each link-state change that occurs for every area in which the router resides. Every area border router is in at least two areas (the backbone and one area). In general, to maximize stability, one router should not be in more than three areas.

Selecting the Designated Router

In general, the DR and BDR on a LAN have the most OSPF work to do. It is a good idea to select routers that are not already heavily loaded with CPU-intensive activities to be the DR and BDR. This can be accomplished using the `ip ospf priority [priority]` command, which will allow you to organize the DRs as needed.

In addition, it is generally not a good idea to select the same router to be the DR on more than one LAN simultaneously. These guidelines will help ensure that no single broadcast link will have too many neighbors with too much hello traffic.

Fully Meshed Versus Partially Meshed Network Topology

Nonbroadcast multiaccess (NBMA) clouds, such as Frame Relay or X.25, are always a challenge. The combination of low bandwidth and too many LSAs is a recipe for problems—even for OSPF. A partially-meshed topology has been proven to behave much better than a fully-meshed network topology. Figure 5-4 shows the benefits and differences between the two topologies.

A carefully laid out point-to-point or point-to-multipoint network can in some cases work much better than multipoint networks that have to deal with DR issues.

The Link-State Database

Although covered in previous chapters, these issues as related to the LSDB are very important and deal directly with its operation in relation to the topology of the network.

- A router has a separate LSDB for each area to which it belongs.
- All routers belonging to the same area have the identical LSDB.

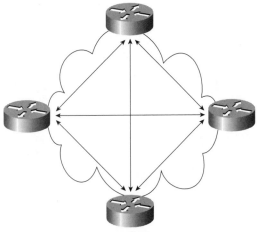

Figure 5–4
*Examples of
fully- and
partially-
meshed
networks.*

fully meshed network
(not recommended)

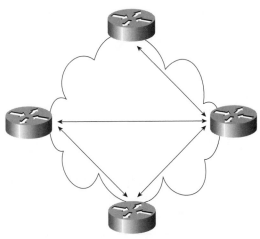

partially meshed network
(recommended)

- SPF calculation is performed separately for each area and its associated LSDB.
- LSA flooding occurs only within the area sending the advertisement.

OSPF Network Scalability

Your ability to scale an OSPF internetwork depends on your overall network structure and IP addressing scheme. As outlined in the discussions concerning network topology and route summarization, adopting a hierarchical addressing environment and a structured address assignment will be the most important factors in determining the scalability of your internetwork. Network scalability is affected by both operational and technical considerations.

Operationally, OSPF networks should be designed so that areas do not need to be split to accommodate growth. Address space should be reserved to permit the addition of new areas. Scalability should always be taken into consideration when designing your network. All routers keep a copy of the LSDB. As the network grows, they will eventually reach a point where the database becomes too large, resulting in inefficiency in your routing. Additionally, the LSAs will be flooded throughout the network, resulting in a congestion problem. The capability of your OSPF network to scale properly is determined by a multitude of factors, including the following:

- Router memory requirements
- CPU requirements
- Available bandwith
- OSPF security

NOTES

In many cases, personnel who work directly with networks are not always in complete control of some of the factors discussed in this section. Of course, bigger is better; unfortunately, it is also more expensive.

Determining Router Memory Requirements

An OSPF router stores all of the link states for all of the areas that it is in. In addition, it can store summary and external routes. Careful use of route summarization techniques and the creation of stub areas can reduce memory use substantially.

It is not easy to determine the exact amount of memory needed for a particular OSPF configuration. Memory issues usually come up when too many external routes are injected in the OSPF domain. A backbone area with 40 routers and a default route to the outside world would have less memory issues compared with a backbone area with 4 routers and 33,000 external routes being injected into OSPF. Router memory could also be conserved by using a good OSPF design. Summarization at the area border routers and use of stub areas could further minimize the number of routes exchanged.

The total memory used by OSPF is the sum of the memory used in the routing table (show ip route summary) and the memory used in the LSDB. The following numbers are a "rule of thumb" estimate. Each entry in the routing table will consume between approximately 200 and 280 bytes plus 44 bytes per extra path. Each LSA will consume a 100 byte overhead plus the size of the actual LSA, possibly another 60 to 100 bytes (For router links, this depends on the number of interfaces on the router). These amounts should be added to memory already used by other processes and by the IOS itself.

If you really want to know the exact number, you can do a show memory with and without OSPF being turned on. The difference in the processor memory used would be the answer.

TIPS

Consider getting and keeping available a backup copy of the router configuration beforehand, of course.

Normally, a routing table using less than 500K bytes could be accommodated with 2 to 4MB of RAM; large networks that have routing tables greater than 500K might need 8 to 16MB. They might even need 32 to 64MB if full routes are injected from the Internet.

CPU Requirements

An OSPF router uses CPU cycles whenever a link-state change occurs. Thus, keeping the OSPF areas small and using route summarization dramatically reduces usage of the router's CPU and creates a more stable environment within which OSPF can operate.

Available Bandwidth

OSPF sends partial LSA updates when a link-state change occurs. The updates are flooded to all routers in the area. In a quiet network, OSPF is a quiet protocol, go figure; aren't all protocols that way? Sorry, it had to be said. In a network with substantial topology changes, OSPF minimizes the amount of bandwidth used for customer traffic.

OSPF Security

The two kinds of security applicable to routing protocols are as follows:

- The routers that participate in an OSPF network are controlled.
- OSPF contains an optional authentication field.

All routers within an area must agree on the value of the authentication field. Because OSPF is a standard protocol available on many platforms, including some hosts, using the authentication field prevents the inadvertent startup of OSPF in an uncontrolled platform on your network and reduces the potential for instability.

You might think it is possible to control the routing information within an OSPF area. Remember though, that for OSPF to operate properly, all routers within an area must have the same data. As a result, it is not possible to use route filters in an OSPF network to provide security because OSPF exchanges route information through the use of LSAs, not routes. OSPF then calculates the route to a destination based upon the LSA.

AREA DESIGN CONSIDERATIONS

When creating large-scale OSPF internetworks, the definition of areas and assignment of resources within areas must be done with a pragmatic view of your OSPF internetwork. This assignment of resources includes both physical and logical networking components so that optimal performance will result.

Justifying the Use of Areas and Multiple Areas

Areas are essentially little networks within the larger network, and as such, they route only necessary traffic within themselves, thereby reducing overall network traffic. There are many reasons that using OSPF's capability to create areas would result in benefits for your network. The use of areas is necessary so that OSPF's required hierarchical structure can be put into place. The topology of the network within an area is invisible to anything outside of that area, as demonstrated in Figure 5-5.

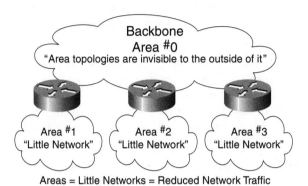

Figure 5–5
Areas serve as little networks, subsequently resulting in reduced network traffic.

Non-Stub Area Characteristics

Non-stub areas carry a default route, static routes, intra-area routes, and external routes. An area must be a non-stub area when it contains a router that uses both OSPF and any other protocol, such as the Routing Information Protocol (RIP). Such a router is known as an autonomous system border router (ASBR). An area must also be a non-stub area when a virtual link is configured across the area. Non-stub areas are the most resource-intensive type of area.

The LSDB Within an Area

The LSDB is everywhere within an OSPF network. When encountered in an area, the LSDB will be identical in each router within the area. The LSDB will also contain a variety of LSAs, as follows:

- Router link advertisements
- Network link advertisements
- Summary link advertisements (IP Network & ASBR)
- Autonomous System, (AS) external advertisements (non-stub areas only)

Area Partitions: Outages or Network Growth?

Area partitions will typically occur within an area. OSPF does not actively attempt to repair area partitions. When an area becomes partitioned the new sections simply become separate areas. As long as the backbone can reach both of them, it will continue to route information to them.

To maintain routing, an IP address range must not be spread across the split area. This assumes that some destinations will now require inter-area routing as a result. If this does occur, then some destinations will become unreachable and routing loops could occur. In an outage condition this information is not very helpful, but when designing areas, assign IP address ranges accordingly so that growth can be handled easier in the future should a new area be needed.

The backbone should never be partitioned, but if it does occur, then consider using a virtual link to temporarily repair the backbone. Virtual links are discussed later in this chapter. Even though partitioning your OSPF backbone is considered bad practice, there are times when it could be beneficial, so OSPF does allow it. For example, a company is trying to merge two separate OSPF networks into one network with a common area 0. In other instances, virtual links are added for redundancy in case some router failure causes the backbone to be split into two. Whatever the reason might be, a virtual link can be configured between separate ABRs that touch area 0 from each side and have a common area (see Figure 5-6).

Figure 5–6
Repairing or joining two backbone areas.

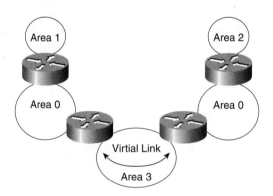

In Figure 5–6, two area 0s are linked together via a virtual link. In case a common area does not exist, an additional area, such as area 3, could be created to become the transit area. In case any area that is different than the backbone becomes partitioned, the backbone will take care of the partitioning without using any virtual links. One part of the partitioned area will be known to the other part via inter-area routes rather than intra-area routes.

The Golden Rules of Area Design

When you begin to design your OSPF network, it will be necessary for you to start with the area 0 the backbone area of every OSPF network. There are two very important rules that, if followed, will get you started properly:

1. A contiguous backbone area must be present.
2. All other areas must have a connection to the backbone area.

The following are more general rules and OSPF capabilities that will help ensure that your OSPF network remains flexible and provides the kind of performance needed to deliver reliable service to all of its users:

- Consider physical proximity when defining areas.
- Reduce the maximum size of areas if links are unstable.
- Ensure contiguous individual areas.
- Use tunable OSPF parameters.

Considering Physical Proximity When Defining Areas

If a particular location is densely connected, create an area specifically for nodes at that location. This will enable OSPF to better handle a large, dense cluster of nodes, and it will enable more efficient management and routing.

Reducing the Maximum Size of Areas if Links Are Unstable

If your internetwork includes unstable links, consider implementing smaller areas to reduce the effects of route flapping. Whenever a route is lost or comes online, each affected area must converge on the new topology. The Dijkstra algorithm will run on all the affected routers. By segmenting your network into smaller or multiple areas, you can isolate unstable links and deliver more reliable overall service. This is always of benefit to everyone concerned.

Ensuring Contiguous Individual Areas

A contiguous OSPF area is one in which a continuous path can be traced from any router in an area to any other router in the same area. This does not mean that all routers must share a common network media (like Ethernet). Refer to Figure 5-7 which demonstrates both concepts.

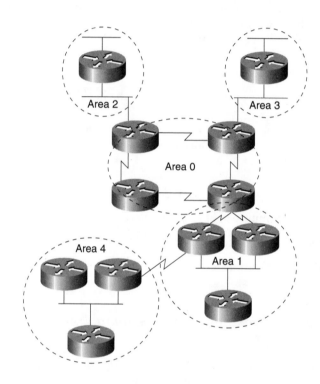

Ideally, areas should have multiple redundant internal and external links to prevent partitioning.

Using Tunable OSPF Parameters

There is a group of tunable OSPF parameters that can help you design an area that will more readily meet your network's specific needs. All of these commands and their associated values generally default to good values. If you are considering changing them, it is good practice to change them in all routers.

TIPS

Remember, Cisco routers will not show default values in their configuration files.

The tunable OSPF parameters are as follows:

- `ip ospf hello-interval {seconds}`. This command defaults to a value of 10 seconds. By modifying this value you can specify the transmission interval between hello packets sent out an interface.

- `ip ospf dead interval {seconds}`. This command defaults to a value four times the hello interval. This command specifies how long a router's hello packets must not have been seen before its neighbors declare the router down.

- `ip ospf retransmission-interval {seconds}`. This command defaults to a value of five seconds. By modifying this value, you can specify the number of seconds between LSA retransmissions.

- `ip ospf transmit-delay {seconds}`. This command defaults to a value of one second. By modifying this value, you are able to set the time to delay before transmitting a LSA from an interface.

Critical Aspects of Area Design

The two most critical aspects of designing an area include determining how the area is addressed and determining how the area is connected to the backbone. Areas should have a contiguous set of network and/or subnet addresses whenever possible. You can have an area with any combination of networks and subnets, but it is strongly discouraged. Whenever possible, you should have an area consist of grouped networks and subnets so that route summarization can be easily accomplished. Without a contiguous address space, the implementation of route summarization is impossible.

The routers that connect an area to the backbone are called ARBs. Areas can have a single ABR or they can have multiple ABRs. In general, you should have more than one ABR per area to minimize the chance of the area becoming disconnected from the backbone.

Designing the Backbone Area

The OSPF backbone (also known as area 0) is extremely important. If more than one area is configured in an OSPF network, one of these areas has to be area 0. When designing networks, it is good practice to start with area 0 and then expand into other areas later on. To summarize, the OSPF backbone is the part of the OSPF network that acts as the primary path for traffic that is destined to other areas or networks.

Accepted network design theory recommends a three-tiered approach (see Figure 5-8). This theory states that there should never be more than three tiers with a maximum of six router hops across the farthest points of the network. This type of design suits OSPF very well because of its area concepts and need for hierarchical routing. This design also reduces convergence time and facilitates route summarization.

Figure 5–8
The three-tiered network design model.

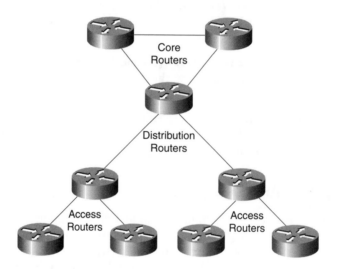

Backbone Design Golden Rules

You should stick to the following guidelines when designing an OSPF backbone (area 0):

- Ensure the stability of the backbone.
- Ensure redundancy, as this is definitely called for in such a critical area.

- Ensure that OSPF backbones are contiguous.

- Keep this area simple. The fewer the routers the better.

- Keep the bandwidth symmetrical so that OSPF can maintain load balancing.

- Ensure all other areas connect directly to area 0.

- Restrict all enduser (host) resources from area 0.

The backbone has to be at the center of all other areas, that is, all areas have to be physically connected to the backbone. The reasoning behind this is that OSPF expects all areas to inject routing information into the backbone and, in turn, the backbone will disseminate that routing information into other areas. Figure 5-9 illustrates the flow of routing information in an OSPF network.

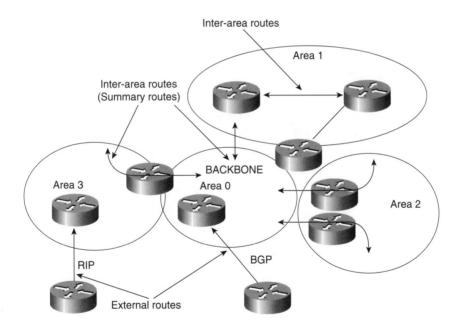

Figure 5-9
The flow of information in an OSPF network, in which the backbone is the key.

In Figure 5-9, all areas are directly connected to the backbone. Stability and redundancy are the most important criteria for the backbone. Keeping the size of the backbone reasonable results in stability. This is very desirable because every router in the backbone needs to recompute its routes after every link-state change. Keeping the backbone small reduces the likelihood of a change and reduces the amount of CPU cycles required to recompute routes.

Redundancy is important in the backbone to prevent partition when a link fails. Good backbones are designed so that no single link failure can cause a partition (that is, the backbone becomes isolated). OSPF backbones must be contiguous. All routers in the backbone should be directly connected to other backbone routers. Avoid placing hosts (such as workstations, file servers, or other shared resources) in the backbone area. Keeping hosts out of the backbone area simplifies internetwork expansion and creates a more stable environment because a host's normal operation (morning/evening, power up/down) will cause unnecessary LSA traffic.

Virtual Links: Bane or Benefit?

OSPF includes the concept of virtual links. In the rare situations that a new area is introduced that cannot have a direct physical access to the backbone, a virtual link will have to be configured. A virtual link creates a path between two ABRs that are not directly connected. Accepted network design theory considers the use of virtual links the result of a poorly designed backbone.

A virtual link is able to connect an ABR to the backbone (area 0) even though it is not directly connected (see Figure 5-10). Through the use of a virtual link, which is similar to a tunnel, this can be accomplished.

Figure 5–10
Virtual links: bane or benefit?

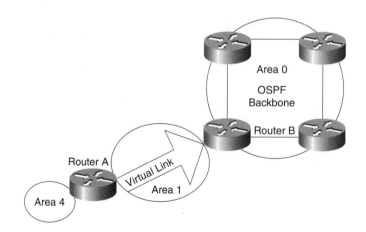

Some of the characteristics and suggested uses for virtual links include the following:

- Their stability is determined by the stability of the area they traverse.
- They can only be configured on ABRs.
- They cannot run across stub areas.
- They assist in solving short-term network connectivity problems.
- They can be used to assist in providing redundancy.
- OSPF treats two routers joined by a virtual link as if they were connected by an unnumbered point-to-point network.
- Virtual links cannot be configured on unnumbered links or through stub areas.

TIPS

Using the `show ip ospf virtual-links` command in enable (EXEC) mode, you can see the virtual links configured on a router.

Stub Areas

A stub area in OSPF is an area that carries a default route, and inter-area routes but does not carry any external routes. Stub areas reduce network overhead by placing sections of the network into dead end areas, also known as stub areas. This reduces the routes being advertised across the network.

Because default routing is used, the LSDB is reduced in size, which in turn also reduces the load being placed on the router's CPU and memory. Routing updates are also reduced because specific link flaps will not be injected across the network; instead, they are confined to the area or they don't even enter the area, depending on where they occurred.

There are three different types of stub areas: normal stub, totally stubby area (TSA), and NSSAs. Each stub area and the corresponding characteristics will be discussed in the sections that follow.

Stub Area Design Golden Rules

Many stub area design rules are in place because a stub area is designed and configured not to carry external routers. If a situation occurred within a stub area that caused external links to be injected into the area, then its usefulness is ruined. The following are the rules:

- Only a single ABR can be in a stub area, but if there is more than one, then accept non-optimal routing paths.

- No ASBRs can be within a stub area.

- No virtual links area is allowed.

- All routers within any type of stub area must be configured to recognize their location (that is, what area they are in and any specific OSPF settings for that area). If the routers do not all agree on their location, then they will not become neighbors and routing will not take effect.

- The backbone area cannot be configured as a stub area.

Normal Stub Areas

The configuration command area # stub turns on stub area routing. External routes being advertised into OSPF must be done via the summary-address command; this is typically done at the ASBR.

Normal stub areas only block external routes; however, they do allow summary routes. For example, LSA Types 1–4 are allowed and 5–7 are blocked. This is the difference between normal stub areas and the other types of stub areas.

The command that configures an area as stub is as follows:

```
area <area-id> stub [no-summary]
```

The command that configures a default-cost into an area is as follows:

```
area area-id default-cost cost
```

If the cost is not set using the **area** area-id **default-cost** cost command, a cost of one will be advertised by the ABR. Figure 5-11 shows a very good example of stub areas. In the examples that follow, the router configuration files will be presented based upon the setup in Figure 5-11.

Assume that area 2 is to be configured as a stub area. The following examples show the routing table of RTE before and after configuring area 2 as a stub area.

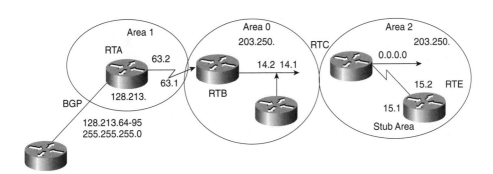

Figure 5–11
Configuring an OSPF area as a stub area.

Before Becoming a Stub Area

```
RTC#
interface Ethernet 0
ip address 203.250.14.1 255.255.255.0
interface Serial1
ip address 203.250.15.1 255.255.255.252
router ospf 10
network 203.250.15.0 0.0.0.255 area 2
network 203.250.14.0 0.0.0.255 area 0


RTE#sh ip route
Codes: C - connected, S - static, I - IGRP, R - RIP, M - mobile, B - BGP
D - EIGRP, EX - EIGRP external, O - OSPF, IA - OSPF inter area
E1 - OSPF external type 1, E2 - OSPF external type 2, E - EGP
i - IS-IS, L1 - IS-IS level-1, L2 - IS-IS level-2, * - candidate
default
Gateway of last resort is not set
203.250.15.0 255.255.255.252 is subnetted, 1 subnets
C 203.250.15.0 is directly connected, Serial0
O IA 203.250.14.0 [110/74] via 203.250.15.1, 00:06:31, Serial0
128.213.0.0 is variably subnetted, 2 subnets, 2 masks
O E2 128.213.64.0 255.255.192.0
[110/10] via 203.250.15.1, 00:00:29, Serial0
O IA 128.213.63.0 255.255.255.252
[110/84] via 203.250.15.1, 00:03:57, Serial0
131.108.0.0 255.255.255.240 is subnetted, 1 subnets
O 131.108.79.208 [110/74] via 203.250.15.1, 00:00:10, Serial0
```

RTE has learned the inter-area routes (O IA) 203.250.14.0 and 128.213.63.0, and it has learned the intra-area route (O) 131.108.79.208 and the external route (O E2) 128.213.64.0. If you configure area 2 as stub, you need to do the following:

After Becoming a Stub Area

```
RTC#
interface Ethernet 0
ip address 203.250.14.1 255.255.255.0
interface Serial1
ip address 203.250.15.1 255.255.255.252
router ospf 10
network 203.250.15.0 0.0.0.255 area 2
network 203.250.14.0 0.0.0.255 area 0
area 2 stub

RTE#
interface Ethernet0
ip address 203.250.14.2 255.255.255.0
interface Ethernet1
ip address 131.108.79.209 255.255.255.240
interface Serial1
ip address 203.250.15.1 255.255.255.252
router ospf 10
network 203.250.15.0 0.0.0.255 area 2
network 203.250.14.0 0.0.0.255 area 0
network 131.108.0.0 0.0.255.255 area 2
area 2 stub
```

NOTES

Note that the stub command is configured on RTE also; otherwise, RTE will never become a neighbor to RTC. The default cost was not set, so RTC will advertise 0.0.0.0 to RTE with a metric of 1.

```
RTE#sh ip route
Codes: C - connected, S - static, I - IGRP, R - RIP, M - mobile, B - BGP
D - EIGRP, EX - EIGRP external, O - OSPF, IA - OSPF inter area
E1 - OSPF external type 1, E2 - OSPF external type 2, E - EGP
i - IS-IS, L1 - IS-IS level-1, L2 - IS-IS level-2, * - candidate default

Gateway of last resort is 203.250.15.1 to network 0.0.0.0
203.250.15.0 255.255.255.252 is subnetted, 1 subnets
C 203.250.15.0 is directly connected, Serial0
O IA 203.250.14.0 [110/74] via 203.250.15.1, 00:26:58, Serial0
128.213.0.0 255.255.255.252 is subnetted, 1 subnets
O IA 128.213.63.0 [110/84] via 203.250.15.1, 00:26:59, Serial0
131.108.0.0 255.255.255.240 is subnetted, 1 subnets
O 131.108.79.208 [110/74] via 203.250.15.1, 00:26:59, Serial0
O*IA 0.0.0.0 0.0.0.0 [110/65] via 203.250.15.1, 00:26:59, Serial0
```

Note that all the routes show up except the external routes that were replaced by a default route of 0.0.0.0. The cost of the route happened to be 65 (64 for a T1 line+1 advertised by RTC). You will now configure area 2 to be totally stubby and change the default cost of 0.0.0.0 to 10:

```
RTC#
interface Ethernet 0
ip address 203.250.14.1 255.255.255.0
interface Serial1
ip address 203.250.15.1 255.255.255.252
router ospf 10
network 203.250.15.0 0.0.0.255 area 2
network 203.250.14.0 0.0.0.255 area 0
area 2 stub no-summary

RTE#sh ip route
Codes: C - connected, S - static, I - IGRP, R - RIP, M - mobile, B - BGP
D - EIGRP, EX - EIGRP external, O - OSPF, IA - OSPF inter area
E1 - OSPF external type 1, E2 - OSPF external type 2, E - EGP
i - IS-IS, L1 - IS-IS level-1, L2 - IS-IS level-2, * - candidate default

Gateway of last resort is not set
203.250.15.0 255.255.255.252 is subnetted, 1 subnets
C 203.250.15.0 is directly connected, Serial0
131.108.0.0 255.255.255.240 is subnetted, 1 subnets
O 131.108.79.208 [110/74] via 203.250.15.1, 00:31:27, Serial0
O*IA 0.0.0.0 0.0.0.0 [110/74] via 203.250.15.1, 00:00:00, Serial0
```

Note that the only routes that show up are the intra-area routes (O) and the default-route 0.0.0.0. The external and inter-area routes have been blocked. The cost of the default route is now 74 (64 for a T1 line+10 advertised by RTC). No configuration is needed on RTE in this case. The area is already stub, and the no-summary command does not affect the hello packet at all as the stub command does.

Totally Stubby Areas (TSA)

Cisco indicates a TSA when configuring the routers by adding the no summary keyword to the configuration command. Thus, the configuration command needed is area # stub no summary.

A TSA blocks external routes and summary routes from entering the area. This leaves the default route and intra-area routes as the only types being advertised throughout the area. This is most complete summarization technique possible in OSPF and results in extremely small routing tables made up only of networks found with the area.

Not-So-Stubby Areas (NSSA)

As mentioned in Chapter 4, "Introduction to OSPF," NSSAs have their own RFC and are a rather new concept to OSPF. The advent of this new type of hybrid stub area also introduced a new LSA, Type 7, which is responsible for carrying external route information.

TIPS

NSSAs are not supported until Cisco IOS version 11.2 and later.

The two main benefits of the Type-7 LSA are that it can be filtered and flexibly summarized. Generally speaking, the use of a NSSA is advised when it lies between a ASBR and ABR, where the ASBR is connected to different routing protocol and the ABR is connected to OSPF's area 0.

NOTES

In Chapter 4, under RFC 1587 you will find a detailed description of the reasons you would want to use an NSSA. You should also read the RFC itself for detailed information.

The operation of an NSSA is rather straightforward. You have an ASBR connected to a network running RIP. This router is also configured as part of an NSSA. The router will redistribute the routes learned from RIP into an OSPF Type-6 LSA for transmission into the NSSA. The NSSA ABR will see these advertisements and want to forward them onto area 0 for distribution throughout the network. The ABR will then redistribute the Type-7 LSAs into Type-5 LSAs.

OSPF ROUTE SELECTION

When designing an OSPF internetwork for efficient route selection, you need to consider three important topics:

- Tuning OSPF metrics
- Controlling inter-area traffic
- Load balancing in OSPF internetworks

Tuning OSPF Metrics

The default value for OSPF metrics (cost) is based on bandwidth. The following characteristics show how OSPF metrics are generated:

- Each link is given a metric value based on its bandwidth.
- The metric for a specific link is the inverse of the bandwidth for that link.
- Link metrics are normalized to give FDDI a metric of 1.
- The metric for a route is the sum of the metrics for all the links in the route.

In some cases, your network might implement a media type that is faster than the fastest default media configurable for OSPF (FDDI). An example of a faster media is ATM. By default, a faster media will be assigned a cost equal to the cost of an FDDI link—a link-state metric cost of 1. Given an environment with both FDDI and a faster media type, you must manually configure link costs to configure the faster link with a lower metric. Configure any FDDI link with a cost greater than 1, and configure the faster link with a cost less than the assigned FDDI link cost. Use the `ip ospf cost` interface configuration command to modify link-state cost.

When route summarization is enabled, OSPF uses the metric of the best route in the summary.

TIPS

Found within Cisco's IOS version 11.3 is a new OSPF command, `ospf auto-cost reference bandwidth`, which can assist you in route summarization.

Types of External Metrics: E1 and E2

Routes that originate from other routing protocols (or different OSPF processes) and that are injected into OSPF via redistribution are called *external routes*. There are two forms of external metrics: type 1 (E1) and type 2 (E2). These routes are represented by O E2 or O E1 in the IP routing table. They are examined after the router is done building its internal routing table. After they are examined, they are flooded throughout the Autonomous System (AS), unaltered. External information could come from a variety of sources, such as another routing protocol.

E1 metrics result in routes adding the internal OSPF metric to the external route metric; they are also expressed in the same terms as an OSPF link-state metric. The internal OSPF metric is the total cost of reaching the external destination, including whatever internal OSPF network costs are incurred to get there. These costs are calculated by the router wanting to reach the external route.

E2 metrics do not add the internal OSPF metric to the cost of external routes; they are also the default type used by OSPF. The E1 metric is generally preferred. The use of E2 metrics assumes that you are routing between AS; therefore, the cost is considered greater than any internal metrics. This eliminates the need to add the internal OSPF metrics. Figure 5-12 shows a nice comparison of the two metrics.

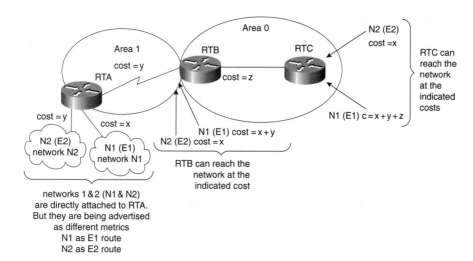

Figure 5–12
*E1 versus E2
External metric
(routes) types.*

For example, suppose you have two routers (cost 10 and 80, respectively) advertising the same external route, which one do you take? OSPF will determine the link metric going to those external networks. In this case of 10 and 80, because 10 is lower, that is the route that will be chosen. But what if the cost was equal? Then OSPF will use the internal metric to determine the lowest cost, thus breaking the tie.

Controlling Inter-Area Traffic

When an area has only a single ABR, all traffic that does not belong in the area will be sent to the ABR. In areas that have multiple ABRs, two choices are available for traffic that needs to leave the area:

- Use the ABR closest to the originator of the traffic. This results in traffic leaving the area as soon as possible.

- Use the ABR closest to the destination of the traffic. This results in traffic leaving the area as late as possible. But if the ABRs are only injecting a default route, the traffic goes to the ABR that is closest to the source of the traffic.

Generally, the latter behavior is desirable because the backbone typically has higher bandwidth lines available. Also, the faster packets get there, the quicker they can be routed to their destination. However, if you want the traffic to use the ABR that is nearest the destination (so that traffic leaves the area as late as possible), the ABRs should inject route summaries into the area instead of just injecting the default route.

Most network designers prefer to avoid asymmetric routing (that is, using a different path for packets that are going from A to B than for those packets that are going from B to A.) It is important to understand how routing occurs between areas so you can avoid asymmetric routing if at all possible.

Routes that are generated from within an area (the destination belongs to the area) are called *intra-area routes*. These routes are represented by the letter O in the IP routing table. Routes that originate from other areas are called *inter-area* routes or *summary routes*. The notation for these routes is O IA in the IP routing table.

Load Balancing in OSPF Internetworks

As part of your design, you will need to consider the traffic flow across the network and whether or not to use load balancing. The use of this OSPF feature can be very helpful to your network's overall health. This section discusses how to best utilize the OSPF load balancing feature with a network.

In routing, load balancing is the capability of a router to distribute traffic over all its network ports that are the same distance from the destination address. Good load-balancing algorithms use both line speed and reliability information. Load balancing increases the utilization of network segments, thus increasing effective network bandwidth.

Internetwork topologies are typically designed to provide redundant routes in order to prevent a partitioned network. Redundancy is also useful to provide additional bandwidth for high traffic areas. If equal-cost paths between nodes exist, Cisco routers automatically load balance in an OSPF environment.

TIPS

Fast-switching is a Cisco feature whereby a route cache is used to expedite packet switching through a router. For line speeds of 56Kbps and faster, it is recommended that you enable fast-switching.

Cisco routers can use up to four equal-cost paths for a given destination. Packets might be distributed either on a per-destination (when fast-switching) or a per-packet basis. Per-destination load balancing is the default behavior. Per-packet load balancing can be enabled by turning off fast-switching using the `no ip route-cache` interface configuration command.

OSPF IP Addressing & Route Summarization

IP address assignment and route summarization are inextricably linked when designing OSPF networks. To create a scalable OSPF network, you should implement route summarization. To create an environment capable of supporting route summarization, you must implement an effective hierarchical addressing scheme. The addressing structure that you implement can have a profound impact on the performance and scalability of your OSPF network. The ultimate goal is to put as few routes as possible into the routing tables and reduce the number of updates.

Figure 5-13 illustrates the benefits of route summarization on a routing table. Without summarization, only three entries exist in the routing table, and with summarization, only one entry exists in the routing table.

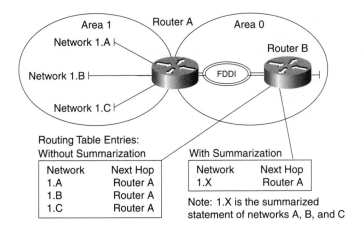

Figure 5–13
Benefits of route summarization.

IP Addressing & Route Summarization Design Golden Rules

When planning your OSPF network, consider the following golden rules of design for IP addressing and route summarization:

- The network's IP addressing scheme should be configured so that the range of subnets assigned within an area is contiguous.

- Allocate your IP address space within each area so that it will permit you to easily split areas as your network grows.

- Whenever possible, assign subnets according to simple octet boundaries.

- Thoroughly define your network's addressing structure. This will enable you to allocate and plan more effectively and keep your IP addressing scheme structured and simple.

- Determine the correct locations of each type of router, area, backbone, and so forth. This will assist you in determining which router should summarize.

OSPF Route Summarization Techniques

Route summarization is particularly important in an OSPF environment because it increases the stability and efficiency of the network. Summarizing is the consolidation of multiple routes into one single advertisement. This is normally done at the boundaries of ABRs or ASBRs. Although summarization could be configured between any two areas, it is better to summarize in the direction of the backbone. This way the backbone receives all the aggregate addresses and, in turn, will inject them, already summarized, into other areas. If route summarization is being used, routes within an area that change do not need to be changed in the backbone or in other areas. There are two types of summarization:

- Inter-area route summarization
- External route summarization

Inter-Area Route Summarization

Inter-area route summarization is done on ABRs, and it applies to routes from within the AS. It does not apply to external routes injected into OSPF via redistribution. To take advantage of summarization, network numbers in areas should be assigned in a contiguous way so that you can lump these addresses into one range when summarizing them.

To specify an address range, perform the following task in router configuration mode:

> **area** *area-id* **range** *address mask*

The area-id is the area containing networks to be summarized. The address and mask will specify the range of addresses to be summarized in one range. Figure 5-14 illustrates an example of summarization.

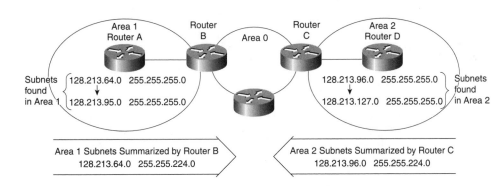

Figure 5–14
An example of inter-area route summarization.

In Figure 5-14, Router B is summarizing the range of subnets found within area 1 from 128.213.64.0 to 128.213.95.0 into one range: 128.213.64.0 with a mask of 255.255.224.0 into the backbone. This is achieved by masking the first three left-most bits of 64, using a mask of 255.255.224.0.

In the same way, Router C is generating the summary address 128.213.96.0 255.255.224.0 into the backbone. Note that this summarization was successful because you have two distinct ranges of subnets, 64–95 and 96–127 in areas 1 and 2 respectively.

It would be hard to summarize if the subnets between area 1 and area 2 were overlapping. The backbone area would receive summary ranges that overlap and routers in the middle would not know where to send the traffic based on the summary address. The following is the relative configuration of Router B, and you can extrapolate Router C's configuration as well:

```
Router B#
router ospf 100
area 1 range 128.213.64.0 255.255.224.0
```

External Route Summarization

External route summarization is specific to external routes that are injected into OSPF via redistribution done by ASBRs. Also, make sure that external ranges being summarized are contiguous. Summarization that overlaps ranges from two different routers could cause packets to be sent to the wrong destination. Summarization is done via the following `router ospf` subcommand:

> **summary-address** *ip-address mask*

This command is effective only on ASBRs doing redistribution into OSPF.

In Figure 5-15, Router A and Router D (both ASBRs) are injecting external routes into OSPF by redistribution. Router A is injecting subnets in the range `128.213.64–95` and Router D is injecting subnets in the range `128.213.96–127`.

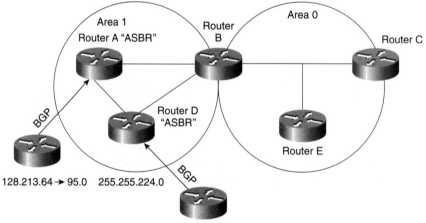

Figure 5–15
An example of external route summarization.

To properly summarize the subnets into one range on each router, you can configure the routers as follows:

```
Router A#
router ospf 100
summary-address 128.213.64.0 255.255.224.0
redistribute bgp 50 metric 1000 subnets

Router D#
router ospf 100
summary-address 128.213.96.0 255.255.224.0
redistribute bgp 20 metric 1000 subnets
```

This will cause Router A to generate one external route 128.213.64.0 with a mask of 255.255.224.0 and will cause Router D to generate one external route 128.213.96.0 with a mask of 255.255.224.0. Note that the summary-address command has no effect if used on Router B because Router B is not doing the redistribution into OSPF, nor is it an ASBR.

Route Summarization and Route Distribution

Route summarization addresses two important questions of route information distribution:

- **What information does the backbone need to know about each area?** The answer to this question focuses attention on area-to-backbone routing information.

- **What information does each area need to know about the backbone and other areas?** The answer to this question focuses attention on backbone-to-area routing information.

If you know the answers to these questions, you will be able to effectively design how you need to summarize routes within your OSPF network.

Area-to-Backbone Route Advertisements

There are several key considerations when setting up your OSPF areas for proper summarization. OSPF route summarization occurs in the ABRs. OSPF supports variable length subnet masks (VLSM), so it is possible to summarize on any bit boundary in a network or subnet address. OSPF requires manual summarization. As you design the areas, you need to determine summarization at each ABR.

Backbone-to-Area Route Advertisements

Four potential types of routing information exist in an area and are listed in Table 5-2, which shows the different types of areas according to the routing information that they use.

Table 5-2   *OSPF area route types*

Area Type	Default	Intra-Area	Inter-Area	External
Non-stub	Yes	Yes	Yes	Yes
Stub	Yes	Yes	Yes	No
TSA	Yes	Yes	No	No
NSSA	Yes	Yes	Yes	Yes

The types of routes defined in Table 5-2 for OSPF areas are as follows:

- **Default Routes.** If an explicit route cannot be found for a given IP network or subnetwork, the router will forward the packet to the destination specified in the default route.

- **Intra-Area Routes.** Explicit network or subnet routes must be carried for all networks or subnets inside an area.

- **Inter-Area Routes.** Areas may carry explicit network or subnet routes for networks or subnets that are in this AS but not in this area.

- **External Routes.** When different ASs exchange routing information, the routes they exchange are referred to as external routes.

OSPF Addressing and Summarization Scenarios

The following sections discuss OSPF route summarization and the three most commonly encountered IP addressing scenarios:

- Scenario 1: Assigning Unique Network Numbers to Each OSPF Area
- Scenario 2: Complex Address Assignment with Only a Single NIC Address
- Scenario 3: Using Private IP Addresses

Scenario 1: Assigning Unique Network Numbers to Each OSPF Area

In this scenario each OSPF area has its own unique NIC-assigned IP address range. This can be as grand as a Class A address for the entire network with multiple Class Bs assigned to each area, or more realistically, you can be using a group of Class C addresses. This example is demonstrated in Figure 5-15. The benefits of this method are as follows:

- Address assignment is very simple.

- Configuration of the routers is easy and mistakes unlikely.

- Network operations are streamlined because each area has a simple unique address prefix.

The following two steps are the basic steps for creating such a network:

1. Define your structure (identify areas and allocate nodes to areas).

2. Assign addresses to networks, subnets, and end stations as demonstrated in Figure 5-16.

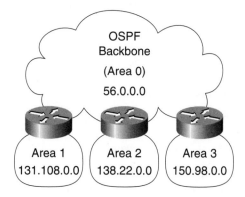

Figure 5–16
Assigning unique network numbers to each OSPF area.

As an example, the route summarization configuration at the ABRs is greatly simplified. Routes from area 4 injected into the backbone would be summarized as "all routes starting with 150.98 are found in area 4." This can be accomplished on a Cisco router with the following command:

```
area 4 range 150.98.0.0 255.255.0.0
```

The main drawback of this approach is that it can be very wasteful with important IP address space. Of course, this space could also be very difficult to obtain, at least until IPv6.

Scenario 2: Complex Address Assignment with Only a Single NIC Address

There might be a situation where you only have one NIC address (a single Class B for example) to allocate for all areas of your multi-area OSPF network. You might also wish to save some address space by using VLSM such that the point-to-point serial links in each area have a subnet mask that allows two hosts per subnet.

This example uses part of the address space for the NIC address 150.100.0.0. It is meant to illustrate both the concept of "area masks" and also the breakdown of large subnets into smaller ones (VLSMs).

The points that follow list the assumptions made and describe the process used to allocate addresses:

1. Determine how many areas you will have in your OSPF network. A value of 500 has been chosen for this example. (A 500 area OSPF network is not realistic, but it will help to illustrate the methodology used.)

2. Create an artificial "area mask boundary" in your address space. The dotted lines in Figure 5-17 indicate that you will be using 9 bits of the subnetable portion of the address to identify the areas uniquely. Note that 2exp9=512 meets the requirement of 500 areas. Only the address space for two of the 512 areas is documented in this example.

3. Determine the number of subnets required in each area and the number of hosts (maximum) required per subnet. In this example, you require seven subnets with 14 hosts each and four subnets with 2 hosts each (the serial lines).

4. Step 3 enables you to decide where to draw the dividing line between the subnet and host (called subnet mask) within each area. Note that you have only 7-bits left to use because of the creation of the artificial area mask. In fact, the 9-bits of the area mask are part of the subnet portion of the address, but you have restricted their flexibility so that you can summarize all the subnets of an area with one range command.

The portion of the address space that has the 2-bit host field (subnet mask of 255.255.255.252) was chosen arbitrarily from one of the larger subnet fields. This method of assigning addresses for the VLSM portion of the address space is done to guarantee no address overlap. Alternatively, if the requirement had been different, you could have chosen any number of the larger subnets (with mask 255.255.255.240) and broken them up into smaller ranges with fewer hosts, or combined several of them to create subnets with more hosts.

Realistic Summarization Design Guidelines

It is important to note that the sample of addresses and mask boundary choices in scenario 2 were chosen simply so that the entire address space of a single area could be shown on a single page. **It is not realistic to have an OSPF network designed with 500 areas.**

A realistic design might include the following:

- About 20–30 areas (maximum) for the entire AS

- Approximately 20–30 routers per OSPF area

- One or more Class B addresses with several Class C networks to allocate for the AS

Real World Route Summarization Example

Now that you know about segmenting the IP address space for 500 areas, you can take a more realistic approach. Assume that you have the following design criteria and IP addresses to work with:

- 18 OSPF areas including the backbone area

- The following assigned network addresses:

- Class B: 156.77.0.0

- Class C: 198.22.33.0 198.22.34.0

Area Assignment

Here, each Class C network will be used entirely in its own area (similar to scenario 1) and the Class B address will be subdivided using an *area mask* and distributed among the remaining 16 areas.

The Class B network, 156.77.0.0, could be subdivided as follows:

```
156.77. x x x x y y y y . y z
        area mask boundary
```

The letters x, y and z represent bits of the last two octets of the Class B.

The four x bits are used to identify 16 areas.

The five y bits represent up to 32 subnets per area.

The seven z bits allow for 126 (128–2) hosts per subnet.

All of the principles used for summarization and VLSM shown in scenarios 1 and 2 also apply for this more realistic example.

Route summarization is extremely desirable for a reliable and scalable OSPF internetwork. The effectiveness of route summarization, and your OSPF implementation in general, hinges on the addressing scheme that you adopt. Summarization in an OSPF internetwork occurs between each area and the backbone area. Summarization must be configured manually in OSPF.

Because of the careful assignment of addresses, each area can be summarized with a single range command. This is a *requirement* to be able to scale an OSPF network. The first set of addresses starting with 150.100.2.0xxxxxxx (the last octet is represented in binary) can be summarized into the backbone with the following command:

```
area 8 range 150.100.2.0 255.255.255.128
```

This means that all addresses starting with 150.100.2.0xxxxxxx can be found in area 8.

Similarly, with the second area shown, the range of addresses starting with

```
150.100.2.1xxxxxxx
```

can be summarized as follows:

```
area 17 range 150.100.2.128 255.255.255.128
```

This design methodology is extensible such that the area mask boundary and the subnet masks may be drawn at any point in the address space. This might be required if you had originally planned for 32 areas in your network but then later decided that you needed more. Here, you may decide to have a variable-length area mask boundary. This becomes much more complex to manage and is beyond the scope of this book. Strategy 2 is meant to show one approach that tries to simplify something that is inherently complicated for people to deal with. Keep in mind that if you had displayed the entire address space for 150.100.0.0, there would be an additional 510 pages to the document.

Bit-Wise Subnetting and VLSM Example

Bit-wise subnetting and variable-length subnet masks (VLSMs) can be used in combination to save address space. Consider a hypothetical network where a Class B address is subdivided using an area mask and distributed among 16 areas. The Class B network, 156.77.0.0, might be subdivided as illustrated in Figure 5-17.

In Figure 5-17, the letters x, y, and z represent bits of the last two octets of the Class B network as follows:

- The four x bits are used to identify 16 areas.

- The five y bits represent up to 32 subnets per area.

- The seven z bits allow for 126 (128-2) hosts per subnet.

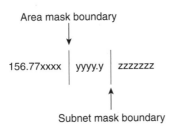

Area mask boundary

156.77xxxx | yyyy.y | zzzzzzz

Subnet mask boundary

Figure 5–17
Bit-wise subnetting and VLSM example.

Scenario 3: Using Private IP Addresses

Private addressing is another option often cited as simpler than developing an area scheme using bit-wise subnetting. Although private address schemes provide an excellent level of flexibility and do not limit the growth of your OSPF internetwork, they have certain disadvantages.

For instance, developing a large-scale internetwork of privately addressed IP nodes limits total access to the Internet and mandates the implementation of what is referred to as a demilitarized zone (DMZ). If you need to connect to the Internet, Figure 5-18 illustrates the way in which a DMZ provides a buffer of valid NIC nodes between a privately addressed network and the Internet.

All nodes (end systems and routers) on the network in the DMZ must have NIC-assigned IP addresses. The NIC might, for example, assign a single Class C network number to you. The DMZ shown in Figure 5-18 has two routers and a single application gateway host (ApGate).

Router A provides the interface between the DMZ and the Internet, and Router B provides the firewall between the DMZ and the private address environment. All applications that need to run over the Internet must access the Internet through the application gateway.

NOTES

Firewalls can take many forms. They can be a router specially configured through the use of the Cisco firewall feature set or a dedicated machine designed from the ground up to perform firewall duties, such as a PIX Firewall, Raptor Eagle, or Firewall-1.

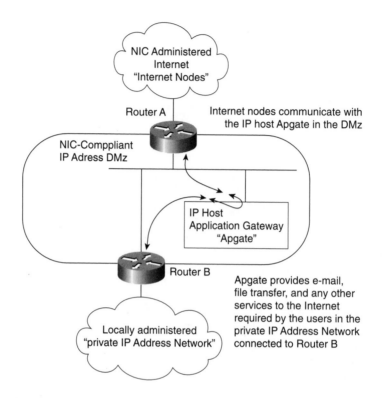

Figure 5–18
Connecting to the Internet from a privately addressed network.

VLSM in OSPF

IP networks are divided into Class A, B, and C addresses. You can define a mask that specifies which bits in the address define the subnet and which define the host. OSPF supports a concept called variable-length subnet masks (VLSM) which enables an administrator to use different masks for the same network number on different interfaces.

VLSM Functionality

You might want to use VLSM if you are concerned about running out of IP address space. VLSM enables you to get more use out of your available space. VLSM offers the flexibility to handle subnets with different numbers of hosts. For example, a customer who has not implemented VLSM has some interfaces with only a few hosts and other interfaces with many hosts may choose to use a long mask on the first interface and a short mask on the second interface. This address space must be assigned very carefully. It is very likely that existing networks will need to re-number their networks in order to be able to take advantage of this feature.

With VLSM, you don't have to waste network numbers on serial interfaces because you can support unnumbered IP interfaces. Also, VLSM supports discontinuous subnets. An example of a discontinuous subnet application is where a customer has two Class B addresses. One is used in the backbone, and one is used by sites. The site network number is discontinuous if there is more than one site with the same network number. The existing solution is to use secondary IP addresses on the same interface. In this way, you can provide a set of network numbers across the backbone and, thus, connect the discontinuous subnets.

VLSM Pitfalls

Some of the disadvantages of VLSM include the following:

- It is easy to make mistakes in address assignment.
- It is more difficult to monitor your network.

When using VLSM, be very careful about assigning addresses. For example, Cisco's internal Class B network number is 131.108.0.0.

First a little math to help show some common masks:

Table 5-3 *Common masks and hosts*

Mask	Number of hosts
255.255.255.252	2
255.255.255.248	6
255.255.255.240	14
255.255.255.224	30
255.255.255.192	62
255.255.255.128	126
255.255.255.0	254

Suppose that you had two labs to which you want to assign subnet numbers. The first lab is very small and will never have more than six hosts. The second lab is large and might need to support up to 126 hosts. The obvious thing to do is to assign the masks appropriately. However, it is easy to make mistakes when doing this.

Table 5-4   *Mask assignments*

IDs	Network Number	Mask	Legal Host
Lab A	131.108.13.248	255.255.255.248	249–254
Lab B	131.108.13.128	255.255.255.128	129–254

This is an illegal configuration because one of the network/mask pairs is a bit-wise subset of the other. Watch what can happen.

The owners of those labs are allowed to assign their IP addresses within the labs themselves. Let's say that the owner of Lab A assigns a host the IP address of 131.108.13.250—this is host '2' in network 131.108.13.248. Meanwhile, the owner of Lab B assigns a host the IP address 131.108.13.250—this is host '122' in network 131.108.13.128. Both of these are legal addresses.

However, it is impossible for a router to tell which host should get packets that are sent to that IP address. Worse yet, neither of the lab owners realizes that they have created a problem. To make this even harder to keep straight, the following configuration in Table 5-5 shows other legal possibilities:

Table 5-5   *IP configurations*

IDs	Network Number	Mask	Legal Host
Lab A	131.108.13.248	255.255.255.248	249–254
Lab B	131.108.13.0	255.255.255.128	1–127

A final pitfall to watch out for is the use of subnet zero, which isn't legal. If you use subnet masks that don't fall on 8-bit boundaries, you can end up creating a non-obvious subnet zero.

For example, network 192.111.108.0 mask 255.255.255.0 has eight hosts on it (192.111.108.[1-8]). You can try to expand the number of networks by stretching the mask: network 192.111.108.0 mask 255.255.255.240 (15 nets with 14 hosts each)

However, this leaves all of the existing hosts in subnet zero, which doesn't work. The hosts need to be renumbered (17–24, for example). This problem exists even when VLSMs are *not* used. However, VLSM makes it more likely to occur.

TIPS

According to RFC 795, the only illegal number is subnet zero. The all ones subnet is fair game. In fact, the `ip subnet zero` IOS command gets around the first restriction.

Proper Implementation of VLSM

The best way to use VLSM is to keep the existing numbering plan in place and gradually migrate some networks in order to recover address space. In Cisco's network, the Class B address is 131.108.0.0. You use a mask of 255.255.255.0. You could take one address and decide to use it for all serial lines, for example:

Existing addressing: network number: 131.108.0.0, mask: 255.255.255.0

Reserve one existing subnet for all serial lines: network number: 131.108.254.0, mask: 255.255.255.252

The use of VLSM allows 6-bits or 64 subnets for serial lines. These subnets would be
> 131.108.254.1 and 131.108.254.2
> 131.108.254.5 and 131.108.254.6
> 131.108.254.9 and 131.108.254.10
>
> . . .

Note that host numbers with all zeros or all ones are not supported. This achieves a 64:1 improvement in address space allocation on serial lines. It also assumes that you are including subnet zero and the broadcast.

Inter-Operability Issues with VLSM

Routers in a single area *must* agree on the network mask. IGRP does not support VLSM. So when information is redistributed from OSPF to IGRP, only a single mask will be used. The best way to make this work is to hide all VLSMs from IGRP. OSPF should summarize the networks to achieve one mask per network number.

The idea behind VLSMs is to offer more flexibility in dealing with dividing a major network into multiple subnets and still being able to maintain an adequate number of hosts in each subnet. Without VLSM, one subnet mask can only be applied to a major network. This would restrict the number of hosts given the number of subnets required. If you pick the mask such that you have enough subnets, you wouldn't be able to allocate enough hosts in each subnet. The same is true for the hosts: a mask that allows enough hosts might not provide enough subnet space.

For example, suppose you were assigned a Class C network 192.214.11.0, and you need to divide that network into three subnets with 100 hosts in one subnet and 50 hosts for each of the remaining subnets. Ignoring the two end limits 0 and 255, you theoretically have available to you 256 addresses (192.214.11.0–192.214.11.255). This cannot be done without VLSM. Figure 5-19 shows an example of how you can use VLSM to segment a Class C address.

Figure 5–19
VLSM example.

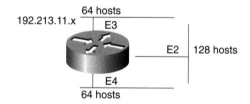

There are a handful of subnet masks that can be used; remember that a mask should have a contiguous number of ones starting from the left and the rest of the bits being all zeros. As an example, some common VLSM configurations include the following:

- For . . . 252 (1111 1100), the address space is divided into 64.

- For . . . 248 (1111 1000), the address space is divided into 32.

- For . . . 240 (1111 0000), the address space is divided into 16.

- For . . . 224 (1110 0000), the address space is divided into 8.

- For . . . 192 (1100 0000), the address space is divided into 4.

- For . . . 128 (1000 0000), the address space is divided into 2.

Without VLSM, you have the choice of using mask 255.255.255.128 and dividing the addresses into two subnets with 128 hosts each or using 255.255.255.192 and dividing the space into four subnets with 64 hosts each.

This would not meet the requirement. By using multiple masks you can use mask 128 and further subnet the second chunk of addresses with mask 192. Figure 5-20 shows the proper division of address space.

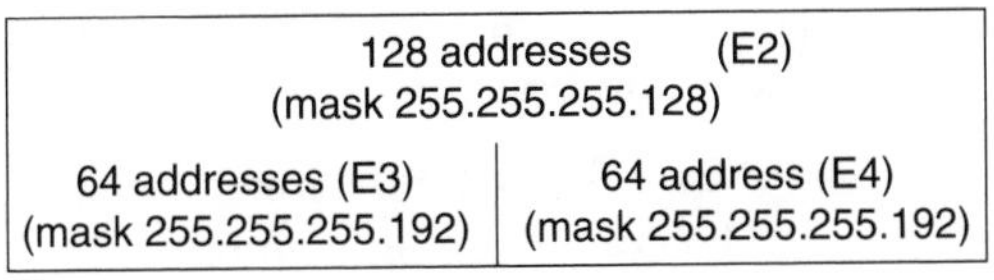

128 addresses (E2) (mask 255.255.255.128)	
64 addresses (E3) (mask 255.255.255.192)	64 address (E4) (mask 255.255.255.192)

Figure 5–20
VLSM address
distribution.

Now, be careful in allocating the IP addresses to each mask. After you assign an IP address to the router or to a host, you have used up the whole subnet for that segment. For example, if you assign 192.214.11.10 255.255.255.128 to E2, the whole range of addresses between 192.214.11.0 and 192.214.11.127 is consumed by E2. In the same way if you assign 192.214.11.160 255.255.255.128 to E2, the whole range of addresses between 192.214.11.128 and 192.214.11.255 is consumed by the E2 segment.

The following is an illustration of how the router will interpret these addresses. Please remember that any time you are using a mask different than the natural mask, the router will complain if the combination IP address and mask result in a subnet zero. To resolve this issue, use the ip subnet-zero commandon the router:

```
RTA#
ip subnet-zero
interface Ethernet2
ip address 192.214.11.10 255.255.255.128
interface Ethernet3
ip address 192.214.11.160 255.255.255.192
interface Ethernet4
ip address 192.214.11.226 255.255.255.192

RTA# show ip route connected
```

```
192.214.11.0 is variably subnetted, 3 subnets, 2 masks
C 192.214.11.0 255.255.255.128 is directly connected, Ethernet2
C 192.214.11.128 255.255.255.192 is directly connected, Ethernet3
C 192.214.11.192 255.255.255.192 is directly connected, Ethernet4
```

CHAPTER SUMMARY

This chapter completes the discussion on the mathematics surrounding the SPF algorithm and its operation within OSPF. The various "golden rules of design" were provided for all of the essential portions of an OSPF network. Included within those discussions was the ability of OSPF to summarize routes and the benefits of using such a strong feature of the protocol. The discussion concluded with a demonstration of VLSM's usefulness within the OSPF environment.

In conclusion, many of the OSPF-specific configuration commands will be presented in detail in the next chapter. All of the configuration commands are grouped together for your ease of reference In addition, a complete list and definition of the commands will be provided in Chapter 7, "Designing & Implementing an OSPF Network."

OSPF CASE STUDY: POINT-TO-MULTIPOINT LINK NETWORKS

The objective of this case study is to demonstrate how to design, configure, and troubleshoot an OSPF point-to-multipoint link network.

This feature's importance is linked with the increased use of Frame Relay due to reduced cost for the service. As customers used point-to-multipoint on nonbroadcast media (Frame Relay), they found that their routers could not dynamically discover their neighbors. The OSPF point-to-multipoint link feature allows the `neighbor` command to be used on point-to-multipoint interfaces. The use of point-to-multipoint can be used to minimize the number of IP addresses that are used and basically enable the user to configure a nonbroadcast media similarly to a LAN.

Before the OSPF point-to-multipoint link feature, some OSPF point-to-multipoint protocol traffic was treated as multicast traffic. This meant that the `neighbor` command was not needed for point-to-multipoint interfaces because multicast took care of the traffic. In particular, multicast hellos discovered all neighbors dynamically.

Also, on any point-to-multipoint interface (broadcast or not), the Cisco IOS software assumed that the cost to each neighbor was equal. In reality, the bandwidth to each neighbor can be different; therefore, the cost should be different because the OSPF point-to-multipoint link enables you to configure a separate cost for each neighbor.

NOTES

One method of increasing your understanding of this feature is to become familiar with the following document: `http://www.cisco.com/univercd/cc/td/doc/product/software/ios113ed/113aa/ospfpmp.htm`.

Another advantage is that you do not need to use subinterfaces with this feature. Subinterfaces count toward the practical upper limit of 300 IDBs (Interface Descriptor Blocks). There is an IDB assigned for each physical and software interface that is configured on the router. This includes any subinterfaces. There is no command that will tell you how many IDBs have been used. In other words, Cisco IOS currently supports less then 300 interfaces on the router (real or virtual) unless you have an 11.1CA or CC image which has 1,024 IDBs, but this only runs on the high end routers.

How many DLCIs can one configure per physical interface? How many DLCIs can one configure in a specific router? These two questions are frequently asked. Disappointingly, the answer is, "It depends."

DLCI address space: Approximately 1,000 DLCIs can be configured on a single physical link, given a 10-bit address. Because certain DLCIs are reserved (vendor implementation dependent), the maximum is about 1,000.

Local Management Interface (LMI) status update: The LMI protocol (ANSI Annex D, and ITU-T standards also) requires that all PVC status reports fit into a single packet and generally limits the number of DLCIs to less than 800, depending on the maximum transmission unit (MTU) size. This limit does not apply to Cisco LMI (also known as the "Gang of Four" LMI), which allows fragmentation of the PVC status report.

Configuring NBMA networks as either broadcast or nonbroadcast assumes that there are VCs from every router to every other router. This is often not true due to real world cost constraints. In these cases, you can configure the OSPF network type as point-to-multipoint. This will enable routing between two routers that are not directly connected to go through the router that has the VCs to each.

Figure 5-21 illustrates the network topology considered in this case study.

As illustrated in Figure 5-21, Hub Router R1 has virtual circuits to Spoke Routers R2, R3, and R4. But the other three routers do not have direct circuits to each other. This will be configured as a single subnet and point-to-multipoint links rather than multiple subnets and point-to-point links.

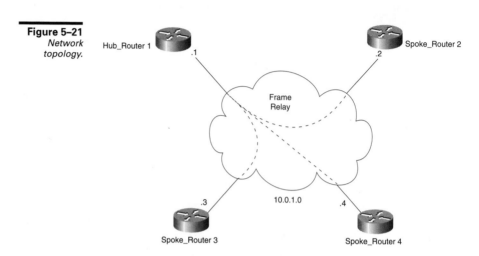

Figure 5-21
Network topology.

To configure an interface as point-to-multipoint broadcast and assign a cost to each neighbor, you will need to perform the following tasks on each interface while in configuration mode:

1. Configure an interface as point-to-multipoint for broadcast media using the `ip ospf network point-to-multipoint` command.

2. Configure an OSPF routing process and enter router configuration mode with `router ospf process-id`.

3. Specify a neighbor and assign a cost to the neighbor using `neighbor ip-address cost number`.

4. Repeat Step 3 for each neighbor if you want to specify a cost. Otherwise, neighbors will assume the cost of the interface, based on the `ip ospf cost` command.

Router Configuration Examples

The following are examples of the configurations contained within the routers shown in Figure 5-21. These configurations weere built with IOS version 11.3. They will not work with older IOS versions. For the older IOS versions please add the command `frame-relay map ip <address> <dlci> broadcast`.

```
Hub_Router1#
interface Serial 0
    ip address 10.0.1.1 255.255.255.0
    encapsulation frame-relay
```

```
    ip ospf network point-to-multipoint non-broadcast
    frame-relay local-dlci 100
!
router ospf 1
  network 10.0.1.0 0.0.0.255 area 0
  neighbor 10.0.1.2 10
  neighbor 10.0.1.3 10
  neighbor 10.0.1.4 10
```

Spoke_Router2#
```
interface Serial 0
  ip address 10.0.1.2 255.255.255.0
  encapsulation frame-relay
  ip ospf network point-to-multipoint non-broadcast
  frame-relay local dlci 101
!
router ospf 1
  network 10.0.1.0 0.0.0.255 area 0
  network 10.2.0.0 0.0.255.255 area 2
  neighbor 10.0.1.1 10
```

Spoke_Router3#
```
interface Serial 0
  ip address 10.0.1.3 255.255.255.0
  encapsulation frame-relay
  ip ospf network point-to-multipoint non-broadcast
  frame-relay local-dlci 103
!
router ospf 1
  network 10.0.1.0 0.0.0.255 area 0
  network 10.3.0.0 0.0.255.255 area 3
  neighbor 10.0.1.1 10
```

Spoke_Router4#
```
interface Serial 0
  ip address 10.0.1.4 255.255.255.0
  encapsulation frame-relay
  ip ospf network point-to-multipoint non-broadcast
  frame-relay local-dlci 104
!
router ospf 1
  network 10.0.1.0 0.0.0.255 area 0
  network 10.4.0.0 0.0.255.255 area 4
  neighbor 10.0.1.1 10
```

NOTES

Note that no static frame relay map statements were configured. This is because Inverse ARP will take care of the DLCI to IP resolution and mapping.

You will not be able to ping your own IP address on a multipoint Frame Relay interface. This is because FR multipoint (sub)interfaces are nonbroadcast (unlike Ethernet and point-to-point interfaces (HDLC) and Frame Relay point-to-point sub-interfaces). Furthermore, you will not be able to ping from one spoke router to another spoke router in a hub and spoke configuration. This is because there is no mapping for your own IP address (and none was learned via inverse-arp). However, if you configure a static map (frame-relay map) for your own IP address (or one for the remote spoke) to use the local DLCI, you can ping yourself to your heart's content.

The following capture from a router occurred before the circuit went active. Check the State. The following example highlights the important fields that you would use in troubleshooting an OSPF link-state problem:

```
Hub_router1#show ip ospf interface serial 0
Serial0 is up, line protocol is up
    Internet Address 10.0.1.1/24, Area 0
    Process ID 10, Router ID 10.0.1.1, Network Type POINT_TO_MULTIPOINT,
    Cost: 64
    DoNotAge LSA allowed.
    Transmit Delay is 1 sec, State DOWN,
    Timer intervals configured, Hello 10, Dead 40, Wait 40, Retransmit 5
```

After the OSPF state goes active, the capture from the router is as follows:

```
Hub_router1#show ip ospf interface serial 0
Serial0 is up, line protocol is up
    Internet Address 10.0.1.1/24, Area 0
    Process ID 10, Router ID 10.0.1.1, Network Type POINT_TO_MULTIPOINT,
    Cost: 64
    DoNotAge LSA allowed.
    Transmit Delay is 1 sec, State POINT_TO_MULTIPOINT,
    Timer intervals configured, Hello 10, Dead 40, Wait 40, Retransmit 5
      Hello due in 00:00:01
    Neighbor Count is 1, Adjacent neighbor count is 1
    Adjacent with neighbor 10.0.1.2
    Suppress hello for 0 neighbor(s)
```

Taking a look at the show ip ospf neighbor command for each of the routers will show the following:

```
Hub_Router1#show ip ospf neighbor

Neighbor ID  Pri   State        Dead Time   Address     Interface
10.0.1.2      1    FULL/  -     00:01:30    10.0.1.1    Serial0
10.0.1.3      1    FULL/  -     00:01:30    10.0.1.1    Serial0
10.0.1.4      1    FULL/  -     00:01:30    10.0.1.1    Serial0
```

The preceding command shows that the state is a full adjacency. Notice that there is no DR or ADR, which is normal and expected behavior for a NBMA media. If the state is anything but FULL, then the adjacencies have not been completely built and there might be a problem with the multicast LSA packets being passed through the interface. Perform the following command to check the state:

```
Spoke_Router2#show ip ospf neighbor

Neighbor ID  Pri   State        Dead Time   Address     Interface
10.0.1.1      1    FULL/  -     00:01:52    10.0.1.2    Serial0


Spoke_Router3#show ip ospf neighbor

Neighbor ID  Pri   State        Dead Time   Address     Interface
10.0.1.1      1    FULL/  -     00:01:52    10.0.1.3    Serial0


Spoke_Router4#show ip ospf neighbor
Neighbor ID  Pri   State        Dead Time   Address     Interface
10.0.1.1      1    FULL/  -     00:01:52    10.0.1.4    Serial0
```

The following sections provide a definition of the different OSPF states.

The Neighbor State Changes (Hello Protocol)

The following is a brief description of the possible OSPF neighbor state changes:

- **Down.** This is the initial state of a neighbor conversation.

- **Attempt.** This is valid only for neighbors attached to nonbroadcast networks.

- **Init.** Hello packet has been seen, but bi-directional communication has not yet been established with the neighbor.

- **2-Way.** Communication between the two routers is bi-directional. On Cisco routers, you see the router, in this state, when you give a priority of 0 for that interface.

NOTES

Typically you will see OSPF go from *2-Way* to *full*; however, when a full state is reached, this reflects that the LSDBs (that is, all database exchanges) have been completely exchanged between the two routers in question. This process differs from the Hello protocol and is the subtle difference between the two.

The Neighbor State Changes (Database Exchange)

The following is a brief description of the possible OSPF neighbor state changes:

- **ExStart.** This state indicates the first step in creating adjacency, the goal of which is to decide which router is the master and to decide upon the initial DD sequence number.

- **Exchange.** In this state, the router is describing its entire LSDB by sending Database Description packets to the neighbor.

- **Loading.** This state indicates that the LSR packets are sent to the neighbor asking for the more recent advertisements that are not yet received in the Exchange state.

- **Full.** This state indicates that the neighboring routers are fully adjacent.

It is important to note that there is no DR/BDR election on a point-to-multipoint interface and that you can confirm that with the appropriate show command.

If you do not see full adjacencies, then the packet negotiation sequence that occurs can be seen through the use of a debug ip ospf events command. This can be essential in identifying problems with the OSPF process by looking at the packets with the debug command as follows:

```
HUB_ROUTER1#term monitor
HUB_ROUTER1#debug ip ospf events

%FR-5-DLCICHANGE: Interface Serial0 - DLCI 100 state changed to ACTIVE
OSPF: rcv. v:2 t:1 l:44 rid:10.0.1.2

     Field definitions:
         aid:0.0.0.0 chk:EE35 aut:0 auk: from Serial0
         rcv - received packet
         v:2 - OSPF v2
         1:44
         rid: - Router ID
         aid: - Area ID
         chk: -
         aut: - Authentication
         auk: - physical interface packet was received through
OSPF: rcv. v:2 t:2 l:32 rid:10.0.1.2
         aid:0.0.0.0 chk:D363 aut:0 auk: from Serial0
OSPF: Receive dbd from 10.0.1.2 seq 0x1A6E --- begin of database exchange
OSPF: 2 Way Communication to neighbor 10.0.1.2 - building of adjacency
OSPF: send DBD packet to 10.0.1.2 seq 0x995
OSPF: rcv. v:2 t:2 l:72 rid:10.0.1.2
         aid:0.0.0.0 chk:36C4 aut:0 auk: from Serial0
OSPF: Receive dbd from 10.0.1.2 seq 0x995
OSPF: NBR Negotiation Done We are the MASTER - neighbor negotiation
OSPF: send DBD packet to 10.0.1.2 seq 0x996
OSPF: Database request to 10.0.1.2
OSPF: sent LS REQ packet to 10.0.1.2, length 12 - we are sending a request
   to 10.0.1.2 for link state data.
OSPF: rcv. v:2 t:2 l:32 rid:10.0.1.2
         aid:0.0.0.0 chk:E442 aut:0 auk: from Serial0
OSPF: Receive dbd from 10.0.1.2 seq 0x996
OSPF: send DBD packet to 10.0.1.2 seq 0x997
OSPF: rcv. v:2 t:3 l:48 rid:10.0.1.2
         aid:0.0.0.0 chk:5E71 aut:0 auk: from Serial0
```

```
OSPF: rcv. v:2 t:4 1:64 rid:10.0.1.2
      aid:0.0.0.0 chk:98D8 aut:0 auk: from Serial0
OSPF: rcv. v:2 t:2 1:32 rid:10.0.1.2
      aid:0.0.0.0 chk:E441 aut:0 auk: from Serial0
OSPF: Receive dbd from 10.0.1.2 seq 0x997
OSPF: Exchange Done with neighbor 10.0.1.2
OSPF: Synchronized with neighbor 10.0.1.2, state:FULL - completion of
   the adjacency process
```

Explanation of the fields is included with the first packet, and they are also shown in Table 5-6:

Table 5-6   *Fields in the* `debug ip ospf events` *command*

Field	Description
v	ospf_version
t	ospf_type
1 Hello	To maintain neighbors
2 Database	Exchange to bring up adjacency
3 Link State Request	
4 Link State Update	
5 Link State Ack.	
l	ospf_length
rid	ospf_rtr_id
aid	ospf_area_id
chk	ospf_checksum
aut	ospf_autype

This sequence shows the distribution of the LSA packets and the building of the database. It also shows the building of the OSPF adjacency. The `debug ip ospf events` command is very useful in discovering the problems that might be causing an OSPF adjacency problem on the network.

The output from a `debug ip ospf events` command shows both the received and transmitted packets, the building of the OSPF adjacency, and the exchange of database information. If you are having a problem with building the OSPF adjacency or there are OSPF database problems, then this debug command can help you identify whether the packets are being received or sent.

The following example illustrates a nonbroadcast point-to-multipoint network using the frame relay map statement for clarification of the PVCs. This enables you to identify both ends of the PVC and if you need to define multiple DLCIs for a split DLCI —one PVC for receiving and one PVC for transmitting. This enables you to work with your provider in setting the committed information rate (CIR) for each of the PVCs. As customers need to shape their user and application traffic across their frame relay circuits, the use of this kind of mapping is necessary.

```
HUB_ROUTER1#
interface Serial0
ip address 10.0.1.1 255.255.255.0
ip ospf network point-to-multipoint non-broadcast
encapsulation frame-relay
frame-relay local-dlci 100
frame-relay map ip 10.0.1.2 102
frame-relay map ip 10.0.1.3 103
frame-relay map ip 10.0.1.4 104
no shut
!
router ospf 1
network 10.0.1.0 0.0.0.255 area 0
neighbor 10.0.1.3
neighbor 10.0.1.4
neighbor 10.0.1.5
```

The preceding code also illustrates the use of the neighbor command to force the configured OSPF routers interconnecting to nonbroadcast networks. The neighbor statements are used to form OSPF adjacency. This also enables the user to dictate upon which connections the router will attempt to form an OSPF adjacency.

Without the neighbor command, the OSPF adjacency might have problems being attained. With the command, you know which routers you should make an OSPF adjacency with and, therefore, know what to look for if there are problems.

Because OSPF performs an election process for a DR and BDR, which acts as a "central distribution" point for routing information, the setting up of neighbors can be important. Also, OSPF routers will only form a full adjacency to the DR and BDR. Therefore, OSPF can efficiently support a full mesh of neighboring routers per interface. This will enable the point-to-multipoint feature to provide the connectivity that is needed for a non–fully-meshed network.

Another command used to troubleshoot the connection is `show frame-relay map`. It can be used to confirm the Layer 1 and 2 connectivity between the routers. This enables you to eliminate this as a problem before you begin concentrating on the Layer 3 issues. This command is available for use and is shown in the following example:

```
HUB_ROUTER1#show frame map
Serial0 (up): point-to-point dlci, dlci 101(0x12,0x420), broadcast
Serial0 (up): point-to-point dlci, dlci 102(0x10,0x400), broadcast
Serial0 (up): point-to-point dlci, dlci 103(0x12,0x420), broadcast
```

This shows the connection from serial 0 to three different DLCIs; it shows that they are enabled for broadcast; and it will also show if the mapping is dynamic or static.

If there is no mapping to the other end, then the PVC has not been fully made. Therefore, there is a problem with the Frame Relay circuit and any associated problems with routing or with the OSPF process are not important until the physical layer problem has been taken care of.

Also, `show ip ospf interface serial 0` will show the following:

```
Spoke_R2#show ip ospf interface serial 0
Serial0 is up, line protocol is up
  Internet Address 10.0.1.2/24, Area 0
  Process ID 1, Router ID 10.0.1.2, Network Type POINT_TO_MULTIPOINT,
  Cost: 64
  Transmit Delay is 1 sec, State POINT_TO_MULTIPOINT,
  Timer intervals configured, Hello 10, Dead 40, Wait 40, Retransmit 5
    Hello due in 00:00:07
  Neighbor Count is 1, Adjacent neighbor count is 1
    Adjacent with neighbor 10.0.2.1
```

The preceding command shows the network type and state. It also lets you confirm that different timers that are set in OSPF. These should be identical between your routers. If these are not, or there is a problem with the subnet masks between the two routers, then a `debug ip ospf events` will show the following:

```
OSPF: Mismatched hello parameters from 200.1.3.2
Dead R 40 C 40, Hello R 10 C 10 Mask R 255.255.255.248 C 255.255.255.0
OSPF: Mismatched hello parameters from 200.1.3.2
Dead R 40 C 40, Hello R 10 C 10 Mask R 255.255.255.248 C 255.255.255.0
```

What is happening in the preceding output?

- The mask is not matching.

- R indicates what you are receiving.

- C indicates what is configured.

If one end of a Frame Relay link is configured to be a multipoint link type and the other end point-to-point, the multipoint interface would advertise the link as a `Nonbroadcast` and the point-to-point would interface the link as a point-to-point, which creates a conflict in the LSDB. It might cause the router to learn none of the routes through that link.

One possible fix for this is to change the point-to-point interface to a multipoint interface or change the interface type to `broadcast` by using the command `ip ospf network broadcast`.

OSPF and multipoint can be dangerous. OSPF needs a DR and if you start missing PVCs, then some routers might loose connectivity and want to become the DR. This can become a serious problem even though other routers still see the old DR. So your OSPF process will go a little crazy. Overhead associated with OSPF is not as obvious and predictable as that with traditional distance vector-routing protocols. The unpredictability comes from whether or not the OSPF network links are stable. If all adjacencies to a Frame Relay router are stable, only neighbor hello packets (keepalives) will flow, which is comparatively much less overhead than that incurred with a distance vector protocol (RIP, IGRP). If, however, routes (adjacencies) are unstable, link-state flooding will occur, and bandwidth can quickly be consumed. OSPF also is very processor-intensive when running the Dijkstra algorithm, which is used for computing routes.

Case Study Conclusion

The objective of this case study was to demonstrate how to use, configure, and troubleshoot an OSPF point-to-multipoint link. You have an example and explanation for the configuration, which should help you in both design considerations and implementation. The different `show` commands and `debug` commands reviewed will assist you in troubleshooting the point-to-multipoint configuration and, by understanding the data, should be helpful in troubleshooting more general OSPF problems as well.

A summary of appropriate `show` and `debug` commands for OSPF point-to-multipoint use, configuration, and troubleshooting is as follows:

- `show ip ospf neighbor`
- `show ip ospf interface`
- `show ip ospf virtual`
- `debug ip ospf packet`
- `debug ip ospf events`
- `show frame-relay map`
- `show frame-relay PVC`

FREQUENTLY ASKED QUESTIONS

Q— *OSPF is an IP based protocol which means it runs directly over IP but what value is placed in the IP packet header to identify it as a OSPF packet?*

A— Protocol 89

Q— *OSPF uses the class D multicast addresses in the range 224.0.0.0 through 239.255.255.255. with specially reserved address as follows 224.0.0.5 for all OSPF routers and 224.0.0.6 for all DRs and BDRs. However, is the multicasting on the IP layer alone sufficient?*

A— No, sometimes the link layer protocol might also require special multicast MAC addresses so as to route the info properly.

CHAPTER 6

Advanced OSPF Design Concepts

"Life: Be glad of life because it gives you the chance to love and to work and to play and to look up at the stars."—Henry Van Dyke

This chapter covers the following topics in-depth:

- OSPF redistribution

- Designing OSPF on-demand circuits

- OSPF configuration commands

- OSPF error messages

Redistribution is probably one of the most talked about and used but least understood concepts in routing. Redistribution is the process through which routing information discovered by one routing protocol is to be distributed in the update messages of another routing protocol. There are not very many networks left that do not perform some type of redistribution. A series of golden rules to follow is presented so that you may seamlessly learn the concepts behind this complicated task. This chapter will discuss several examples and techniques on how to avoid the dreaded formation of routing loops within an OSPF network. After you understand redistribution, this chapter will discuss how to perform mutual redistribution between multiple protocols.

One of the most under-funded routes, although it is just as mission critical as the networks themselves, is back up routes. Although many of today's networks have become critical to the success and operation of many corporations both large and small, these requirements often go overlooked until it's too late. This chapter will discuss the golden rules for designing demand circuits and go through several design scenarios that demonstrate both good and bad designs.

The section on OSPF configuration commands was an absolute joy to include and to write. Many networking professionals are distinguished by their manuals or stacks of compact discs detailing the various router commands. In this section, the objective was to include every OSPF configuration-related command from whatever source was available and then compile them into one section, complete with examples and explanations of their uses. This section is intended to be the one stop for anyone configuring an OSPF network.

Everyone also has encountered error messages. But what do you do with them while troubleshooting an OSPF problem? Typically, they are filed away for later use or you memorize them. This section will be a boon for those who would rather memorize other things like anniversaries. During the configuration of your OSPF network, you will encounter error messages. The section, "OSPF Error Messages," will help you decipher these messages and to use the necessary configuration commands to correct the problem.

OSPF REDISTRIBUTION

Most, if not all, OSPF networks are going to have to perform redistribution at some point in their evolution. Whether you are converting a RIP network to OSPF or you are using BGP and OSPF together, the ability to accurately and effectively redistribute routes is going to be needed. This section will discuss a variety of the different issues surrounding redistribution.

Redistributing Routes into OSPF

The redistribution of routes in networking is the process of taking routes from one routing protocol and allowing a different protocol to distribute them as new routes. Figure 6-1 illustrates this concept.

Figure 6–1
Redistribution of routing information.

Redistribution consists of more than just translating routes between protocols. In addition to routes, metrics and routing updates need to be shared to ensure accurate routing.

Golden Rules of Redistributing OSPF Routes

In general, redistribution with any type of protocol can be very tricky. The following list highlights some of the more important rules to follow when redistributing routes in an OSPF network.

- The most important rule is to NEVER allow routes from one protocol to be redistributed back into the originating protocol. The results of this are discussed later in this chapter.

- On an autonomous system border router (ASBR), use the `distribute-list out` command to filter redistributed routes into other protocols.

- The command `distribute-list in` stops routes from being inserted in routing tables, but it does NOT stop link-state advertisements (LSAs) from being sent. As a result all downstream routers will learn about the networks that were supposed to be filtered by these LSAs.

- Try to avoid using filters (access lists) under the *Router OSPF* section of the router's configuration.

- Whenever you redistribute OSPF into other protocols, you have to respect the rules of operation for those other protocols.

Redistributing routes into OSPF from other routing protocols or from static routes will cause these routes to become OSPF external routes. To redistribute routes into OSPF, use the redistribution command in the router configuration mode. Several examples are given to further assist in demonstrating the concept of redistribution.

Example #1: Redistributing RIP into OSPF

This example illustrates a common occurrence and that redistributing RIP into OSPF as shown in Figure 6-2. The router configuration commands are also included to further illustrate this example.

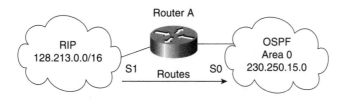

Figure 6–2
Redistributing RIP into OSPF.

```
Router A(config)#
router ospf 10
    redistribute rip subnets metric-type 1 metric 12
    network 128.130.0.0
    router rip
    network 128.130.0.0
    passive interface s 0
    default-metric 5
```

NOTES

All the configuration commands used will be discussed in context later in this chapter in the section titled, "OSPF Configuration Commands."

Example #2: Redistributing IGRP into OSPF

This example illustrates how to redistribute IGRP into OSPF as shown in Figure 6-3. The router configuration commands are also included to further illustrate this example.

Figure 6-3
Redistributing IGRP into OSPF.

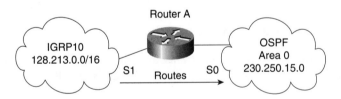

```
Router A(config)#
router ospf 10
    redistribute igrp subnets metric-type 1 metric 12
    network 128.130.0.0
    router igrp
    network 128.130.0.0
    passive-interface s 0
    default-metric k1 k2 k3 k4 k5
```

This example is very similar to the one shown for RIP, but IGRP has a multitude of metrics (k1–k5) that must be set in order for distribution to work properly. The five IGRP metrics are as follows:

- k1: bandwidth

- k2: delay

- k3: reliability

- k4: network utilization

- k5: maximum transmission unit (mtu)

TIPS

OSPF puts a default value of 20 when redistributing routes from all protocols except BGP routes, which get a metric of 1. If you are redistributing from OSPF to OSPF, the metrics are preserved.

Redistributing Routes Between Domains

Use route maps when you want detailed control over how routes are redistributed between routing processes. The destination routing protocol is the one you specify with the router global configuration command. The source routing protocol is the one you specify with the redistribute router configuration command. See the following example as an illustration of how route maps are configured.

The route map is a method used to control the redistribution of routes between routing domains. The format of a route map is as follows:

```
route-map map-tag [[permit ¦ deny] ¦ [ sequence-number]]
```

When you are passing routes through a route map, a route map can have several parts. Any route that does not match at least one match clause relating to a route-map command will be ignored; that is, the route will not be advertised for outbound route maps and will not be accepted for inbound route maps. If you want to modify only some data, you must configure a second route map section with an explicit match specified or you may use a permit depending upon your requirements.

When redistributing routes into OSPF, only routes that are not subnetted are redistributed if the subnets keyword is not specified.

Avoiding Redistribution Loops

Even though trying to avoid this situation is a golden rule for route redistribution, it does happen. To summarize what exactly is occurring, realize that Router A is distributing network 230.250.15.0 into the RIP network. Router B then sees it advertised by RIP as a valid destination, so it tells the OSPF network that it can reach it. This results in a very nasty routing loop as illustrated in Figure 6-4.

Figure 6–4
Example of a redistribution loop.

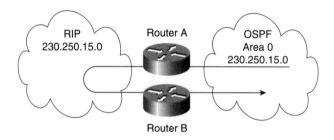

The initial configuration of Router A would have been as follows:
```
Router A (config)#
router ospf 10
   redistribute rip subnets
   network 230.250.0.0 0.0.255.255 area 0
```

As already mentioned, this configuration would result in a routing loop caused by the uncontrolled redistribution. To prevent this, some modifications will have to be made as indicated below, this time to Router B:
```
Router B (config)#
router ospf 10
   redistribute rip subnets
   network 230.250.0.0 0.0.255.255 area 0
   distribute-list 1 out rip

   access-list 1 deny 230.250.0.0
   access-list 1 permit any
```

The distribute-list commands were designed specifically to filter routing updates based upon an access list, in this case access list 1.

But what did these commands actually do? Simply put, the `distribute-list 1` command is invoked under the OSPF process and it applies `access-list 1` to the outbound updates from OSPF, and `rip` means all of this is applied if the redistribution source is the RIP network. In summary, this filter (`access-list`) will prevent the network `230.250.0.0` from being advertised back into the OSPF network. It is recommended that this solution be applied to all routers advertising this network.

E1 & E2 External Routes

The characteristics and definitions of E1 and E2 routes were discussed in Chapter 5, "The Fundamentals of OSPF Routing & Design," but here's a review of their operation before how they are redistributed is discussed.

External routes fall under two categories: external type 1 (E1) and external type 2 (E2). The difference between the two is in the way the cost (metric) of the route is calculated, as illustrated in the following bulleted points:

- **E1 Routes.** A type 1 cost is the addition of the external cost and the internal cost used to reach that route.

- **E2 Routes.** The cost of a type 2 route is always the external cost, irrespective of the interior cost to reach that route.

A type 2 route is always preferred over a type 1 route for the *same destination* as shown in Figure 6-5. You may recognize Figure 6-5 from Chapter 5 (Figure 5-12), where external routes were first discussed.

As Figure 6-5 shows, Router A redistributes two external routes into OSPF. Networks 1 and 2 (N1, N2) both have an external cost of x. The only difference is that N1 is redistributed into OSPF with a metric-type 1, and N2 is redistributed with a metric-type 2. If you follow the routes as they flow from Area 1 to Area 0, the cost to reach N2 as seen from RTB or RTC will always be x. The internal cost along the way is not considered because they are external route type E2.

On the other hand, the cost to reach N1 is incremented by the internal cost. The cost is x+y as seen from RTB and x+y+z as seen from RTC. Type 2 routes are preferred over type 1 routes in case two same cost routes exist to the destination. The default is type 2 (see Figure 6-6).

Figure 6–5
*E1 & E2
external route
redistribution.*

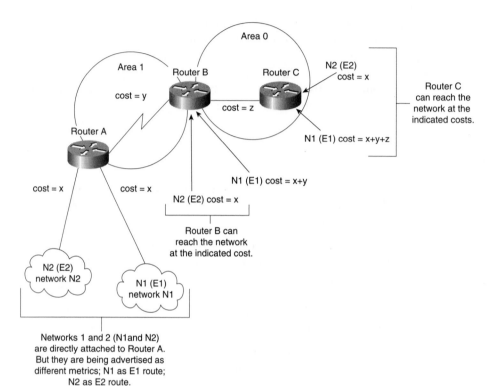

Figure 6–6
E2 preference.

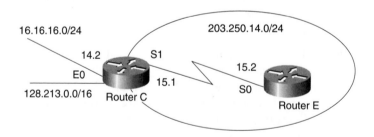

Example of Redistributing External Routes

Suppose you added two static routes pointing to E0 on Router C: 16.16.16.0
255.255.255.0 (the /24 notation indicates a 24-bit mask starting from the far left) and
128.213.0.0 255.255.0.0. The following example shows the different Area 0 and Area

1 behaviors when different parameters are used in the redistribute command on Router C:

```
Router C#
   interface Ethernet0
     ip address 203.250.14.2 255.255.255.0
   interface Serial1
     ip address 203.250.15.1 255.255.255.252
   router ospf 10
     redistribute static
     network 203.250.15.0 0.0.0.255 area 2
     network 203.250.14.0 0.0.0.255 area 0
 ip route 16.16.16.0 255.255.255.0 Ethernet0
 ip route 128.213.0.0 255.255.0.0 Ethernet0
```

```
Router E#
   interface Serial0
     ip address 203.250.15.2 255.255.255.252
   router ospf 10
     network 203.250.15.0 0.0.0.255 area 2
```

The following is the output of show ip route on Router E:

```
Router E# show ip route
Codes: C - connected, S - static, I - IGRP, R - RIP, M - mobile, B - BGP
D - EIGRP, EX - EIGRP external, O - OSPF, IA - OSPF inter area
E1 - OSPF external type 1, E2 - OSPF external type 2, E - EGP
i - IS-IS, L1 - IS-IS level-1, L2 - IS-IS level-2, * - candidate
default
Gateway of last resort is not set
203.250.15.0 255.255.255.252 is subnetted, 1 subnets
C 203.250.15.0 is directly connected, Serial0
O IA 203.250.14.0 [110/74] via 203.250.15.1, 00:02:31, Serial0
O E2 128.213.0.0 [110/20] via 203.250.15.1, 00:02:32, Serial0
```

Notice that the only external route that has appeared is 128.213.0.0, because you did not use the subnets keyword in Router C's configuration. If the subnets keyword is not used, only routes that are not subnetted, will be redistributed. In this case, 16.16.16.0 is a class A route that is subnetted and it did not get redistributed. Because the metric keyword was not used (or a default-metric statement under router OSPF), the cost allocated to the external route is 20 (the default is 1 for bgp). Watch what happens when you use the redistribute static metric 50 subnets command in Router C's configuration:

```
Router E# show ip route
Codes: C - connected, S - static, I - IGRP, R - RIP, M - mobile, B - BGP
D - EIGRP, EX - EIGRP external, O - OSPF, IA - OSPF inter area
E1 - OSPF external type 1, E2 - OSPF external type 2, E - EGP
i - IS-IS, L1 - IS-IS level-1, L2 - IS-IS level-2, * - candidate
default
Gateway of last resort is not set
16.0.0.0 255.255.255.0 is subnetted, 1 subnets
O E2 16.16.16.0 [110/50] via 203.250.15.1, 00:00:02, Serial0
203.250.15.0 255.255.255.252 is subnetted, 1 subnets
C 203.250.15.0 is directly connected, Serial0
O IA 203.250.14.0 [110/74] via 203.250.15.1, 00:00:02, Serial0
O E2 128.213.0.0 [110/50] via 203.250.15.1, 00:00:02, Serial0
```

Notice that network 16.16.16.0 has shown up now, and the cost to external routes is 50. Because the external routes are of type 2 (E2), the internal cost has not been added. Suppose now, you change the external route type to E1 through the use of the redistribute static metric 50 metric-type 1 subnets command, which is added to Router C's configuration:

```
Router E# show ip route
Codes: C - connected, S - static, I - IGRP, R - RIP, M - mobile, B - BGP
D - EIGRP, EX - EIGRP external, O - OSPF, IA - OSPF inter area
E1 - OSPF external type 1, E2 - OSPF external type 2, E - EGP
i - IS-IS, L1 - IS-IS level-1, L2 - IS-IS level-2, * - candidate
default
Gateway of last resort is not set
16.0.0.0 255.255.255.0 is subnetted, 1 subnets
O E1 16.16.16.0 [110/114] via 203.250.15.1, 00:04:20, Serial0
203.250.15.0 255.255.255.252 is subnetted, 1 subnets
C 203.250.15.0 is directly connected, Serial0
O IA 203.250.14.0 [110/74] via 203.250.15.1, 00:09:41, Serial0
O E1 128.213.0.0 [110/114] via 203.250.15.1, 00:04:21, Serial0
```

Notice that the external route type for network 16.16.16.0 has changed to E1, and the cost has been incremented by the internal cost of S0, which is 64. The total cost is 64+50=114. Assuming that you add a route map to Router C's configuration, you will get the following:

```
Router C#
    interface Ethernet0
        ip address 203.250.14.2 255.255.255.0
    interface Serial1
        ip address 203.250.15.1 255.255.255.252
```

```
router ospf 10
  redistribute static metric 50 metric-type 1 subnets route-map
  network 203.250.15.0 0.0.0.255 area 2
  network 203.250.14.0 0.0.0.255 area 0
ip route 16.16.16.0 255.255.255.0 Ethernet0
ip route 128.213.0.0 255.255.0.0 Ethernet0
access-list 1 permit 128.213.0.0 0.0.255.255
route-map permit 10
match ip address 1
```

The preceding route map will only permit 128.213.0.0 to be redistributed into OSPF and will deny the rest. This is why 16.16.16.0 does not show up in Router E's routing table anymore, as shown in the following:

```
Router E# show ip route
Codes: C - connected, S - static, I - IGRP, R - RIP, M - mobile, B - BGP
D - EIGRP, EX - EIGRP external, O - OSPF, IA - OSPF inter area
E1 - OSPF external type 1, E2 - OSPF external type 2, E - EGP
i - IS-IS, L1 - IS-IS level-1, L2 - IS-IS level-2, * - candidate
default
Gateway of last resort is not set
203.250.15.0 255.255.255.252 is subnetted, 1 subnets
C 203.250.15.0 is directly connected, Serial0
O IA 203.250.14.0 [110/74] via 203.250.15.1, 00:00:04, Serial0
O E1 128.213.0.0 [110/114] via 203.250.15.1, 00:00:05, Serial0
```

Redistributing OSPF into Other Protocols

The most important rule when redistributing OSPF into other protocols is that you respect the rules of operation for those other protocols. In particular, the metric applied should match the metric used by that protocol.

For example, the RIP metric is a hop count ranging between 1 and 16, where 1 indicates that a network is one hop away and 16 indicates that the network is unreachable. On the other hand IGRP and EIGRP require a series of metrics as demonstrated in the command:

```
Router eigrp
default-metric bandwidth delay reliability loading mtu
```

Variable-Length Subnet Masking (VLSM)

Another issue to consider is VLSM. OSPF can carry multiple subnet information for the same major network, but other protocols such as RIP and IGRP (EIGRP is okay with VLSM) cannot.

If the same major network crosses the boundaries of an OSPF and RIP domain, VLSM information redistributed into RIP or IGRP will be lost and static routes will have to be configured in the RIP or IGRP domains as illustrated in Figure 6-7.

Figure 6–7
Losing VLSM information.

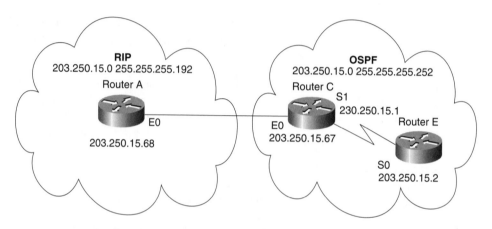

In Figure 6-7, Router E is running OSPF and Router A is running RIP. Router C is doing the redistribution between the two protocols.

The problem is that the class C network 203.250.15.0 is variably subnetted; it has two different masks: 255.255.255.252 and 255.255.255.192. Here are the configuration and the routing tables of both Router A and Router C:

```
Router A#
    interface Ethernet0
        ip address 203.250.15.68 255.255.255.192
    router rip
        network 203.250.15.0

Router C#
    interface Ethernet0
        ip address 203.250.15.67 255.255.255.192
    interface Serial1
        ip address 203.250.15.1 255.255.255.252
```

```
router ospf 10
   redistribute rip metric 10 subnets
   network 203.250.15.0 0.0.0.255 area 0
router rip
   redistribute ospf 10 metric 2
   network 203.250.15.0
```

Router A# show ip route
```
Codes: C - connected, S - static, I - IGRP, R - RIP, M - mobile, B - BGP
D - EIGRP, EX - EIGRP external, O - OSPF, IA - OSPF inter area
E1 - OSPF external type 1, E2 - OSPF external type 2, E - EGP
i - IS-IS, L1 - IS-IS level-1, L2 - IS-IS level-2, * - candidate
default
Gateway of last resort is not set
   203.250.15.0 255.255.255.192 is subnetted, 1 subnets
   C 203.250.15.64 is directly connected, Ethernet0
```

Router E# show ip route
```
Codes: C - connected, S - static, I - IGRP, R - RIP, M - mobile, B - BGP
D - EIGRP, EX - EIGRP external, O - OSPF, IA - OSPF inter area
E1 - OSPF external type 1, E2 - OSPF external type 2, E - EGP
i - IS-IS, L1 - IS-IS level-1, L2 - IS-IS level-2, * - candidate
default
Gateway of last resort is not set
   203.250.15.0 is variably subnetted, 2 subnets, 2 masks
   C 203.250.15.0 255.255.255.252 is directly connected, Serial0
   O 203.250.15.64 255.255.255.192
      [110/74] via 203.250.15.1, 00:15:55, Serial0
```

Notice that Router E has recognized that 203.250.15.0 has two subnets while Router A thinks that it has only one subnet (the one configured on its Ethernet interface). Information about subnet 203.250.15.0 255.255.255.252 is lost in the RIP domain. To reach that subnet, a static route needs to be configured on Router A as follows:

Router A#
```
   interface Ethernet0
      ip address 203.250.15.68 255.255.255.192
   router rip
      network 203.250.15.0
   ip route 203.250.15.0 255.255.255.0 203.250.15.67
```

With the addition of the static route as shown above, Router A will now be able to reach the other subnets within the OSPF network.

Mutual Route Redistribution

Mutual route redistribution between multiple routing protocols should be done very carefully and in a controlled manner. As previously mentioned, incorrect configuration could lead to routing loops. A golden rule for mutual redistribution is *not* to allow information learned from a protocol to be injected back into the same protocol.

TIPS

Passive interfaces and distribute lists should be applied on the redistributing routers to prevent routing loops.

The `distribute-list out` command works on the ASBR to filter redistributed routes into other protocols. The `distribute-list in` command works on any router to prevent routes from being put in the routing table, but it does not prevent link-state packets (LSPs) from being propagated; downstream routers would still have the routes. It is better to avoid OSPF filtering as much as possible if filters can be applied on the other protocols to prevent loops.

To demonstrate this, suppose Router A, Router C, and Router E are all running RIP. Router C and Router A are also running OSPF. This network configuration is shown in Figure 6-8.

Figure 6–8
Mutual route redistribution.

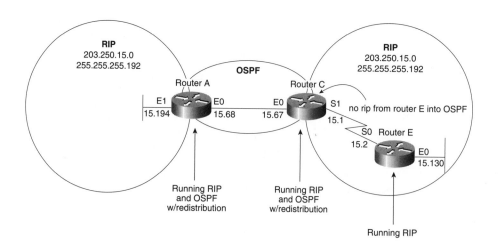

Both Router C and Router A are doing mutual redistribution between RIP and OSPF. Assume that you do not want the RIP coming from Router E to be injected into the OSPF domain, so you put a passive interface for RIP on the Ethernet 0 interface of Router C. However, you allow the RIP coming from Router A to be injected into OSPF. The routers would need to be configured as follows in order for this to occur, but as you review the following configurations, review them closely.

```
Router E#
    interface Ethernet0
        ip address 203.250.15.130 255.255.255.192
    interface Serial0
        ip address 203.250.15.2 255.255.255.192
    router rip
        network 203.250.15.0

Router C#
    interface Ethernet0
        ip address 203.250.15.67 255.255.255.192
    interface Serial1
        ip address 203.250.15.1 255.255.255.192
    router ospf 10
        redistribute rip metric 10 subnets
        network 203.250.15.0 0.0.0.255 area 0
    router rip
        redistribute ospf 10 metric 2
        passive-interface Ethernet0
        network 203.250.15.0

Router A#
    interface Ethernet0
        ip address 203.250.15.68 255.255.255.192
    router ospf 10
        redistribute rip metric 10 subnets
        network 203.250.15.0 0.0.0.255 area 0
    router rip
        redistribute ospf 10 metric 1
        network 203.250.15.0
```

Did you see the routing loop? Well, looking at the routes as seen from Router C clearly shows the routing loop. Please do not use the preceding configuration!

```
Router C# show ip route
Codes: C - connected, S - static, I - IGRP, R - RIP, M - mobile, B - BGP
D - EIGRP, EX - EIGRP external, O - OSPF, IA - OSPF inter area
E1 - OSPF external type 1, E2 - OSPF external type 2, E - EGP
i - IS-IS, L1 - IS-IS level-1, L2 - IS-IS level-2, * - candidate
default
Gateway of last resort is not set
203.250.15.0 255.255.255.192 is subnetted, 4 subnets
C 203.250.15.0 is directly connected, Serial1
C 203.250.15.64 is directly connected, Ethernet0
R 203.250.15.128 [120/1] via 203.250.15.68, 00:01:08, Ethernet0
  [120/1] via 203.250.15.2, 00:00:11, Serial1
O 203.250.15.192 [110/20] via 203.250.15.68, 00:21:41, Ethernet0
```

Notice that Router C has *two* paths to reach the 203.250.15.128 subnet: Serial1 and Ethernet0 (E0 is obviously the wrong path).

This happened because Router C gave that entry to Router A via OSPF, and Router A gave it back via RIP because Router A did not learn it via RIP. This is a very small example of the loops that can occur because of an incorrect configuration or partial configuration. In larger networks, this situation gets even more aggravated.

To fix the situation in this example, you could stop RIP from being sent on Router A's Ethernet0 via a passive interface. This might not be suitable in case some routers on the Ethernet are RIP only routers. In this case, you could allow Router C to send RIP on the Ethernet; this way Router A will not send it back on the wire because of split horizon. (This might not work on NBMA media if split horizon is off.)

Split horizon does not allow updates to be sent back on the same interface from which they were learned (via the same protocol). Another good method is to apply distribute-lists on Router A to deny subnets learned via OSPF from being put back into RIP on the Ethernet. The latter is the one you will be using:

```
Router A#
    interface Ethernet0
        ip address 203.250.15.68 255.255.255.192
    router ospf 10
        redistribute rip metric 10 subnets
        network 203.250.15.0 0.0.0.255 area 0
    router rip
        redistribute ospf 10 metric 1
        network 203.250.15.0
        distribute-list 1 out ospf 10
```

The correct routing table that is seen in Router C would be as follows:

```
Router C# show ip route
Codes: C - connected, S - static, I - IGRP, R - RIP, M - mobile, B - BGP
D - EIGRP, EX - EIGRP external, O - OSPF, IA - OSPF inter area
E1 - OSPF external type 1, E2 - OSPF external type 2, E - EGP
i - IS-IS, L1 - IS-IS level-1, L2 - IS-IS level-2, * - candidate
default
Gateway of last resort is not set
203.250.15.0 255.255.255.192 is subnetted, 4 subnets
C 203.250.15.0 is directly connected, Serial1
C 203.250.15.64 is directly connected, Ethernet0
R 203.250.15.128 [120/1] via 203.250.15.2, 00:00:19, Serial1
O 203.250.15.192 [110/20] via 203.250.15.68, 00:21:41, Ethernet0
```

Injecting Default Routes into OSPF

The capability to generate and redistribute default routes is of extreme importance within any large network.

An ASBR can be forced to generate a default route into an OSPF Network (domain). As discussed earlier, a router becomes an ASBR whenever routes are redistributed into an OSPF network (domain). However, an ASBR does not, by default, generate a default route into an OSPF network (domain).

NOTES

In this section, the use of the words "network" and "domain" are used interchangeably so that the different definitions regarding them are not confused. But "domain" is typically used to refer to groupings of networks on the Internet.

There are several ways to generate a default route within an OSPF network.

The first is to advertise 0.0.0.0 inside the domain, but only if the ASBR itself already has a default route.

The second is to advertise 0.0.0.0 regardless of whether the ASBR has a default route. This can be set by adding the keyword always. Be very careful when using the always keyword. If your router advertises a default (0.0.0.0) inside the domain and does not have a default itself or a path to reach the destinations, routing will be broken.

The third is to be in an OSPF stub area that needs a default exit, hence the default route is used.

To have OSPF generate a default route, use the following configuration command:

```
default-information originate [always] [metric metric-value]
[metric-type type-value] [route-map map-name]
```

The metric and metric-type are the cost and route type (E1 or E2) assigned to the default route. The route-map specifies the set of conditions that need to be satisfied in order for the default to be generated. Figure 6-9 shows a sample network and an example demonstrates how a default route will be determined.

Figure 6–9
Injecting a default route.

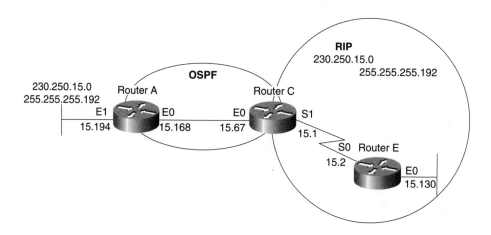

Referring to Figure 6-9 and assuming that Router E is injecting a default route of 0.0.0.0 into the RIP network and Router C will have a gateway of last resort of 203.250.15.2, the following is true of Routers A, C, and E:

- Router A only knows what Router C tells it about the default route.

- Router C sees the default route, but will not share the information with other routers until told to by the default-information originate command.

- Router E knows a default route of 0.0.0.0.

The following example shows that Router C knows about the default route, but it will not tell anyone else until told to do so with the `default-information originate` command.

```
Router C# show ip route
Codes: C - connected, S - static, I - IGRP, R - RIP, M - mobile, B - BGP
D - EIGRP, EX - EIGRP external, O - OSPF, IA - OSPF inter area
E1 - OSPF external type 1, E2 - OSPF external type 2, E - EGP
i - IS-IS, L1 - IS-IS level-1, L2 - IS-IS level-2, * - candidate
default
Gateway of last resort is 203.250.15.2 to network 0.0.0.0
203.250.15.0 255.255.255.192 is subnetted, 4 subnets
C 203.250.15.0 is directly connected, Serial1
C 203.250.15.64 is directly connected, Ethernet0
R 203.250.15.128 [120/1] via 203.250.15.2, 00:00:17, Serial1
O 203.250.15.192 [110/20] via 203.250.15.68, 2d23, Ethernet0
R* 0.0.0.0 0.0.0.0 [120/1] via 203.250.15.2, 00:00:17, Serial1
[120/1] via 203.250.15.68, 00:00:32, Ethernet0
interface Ethernet0
    ip address 203.250.15.67 255.255.255.192

interface Serial1
    ip address 203.250.15.1 255.255.255.192

router ospf 10
    redistribute rip metric 10 subnets
    network 203.250.15.0 0.0.0.255 area 0
    default-information originate metric 10

router rip
    redistribute ospf 10 metric 2
    passive-interface Ethernet0
    network 203.250.15.0
```

Now that Router C has been configured to tell Router A about the default route, you can check Router A's routing table. You will quickly see that the default route is known by the router:

```
Router A# show ip route
Codes: C - connected, S - static, I - IGRP, R - RIP, M - mobile, B - BGP
D - EIGRP, EX - EIGRP external, O - OSPF, IA - OSPF inter area
E1 - OSPF external type 1, E2 - OSPF external type 2, E - EGP
i - IS-IS, L1 - IS-IS level-1, L2 - IS-IS level-2, * - candidate
default
```

```
Gateway of last resort is 203.250.15.67 to network 0.0.0.0
203.250.15.0 255.255.255.192 is subnetted, 4 subnets
O   203.250.15.0 [110/74] via 203.250.15.67, 2d23, Ethernet0
C   203.250.15.64 is directly connected, Ethernet0
O E2 203.250.15.128 [110/10] via 203.250.15.67, 2d23, Ethernet0
C   203.250.15.192 is directly connected, Ethernet1
O*E2 0.0.0.0 0.0.0.0 [110/10] via 203.250.15.67, 00:00:17, Ethernet0
```

Notice that Router A has learned about 0.0.0.0 as an external route with metric of 10. The gateway of last resort is set to 203.250.15.67 as expected. Thus, its default route is the E0 interface of Router C that has a default route in Router E.

DESIGNING OSPF ON-DEMAND CIRCUITS

On-demand circuits can come in many different forms, from ISDN to SVCs. They tend to be implemented in one of two ways. First, they are put in place as a backup for the dedicated circuit, or second, they are for sites that require connectivity, just not all the time.

The OSPF on-demand circuits is an enhancement to the original OSPF protocol that allows efficient operation over on-demand circuits like ISDN, X.25 SVCs, and dial-up lines. This feature was first introduced in RFC 1793, "Extending OSPF to Support Demand Circuits." It is fully supported by Cisco in all releases of their IOS.

This feature is useful when you want to connect telecommuters or branch offices to an OSPF backbone at a central site. As the pricing of demand circuits has gone down and the criticality of networks has increased, many network designers are turning to demand circuits as a means of back up.

Prior to this feature, OSPF periodic hello and LSAs updates would be exchanged between routers that connected via the on-demand link, even when no changes occurred in the hello or LSA information. This is, of course, normal operation for the OSPF protocol, but it has the unwanted side effect of causing the demand circuit to remain active because there was always interesting traffic to route across it.

However, with this new RFC, periodic hellos are suppressed and the periodic refreshes of LSAs are not flooded over the demand circuit. These packets bring up the link only when they are exchanged for the first time, or when a critical change occurs in the information they contain.

This suppression allows the demand circuit to be released. This is extremely important because most of the demand circuits have usage fees relating to them in either the length of use or amount of use and sometimes even both.

In this case, OSPF for on-demand circuits allows the benefits of OSPF over the entire domain, without excess connection costs. Periodic refreshes of hello updates, LSA updates, and other protocol overhead traffic is prevented from enabling the on-demand circuit when there is no "real" data to transmit.

Golden Rules for Designing Demand Circuits

As with every configuration of OSPF, there are a series of golden rules that you must be aware of before proceeding on. This is a list of them for demand circuits:

- Because LSAs that include topology changes are flooded over an on-demand circuit, it is advised to put demand circuits within OSPF stub areas or within NSSAs to isolate the demand circuits from as many topology changes as possible.

- To take advantage of the on-demand circuit functionality within a stub area or NSSA, every router in the area must have this feature loaded. If this feature is deployed within a regular area, all other regular areas must also support this feature before the demand circuit functionality can take effect. This is because Type 5 external LSAs are flooded throughout all areas.

- You do not want to implement this on a broadcast-based network topology because the overhead protocols (such as hellos and LSAs) cannot be successfully suppressed, which means the link will remain up.

Dial On-Demand Design Scenarios

There are a number of common scenarios that will be encountered if you are planning on using this feature of OSPF. The first two are ways (NOT the best ways!) to implement OSPF. In the following scenarios, Site Router A is the router equipped with on-demand dialing.

Design Scenario #1: Site Router Is in Two Areas (Neither Is Area 0)

This approach does not work as the LAN interface cannot be in more than one area, as shown in Figure 6-10. There is no exchange of link-state information between areas 1 and 2.

As shown in Figure 6-10, the site router is located in two different OSPF areas with neither of them being area 0. However, if the site LAN is not included in the OSPF routing, and its routing information is injected with a static route either at the site router or at the distribution router, this could be made to work, although it is not the most optimal OSPF network design.

Figure 6–10
Site Router is in two areas (neither area is area 0).

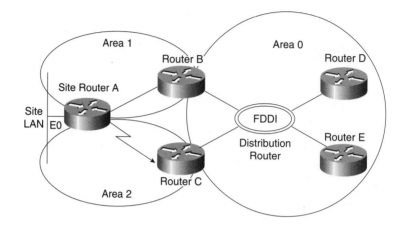

Design Scenario #2: Site Router Is in Two Areas (One Is Area 0)

This approach makes the Site Router (Router A) an area border router (ABR) under failure. It does work; however, it is not considered an acceptable design because it would make the Site Router part of area 0. This design would require more resources than would be cost-effective in all but the smallest networks (see Figure 6-11).

Figure 6–11
Site Router is in two areas (one is area 0).

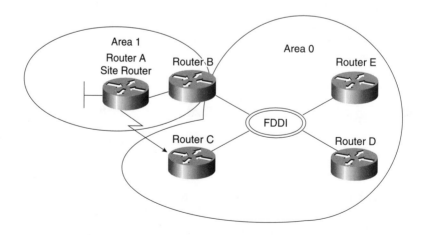

Design Scenario #3: Site Router Is in One Area

This approach is the most suitable and works even if the backup server ("C" in Figure 6-12) is located elsewhere. The secret is that "C" does not summarize for its attached areas; thus, more specific prefixes are originated by "C" for those sites in failure. The disadvantage is that dedicated backup interfaces are required for each area.

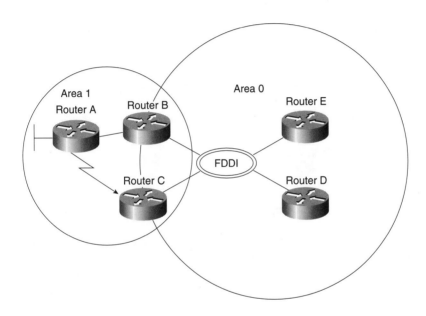

Figure 6–12
Site Router is in one area.

The following are some sample configurations for this design scenario:

Site Router A Configuration

```
Interface ethernet 0
   ip address 132.32.12.193 255.255.255.224
interface serial 0
   ip address 132.32.12.254 255.255.255.252
backup interface serial 1
   backup delay 0 5
interface serial 1
   ip address 132.32.12.250 255.255.255.252
router ospf 1
   network 132.32.0.0 0.0.255.255 area 1
```

Site Router B Configuration
```
interface fddi 0
    ip address 132.32.1.1 255.255.255.248
interface serial 0
    ip address 132.32.12.253 255.255.255.252
router ospf 1
    network 132.32.12.0 0.0.3.255 area 1
    area 1 range 132.32.12.0 255.255.252.0
    network 132.32.0.0 0.0.255.255 area 0
```

Site Router C Configuration
```
interface fddi 0
    ip address 132.32.1.2 255.255.255.248
interface serial 0
    ip address 132.32.12.249 255.255.255.252
router ospf 1
    network 132.32.12.0 0.0.3.255 area 1
    network 132.32.0.0 0.0.255.255 area 0
```

Design Scenario #4: Site Router Is in Two Routing Domains

This approach relies on one-way redistribution of multiple instances of a separate routing protocol into OSPF as shown in Figure 6-13. Auto-summarization must also be disabled in this scenario. Administrative distances should be tweaked to ensure that OSPF is the favored routing protocol. This approach has the advantage that interfaces may be shared among areas; that is, a dedicated set of interfaces for each area is not required.

Figure 6–13
Site Router in two routing domains.

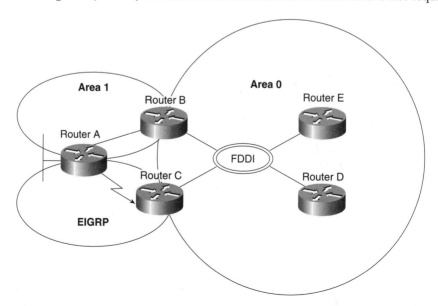

Included are some sample configurations for this design scenario.

Router A Configuration

```
interface ethernet 0
  ip address 132.132.132.193 255.255.255.224
interface serial 0
  ip address 132.132.132.254 255.255.255.252
backup interface serial 1
  backup delay 0 5
interface serial 1
  ip address 132.132.132.250 255.255.255.252
router ospf 1
  network 132.132.132.192 0.0.0.31 area 1
  network 132.132.132.252 0.0.0.3 area 1
router eigrp 1
  network 132.132.0.0 distance 200 0.0.0.0 255.255.255.255
```

Router B Configuration

```
interface fddi 0
  ip address 132.132.1.1 255.255.255.248
interface serial 0
  ip address 132.132.132.253 255.255.255.252
router ospf 1
  network 132.132.132.0 0.0.3.255 area 1
  area 1 range 132.132.132.0 255.255.252.0
  network 132.132.0.0 0.0.255.255 area 0
```

Router C Configuration

```
interface fddi 0
  ip address 132.132.1.2 255.255.255.248
interface serial 0
  ip address 132.132.132.249 255.255.255.252
router ospf 1
  network 132.132.1.0 0.0.0.7 area 0
  redistribute eigrp 1 subnets metric 32000
router eigrp 1
  network 132.132.0.0
passive-interface fddi 0
  distance 200 0.0.0.0 255.255.255.255
```

The preceding examples work with dial-on-demand routing as well as dial-backup. One should set the metric on the backup interface to be less favorable than that on the primary. Also, be certain to set the administrative distance on the backup routing protocol to be greater than that of the primary (both of these so as to allow the idle timer to work). The redistribution of a static route for the backed-up site is absolutely necessary. Not only does it speed convergence somewhat, it is the controlling factor in directing traffic at the upstream dial-on-demand interface to trigger dialing. After the primary interface goes down, all knowledge of the site LAN is lost. If the backup server is originating routes for the site LANs at a much higher cost, these will now come into effect.

OSPF CONFIGURATION COMMANDS

There are literally thousands of documented and undocumented commands that can be used on Cisco equipment. These commands are found in several different areas and, of course, differ by IOS. These differences might not be major in the case of OSPF, but I recommend you have a set for each version of IOS in your network.

- IOS Documentation Set (a minimum of 16 books)

- Technical Compact Disc (updated every month)

- World Wide Web (http://www.cisco.com)

- Command-line help (effectiveness varies by equipment)

At first glance, it might seem that the variety of information sources available is wonderful. But what the uninitiated does not realize is that the various commands are spread out within each source. There is no one link that takes you to all the OSPF commands that Cisco routers have available.

This chapter is concerned about OSPF and only the commands associated with its configuration, design, and operation. Specifically, this chapter deals with the various commands that can set up or alter the performance of OSPF within a network. This section will provide you with an exhaustive list of Cisco router configuration commands dealing specifically with the OSPF protocol. Hopefully, you will find this section to be a valuable resource. Of course, all of this information can be found with various Cisco sources as detailed above, but not all in one place!

The following section covers the various commands used within a Cisco router to configure OSPF authentication. These entries follow a specific format (where applicable):

- Command syntax

- Syntax description

- Default settings

- Command mode

- Usage guidelines

- Examples

- Related commands

area authentication

To enable authentication for an OSPF area, use the `area authentication` router configuration command. To remove an area's authentication specification or a specified area from the configuration, use the no form of this command.

```
area area-id authentication [message-digest]
no area area-id authentication
no area area-id
```

Syntax Description:

area-id. Identifier of the area for which authentication is to be enabled. The identifier can be specified as either a decimal value or an IP address.
message-digest (**optional**). This enables MD5 authentication on the area specified by area-ID.

TIPS

When dealing with a multi-vendor network, you might have to disable the MD5 OSPF Authentication for proper operation. You will also want to remember that the authentication must be configured on the opposing side's router for proper operation.

---

area default-cost

To specify a cost for the default summary route sent into a stub area, use the `area default-cost` router configuration command. To remove the assigned default route cost, use the no form of this command. The syntax for this command (and the no form) is as follows:

```
area area-id default-cost cost
no area area-id default-cost cost
```

Syntax Description:

area-id. Identifier for the stub area. The identifier can be specified as either a decimal value or as an IP address.

cost. Cost for the default summary route used for a stub area. The acceptable value is a 24-bit number.

Default: Cost of 1.

Command Mode: Router configuration.

Usage Guidelines: This command is used only on an area border router attached to a stub area. There are two stub area router configuration commands: the stub and default-cost options of the area command. In all routers and access servers attached to the stub area, the area should be configured as a stub area using the stub option of the area command. Use the default-cost option only on an ABR attached to the stub area. The default-cost option provides the metric for the summary default route generated by the ABR into the stub area.

Example: The following example assigns a default-cost of 20 to stub network 36.0.0.0:

```
interface ethernet 0
ip address 36.56.0.201 255.255.0.0
!
router ospf 201
network 36.0.0.0 0.255.255.255 area 36.0.0.0
area 36.0.0.0 stub
area 36.0.0.0 default-cost 20
```

Related Commands: area authentication, area stub

area-id

area-id refers to the area that is to be associated with the OSPF address range. It can be specified as either a decimal value or as an IP address. If you intend to associate areas with IP subnets, you can specify a subnet address as the area-id.

Default: Disabled.

Command Mode: Router configuration.

Usage Guidelines: The address and wildcard-mask arguments together enable you to define one or multiple interfaces to be associated with a specific OSPF area using a single command. Using the wildcard-mask enables you to define one or multiple interfaces to be associated with a specific OSPF area using a single command. If you intend to associate areas with IP subnets, you can specify a subnet address as the area-id.

The Cisco IOS software sequentially evaluates the address/wildcard-mask pair for each interface as follows:

1. The wildcard-mask is enabled logically with the interface IP address.

2. The wildcard-mask is enabled logically with the address in the network command.

3. The software compares the two resulting values.

4. If they match, OSPF is enabled on the associated interface logically and this interface is attached to the OSPF area specified.

NOTES

Any individual interface can only be attached to a single area. If the address ranges specified for different areas overlap, the software will adopt the first area in the network command list and ignore the subsequent overlapping portions. In general, it is recommended that you devise address ranges that do not overlap to avoid inadvertent conflicts.

Example: In the following partial example, OSPF routing process 109 is initialized, and four OSPF areas are defined: 10.9.50.0, 2, 3, and 0. Areas 10.9.50.0, 2, and 3 mask specific address ranges, while area 0 enables OSPF for all other networks.

```
router ospf 109
network 131.108.20.0 0.0.0.255 area 10.9.50.0
network 131.108.0.0 0.0.255.255 area 2
network 131.109.10.0 0.0.0.255 area 3
network 0.0.0.0 255.255.255.255 area 0
```

Related Commands: router ospf

area nssa

To configure an area as a not-so-stubby area (NSSA), use the area nssa router config-uration command. To remove the NSSA distinction from the area, use the no form of this command. The syntax for this command (and the no form) is as follows:

```
area area-id nssa [no-redistribution] [default-information-originate]
no area area-id nssa
```

Syntax Description:

> **area-id**. Identifier of the area for which authentication is to be enabled. The identifier can be specified as either a decimal value or an IP address.
>
> **no-redistribution** (optional). This is used when the router is a NSSA ABR and you want the redistribute command to import routes only into the nor-mal areas, but not into the NSSA area.
>
> **default-information-originate** (optional). Used to generate a Type 7 default into the NSSA area. This command only takes effect on NSSA ABR.

area range

To consolidate and summarize routes at an area boundary, use the area range router configuration command. To disable this function, use the no form of this command. The syntax for this command (and the no form) is as follows:

```
area area-id range address mask
no area area-id range address mask
```

Syntax Description:

> **area-id**. Identifier of the area about which routes are to be summarized. It can be specified as either a decimal value or as an IP address.
>
> **address**. IP address.
>
> **mask**. IP mask.

Default: Disabled.

Command Mode: Router configuration.

Usage Guidelines: The area range command is used only with area border routers. It is used to consolidate or summarize routes for an area. The result is that a single summary route is advertised to other areas by the area border router. Routing information is con-densed at area boundaries. External to the area, a single route is advertised for each address range. This is called route summarization.

Multiple area router configuration commands specifying the range option can be configured. Thus, OSPF can summarize addresses for many different sets of address ranges.

Example: The following example specifies one summary route to be advertised by the ABR to other areas for all subnets on network `36.0.0.0` and for all hosts on network `192.42.110.0`:

```
interface ethernet 0
ip address 192.42.110.201 255.255.255.0
!
interface ethernet 1
ip address 36.56.0.201 255.255.0.0
!
router ospf 201
network 36.0.0.0 0.255.255.255 area 36.0.0.0
network 192.42.110.0 0.0.0.255 area 0
area 36.0.0.0 range 36.0.0.0 255.0.0.0
area 0 range 192.42.110.0 255.255.255.0
```

area stub

To define an area as a stub area, use the `area stub` router configuration command. To disable this function, use the no form of this command. The syntax for this command (and the no form) is as follows:

```
area area-id stub [no-summary]
no area area-id stub
```

Syntax Description:

> *area-id*. Identifier for the stub area. The identifier can be either a decimal value or an IP address.
>
> *no-summary* (optional). This prevents an ABR from sending summary link advertisements into the stub area.

Default: No stub area is defined.

Command Mode: Router configuration.

Usage Guidelines: You must configure the `area stub` command on all routers and access servers in the stub area.

Use the `area router` configuration command with the `default-cost` option to specify the cost of a default internal router sent into a stub area by an ABR.

There are two stub area router configuration commands: the stub and default-cost options of the area router configuration command. In all routers attached to the stub area, the area should be configured as a stub area using the stub option of the area command. Use the default-cost option only on an ABR attached to the stub area. The default-cost option provides the metric for the summary default route generated by the ABR into the stub area.

To further reduce the number of link-state advertisements (LSAs) sent into a stub area, you can configure no-summary on the ABR to prevent it from sending summary LSAs (LSA type 3) into the stub area.

Example: The following example assigns a default cost of 20 to stub network 36.0.0.0:

```
interface ethernet 0
ip address 36.56.0.201 255.255.0.0
!
router ospf 201
network 36.0.0.0 0.255.255.255 area 36.0.0.0
area 36.0.0.0 stub
area 36.0.0.0 default-cost 20
```

Related Commands: area authentication, area default-cost

area virtual-link

To define an OSPF virtual link, use the area virtual-link router configuration command with the optional parameters. To remove a virtual link, use the no form of this command. The syntax for this command (and the no form) is as follows:

```
area area-id virtual-link router-id [hello-interval seconds]
[retransmit-interval seconds] [transmit-delay seconds]
[dead-interval seconds] [[authentication-key key] ¦
[message-digest-key keyid md5 key]]
no area area-id virtual-link router-id [hello-interval seconds]
[retransmit-interval seconds] [transmit-delay seconds]
[dead-interval seconds] [[authentication-key key] ¦
[message-digest-key keyid md5 key]]
```

Syntax Description:

area-id. Area ID assigned to the transit area for the virtual link. This can be either a decimal value or a valid IP address. There is no default.
router-id. Router ID associated with the virtual link neighbor. The router ID appears in the show ip ospf display. It is internally derived by each router from

the router's interface IP addresses. This value must be entered in the format of an IP address. There is no default.

hello-interval seconds (optional). Time in seconds between the hello packets that the Cisco IOS software sends on an interface. Unsigned integer value to be advertised in the software's hello packets. The value must be the same for all routers and access servers attached to a common network. The default is 10 seconds.

retransmit-interval seconds (optional). Time in seconds between LSA retransmissions for adjacencies belonging to the interface. Expected round-trip delay between any two routers on the attached network. The value must be greater than the expected round-trip delay. The default is 5 seconds.

transmit-delay seconds (optional). Estimated time in seconds it takes to transmit a link-state update packet on the interface. Integer value that must be greater than zero. LSAs in the update packet have their age incremented by this amount before transmission. The default value is 1 second.

dead-interval seconds (optional). Time in seconds that a software's hello packets are not seen before its neighbors declare the router down. Unsigned integer value. The default is four times the hello interval, or 40 seconds. As with the hello interval, this value must be the same for all routers and access servers attached to a common network.

authentication-key key (optional). Password to be used by neighboring routers. The password can be any continuous string of characters that you can enter from the keyboard up to eight bytes long. This string acts as a key that will allow the authentication procedure to generate or verify the authentication field in the OSPF header. This key is inserted directly into the OSPF header when originating routing protocol packets. A separate password can be assigned to each network on a per-interface basis.

All neighboring routers on the same network must have the same password to be able to route OSPF traffic. The password is encrypted in the configuration file if the service password-encryption command is enabled. There is no default value.

message-digest-key, keyid md5 key (optional). Key identifier and password to be used by neighboring routers and this router for MD5 authentication. The keyid is a number in the range 1 through 255. The key is an alphanumeric string of up to 16 characters. All neighboring routers on the same network must have the same key identifier and key to be able to route OSPF traffic. There is no default value.

Default Values

> *area-id*. No area ID is predefined.
> *router-id*. No router ID is predefined.
> *hello-interval seconds*. 10 seconds.
> *retransmit-interval seconds*. 5 seconds.
> *transmit-delay seconds*. 1 second.
> *dead-interval seconds*. 40 seconds.
> *authentication-key key*. No key is predefined.
> *message-digest-key, keyid md5 key*. No key is predefined.

TIPS

If area authentication is configured, but no key is specified, an empty key is used. For simple-text key, it is the NULL string. For MD5, Cisco uses key 0 with NULL string.

Command Mode: Router configuration.

Usage Guidelines: In OSPF, all areas must be connected to a backbone area. If the connection to the backbone is lost, it can be repaired by establishing a virtual link. The smaller the hello interval, the faster topological changes will be detected, but more routing traffic will ensue. The setting of the retransmit interval should be conservative, or needless retransmissions will result. The value should be larger for serial lines and virtual links. The transmit delay value should take into account the transmission and propagation delays for the interface.

The Cisco IOS software will use the specified authentication key only when authentication is enabled for the backbone with the area area-id authentication router configuration command. The two authentication schemes, simple text and MD5 authentication, are mutually exclusive. You can specify one or the other or neither. Any keywords and arguments you specify after authentication-key key or message-digest-key keyid md5 key are ignored. Therefore, specify any optional arguments before such a keyword-argument combination.

> **NOTES**
>
> Each virtual link neighbor must include the transit area ID and the corresponding virtual link neighbor's router ID in order for a virtual link to be properly configured. Use the `show ip ospf` EXEC command to see the router ID.

Example 1: The following example establishes a virtual link with default values for all optional parameters:

```
router ospf 201
network 36.0.0.0 0.255.255.255 area 36.0.0.0
area 36.0.0.0 virtual-link 36.3.4.5
```

Example 2: The following example establishes a virtual link with MD5 authentication:

```
router ospf 201
network 36.0.0.0 0.255.255.255 area 36.0.0.0
area 36.0.0.0 virtual-link 36.3.4.5 message-digest-key 3 md5 sa5721bk47
```

Related Commands: `area authentication`, `service password-encryption`, `show ip ospf`

default-information originate

To generate a default route into an OSPF routing domain, use the `default-information originate` router configuration command. To disable this feature, use the no form of this command. The syntax for this command (and the no form) is as follows:

```
default-information originate [always] [metric metric-value]
[metric-type type-value] {level-1 ¦ level-1-2 ¦ level-2}
[route-map map-name]
no default-information originate [always] [metric metric-value]
[metric-type type-value] {level-1 ¦ level-1-2 ¦ level-2}
[route-map map-name]
```

Syntax Description:

originate. Causes the Cisco IOS software to generate a default external route into an OSPF domain if the software already has a default route and you want to propagate to other routers.

always (optional). Advertises the default route regardless of whether the software has a default route.

metric metric-value (optional). Metric used for generating the default route. If you omit a value and do not specify a value using the `default metric` router configuration command, the default metric value is 10. The value used is specific to the protocol.

metric-type type-value (optional). External link type associated with the default route advertised into the OSPF routing domain. The values can be either 1 (Type 1 external route) or 2 (Type 2 external route). The default is 2

level-1. Level 1 routes are redistributed into other IP routing protocols independently. It specifies if IS-IS advertises network `0.0.0.0` into the Level 1 area.

level-1-2. Both Level 1 and Level 2 routes are redistributed into other IP routing protocols. It specifies if IS-IS advertises network `0.0.0.0` into both levels in a single command.

level-2. Level 2 routes are redistributed into other IP routing protocols independently. It specifies if IS-IS advertises network `0.0.0.0` into the Level 2 subdomain.

route-map map-name (optional). Routing process will generate the default route if the route-map is satisfied.

Default: Disabled.

Command Mode: Router configuration.

Usage Guidelines: Whenever you use the `redistribute` or the `default-information` router configuration commands to redistribute routes into an OSPF routing domain, the Cisco IOS software automatically becomes an ASBR. However, an ASBR does not, by default, generate a default route into the OSPF routing domain. The software still needs to have a default route for itself before it generates one, except when you have specified the `always` keyword.

When you use this command for the OSPF process, the default network must reside in the routing table and you must satisfy the `route-map map-name` keyword. Use the `default-information originate always route-map map-name` form of the command when you do not want the dependency on the default network in the routing table.

Example: The following example specifies a metric of 100 for the default route redistributed into the OSPF routing domain and an external metric type of type 1:

```
router ospf 109
    redistribute igrp 108 metric 100 subnets
    default-information originate metric 100 metric-type 1
```

Related Commands: `redistribute`

default-metric

To set default metric values for the BGP, EGP, OSPF, and RIP routing protocols, use this form of the `default-metric` router configuration command. To return to the default state, use the no form of this command. The syntax for this command (and the no form) is as follows:

```
default-metric number
no default-metric number
```

Syntax Description:

> *number*. Default metric value appropriate for the specified routing protocol.

distance

To define an administrative distance, use the `distance` router configuration command. To remove a distance definition, use the no form of this command. The syntax for this command (and the no form) is as follows:

```
distance weight [address mask [access-list-number ¦ name]] [ip]
no distance weight [address mask [access-list-number]] [ip]
```

Syntax Description:

> *weight*. Administrative distance. This can be an integer from 10 to 255. (The values 0 through 9 are reserved for internal use.) Used alone, the argument weight specifies a default administrative distance that the Cisco IOS software uses when no other specification exists for a routing information source. Routes with a distance of 255 are not installed in the routing table.
>
> *address* (optional). IP address in four-part dotted notation.
>
> *mask* (optional). IP address mask in four-part dotted-decimal format. A bit set to 1 in the mask argument instructs the software to ignore the corresponding bit in the address value.
>
> *access-list-number* (optional). Number of a standard IP access list to be applied to incoming routing updates.
>
> *ip* (optional). IP-derived routes for IS-IS. It can be applied independently for IP routes and ISO CLNS routes.

Default Distance Weights: Table 6-1 provides you with the accepted default values for weights.

Command Mode: Router configuration.

Table 6-1   *Default distance weights*

Route Source	Default Distance
Connected interface	0
Static route	1
Enhanced IGRP summary route	5
External BGP	20
Internal Enhanced IGRP	90
IGRP	100
OSPF	110
IS-IS	115
RIP	120
EGP	140
Internal BGP	200
Unknown	255

Usage Guidelines: Numerically, an administrative distance is an integer between 0 and 255. In general, the higher the value, the lower the trust rating. An administrative distance of 255 means the routing information source cannot be trusted at all and should be ignored.

When the optional access list number is used with this command, it is applied when a network is being inserted into the routing table. This behavior allows filtering of networks according to the IP address of the router supplying the routing information. This could be used, as an example, to filter out possibly incorrect routing information from routers not under your administrative control.

The order in which you enter distance commands can affect the assigned administrative distances in unexpected ways (see "Example" for further clarification). Weight values are also subjective; there is no quantitative method for choosing weight values.

For BGP, the distance command sets the administrative distance of the External BGP route. The show ip protocols EXEC command displays the default administrative distance for a specified routing process.

Example: In the following example, the router igrp global configuration command sets up IGRP routing in autonomous system number 109. The network router configuration commands specify IGRP routing on networks 192.31.7.0 and 128.88.0.0. The first distance router configuration command sets the default administrative distance to 255, which instructs the Cisco IOS software to ignore all routing updates from routers for which an explicit distance has not been set. The second `distance` command sets the administrative distance for all routers on the Class C network `192.31.7.0` to `90`. The third `distance` command sets the administrative distance for the router with the address `128.88.1.3` to `120`.

```
router igrp 109
 network 192.31.7.0
 network 128.88.0.0
 distance 255
 distance 90 192.31.7.0 0.0.0.255
 distance 120 128.88.1.3 0.0.0.0
```

distribute-list out

To suppress networks from being advertised in updates, use the `distribute-list out` router configuration command. To cancel this function, use the no form of this command. The syntax for this command (and the no form) is as follows:

```
distribute-list access-list-number out [interface-name ¦
routing-process ¦ autonomous-system-number]
no distribute-list access-list-number out [interface-name ¦
routing-process ¦ autonomous-system-number]
```

Syntax Description:

> *access-list-number*. Standard IP access list number. The list defines which networks are to be sent and which are to be suppressed in routing updates.
> *out*. Applies the access list to outgoing routing updates.
> *interface-name* (optional). Name of a particular interface.
> *routing-process* (optional). Name of a particular routing process, or the keyword `static` or `connected`.
> *autonomous-system-number* (optional). Autonomous system number.

Default: Disabled.

Command Mode: Router configuration.

Usage Guidelines: When redistributing networks, a routing process name can be specified as an optional trailing argument to the `distribute-list` command. This causes the access list to be applied to only those routes derived from the specified routing process. After the process-specific access list is applied, any access list specified by a `distribute-list` command without a process name argument will be applied. Addresses not specified in the `distribute-list` command will not be advertised in outgoing routing updates.

> **NOTES**
>
> To filter networks received in updates, use the `distribute-list` in command.

Example: The following example would cause only one network to be advertised by a RIP router and will not work for OSPF.

```
process: network 131.108.0.0.
  access-list 1 permit 131.108.0.0
  access-list 1 deny 0.0.0.0 255.255.255.255
router rip
  network 131.108.0.0
  distribute-list 1 out
```

ip ospf authentication-key

To assign a password to be used by neighboring routers that are using OSPF's simple password authentication, use the `ip ospf authentication-key` interface configuration command. To remove a previously assigned OSPF password, use the no form of this command. The syntax for this command (and the no form) is as follows:

```
ip ospf authentication-key password
no ip ospf authentication-key
```

Syntax Description:

password. Any continuous string of characters that can be entered from the keyboard up to eight bytes in length.

Default: No password is specified.

Command Mode: Interface configuration.

Usage Guidelines: The password created by this command is used as a "key" that is inserted directly into the OSPF header when the Cisco IOS software originates routing protocol packets. A separate password can be assigned to each network on a per-interface basis. All neighboring routers on the same network must have the same password to be able to exchange OSPF information.

NOTES

The Cisco IOS software will use this key only when authentication is enabled for an area with the area authentication router configuration command.

Example: In the following example, the authentication key is enabled with the string yourpass:

```
ip ospf authentication-key yourpass
```

Related commands: `area authentication`

ip ospf cost

To explicitly specify the cost of sending a packet on an interface, use the `ip ospf cost` interface configuration command. To reset the path cost to the default value, use the `no` form of this command. The syntax for this command (and the `no` form) is as follows:

```
ip ospf cost cost
no ip ospf cost
```

Syntax Description:

cost. Unsigned integer value expressed as the link-state metric. It can be a value in the range 1 to 65535.

Default: The default cost is 10^8/bandwidth.

Command Mode: Interface configuration.

Usage Guidelines: Unlike IGRP, you must set this metric manually using this command, if you need to change the default. Changing the bandwidth will change the link cost.

The link-state metric is advertised as the link cost in the router link advertisement. Cisco does not support type of service (TOS), so you can assign only one cost per interface.

In general, the path cost is calculated using the following formula:

108 √ Bandwidth

The default of reference-bandwidth is 10^8.

Using the preceding formula, the default path costs were calculated as noted in Table 6-2. If these values do not suit your network, you can use your own method of calculating path costs as demonstrated in Table 6-2.

Table 6-2   *Calculating path costs based on network type*

Network type	Default cost
56kbps serial link	1,785
64kbps serial link	1,562
T1 (1.544Mbps serial link)	65
E1 (2.048Mbps serial link)	48
4Mbps Token Ring	25
Ethernet	10
16Mbps Token Ring	6
FDDI	1

Example: The following example sets the interface cost value to 65:

```
ip ospf cost 65
```

ip ospf dead-interval

To set how long hello packets must not have been seen before its neighbors declare the router down, use the ip ospf dead-interval interface configuration command. To return to the default time, use the no form of this command. The syntax for this command (and the no form) is as follows:

```
ip ospf dead-interval seconds
no ip ospf dead-interval
```

Syntax Description:

> **seconds.** Unsigned integer that specifies the interval in seconds; the value must be the same for all nodes on the network.

Default: Four times the interval set by the ip ospf hello-interval command.

Command Mode: Interface configuration.

Usage Guidelines: The interval is advertised in the router's hello packets. This value must be the same for all routers and access servers on a specific network.

Example: The following example sets the OSPF dead interval to 60 seconds:
```
interface ethernet 1
ip ospf dead-interval 60
```

Related commands: ip ospf hello-interval

ip ospf demand circuit

To configure OSPF to treat the interface as an OSPF demand circuit, use the ip ospf demand-circuit interface configuration command. To remove the demand circuit designation from the interface, use the no form of this command. The syntax for this command (and the no form) is as follows:
```
ip ospf demand-circuit
no ip ospf demand-circuit
```

ip ospf hello-interval

To specify the interval between hello packets that the Cisco IOS software sends on the interface, use the ip ospf hello-interval interface configuration command. To return to the default time, use the no form of this command. The syntax for this command (and the no form) is as follows:
```
ip ospf hello-interval seconds
no ip ospf hello-interval
```

Syntax Description:

>   *seconds*. Unsigned integer that specifies the interval in seconds. The value must be the same for all nodes on a specific network.

Default: 10 seconds.

Command Mode: Interface configuration.

Usage Guidelines: This value is advertised in the hello packets. The smaller the hello interval, the faster topological changes will be detected, but more routing traffic will ensue. This value must be the same for all routers and access servers on a specific network.

Example: The following example sets the interval between hello packets to 15 seconds:
```
interface ethernet 1
ip ospf hello-interval 15
```

Related Commands: ip ospf dead-interval

ip ospf message-digest-key

To enable OSPF MD5 authentication, use the `ip ospf message-digest-key` interface configuration command. To remove an old MD5 key, use the no form of this command. The syntax for this command (and the no form) is as follows:

```
ip ospf message-digest-key keyid md5 key
no ip ospf message-digest-key keyid
```

Syntax Description:

> **keyid.** An identifier in the range 1 through 255.
> **key.** An alphanumeric password of up to 16 bytes.

Default: OSPF MD5 authentication is disabled.

Command Mode: Interface configuration.

Usage Guidelines: Usually there is one key per interface, which is used to generate authentication information when sending packets and to authenticate incoming packets. The same key identifier on the neighbor router must have the same key value.

The process of changing keys is as follows. Suppose the current configuration is

```
interface ethernet 1
ip ospf message-digest-key 100 md5 OLD
```

You change the configuration to the following:

```
interface ethernet 1
ip ospf message-digest-key 101 md5 NEW
```

The system assumes its neighbors do not have the new key yet, so it begins a rollover process. It sends multiple copies of the same packet, each authenticated by different keys. In this example, the system sends out two copies of the same packet—the first one authenticated by key 100 and the second one authenticated by key 101.

Rollover allows neighboring routers to continue communication while the network administrator is updating them with the new key. Rollover stops once the local system finds that all its neighbors know the new key. The system detects that a neighbor has the new key when it receives packets from the neighbor authenticated by the new key.

After all neighbors have been updated with the new key, the old key should be removed. In this example, you would enter the following:

```
interface ethernet 1
no ip ospf message-digest-key 100
```

Then, only key 101 is used for authentication on Ethernet interface 1. You should not keep more than one key per interface, as recommended by Cisco. Every time you add a new key, you should remove the old key to prevent the local system from continuing to communicate with a hostile system that knows the old key. Removing the old key also reduces overhead during rollover.

Example: The following example sets a new key 19 with the password 8ry4222:

```
interface ethernet 1
ip ospf message-digest-key 10 md5 xvv560qle
ip ospf message-digest-key 19 md5 8ry4222
```

Related Commands: `area authentication`

ip ospf name-lookup

To configure OSPF to look up Domain Name System (DNS) names for use in all OSPF SHOW EXEC command displays, use the `ip ospf name-lookup` global configuration command. To disable this feature, use the no form of this command. The syntax for this command (and the no form) is as follows:

```
ip ospf name-lookup
no ip ospf name-lookup
```

Syntax Description: This command has no arguments or keywords.

Default: Disabled.

Command Mode: Global configuration.

Usage Guidelines: This feature makes it easier to identify a router because it is displayed by name rather than by its router ID or neighbor ID.

Example: The following example configures OSPF to look up DNS names for use in all OSPF SHOW EXEC command displays:

```
ip ospf name-lookup
```

Sample Display: The following is sample output from the `show ip ospf database` EXEC command, for example, after you have enabled the DNS name lookup feature:

```
Router# show ip ospf database
OSPF Router with id (160.89.41.1) (Autonomous system 109)
Router Link States (Area 0.0.0.0)
Link ID ADV Router Age Seq# Checksum Link count
160.89.41.1 router 381 0x80000003 0x93BB 4
160.89.34.2 neon 380 0x80000003 0xD5C8 2
Net Link States (Area 0.0.0.0)
Link ID ADV Router Age Seq# Checksum
160.89.32.1 router 381 0x80000001 0xC117
```

ip ospf network

To configure the OSPF network type to a type other than the default for a given media, use the `ip ospf network` interface configuration command. To return to the default value, use the no form of this command. The syntax for this command (and the no form) is as follows:

```
ip ospf network {broadcast | non-broadcast | point-to-multipoint}
no ip ospf network
```

Syntax Description:

> *broadcast*. Sets the network type to broadcast.
> *non-broadcast*. Sets the network type to nonbroadcast.
> *point-to-multipoint*. Sets the network type to point-to-multipoint.

Default: Depends on the network type.

Command Mode: Interface configuration.

Usage Guidelines: Using this feature, you can configure broadcast networks as non-broadcast multiaccess networks when, for example, you have routers in your network that do not support multicast addressing.

You can also configure nonbroadcast multiaccess networks, such as X.25, Frame Relay, and SMDS, as broadcast networks. This feature saves you from having to configure neighbors.

Configuring nonbroadcast multiaccess networks as either broadcast or nonbroadcast assumes that there are virtual circuits from every router to every router or fully-meshed network. This is not true for some cases, for example, due to cost constraints or when you have only a partially-meshed network. In these cases, you can configure the OSPF network type as a point-to-multipoint network. Routing between two routers that are not directly connected will go through the router that has virtual circuits to both routers. Note that you do not need to configure neighbors when using this feature.

If this command is issued on an interface that does not allow it, it will be ignored.

Example: The following example sets your OSPF network as a broadcast network:

```
interface serial 0
ip address 160.89.77.17 255.255.255.0
ip ospf network broadcast
encapsulation frame-relay
```

Related Commands: `neighbor` (OSPF)

ip ospf priority

To set the router priority, which helps determine the designated router for this network, use the `ip ospf priority` interface configuration command. To return to the default value, use the no form of this command. The syntax for this command (and the no form) is as follows:

```
ip ospf priority number
no ip ospf priority
```

Syntax Description:

> *number*. 8-bit unsigned integer that specifies the priority. The range is from 0 to 255.

Default: Priority of 1.

Command Mode: Interface configuration.

Usage Guidelines: When two routers attached to a network, both attempt to become the designated router; the one with the higher router priority takes precedence. If there is a tie, the router with the higher router ID takes precedence. A router with a router priority set to zero is ineligible to become the DR or BDR. Router priority is only configured for interfaces to multiaccess networks (in other words, not point-to-point networks).

This priority value is used when you configure OSPF for nonbroadcast networks using the neighbor router configuration command for OSPF.

Example: The following example sets the router priority value to 4:

```
interface ethernet 0
ip ospf priority 4
```

Related Commands: `ip ospf network`, `neighbor` (OSPF)

ip ospf retransmit-interval

To specify the time between LSA retransmissions for adjacencies belonging to the interface, use the `ip ospf retransmit-interval` interface configuration command. To return to the default value, use the no form of this command. The syntax for this command (and the no form) is as follows:

```
ip ospf retransmit-interval seconds
no ip ospf retransmit-interval
```

Syntax Description:

> **seconds.** Time in seconds between retransmissions. It must be greater than the expected round-trip delay between any two routers on the attached network. The range is 1 to 65535 seconds. The default is 5 seconds.

Default: 5 seconds.

Command Mode: Interface configuration.

Usage Guidelines: When a router sends a LSA to its neighbor, it keeps the LSA until it receives back the acknowledgment. If it receives no acknowledgment in seconds, it will retransmit the LSA.

The setting of this parameter should be conservative, or needless retransmission will result. The value should be larger for serial lines and virtual links.

Example: The following example sets the `retransmit-interval` value to eight seconds:

```
interface ethernet 2
ip ospf retransmit-interval 8
```

ip ospf transmit-delay

To set the estimated time it takes to transmit a link-state update packet on the interface, use the `ip ospf transmit-delay` interface configuration command. To return to the default value, use the no form of this command. The syntax for this command (and the no form) is as follows:

```
ip ospf transmit-delay seconds
no ip ospf transmit-delay
```

Syntax Description:

> **seconds.** Time in seconds that it takes to transmit a link-state update. It can be an integer in the range is 1 to 65,535 seconds. The default is 1 second.

Default: 1 second.

Command Mode: Interface configuration.

Usage Guidelines: LSAs in the update packet must have their age incremented by the amount specified in the seconds argument before transmission. The value assigned should take into account the transmission and propagation delays for the interface.

If the delay is not added before transmission over a link, the time in which the LSA propagates over the link is not considered. This setting has more significance on very low speed links.

Example: The following example sets the retransmit-delay value to three seconds:
```
interface ethernet 0
ip ospf transmit-delay 3
```

ip policy route-map

To identify a route map to use for policy routing on an interface, use the `ip policy route-map` interface configuration command. To disable policy routing on the interface, use the no form of this command. The syntax for this command (and the no form) is as follows:
```
ip policy route-map map-tag
no ip policy route-map map-tag
```

Syntax Description:

> ***map-tag***. Name of the route map to use for policy routing. Must match a map-tag specified by a route-map command.

Default: No policy routing occurs on the interface.

Command Mode: Interface configuration.

Usage Guidelines: You might enable policy routing if you want your packets to take a route other than the obvious shortest path. The `ip policy route-map` command identifies a route map to use for policy routing. Each route-map command has a list of match and set commands associated with it. The match commands specify the match criteria—the conditions under which policy routing is allowed for the interface. The set commands specify the set actions—the particular policy routing actions to perform if the criteria enforced by the match commands are met. The `no ip policy route-map` command deletes the pointer to the route map.

Example: In the following example, packets with the destination IP address of 174.95.16.18 are sent to a router at IP address 174.21.3.20:
```
interface serial 0
ip policy route-map wethersfield
!
route-map wethersfield
match ip address 174.95.16.18
set ip next-hop 174.21.3.20
```

Related Commands: match ip address, match length, route-map, set default interface, set interface, set ip default next-hop, set ip next-hop

neighbor (OSPF)

To configure OSPF routers and access servers interconnecting to nonbroadcast networks, use this form of the neighbor router configuration command. To remove a configuration, use the no form of this command. The syntax for this command (and the no
form) is as follows:

    neighbor ip-address [priority number] [poll-interval seconds]
    no neighbor ip-address [priority number] [poll-interval seconds]

TIPS

The command neighbor <address> cost <value> can be used to specify per neighbor
cost on a point-to-multipoint network. This value takes precedence over the interface cost.

Syntax Description:

> **ip-address.** Interface IP address of the neighbor.
> **priority number** (optional). 8-bit number indicating the router priority value
> of the nonbroadcast neighbor associated with the IP address specified. The de-
> fault is 0.
> **poll-interval seconds** (optional). Unsigned integer value reflecting the poll
> interval. RFC 1247 recommends that this value be much larger than the hello
> interval. The default is two minutes (120 seconds).

Default: No configuration is specified.

Command Mode: Router configuration.

Usage Guidelines: X.25 and Frame Relay provide an optional broadcast capability that
can be configured in the map to allow OSPF to run as a broadcast network. At the OSPF
level you can configure the router as a broadcast network. See the x25 map and
frame-relay map commands in "X.25 Commands" and "Frame Relay Commands"
chapters, respectively, in the *Wide-Area Networking Command Reference* for more
detail.

One neighbor entry must be included in the Cisco IOS software configuration for each known nonbroadcast network neighbor. The neighbor address has to be on the primary address of the interface.

If a neighboring router has become inactive (hello packets have not been seen for the Router Dead Interval period), it might still be necessary to send hello packets to the dead neighbor.

These hello packets will be sent at a reduced rate called Poll Interval. When the router first starts up, it sends only hello packets to those routers with non-zero priority, that is, routers that are eligible to become DR and BDR. After the DR and BDR are selected, the DR and BDR will then start sending hello packets to all neighbors in order to form adjacencies.

Example: The following example declares a router at address `131.108.3.4` on a non-broadcast network, with a priority of 1 and a poll-interval of 180:

```
router ospf
neighbor 131.108.3.4 priority 1 poll-interval 180
```

Related Commands: `ip ospf priority`

network area

To define the interfaces on which OSPF runs and to define the area ID for those interfaces, use the `network area` router configuration command. To disable OSPF routing for interfaces defined with the *address wildcard-mask* pair, use the no form of this command. The syntax for this command (and the no form) is as follows:

```
network address wildcard-mask area area-id
no network address wildcard-mask area area-id
```

Syntax Description:

> *address*. IP address.
> *wildcard-mask*. IP-address-type mask that includes "don't care" bits
> *area-id*. Area that is to be associated with the OSPF address range. It can be specified as either a decimal value or as an IP address. If you intend to associate areas with IP subnets, you can specify a subnet address as the area-id.

ospf auto-cost-determination

To control how OSPF calculates default metrics for the interface, use the ospf auto-cost-determination router configuration command. To disable this feature, use the no form of this command. The syntax for this command (and the no form) is as follows:

```
ospf auto-cost-determination
no ospf auto-cost-determination
```

Syntax Description: This command has no arguments or keywords.

Default: Enabled.

Command Mode: Router configuration.

Usage Guidelines: In Cisco IOS Release 10.2 and earlier, OSPF assigns default OSPF metrics to interfaces regardless of the interface bandwidth. It gives both 64K and T1 links the same metric (1562) and, thus, requires an explicit ip ospf cost command in order to take advantage of the faster link.

In Cisco IOS Release 10.3 and later, by default OSPF will calculate the OSPF metric for an interface according to the bandwidth of the interface. For example, a 64K link will get a metric of 1562, while a T1 link will have a metric of 64.

The OSPF metric is calculated as metric-scale / bandwidth, with metric-scale equal to 10 to a power of 8 by default, giving FDDI a metric of 1.

Example: The following example causes a fixed default metric assignment, regardless of interface bandwidth:

```
router ospf 1
no ospf auto-cost-determination
```

Related Command: ip ospf cost

ospf log-adj-changes

To configure the router to send a SYSLOG message when an OSPF neighbor state changes, perform the following task in router configuration mode:

```
ospf log-adj-changes
```

Configure this command if you want to know about OSPF neighbor changes without turning on the debugging command debug ip ospf adjacency. The ospf log-adj-changes command provides a higher level view of changes to the state of the peer relationship with less output.

passive-interface

To disable sending routing updates on an interface, use the `passive-interface` router configuration command. To re-enable the sending of routing updates, use the no form of this command. The syntax for this command (and the no form) is as follows:

```
passive-interface type number
no passive-interface type number
```

Syntax Description:

> *type*. Interface type.
> *number*. Interface number.

Default: Routing updates are sent on the interface.

Command Mode: Router configuration.

Usage Guidelines: If you disable the sending of routing updates on an interface, the particular subnet will continue to be advertised to other interfaces, and updates from other routers on that interface continue to be received and processed.

For OSPF, OSPF routing information is neither sent nor received through the specified router interface. The specified interface address appears as a stub network in the OSPF domain.

For IS-IS, this command instructs IS-IS to advertise the IP addresses for the specified interface without actually running IS-IS on that interface. The no form of this command for IS-IS disables advertising IP addresses for the specified address.

Enhanced IGRP is disabled on an interface that is configured as passive although it advertises the route.

Example 1: The following example sends IGRP updates to all interfaces on network `131.108.0.0` except Ethernet interface 1:

```
router igrp 109
network 131.108.0.0
passive-interface ethernet 1
```

Example 2: The following configuration enables IS-IS on interfaces Ethernet 1 and serial 0 and advertises the IP addresses of Ethernet 0 in its link-state PDUs:

```
router isis Finance
passive-interface Ethernet 0
interface Ethernet 1
ip router isis Finance
interface serial 0
ip router isis Finance
```

redistribute

To redistribute routes from one routing domain into another routing domain, use the redistribute router configuration command. To disable redistribution, use the no form of this command. The syntax for this command (and the no form) is as follows:

> **redistribute** *protocol* [*process-id*] {**level-1** ¦ **level-1-2** ¦ **level-2**}
> [**metric** *metric-value*]
> [**metric-type** type-value] [**match** {**internal** ¦ **external 1** ¦ **external 2**}]
> [**tag** *tag-value*] [**route-map** map-tag] [**weight** *weight*] [**subnets**]
> **no redistribute** protocol [*process-id*] {**level-1** ¦ **level-1-2** ¦ **level-2**}
> [**metric** *metric-value*] [**metric-type** *type-value*] [**match** {**internal** ¦
> **external 1** ¦ **external 2**}]
> [**tag** *tag-value*] [**route-map** map-tag] [**weight** *weight*] [**subnets**]

Syntax Description:

> ***protocol***. Source protocol from which routes are being redistributed. It can be one of the following keywords: bgp, egp, igrp, isis, ospf, static [ip], connected, and rip. The keyword static [ip] is used to redistribute IP static routes. The optional ip keyword is used when redistributing into IS-IS. The keyword connected refers to routes that are established automatically by the virtue of having enabled IP on an interface. For routing protocols such as OSPF and IS-IS, these routes will be redistributed as external to the autonomous system.
>
> ***process-id*** (optional). For bgp, egp, or igrp, this is an autonomous system number, which is a 16-bit decimal number. For isis, this is an optional tag that defines a meaningful name for a routing process. You can specify only one IS-IS process per router. Creating a name for a routing process means that you use names when configuring routing or ospf, this is an appropriate OSPF process ID from which routes are to be redistributed. This identifies the routing process. This value takes the form of a nonzero decimal number. For rip, no process-id value is needed.
>
> **level-1**. For IS-IS, Level 1 routes are redistributed into other IP routing protocols independently.
>
> **level-1-2**. For IS-IS, both Level 1 and Level 2 routes are redistributed into other IP routing protocols.
>
> **level-2**. For IS-IS, Level 2 routes are redistributed into other IP routing protocols independently.
>
> metric *metric-value* (optional). Metric used for the redistributed route. If a value is not specified for this option, and no value is specified using the default-metric command, the default metric value is 0. Use a value consistent with the destination protocol.

metric-type *type-value* (optional). For OSPF, the external link type associated with the default route advertised into the OSPF routing domain. It can be either of the following two values: 1 (Type 1 external route) or 2 (Type 2 external route). If a metric-type is not specified, the Cisco IOS software adopts a Type 2 external route. For IS-IS, it can be one of two values: internal (IS-IS metric which is < 63) or external (IS-IS metric which is > 64 < 128). The default is internal.

match {internal ¦ external 1 ¦ external 2} (optional). For OPSF, the criteria by which OSPF routes are redistributed into other routing domains. It can be one of the following: internal (routes that are internal to a specific autonomous system), external 1 (routes that are external to the autonomous system, but are imported into OSPF as type 1 external route), external 2 (routes that are external to the autonomous system but are imported into OSPF as type 2 external route).

tag *tag-value* (optional). 32-bit decimal value attached to each external route. This is not used by the OSPF protocol itself. It may be used to communicate information between ASBRs. If none is specified, then the remote autonomous system number is used for routes from BGP and EGP; for other protocols, zero is used.

route-map (optional). Route map should be interrogated to filter the importation of routes from this source routing protocol to the current routing protocol. If not specified, all routes are redistributed. If this keyword is specified, but no route map tags are listed, no routes will be imported.

map-tag (optional). Identifier of a configured route map.

weight *weight* (optional). Network weight when redistributing into BGP. An integer from 0 to 65,535.

subnets (optional). For redistributing routes into OSPF, the scope of redistribution for the specified protocol.

Command Mode: Router configuration.

Usage Guidelines: Changing or disabling any keyword will not affect the state of other keywords.

A router receiving a LSP with an internal metric will consider the cost of the route from itself to the redistributing router plus the advertised cost to reach the destination. An external metric only considers the advertised metric to reach the destination. Routes learned from IP routing protocols can be redistributed at level-1 into an attached area or at level-2. The keyword level-1-2 allows both in a single command.

Redistributed routing information should always be filtered by the `distribute-list` out router configuration command. This ensures that only those routes intended by the administrator are passed along to the receiving routing protocol.

Whenever you use the `redistribute` or the `default-information` router configuration commands to redistribute routes into an OSPF routing domain, the router automatically becomes an ASBR. However, an ASBR does not, by default, generate a default route into the OSPF routing domain. When routes are redistributed between OSPF processes, no OSPF metrics are preserved.

When routes are redistributed into OSPF and no metric is specified in the `metric` keyword, the default metric that OSPF uses is 20 for routes from all protocols except BGP route, which gets a metric of 1. When redistributing routes into OSPF, only routes that are not subnetted are redistributed if the `subnets` keyword is not specified.

The only connected routes affected by this redistribute command are the routes not specified by the network command. You cannot use the `default-metric` command to affect the metric used to advertise connected routes.

NOTES

The metric value specified in the redistribute command supersedes the metric value specified using the `default-metric` command.

Default redistribution of IGPs or EGP into BGP is not allowed unless `default-information originate` is specified.

When routes are redistributed into OSPF and no metric is specified in the `metric` keyword, the default metric that OSPF uses is 20 for routes from all protocols except BGP route, which gets a metric of 1.

Examples: The following are examples of the various configurations you would use to redistribute one routing protocol into another routing protocol. The following example configuration causes OSPF routes to be redistributed into a BGP:

```
domain:
router bgp 109
redistribute ospf...
```

The following example configuration causes IGRP routes to be redistributed into an OSPF:

```
domain:
router ospf 110
redistribute igrp...
```

The following example causes the specified IGRP process routes to be redistributed into an OSPF domain. The IGRP-derived metric will be remapped to 100 and RIP routes to 200:

```
router ospf 109
redistribute igrp 108 metric 100 subnets
redistribute rip metric 200 subnets
```

In the following example, BGP routes are configured to be redistributed into IS-IS. The link-state cost is specified as 5, and the metric type will be set to external, indicating that it has lower priority than internal metrics:

```
router isis
redistribute bgp 120 metric 5 metric-type external
```

Related Commands: `default-information originate` (BGP), `default-information originate` (EGP), `default-information originate` (IS-IS), `default-information originate` (OSPF), `distribute-list out`, `route-map`, `show route-map`

route-map

To define the conditions for redistributing routes from one routing protocol into another, or to enable policy routing, use the `route-map` global configuration command and the `match` and `set route-map` configuration commands. To delete an entry, use the `no route-map` command. The syntax for this command (and the no form) is as follows:

```
route-map map-tag [permit ¦ deny] [sequence-number]
no route-map map-tag [permit ¦ deny] [sequence-number]
```

Syntax Description:

> *map-tag*. Defines a meaningful name for the route map. The `redistribute` router configuration command uses this name to reference this route map. Multiple route maps may share the same map tag name.
>
> *permit* (**optional**). If the match criteria are met for this route map, and `permit` is specified, the route is redistributed as controlled by the set actions. In the case of policy routing, the packet is policy routed.
>
> If the match criteria are not met, and `permit` is specified, the next route map with the same *map-tag* is tested. If a route passes none of the match criteria for the set of route maps sharing the same name, it is not redistributed by that set.

deny (optional). If the match criteria are met for the route map, and deny is specified, the route is not redistributed, or in the case of policy routing, the packet is not policy routed, and no further route maps sharing the same map tag name will be examined. If the packet is not policy routed, it reverts to the normal forwarding algorithm.

sequence-number (optional). Number that indicates the position a new route map is to have in the list of route maps already configured with the same name. If given with the no form of this command, it specifies the position of the route map that should be deleted.

Default: No default is available.

Command Mode: Global configuration.

Usage Guidelines: Use route maps to redistribute routes or to subject packets to policy routing as described in the paragraphs that follow on each, respectively.

Redistribution:

Use the route-map global configuration command and the match and set route-map configuration commands to define the conditions for redistributing routes from one routing protocol into another. Each route-map command has a list of match and set commands associated with it. The match commands specify the match criteria—the conditions under which redistribution is allowed for the current route map. The set commands specify the set actions—the particular redistribution actions to perform if the criteria enforced by the match commands are met. The no route-map command deletes the route map.

The match route-map configuration command has multiple formats. The related match commands are listed in the section "Related Commands for Redistribution." The match commands can be given in any order, and all match commands must "pass" to cause the route to be redistributed according to the set actions given with the set commands. The no forms of the match commands remove the specified match criteria.

Use route maps when you want detailed control over how routes are redistributed between routing processes. The destination routing protocol is the one you specify with the router global configuration command. The source routing protocol is the one you specify with the redistribute router configuration command. See the following example as an illustration of how route maps are configured.

When you are passing routes through a route map, a route map can have several parts. Any route that does not match at least one match clause relating to a route-map command will be ignored; that is, the route will not be advertised for outbound route maps and will not be accepted for inbound route maps. If you want to modify only some data, you must configure a second route-map section with an explicit match specified.

Policy Routing:

Another purpose of route maps is to enable policy routing. Use the `ip policy route-map` command, in addition to the `route-map` command, and the `match` and `set` commands to define the conditions for policy routing packets. The related `match` and `set` commands are listed in the section "Related Commands for Policy Routing." The `match` commands specify the conditions under which policy routing occurs. The `set` commands specify the routing actions to perform if the criteria enforced by the `match` commands are met. You might want to policy route packets some way other than the obvious shortest path.

Example 1: The following example redistributes all OSPF routes into IGRP:

```
router igrp 109
redistribute ospf 110
default metric 1000 100 255 1 1500
```

Example 2: The following example redistributes RIP routes with a hop count equal to 1 into OSPF. These routes will be redistributed into OSPF as external LSAs with a metric of 5, metric type of Type 1 and a tag equal to 1:

```
router ospf 109
redistribute rip route-map rip-to-ospf
route-map rip-to-ospf permit
match metric 1
set metric 5
set metric-type type1
set tag 1
```

Related Commands for Redistribution:

match as-path	set automatic-tag
match community-list	set community
match interface	set level
match ip address	set local-preference
match ip next-hop	set metric
match ip route-source	set metric-type
match metric	set next-hop
match route-type	set origin
match tag	set tag
set as-path	set weight
show route-map	

Related Commands for Policy Routing

```
ip policy route-map                    set interface
match ip address                       set ip default next-hop
match length                           set ip next-hop
set default interface
```

router ospf

To configure an OSPF routing process, use the `router ospf` global configuration command. To terminate an OSPF routing process, use the `no` form of this command. The syntax for this command (and the `no` form) is as follows:

```
router ospf process-id
no router ospf process-id
```

Syntax Description:

> ***process-id.*** Internally used identification parameter for an OSPF routing process. It is locally assigned and can be any positive integer. A unique value is assigned for each OSPF routing process.

Default: No OSPF routing process is defined.

Command Mode: Global configuration.

Usage Guidelines: You can specify multiple OSPF routing processes in each router.

Example: The following example shows how to configure an OSPF routing process and assign a process number of 109:

```
router ospf 109
```

Related Commands: `network area`

set level

To indicate where to import routes, use the `set level` route map configuration command. To delete an entry, use the `no` form of this command. The syntax for this command (and the `no` form) is as follows:

```
set level {level-1 ¦ level-2 ¦ level-1-2 ¦ stub-area ¦ backbone}
no set level {level-1 ¦ level-2 ¦ level-1-2 ¦ stub-area ¦ backbone}
```

Syntax Description:

> *level-1*. Imports routes into a Level-1 area.
> *level-2*. Imports routes into Level-2 subdomain.
> *level-1-2*. Imports routes into Level-1 and Level-2.
> *stub-area*. Imports routes into OSPF NSSA area.
> *backbone*. Imports routes into OSPF backbone area.

set metric

To set the metric value for the destination routing protocol, use the set metric route map configuration command. To return to the default metric value, use the no form of this command. The syntax for this command (and the no form) is as follows:

```
set metric metric-value
no set metric metric-value
```

Syntax Description:

> *metric-value*. Metric value or IGRP bandwidth in kilobits per second. It can be an integer from –294,967,295 through 294,967,295.

Default: Default metric value.

Command Mode: Route map configuration.

Usage Guidelines: Use the route-map global configuration command, and the match and set route-map configuration commands, to define the conditions for redistributing routes from one routing protocol into another. Each route-map command has a list of match and set commands associated with it. The match commands specify the match criteria—the conditions under which redistribution is allowed for the current route map. The set commands specify the set actions—the particular redistribution actions to perform if the criteria enforced by the match commands are met. The no route-map command deletes the route map.

The set route-map configuration commands specify the redistribution set actions to be performed when all of a route map's match criteria are met. When all match criteria are met, all set actions are performed.

Example: In the following example, the metric value for the destination routing protocol is set to 100:

```
route-map set-metric
set metric 100
```

Related Commands:

match as-path	set as-path
match community-list	set automatic-tag
match interface	set community
match ip address	set level
match ip next-hop	set local-preference
match ip route-source	set metric-type
match metric	set next-hop
match route-type	set origin
match tag	set tag
route-map	set weight

set metric-type

To set the metric type for the destination routing protocol, use the set metric-type route map command. To return to the default, use the no form of this command. The syntax for this command (and the no form) is as follows:

    set metric-type {internal ¦ external ¦ type-1 ¦ type-2}
    no set metric-type {internal ¦ external ¦ type-1 ¦ type-2}

Syntax Description:

> *internal*. IS-IS internal metric.
> *external*. IS-IS external metric.
> *type-1*. OSPF external Type 1 metric.
> *type-2*. OSPF external Type 2 metric.

Default: Disabled.

Command Mode: Route map configuration.

Usage Guidelines: Use the route-map global configuration command with match and set route-map configuration commands to define the conditions for redistributing routes from one routing protocol into another. Each route-map command has a list of match and set commands associated with it.

The match commands specify the match criteria—the conditions under which redistribution is allowed for the current route map. The set commands specify the set actions—the particular redistribution actions to perform if the criteria enforced by the match commands are met. The no route-map command deletes the route map.

The set route-map configuration commands specify the redistribution set actions to be performed when all of a route map's match criteria are met. When all match criteria are met, all set actions are performed.

Example: In the following example, the metric type of the destination protocol is set to OSPF external type 1:

```
route-map map-type
set metric-type type-1
```

Related Commands:

match as-path	set as-path
match community-list	set automatic-tag
match interface	set community
match ip address	set level
match ip next-hop	set local-preference
match ip route-source	set metric
match metric	set next-hop
match route-type	set origin
match tag	set tag
route-map	set weight

summary-address

Use the summary-address router configuration command to create aggregate addresses for IS-IS or OSPF. The no summary-address command restores the default. The syntax for this command (and the no form) is as follows:

```
summary-address address mask {level-1 ¦ level-1-2 ¦ level-2} prefix
mask [not-advertise] [tag tag]
no summary-address address mask {level-1 ¦ level-1-2 ¦ level-2}
```

Syntax Description:

> *address.* Summary address designated for a range of addresses.
> *mask.* IP subnet mask used for the summary route.
> **level-1.** Only routes redistributed into Level 1 are summarized with the configured address/mask value. This keyword does not apply to OSPF.
> **level-1-2.** The summary router is injected into both a Level 1 area and a Level 2 subdomain. This keyword does not apply to OSPF.

level-2. Routes learned by Level 1 routing will be summarized into the Level 2 backbone with the configured address/mask value. This keyword does not apply to OSPF.

prefix. IP route prefix for the destination.

not-advertise. Used to suppress routes that match the prefix/mask pair.

tag *tag* (optional). Tag value that can be used as a "match" value for controlling redistribution via route maps.

timers spf

To configure the delay time between when OSPF receives a topology change and when it starts a Shortest Path First (SPF) calculation, and the hold time between two consecutive SPF calculations, use the `timers spf` router configuration command. To return to the default timer values, use the no form of this command. The syntax for this command (and the no form) is as follows:

```
timers spf spf-delay spf-holdtime
no timers spf spf-delay spf-holdtime
```

Syntax Description:

spf-delay. Delay time, in seconds, between when OSPF receives a topology change and when it starts an SPF calculation. It can be an integer from 0 to 65,535. The default time is 5 seconds. A value of 0 means that there is no delay; that is, the SPF calculation is started immediately.

spf-holdtime. Minimum time, in seconds, between two consecutive SPF calculations. It can be an integer from 0 to 65,535. The default time is 10 seconds. A value of 0 means that there is no delay, that is, two consecutive SPF calculations can be done one immediately after the other.

Defaults: For *spf-delay*, the default is 5 seconds; for *spf-holdtime*, the default is 10 seconds.

Router Command Mode: Router configuration.

Usage Guidelines: Setting the delay and hold time low causes routing to switch to the alternate path more quickly in the event of a failure.

Example: The following example changes the delay to 10 seconds and the hold time to 20 seconds.

```
Timers spf 10 20
```

OSPF ERROR MESSAGES

This section consolidates a variety of the available OSPF error messages for Cisco routers and in some cases provides additional support and explanation.

NOTES

The list of system error messages in this section is incomplete. If you encounter an error message for OSPF not listed here, then contact your Cisco representative immediately.

%OSPF-4-BADLENGTH Error Message

The full text for this error message is as follows:

```
%OSPF-4-BADLENGTH: Invalid length [dec] in OSPF packet from [inet]
(ID [inet]], [chars]
```

Explanation: The system received an OSPF packet with a length field of less than normal header size or inconsistent with the size of the IP packet in which it arrived. This indicates an error in the sender of the packet.

Recommended Action: Copy the error message exactly as it appears, and report it to your technical support representative.

%OSPF-4-BADLSATYPE Error Message

The full text for this error message is as follows:

```
%OSPF-4-BADLSATYPE: LOG_WARNING: Invalid lsa type [dec] in LSA [dec],
[dec] from [dec], OSPF_COMPLAIN-IVL
```

Explanation: The router received an LSA with invalid LSA Type. The cause is either memory corruption or unexpected behavior on a router.

Recommended Action: From neighbor address, locate the problem router and reboot it. To determine what is causing this problem, call your technical support representative for assistance.

%OSPF-4-CONFLICTING_LSAID Error Message

The full text for this error message is as follows:
```
%OSPF-4-CONFLICTING_LSAID: Found lsa type [dec] in LSA [inet], [inet]
from [inet], [chars]
```

Explanation: An internal software error occurred.

Recommended Action: Copy the error message exactly as it appears, and report it to your technical support representative.

%OSPF-4-ERRRCV Error Message

The full text for this error message is as follows:
```
%OSPF-4-ERRRCV: Received invalid packet: [chars] from [inet], [chars]
```

Explanation: An invalid OSPF packet was received. Details are included in the error message. The cause might be a misconfigured OSPF or an internal error in the sender.

Recommended Action: Check the OSPF configuration of the receiver and the sender for inconsistency.

%OSPF-3-INTERNALERR Error Message

The full text for this error message is as follows:
```
%OSPF-3-INTERNALERR: Internal error: [chars], OSPF_COMPLAIN_IVL
```

Explanation: An internal software error occurred.

Recommended Action: Copy the error message exactly as it appears, and report it to your technical support representative.

%OSPF-3-NOBACKBONE Error Message

The full text for this error message is as follows:
```
%OSPF-3-NOBACKBONE: Flagged as being an ABR without a backbone
```

Explanation: The router was flagged as an ABR without backbone area in the router.

Recommended Action: Restart the OSPF process.

%OSPF-3-NOCONNDB Error Message

The full text for this error message is as follows:
```
%OSPF-3-NOCONNDB: No database entry for connected address [int]
```

Explanation: While calculating OSPF routes, the router could not find the LSA that represents the connected route in the router.

Recommended Action: Clear the IP routes in the routing table by entering the command `clear ip route`.

%OSPF-3-NOLSA Error Message

The full text for this error message is as follows:
```
%OSPF-3-NOLSA: Failed to find this router LSA in [chars]
```

Explanation: The router is not able to find its own router LSA. This can occur occasionally and self-correct. However, if this message recurs, restart the OSPF process.

Recommended Action: Copy the error message exactly as it appears, and report it to your Cisco technical support representative.

%OSPF-3-NOMEMORY Error Message

The full text for this error message is as follows:
```
%OSPF-3-NOMEMORY: No memory for [chars]
```

Explanation: The requested operation could not be accomplished because of a low memory condition.

Recommended Action: Reduce other system activity to ease memory demands. If conditions warrant, upgrade to a larger memory configuration.

%OSPF-4-NONEIGHBOR Error Message

The full text for this error message is as follows:
```
%OSPF-4-NONEIGHBOR: Received [chars] from unknown neighbor [inet]
```

Explanation: The OSPF hello, database description, or database request packet was received, but the router could not identify the sender.

Recommended Action: This situation should correct itself. If the message recurs, call your technical support representative for assistance.

%OSPF-4-NORTRID Error Message

The full text for this error message is as follows:

```
%OSPF-4-NORTRID: Could not allocate router ID
```

Explanation: OSPF failed while attempting to allocate a router ID from the IP address of one of its interfaces.

Recommended Action: Make sure that there is at least one interface that is up and has a valid IP address. If there are multiple OSPF processes running on the router, each process needs its own unique router ID. You must have enough "up" interfaces so that each of them can obtain a router ID.

%OSPF-6-NOSRCPDB Error Message

The full text for this error message is as follows:

```
%OSPF-6-NOSRCPDB: ex_route_callback(): Can't find the src protocol to
redistribute net [inet] [inet]
```

Explanation: OSPF attempted to redistribute a route but could not fine a valid source protocol.

Recommended Action: No action is required.

%OSPF-6-NOTREDIST1 Error Message

The full text for this error message is as follows:

```
%OSPF-6-NOTREDIST1: ex_route_callback(): do not redistribute net [inet]
[inet], [chars]
```

Explanation: For information only.

Recommended Action: No action is required.

%OSPF-6-NOTREDIST3 Error Message

The full text for this error message is as follows:

```
%OSPF-6-NOTREDIST3: build_ex_route(): don't redistribute net [inet]
[inet], [inet] advertises it already
```

Explanation: For information only.

Recommended Action: No action is required.

%OSPF-4-NOTREDIST4 Error Message

The full text for this error message is as follows:
```
%OSPF-4-NOTREDIST4: Database scanner: external LSA [inet] [inet] is
lost, reinstalls
```

Explanation: The software detected an unexpected condition. The router will take corrective action and continue.

Recommended Action: Record the entire error message and note any OSPF problem you experience. Report the error message to your technical support representative.

%OSPF-4-NOTREDIST5 Error Message

The full text for this error message is as follows:
```
%OSPF-4-NOTREDIST5: db_free: external LSA [inet] [inet],
```

Explanation: An internal software error occurred.

Recommended Action: Copy the error message exactly as it appears, and report it to your technical support representative.

%OSPF-4-OSPFINTDOWN Error Message

The full text for this error message is as follows:
```
%OSPF-4-OSPFINTDOWN: Interface [chars] is up but OSPF state is down.
Clean up, OSPF_COMPLAIN_IVL
```

Explanation: An inconsistency in an internal state was found and corrected.

Recommended Action: Informational message only. No action required.

%OSPF-3-UNKNOWNSTATE Error Message

The full text for this error message is as follows:
```
%OSPF-3-UNKNOWNSTATE: Reached unknown state in neighbor state machine
```

Explanation: An internal software error occurred.

Recommended Action: Copy the error message exactly as it appears, and report it to your technical support representative.

%OSPF-4-VIRTUAL_IN_NON_BACKBONE Error Message

The full text for this error message is as follows:

```
%OSPF-4-VIRTUAL_IN_NON_BACKBONE: Virtual link information found in
non-backbone area: [chars], OSPF_COMPLAIN_IVL
```

Explanation: An internal error occurred.

Recommended Action: Copy the error message exactly as it appears, and report it to your technical support representative.

CHAPTER SUMMARY

The whole section on redistributing OSPF routes both into and out of your OSPF network is designed to once again cover the rules regarding their use and configuration. The chapter then moved into practical low key examples and, as the solid foundation was built, began exploring the tougher aspects of this concept.

The chapter also followed a very similar principle when dealing with the capability of OSPF to operate within a demand-based circuit environment. This time, though, you learned about both optimal and less-than-optimal network designs.

The remaining sections of this chapter gave ideas concerning how router commands should be presented for use. The various OSPF configuration commands and error messages have been presented in as much of a down-to-earth fashion as possible and organized in such away that you will be able to quickly reference them while working online. This last section is a case study and presents the classic RIP and OSPF Redistribution case study.

This chapters contains the contributions of previously existing sources published by Cisco. Many of the sources do not credit authors and such, but everyone involved at Cisco who ensured that a strong internal support framework was built for their products made write this chapter much easier.

CASE STUDY: RIP AND OSPF REDISTRIBUTION

This case study is a classic for those making the transition from RIP to OSPF. It has become extremely popular within networking circles, and I felt it should be reproduced here for everyone. It has been modified and updated slightly, but otherwise the original text and message is identical to when it was a Cisco case study.

This case study addresses the issue of integrating RIP networks with OSPF networks. Most OSPF networks also use RIP to communicate with hosts or to communicate with portions of the internetwork that do not use OSPF.

Cisco supports both the RIP and OSPF protocols and provides a way to exchange routing information between RIP and OSPF networks. This case study provides examples of how to complete the following phases in redistributing information between RIP and OSPF networks:

- Configuring a RIP Network

- Adding OSPF to the Center of a RIP Network

- Adding OSPF Areas

- Setting up Mutual Distribution

Configuring a RIP Network

Figure 6-14 illustrates a RIP network. Three sites are connected with serial lines. The RIP network uses a Class B address and an 8-bit subnet mask. Each site has a contiguous set of network numbers.

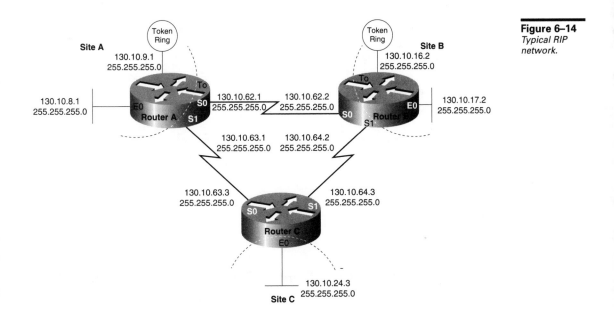

Figure 6–14
Typical RIP network.

Table 6-3 lists the network address assignments for the RIP network, including the network number, subnet range, and subnet masks. All interfaces indicate network 130.10.0.0; however, the specific address includes the subnet and subnet mask. For example, serial interface 0 on Router C has an IP address of 130.10.63.3 with a subnet mask of 255.255.255.0.

Table 6-3   *RIP network assignments.*

Network Number	Subnets	Subnet Masks
130.10.0.0	Site A: 8–15	255.255.255.0
130.10.0.0	Site B: 16–23	255.255.255.0
130.10.0.0	Site C: 24–31	255.255.255.0
130.10.0.0	Serial Backbone: 62–64	255.255.255.0

Configuration File Examples

The following commands in the configuration file for Router A determine the IP address for each interface and enable RIP on those interfaces:

Router A Configuration
```
interface serial 0
   ip address 130.10.62.1 255.255.255.0

interface serial 1
   ip address 130.10.63.1 255.255.255.0

interface ethernet 0
   ip address 130.10.8.1 255.255.255.0

interface tokenring 0
   ip address 130.10.9.1 255.255.255.0

router rip
   network 130.10.0.0
```

The following commands in the configuration file for Router B determine the IP address for each interface and enable RIP on those interfaces:

Router B Configuration
```
interface serial 0
    ip address 130.10.62.2 255.255.255.0

interface serial 1
    ip address 130.10.64.2 255.255.255.0

interface ethernet 0
    ip address 130.10.17.2 255.255.255.0

interface tokenring 0
    ip address 130.10.16.2 255.255.255.0

router rip
    network 130.10.0.0
```

The following commands in the configuration file for Router C determine the IP address for each interface and enable RIP on those interfaces:

Router C Configuration
```
interface serial 0
    ip address 130.10.63.3 255.255.255.0

interface serial 1
    ip address 130.10.64.3 255.255.255.0

interface ethernet 0
    ip address 130.10.24.3 255.255.255.0

router rip
    network 130.10.0.0
```

Adding OSPF to the Center of a RIP Network

A common first step in converting a RIP network to an OSPF network is to add backbone routers that run both RIP and OSPF, while the remaining network devices run RIP. These backbone routers are OSPF ASBRs. Each ASBR controls the flow of routing information between OSPF and RIP. In Figure 6-15, Router A is configured as the ASBR.

Figure 6–15
*RIP with an
OSPF center.*

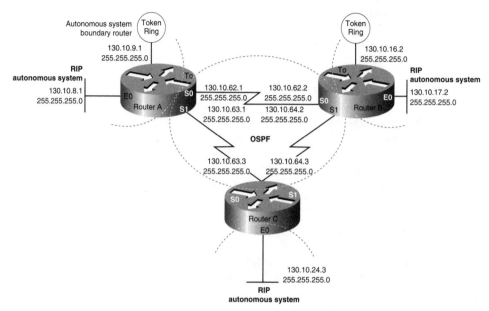

RIP does not need to run between the backbone routers; therefore, RIP is suppressed on
Router A with the following commands:

```
router rip
    passive-interface serial 0
    passive-interface serial 1
```

The RIP routes are redistributed into OSPF by all three routers with the following
commands:

```
router ospf 109
    redistribute rip subnets
    network 13.10.0.0
```

The subnets keyword tells OSPF to redistribute all subnet routes. Without the subnets
keyword, only networks that are not subnetted will be redistributed by OSPF. Redistributed routes appear as external type 2 routes in OSPF. For more detail on route types,
refer to the text earlier in this chapter or see the Cisco Internetwork Operating System
(Cisco IOS) command references.

Each RIP domain receives information about networks in other RIP domains and in the
OSPF backbone area from the following commands that redistribute OSPF routes into
RIP:

```
router rip
    redistribute ospf 109 match internal external 1 external 2
    default-metric 10
```

The `redistribute` command uses the `ospf` keyword to specify that OSPF routes are redistributed into RIP. The keyword `internal` indicates the OSPF intra-area and inter-area routes: external 1 is the external route type 1, and external 2 is the external route type 2. Because the command in the example uses the default behavior, these keywords might not appear when you use the `write terminal` or `show configuration` commands.

Because metrics for different protocols cannot be directly compared, you must specify the default metric in order to designate the cost of the redistributed route used in RIP updates. All routes that are redistributed will use the default metric.

As illustrated in Figure 6-15, there are no paths directly connecting the RIP clouds. However, in typical networks, these paths, or "back doors," frequently exist, allowing the potential for feedback loops. You can use access lists to determine the routes that are advertised and accepted by each router.

For example, access list 11 in the configuration file for Router A allows OSPF to redistribute information learned from RIP only for networks `130.10.8.0` through `130.10.15.0`:

```
router ospf 109
  redistribute rip subnet
  distribute-list 11 out rip

access-list 11 permit 130.10.8.0 0.0.7.255
access-list 11 deny 0.0.0.0 255.255.255.255
```

These commands prevent Router A from advertising networks in other RIP domains onto the OSPF backbone, thereby preventing other boundary routers from using false information and forming a loop.

Configuration File Examples

Compare the partial configuration options with the full configuration files for the routers in question.

Full Configuration for Router A

```
interface serial 0
  ip address 130.10.62.1 255.255.255.0
interface serial 1
  ip address 130.10.63.1 255.255.255.0
interface ethernet 0
  ip address 130.10.8.1 255.255.255.0
interface tokenring 0
  ip address 130.10.9.1 255.255.255.0
```

```
!
router rip
 default-metric 10
 network 130.10.0.0
 passive-interface serial 0
 passive-interface serial 1
 redistribute ospf 109 match internal external 1 external 2
!
router ospf 109
 network 130.10.62.0 0.0.0.255 area 0
 network 130.10.63.0 0.0.0.255 area 0
 redistribute rip subnets
 distribute-list 11 out rip
!
access-list 11 permit 130.10.8.0 0.0.7.255
access-list 11 deny 0.0.0.0 255.255.255.255
```

Full Configuration for Router B

```
interface serial 0
 ip address 130.10.62.2 255.255.255.0
interface serial 1
 ip address 130.10.64.2 255.255.255.0
interface ethernet 0
 ip address 130.10.17.2 255.255.255.0
interface tokenring 0
 ip address 130.10.16.2 255.255.255.0
!
router rip
 default-metric 10
 network 130.10.0.0
 passive-interface serial 0
 passive-interface serial 1
 redistribute ospf 109 match internal external 1 external 2
!
router ospf 109
 network 130.10.62.0 0.0.0.255 area 0
 network 130.10.64.0 0.0.0.255 area 0
 redistribute rip subnets
 distribute-list 11 out rip
access-list 11 permit 130.10.16.0 0.0.7.255
access-list 11 deny 0.0.0.0 255.255.255.255
```

Full Configuration for Router C

```
interface serial 0
 ip address 130.10.63.3 255.255.255.0
interface serial 1
 ip address 130.10.64.3 255.255.255.0
interface ethernet 0
 ip address 130.10.24.3 255.255.255.0
!
router rip
 default-metric 10
!
network 130.10.0.0
 passive-interface serial 0
 passive-interface serial 1
 redistribute ospf 109 match internal external 1 external 2
!
router ospf 109
 network 130.10.63.0 0.0.0.255 area 0
 network 130.10.64.0 0.0.0.255 area 0
 redistribute rip subnets
 distribute-list 11 out rip
 access-list 11 permit 130.10.24.0 0.0.7.255
 access-list 11 deny 0.0.0.0 255.255.255.255
```

Adding OSPF Areas

Figure 6-16 illustrates how each of the RIP clouds can be converted into an OSPF area. All three routers are ABRs. ABRs control network information distribution between OSPF areas and the OSPF backbone. Each router keeps a detailed record of the topology of its area and receives summarized information from the other ABRs on their respective areas.

Figure 6-16 also illustrates VLSMs. VLSMs use different size network masks in different parts of the network for the same network number. VLSM conserves address space by using a longer mask in portions of the network that have fewer hosts.

Table 6-4 lists the network address assignments for the network, including the network number, subnet range, and subnet masks. All interfaces indicate network 130.10.0.0.

Figure 6–16
*Configuring
route
summarization
between OSPF
areas.*

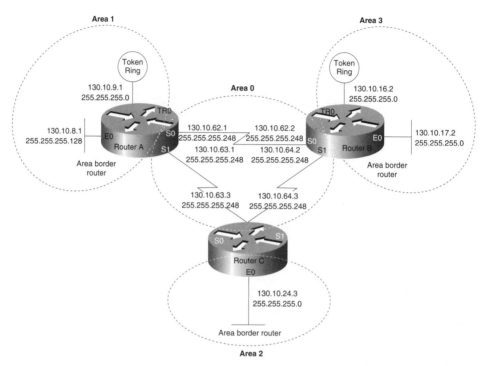

Table 6-4   *SPF address assignments*

Network Number	Subnets	Subnet Masks
130.10.0.0	Area 0: 62–64	255.255.255.248
130.10.0.0	Area 1: 8–15	255.255.255.0
130.10.0.0	Area 2: 16–23	255.255.255.0
130.10.0.0	Area 3: 24–31	255.255.255.0

To conserve address space, a mask of 255.255.255.248 is used for all the serial lines in area 0. If an area contains a contiguous range of network numbers, an ABR uses the range keyword with the area command to summarize the routes that are injected into the backbone:

```
router ospf 109
    network 130.10.8.0 0.0.7.255 area 1
    area 1 range 130.10.8.0 255.255.248.0
```

These commands allow Router A to advertise one route, 130.10.8.0 255.255.248.0 that covers all subnets in Area 1, into Area 0. Without the range keyword in the area command, Router A would advertise each subnet individually; for example, one route for 130.10.8.0 255.255.255.0, one route for 130.10.9.0 255.255.255.0, and so forth.

Because Router A no longer needs to redistribute RIP routes, the router rip command can now be removed from the configuration file; however, it is common in some environments for hosts to use RIP to discover routers. When RIP is removed from the routers, the hosts must use an alternate technique to find the routers. Cisco routers support the IRDP and ARP alternatives to RIP.

The ICMP Router Discovery Protocol (IRDP) technique is illustrated in the example at the end of this section. IRDP is the recommended method for discovering routers. The ip irdp command enables IRDP on the router. Hosts must also run IRDP.

With proxy Address Resolution Protocol (ARP), if the router receives an ARP request for a host that is not on the same network as the ARP request sender, and if the router has the best route to that host, then the router sends an ARP reply packet giving the router's own local data link address. The host that sent the ARP request then sends its packets to the router, which forwards these packets to the intended host. Proxy ARP is enabled on routers by default. Proxy ARP is transparent to hosts.

The proxy ARP alternative is not illustrated in this case study. See the Cisco IOS command references for details on this feature.

Configuration File Examples

The following configuration files reflect the presence of OSPF within the network and on the routers.

Full Configuration for Router A

```
interface serial 0
    ip address 130.10.62.1 255.255.255.248

interface serial 1
    ip address 130.10.63.1 255.255.255.248

interface ethernet 0
    ip address 130.10.8.1 255.255.255.0
    ip irdp

interface tokenring 0
    ip address 130.10.9.1 255.255.255.0
    ip irdp
```

```
router ospf 109
  network 130.10.62.0 0.0.0.255 area 0
  network 130.10.63.0 0.0.0.255 area 0
  network 130.10.8.0 0.0.7.255 area 1
  area 1 range 130.10.8.0 255.255.248.0
```

Full Configuration for Router B

```
interface serial 0
  ip address 130.10.62.2 255.255.255.248

interface serial 1
  ip address 130.10.64.2 255.255.255.248

interface ethernet 0
  ip address 130.10.17.2 255.255.255.0
  ip irdp

interface tokenring 0
  ip address 130.10.16.2 255.255.255.0
  ip irdp

router ospf 109
  network 130.10.62.0 0.0.0.255 area 0
  network 130.10.64.0 0.0.0.255 area 0
  network 130.10.16.0 0.0.7.255 area 2
  area 2 range 130.10.16.0 255.255.248.0
```

Full Configuration for Router C

```
interface serial 0
  ip address 130.10.63.2 255.255.255.248

interface serial 1
  ip address 130.10.64.2 255.255.255.248

interface ethernet 0
  ip address 130.10.24.3 255.255.255.0
  ip irdp

router ospf 109
  network 130.10.63.0 0.0.0.255 area 0
  network 130.10.64.0 0.0.0.255 area 0
  network 130.10.24.0 0.0.0.255 area 3
  area 3 range 130.10.24.0 255.255.248.0
```

Setting Up Mutual Redistribution

It is sometimes necessary to accommodate more complex network topologies such as independent RIP and OSPF clouds that must perform mutual redistribution. In this scenario, it is critically important to prevent potential routing loops by filtering routes. The router in Figure 6-17 is running both OSPF and RIP.

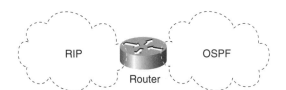

Figure 6–17
Mutual redistribution between RIP and OSPF networks.

With the following commands, OSPF routes will be redistributed into RIP. You must specify the default metric to designate the cost of the redistributed route in RIP updates. All routes redistributed into RIP will have this default metric:

```
! passive interface subcommand from previous example is left out for
clarity!
router rip
default-metric 10
network 130.10.0.0
redistribute ospf 109
```

It is a good practice to strictly control which routes are advertised when redistribution is configured. In the following example, a `distribute-list` out command causes RIP to ignore routes coming from the OSPF that originated from the RIP domain:

```
router rip
distribute-list 10 out ospf 109
!
access-list 10 deny 130.10.8.0 0.0.7.255
access-list 10 permit 0.0.0.0 255.255.255.255
```

Full Configuration for Router A

```
interface serial 0
ip add 130.10.62.1 255.255.255.0
!
interface serial 1
ip add 130.10.63.1 255.255.255.0
!
```

```
interface ethernet 0
ip add 130.10.8.1 255.255.255.0
!
interface tokenring 0
ip add 130.10.9.1 255.255.255.0
!
router rip
default-metric 10
network 130.10.0.0
passive-interface serial 0
passive-interface serial 1
redistribute ospf 109
distribute-list 10 out ospf 109
!
router ospf 109
network 130.10.62.0 0.0.0.255 area 0
network 130.10.63.0 0.0.0.255 area 0
redistribute rip subnets
distribute-list 11 out rip
!
access-list 10 deny 130.10.8.0 0.0.7.255
access-list 10 permit 0.0.0.0 255.255.255.255
access-list 11 permit 130.10.8.0 0.0.7.255
access-list 11 deny 0.0.0.0 255.255.255.255
```

Case Study Conclusion

Because it is common for OSPF and RIP to be used together, it is important to use the practices described here in order to provide functionality for both protocols on an internetwork. You can configure ASBRs that run both RIP and OSPF and redistribute RIP routes into the OSPF and vice versa. You can also create OSPF areas using ABRs that provide route summarizations. Use VLSM to conserve address space.

FREQUENTLY ASKED QUESTIONS

Q— *Are there any outstanding issues with routing OSPF over IP unnumbered interfaces?*

A— Yes, Cisco bug ID: CSCdi46217 discusses problems with IOS 11.3(8) and 11.0(3) where OSPF cannot route packets over ISDN with IP unnumbered on the interface. This problem has been fixed in later versions of the IOS. Consult the TAC if you have any further questions or if you think the IOS is not running OSPF properly.

Q— *I am using OSPF Debugging and the router is giving me an error message:* `authentication-key match fails clear text`. *What does this mean?*

A— This message is being generated by OSPF because it is detecting a neighboring router that has a different authentication key than the router giving the message.

Q— *I have OSPF configured on a X.25 network and it is not routing correctly when looking at the OSPF database in the router. I can see all the correct networks but when executing a* show IP route, *there is no routing table.*

A— Make sure that the command IP OSPF Network Broadcast is applied to all interfaces connected to other OSPF routers.

Q— *I am redistributing routes into OSPF and my subnetted routes are not being redistributed. Why?*

A— When redistributing routes into OSPF, if the keyword subnets is not specified in the router running OSPF, they will not be redistributed. The default in the redistribution command is to only allow unsubnetted routes through.

Q— *When you force OSPF to generate a default route (default-information originate always metric 50 route-map abc), how does OSPF know the IP address of the default gateway?*

A— OSPF does not care. Default route is announced as external route in OSPF and the only information you have about an external route is which router is announcing it (plus the metric).

Q— *Will OSPF work well in an FDDI environment?*

A— Yes. FDDI is what a lot of people use as their backbone (area 0).

Q— *Do we have to manually set up adjacencies for routers on the SMDS cloud with the OSPF* neighbor *subcommand?*

A— In Cisco IOS 9.1, you need the OSPF neighbor command to make OSPF work on SMDS. In Cisco IOS 9.21 and later, you use the multicast capability. Note that neighbors are no longer needed as of IOS 10.3

Q— *Does the* offset-list *subcommand work for OSPF, or is it implemented only for IGRP, RIP, and Hello?*

A— It is implemented only for IGRP, RIP, and Hello. It does not work with OSPF.

Q— *For OSPF, is there a suggested method of determining the lowest possible* ospf dead-interval *to use (and corresponding* ospf hello-interval *to use with the* dead-interval*)? We are currently using the default values and would like to reduce the convergence time.*

A— The default value for the dead-interval is four times the hello interval. In Cisco's implementation, that is 40 seconds for broadcast networks and two minutes for nonbroadcast networks. However, adjusting these parameters might not be sufficient enough to meet your needs, and things like network topology, traffic loading, and keepalive timers on the interfaces also play key roles in determining the speed of the convergence time. As this request can't be answered in a single sentence, you should contact your local support for assistance so that a detailed evaluation can be performed on your network before any OSPF parameter is adjusted. However, if you have decided to do it yourself, keep in mind that if you lower the dead-interval timer, be sure to lower the hello-interval timer as well. In addition, the hello-interval timer must be the same for all nodes on a specific network. This rule also applies to the dead-interval timer.

Q— *Will a Cisco router transform subnet mask information correctly if I redistribute OSPF into IGRP? My users are clamoring for VLSM. I'd like to give them the ability to use OSPF (or other routing protocol of their choosing) in the Ethernet side of their router, while still maintaining IGRP across the WAN. Will this work? We use a 9-bit mask on the WAN side. The mask on the LAN side varies between 4 and 12 bits.*

A— No, it won't work because IGRP doesn't support VLSM. When you are redistributing the VLSM routes into IGRP, some or all of the VLSM routes will be lost. If VLSM is definitely required, then you will have to run either

OSPF or EIGRP on your WAN side to accommodate the VLSM routes from the remote sites. You could run IS-IS, but it is more complicated.

Q— *I have a Cisco 7010 router that is running OSPF and IGRP. OSPF is used to route within my network, and IGRP is used to my service provider. I redistribute between them. I also have two static routes. I have a requirement to advertise one of my static routes out all of my OSPF interfaces and my IGRP interface. The second static route needs to be advertised out all of my OSPF interfaces but needs to be filtered from being advertised to my service provider via IGRP. I think I need to use the* distribute-list *and* access-list *commands in my IGRP process, but I am not sure how to do it.*

A— The best way is to use route-map. Here is an example:

```
!
   router ospf 333
   redistribute static subnets route-map ospf-static
   network 128.30.0.0 0.0.255.255 area 0.0.0.0
!
   router igrp 187
   redistribute static subnets route-map igrp-static
   network 128.99.0.0
!
   ip route 128.30.20.0 255.255.255.0 128.30.28.21
   ip route 128.30.26.0 255.255.255.0 128.30.28.22
   ip route 128.101.0.0 255.255.0.0 128.99.15.2
!
   access-list 7 permit 128.30.20.0 0.0.0.255
   access-list 7 permit 128.30.26.0 0.0.0.255
   access-list 7 deny any
   access-list 8 permit 128.101.0.0 0.0.255.255
   access-list 8 deny any
!
   route-map ospf-static permit 10
   match ip address 7
!
   route-map igrp-static permit 10
   match ip address 8
```

In the preceding example, there are three static routes defined. The first two static routes will be redistributed into the OSPF domain only, and the very last static route will be redistributed into the IGRP domain only.

Q— *Can EIGRP or OSPF give me full connectivity for IP and IPX in a partially-meshed Frame Relay network? Or will I have to configure subinterfaces?*

A— OSPF has a feature called point-to-multipoint interfaces to easily allow full connectivity over a partially-meshed Frame Relay network in Cisco IOS 11.0 and later. It could be done before Cisco IOS 11.0, but it required the hub router to be the designated router and some map statements on each spoke router to all the rest of the spoke routers through the hub router. By the way, OSPF only supports IP. EIGRP does allow it, too, but requires careful configuration, taking the non–fully-meshed nature on the network into consideration.

Q— *I have both OSPF and EIGRP running with default administrative distances. Will the OSPF routing table be ignored because it has a higher cost? If I then add static routes, will the OSPF and EIGRP be ignored until I remove the static routes?*

A— Yes. The default administrative distances are: Static 1; EIGRP 90; OSPF 110. Therefore, static is always preferred over an EIGRP/OSPF route to the same destination. The administrative distance is a measure of the trustworthiness of a routing information source. The default administrative distance can be altered using the distance command, but this is not recommended.

Q— *What is the purpose of the* `ip-ospf-transmit-delay` *command?*

A— If the delay is not added before transmission over a link, the time in which the LSA propagates over the link is not considered. The default value for this command is one second. This parameter has more significance on very low-speed links, where it can alleviate some bandwidth constraint.

Q— *In Cisco IOS 9.1, is the* `neighbor` *command required when running OSPF over X.25 networks?*

A— You need the neighbor command to make OSPF work on X.25 in Cisco IOS 9.1. In 9.21 and later, at OSPF level, an X.25 network can be configured to be a broadcast network, and OSPF treats X.25 as a broadcast network only. X.25 maps with the `broadcast` keyword are be needed to make it work.

Q— *What does* `%OSPF-3-DBEXIST` *mean?*

A— This message appears when the router receives an LSA older than the one in its own database. No action is necessary. A DDT (CSCdi48981) exists to document this message.

Q— *Can I run OSPF with IOS 9.1? I want to change my routing protocol from RIP to OSPF. I have a WAN network with IGS routers running Cisco IOS 9.1 to Cisco 7513s running Cisco IOS 11.0. The network consists of 20 routers.*

A— Yes, running OSPF in 9.1 software is fine. Sites with Cisco IOS 11.0 and Cisco IOS 9.1 together are all running OSPF without any problems.

Q— *I need help to understand Cisco's OSPF network statements. I have a router that I am configuring for OSPF. The router has two interfaces:*
```
e0 - 10.120.175.254 mask 255.255.255.128
s0 - 10.120.173.114 mask 255.255.255.252 (numbered serial, 8
address subnet)
```
Both interfaces belong in the same area. However, when I use the following commands, OSPF does not work:
```
network 10.120.175.128 0.0.0.128 area 0.0.0.2
network 10.120.173.112 0.0.0.252 area 0.0.0.2
```
Cisco IOS appears to have problems resolving the VLSM that I've defined. What am I missing?

A— Your network statements should have been:
```
network 10.120.175.128 0.0.0.127 area 0.0.0.2
network 10.120.173.112 0.0.0.3 area 0.0.0.2
```
OSPF uses inverse masks for defining the VLSM:
```
* 0.0.0.127 is the inverse mask for 128 (127 + 128 = 255)
* 0.0.0.3 is the inverse mask for 252 (252 + 3 = 255)
```
Q— *What is the difference between Type 1 and Type 2 external routes in OSPF?*

A— Type 2 uses only the external cost as set in the ASBR. The cost doesn't change as the route is propagated. Type 1 adds internal OSPF costs as the route is propagated. The default is Type 2, but this can be overridden.

Q—*Does OSPF automatically load balance or are additional commands needed? (I have parallel T1 serial links going between an OSPF Area 0 router and an Area 1 router.)*

A— The router will load balance over two T1 links if it sees equal OSPF costs to a given destination. The default is up to four parallel paths, and in your case, it should be two. You can verify this by doing a `show ip route` and look for two paths to a given destination network across the WAN links.

Also, if IP fast-switching is turned on, the router will load balance on a per-destination basis, and if IP fast-switching is turned off, the router will load balance on a packet-by-packet basis.

PART 3

OSPF Implementation, Troubleshooting & Management

"The Man in the Arena: It is not the critic who counts, not the one who points out how the strong man stumbled or how the doer of deeds might have done them better. The credit belongs to the man who is actually in the arena, whose face is marred with sweat, dust, and blood; who strives valiantly; who errs and comes short again and again; who knows the great enthusiasm, the great devotions, and spends himself in a worthy cause; who if he fails, at least while daring greatly, so that his place shall never be with those cold and timid souls who know neither victory nor defeat."—Anonymous

This section moves into the actual design, implementation, and management of an OSPF network. This information will be presented in three chapters:

Chapter 7, **"Designing & Implementing an OSPF Network,"** covers the actual process of sitting down and designing your OSPF network, including how to configure OSPF on Cisco routers.

Chapter 8, **"Monitoring & Troubleshooting an OSPF Network,"** covers how to about monitoring and ensuring that OSPF is operating correctly and what to do if i not.

Chapter 9, **"Managing Your OSPF Network,"** covers the fundamentals of O network management as well as Simple Network Management Protocol (SNMP) a Management Information Bases (MIBs).

CHAPTER 7

Designing & Implementing an OSPF Network

"Imagination: A mind once stretched by a new idea never regains its original dimensions."—Successories

This chapter covers the actual process of sitting down and designing your OSPF network. The real process of putting the pen to paper and the true process behind it is covered. It is this chapter's intention to take the mystery out of designing any type of network. The concepts and steps discussed have universal application whether your network is BGP or OSPF; of course, the latter is emphasized. Chapter 6, "Advanced OSPF Design Concepts," covered many of the commands necessary for configuring OSPF. In this chapter, you will become familiar with the necessary steps to actually begin the OSPF process on a Cisco router. You already know there are many potential network architectures where you would have to configure OSPF, and the most common are covered in this chapter. This chapter has two specific sections as follows:

- **OSPF Network Design.** This section reviews the specific network design goals that should be the general basis of every network. There are certain issues that you must be aware of as network designers, and they are discussed in this section. The six fundamental steps that make up the Network Design Methodology are covered with special enhancements given to issues regarding OSPF.

- **Configuring OSPF on Cisco Routers.** At this point in the book, you have everything you need to know about how OSPF works and how to go about designing and implementing an OSPF network. But how do you turn on OSPF? This section addresses basic and advanced configuration issues as relate to Cisco routers. A bonus area is covered as well that deals with multi-protocol routers.

OSPF NETWORK DESIGN

This book has discussed the various design techniques for OSPF, from the various golden rules to the number of routers per area. It is now time to actually take this information and begin the process of designing an OSPF network. Let's begin the process by determining what is actually supported by Cisco Systems.

Cisco's Implementation of OSPF

As discussed in Chapter 4, "Introduction to OSPF," there is a variety of RFCs that deal with OSPF. By now, you should be familiar with the many different features available within the OSPF protocol. But which RFCs does Cisco support within its products?

- **RFC 1253: Open Shortest Path First (OSPF) MIB.** This RFC contains the information, which provides management information relating to OSPF.

- **RFC 1583: OSPF Version 2.** Cisco's implementation conforms to the specifications as detailed in this RFC. They support the following key features: stub areas, route redistribution, authentication (covered later), tunable interface parameters, and virtual links.

- **RFC 1587: Not-So-Stubby-Areas (NSSA).** Cisco equipment supports the use of all types of stub areas.

- **RFC 1793: OSPF over Demand Circuits.** Cisco supports this RFC as well.

Network Design Goals

It is not necessary to get into the reasons behind your decision to build an OSPF network or any of the previously covered definitions of what a network is. However, the five basic goals that you should keep in mind while designing your OSPF network (or any network for that matter) should be adhered to:

- Functionality

- Scalability

- Adaptability

- Manageability

- Cost effectiveness

Functionality

"The network must work" is the absolute bottom line. Because networks are an integral part of enabling individual users to do their jobs, this is essential. It is here that the use of Service Level Agreements (SLAs) is essential. You must know what is expected of the network in order to design it properly.

Scalability

As your organization grows, the network must be able to keep pace. Your network and its initial design must enable it to expand accordingly. A network that cannot keep pace with the organization's needs is not much use.

Routing summarization is a major factor in the success of designing your network. If you want to ensure your network can scale properly, the summarization is the biggest factor on your success. Without summarization, you will have a flat address design with specific route information for every host being transmitted across the network, a very bad thing in large networks. To briefly review summarization, remember that routers summarize at several levels, as shown in Figure 7-1. For example, hosts are grouped into subnetworks, subnetworks are then grouped into major networks, and these are then consolidated in areas. The network can then be grouped into an autonomous system.

NOTES

There are many smaller networks that desire to use a "standard" routing protocol such as OSPF. These networks can, for example, have 100 or less routers with a relatively small IP space. In these situations, summarization may not be possible and might not gain much if it were implemented.

Adaptability

Adaptability refers to your network's capability to respond to changes. In most cases, adaptability refers to your network's capability to embrace new technologies in a timely and efficient manner. This becomes extremely important as the network ages because change within networking is racing forward at breakneck speeds. Though it is not necessary to always be on the leading or bleeding edge—there is a lot to be said for letting others find the bugs!

Figure 7–1
*Route
summarization
affects network
scalability.*

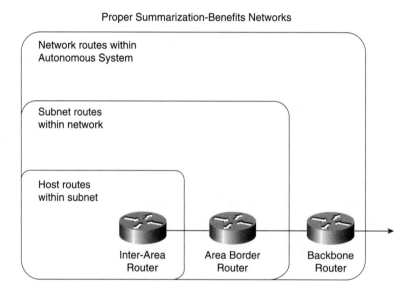

Proper Summarization-Benefits Networks

Manageability

To provide "true" proactive network management is the goal here. The network must have the proper tools and design to ensure you are always aware of its operation and current status.

Cost Effectiveness

In this case, I have saved the true bottom line of network design for last. The reality of life is that budgets and resources are limited, and building or expanding the network while staying within the predetermined budget is always a benefit to your career and proper network design.

Although there are five basic goals of network design that can be followed in any situation, I think there also should be a certain mindset during the process. This mindset is regarding the actual technology you will be using. It is very important to use state-of-the-art technologies whenever possible, though this does not mean to use unproven or inadequately tested technology. The reasoning behind this is that by spending a little extra money up front, you are investing with an eye to the future knowing that the network you are building will be able to grow, from a technological standpoint, longer than otherwise possible.

Network Design Issues

Up until this point, the various network design goals and the methodology needed to make the goals become a reality have been discussed. There are also certain design issues that you must consider when working through the network design process:

- **Reliability.** When designing networks, reliability is usually the most important goal, as the WAN is often the backbone of any network.

- **Latency.** Another big concern with users occurs when network access requests take a long time to be granted. Users should be notified about a latency problem in the network.

- **Cost of WAN resources.** WAN resources are expensive, and as such, frequently involve a tradeoff between cost efficiency and full network redundancy. Usually cost efficiency wins.

- **Amount of traffic.** This is a very straightforward consideration. You must be able to accurately determine the amount of traffic that will be on the network in order to properly size the various components that will make it up. As you implement the network, you should also develop a baseline that can be used to project future growth.

- **Allowing multiple protocols on the WAN.** The simplicity of IP is of great benefit to any network. For example, by only allowing IP-based protocols on the network you will avoid the unique addressing and configuration issues relating to other protocols.

- **Compatibility with standards or legacy systems.** Compatibility is always going to be an issue within your network throughout its life. As a network designer, you need to always keep this in mind as you proceed.

- **Simplicity and easy configuration.** Having been a network engineer for many years and involved in network management, this feature is doubly important to me. You might only be involved in the design and implementation of the network and not the management. In that case, the knowledge you will develop will need to be passed on to those who will manage the network. Ensure that you keep the ideas of simplicity and ease of configuration in mind while you develop your design documents for the network.

- **Support for remote offices and telecommuters.** In today's telecommunications environment, remote satellite offices are becoming commonplace and require network connectivity, so you must plan accordingly. The estimates say that every day you will see companies increase the number of telecommuters. You must keep this in mind as you determine the placement of network components to ensure that they can handle this requirement when it becomes a priority for your organization.

Network Design Methodology

There are six common steps that can be used to design your OSPF network, or any network for that matter. This are not set in stone and will not guarantee the "perfect" network, but they will provide you with realistic steps and considerations that if taken into account will make for well designed network. These steps will also help you avoid getting caught up in all the "bells and whistles" available in the new-enhanced-ultra-secret-turbo-series-network-equipment which is the answer to all your networking needs.

These steps to designing a network have been proven not only over time, but also through countless networks that have been designed and implemented based upon this standard.

1. Analyze the requirements.

2. Develop the network topology.

3. Determine addressing and naming conventions.

4. Provision the hardware.

5. Deploy protocol and IOS features.

6. Implement, monitor, and maintain the network.

Although your network might not have the technology du jour, it might not really need it if you objectively determine the needs of a network by following this design methodology (as shown in Figure 7-2).

Step 1: Analyze the Requirements

This step will detail the process of determining expectations and then converting those into a real network or explaining why everyone can't have video conferencing on the desktop.

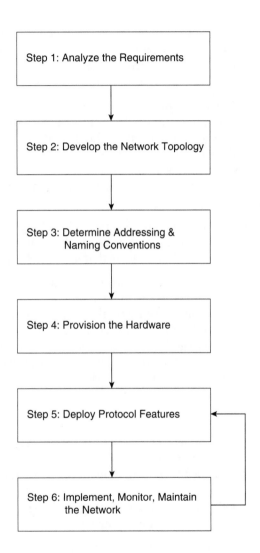

Figure 7–2
Network design methodology.

Step 1: Analyze the Requirements

Step 2: Develop the Network Topology

Step 3: Determine Addressing & Naming Conventions

Step 4: Provision the Hardware

Step 5: Deploy Protocol Features

Step 6: Implement, Monitor, Maintain the Network

NOTES

What do you know? Going into Step 1, you know that an OSPF network is required but not what it will need to accomplish for your users or how you will need to physically design the network.

Granted, the needs of users are always changing, and sometimes they do not even know what they need. There I said it! However, it is true; they know what they want and when they want it, which is always now or yesterday. Nevertheless, from a network design prospective, they do not always know what they need or why they need it.

Nevertheless, you, as the network engineer involved in the design of the network, must still objectively listen and determine user needs. In the end, they are going to be the customers of network, and the customer is always right. You must also take into consideration what the future might hold for them. Therefore, you should ask the users what needs they see themselves having in the future. This question should be directed toward their jobs because it is your responsibility to take their response and turn that into the requirements of the network.

A corporate vision is always important. For example, do the long-range corporate plans include having a Web site? If so, what will it be doing? How about running voice over the network? What about video conferencing; is that going to be a corporate need?

Additional data you might want to consider gathering is the current organization structure, locations, and flow of information within the organization and any internal or external resources available to you. Armed with this information, your networks need analysis, you should then begin determining the cost and benefit analysis. Of course in many cases you will not be able to get all the equipment or bandwidth you think is necessary. Therefore, it is also advisable to create a risk assessment detailing the potential problems or areas of concern regarding the network design.

OSPF Deployment

As you go through the process of determining the network requirements, keep in mind some important questions regarding the requirements of OSPF. The answers to these questions will help you further define the requirements of your OSPF network.

- How should the OSPF Autonomous System be delineated? How many areas should it have and what should the boundaries be?

- Does your network and its data need to have built-in security?

- What information from other Autonomous Systems should be imported into your network?

- Which sites will have links that should be preferred (lower cost)?

- Which sites will have links that should be avoided (higher cost)?

Load Balancing with OSPF

As you go through the process of determining the network requirements, keep in mind the load balancing feature of OSPF. In the Cisco implementation of OSPF, any router can support up to four equal-cost routes to a destination. When a failure to the destination is recognized, OSPF immediately switches to the remaining paths.

OSPF will automatically perform load balancing allow equal-cost paths. The cost associated is determined (default) by the interface bandwidth statement unless otherwise configured to maximize multiple path routing.

Before Cisco's IOS release 10.3, the default cost was calculated by dividing 1,000,000,000 by the default bandwidth of the interface. However, with IOS releases after 10.3, the cost is calculated by dividing 1,000,000,000 by the configured bandwidth of the interface as illustrated in Figure 7-3.

TIPS

In IOS 11.3, this issue has been addressed with the command `ospf auto-cost`

`reference bandwidth`.

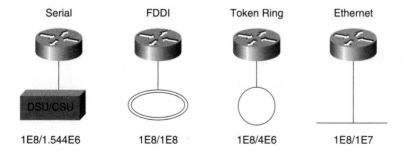

Serial	FDDI	Token Ring	Ethernet
1E8/1.544E6	1E8/1E8	1E8/4E6	1E8/1E7

Figure 7–3
OSPF costs.

OSPF Convergence

OSPF convergence is extremely fast when compared to other protocols; this was one of the main features included within its initial design. To keep this desirable feature fully functional in your network, you need to consider the three components that determine how long it takes for OSPF to converge:

- The length of time it takes OSPF to detect a link or interface failure
- The length of time it takes the routers to exchange routing information via LSAs, rerun the Shortest Path First algorithm, and build a new routing table
- A built-in SPF delay time of five seconds (default value)

Thus, the average time for OSPF to propagate LSAs and rerun the SPF algorithm is approximately 1 second. Then the SPF delay timer of five seconds must elapse. Therefor OSPF convergence can be a anything from 6 to 46 seconds, depending upon the type of failure, SPF timer settings, size of the network, and size of the LSA database. The worst case scenario is when a link fails but the destination is still reachable via an alternate route, because the 40 second default dead timer will need to expire before the SPF is rerun.

Step 2: Develop the Network Topology

This step will cover the process of determining the networks physical layout. There are generally only two common design topologies: meshed or hierarchical. The following sections take a look at each to see which is the most efficient design for today's networks.

NOTES

What do you know? Going into Step 2, you've developed a list of the requirements associated with this OSPF network. You have also begun to lay out the financial costs associated with the network based upon this information. These costs could include equipment, memory, and associated media.

Meshed Topology

In a meshed structure, the topology is flat and all routers perform essentially the same function, so there is no clear definition of where specific functions are performed. Network expansion tends to proceed in a haphazard, arbitrary manner. This type of topology is not acceptable to the operation of OSPF. It will not correctly support the use of areas or designated routers.

Hierarchical Topology

In a hierarchical topology, the network is organized in layers that will have clearly defined functions. In this type of network there are three layers:

- **Core Layer.** This would make an excellent place for OSPF Backbone Routers that are all connected through area 0. All of these routers would be interconnected, and there should not be any host connections. This is because its primary purpose is to provide connectivity between other areas.

- **Distribution Layer.** It is here that you would locate other OSPF areas all connected through Area Border Routers (ABRs) back to the Core Layer (area 0). This is also a good location to begin implementing various network policies such as security, DNS, etc...)

- **Access Layer.** This is where the inter-area routers that provide connections to the users would be located. This layer ID is where the majority of the hosts and servers should be connecting to the network.

By using this type of logical layered network design, you will gain some benefits that will help you design the network as shown in Figure 7-4.

The benefits of the OSPF hierarchical topology as implemented in Figure 7-4 are as follows:

- **Scalable.** Networks can grow easily because functionality is localized so additional sites can be added easily and quickly.

- **Ease of Implementation.** This physical topology fits easily into OSPF's logical hierarchy, making network implementation easier.

- **Ease of Troubleshooting.** Because functionality is localized, it is easier to recognize problem locations and isolate them.

Figure 7–4
*OSPF
hierarchical
topology.*

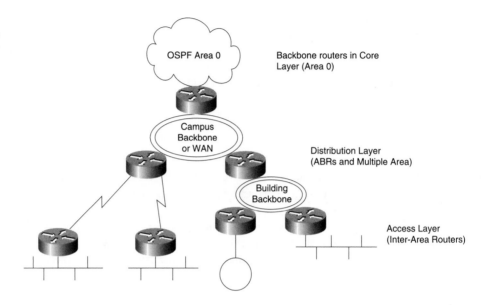

- **Predictability.** Because of the layered approach, the functionality of each layer is much more predictable. This makes capacity planning and modeling that much easier.

- **Protocol Support.** Because an underlying physical architecture is already in place if you want to incorporate additional protocols, such as BGP, or if your organization acquires a network running a different protocol, you will be able to easily add it.

- **Manageability.** The physical layout of the network lends itself towards logical areas that make network management much easier.

There are other variations of the three-layered hierarchical design that are available are one layer—distributed, hub and spoke—and two layers, but they are beyond the scope of this book. At this point, though, you can see that the three layered hierarchical model fits perfectly into OSPF's logical design, and it is this model on which you will be basing your network design. Before discussing how to implement and design this type of model, you need some basic OSPF backbone design suggestions.

OSPF Backbone Design in the Hierarchical Model

The process of designing the backbone area has been previously discussed, so it will be only briefly reviewed here. Always keep the backbone area as simple as possible by avoiding a complex mesh. Consider using a LAN solution for the backbone. The transit across the backbone is always one hop, latency is minimized, and it is a simple design that converges very quickly. Figure 7-5 illustrates a simple OSPF backbone design.

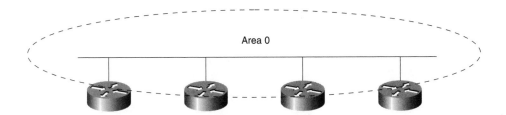

Area 0

Figure 7–5
Simple OSPF backbone design.

You know that you should keep users off the backbone because it is only a transit area, but that is not enough. You also need to consider securing your backbone physically. As a network critical shared resource, the routers need to be physically secure. If you use the previously mentioned LAN backbone solution, then securing your network can be relatively easy; just put it in a secure closet or rack as shown in Figure 7-6.

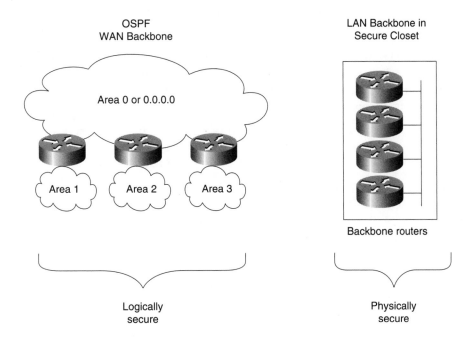

OSPF
WAN Backbone

Area 0 or 0.0.0.0

Area 1   Area 2   Area 3

Logically
secure

LAN Backbone in
Secure Closet

Backbone routers

Physically
secure

Figure 7–6
Isolate the backbone and secure it both physically and logically.

Areas: Stub, Totally Stubby, or Not-So-Stubby

You will have to design your OSPF network with areas to make the network scalable and efficient. Areas have been discussed in previous chapters, but let's briefly review them at this point. Areas should be kept simple, stubby, with less than 100 (optimally 40–50) routers, and have maximum summarization for ease of routing. The network illustrated in Figure 7-7 demonstrates these suggestions.

Figure 7–7
OSPF network with areas.

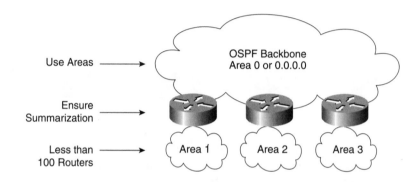

Even though these design suggestions are helpful, what are you really going to gain in your network by adding stub areas? Simply put, they will summarize all external LSAs as one single default LSA that applies only to the external links from outside the autonomous system. The stub area border router sees all the LSAs for the entire network and floods them to other stub area routers. They keep the LSA database for the stub area with this additional information and the default external route. Figure 7-8 illustrates the operations in a stub area.

There are also totally stubby areas that you could design within your network. Totally stubby areas are a Cisco-specific feature available within their implementation of the OSPF standard. You can use totally stubby areas in Cisco IOS Release 9.1 and later.

If an area is configured as totally stubby, only the default summary link is propagated into the area by the ABR. It is important to note that an ASBR cannot be part of a totally stubby area, nor can redistribution of routes from other protocols take place in this area. Figure 7-9 shows the operations in an example totally stubby area.

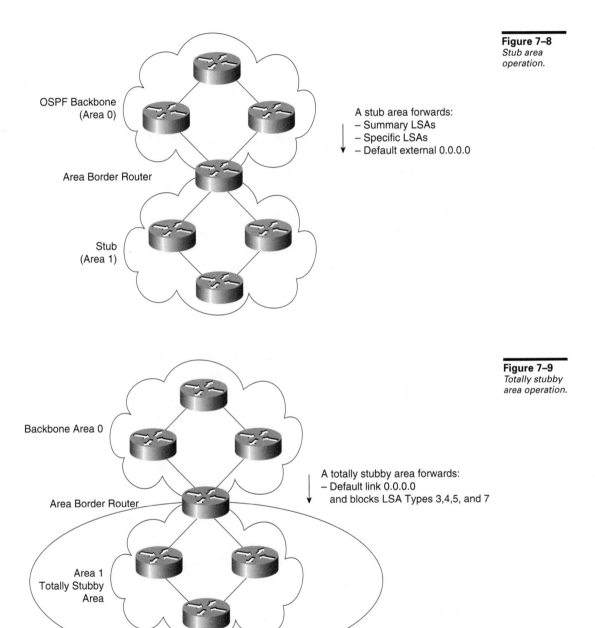

Figure 7–8
Stub area operation.

OSPF Backbone
(Area 0)

A stub area forwards:
– Summary LSAs
– Specific LSAs
– Default external 0.0.0.0

Area Border Router

Stub
(Area 1)

Figure 7–9
Totally stubby area operation.

Backbone Area 0

A totally stubby area forwards:
– Default link 0.0.0.0
  and blocks LSA Types 3,4,5, and 7

Area Border Router

Area 1
Totally Stubby
Area

The main difference between a stub area and a not-so-stubby area (NSSA) is that the NSSA imports a limited number of external routes. The number of routes is limited to only those required to provide connectivity between backbone areas. You may configure areas that redistribute routing information from another protocol to the OSPF Backbone as a NSSA. NSSAs are discussed later in this chapter.

Example of an OSPF Network with a Hierarchical Structure

To design this type of model network, you should gather a list of the different locations requiring network connectivity within your organization. For purposes of this example and ease of understanding, let's consider your organization, as an international corporation, and you have been tasked with building its OSPF network within the United States. You have determined that you have the following divisions (each with various business units within it), as shown in the following hierarchy, which groups the units by location and then by function.

- **Headquarters: Washington D.C. (all in the same building)**
  - United States Executives
  - Legal department
- **Human Resources (located at headquarters but in different building)**
  - Payroll
  - Benefits
  - Corporate Recruiting
- **Sales & Marketing**
  - Northern division (6 offices)
  - Southern division (6 offices)
  - Eastern division (5 offices)
  - Western division (7 offices)
- **Manufacturing**
  - Engineering located in western U.S.
  - Widgets division located in northern U.S. (4 factories)
  - Gidgets division located in southern U.S. (3 factories)
  - Tomgets division located in western U.S. (3 factories)

The listed units will become the basis of OSPF areas. Contained within the areas will be OSPF inter-area routers that connect to the various hosts.

Of these groupings, you should select essential locations at which to locate the backbone routers. For our example, you know that Headquarters will have a backbone router that will be connected to area 0. You have been given several requirements based upon traffic flow and corporate requirements:

- All divisions must be within the same area, regardless of geographic location
- All divisions must be able to connect to headquarters
- In our company, area 0 links all major continental locations throughout the globe
- All region clusters must have alternate routes
- Internet connectivity for entire company
- If backbone router fails, network operation within U.S. division must continue
- Engineering and Manufacturing must communicate quickly and easily

Begin separating the sites into areas and picking one location within each area at which will reside the area border router (ABR). This will result in a proposed set of OSPF routers deployed as follows:

- Backbone router (area 0): Connects to global area 0
- ABR (area 1): Executives and legal department
- ABR (area 2): Human resources
- ABR (area 3): Sales
- ABR (area 4): Manufacturing and Engineering
- ASBR: Internet connectivity

The remaining sites will each be assigned an inter-area router to connect them to the network. One main site within each geographical area will be the hub site for that geographic area, thereby reducing bandwidth costs.

At this point, you should have your organization separated into areas or layers and an overall topology map laid out. Figure 7-10 illustrates the example network described up to this point.

I want to throw out a couple of disclaimers here before people start tearing up my example. First, remember requirement number 1 (All divisions must be within the same area, regardless of geographic location). Second, there are many ways of designing a network and this is just one way and one person's opinion. Third, there is no substitute for actual network design experience, because everyone makes mistakes. Fourth, now that you think you have a solid network design, have someone else look at it and consider modeling it in a software package such as NetSys from Cisco.

Figure 7–10
*Proposed
network
design:
topology map.*

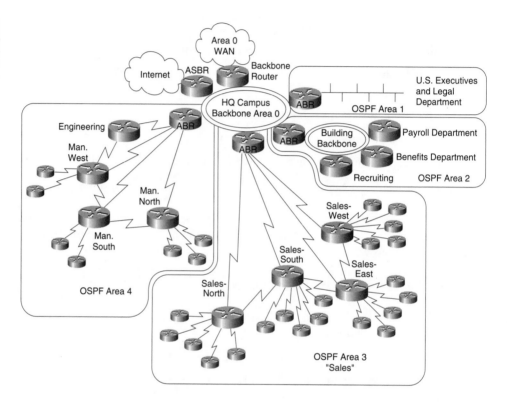

Step 3: Determine Addressing & Naming Conventions

Step 3 covers the actual process of assigning the overall network-addressing scheme. By assigning blocks of addresses to portions of the network, you are able to simplify addressing, administration, routing and increase scalability.

Because OSPF supports variable-length subnet masking (VLSM), you can really develop a true hierarchical addressing scheme. This hierarchical addressing results in very efficient summarization of routes throughout the network. VLSM and CIDR were discussed at great length earlier in the book, and it is in this step of designing your OSPF network that you should begin applying these two techniques.

NOTES

What do you know? Coming into Step 3, you have determined your network's requirements and developed a physical network topology. You have continued to keep track of the costs both one time and recurring while planning. In this step, you will determine the addressing and naming conventions that you plan on using.

Public or Private Address Space

A good rule of thumb to remember when determining whether to use public or private address space is that your address scheme must be able to scale enough to support a larger network because your network will most likely continue to grow.

Now you must determine what range of IP addresses you are going to deploy within your network. The first question you need to answer is: "Do I have public address space assigned to me by the InterNIC or am I going to be using private address space as specified in RFC 1918 and 1597?"

Either choice will have its implications on the design of your network. By choosing to use private address space and with having to connect to the Internet, you will be faced with having to include the capability to do address translation as part of your network design.

To further complicate the issue, you might also have to deal with a preexisting addressing scheme and/or the need to support automatic address assignment through the use of Dynamic Host Configuration Protocol (DHCP) or Domain Naming System (DNS). That type of technology is beyond the scope of this book and will not be covered.

TIPS

DHCP is a broadcast technique used to obtain an IP address for an end station.

DNS is used for translating the names of network nodes into IP addresses.

Figure 7-11 shows a good example of how to lay out the IP addresses and network names for the example network.

Figure 7-11
*Address and
naming
conventions.*

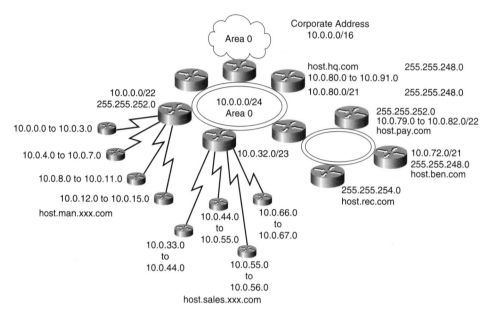

Plan Now for OSPF Summarization

The operation and benefits of route summarization have been discussed in previous chapters. At this point though, you should realize the importance of proper summarization on your network. The OSPF network in Figure 7-12 does not have summarization turned on. Notice that by not using summarization, every specific-link LSA will be propagated into the OSPF backbone and beyond, causing unnecessary network traffic and router overhead. Whenever an LSA is sent, all affected OSPF routers will have to recompute their LSA database and routes using the SPF algorithm.

OSPF will provide some added benefits if you design the network with summarization. For example, only summary-link LSAs will propagate into the backbone (area 0). This is very important because it prevents every router from having to rerun the SPF algorithm, increases the network's stability, and reduces unnecessary traffic. Figure 7-13 demonstrates this principle.

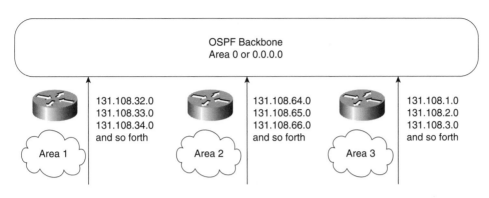

Figure 7–12
No route summarization will cause network problems.

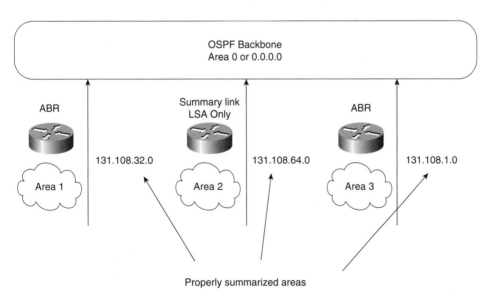

Figure 7–13
Proper route summarization improves OSPF network stability.

IP addresses in an OSPF network should be grouped by area, and you can expect to see areas with some or all of the following characteristics:

- Major network number(s)

- Fixed subnet mask(s)

- Random combination of networks, subnets, and host addresses

It is important that hosts, subnets, and networks be allocated in a controlled manner during the design and implementation of your OSPF network. The allocation should be in the form of contiguous blocks that are adjacent so OSPF LSAs can easily represent the address space. Figure 7-14 shows an example of this.

Figure 7–14
*Configure
OSPF for
summarization.*

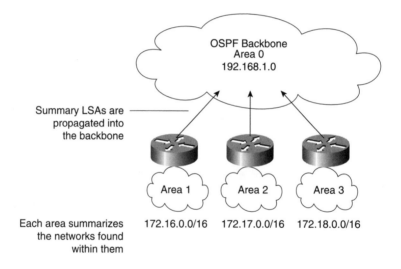

TIPS

Allocation of IP addresses should be done in powers of two so that these "blocks" can be represented by a single summary link advertisement. Through the use of the **area range** command you will be able to summarize large contiguous blocks of addresses. In order to minimize the number of blocks you should make them as large as possible.

Bit Splitting

Bit splitting is also a very useful technique discussed in previous chapters, and you might now want to consider using it if you have to split a large network number across more than one OSPF area. Simply put, bit splitting borrows some subnet bits for designated areas, as discussed in Chapter 5, "The Fundamentals of OSPF Routing & Design."

To differentiate two areas, split one bit.

To differentiate 16 areas, split four bits.

Figure 7-15 demonstrates this bit splitting technique.

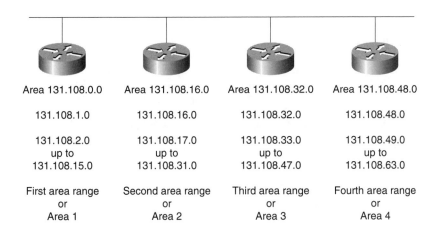

Figure 7–15
Bit splitting address space.

Area 131.108.0.0	Area 131.108.16.0	Area 131.108.32.0	Area 131.108.48.0
131.108.1.0	131.108.16.0	131.108.32.0	131.108.48.0
131.108.2.0 up to 131.108.15.0	131.108.17.0 up to 131.108.31.0	131.108.33.0 up to 131.108.47.0	131.108.49.0 up to 131.108.63.0
First area range or Area 1	Second area range or Area 2	Third area range or Area 3	Fourth area range or Area 4

The example uses four bits for the area and uses 32-bit numbers to represent four of the 16 possible areas. The area numbers appear in dotted decimal notation and look like subnet numbers. In fact, the 32-bit area numbers correspond to the summary advertisement that represents the area.

Map OSPF Addresses for VLSM

Variable-length subnet masking (VLSM) has been discussed previously, so this section will not dwell on it too deeply. But suffice it to say that the reasons behind it are similar to bit splitting. Remember to keep small subnets in a contiguous block and increase the number of subnets for a serial meshed network. Figure 7-16 provides a good example of VLSM OSPF mappings.

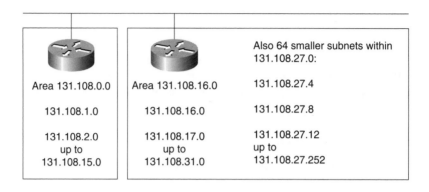

Figure 7–16
VLSM OSPF mappings.

Discontiguous Subnets

Subnets become discontiguous when they are separated by one or more segments represented by a different major network number. Discontiguous subnets are supported by OSPF because subnets masks are part of the link-state database.

Consider the following example: The OSPF backbone area 0 could be a class C address, while all the other areas could consist of address ranges from a class B major network as illustrated in Figure 7-17.

Figure 7–17
OSPF network with discontiguous subnets.

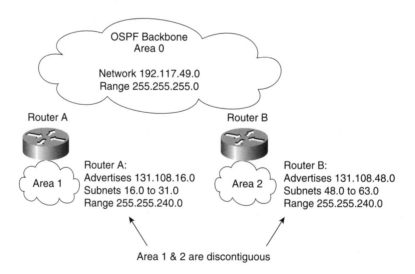

TIPS

OSPF supports discontiguous subnets regardless of whether summarization is configured within the network. Although, everything within your network will route better and have a more stable design if summarization is configured.

Naming Schema

The naming scheme used in your network should also be designed in a systematic way. By using common prefixes for names within an organization, you will make the network much easier to manage and more scalable. All of this is shown in Figure 7-11.

It is also important to carry a naming convention into your routers as well. This will assist everyone dealing with your network because the router names actually hold some meaning, instead of an abstract like an order number.

Step 4: Provision the Hardware

In Step 4, you must use vendor documentation, salesmen, and system engineers to determine the hardware necessary for your network. This is for both LAN and WAN components.

For LANs, you must select and provision router models, switch models, cabling systems, and backbone connections.

For WANs, you must select and provision router models, modems, CSUs/DSUs, and remote access servers.

NOTES

What do you know? Coming into Step 4 you have determined your network requirements, developed a physical network topology, and laid out your addressing and naming scheme for the network. In this step, you will begin selecting and provisioning the necessary network equipment to implement the design.

When selecting and provisioning routing or switching hardware, consider the following areas:

- Expected CPU usage

- Minimum RAM

- BUS budget

- Forwarding budget

- Required Interface Types and Density

Step 5: Deploy Protocol and IOS Features

In Step 5, you will need to deploy the more specific features possible by the OSPF protocol and the routers IOS. It is not necessary to have a network with every single option turned, nor is it something you are likely to see. Some of the features you should consider implementing are covered in the two sections that follow.

NOTES

What do you know? Coming into Step 5 you have determined your network requirements, developed a physical network topology, laid out your addressing and naming scheme, and begun the provisioning of the network equipment. In this step, you will begin deploying the OSPF and IOS features that you will be using within the network.

OSPF Features

This area covers some of the features of OSPF (authentication and route redistribution between protocols) that you should consider deploying within your network. There can be only one choice concerning which feature should be first for you to consider.

Protecting corporate resources, security, policing the network, ensuring correct usage of the network, authentication—they are all different labels for a similar need within every network: network security. Network security should be built into the network from day one, not added as an afterthought. Mistakes have already happened in the networking environment you know today. Nevertheless, how could they not with the almost required Internet presence and "www" logo seen on almost every business card? The open unsecure protocols such as Simple Mail Transfer Protocol (SMTP) or Simple Network Management Protocol (SNMP) are essential for business and network management, though they are also vulnerable for exploitation. Hopefully, the respective working groups will get moving towards solving this problem. All is not doom and gloom though, as OSPF comes with built-in authentication—the way it should be!

OSPF's built-in authentication set is extremely useful and flexible. In the OSPF specification, MD5 is the only cryptographic algorithm that has been completely specified. The overall implementation of security within OSPF is rather straightforward. For example, you assign a *key* to OSPF. This key can either be the same throughout your network or different on each router's interface or a combination of the two. The bottom line is that each router directly connected to each other must have the same key for communication to take place. Further detailed discussion of this OSPF feature will take place in later chapters.

Route redistribution is another very useful Cisco IOS software feature. To review redistribution is the exchange of routing information between two different routing processes (protocols). This feature should be turned on in your routers if you have separate routing domains within your Autonomous System and you need to exchange routes between them.

For example, the engineering department might be running OSPF and the accounting department might be running IGRP as shown in Figure 7-18.

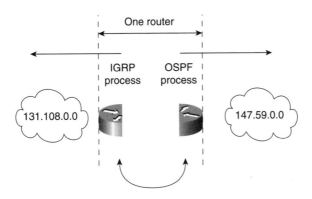

Figure 7–18
Redistributing routing information between protocols.

Figure 7-18 depicts one router connecting the two separate touring processes (protocols), which need to share routing information. This sharing process is called redistribution. The router shown in Figure 7-18 is configured to run both IGRP and OSPF routing.

TIPS

When routes are redistributed between major networks, no subnet information is required.

IOS Features

Some of the features of the IOS that you should consider deploying within your network are as follows:

- Access lists
- Queuing
- Route maps
- Limit of certain routes from being propagated

Step 6: Implement, Monitor, and Manage the Network

The last step is also the first step to continually managing the growth of your network. Some time is spent on this subject later in the chapter, but Chapter 9, "Managing Your OSPF Network," will delve more deeply into the network management arena. In the context of this step you should consider the following actions:

- Using network management tools for monitoring
- Performing proactive data gathering
- Knowing when to scale the network to meet new demands (new hardware, upgrade circuit speeds, support new applications)

NOTES

What do you know? Coming into Step 6 you have determined your network requirements, developed a physical network topology, laid out your addressing and naming scheme, provisioned your network equipment, and deployed the necessary OSPF and IOS features. In this step, you will begin to implement the network, institute monitoring, and engage in proactive network management.

Network Management and Monitoring Applications

Network management applications that use Simple Network Management Protocol (SNMP) provide a useful array of tools to control internetwork support costs:

- Cisco debug and show commands
- Syslogd
- Protocol analyzers
- DNS
- TFTP and FTP
- DHCP and BOOTP
- Telnet
- TACACS
- Cisco Works (Router configuration management, network analysis)

CONFIGURING OSPF ON CISCO ROUTERS

OSPF typically requires coordination among many internal routers, *area border routers* (routers connected to multiple areas), and autonomous system boundary routers. At a minimum, OSPF-based routers, or access servers, can be configured with all default parameter values, no authentication, and interfaces assigned to areas. If you intend to customize your environment, you must ensure coordinated configurations of all routers.

To configure OSPF, complete the tasks in the following sections. Enabling OSPF is mandatory; the other tasks are optional, but they might be required for your network.

Enabling OSPF on an Inter-Area Router

As with other routing protocols, the enabling of OSPF on Cisco routers requires a few steps before the process begins:

1. You must determine the *Process ID* under which OSPF will be running within your network. It is suggested that this *Process ID* be unique from any other OSPF network to which you might be connecting.

2. You must specify the range of addresses that are to be associated with the OSPF routing process. This is part of one command that must also include the area with which this range of addresses is to be associated.

Now that you have determined how the OSPF process should be configured, you need to start configuring the router. Perform the following tasks, starting in global configuration mode:

1. Enable OSPF routing, which places you in router configuration mode. You will do this with the following command: **router ospf** *process-id*.

2. Define an interface on which OSPF runs, and define the area ID for that interface. You will do this with the following command: **network** *address* *wildcard-mask* **area** *area-id*.

If this was an inter-area OSPF router, then the process for configuring it for OSPF would now be complete. There are a few subtle differences when configuring the different types of OSPF routers, as described in the next few sections.

Configuring an Area Border Router (ABR)

The process for configuring an ABR for OSPF is essentially the same as described in the preceding section "Enabling OSPF on an Inter-Area Router" with just a few minor additions:

1. Before starting the OSPF routing process, you need to decide on a few things about how OSPF is going to be configured for OSPF in your network. These considerations include: Deciding what OSPF routing process ID you want to assign to your network and deciding if you want OSPF to determine which router becomes the Designated Router (DR) and Backup Designated Router

(BDR). The second consideration might require you to decide upon setting a loopback interface. If you do decide to configure a loopback interface then please refer to the section "Creating A Loopback Interface" later in this chapter for specific details.

2. Turn on the OSPF routing process with the router ospf *process-id* command as described in the previous section on "Enabling OSPF on an Inter-Area Router."

3. Assign the appropriate network statements to the OSPF routing process with the correct area ID, for example:

```
router ospf 109
    network 130.10.8.0 0.0.0.255 area 0
    network 172.25.64.0 0.0.0.255 area 1
```

4. Is the area going to be a stub area? If so, enter the area *area-id* stub [no-summary] command, which defines a stub area. You will also need to enter the area *area-id* default-cost *cost* command, which assigns a specific cost. Some additional commands for areas that you might want to consider are covered in Chapter 6.

5. You will want to add the *area range* command so that the networks within each area can be properly summarized, for example:

```
router ospf 109
    network 130.10.8.0 0.0.0.255 area 0
    network 172.25.64.0 0.0.0.255 area 1
    area 1 range 130.10.8.0 255.255.255.0
```

6. Determine if you are going to use any optional OSPF parameters. You do not need to decide now to use any of these options, but be aware of them as they can help your OSPF network. Although many of these have been discussed already, the following list highlights a few of the more significant optional parameters in command syntax:

```
area area-id authentication
area area-id authentication message-digest
ip ospf authentication-key
ip ospf hello-interval
ip ospf dead-interval
timers spf spf-delay spf-holdtime
```

You can use the *show ip ospf border-routers* command to see the area border routers within your network. This command is explained in more detail in Chapter 8, "Monitoring & Troubleshooting an OSPF Network."

Configuring an Autonomous System Boundary Router (ASBR)

The process of configuring an autonomous system boundary router (ASBR) for OSPF is very similar to how you would configure an ABR:

1. You should already know the OSPF Process ID, whether or not you need a loopback interface, and which optional OSPF parameters you are going to be using.

2. Turn on the OSPF routing process as described previously in the section "Enabling OSPF on a Router." Again, you will use the router ospf *process-id* command.

3. Assign the appropriate network statements to the OSPF routing process with the correct Area ID, for example:

```
router ospf 109
    network 130.10.8.0 0.0.0.255 area 0
    network 172.25.64.0 0.0.0.255 area 1
```

4. Then you will want to add the *area range* command so that the networks within each area can be properly summarized, for example:

```
router ospf 109
    network 130.10.8.0 0.0.0.255 area 0
    network 172.25.64.0 0.0.0.255 area 1
    area 1 range 130.10.8.0 255.255.255.0
```

5. At this point, you will want to begin the redistribution process between your OSPF autonomous system and the external autonomous system to which the ASBR is providing connectivity, for example:

```
router ospf 109
    redistribute rip subnets metric-type 1 metric 12
    network 130.10.8.0 0.0.0.255 area 0
    network 172.25.64.0 0.0.0.255 area 1
    area 1 range 130.10.8.0 255.255.255.0
router rip
    network 128.130.0.0
    passive interface s 0
    default-metric 5
```

You can use the *show ip ospf border-routers* command to see the area border routers within your network. This command is explained in more detail in Chapter 8.

Configuring a Backbone Router

The process of configuring an OSPF backbone router for OSPF is very similar to how you would configure an ABR:

1. You should already know the OSPF Process ID, whether or not you need a loopback interface, and which optional OSPF parameters you are going to be using.

2. Turn on the OSPF routing process as described previously in the section "Enabling OSPF on a Router." Again, you will use the `router ospf process-id` command.

3. Assign the appropriate network statements to the OSPF routing process with the correct Area ID, for example:

```
router ospf 109
  network 130.10.8.0 0.0.0.255 area 0
  network 172.25.64.0 0.0.0.255 area 1
```

4. Then you will want to add the *area range* command so that the networks within each area can be properly summarized, for example:

```
router ospf 109
  network 130.10.8.0 0.0.0.255 area 0
  network 172.25.64.0 0.0.0.255 area 1
  area 1 range 130.10.8.0 255.255.255.0
```

Configuring a Simplex Ethernet or Serial Interface

Because simplex interfaces between two devices on an Ethernet represent only one network segment, for OSPF you must configure the transmitting interface to be a passive interface. This prevents OSPF from sending hello packets for the transmitting interface. Both devices are able to see each other via the hello packet generated for the receiving interface.

This means that the suppression of sending hello packets is required on the specified interface. This is accomplished using the following command:

```
passive interface type number
```

> ⬤ **TIPS** ───
>
> Why are they called simplex interfaces? Simplex means half duplex, and this means they typically have one transmitter. However, the newer devices have interfaces that allow full duplex, which means fewer collisions during transmissions. Most interfaces default to simplex.

Configuring OSPF Tunable Parameters

Cisco's OSPF implementation enables you to alter certain interface-specific OSPF parameters, as needed. You are not required to alter any of these parameters, but some interface parameters must be consistent across all routers in an attached network. Those are the parameters set by the following commands:

```
ip ospf hello-interval
ip ospf dead-interval
ip ospf authentication-key
timers spf spf-delay spf-holdtime
```

Therefore, be sure that if you do configure any of these parameters, the configurations for all routers on your network have compatible values.

More detailed information regarding tunable OSPF parameters was previously covered in Chapter 6. Remember that the hello packet defaults to being sent every 10 seconds on broadcast networks (Ethernet) and every 30 seconds on nonbroadcast networks (Frame Relay).

In interface configuration mode, specify any of the interface parameters as needed for your network as shown in Table 7-1.

Configuring Route Calculation Timers

You can configure the delay time between when OSPF receives a topology change and when it starts a shortest path first (SPF) calculation. You can also configure the hold time between two consecutive SPF calculations. This command was added to prevent routers from computing new routing tables. This is important if you are running OSPF in a very active network that experiences a lot of interface changes or other occurrences which would cause an LSA to be sent, such as a rapidly flapping serial line.

To set the values, perform the following task in router configuration mode:

```
timers spf spf-delay spf-holdtime
```

Table 7-1 *Tunable OSPF parameters*

Command	Task
`ip ospf cost cost`	Explicitly specify the cost of sending a packet on an OSPF interface
`ip ospf retransmit-interval seconds`	Specify the number of seconds between link-state advertisement retransmissions for adjacencies belonging to an OSPF interface
`ip ospf transmit-delay seconds`	Set the estimated number of seconds it takes to transmit a link-state update packet on an OSPF interface
`ip ospf priority number`	Set priority to help determine the OSPF designated router for a network
`ip ospf hello-interval seconds`	Specify the length of time, in seconds, between hello packets the Cisco IOS software sends on an OSPF interface
`ip ospf dead-interval seconds`	Set the number of seconds that a device's hello packets must not have been seen before its neighbors declare the OSPF router down
`ip ospf authentication-key key`	Assign a specific password to be used by neighboring OSPF routers on a network segment that is using OSPF's simple password authentication
`ip ospf message-digest-key keyid md5 key`	Enable OSPF MD5 authentication

Creating a Loopback Interface

As previously discussed, the use of a loopback interface will force the selection by OSPF of its router ID. The default for Cisco routers is loopback interface and then the highest IP address assigned to an interface. The use of a loopback interface enables you to assign the router ID. This can be very beneficial. Because a loopback interface is not a physical interface, like Ethernet, you must create it.

You can configure a loopback interface by entering the *interface loopback 0* command in the router configuration mode. The following example demonstrates the process:

```
OSPF_Router# conf t
Enter configuration commands, one per line. End with CNTL/Z.
OSPF_Router(config)# interface loopback 0
OSPF_Router(config-if)# ip address 10.251.11.1 255.255.255.255
OSPF_Router(config-if)# description Configured to be OSPF Router ID
```

Configuring OSPF for Different Network Types

As previously discussed, OSPF classifies different media into three types of networks as a default. Each of these networks requires a slightly different configuration to optimize the performance of OSPF. This section covers the methods and procedures that are needed in order to configure OSPF over different physical networks, such as the following:

- Broadcast networks (Ethernet, Token Ring, FDDI)
- Nonbroadcast multiaccess networks (SMDS, Frame Relay, X.25)
- Point-to-point networks (HDLC, PPP)

One of the most flexible features of OSPF is that you can configure your network as either a broadcast or a nonbroadcast multiaccess network. OSPF will respond accordingly.

X.25 and Frame Relay provide an optional broadcast capability that can be configured using the *map* command to allow OSPF to run as a broadcast network. This command is useful if you are running a meshed network.

The specific X.25 and Frame Relay commands are outside the scope of this book. If additional information is required, see the `x25 map` and `frame-relay map` command descriptions in *Cisco's Wide-Area Networking Command Reference* for more details.

Configuring your OSPF network type is one of the most functional features of OSPF. Everyone realizes that OSPF is not the perfect protocol, in fact, there will be never a protocol suitable for every situation. The strength of OSPF lies in its capability to be customized to meet certain network design requirements. The following sections will assist your understanding of customizing OSPF to your network's design.

Configuring OSPF for Broadcast or Nonbroadcast Multiaccess Networks

You have the choice of configuring your OSPF network type as either broadcast or nonbroadcast multiaccess (X.25), regardless of the default media type. For example, it does not matter if you have a broadcast media type, such as Ethernet, because you can still configure it as nonbroadcast if you so desire.

Using this feature, you can configure broadcast networks as nonbroadcast multiaccess networks when, for example, you have routers in your network that do not support multicast addressing.

You also can configure nonbroadcast multiaccess networks (such as X.25, Frame Relay, and SMDS) as broadcast networks. This feature saves you from having to configure neighbors, as described in the section "Configuring OSPF for Nonbroadcast Networks," later in this chapter.

Why would it be beneficial not to have a neighbor? This is a very odd statement because OSPF utilizes neighbors quite extensively. Assume, for example, that you have a point-to-point network. By not using neighbors you can reduce router memory and processor usage since there is only one other router to talk with.

Configuring OSPF for Nonbroadcast Networks

Because there might be many routers attached to an OSPF network, a *designated router* is selected for the network. You must use special configuration parameters in the designated router selection if the broadcast capability is not configured.

These parameters need only be configured in those devices that are eligible to become the Designated Router (DR) or Backup Designated Router (BDR).

NOTES

Any device running OSPF is eligible to become the DR or BDR unless its *priority value* is set to zero.

To configure routers that connect to nonbroadcast networks, you can specify the following neighbor parameters, as required:

- Priority value for a neighboring router
- Nonbroadcast poll interval
- Interface (via IP Address) through which the neighbor is reachable

These features enable you to determine several OSPF operating variables in just one router that will be propagated to its neighbors that are identified in the following configuration command:

```
neighbor ip-address [priority number] [poll-interval seconds]
```

Configuring OSPF for Point-to-Multipoint Networks

An OSPF point-to-multipoint interface is defined as a numbered point-to-point interface with the router having one or more OSPF neighbors. Because of this, OSPF will create multiple host routes.

An OSPF point-to-multipoint network has the following benefits compared to nonbroadcast multiaccess and point-to-point networks:

- Point-to-multipoint is easier to configure because it requires no configuration of neighbor commands, it consumes only one IP subnet, and it requires no designated router election.

- Point-to-multipoint has fully-meshed topology.

- Point-to-multipoint is more reliable because it maintains connectivity in case of virtual circuit failure.

When you decide to configure nonbroadcast, multiaccess networks as either broadcast or nonbroadcast networks, OSPF assumes that there are virtual circuits from every router to every router or that you are running a fully-meshed network.

This is not true in many cases because you might only have a partially-meshed network because the cost required to fully mesh the network is prohibitive. In this case, you can configure the OSPF network type as a point-to-multipoint network. Routing between two routers not directly connected will go through the router that has virtual circuits to both routers.

TIPS

If you are going to configure OSPF's network type as point-to-multipoint then you should not configure any neighbors. Because of the presence of virtual links, this will cause additional unneeded traffic and potential routing problems. You might want to refer to the case study provided in Chapter 5 for more information.

To configure your OSPF network type on a specific interface (int s0), enter the following command in interface configuration mode:

ip ospf network {*broadcast¦non-broadcast¦point-to-multipoint*}

Figure 7-19 shows an example of OSPF in a point-to-multipoint networking environment.

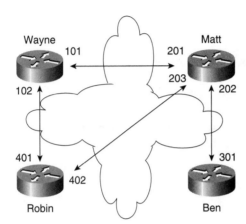

Figure 7–19
Point-to-multipoint network example.

TIPS

Remember there are no Designated Routers or Backup Designated Routers on a point-to-multipoint subnet. The OSPF Hello protocol will find neighbors.

Referring to the setup in Figure 7-19 and for demonstration purposes, assume the following scenario:

- Matt uses DLCI 201 to communicate with Wayne, DLCI 202 to Ben, and DLCI 203 to Robin.

- Wayne uses DLCI 101 to communicate with Matt and DLCI 102 to communicate with Robin.

- Robin communicates with Wayne (DLCI 401) and Matt (DLCI 402).

- Ben communicates with Matt (DLCI 301).

Given this setup, the configurations for Matt, Wayne, Robin, and Ben would be as follows:

Matt's Configuration

```
hostname Matt
!
interface serial 1
ip address 10.0.0.2 255.0.0.0
ip ospf network point-to-multipoint
encapsulation frame-relay
frame-relay map ip 10.0.0.1 201 broadcast
frame-relay map ip 10.0.0.3 202 broadcast
frame-relay map ip 10.0.0.4 203 broadcast
!
router ospf 1
network 10.0.0.0 0.0.0.255 area 0
```

Wayne's Configuration

```
hostname Wayne
!
interface serial 0
ip address 10.0.0.1 255.0.0.0
ip ospf network point-to-multipoint
encapsulation frame-relay
frame-relay map ip 10.0.0.2 101 broadcast
frame-relay map ip 10.0.0.4 102 broadcast
!
router ospf 1
network 10.0.0.0 0.0.0.255 area 0
```

Robin's Configuration

```
hostname Robin
!
interface serial 3
ip address 10.0.0.4 255.0.0.0
ip ospf network point-to-multipoint
encapsulation frame-relay
clockrate 1000000
frame-relay map ip 10.0.0.1 401 broadcast
```

```
frame-relay map ip 10.0.0.2 402 broadcast
!
router ospf 1
network 10.0.0.0 0.0.0.255 area 0
```

Ben's Configuration

```
hostname Ben
!
interface serial 2
ip address 10.0.0.3 255.0.0.0
ip ospf network point-to-multipoint
encapsulation frame-relay
clockrate 2000000
frame-relay map ip 10.0.0.2 301 broadcast
!
router ospf 1
network 10.0.0.0 0.0.0.255 area 0
```

Configuring OSPF Area Parameters

Cisco OSPF software enables you to configure several area parameters. These area parameters include authentication, defining stub areas, and assigning specific costs to the default summary route.

Authentication allows password-based or key-based protection against unauthorized access to an area.

Stub areas are areas into which information on external routes is not sent. Instead, there is a default external route generated by the area border router, into the stub area for destinations outside the autonomous system.

To further reduce the number of link-state advertisements sent into a stub area, you can configure *no-summary* on the ABR to prevent it from sending summary link advertisement (LSA Type 3) into the stub area.

In router configuration mode, specify any of the following area parameters as needed for your network:

- **area *area-id* authentication**. Enables authentication
- **area *area-id* authentication message-digest**. Enables MD5
- **area *area-id* stub [no-summary]**. Defines a stub area
- **area *area-id* default-cost** *cost*. Assigns specific cost

Configuring OSPF Not-So-Stubby Areas (NSSAs)

NSSAs are similar to regular OSPF stub areas, except that an NSSA does not flood Type 5 external LSAs from the core into the not so stubby area, but it has the capability to import AS external routes in a limited fashion within the area.

Prior to NSSA, the connection between the corporate site border router and the remote router could not be run as OSPF stub area because routes for the remote site cannot be redistributed into stub area. A simple protocol like RIP is usually run to handle the redistribution. This has meant maintaining two routing protocols. With NSSA, you can extend OSPF to cover the remote connection by defining the area between the corporate router and the remote router as an NSSA. Figure 7-20 illustrates the overall operation of an OSPF NSSA.

Figure 7–20
OSPF NSSA overview.

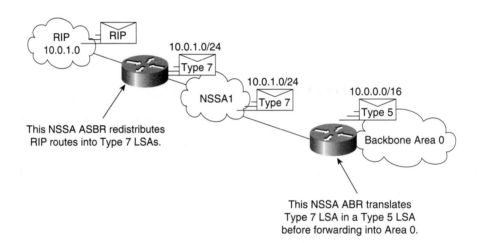

NSSA allows importing of Type 7 AS external routes within NSSA area by redistribution. These Type 7 LSAs are translated into Type 5 LSAs by NSSA ABR which are flooded throughout the whole routing domain. Summarization and filtering are supported during the translation.

If you are an Internet Service Provider (ISP), or a network administrator who has to connect a central site using OSPF to a remote site that is using a different protocol, such as RIP or EIGRP, you can use NSSA to simplify the administration of this kind of topology. Before NSSA, the connection between the corporate site ABR and the remote router used RIP or EIGRP. This meant maintaining two routing protocols. Now, with NSSA, you can extend OSPF to cover the remote connection by defining the area between the corporate router and the remote router as an NSSA, as shown in Figure

7-21. You cannot expand the normal OSPF area to the remote site because the Type 5 external will overwhelm both the slow link and the remote router.

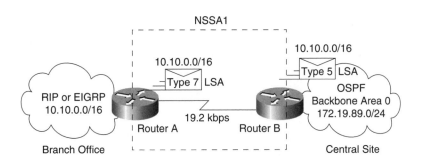

Figure 7–21
Reasons to use the OSPF NSSA option.

NSSA Implementation Considerations

Evaluate the following considerations before implementing NSSA:

- You can set a Type 7 default route that can be used to reach external destinations. When configured, the router generates a Type 7 default into the NSSA by the NSSA ABR.

- Every router within the same area must agree that the area is NSSA; otherwise, the routers will not be able to communicate with each other.

If possible, avoid using explicit redistribution on NSSA ABRs because confusion might result over which packets are being translated by which router.

In router configuration mode, specify the following area parameters as needed to configure and define the OSPF NSSA:

```
area area-id nssa [no-redistribution] [default-information-originate]
```

In router configuration mode on the ABR, specify the following command to control summarization and filtering of Type 7 LSA into Type 5 LSA during the translation process:

```
summary address prefix mask [not advertise] [tag tag]
```

Configuring Route Summarization Between OSPF Areas

In OSPF, an ABR will advertise addresses that describe how to reach networks (routes) from one area into another area. *Route summarization* is the consolidation of these advertised addresses. This feature causes a single summary route to be advertised to other areas by an ABR, thereby representing multiple routes in a single statement. This has several benefits, but the primary one is a reduction in the size of routing tables.

If the network numbers in an area are assigned in such a way that they are contiguous, you can configure the ABR to advertise a summary route that covers all the individual networks within the area that fall into the range specified by the summary route.

To specify an address range, perform the following task in router configuration mode:

```
area area-id range address mask
```

Configuring Route Summarization when Redistributing Routes into OSPF

When redistributing routes from other protocols into OSPF, each route is advertised individually in an external link-state advertisement (LSA). However, you can configure OSPF to advertise a single route for all the redistributed routes that are covered by a specified network address and mask. Doing so helps decrease the size of the OSPF link-state databases and in turn the routing table. The same benefits discussed in route summarization between areas is applicable here, only now the routes are coming from an external source.

To have OSPF advertise one summary route for all redistributed routes covered by a network address and mask, perform the following task in router configuration mode:

```
summary-address address mask
```

Generating a Default OSPF Route during Redistribution

Whenever you specifically configure redistribution of routes from a different routing protocol or autonomous system into an OSPF routing domain, the router in question automatically becomes an autonomous system boundary router (ASBR) because it is doing the redistribution. You can force an ASBR to generate a default route into an OSPF routing domain as illustrated in Figure 7-22.

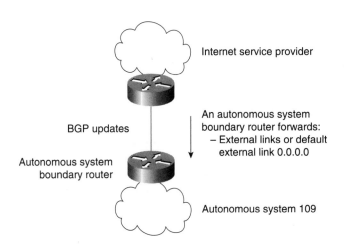

Figure 7–22
ASBRs
consolidate
routes.

Internet service provider

BGP updates

An autonomous system
boundary router forwards:
– External links or default
external link 0.0.0.0

Autonomous system
boundary router

Autonomous system 109

However, an ASBR does not, by default, generate a *default route* into the OSPF routing domain. To force the ASBR to generate a default route, perform the following task in router configuration mode:

default-information originate [**always**] [**metric** *metricvalue*]
[**metric-type** *type-value*] [**route-map** map-name]

Figure 7-23 shows a good example of when you would generate a default during the use of an OSPF stub area.

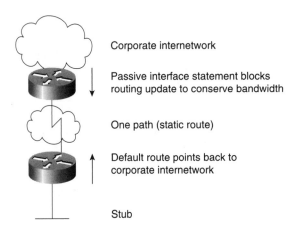

Figure 7–23
Manually
configuring a
path to the
OSPF stub
network.

Corporate internetwork

Passive interface statement blocks
routing update to conserve bandwidth

One path (static route)

Default route points back to
corporate internetwork

Stub

The most common method of generating a default route is through the use of a static route statement within the router. When using a static route paired with a passive interface, you will stop routing updates and enable the path to have a lower administrative distance.

Configuring Lookup of DNS Names

You can configure OSPF to look up Domain Naming System (DNS) names for use in all OSPF show command displays. This feature makes it easier to identify a router, because it is displayed by name rather than by its router ID or neighbor ID. Through the use of this command you will find that some of the more cryptic components displayed by OSPF will make a bit more sense, especially if you have used a good naming system, as previously discussed.

To configure OSPF to do a DNS name lookup, perform the following task in the routers global configuration mode:

```
ip ospf name-lookup
```

Forcing the Router ID Choice with a Loopback Interface

OSPF uses the largest IP address configured on the interfaces as its router ID. If the interface associated with this IP address is ever unavailable, or if the address is removed, the OSPF process must recalculate a new router ID and flood all its routing information out its interfaces.

If a loopback interface is configured with an IP address, OSPF will default to using this IP address as its router ID, even if other interfaces have larger IP addresses. Because loopback interfaces never go down, greater stability throughout your OSPF network is achieved.

TIPS

You cannot tell OSPF to use a particular interface as its router ID. It has built in defaults that force it to accept a loopback interface first then the highest IP address on any interface.

Disable Default OSPF Metric Calculation Based on Bandwidth

In Cisco IOS Release 10.2 and earlier, OSPF assigned default metrics to router interfaces regardless of the interface bandwidth. It gave both 64K and T1 links the same metric (1562), and thus required an explicit ip ospf cost command in order to take advantage of the faster link.

In Cisco IOS Release 10.3 and later, by default, OSPF calculates the OSPF metric for an interface according to the bandwidth statement of the interface. You can see this in the following excerpt from a router:

```
OSPF_Router# sho int s0
Serial0 is down, line protocol is down
   Hardware is QUICC Serial (with onboard CSU/DSU)
   Description: OSPF uses the Bandwidth Statement on EVERY Interface
   Internet address is 10.251.20.1/24
   MTU 1500 bytes, BW 56 Kbit, DLY 20000 usec, rely 255/255, load 1/255
   Encapsulation FRAME-RELAY IETF, loopback not set, keepalive set (10 sec)
   LMI enq sent 0, LMI stat recvd 0, LMI upd recvd 0, DTE LMI down
   LMI enq recvd 0, LMI stat sent 0, LMI upd sent 0
   LMI DLCI 0 LMI type is ANSI Annex D frame relay DTE
   Broadcast queue 0/64, broadcasts sent/dropped 0/0, interface broadcasts 0
   Last input never, output never, output hang never
   Last clearing of "show interface" counters 00:02:17
   Queueing strategy: fifo
   Output queue 0/40, 0 drops; input queue 0/75, 0 drops
   5 minute input rate 0 bits/sec, 0 packets/sec
   5 minute output rate 0 bits/sec, 0 packets/sec
      0 packets input, 0 bytes, 0 no buffer
      Received 0 broadcasts, 0 runts, 0 giants
      0 input errors, 0 CRC, 0 frame, 0 overrun, 0 ignored, 0 abort
      0 packets output, 0 bytes, 0 underruns
      0 output errors, 0 collisions, 5 interface resets
      0 output buffer failures, 0 output buffers swapped out
      0 carrier transitions
      DCD=down DSR=down DTR=up RTS=up CTS=up
```

For example, a 64K link gets a metric of 1562, and a T1 link gets a metric of 64.

TIPS

Remember that OSPF will load balance over multiple equal-cost links, so if you use the defaults, this feature will be on automatically.

To disable this feature, perform the following task in router configuration mode:
```
no ospf auto-cost-determination
```

Configuring OSPF Over On-Demand Circuits

The OSPF on-demand circuit operational capability is an enhancement to the OSPF protocol that allows efficient operation over on-demand circuits like ISDN, X.25, switched virtual circuits (SVCs) and dial-up lines. This feature set is fully supported by Cisco and follows the standard as described in RFC 1793, *Extending OSPF to Support Demand Circuits*. This is one of the better RFCs and is worth consulting if you plan to configure OSPF to operate within this type of networking environment.

Prior to this RFC, periodic OSPF hello and link-state advertisements (LSAs) would be exchanged between routers that were connected on the demand link, even when no changes were being reported in the hello or LSA information. This would cause the costs involved with these types of connectivity to skyrocket.

However, with this enhancement to OSPF, periodic hellos are suppressed and the periodic refreshes of LSAs are not flooded over the demand circuit. These packets bring up the link only under tightly controlled circumstances:

- When they are exchanged for the first time.
- When a change occurs in the information they contain.

This operation allows the underlying Data Link layer to be closed when the network topology is stable. Thus saving on unnecessary costs. This is very useful because if your company is paying ISDN costs every time a call is placed, you want to ensure that the call is necessary. Consider it an automatic feature that restricts your teenage daughter from using the telephone unless it is necessary . . . very useful isn't it.

This feature is also very useful when you want to connect telecommuters or branch offices to an OSPF backbone at a central site. In this case, OSPF for on-demand circuits allows the benefits of OSPF over the entire domain, without excess connection costs.

Periodic refreshes of hello updates, LSA updates, and other protocol overhead are prevented in this configuration from enabling the on-demand circuit when there is no "real" data to transmit. Figure 7-24 illustrates this type of OSPF setup.

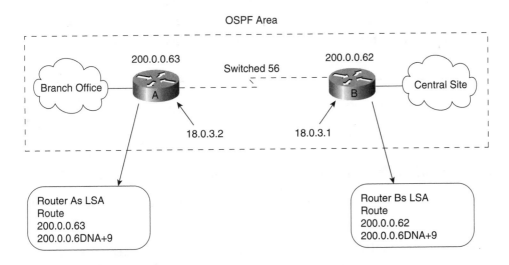

Figure 7–24
*OSPF
on-demand
circuit
operation.*

Overhead protocols within OSPF such as hellos and LSAs are transferred over the on-demand circuit only upon initial setup and when they reflect a change in the network topology. This means that critical changes to the topology that require new SPF calculations are transmitted in order to maintain network topology integrity. Periodic refreshes that do not include changes, however, are not transmitted across the link.

To configure OSPF for on-demand circuits, enter the following command within the interface configuration mode:

```
ip ospf demand-circuit
```

This command is also shown in the following example:

```
OSPF_Router(config)#router ospf 200
OSPF_Router(config-if)#ip ospf demand circuit
```

> **TIPS**
>
> If the router is part of a point-to-point topology, then only one end of the demand circuit must be configured with this command. However, all routers must have this feature loaded within the area and must be configured with the `ip ospf demand-circuit` command. If the router is part of a point-to-multipoint topology, only the multipoint end must be configured with this command.

Implementation Considerations for OSPF over On-Demand Circuits

Please evaluate the following considerations before implementing on-demand circuits on a Cisco router:

- Because LSAs that include topology changes are flooded over an on-demand circuit, it is advised to put demand circuits within OSPF stub areas, or within NSSAs to isolate the demand circuits from as many topology changes as possible.

- To take advantage of the on-demand circuit functionality within a stub area or NSSA, every router in the area must have this feature loaded. If this feature is deployed within a regular area, all other regular areas must also support this feature before the demand circuit functionality can take effect. This is because Type 5 external LSAs are flooded throughout all areas.

- You do not want to implement this OSPF feature on a broadcast-based network topology because the overhead protocols (such as hellos and LSAs) cannot be successfully suppressed, which means the link will remain up.

Multicast OSPF

Multicast OSPF (MOSPF) was defined as an extension to the OSPF unicast routing protocol in RFC 1584. Multicast OSPF works by ensuring each router in a network understands all the available links in the network. Each OSPF router calculates routes from itself to all possible destinations.

Before discussing MOSPF any further, it is important to note that Cisco Systems does NOT support this feature of OSPF. Nevertheless, because many networks will have multiple router manufacturers in them or connect to other manufacturers, it is important to discuss this OSPF feature, as you will probably encounter it if your network has a blend of routers within it. This section will later discuss the reasons why Cisco does not support Multicast OSPF.

NOTES

If you have a need to run MOSPF, then you will need to contact one of these five router vendors: 3Com, Bay Networks, IBM, Proteon, and Xyplex as they are the only manufacturers to have implemented MOSPF.

MOSPF works by including multicast information in OSPF link-state advertisements. A MOSPF router learns which multicast groups are active on which LANs.

MOSPF then builds a distribution tree for each source/group pair and computes a tree for active sources sending to the group. The tree state is cached on all routers, and trees must be re-computed when a link-state change occurs or when the cache times out. This eventuality in turn can hinder multicast performance, depending upon the size of the network and the volatility of the multicast groups.

As expected, MOSPF works only in internetworks that are using OSPF and have implemented routers manufactured by a company other than Cisco Systems.

MOSPF is best suited for environments that have relatively few source/group pairs active at any given time. It will work less well in environments that have many active sources or environments that have unstable links.

Some multicast group addresses are assigned as well-known addresses by the Internet Assigned Numbers Authority (IANA). These groups are called permanent host groups, similar in concept to the well-known TCP and User Datagram Protocol (UDP) port numbers.

Why doesn't Cisco Systems support this powerful enhancement to the OSPF protocol? You will not find this information on CCO nor in any of their corporate literature, and I had to open a trouble ticket with the TAC to find it. Various engineers within Cisco were consulted, and the problem with MOSPF is that every OSPF router in your network must have it turned on. Every router will then have to run the Dijkstra algorithm for *every* multicast source and group within the network. This feature will work properly within a multicast network that is *very* small but it will melt down routers as the number of multicast routers grows.

For example, this means that every receiver of a multicast is also a sender and will therefore cause another instance of the Dijkstra algorithm to be run within every router in the network. As the use of your multicast application grows, this would cause an increased load to be placed on the CPUs of your routers. Simply put, imagine if you have an ABR that was connected to multiple areas and every area had several hundred routers. Your ABR would have to run the Dijkstra algorithm for every router in every area, thus a network melt down would result.

Now extend that to every router in your network.

NOTES

A nice example of the added load MOSPF will put on your network are some figures surrounding Proteon's implementation of MOSPF. When adding MOSPF into the base OSPF code, it caused a 30 percent increase in its size. Extra load will be placed upon a router to support such a jump in size and the operational requirements of MOSPF. My suggestion is: be very sure of the benefits you expect to gain if ever you decide to implement this feature. Due to scalability issues, Cisco does not see a need to go to MOSPF right now. Additionally, PIM is getting pushed now as the multicast protocol of choice.

OSPF and the Multi-Protocol Router (MPR)

I considered long and hard about whether to include this section in the book, and I decided I would. Because it is important to note the extent to which OSPF has been implemented throughout the networking arena.

Not too long ago, routers were by default very expensive pieces of hardware that always received the blame for network outages. You are probably aware that the Cisco router is usually very reliable and easy to understand—at least when compared to the competition. Imagine that—reliable and easy to operate, and they are the market leader—seems like Business 101 to me, but I digress.

Today routers are relatively inexpensive and self-configuring to a certain degree. It is acknowledged that the IOS is the soul of the router because it examines and makes routing decisions, which the hardware executes. There are now a variety of router manufacturers such as Cisco Systems, Bay Networks, Ascend, 3Com, and many others. However, Novell made a truly astounding move by introducing the Multi-Protocol Router (MPR) as a software service within their NetWare Software Suite. This MPR delivers routing services, and it can operate on any machine that can run NetWare server. Novell's move indicates a move within networking away from traditional router design. It was not long before Microsoft also offered an MPR within Windows NTv4. Adding this routing ability is an excellent move on their part because it further enhances the usefulness of their operating systems. You can argue all day about the good and bad regarding software routers or specialized routers. Nevertheless, the bottom line for many is economics and being able to use a PC as a router has its appeal. While Cisco and others have many office or campus routers on the market, they still have not recognized the need to make a PC a router, so this market remains the sole property of Novell and Microsoft.

To be fair, I should discuss both Microsoft's and Novell's MPRs, but this is a book about OSPF networks and only Novell recommends configuring your MPR using the OSPF standard. In this case, it is beyond the scope of this book to discuss Microsoft's MPR. Sorry Bill, but you should consider OSPF as the default in WIN NTv5.

OSPF & Novell's MPR

When configuring OSPF within Novell's MPR it is important to note that by default OSPF is turned on—they are so smart! The MPR uses the standards for OSPF in its design. It is not as configurable as a normal router but then it was not meant to be. You will find that the MPR has the following configurable options:

- Area ID that can be configured up to 32 bits

- Cost option with an upper limit of 65.535

- Priority option to determine which router becomes the Designated Router (DR)

- Authentication key that is eight bytes in length

- Hello Interval timer

- Router Dead Interval timer

- Neighbor list

NOTES

MPR is good because you don't need a dedicated router. You can use a Novell server to do the routing for you in addition to serving files and giving print services.

Considering that you would likely use an MPR within a stub area, at a very small location not rating a real router, or in case of emergencies, it can be configured surprisingly well. The MPR is not the means to build today's Enterprise networks but, it certainly should not be discarded out of hand because it does have its place in the grand scheme of networking. It is going to be interesting to see what the future is going to bring us regarding this area of networking. I suggest watching it very closely.

CHAPTER SUMMARY

This chapter covered the common set of network design goals to ensure that your network is of enterprise quality. There are always some unique issues surrounding every type of network and these were discussed as well. To review, the six steps of designing a network with special emphasis on the areas that are essential to OSPF are as follows:

1. Analyze the requirements.

2. Develop the network topology.

3. Determine addressing and naming conventions.

4. Provision the hardware.

5. Deploy the protocol and IOS features.

6. Implement, monitor, and manage the network.

Answering the question of "how to actually make my Cisco router do all this" was then covered in the "Configuring OSPF on Cisco Routers" section. The overall process of implementing OSPF on your routers as well as the different types of OSPF routers (inter-area, intra-area, ABR, ASBR, and backbone), was discussed. Then, a variety of different scenarios that you might encounter within your network were discussed, as well as how best to implement OSPF to meet these scenarios. The chapter concluded with the "IOS on a PC" or Multi-Protocol Router (MPR) that are beginning to see more wide-spread application within the industry and, of course, they also support OSPF, so their roles as they relate to OSPF were discussed.

CASE STUDY: DESIGNING AN OSPF FRAME RELAY NETWORK

Terrapin Pharmaceuticals has 25 regional sales offices dispersed throughout the eastern United States. The main corporate headquarters and the data center for Terrapin Pharmaceuticals is located in Tennessee. The following list details some of the network attributes of the Terrapin Pharmaceuticals setup.

- Network computing of these sales offices primarily consists of IBM Systems Network Architecture (SNA) Mainframe Access over dedicated 56KB leased lines.

- IBM 3174 cluster controllers connect directly to the 56KB modems using Synchronous Data Link Control (SDLC) modules.

- Each branch office also has small Novell NetWare 3.11 networks installed on a standalone Ethernet Local Area Network (LAN) for local file sharing and printing.

- All PCs have Ethernet cards for LAN connectivity and 3270-type coaxial (dumb terminal) cards for IBM Host connectivity.

Figure 7-25 shows the existing Terrapin Pharmaceutical network.

Wide Area Network Design Requirements

Terrapin wants to remove the leased lines and 3174 cluster controllers and network its sales offices using public Frame Relay service. The new WAN must seamlessly integrate into the existing corporate internetwork.

- The existing corporate campus network infrastructure is 10MB Ethernet with an established router base of 25 Cisco's. Enterprise network protocols are IPX/RIP and TCP/IP with IGRP as the routing protocol.

- The new WAN must implement OSPF as the IP routing protocol, as that is the future direction of the campus network.

As the design engineer, you are responsible for the OSPF design and implementation, TCP/IP addressing scheme, and router implementation of this frame relay network. To construct a scalable OSPF network capable of meeting both the present and future requirements, you need to gather the necessary information from the appropriate

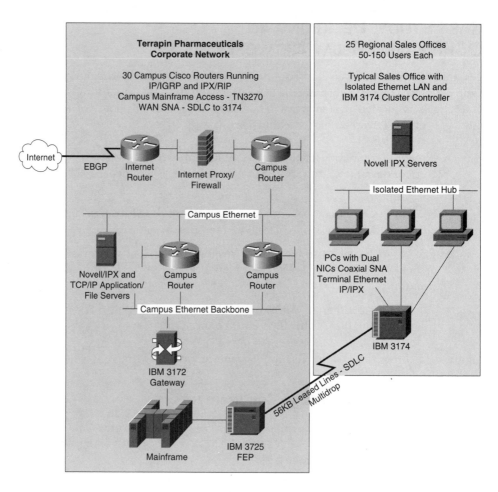

Figure 7–25
*Terrapin
Pharmaceuticals'
existing network.*

company decision-makers. This information will consist of determining the customer's requirements as discussed in the following section.

Determining the Frame Relay PVC Architecture

The corporate engineering group has control of all circuit and transmission architectural decisions such as the planning and ordering of all data and voice lines, as well as equipment procurement and installation. You are told that the new frame relay topology will be a partially-meshed hub and spoke. Figure 7-26 illustrates this topology.

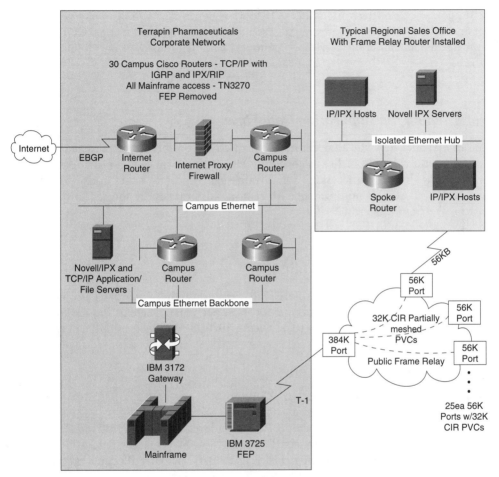

Figure 7–26
Partially-meshed hub and spoke PVC topology.

Each spoke or remote sales office will have a 56KB local circuit installed into the frame relay POP with a single 32K CIR PVC provisioned to a T1 circuit which will be installed on a central hub router at the corporate Headquarters and data center facility in Tennessee. The CIR on the T1 circuit will be 384K.

Determining if There Will Be Multi-Protocol Support

The WAN network must support Novell IPX in addition to TCP/IP since it is on the customers' LANs. The corporate IS manager indicates that no native SNA will need to be supported on this network as all the IBM 3174 controllers will be removed after conversion to frame relay. Mainframe access will be accomplished using TCP/IP directly from terminal emulation software running TN3270 (Telnet) at the Regional Sales Offices

Determining the Application Data Flow

The IS manager tells you that the majority of traffic on this frame relay network will flow from individual branches to corporate HQ, in the form of PC-to-mainframe communications. It will be necessary for certain sales offices to share and print files on remote Novell Servers and printers. All remote sales offices are located in the Northeastern and Southeastern US.

Determining the Number of Routers

There will be 25 routers on this frame relay network with a potential 10% increase (3 routers) over the next three years (one location per year). The existing corporate network has 30 Cisco routers deployed, servicing 50 TCP/IP subnets and IPX networks on an Ethernet infrastructure.

Determining TCP/IP Addressing

Terrapin Pharmaceuticals is allocating TCP/IP addresses from the private RFC 1918 space. All existing LANs are subnetted out of 172.17.0.0 space using 24 bit prefixes. (/24 prefix or 255.255.255.0 subnet mask). IP subnets currently allocated on the corporate network are 172.17.1.0–172.17.55.0. You are told that you must support between 50 and 150 IP hosts per remote Sales LAN from unused subnets out of this same address space.

Determining Internet Connectivity

Terrapin Pharmaceuticals currently has Internet connectivity through a firewall segment. The default route or "gateway of last resort" is propagated into IGRP from a central router on the internal network to all other IGRP-speaking routers. A registered class C address has been obtained and is deployed as the Internet DMZ segment. This is the only address that is announced to the Internet from Terrapin's Internet Cisco 4700 router, as the firewall has proxy and Network Address Translation (NAT) capabilities.

Determining Enterprise Routing Policies

After speaking with the managers of the IS department, you discover that they intend to migrate the network from IGRP to OSPF on the existing Cisco router base in the near future. Thus, the frame relay network must run OSPF and integrate seamlessly into the eventual corporate OSPF network architecture. Because no timeframe for the campus OSPF conversion can be determined, your network must integrate into the IGRP network upon installation for an undetermined period of time.

Establishing Security Concerns

The company plans to use OSPF password-authentication when the network is converted to OSPF from IGRP. The security manager indicates that a single password will be sufficient across all OSPF-speaking router links.

After evaluating all of Terrapin's requirements, Figure 7-27 illustrates the proposed OSPF network design.

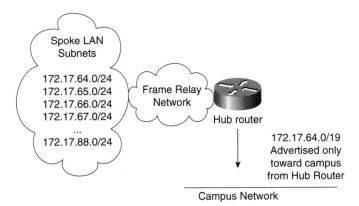

Figure 7–27
Proposed Terrapin Pharmaceutical OSPF Frame Relay network.

OSPF Network Design

This section will discuss some of the design topics to consider within this case study.

TCP/IP Addressing

You are able to obtain a contiguous block of 32 "class C" (/24 or 255.255.255.0 mask) subnets for this network from the IP address manager. The address block is 172.17.64.0/19, which will allow clean summarization into the backbone area once the corporate network converts to OSPF. (This occurs because all of the frame relay network LAN and WAN addresses will be summarized as one route (172.17.64.0/19) once the backbone routers are converted to OSPF as show in Figure 7-28.)

Figure 7–28
OSPF summarization with TCP/IP.

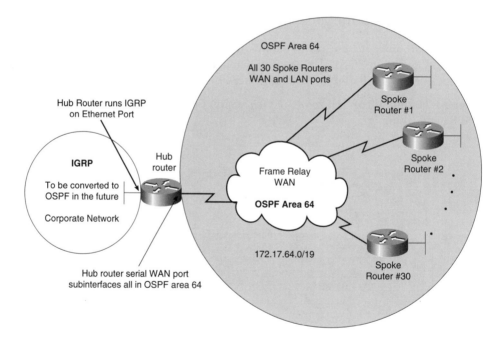

Sales Office LAN Addressing

Given the host requirements of 50–150 nodes per remote LAN and the existing subnetting scheme of /24 (class C mask) on the corporate network, it makes sense to assign /24 subnets of the 172.17.64.0/19 space to every one of the 25 spoke LANs. Every LAN will have addressing space for up to 254 nodes with this subnetting scheme that will facilitate future growth requirements at each site. This fulfills the earlier requirement concerning network growth and planning. This masking scheme will be easily understood by the desktop support staff and will work with existing routers running the IGRP routing protocol.

NOTES

IGRP does not carry subnet information in routing updates and routers require a uniform masking scheme enterprise-wide.

The spoke router LAN subnets on this network will be assigned out of the range 172.17.64.0–172.17.88.255.

The hub router will attach to an existing corporate backbone Ethernet segment, and will be assigned an IP address from that subnet, which does not fall within the 172.17.64.0/19 range. You are given 172.17.10.240/24 for the Hub router Ethernet IP address.

WAN Addressing

Before the WAN IP address plan can be devised for the routers on this network, the decision must be made as to whether to treat the frame relay PVCs as a single multipoint subnet or a collection of point-to-point links on the Cisco routers.

NOTES

Multipoint mode models the Frame Relay cloud as a LAN subnet, whereas the point-to-point mode models each PVC as a separate WAN point-to-point link in terms of addressing and routing

Given the additional requirements to support the IPX protocol in an any-to-any fashion, the point-to-point model is the only option.

TIPS

IPX RIP is a distance-vector routing protocol with limitations of the split-horizon behavior of not sending routing updates out an interface on which they were received. The multipoint model would not facilitate IPX any-to-any as the router would not send IPX routing updates out to any of the remote routers.

To support the point-to-point model, you must define individual router serial port logical interfaces or subinterfaces, each of which will represent a discrete IP subnet and IPX network. TCP/IP addressing can accommodate this model most efficiently by assigning each of the subinterfaces with a /30 subnet. IP address space for these WAN links will be derived from further subnetting of a single /24 bit subnet (172.17.95.0) The example Hub router configuration (TENN) that follows provides more details:

```
TENN#
interface serial 0
        encapsulation frame-relay ietf
        frame-relay lmi-type ansi
        no ip address

        interface serial 0.1 point-to-point
        description PVC to Cumberland router
        ip address 172.17.95.1 255.255.255.252
```

```
ipx network 179500
frame-relay interface-dlci 401 broadcast

interface serial 0.2 point-to-point
description PVC to west LA router
ip address 172.17.95.5 255.255.255.252
ipx network 179504
frame-relay interface-dlci 402 broadcast
```

OSPF Area Organization

Given the relatively small size of this network (less than 50 routers), it will be practical to include all routers into one single OSPF area. This will create a "portable" OSPF network that can be easily integrated into the enterprise corporate OSPF network once converted from IGRP. Because you do not know the future location of the OSPF backbone, you decide to be safe and put all routers in this network into a non-zero area. Putting this network into a non-zero area will allow you to avoid a future mass router reconfiguration after the corporate network is converted to OSPF. You assign this non-zero OSPF area an identifier of 64, because this number is the base number of the /19 CIDR block which is a logical representation of the addressing. You decide to use the company's registered BGP AS# of 5775 as the OSPF process ID# for this network:

```
router ospf 5775
```

The hub router in Tennessee will be the sole ASBR in this network, as it must run OSPF and IGRP to support mutual redistribution of routes between the Campus and WAN networks.

Because all routers in the frame relay network will be in area 64, no backbone area (area 0) will be created, and subsequently no routers will be configured as ABRs or backbone routers at this point.

Figure 7-29 shows the OSPF area architecture established for Terrapin.

Specifying the OSPF Network Type

Use the default OSPF network type of point-to-point because you are modeling the router frame-relay cloud as individual point-to-point subinterfaces. The initial step of DR/BDR election is not required because only two routers exist on point-to-point networks, resulting in quick adjacency formation upon startup.

Figure 7–29
OSPF Frame
Relay network
area
architecture.

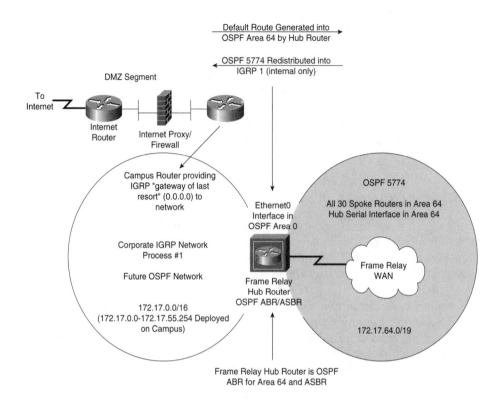

Implementing Authentication

The IS security manager insists that you use OSPF authentication to provide a low level of security on this network. You implement simple password authentication by assigning a key of "watchtower" to your OSPF area 64. All OSPF routers added to this frame relay network need to have this key configured in order to form an OSPF adjacency with the Hub router. This authentication will need to be entered under the OSPF process ID and on each serial interface as follows:

```
interface serial 0.1 point-to-point
   description PVC to Cumberland router
   ip address 172.17.95.1 255.255.255.252
   ip ospf authentication-key watchtower
   ipx network 179500
   frame-relay interface-dlci 401 broadcast
```

```
!
router ospf 5775
   area 64 authentication
```

NOTES

If you are planning on implementing OSPF authentication, you should also enable the Cisco Password encryption option through the use of the `service password-encryption` command.

Configuring Link Cost

Because all spoke routers will only have one PVC provisioned to the hub router, there is no need to configure specific OSPF costs to links to engineer traffic patterns in a particular matter. Use the defaults by not assigning costs in router configurations.

Tuning OSPF Timers

Because all routers are Cisco and running the same version of code, there is no reason to tune individual HELLO, DEAD, or RETRANSMIT timers. Cisco's default WAN values of 10, 40 and 120, respectively, will provide fast convergence times and ensure consistency across all routers:

```
TENN#
        interface Ethernet 0
        description LAN connection to campus backbone
        ip address 172.17.10.240 255.255.255.0
        !
        interface serial 0.1 point-to-point
        description PVC to Cumberland router
        ip address 172.17.95.1 255.255.255.252
        ip ospf authentication-key watchtower
        ipx network 179500
        frame-relay interface-dlci 401 broadcast
```

```
!
interface serial 0.2 point-to-point
description PVC to west LA router
ip address 172.17.95.5 255.255.255.252
ip ospf authentication-key watchtower
ipx network 179504
frame-relay interface-dlci 401 broadcast
!
router ospf 5775
network 172.17.95.0 0.0.0.255 area 64
area 64 authentication
```

Strategizing Route Redistribution

Redistribution of routes between the OSPF and IGRP domains will be done at the frame-relay hub router (ASBR) in Tennessee. To learn of routes from both domains, the hub router must run both an OSPF and IGRP routing process. Redistribution of routes must address all of the issues detailed in the sections that follow.

Campus Routing to Frame Relay WAN

This section discusses how the existing campus routers will dynamically learn about the new Frame Relay networks, specifically examining the following issues:

- OSPF Route Redistribution into IGRP
    - Static Route aggregation and redistribution into IGRP
    - OSPF Route aggregation and redistribution into IGRP
- Testing of OSPF route redistribution into IGRP

Redistribution of OSPF routes into the IGRP process will cause the hub router to send IGRP advertisements of all /24 subnets known to OSPF. This will allow all spoke router LAN subnets to be learned by IGRP routers.

Use the "internal" keyword when performing this redistribution on the Hub Cisco router to allow only OSPF "internal" routes to be redistributed into IGRP. This will prevent a possible router loop in the future if more routers are installed and running "two-way" OSPF/IGRP redistribution. (All of the frame relay LAN/WAN networks will be known as OSPF "internal" routes because they originated from this same domain.)

The WAN subnets cannot be redistributed into IGRP this simply, however, due to the "classless" IP subnetting scheme of /30. IGRP only supports "classful" subnetting, and routers would ignore all /30 subnets when redistributing. Although this would not affect host-to-host IP connectivity, it could potentially cause a problem with network management tools, subsequently causing routing holes when accessing the router's WAN IP address directly to/from frame-relay.

Two possible strategies for handling the WAN link advertisements into IGRP are possible: static route aggregation and redistribution into IGRP and OSPF Route aggregation and redistribution into IGRP.

With static route aggregation and redistribution into IGRP, you must represent all /30 WAN subnets into an aggregate 24-bit summary and then redistribute them because only /24 prefixed routes will be announced into IGRP. Configure a static route on the Hub router for 172.17.95.0 255.255.255.0, with the next hop as the "Null 0" interface (a.k.a. the hub router). Now, redistribute static routes into IGRP and all IGRP routers will be able to route traffic to these WAN links. Control redistribution of routes to just the 172.17.95.0/24 network by defining an access list that will only allow redistribution of this route. Defining an access list may prevent future routing problems if additional static routes are added to the hub router, which the campus need not know about through IGRP. The following configuration demonstrates how to control redistribution of routes.

```
TENN#
router igrp 10
network 172.17.0.0
passive-interface serial0.1:0.30
default-metric 10000 100 255 1 1500
redistribute ospf 5774 match internal
redistribute static
distribute-list 3 out static

ip route 172.17.95.0 255.255.255.0 null0
access-list 3 permit 172.17.95.0
```

The passive-interface command stops IGRP updates from being broadcasted unnecessarily across all wan PVCs.

The default-metric command assigns IGRP metrics to routes known from all other route sources (in this case static routes) that need redistribution into IGRP.

NOTES

IGRP uses Bandwidth, Delay, Reliability, Load, and MTU components to calculate route metrics across specific interfaces. The values `10000 100 255 1 1500` are defaults for 10MB Ethernet.

An alternative to static route aggregation of the WAN subnets would be to employ OSPF route aggregation and redistribution into IGRP to accomplish this task. This is the preferred solution, and the one chosen for this case study, as OSPF is already currently being redistributed into the IGRP process in order to propagate the LAN subnets.

To accomplish OSPF route summarization, the Hub router will need to be configured as an ABR. This is required because OSPF inter-area summarization can only be accomplished at area boundaries towards the backbone. You can accomplish this by adding the Ethernet interface into OSPF area 0. Now that the hub router (TENN) is an ABR, you can summarize the WAN subnets as one /24 network (`172.17.95.0/24`). This network falls on the established 24-bit boundary and will be redistributed into IGRP and understood by all interior IGRP-speaking routers as shown in the following configuration example.

```
TENN#
router igrp 10
network 172.17.0.0
passive-interface serial0.1:0.30
default-metric 10000 100 255 1 1500
redistribute ospf 5775 match internal

router ospf 5775
summary-address 172.17.95.0 255.255.255.0
network 172.17.95.0 0.0.0.255 area 64
network 172.17.10.240 0.0.0.0 area 0
area 64 range 172.17.95.0 255.255.255.0
area 64 authentication
```

To test the OSPF route redistribution into IGRP, you can display the routing table of any IGRP internal router, which will indicate the success or failure of the redistribution of OSPF routes into IGRP. If problems arise, debugging on IGRP transactions on the ASBR (hub) router may provide information as to what is going wrong.

CAMPUS to WAN Routing

Now that all WAN routes are available on the campus IGRP backbone, it will be necessary to advertise routing information to the WAN routers such that all campus subnets can be reached. This can be accomplished in two ways:

- Redistributing IGRP routes into OSPF
- Generating a default route into OSPF

All known IGRP subnets can be redistributed into OSPF at the Hub router with the following:

```
TENN#
router ospf 5775
redistribute igrp 10 metric 100 metric-type 1 subnets
```

`metric 100` is an arbitrary default metric that will be attached to IGRP routes redistributed into OSPF.

`metric-type 1` will make redistributed IGRP routes external Type 1, which will allow the OSPF spoke routers to add individual link costs in order to calculate OSPF metrics.

`subnets` is necessary to allow subnets of natural class B address `172.17.0.0` to be redistributed into OSPF.

You should take note that the IGRP "gateway of last resort," default route or `0.0.0.0`, will be automatically redistributed into OSPF because it appears as an IGRP route on the Hub router. This default route will be propagated to all frame-relay routers as an external 0.0.0.0/0 route.

When generating a default route into OSPF, because all spoke routers only have a single path (one PVC) out to the WAN, all destinations, which are not locally connected, would have to traverse that path. A default route (`0.0.0.0/0.0.0.0`) can be sent from the ASBR Hub router in lieu of specific subnet routes. This is the preferred method in this case, since the routing tables on remote routers become smaller, and potential routing loops which sometimes result from two-way redistribution can be avoided altogether. The syntax that follows demonstrates this procedure.

```
TENN#
router ospf 5775
default information originate metric 100 metric-type 1
```

NOTES

In order to use the default route method, it is necessary to enable classless interdomain routing (CIDR) on all OSPF routers. This is done using the "ip classless" command on all routers:

```
Router#
ip classless
```

Without this command, remote routers will not use the default route as a possible path for any destination networks, which are subnetted out of the "native class" 172.17.0.0 network.

Refer to Figure 7-29 to see the implementation of the techniques covered in this section for Campus-to-WAN routing.

CASE STUDY CONCLUSIONS

Although the Terrapin OSPF network design was fairly simple in terms of IP addressing and OSPF architecture, integration into the IGRP network presented a number of challenges. Adding OSPF into existing networks running other routing protocols is often a difficult task, and must be carefully planned out; otherwise sub-optimal routing or even loops may occur.

FREQUENTLY ASKED QUESTIONS

Q— *What is the benefit of a one-layer distributed network design?*

A— They are good for smaller networks and are useful from a survivability aspect if you plan to distribute servers throughout the network. The downside is a tendency to have duplicated functions at the various sites, which results in higher costs.

Q— *I have a server farm type of LAN within my networking environment. How should I design the network to maximize their placement?*

A— The standard hub and spoke network design would be good for locations having a server farm. You might also want to consider using the higher bandwidth LANs (FDDI and fast Ethernet) to connect the servers.

Q— *Why shouldn't I put hosts and users on the backbone of my network?*

A— To facilitate effective routing at the backbone, users should not be directly connected to it. Ideally, about 80 percent of LAN traffic should remain there. By following the guidelines, you will increase the backbone's reliability, facilitate proper traffic management, and be able to easily plan for backbone equipment or bandwidth upgrades.

Q— *Where can you get OSPF software?*

A— The first thing that comes to mind is Cisco routers. However, there are other places to find the software such as other router manufactures. In addition, Merit Networks of Ann Arbor, MI currently maintains a program known as GATED. This program is among other things a routing daemon for Unix platforms and it contains OSPF. The original implementation of OSPF has been incorporated into GATED. For additional information on these two sources, refer to the following sites: `http://www.cisco.com` and `http://www.gated.com`.

Q— *How can I learn more about networking and OSPF in particular?*

A— I would recommend two mailing lists. The first is a mailing list regarding Cisco networking equipment as a whole. You can join it by sending a subscription request to: `cisco-request@spot.colorado.edu`.

The other mailing list that I would recommend concerns the OSPF protocol as a whole. The OSPF Working Group has a mailing list that holds discussions on various OSPF topic. You can join it by sending a subscription request to: ospf-request@gated.cornell.edu.

You can also go to the IETF and learn more about the IETF Working Groups and the areas of networking that they monitor and such: http://www.ietf.com.

Cisco also has a very extensive Web page that contains an impressive amount of information on networking, although to access the majority of it, you need a Cisco Connection Online (CCO) account. This information can be found at http://www.cisco.com.

Q— *I need an explanation of OSPF link types. Could you please summarize and explain the differences between the following:*

- OSPF router links
- OSPF net links
- OSPF summary net links
- OSPF exterior links

A— RFC 1583 describes what those links are. The following information is in RFC 1583:

- **List of router link advertisements.** A router link's advertisement is generated by each router in the area. It describes the state of the router's interfaces to the area.

- **List of network link advertisements.** One network links advertisement is generated for each transit multi-access network in the area. A network link's advertisement describes the set of routers currently connected to the network.

- **List of summary link advertisements.** Summary link advertisements originate from the area's area border routers. They describe routes to destinations internal to the Autonomous System, yet external to the area.

- **List of external routes.** These are routes to destinations external to the Autonomous System that have been gained either through direct experience with another routing protocol (such as EGP), through configuration information, or through a combination of the two (for example, dynamic external information to be advertised by OSPF with configured metric). Any router having these external routes is called an AS boundary router. These routes are advertised by the router into the OSPF routing domain via AS external link advertisements.

- **List of AS external link advertisements.** Part of the topological database, these have originated from the AS boundary routers, and they comprise routes to destinations external to the Autonomous System. Note that if the router is itself an AS boundary router, some of these AS external link advertisements have been self-originated.

Q— *I want to run OSPF over ISDN (DDR). How can I suppress that the connection is established for every hello packet? Does snapshot routing work with OSPF, or just with distance vector protocols?*

A— Snapshot will not work with OSPF because it is a link-state protocol. However, OSPF over DDR links is supported in Cisco IOS 11.2. This feature enables you to suppress hellos and updates after the updates and hellos are passed initially.

Q— *What is the best way to implement an IP default network (0.0.0.0) in a mixed RIP/OSPF network? I have inherited a network that has an OSPF backbone and is redistributed into RIP on the boundary routers. There are static routes to 0.0.0.0 scattered throughout the network, and they are redistributed in OSPF and RIP. In fact, there is a static route to 0.0.0.0 pointing to the next hop for Frame Relay defined on every router. There are IP default network statements on every local campus router, and there is an OSPF default-information originate statement. What is the best, most fault tolerant methodology to introduce a simple clean default route in this environment?*

A— Remove all the static routes. Watch where you dynamically get a default route. Make sure you have the default-info originate command on the correct router that you want to generate the 0.0.0.0 route. Let this go to every area dynamically. When you redistribute OSPF into RIP, this route will also go dynamically. Remember that you cannot originate default on every OSPF router: 1) Stub areas do this automatically; 2) Only ABR can generate this by using the default-information command.

Q— *Can OSPF give me full connectivity for IP in a partially-meshed Frame Relay network? Or, will I have to configure subinterfaces?*

A— OSPF has a feature called point-to-multipoint interfaces to easily allow full connectivity over a partially meshed Frame Relay network in Cisco IOS 11.0 and later. It could be done before Cisco IOS 11.0, but it required the hub router to be the Designated Router and some map statements on each spoke router to all the rest of the spoke routers through the hub router.

Q— *Can the* `ip ospf network point-to-multipoint` *command be used with Frame Relay subinterfaces?*

A— Yes, that is exactly what it was designed for.

Q— *Can IPX be routed using OSPF?*

A— No, OSPF is for IP. NetWare Link Services Protocol (NLSP) is Novell's answer to link-state routing protocol for IPX.

Q— *I have a serial link between Router A and Router B. They will use an ISDN link for bandwidth-on-demand and backup, as indicated here:*

```
backup interface bri 0
backup load 25 5
backup delay 10 60
```

The serial link has OSPF and IPX configured. Is it possible to have all the IPX and OSPF perimeters transferred to the ISDN link when the serial reaches 25 percent, or must I configure OSPF and IPX on the BRI?

A— You need to configure both the IP and IPX parameters on the BRI interface also. After all, bringing up another link means another physical path to the destination and this path must contain the IP and IPX information before the router can put IP and IPX traffic onto this link.

Q— *Does OSPF support secondary addressing? Is there anything special I have to configure?*

A— Yes, secondary addressing is supported. The secondary address needs to be in the same area as the primary interface. In addition, OSPF cannot be configured on a secondary interface without being enabled on the primary.

Q— *Can I redistribute interior BGP routes into OSPF?*

A— Yes, but it is really not allowed and is *strongly discouraged*. Otherwise, you might cause routing loops.

Q— *My ASBR router is running OSPF as well as BGP. The router knows about my network's IP addresses through OSPF—the* sh ip route *command shows all my OSPF routes. But the BGP process does not exchange these routes with its peer, even if I use the BGP command:* network <number> <mask>, *where* <number> <mask> *are the aggregated IP addresses and corresponding masks of networks known by the ASBR router's OSPF process. If I redistribute the OSPF routes into the BGP process using the* redistribute ospf <id> route-map <ospf-to-bgp> *command, then only BGP will start redistributing my networks to its peer. I have taken care to use the proper access list associated with the* redistribute *command. The Cisco manuals recommend not to redistribute IGP into BGP, however, and state that the better way to do this is to use the BGP* network *command, which does not seem to work for me. How can I resolve this problem?*

A— For the network command to work, you need to have the *exact* route specified in it contained in your routing table. Make sure that your IP routing table has the exact routes that are mentioned in the network statement. Refer to BGP Technical Tips at: http://www.cisco.com/warp/customer/459/ 18.html or the Cisco troubleshooting engine which is found at: http://www.cisco.com/diag/te_start.html.

Q— *Can you use the* distribute-list out *command to filter static routes that are being redistributed into OSPF? I have a network running OSPF. On some of my routers, I have static routes that are being redistributed into OSPF; however, I do not want all of the static routes to be redistributed. I used the* distribute-list out *command, and this appears to have worked, but I have found that if I add another* access-list *command to permit an additional static route to be redistributed, the new access-list has no effect until I remove the* distribute-list out *command from the OSPF routing process and then re-insert it.*

A— What you have done is fine. You can also use the clear ip ospf redistribution command to refresh the redistribution process.

Q— *When implementing an OSPF network, what are the advantages and disadvantages in establishing Area 0 for the whole network?*

A— Generally, it depends on the total number of routers in the network and the topology of the network. If you are going to have fewer than 40 routers in the network, you should be able to get away with having all routers in area 0. For larger networks, you will want to subdivide your network to break it up into areas.

Q— *Can you set an OSPF dead interval timer in Cisco IOS 11.0 on a 4500 series router? I configured a core router (FDDI-attached) with the same configuration as a local router, but the users could not see out of their LAN. Both of the interfaces configured are Ethernet. There was an OSPF hello interval statement and network statements in the one router, and both had area statements.*

A— Yes, you can change the dead interval using the `ip ospf dead-interval` command. If this timer is not manually set, it will take a value of four times the Hello interval, by default.

Q— *What is the command to enable the serial interface learn routes only (listen) and not send the updates? I am running OSPF in a Cisco 7000 router.*

A— You will not be able to do this. The command `passive-interface serial` *x* with OSPF will disable both incoming and outgoing routing updates. The command `distribute-list out` cannot be used, unless this is an autonomous system border router (ASBR), and you only want to filter external routes (from other routing protocols).

On the other router, the most you can do is filter incoming updates from the serial link with `distribute-list in`. This will affect only those routers coming into that particular router's routing table. It will not alter the OSPF database.

Thus, that router will pass the LSAs on to its other neighbors, so even this is not a very good solution. You would need a `distribute-list in` on each subsequent router to block the LSAs from getting into each router's routing table.

Q— *If area1=NJ, area2=Delaware, and area0=NYC, will routing ever take place between area 1 and area 2 without traversing the backbone (as it will be the shortest path)?*

A— In the migration of RIP to OSPF, there seems to be a case where two non-backbone areas are going to be connected, such as area 1 to area 2. This is in place for redundancy. In OSPF, all areas must touch the backbone area 0. You can, however, use virtual links to get from area 1 to the backbone and then to area 2. The virtual links are tunnels to the backbone.

Q— *What is the recommended maximum number of routers in an OSPF area, specifically the backbone area?*

A— It depends on how stable your network is. If it is extremely stable, with no flapping links, you can get by with more routers in an area. 40 is a conservative estimate.

Q— *What is the correct wildcard mask for an OSPF network with mask 255.255.255.252? We are using Class C network addresses, on Loopback interfaces for DLSw, subnetted 255.255.255.252. From the three proposals that follow, what is the correct wildcard mask to use on the OSPF network definition statement* router ospf 1234:

1. network 192.168.1.4 0.0.0.2 area 0 (two hosts)

2. network 192.168.1.4 0.0.0.3 area 0 (two hosts and broadcast)

3. network 192.168.1.4 0.0.0.4 area 0 (network, two hosts, and broadcast)

A— The third wildcard mask is the best method. For the loopback interface, you can use a 255.255.255.255 mask to save address space because OSPF supports host-route. To answer your question, if your loopback is 192.168.1.9 255.255.255.252, then under OSPF you would have: network 192.168.1.8 0.0.0.3 area 0. In other words, #2 in your question is the correct choice.

Q— *How does OSPF handle multiple exit points? I am running OSPF between areas and RIP within areas. I also have multiple exit points to some destinations. How do I tell OSPF to use the preferred path? Do I need static route statements to force it?*

A— OSPF will use the lowest cost to the end destination. You can find the total cost by adding up all the costs on individual links to the exit points. If you want, you can manipulate the OSPF costs with the ip ospf cost command. The administrative distance of RIP is 120 and OSPF is 110.

Q— *Is there anything I should look out for with Dial Backup using OSPF?*

A— It will work well as long as you obey the general rules of OSPF, such as never dial between areas (from area 1 to area 2, for example). Also, make your backup delay intervals long enough so you don't end up causing route flaps in the OSPF, which will cause routing storms.

Q— *If I inject some external routes into OSPF, can I then summarize those routes into one route on some router downstream in the network? It seems that the only way to summarize the external routes is by summarizing on the router that first injected (redistributed) the external routes. I am using the* summary-address *command. I do not think the area range command will work either because this summarizes only internal OSPF routes.*

A— You must summarize the external routes at the ASBR router (the router where the redistribution of external routes into OSPF is taking place). Please see the OSPF Design Guide for details.

Q— *While testing OSPF, I ran OSPF on one of my routers and used the OSPF* default-information originate metric-type 1 *command. This same router had a static route* ip route 0.0.0.0 0.0.0.0 xxx.xxx.xxx.xxx, *where xxx.xxx.xxx.xxx was the opposite directly connected interface on s0 of my test router. When I shut down s0, the default route generated by the* default-information originate *command disappeared. Does that mean that the OSPF* default-information originate *command polls the interface defined in the static route?*

A— If the next hop in a static route is unreachable or down, the static route will no longer be installed. In addition, because that static route is no longer in the router, OSPF is not originating default. For the router to originate a default without any regard to the availability of a default route in the router, use the command default-information originate always.

Q— *When using OSPF, is area* 0.0.0.0 *the same as area 0? Should the backbone always be area 0?*

A— Yes. Area 0 is also displayed as area 0.0.0.0. Yes. Area 0 is the backbone area, and it is mandatory.

Q— *Do Cisco routers support OSPF for secondary addresses? We would like to run OSPF for both the primary and secondary addresses, but have that interface as passive. A second scenario (but not yet needed) is OSPF on the LAN with OSPF neighbor as primary IP address, with neighbor as secondary IP address—is that possible?*

A— Cisco routers treat secondary addresses as stub networks under OSPF. They also do not form adjacencies on secondary addresses. It has to be the primary for that to happen.

Q— *Is it possible to create an OSPF virtual link through two or more areas to connect to area 0?*

A— That is not a supported function according to the RFC. You cannot create an OSPF virtual link across more than one area.

Q— *How do I set the hub router on a hub and spoke Frame Relay network to be the designated router (DR) in an OSPF routing environment?*

A— Most hub-and-spoke architectures do not have any broadcast capability to emulate shared media between remote nodes, but instead are made up of a set of point-to-point links converging on one central router. In any point-to-point topology, even with a large set of neighbors, the DR concept is irrelevant and not used. The routers will establish a complete adjacency without electing a DR. In many cases, the above might require that each sub-interface be set up as an explicitly point-to-point subinterface and/or the use on a per-interface basis of: `ip ospf network point-to-point`. If, for some reason, you want to establish DR/BDR relationships on point-to-point links, you may still implement `ip ospf priority < number >`, where `< number >` is greater than one and applied on the local interfaces to the hub router. In such a topology, however, this is not recommended.

Q— *How do I advertise a single summary route to other OSPF areas? I have subnetted a Class C network no. With a* `255.255.255.252` *mask for my Frame Relay backbone. For each of my point-to-point connections, I am using a subnet, and on the Frame Relay backbone all subnets are contiguous. How would I summarize all routes using OSPF to advertise a single summary route to other OSPF areas? For example, based on a* `207.105.207.0` *network no., is the following correct?*

    Network no.: 207.105.207.0
    Subnet mask: 255.255.255.252

A— Summarize all addresses between `207.105.207.4` through `207.105.207.44` with the following: `area 12 range 207.105.207.4 255.255.255.47`. The `area range` command summarizes a block of addresses in an area to the backbone. This command should be configured on the backbone area border router. For example, if you were to summarize a block of addresses `131.108.32.0–131.108.47.255` in area 12 to the backbone; the required command would be `area 12 range 131.108.32.0 255.255.240.0`.

Q— *If a router (router 1) has a default route specified to be to a router (router 2, which is not talking OSPF) on a network on which router 1 has an interface, and router 1 has* default-information originate *set so that it propagates a default route, will the default route advertisements have a forwarding address set to the address of router 2 so as to avoid ICMP redirects?*

A— The OSPF updates should contain database information including the IP address of the location of the default router. The OSPF router receiving the update should independently decide the best "next-hop" to get to the network where that address resides. If it is directly connected to the subnet in common with router 1 and router 2, it should send the packet directly to router 2 even though router 2 does not speak OSPF. Unlike classic distance-vector protocols, the "next-hop" address is independent of the advertising router.

Q— *When using floating static routes on a link backup over ISDN, how can I ensure that the floating route stays active until the OSPF table is built?*

A— Floating static routes have administrative distances greater than the other routing protocols (higher than 120). This means that a route learned via any routing protocol will take precedence, regardless of the metric. When the link is restored, the router will use the OSPF route as soon as it is available. The backup link will stay up until the backup delay timer expires, but IP traffic will use the OSPF route.

Q— *I have a network (Frame Relay) in which every remote site has a primary and a secondary link. I want the secondary link to be used only if the primary becomes inaccessible; OSPF is my routing protocol. When I do trace route, the path taken to reach the destination is through the secondary link. Why does this happen?*

A— I think you mean that both links are connected to the same router. The best way is to use different ip ospf cost on the links or use static routing for the backup link with a higher distance than OSPF.

Q— *How do I resolve discontiguous networks?*

A— You can use secondary IP addresses to link the address space or you can use OSPF EIGRP, IS-IS or BGP4 with auto summarization turned off.

Q— *In 9.1, why must the* neighbor *command be used when running OSPF over X.25 networks?*

A— You need the neighbor command to make OSPF work on X.25 in 9.1. In 9.21 and later, at OSPF level, an X.25 network can be configured to be a broadcast network, and OSPF would treat X.25 as a broadcast network only. X.25 maps with the broadcast keyword would be needed to make it work.

Q— *How can an OSPF default be originated into the system based on the existence of certain external information (i.e., routes learned from some exterior protocol) on a router which does not itself have a default?*

A— OSPF will generate a default only if it is configured using the command default-information originate and if there is a default network in the box from a different process.

CHAPTER 8

Monitoring & Troubleshooting an OSPF Network

> *"Perseverance: The difference between a successful person and others is not a lack of strength, not a lack of knowledge, but rather a lack of will."*—Successories

This chapter builds upon the design theories and processes discussed in Chapter 7, "Designing & Implementing an OSPF Network." This chapter assumes that you have designed and implemented an OSPF network as detailed in the process in Chapter 7. The basis for this chapter is how to go about monitoring and ensuring OSPF is operating correctly and what to do if it is not. There are certain troubleshooting procedures and techniques that you can use to determine the causes of a network problem, which are covered as well. This chapter consists of three major sections, which are as follows:

- **Monitoring OSPF.** This section covers how to go about determining if OSPF is configuring and operating as you designed it to. This is one of the most important areas of the book. It is essential to master the techniques and commands used to this section. By doing so, you will be able to more effectively implement, monitor, and manage your OSPF network.

- **Troubleshooting OSPF.** This section provides you with the techniques needed to troubleshoot more effectively when an OSPF-related network problem occurs. This section also assists you in developing your network and its related management structure to allow you to reduce the length of any network problem. This information is supplemented by in-depth discussions on various network troubleshooting commands.

- **Cisco Technical Support.** This section explores the many different ways of finding and gaining access to the resources available. These resources include deciphering Cisco's Connection Online (CCO) and how technical support information is available for engineers at all levels of knowledge.

MONITORING OSPF

Now that your OSPF network has been designed and implemented, or will soon be implemented, there are some important questions to ask yourself before proceeding:

- Is OSPF operating properly and in accordance with your design?

- Are you sure or unsure?

- How and why are you sure or unsure?

- What do you know about how OSPF is operating?

The true test of your design will be in how well it operates. This section will concentrate on the methods needed to determine how well the OSPF design is operating and provide you with the tools necessary to answer the previously cited questions. Many people follow the belief that the network "must be up," but I think that going a step further is more accurate in that the network "must be up and operational."

Monitoring the Operation of OSPF

Having the ability and knowledge to properly monitor OSPF will be a crucial part of your network's success or failure. An essential requirement to your network operation is that the status of your routers and their routing protocols are monitored to ensure network availability for all users. Although many different types of network management platforms are available to assist you in this endeavor, there are tools to make this management task easier. At some level, every management platform will be based upon the following three methods of monitoring:

- SHOW commands

- Router SYSLOG files

- SNMP and MIBs

Each of these three monitoring techniques requires a different area of understanding in order to use it. This chapter discusses the various OSPF SHOW commands and how to configure the Router SYSLOG file to provide you with information regarding OSPF. Chapter 9, "Managing Your OSPF Network," discusses SNMP and OSPF MIBs.

OSPF SHOW Commands

This section is similar to the OSPF configuration commands provided in Chapter 6, "Advanced OSPF Design Concepts." This section has a list of the most useful OSPF SHOW commands and definitions of their output. This information is essential for you as you begin implementing your network design. By this point in your network implementation, you should be ready to see if your OSPF network is working as you designed it to.

This section discusses many of the SHOW commands available for use within Cisco routers. Before going on, review the OSPF actions that will demand resources from the router, as illustrated in Figure 8-1.

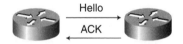

Hello

ACK

• Hello timer 10 seconds by default
• No LSAs if no link changes state
• CPU utilization determined by SPF frequency

Figure 8–1
OSPF resource utilization.

show ip ospf ? *Command*

The show ip ospf ? command provides you with the means to determine exactly what OSPF SHOW commands are available for you within a Cisco router. This is very useful, as available commands differ per Cisco IOS release. Any time you use a question mark, it invokes a help menu as shown below of the available commands.

Example:
```
OSPF_Router# show ip ospf ?
<1-4294967295>     Process ID number(s) that are running on the router
   border-routers          Border and Boundary Router Information
   database                LSA Database summary
   interface               Interface information
   neighbor                Neighbor list
```

```
request-list                Link state request list
retransmission-list         Link state retransmission list
summary-address             Summary-address redistribution Information
virtual-links               Virtual link information
```

show ip ospf *Command*

The show ip ospf command displays a variety of general information about the routing process. To display general information about OSPF routing processes, use the show ip ospf EXEC command. The syntax for this command is as follows:

```
show ip ospf [process-id]
```

Syntax Description:

> ***process-id.*** If the optional process-id argument (which represents the Process ID) is included, only information for the specified OSPF routing process is included.

Usage Guidelines: The full SPF algorithm is run only when there is a topology change, as expressed in a router link-state advertisements (LSAs), not for summary LSAs; they cause a partial spf to be run. This command can be used to determine the number of times the SPF algorithm has been executed. It also shows the link-state update interval, assuming no topological changes have occurred.

Example: The following command syntax will provide you with a wealth of relevant information regarding the OSPF processes that are currently running on your Cisco router. The entries in this output are defined in Table 8-1 that follows.

```
OSPF_ROUTER> show ip ospf
 Routing Process ''ospf 5774'' with ID 156.20.16.6
 Supports only single TOS (TOS0) routes
 It is an area border and autonomous system boundary router
 Summary Link update interval is 00:30:00 and the update due in 00:00:54
 External Link update interval is 00:30:00 and the update due in 00:02:43
 Redistributing External Routes from,
    connected with metric mapped to 100, includes subnets in redistribution
    bgp 5754 with metric mapped to 50, includes subnets in redistribution
 SPF schedule delay 5 secs, Hold time between two SPFs 10 secs
 Number of areas in this router is 2. 2 normal 0 stub
    Area BACKBONE(0)
        Number of interfaces in this area is 3
        Area has no authentication
        SPF algorithm executed 9778 times
```

```
        Area ranges are
          156.20.16.0/24 Active(1)
        Link State Update Interval is 00:30:00 and due in 00:02:43
        Link State Age Interval is 00:20:00 and due in 00:02:43
    Area 14
        Number of interfaces in this area is 2
        Area has no authentication
        SPF algorithm executed 30 times
        Area ranges are
        Link State Update Interval is 00:30:00 and due in 00:00:50
        Link State Age Interval is 00:20:00 and due in 00:00:43
```

Table 8-1 describes some fields that are useful in a troubleshooting environment.

Table 8-1   *show ip ospf output definitions*

Field	Description
Routing Process "ospf 5774" with ID 56.0.16.6	OSPF Process ID and OSPF router ID
Type of Service	Number of Types of Service supported (Type 0 only)
Type of OSPF Router	Possible types are internal, area border, or autonomous system boundary
Summary Link update interval	Specify summary update interval in hours:minutes:seconds, and time to next update
External Link update interval	Specify external update interval in hours:minutes:seconds, and time to next update
Redistributing External Routes	Lists of redistributed from routes, by protocol
Number of areas	Number of areas in the router, area addresses, and so on
SPF Algorithm	This is run only for route link-state advertisements (LSAs), not for summary LSAs. This command shows the number of times the full SPF algorithm has been run.
Link State Update Interval	Specify router and network link-state update interval in hours:minutes:seconds, and time to next update
Link State Age Interval	Specify max-aged update deletion interval and time until next database cleanup in hours:minutes:seconds

show ip ospf interface *Command*

You can gain an extensive amount of useful information from the show ip ospf inter-face command. In this use of the command, a specific interface was selected, but if used as shown here, then it will provide you with information on all interfaces. To display OSPF-related interface information, use the show ip ospf interface EXEC command. The syntax for this command is as follows:

```
show ip ospf interface [type number]
```

Syntax Description:

type: This optional argument represents the interface type.
number: This optional argument represents the interface number.

Usage Guidelines: You can verify that interfaces have been configured in the intended areas. In the example that follows, the serial interface has been placed in area 0.

The show ip ospf interface command also gives the timer intervals including the hello interval. These values must match if the OSPF routers are to become neighbors.

Example: The following is sample output from the show ip ospf interface command when Serial2/0.1 is specified.

```
OSPF_ROUTER# show ip ospf interface s2/0.1
Serial2/0.1 is up, line protocol is up
   Internet Address 156.20.16.65/27, Area 0
   Process ID 5774, Router ID 156.20.16.1, Network Type BROADCAST, Cost: 64
   Transmit Delay is 1 sec, State DROTHER, Priority 10
   Designated Router (ID) 156.20.16.8, Interface address 156.20.16.72
   Backup Designated router (ID) 156.20.16.9, Interface address 156.20.16.73
   Timer intervals configured, Hello 10, Dead 40, Wait 40, Retransmit 5
     Hello due in 00:00:09
   Neighbor Count is 8, Adjacent neighbor count is 2
     Adjacent with neighbor 156.20.16.8 (Designated Router)
     Adjacent with neighbor 156.20.16.9 (Backup Designated Router)
```

Table 8-2 describes some fields that are useful in a troubleshooting environment.

Table 8-2 *show ip ospf int* output definitions

Field	Description
Serial	The serial interface about which you requested information. The status of the physical link and operational status of protocol.
Internet Address	Interface IP address, subnet mask, and area address
process ID	OSPF process ID (ex: Autonomous System number), router ID, link-state cost
Transmit Delay	Transmit delay, interface state (is it the DR or BDR?), and router priority to be used in determining the DR and BDR
Network Type	Indicates the network type; in this case, broadcast
State DROTHER	This command means that this router is not acting as either the Designated Router (DR) nor the Backup Designated Router (BDR). Both of these conditions are also possible in this field and these values are typically only seen on broadcast media.
Priority 10	This value indicates the priority of this router in the DR/BDR election. The default value is 1.
State DROTHER	This command means that this router is acting as neither the Designated Router (DR) nor the Backup Designated Router (BDR). Both of these conditions are also possible in this field.
Designated Router	Designated Router ID and its respective interface IP address
Backup Designated router	Backup Designated Router ID and its respective interface IP address
Timer intervals configured	Configuration of OSPF tunable timer intervals
Hello	Number of seconds until next hello packet is sent out from this interface
Wait	Indicates how long to wait if the Designated Router (DR) fails until the election process begins in order to replace the DR
Retransmit	If a link-state retransmission list (flooded LSAs but not yet acknowledged) exists, this is the amount of time until it they are retransmitted.
Neighbor Count	Count of network neighbors and list of adjacent neighbors
Adjacent neighbors	Shows all routers that are adjacent to this one. This core router has two adjacencies, each of the ASBRs within an Autonomous System.

show ip ospf border-routers *Command*

To display the internal OSPF routing table entries to an Area Border Router (ABR) and Autonomous System Boundary Router (ASBR), use the show ip ospf border-routers privileged EXEC command.

Example:

```
OSPF_ROUTER#show ip ospf border-routers
OSPF Process 5774 internal Routing Table
Codes: i - Intra-area route, I - Inter-area route
 i 156.20.18.5 [64] via 156.20.18.1, Serial3/0.1, ASBR, Area 5, SPF 1020
 i 56.88.5.17 [64] via 156.20.18.9, Serial3/0.2, ASBR, Area 5, SPF 1020
 I 156.20.18.97 [128] via 156.20.16.40, Serial1/0.1, ASBR, Area 0, SPF 9819
 I 156.20.18.97 [128] via 156.20.16.72, Serial2/0.1, ASBR, Area 0, SPF 9819
 I 156.20.18.97 [128] via 156.20.16.41, Serial1/0.1, ASBR, Area 0, SPF 9819
 I 156.20.18.97 [128] via 156.20.16.73, Serial2/0.1, ASBR, Area 0, SPF 9819
 I 156.20.18.96 [128] via 156.20.16.40, Serial1/0.1, ASBR, Area 0, SPF 9819
 I 156.20.18.96 [128] via 156.20.16.72, Serial2/0.1, ASBR, Area 0, SPF 9819
 I 156.20.18.96 [128] via 156.20.16.41, Serial1/0.1, ASBR, Area 0, SPF 9819
 I 156.20.18.96 [128] via 156.20.16.73, Serial2/0.1, ASBR, Area 0, SPF 9819
 I 56.224.10.16 [128] via 156.20.16.36, Serial1/0.1, ASBR, Area 0, SPF 9819
 I 56.224.10.16 [128] via 156.20.16.68, Serial2/0.1, ASBR, Area 0, SPF 9819
 I 56.224.10.16 [128] via 156.20.16.38, Serial1/0.1, ASBR, Area 0, SPF 9819
 I 56.224.10.16 [128] via 156.20.16.70, Serial2/0.1, ASBR, Area 0, SPF 9819
 I 56.224.10.17 [128] via 156.20.16.36, Serial1/0.1, ASBR, Area 0, SPF 9819
 I 56.224.10.17 [128] via 156.20.16.68, Serial2/0.1, ASBR, Area 0, SPF 9819
 I 56.224.10.17 [128] via 156.20.16.38, Serial1/0.1, ASBR, Area 0, SPF 9819
 I 56.224.10.17 [128] via 156.20.16.70, Serial2/0.1, ASBR, Area 0, SPF 9819
```

Table 8-3 describes some fields that are useful in a troubleshooting environment.

Table 8-3 *show ip ospf border-routers* output definitions

Field	Description
Rte Type	The type of this route; it is either an intra-area or inter-area route
Destination	Destination's router ID
Next Hop	Next hop toward the destination
Cost	Cost of using this route

Table 8-3	*show ip ospf border-routers* output definitions, continued
Field	**Description**
Type	The router type of the destination; it is either an Area Border Router (ABR), an Autonomous System Boundary Router (ASBR), or both.
Area	The area ID of the area from which this route is learned
SPF No	The internal number of SPF calculation that installs this route

show ip ospf database *Command*

The show ip ospf database command displays the contents of the topological database maintained by the router. The command shows the router ID and the OSPF Process ID. The use of an easy-to-recognize router ID, such as a fictitious ID established for a loopback interface, can make troubleshooting more straightforward. Use the show ip ospf database EXEC command to display lists of information related to the OSPF database for a specific router. The various forms of this command deliver information about different OSPF link-state advertisements. The syntax for the various forms of the show ip ospf database EXEC command are as follows:

```
show ip ospf [process-id area-id] database
show ip ospf [process-id area-id] database [router] [link-state-id]
show ip ospf [process-id area-id] database [network] [link-state-id]
show ip ospf [process-id area-id] database [summary] [link-state-id]
show ip ospf [process-id area-id] database [asbr-summary] [link-state-id]
show ip ospf [process-id] database [external] [link-state-id]
show ip ospf [process-id area-id] database [database-summary]
```

Syntax Description:

process-id. This optional argument represents an internally used identification parameter. It is locally assigned and can be any positive integer number. The number used here is the number assigned administratively when enabling the OSPF routing process.

area-id. This option argument represents an area number associated with the OSPF address range defined in the network router configuration command used to define the particular area.

link-state-id. This optional argument identifies the portion of the Internet environment that is being described by the advertisement. The value entered depends on the advertisement's LS type. It must be entered in the form of an IP address. When the link-state advertisement is describing a network, the *link-state-id* can take one of two forms: the network's IP address (as in type 3 summary-link advertisements and in Autonomous System external link advertisements); a derived address obtained from the link state ID. (Note that masking a network link advertisement's link state ID with the network's subnet mask yields the network's IP address.) When the link-state advertisement is describing a router, the link state ID is always the described router's OSPF router ID. When an Autonomous System external advertisement (LS Type = 5) is describing a default route, its link state ID is set to Default Destination (0.0.0.0).

Example: The following command syntax will provide you with a wealth of relevant information regarding the OSPF database that is currently running on your Cisco router. The entries in this output are defined in the Table 8-4 that follows the example syntax.

```
OSPF_Router# show ip ospf database
OSPF Router with id(190.20.239.66) (Process ID 300)


             Displaying Router Link States(Area 0.0.0.0)


     Link ID       ADV Router      Age    Seq# Checksum Link count
   155.187.21.6   155.187.21.6    1731   0x80002CFB  0x69BC    8
   155.187.21.5   155.187.21.5    1112   0x800009D2  0xA2B8    5
   155.187.1.2    155.187.1.2     1662   0x80000A98  0x4CB6    9
   155.187.1.1    155.187.1.1     1115   0x800009B6  0x5F2C    1
   155.187.1.5    155.187.1.5     1691   0x80002BC   0x2A1A    5
   155.187.65.6   155.187.65.6    1395   0x80001947  0xEEE1    4
   155.187.241.5  155.187.241.5   1161   0x8000007C  0x7C70    1
   155.187.27.6   155.187.27.6    1723   0x80000548  0x8641    4
   155.187.70.6   155.187.70.6    1485   0x80000B97  0xEB84    6


             Displaying Net Link States(Area 0.0.0.0)


     Link ID       ADV Router      Age    Seq#        Checksum
   155.187.1.3    192.20.239.66   1245   0x800000EC  0x82E
```

```
                    Displaying Summary Net Link States(Area 0.0.0.0)

        Link ID       ADV Router      Age    Seq#         Checksum
    155.187.240.0  155.187.241.5  1152  0x80000077    0x7A05
    155.187.241.0  155.187.241.5  1152  0x80000070    0xAEB7
    155.187.244.0  155.187.241.5  1152  0x80000071    0x95CB
```

Table 8-4 describes some fields that are useful in a troubleshooting environment.

Table 8-4   *show ip ospf database* output definitions

Field	Description
Link ID	Router ID number
ADV Router	Advertising router's ID
Age	Link state age
Seq#	Link state sequence number (detects old or duplicate link-state advertisements)
Checksum	Fletcher checksum of the complete contents of the link-state advertisement
Link count	Number of interfaces detected for router

show ip ospf database asbr-summary *Command*

The following command syntax will provide you with a wealth of relevant information regarding the OSPF database on an ASBR. The entries in this output are defined in the table below.

Example: The following is sample output from the show ip ospf database asbr-summary command when no optional arguments are specified:

```
OSPF_Router# show ip ospf database asbr-summary
OSPF Router with id(190.20.239.66) (Autonomous system 300)
                Displaying Summary ASB Link States(Area 0.0.0.0)
LS age: 1463
Options: (No TOS-capability)
LS Type: Summary Links(AS Boundary Router)
Link State ID: 155.187.245.1 (AS Boundary Router address)
```

```
Advertising Router: 155.187.241.5
LS Seq Number: 80000072
Checksum: 0x3548
Length: 28
Network Mask: 0.0.0.0 TOS: 0 Metric: 1
```

Table 8-5 describes some fields that are useful in a troubleshooting environment.

Table 8-5   *show ip ospf database asbr-summary* output definitions

Field	Description
Router ID	Router ID number
Process ID	OSPF process ID
LS age	Link-state age
Options	Type of Service options (Type 0 only)
LS Type	Link-state type
Link State ID	Link-state ID (autonomous system boundary router)
Advertising Router	Advertising router's ID
LS Seq Number	Link-state sequence (detects old or duplicate link-state advertisements)
Checksum	LS checksum (Fletcher checksum of the complete contents of the link-state advertisement)
Length	Length in bytes of the link-state advertisement
Network Mask	Network mask implemented. The network mask for type 4 LSA is always 0.0.0.0.
TOS	Type of Service
Metric	Link-state metric

show ip ospf database external *Command*

The following command syntax will provide you with a wealth of relevant information regarding the OSPF database external LSAs. The entries in this output are defined in the table below.

Example: The following is sample output from the `show ip ospf database external` command when no optional arguments are specified:

```
OSPF_Router# show ip ospf database external

OSPF Router with id(190.20.239.66) (Process ID 300)


  AS External Link States
  Routing Bit Set on this LSA
  LS age: 280
  Options: (No TOS-capability)
  LS Type: AS External Link
  Link State ID: 143.105.0.0 (External Network Number)
  Advertising Router: 155.187.70.6
  LS Seq Number: 80000AFD
  Checksum: 0xC3A
  Length: 36
  Network Mask: 255.255.0.0
          Metric Type: 2 (Larger than any link state path)
          TOS: 0
          Metric: 1
          Forward Address: 0.0.0.0
          External Route Tag: 0
```

Table 8-6 describes some fields that are useful in a troubleshooting environment.

Table 8-6 *show ip ospf database external* output definition

Field	Description
Router ID	Router ID number
Process ID	OSPF process ID
Routing Bit Set On this LSA	This statement will appear if OSPF has used the LSA to create a route.
LS age	Link-state age
Options	Type of Service options (Type 0 only)
LS Type	Link-state type
Link State ID	Link-state ID (External Network Number)
Advertising Router	Advertising router's ID

Table 8-6   *show ip ospf database external output definition, continued*

Field	Description
LS Seq Number	Link-state sequence number (detects old or duplicate link-state advertisements)
Checksum	LS checksum (Fletcher checksum of the complete contents of the link-state advertisement)
Length	Length in bytes of the link-state advertisement
Network Mask	Network mask implemented
Metric Type	External Type
TOS	Type of Service
Metric	Link-state metric
Forward Address	Forwarding address. Data traffic for the advertised destination will be forwarded to this address. If the forwarding address is set to 0.0.0.0, data traffic will be forwarded instead to the advertisement's originator.
External Route Tag	External route tag, a 32-bit field attached to each external route. This is not used by the OSPF protocol itself.

show ip ospf database network *Command*

The following command syntax will provide you with a wealth of relevant information regarding the OSPF database network LSAs. The entries in this output are defined in Table 8-7 that follows the example output.

Example: The following is sample output from the show ip ospf database network command when no optional arguments are specified:

```
OSPF_Router# show ip ospf database network
OSPF Router with id(190.20.239.66) (Process ID 300)

            Displaying Net Link States(Area 0.0.0.0)

LS age: 1367
Options: (No TOS-capability)
LS Type: Network Links
Link State ID: 155.187.1.3 (address of Designated Router)
```

```
Advertising Router: 190.20.239.66
LS Seq Number: 800000E7
Checksum: 0x1229
Length: 52
Network Mask: 255.255.255.0
        Attached Router: 190.20.239.66
        Attached Router: 155.187.241.5
        Attached Router: 155.187.1.1
        Attached Router: 155.187.54.5
        Attached Router: 155.187.1.5
```

Table 8-7 describes some fields that are useful in a troubleshooting environment.

Table 8-7   *show ip ospf database network* output definitions

Field	Description
OSPF Router with id	Router ID number
Process ID	OSPF process ID
LS age:	Link state age
Options:	Type of Service options (Type 0 only)
LS Type:	Link-state type
Link State ID	Link-state ID of designated router
Advertising Router	Advertising router's ID
LS Seq Number	Link state sequence (detects old or duplicate link-state advertisements)
Checksum	LS checksum (Fletcher checksum of the complete contents of the link-state advertisement)
Network Mask	Network mask implemented
Attached Router	List of routers attached to the network, by IP address

show ip ospf database router *Command*

The following command syntax will provide you with a wealth of relevant information regarding the OSPF database router LSAs. The entries in this output are defined in Table 8-8 that follows the example output.

Example: The following is sample output from the show ip ospf database router command when no optional arguments are specified.

```
OSPF_Router# show ip ospf database router

OSPF Router with id(190.20.239.66) (Process ID 300)

                    Displaying Router Link States(Area 0.0.0.0)

    LS age: 1176
    Options: (No TOS-capability)
    LS Type: Router Links
    Link State ID: 155.187.21.6
    Advertising Router: 155.187.21.6
    LS Seq Number: 80002CF6
    Checksum: 0x73B7
    Length: 120
    AS Boundary Router
    155 Number of Links: 8

    Link connected to: another Router (point-to-point)
     (link ID) Neighboring Router ID: 155.187.21.5
     (Link Data) Router Interface address: 155.187.21.6
    Number of TOS metrics: 0
    TOS 0 Metrics: 2
```

Table 8-8 describes some fields that are useful in a troubleshooting environment.

Table 8-8   *show ip ospf database router* output definitions

Field	Description
OSPF Router with id	Router ID number
Process ID	OSPF process ID
LS age	Link-state age
Options	Type of Service options (Type 0 only)

Table 8-8 *show ip ospf database router* output definitions, continued

Field	Description
LS Type	Link-state type
Link State ID	Link-state ID
Advertising Router	Advertising router's ID
LS Seq Number	Link-state sequence (detects old or duplicate link-state advertisements)
Checksum	LS checksum (Fletcher checksum of the complete contents of the link-state advertisement)
Length	Length in bytes of the link-state advertisement
AS Boundary Router	Definition of router type
Number of Links	Number of active links
link ID	Link type
Link Data	Router interface address
TOS	Type of Service metric (Type 0 only)

show ip ospf database summary *Command*

The following is sample output from show ip ospf database summary command when no optional arguments are specified.

```
OSPF_Router# show ip ospf database summary

        OSPF Router with id(190.20.239.66) (Process ID 300)

            Displaying Summary Net Link States(Area 0.0.0.0)

    LS age: 1401
    Options: (No TOS-capability)
    LS Type: Summary Links(Network)
    Link State ID: 155.187.240.0 (summary Network Number)
    Advertising Router: 155.187.241.5
    LS Seq Number: 80000072
    Checksum: 0x84FF
    Length: 28
    Network Mask: 255.255.255.0 TOS: 0 Metric: 1
```

Table 8-9 describes some fields that are useful in a troubleshooting environment.

Table 8-9   `show ip ospf database summary` output definition

Field	Description
OSPF Router with id	Router ID number
Process ID	OSPF process ID
LS age	Link-state age
Options	Type of Service options (Type 0 only)
LS Type	Link-state type
Link State ID	Link-state ID (summary network number)
Advertising Router	Advertising router's ID
LS Seq Number	Link-state sequence (detects old or duplicate link-state advertisements)
Checksum	LS checksum (Fletcher checksum of the complete contents of the link-state advertisement)
Length	Length in bytes of the link-state advertisement
Network Mask	Network mask implemented
TOS	Type of Service
Metric	Link-state metric

show ip ospf database database-summary *Command*

Example: The following is sample output from `show ip ospf database data-base-summary` command when no optional arguments are specified:

```
OSPF_Router# show ip ospf database database-summary

        OSPF Router with ID (172.19.65.21) (Process ID 1)

Area ID Router Network Sum-Net Sum-ASBR Subtotal Delete   Maxage
202     1      0       0       0        1        0      0
AS External            0       0        0
Total   1      0       0       0        1
```

Table 8-10 describes some fields that are useful in a troubleshooting environment.

Table 8-10 *show ip ospf database database-summary output definition*

Field	Description
Area ID	Area number
Router	Number of router link-state advertisements in that area
Network	Number of network link-state advertisements in that area
Sum-Net	Number of summary link-state advertisements in that area
Sum-ASBR	Number of summary autonomous system boundary router (ASBR) link-state advertisements in that area
Subtotal	Sum of Router, Network, Sum-Net, and Sum-ASBR for that area
Delete	Number of link-state advertisements that are marked "Deleted" in that area
Maxage	Number of link-state advertisements that are marked "Maxaged" in that area
AS External	Number of external link-state advertisements

show ip ospf neighbor *Command*

To display OSPF-neighbor information on a per-interface basis, use the `show ip ospf neighbor` EXEC command. The syntax for this command is as follows:

> `show ip ospf neighbor` [*type number*] [*neighbor-id*] `detail`

Syntax Description:

> *type*. This optional argument represents the Interface type.
> *number*. This optional argument represents the Interface number.
> *neighbor-id*. This optional argument represents the Neighbor ID.
> *detail*. Displays all neighbors given in detail (list all neighbors).

Example: The following command shows the OSPF neighbors from the router's perspective in which it was executed.

```
OSPF_Router# show ip ospf neighbor
Neighbor ID Pri  State          Dead Time  Address      Interface
76.0.16.4    1   FULL/DROTHER   00:00:39   76.0.16.36   Serial1/0.1
76.0.16.8    1   FULL/DROTHER   00:00:36   76.0.16.40   Serial1/0.1
76.0.16.7    1   FULL/DROTHER   00:00:38   76.0.16.39   Serial1/0.1
76.0.16.9    1   FULL/BDR       00:00:38   76.0.16.41   Serial1/0.1
76.0.16.5    1   FULL/DROTHER   00:00:38   76.0.16.37   Serial1/0.1
76.0.16.2    1   FULL/DROTHER   00:00:38   76.0.16.34   Serial1/0.1
76.0.16.6    1   FULL/DROTHER   00:00:39   76.0.16.38   Serial1/0.1
76.0.16.3    1   FULL/DROTHER   00:00:38   76.0.16.35   Serial1/0.1
76.0.16.4    1   2WAY/DROTHER   00:00:39   76.0.16.68   Serial2/0.1
76.0.16.6    1   2WAY/DROTHER   00:00:39   76.0.16.70   Serial2/0.1
76.0.16.2    1   2WAY/DROTHER   00:00:38   76.0.16.66   Serial2/0.1
76.0.16.3    1   2WAY/DROTHER   00:00:38   76.0.16.67   Serial2/0.1
76.0.16.8    1   FULL/DR        00:00:36   76.0.16.72   Serial2/0.1
76.0.16.5    1   2WAY/DROTHER   00:00:34   76.0.16.69   Serial2/0.1
76.0.16.7    1   2WAY/DROTHER   00:00:36   76.0.16.71   Serial2/0.1
76.0.16.9    1   FULL/BDR       00:00:38   76.0.16.73   Serial2/0.1
76.0.18.5    1   FULL/ -        00:00:35   76.0.18.1    Serial3/0.1
76.88.5.17   1   FULL/ -        00:00:39   76.0.18.9    Serial3/0.2
76.0.18.36   1   FULL/ -        00:00:35   76.0.18.21   Serial3/0.3
76.0.18.37   1   FULL/ -        00:00:38   76.0.18.29   Serial3/0
```

Table 8-11 describes some fields that are useful in a troubleshooting environment.

Table 8-11 *show ip ospf neighbor* output definitions

Field	Description
Neighbor x.x.x.x	Neighbor router ID
interface address x.x.x.x	IP address of the interface
Neighbor priority	Router priority of neighbor, neighbor state
State	OSPF state
Dead timer	Expected time before Cisco IOS software will declare neighbor dead

show ip ospf neighbor <ip address> *Command*

The `show ip ospf neighbor <ip address>` command provides you with detailed information regarding a specific OSPF neighbor as specified by the IP address.

Example: The following is sample output showing summary information about the neighbor that matches the neighbor ID:

```
OSPF_Router# show ip ospf neighbor 199.199.199.137

Neighbor 199.199.199.137, interface address 160.89.80.37
    In the area 0.0.0.0 via interface Ethernet0
    Neighbor priority is 1, State is FULL
    Options 2
    Dead timer due in 0:00:32
    Link State retransmission due in 0:00:04
  Neighbor 199.199.199.137, interface address 192.31.48.189
    In the area 0.0.0.0 via interface Fddi0
    Neighbor priority is 5, State is FULL
    Options 2
    Dead timer due in 0:00:32
    Link State retransmission due in 0:00:03
```

Table 8-12 describes some fields that are useful in a troubleshooting environment.

Table 8-12 *show ip ospf neighbor <ip address>* output

Field	Description
Neighbor x.x.x.x	Neighbor router ID
interface address x.x.x.x	IP address of the interface
In the area	Area and interface through which OSPF neighbor is known
Neighbor priority	Router priority of neighbor, neighbor state
State	OSPF state
Options	Hello packet options field contents (E-bit only; possible values are 0 and 2; 2 indicates area is not a stub; 0 indicates area is a stub)
Dead timer	Expected time before Cisco IOS software will declare neighbor dead
Link State Retransmission	How long until the next LSA transmission occurs

`show ip ospf neighbor <int> <ip address>` *Command*

The `show ip ospf neighbor <int> <ip address>` command provides you with detailed information regarding a specific OSPF neighbor as specified by the interface number and IP address.

Example: If you specify the interface along with the Neighbor ID, the Cisco IOS software displays the neighbors that match the neighbor ID on the interface, as in the following sample display:

```
OSPF_Router# show ip ospf neighbor e0 199.199.199.137

Neighbor 199.199.199.137, interface address 160.89.80.37
    In the area 0.0.0.0 via interface Ethernet0
    Neighbor priority is 1, State is FULL

    Options 2
    Dead timer due in 0:00:37
    Link State retransmission due in 0:00:04
```

Table 8-13 describes some fields that are useful in a troubleshooting environment.

Table 8-13   *show ip ospf neighbor <int> <ip address>* output

Field	Description
Neighbor x.x.x.x	Neighbor router ID
interface address x.x.x.x	IP address of the interface
In the area	Area and interface through which OSPF neighbor is known
Neighbor priority	Router priority of neighbor, neighbor state
State	OSPF state
Options	Hello packet options field contents (E-bit only; possible values are 0 and 2; 2 indicates area is not a stub; 0 indicates area is a stub)
Dead timer	Expected time before Cisco IOS software will declare neighbor dead

show ip ospf neighbor detail *Command*

The show ip ospf neighbor detail command provides you with detailed information regarding OSPF neighbors. The actual information output from the command is defined in the example that follows.

Example: The following is sample output from the show ip ospf neighbor detail command:

```
OSPF_Router# show ip ospf neighbor detail

Neighbor 160.89.96.54, interface address 160.89.96.54
    In the area 0.0.0.3 via interface Ethernet0
    Neighbor priority is 1, State is FULL
    Options 2
    Dead timer due in 0:00:38
Neighbor 160.89.103.52, interface address 160.89.103.52
    In the area 0.0.0.0 via interface Serial0
    Neighbor priority is 1, State is FULL
    Options 2
    Dead timer due in 0:00:31
```

Table 8-14 describes some fields that are useful in a troubleshooting environment.

Table 8-14   *show ip ospf neighbor detail* output definition

Field	Description
Neighbor x.x.x.x	Neighbor router ID
interface address x.x.x.x	IP address of the interface
In the area	Area and interface through which OSPF neighbor is known
Neighbor priority	Router priority of neighbor, neighbor state
State	OSPF state
Options	Hello packet options field contents (E-bit only; possible values are 0 and 2; 2 indicates area is not a stub; 0 indicates area is a stub)
Dead timer	Expected time before Cisco IOS software will declare neighbor dead

show ip ospf virtual-links *Command*

To display parameters about and the current state of OSPF virtual links, use the show ip ospf virtual-links EXEC command. This command provides you with detailed information regarding OSPF virtual links. The actual information output from the command is defined in the example that follows.

Usage Guidelines: The information displayed by show ip ospf virtual-links is useful in debugging OSPF routing operations.

Example:

```
OSPF_Router# show ip ospf virtual-links
Virtual Link to router 160.89.101.2 is up
Transit area 0.0.0.1, via interface Ethernet0, Cost of using 10
Transmit Delay is 1 sec, State POINT_TO_POINT
Timer intervals configured, Hello 10, Dead 40, Wait 40, Retransmit 5
Hello due in 0:00:08
Adjacency State FULL
```

Table 8-15 describes some fields that are useful in a troubleshooting environment.

Table 8-15   *show ip OSPF virtual-links output definition*

Field	Description
Virtual Link to router 160.89.101.2 is Up	Specifies the OSPF neighbor, and if the link to that neighbor is Up or Down
Transit area 0.0.0.1	The transit area through which the virtual link is formed
via interface Ethernet0	The interface through which the virtual link is formed
Cost of using 10	The cost of reaching the OSPF neighbor through the virtual link
Transmit Delay is 1 sec	The transmit delay on the virtual link
State POINT_TO_POINT	The state of the OSPF neighbor
Timer intervals...	The various timer intervals configured for the link
Hello due in 0:00:08	When the next hello is expected from the neighbor
Adjacency State FULL	The adjacency state between the neighbor

show ip ospf summary-address *Command*

Example syntax for the show ip ospf summary-address command is as follows:

```
AST7401#sho ip ospf summary-address
OSPF Process 5774, Summary-address
```

TROUBLESHOOTING OSPF

This section deals with the inevitable network routing problems. These problems can take many forms, from straightforward loss of connectivity to the more complex routing loops. Even though additional problems exist, such as access list configuration, buffer usage, and queue sizes, they are beyond the scope of this book. The reader is referred to CCO (http://www.cisco.com) for information regarding these subjects.

This section provides a variety of resources that can assist in resolving these issues and briefly mentions other issues that are not within the scope of this book.

As with any potentially complex problem, certain techniques or methodology have evolved to deal with troubleshooting network-related problems. This troubleshooting methodology is not only applicable to OSPF, it can also be used to assist you with any network problem.

As this book deals primarily with OSPF, a routing protocol, take a minute to review how and what the routing process uses for sources of input on a larger scale (that is, not just OSPF LSAs). This information will greatly assist you as routing problems can be many layered or give you false indications. For purposes of the discussion here, consider how Cisco routers build their IP routing tables. Figure 8-2 illustrates an example of the many types of inputs into the routing process that are discussed.

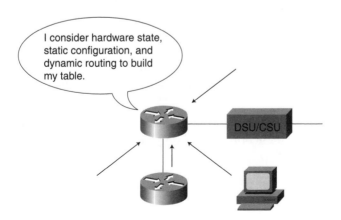

Figure 8–2
Static and dynamic inputs to routing.

Proper routing will be achieved based upon the following sources of information gained from the network:

- Dynamic routing protocols and their associated metrics (cost)

- Redistribution between routing protocols

- Static routes which might differ from dynamic routes

- Policy decisions implemented via access lists

- ARP and Inverse ARP

- Local interface configuration

- Local interface status via counters, timers, and carrier detection

Preparing for Network Failure

You can always recover from a network failure easier if you are prepared ahead of time. To see if you are prepared for a network failure, answer the following questions:

- **Do you have an accurate physical and logical map of your internetwork?** Does your organization or department have an up-to-date internetwork map that outlines the physical location of all of the devices on the network and how they are connected, as well as a logical map of network addresses, network numbers, subnetworks, router interfaces, and so forth?

- **Do you have a list of all network protocols implemented in your network?** For each of the protocols implemented, do you have a list of the network numbers, IP addresses, DLCIs, subnetworks, zones, areas, and so on that are associated with them?

- **Do you know which protocols are being routed?** For each of these protocols, do you have a correct, updated router configuration? You also need to keep router configuration files before and after major network changes. This helps ensure that a readily available backup exists in case the change must be reversed.

- **Do you know which protocols are being bridged?** Are there any filters configured in any of these bridges, and do you have a copy of these configurations?

- **Do you know all the points of contact to external networks, including any connections to the Internet?** For each external network connection, do you know what routing protocol is being used? Do you have adequate security in place and documented? How are the external networks being advertised into your OSPF network?

- **Do you have an established baseline for your network?** Has your organization documented the baseline or normal network behavior and performance so that you can compare current problems with a baseline? This documentation is essential to understanding the network and judging the impact of changes to your network. These changes can be related to either a network failure or the introduction of new network service.

- **Is this information stored in a central location so that it is accessible to everyone concerned with the network operation and management?** Having the information is only half the battle. The information must be available so that if needed, it can be readily accessed in order to reduce network downtime.

Troubleshooting Methodology

Internetworks come in a variety of topologies and levels of complexity; from single-protocol, point-to-point links connecting cross-town campuses, to highly-meshed, large-scale WANs traversing multiple time zones and international boundaries. The industry trend is toward increasingly complex environments, involving multiple types of media, multiple protocols, and often providing interconnection to "unknown" networks.

Consequently, the potential for connectivity and performance problems in internetworks is high, and the sources of such problems are often elusive. The goal of this section is to help you isolate and resolve the most common connectivity and performance problems within your OSPF Network.

Symptoms, Problems, and Solutions

Failures in internetworks are characterized by certain symptoms. These symptoms might be general (such as clients being unable to access specific servers) or more specific (routes not in the routing table). Each symptom can be traced to one or more problems or causes by using specific troubleshooting tools and techniques. After they are identified, each problem can be remedied by implementing a solution consisting of a series of actions.

The section that follows describes how to define symptoms, identify problems, and implement solutions as apply to a OSPF network but the basics can also apply to any generic network environment. Always apply the specific context in which you are troubleshooting to determine how to detect symptoms and diagnose problems for your specific environment.

General Problem-Solving Model

When troubleshooting problems within an OSPF networked environment, a systematic approach works best. Define the specific symptoms, identify all potential problems that could be causing the symptoms, and then systematically eliminate each potential problem (from most likely to least likely) until the symptoms disappear.

This process is not a rigid outline for troubleshooting an internetwork. Rather, it is a solid foundation from which you can build a problem-solving process to suit the particular needs of your OSPF environment.

The following seven steps detail the problem-solving process:

1. Clearly define the problem.

2. Gather facts.

3. Consider possible problems.

4. Create an action plan.

5. Implement the action plan.

6. Gather results.

7. Reiterate the process.

Step 1: Clearly Define the Problem

When analyzing a network problem, make a clear problem statement. You should define the problem in terms of a set of symptoms and potential causes. To do this, identify the general symptoms and then ascertain what kinds of problems (causes) could result in these symptoms.

For example, hosts might not be responding to service requests from clients (a symptom). Possible causes might be a misconfigured host, bad interface cards, or missing router configuration commands.

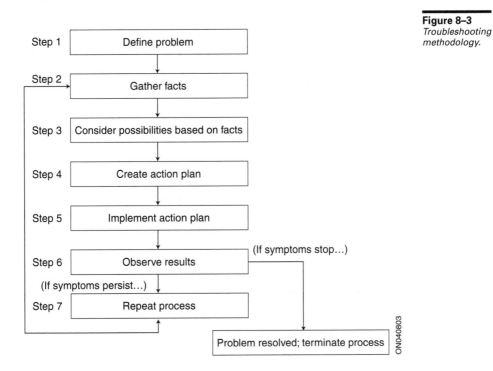

Figure 8–3
*Troubleshooting
methodology.*

Step 1 — Define problem

Step 2 — Gather facts

Step 3 — Consider possibilities based on facts

Step 4 — Create action plan

Step 5 — Implement action plan

Step 6 — Observe results   (If symptoms stop...)

(If symptoms persist...)

Step 7 — Repeat process

Problem resolved; terminate process

ON040803

Step 2: Gather Facts

Gather the facts you need to help isolate possible causes by asking questions of your peers and others such as:

Users that are affected. What type of problems are they experiencing?

Network Administrators. Has anything changed or been added to the network?

Your Peers and Associates. Have they seen this problem before, or do they know something that might help?

Asking questions is a good method of gathering facts, but it is not the only resource available to you. Consider collecting information from other sources such as:

- **Network Management System.** What are the indications being reported by your NMS?

- **Protocol Analyzer Traces.** What are the characteristics of the traffic? Are you missing LSAs that should be happening but are not? In this case, it might not be what you see that is important, but what you don't see.

- **Router Diagnostic Commands.** What does the router tell you is wrong? What do the routers near the affected area report?

- **Cisco IOS Release Notes.** Is what you are experiencing related to new or altered features within the IOS?

- **Cisco Bug Search.** Could what you are experiencing be caused by a bug that has already been reported? If so, is there a fix for it, or did you just discover it?

- **RMON Probes.** Can you dispatch a probe to reach the location having the problem?

- **Performance Analysis Tools.** Is this a capacity or utilization related issue? Is there a trend of some sort going on that long-term monitoring would identify?

There are a variety of different sources upon which you can draw to assist you in gathering the facts. A good rule of thumb is that the only dumb question is the one never asked. So ask people, look at what the network is telling you, and use the money spent on various networking-related tools.

Step 3: Consider Possible Problems

The basis for considering a possible problem is tied to the facts you gathered. By using the facts you gathered, you could eliminate potential problems from your list. Armed with your findings and the facts surrounding the problem, you should then use them to discard potential causes of the problem.

For example, depending on the data, you might be able to eliminate hardware as a problem, allowing you to focus on software problems.

At every opportunity, try to narrow the number of potential problems so that you can create an efficient plan of action. Narrowing down the number of possibilities is key to this step. Analyze the data gathered and use it reduce the potential causes. This will greatly reduce the downtime of the network and increase your accuracy when engaging Step 4.

Step 4: Create an Action Plan

Create an action plan based on the remaining potential causes. Begin with the most likely cause and devise a plan to either prove or disprove that the cause selected was, in fact, the culprit. When creating an action remember to proceed in steps in which only one variable will be manipulated at a time.

For example, I do not see routes to the Internet in my OSPF routing table. I know they are external routes, so I look at my ASBR. I will verify that my ISP is providing me with the correct routes. If they are, then that removes the possibility of an external configuration error as the cause. I can then move onto the next likely cause of my problem.

This approach allows you to reproduce a given solution to a specific problem. If you alter more than one variable simultaneously, you might solve the problem, but identifying the specific change that eliminated the symptom becomes more difficult.

Step 5: Implement the Action Plan

Implement the action plan, performing each step carefully while testing to see if the symptom disappears. I would also recommend that you have a means of recording your steps during this process. This serves multiple purposes during your troubleshooting.

- It provides you with a record of your actions in case you need to recall what was done.

- It ensures that a back out plan can be implemented immediately, if needed.

- Technical support, if needed, will probably request the very information you have been researching.

- After action, reports are always going to require supporting information and this is a great means of providing it. These reports will also help you to write down and learn from the lessons you experienced.

Step 6: Gather Results

Whenever you change a variable, be sure to gather the results because these are the facts of what is now occurring. Generally, you should use the same method of gathering facts that you used in Step 2.

Analyze the results to determine whether the problem has been resolved. If it has, then the process is complete. If the problem has not been resolved, then continue on to Step 7.

Step 7: Reiterate the Process

If the problem has not been resolved by this step, you must create another action plan based on the next most likely problem in your list. Return to Step 4 and reiterate the process until the problem is solved. Make sure to undo any "fixes" you made in implementing your first action plan. Remember that you want to change only one variable at a time.

Figure 8-3 illustrates the seven-step, problem-solving methodology just discussed.

System Logging (SYSLOG)

Logging is an extremely useful troubleshooting tool that enables the router to keep track of events that occur within the router. There are several different options available when configuring this feature. The two major options are allowing the router to have the capability to record events in either the router's buffer or to send them to a SYSLOG server or both.

This flexibility is very useful, as it enables you to see if events that are occurring within your network are related to the router's operation or if the router has detected a network event. This can help you find trends, system error messages, outages, and a variety of other network events.

Configuring SYSLOG

The first step in getting the router to start logging requires a decision on your part. Eight possible level settings enable you to limit how the events within the router are logged. To configure the router option, you will need to enter the global configuration mode as shown in the following example.

```
OSPF_Router(config)#logging console ?
  alerts          Immediate action needed
  critical        Critical conditions
  debugging       Debugging messages
  emergencies     System is unusable
  errors Error    conditions
  informational   Informational messages
  notifications   Normal but significant conditions
  warnings        Warning conditions
```

TIPS

When comparing the preceding example from a router that uses the built-in `help` command to the actual levels of logging listed in Table 8-16, note the router provides its output in alphabetical order, not level of functionality.

To limit messages logged to the console based on severity, use the logging console global configuration command. The *no* form of this command disables logging to the console terminal.

```
logging console level
no logging console
```

Specifying a *level* causes messages at that level and numerically lower levels to be displayed at the console terminal. Table 8-16 shows these priority levels.

Table 8-16 *Logging message priorities*

Level Name	Level	Level Description	SYSLOG Definition
emergencies	0	System unusable	LOG_EMERG
alerts	1	Immediate action needed	LOG_ALERT
critical	2	Critical conditions	LOG_CRIT
errors	3	Error conditions	LOG_ERR
warnings	4	Warning conditions	LOG_WARNING
notifications	5	Normal but significant condition	LOG_NOTICE
informational	6	Informational messages only	LOG_INFO
debugging	7	Debugging messages	LOG_DEBUG

TIPS

The effect of the log keyword with the `ip access-list` (extended) command depends on the setting of the logging console command. The log keyword takes effect only if the logging console level is set to 6 or 7. If you change the default to a level lower than 6 and specify the log keyword with the `ip access-list` (extended) command, no information is logged or displayed. Although you cannot specify your level numerically in the router, it must be done textually:

```
OSPF_Core(config)#logging console ?
    alerts        Immediate action needed
    critical      Critical conditions
    debugging     Debugging messages
    emergencies   System is unusable
    errors        Error conditions
    informational Informational messages
    notifications Normal but significant conditions
    warnings      Warning conditions
```

The EXEC command `show logging` displays the addresses and levels associated with the current logging setup, as well as any other logging statistics. The following example shows a wide variety of events that can be reflected within the router's log file.

```
OSPF_Router# show logging
Syslog logging: enabled (0 messages dropped, 0 flushes, 0 overruns)
    Console logging: level debugging, 66 messages logged
    Monitor logging: level debugging, 0 messages logged
    Trap logging: level informational, 70 message lines logged

%QUICC_ETHER-1-LOSTCARR: Unit 0, lost carrier. Transceiver problem?
%LINEPROTO-5-UPDOWN: Line protocol on Interface Ethernet0, changed state to down
%LINEPROTO-5-UPDOWN: Line protocol on Interface Serial0, changed state to down
%LINEPROTO-5-UPDOWN: Line protocol on Interface Serial1, changed state to down
*Mar 1 00:00:08 UTC: %LINK-3-UPDOWN: Interface Ethernet0, changed state to up
*Mar 1 00:00:08 GMT: %LINK-3-UPDOWN: Interface Serial0, changed state to down
*Mar 1 00:00:08 GMT: %LINK-3-UPDOWN: Interface Serial1, changed state to down
*Mar 1 00:00:09 GMT: %LINEPROTO-5-UPDOWN: Line protocol on Interface Loopback0, changed state to up
*Mar 1 00:00:10 GMT: %LINEPROTO-5-UPDOWN: Line protocol on Interface Serial0.1, changed state to down
*Mar 1 00:00:12 GMT: %LINK-5-CHANGED: Interface Serial1, changed state to administratively down
*Mar 1 00:00:12 GMT: %SYS-5-CONFIG_I: Configured from memory by console
*Mar 1 00:00:12 GMT: %SYS-5-RESTART: System restarted --
Cisco Internetwork Operating System Software
IOS (tm) 1600 Software (C1600-Y-L), Version 11.1(7)AA, EARLY DEPLOYMENT RELEASE SOFTWARE (fc2)
Copyright (c) 1986-1996 by cisco Systems, Inc.
Compiled Thu 24-Oct-96 02:26 by kuong
*Mar 1 00:01:08 GMT: %QUICC_ETHER-1-LOSTCARR: Unit 0, lost carrier. Transceiver problem?
*Mar 1 00:02:07 GMT: %QUICC_ETHER-1-LOSTCARR: Unit 0, lost carrier. Transceiver problem?
*Mar 1 00:03:07 GMT: %QUICC_ETHER-1-LOSTCARR: Unit 0, lost carrier. Transceiver problem?
*Mar 1 00:04:06 GMT: %QUICC_ETHER-1-LOSTCARR: Unit 0, lost carrier. Transceiver problem?
*Mar 1 00:05:06 GMT: %QUICC_ETHER-1-LOSTCARR: Unit 0, lost carrier. Transceiver problem?
*Mar 1 00:06:06 GMT: %QUICC_ETHER-1-LOSTCARR: Unit 0, lost carrier. Transceiver problem?
*Mar 1 00:07:05 GMT: %QUICC_ETHER-1-LOSTCARR: Unit 0, lost carrier. Transceiver problem?
*Mar 1 00:49:50 GMT: %QUICC_ETHER-1-LOSTCARR: Unit 0, lost carrier. Transceiver problem?
*Mar 1 00:50:21 GMT: %SYS-5-CONFIG_I: Configured from console by console
*Mar 1 00:50:49 GMT: %QUICC_ETHER-1-LOSTCARR: Unit 0, lost carrier. Transceiver problem?
*Mar 1 00:51:43 GMT: %SYS-5-CONFIG_I: Configured from console by console
*Mar 1 00:51:43 GMT: %LINK-5-CHANGED: Interface Ethernet0, changed state to administratively down
```

Notice the first four lines after the header start with % followed by system error information, then a brief English statement of the event being logged. Within the system error information is a number with hyphens of either side of it. This number corresponds to the levels as shown in Table 8-16.

Date and Time Stamping

In the preceding example, the first four lines are not date and time stamped. When did those events occur? Did they happen recently? Are they related to problems that are now occurring within the network? Unless you were closely monitoring events in the SYSLOG, it is unlikely that you would be able to answer these questions. The remaining SYSLOG entries are stamped with the month, date, hour, minute, second, and timezone (programmed into the router) of when the event occurred.

As is readily apparent throughout the remainder of the example, having this information before each entry would be of great benefit when using the SYSLOG entries to assist you in troubleshooting. For instance, in the preceding example, consider that shortly after midnight this router went down for no apparent reason and severe network impact resulted. One of the first questions you will need to answer is why did this happen? This answer is readily found in the router's SYSLOG as shown in the following example.

```
*Mar 1 00:00:12 GMT: %SYS-5-RESTART: System restarted --
Cisco Internetwork Operating System Software
IOS (tm) 1600 Software (C1600-Y-L), Version 11.1(7)AA, EARLY
        DEPLOYMENT RELEASE SOFTWARE (fc2)
Copyright (c) 1986-1996 by cisco Systems, Inc.
Compiled Thu 24-Oct-96 02:26 by kuong
```

By looking into the router's SYSLOG, you will realize that the outage was caused by the router restarting. This enables you to immediately narrow your search for the root cause. Through the use of the router's SYSLOG with date and time stamping, you now see the benefits of troubleshooting your network. You should familiarize yourself with how to see what time the router thinks it is and how to configure the router to operate as previously discussed.

What is the current time and date in the router? Through the use of the *show clock* command this can quickly and easily be determined as shown in the following example:

```
OSPF_Router# show clock
*02:16:54.592 GMT Mon Mar 1 1993
```

How do I set the date and time in the router? Through the use of the following command in the router's EXEC mode:

```
OSPF_Router# clock set ?
  hh:mm:ss Current Time

OSPF_Router# clock set 22:15:00 ?
  <1-31>  Day of the month
  MONTH   Month of the year

OSPF_Router# clock set 22:15:00 19 April ?
  <1993-2035> Year

OSPF_Router# clock set 22:15:00 19 April 1998
```

The next item you want to configure is the time zone for the router. The process of setting the router to automatically recognize daylight savings time is also provided in the following example.

```
OSPF_Router# clock timezone GMT 0
OSPF_Router# clock summer-time EST recurring
```

A good rule of thumb is to have all routers on the same time and in the same time zone regardless of their physical location.

The final and most important area that you need to cover on this subject is how to get the router SYSLOG to apply the date and time you just finished configuring in the router? The following example demonstrates how to do this.

```
OSPF_Router# configuration terminal
Enter configuration commands, one per line. End with CNTL/Z.
OSPF_Router(config)#service timestamps log datetime localtime show-timezone
```

NOTES

If you plan on date and time stamping your log entries it would be a good idea to consider also using Network Time Protocol (NTP) to synchronize all the router clocks. This command is out of the scope of this book; however, it can be found in the Cisco documentation.

Log OSPF Neighbor Changes

Configure your OSPF router with the debug ip ospf adjacency command if you want to know when an OSPF neighbor changes without turning on the debugging command. To configure the router to generate a SYSLOG message when an OSPF neighbor changes state, enter the following command in router configuration mode:

```
OSPF_Router(config)# ospf log-adj-changes
```

The *ospf log-adj-changes* command provides a high-level view of changes to the state of the OSPF peer relationships with less output and router overhead if debug was used.

Logging to the Router's Buffer

To log messages to the router's internal buffer, use the logging buffered command while in the router's global configuration mode. This command copies logging messages to an internal buffer instead of writing them to the console terminal. The buffer is circular (that is, FIFO) in nature, so newer messages overwrite older messages after the buffer is filled. The no form of this command cancels the use of the buffer and writes messages to the console terminal, which is the default.

```
logging buffered [size]
no logging buffered
```

The *size* argument (optional) sets the size of the buffer from 4,096 to 4,294,967,295 bytes. The default is 4,096 bytes (4K).

NOTES

To display the messages that are logged in the buffer, use the EXEC command show logging. The first message displayed is the oldest message in the buffer.

Ensure that you do not make the buffer size too large because the router could run out of memory and not be able to perform other tasks.

TIPS

You can use the *show memory* command to view the free processor memory on the router; however, this is the maximum available after the router has loaded the IOS and so forth, and should not be considered completely available for use. You should begin by just taking the default and seeing if that first meets your needs.

Logging to a SYSLOG Server

The capability to record, at a central location, the information from a router's SYSLOG is extremely useful in determining problems that might be occurring or those that did occur on a router you can no longer reach.

To log messages to a SYSLOG server host, use the *logging* command in the router's global configuration command mode. This command identifies a SYSLOG server host to receive logging messages. The no form of this command deletes the SYSLOG server with the specified address from the list of SYSLOG servers in the router's configuration file. The following is the syntax for the logging command as well as its no form:

```
logging host ip address
no logging host ip address
```

If you are interested, there are a variety of places to get this software. Some SYSLOG server manufacturers make you pay for it, and others will give it away. The CLS syslog daemon for Win95 and WinNT can be found at the following URL: http://www.cls.de/syslog.

By issuing the logging command more than once, you build a list of SYSLOG servers that receive logging messages. The following example shows a section of a router's configuration file.

```
logging buffered 8191
logging console critical
logging 175.82.45.6
logging 175.82.56.10
logging 175.82.77.35
```

This particular router has been configured to allocate 8,191 bytes to an internal buffer, which will record the SYSLOG events. The router has also been configured to send critical events to three SYSLOG servers.

There are a variety of other options and settings for performing syslogging within a router. The example that follows shows these options through the use of the built-in help feature. Please note some of the ones already discussed. Further discussion on these features is beyond the scope of this book. If additional information is required, the reader is referred to the Cisco *Network Protocol Command Reference Guide.*

```
OSPF_Router(config)#logging ?
  WORD      IP address of the logging host
  buffered  Copy logging messages to an internal buffer
  console   Set console logging level
  facility  Facility parameter for syslog messages
  monitor   Set terminal line (monitor) logging level
  on        Enable logging to all supported destinations
  trap      Set syslog server logging level
```

OSPF debug Commands

The debug privileged EXEC commands can provide a wealth of information about the traffic and events being seen (or *not* seen) to include but not limited to, interface traffic, error messages generated by nodes on the network, protocol-specific diagnostic packets, and other useful troubleshooting data.

NOTES

Exercise extreme care when using debug commands. Many of these commands are processor-intensive and can cause serious network problems (such as degraded performance or loss of connectivity) if they are enabled on an already heavily loaded router. When you finish using a debug command, remember to disable it with its specific no debug command (or use the no debug all command to turn off all debugging).

When to Use debug Commands

Only use debug commands to isolate problems, not to monitor normal network operation. Because the high overhead of debug commands can disrupt router operation, you should use debug commands only when you are looking for specific types of traffic or problems and have narrowed your problems to a likely subset of causes.

There are a quite a few debug commands available to you. The following is an example of only the IP-based debug commands that you might use.

```
OSPF_Router# debug ip ?
    bgp        BGP information
    cache      IP cache operations
    cgmp       CGMP protocol activity
    dvmrp      DVMRP protocol activity
    egp        EGP information
    eigrp      IP-EIGRP information
    error      IP error debugging
    http       HTTP connections
    icmp       ICMP transactions
    igmp       IGMP protocol activity
    igrp       IGRP information
    mcache     IP multicast cache operations
    mobile     Mobility protocols
    mpacket    IP multicast packet debugging
    mrouting   IP multicast routing table activity
    ospf       OSPF information
    packet     General IP debugging and IPSO security transactions
    peer       IP peer address activity
    pim        PIM protocol activity
    policy     Policy routing
    rip        RIP protocol transactions
    routing    Routing table events
    sd         Session Directory (SD)
    security   IP security options
    tcp        TCP information
    udp        UDP based transactions
```

The format of the output varies with each different debug command:

- Some debug commands generate a single line of output per packet, and others generate multiple lines of output per packet.

- Some debug commands generate large amounts of output, and others generate only occasional output.

- Some debug commands generate lines of text, and others generate information in field format.

How to Use debug *Commands*

Adhering to the following procedure minimizes the load created by using debug commands because the console port no longer has to generate character-by-character processor interrupts.

To minimize the negative impact on your router of using debug commands, follow this procedure:

1. Use the no logging console global configuration command on your router. This command disables all logging to the console terminal.

2. Telnet to a router port and enter the enable EXEC mode.

3. Use the terminal monitor command to copy debug command output and system error messages to your current terminal display. This permits you to view debug command output remotely, without being connected through the console port.

4. Open another Telnet session with the router and type the command undebug all in this second session but do not hit return. Then you start the debug session in the first session. When you are ready to stop the debug session go back to the second session and just press return to send the command. Eventually the router's CPU will process the command and shut off debug.

If you intend to keep the output of the debug command, spool the output to a file. The procedure for setting up such a debug output file is described in *Cisco's Debug Command Reference* publication. There are also certain programs that offer the capability to log everything displayed in your current Telnet session. The Windows Telnet application is a good example of a program with this capability.

Complete OSPF debug *Commands*

This book refers to specific debug commands that are useful when troubleshooting OSPF-specific related problems. Complete details regarding the function and output of debug commands are provided in *Cisco's Debug Command Reference* publication.

TIPS

debug is a useful command that has many different options available for its use. It also provides you with a lot of information on what is going on within a router. However, it also can hurt the routing processes and normal operation of the router, so use it wisely.

The following is a list of the different types of debug commands:

- **debug ip ospf ?**. Provides help for debug ip ospf commands
- **debug ip ospf adj**. Deals with OSPF adjacency events
- **debug ip ospf events**. Deals with OSPF events
- **debug ip ospf flood**. Deals with OSPF flooding
- **debug ip ospf lsa-generation**. Deals with OSPF lsa generation
- **debug ip ospf packet**. Deals with OSPF packets
- **debug ip ospf retransmission**. Deals with OSPF retransmission events
- **debug ip ospf spf**. Deals with OSPF spf
- **debug ip ospf tree**. Deals with OSPF database tree

debug ip ospf adjacency Command

The debug ip ospf adjacency command will report to you the various events occurring in relation to the various adjacencies within OSPF. The following example shows that the router detected OSPF adjacency problems on the network to which it is connected. The no form of this command disables debugging output.

```
OSPF_Router#debug ip ospf adj
OSPF adjacency events debugging is on

Feb 21 22:48:46.227: OSPF: Rcv pkt from 156.35.254.45, Ethernet1, area 0.0.0.0 : src not on the same network
Feb 21 22:48:56.227: OSPF: Rcv pkt from 156.35.254.45, Ethernet1, area 0.0.0.0 : src not on the same network
Feb 21 22:49:06.227: OSPF: Rcv pkt from 156.35.254.45, Ethernet1, area 0.0.0.0 : src not on the same network
Feb 21 22:49:16.228: OSPF: Rcv pkt from 156.35.254.45, Ethernet1, area 0.0.0.0 : src not on the same network
Feb 21 22:49:26.228: OSPF: Rcv pkt from 156.35.254.45, Ethernet1, area 0.0.0.0 : src not on the same network
Feb 21 22:49:36.228: OSPF: Rcv pkt from 156.35.254.45, Ethernet1, area 0.0.0.0 : src not on the same network
Feb 21 22:49:46.228: OSPF: Rcv pkt from 156.35.254.45, Ethernet1, area 0.0.0.0 : src not on the same network
```

The debug message can be interpreted as follows:

- **Feb 21 22:48:46.227:**. The date and time stamp indicates when the reported event occurred.

- **OSPF:**. The IP protocol to which the debug message is related.

- **Rcv pkt from 156.35.254.45, Ethernet1, area 0.0.0.0 :**. The event that occurred which caused debug to report it to you.

- **src not on the same network**. It defines that the exact problem is.

debug ip ospf events Command

Use the debug ip ospf events EXEC command to display information on Open Shortest Path First (OSPF)-related events, such as adjacencies, flooding information, designated router selection, and shortest path first (SPF) calculation, and so forth. The no form of this command disables debugging output. The basic syntax for this command is as follows:

```
[no] debug ip ospf events
```

The following is example output generated by the debug ip ospf events command:

```
OSPF_router# debug ip ospf events

OSPF:hello with invalid timers on interface Ethernet0
hello interval received 10 configured 10
net mask received 255.255.255.0 configured 255.255.255.0
dead interval received 40 configured 30
```

The example *debug ip ospf events* output might appear if any of the following occurs:

- The IP subnet masks for routers on the same network do not match.

- The OSPF hello interval for the router does not match that configured for a neighbor.

- The OSPF dead interval for the router does not match that configured for a neighbor.

If a router configured for OSPF routing is not seeing an OSPF neighbor on an attached network, do the following:

- Make sure that both routers have been configured with the same IP mask, OSPF hello interval, and OSPF dead interval.

- Make sure that both neighbors are part of the same area type.

`debug ip ospf flood` Command

This `debug` command enables you to view the actions and events being generated by OSPF's Flooding protocol. The `no` form of this command disables debugging output. The basic syntax for this command is as follows:

[no] debug ip ospf flood

This debug command allows for several options to include access lists:

```
OSPF_Router# debug ip ospf flood ?
  <1-99> Access list
  <cr>
```

Access list is used to match the LSA ID and only LSA which LSA ID is permitted by the access-list will be displayed. It is used to reduce the debug message generated and make it more useful. For example, if you suspect that the flooding of external LSA is not working, then choose one or two external LSA and use the access list to filter it out with the debug to watch the exact operation of flooding on those LSA.

In the following example, you can see the OSPF Flooding protocol provides a plethora of information on its operation. The `debug ip ospf flood` command generates information about flooding, which includes sending/receiving update/acknowledgement packet. The Received and Sending line means that the router has received or sent a packet; the lines that follow give you detailed information about the content of that packet.

```
OSPF_Router# debug ip ospf flood
OSPF flooding debugging is on
Feb 21 22:52:57.973: OSPF: received update from 56.82.197.2, Ethernet1
Feb 21 22:52:57.973: OSPF: Rcv Update Type 1, LSID 156.35.254.43, Adv rtr 156.35.254.43, age 2, seq 0x80003162
Feb 21 22:52:57.973: OSPF: Sending update on Ethernet0 to 224.0.0.6
Feb 21 22:52:57.973: OSPF: Send Type 1, LSID 156.35.254.43, Adv rtr 156.35.254.43, age 3, seq 0x80003162
Feb 21 22:52:57.973: OSPF: received update from 56.82.197.2, Ethernet0
Feb 21 22:52:57.973: OSPF: Rcv Update Type 1, LSID 156.35.254.43, Adv rtr 156.35.254.43, age 2, seq 0x80003162
Feb 21 22:52:57.973: OSPF: Received same lsa
Feb 21 22:52:57.973:        Remove LSA from retransmission list
Feb 21 22:52:57.973: OSPF: received update from 156.35.255.76, Ethernet1
Feb 21 22:52:57.973: OSPF:Rcv Update Type 1, LSID 156.35.254.43, Adv rtr 156.35.254.43, age 3, seq 0x80003162
Feb 21 22:52:57.973: OSPF: Received same lsa
Feb 21 22:52:57.973:        Remove LSA from retransmission list
Feb 21 22:52:59.973: OSPF: Received ACK from 56.82.127.3
Feb 21 22:52:59.973: OSPF: Rcv Ack Type 1, LSID 156.35.254.43, Adv rtr 156.35.254.43, age 2, seq 0x80003162
Feb 21 22:52:59.973:        Remove LSA from retransmission list
Feb 21 22:52:59.973: OSPF: Received ACK from 56.82.197.2
Feb 21 22:52:59.973: OSPF: Rcv Ack Type 1, LSID 156.35.254.43, Adv rtr 156.35.254.43, age 3, seq 0x80003162
Feb 21 22:53:00.473: OSPF: Sending delayed ACK on Ethernet1
Feb 21 22:53:00.473: OSPF: Ack Type 1, LSID 156.35.254.43, Adv rtr 156.35.254.43, age 2, seq 0x80003162
Feb 21 22:54:21.143: OSPF: received update from 56.82.197.2, Ethernet1
Feb 21 22:54:21.143: OSPF: Rcv Update Type 1, LSID 156.35.254.41, Adv rtr 156.35.254.41, age 2, seq 0x80003168
Feb 21 22:54:21.143: OSPF: Sending update on Ethernet0 to 224.0.0.6
```

```
Feb 21 22:54:21.143: OSPF: Send Type 1, LSID 156.35.254.41, Adv rtr 156.35.254.41, age 3, seq 0x80003168
Feb 21 22:54:21.143: OSPF: received update from 56.82.197.2, Ethernet0
Feb 21 22:54:21.143: OSPF: Rcv Update Type 1, LSID 156.35.254.41, Adv rtr 156.35.254.41, age 2, seq 0x80003168
Feb 21 22:54:21.143: OSPF: Received same lsa
Feb 21 22:54:21.143:        Remove LSA from retransmission list
Feb 21 22:54:23.139: OSPF: Received ACK from 156.35.255.76
Feb 21 22:54:23.139: OSPF: Rcv Ack Type 1, LSID 156.35.254.41, Adv rtr 156.35.254.41, age 2, seq 0x80003168
Feb 21 22:54:23.139:        Remove LSA from retransmission list
Feb 21 22:54:23.143: OSPF: Received ACK from 56.82.127.3
Feb 21 22:54:23.143: OSPF: Rcv Ack Type 1, LSID 156.35.254.41, Adv rtr 156.35.254.41, age 2, seq 0x80003168
Feb 21 22:54:23.143:        Remove LSA from retransmission list
Feb 21 22:54:23.643: OSPF: Sending delayed ACK on Ethernet1
Feb 21 22:54:23.643: OSPF: Ack Type 1, LSID 156.35.254.41, Adv rtr 156.35.254.41, age 2, seq 0x80003168
```

`debug ip ospf lsa-generation` Command

This `debug` command enables you to view the actions and events being generated by OSPF's Flooding protocol. The no form of this command disables debugging output. The basic syntax for this command is as follows:

```
[no] debug ip ospf lsa-generation ?
```

This `debug` command allows several options to include access lists, as previously discussed:

```
OSPF_Router# debug ip ospf lsa-generation ?
  <1-199> Access list
  <cr>
```

In the following example, you can see the OSPF Flooding protocol providing a plethora of information on its operation and LSA generation.

```
OSPF_Router# debug ip ospf lsa-generation
OSPF summary lsa generation debugging is on
```

`debug ip ospf packet` Command

Use the `debug ip ospf packet` EXEC command to display information about each Open Shortest Path First (OSPF) packet received. The no form of this command disables debugging output. The basic syntax for this command is as follows:

```
[no] debug ip ospf packet
```

The *debug ip ospf packet* command produces one set of information for each packet received. The output varies slightly depending on which type of authentication is used. The following example shows the OSPF packet being seen by the router.

```
OSPF_Router# debug ip ospf packet
Feb 21 22:59:43.442: OSPF: rcv. v:2 t:1 l:84 rid:156.83.197.2 aid:0.0.0.0 chk:2D83 aut:0 auk: from Ethernet0
Feb 21 22:59:43.446: OSPF: rcv. v:2 t:1 l:68 rid:156.83.197.2 aid:0.0.0.0 chk:200 aut:0 auk: from Ethernet1
Feb 21 22:59:48.974: OSPF: rcv. v:2 t:1 l:84 rid:156.82.197.2 aid:0.0.0.0 chk:2D83 aut:0 auk: from Ethernet0
```

```
Feb 21 22:59:50.138: OSPF: rcv. v:2 t:1 l:84 rid:156.82.127.3 aid:0.0.0.0 chk:2D83 aut:0 auk: from Ethernet0
Feb 21 22:59:51.222: OSPF: rcv. v:2 t:1 l:68 rid:156.82.197.2 aid:0.0.0.0 chk:200 aut:0 auk: from Ethernet1
Feb 21 22:59:51.494: OSPF: rcv. v:2 t:1 l:68 rid:156.82.127.3 aid:0.0.0.0 chk:200 aut:0 auk: from Ethernet1
Feb 21 22:59:53.442: OSPF: rcv. v:2 t:1 l:84 rid:156.83.197.2 aid:0.0.0.0 chk:2D83 aut:0 auk: from Ethernet0
Feb 21 22:59:53.446: OSPF: rcv. v:2 t:1 l:68 rid:156.83.197.2 aid:0.0.0.0 chk:200 aut:0 auk: from Ethernet1
Feb 21 22:59:58.974: OSPF: rcv. v:2 t:1 l:84 rid:156.82.197.2 aid:0.0.0.0 chk:2D83 aut:0 auk: from Ethernet0
Feb 21 23:00:00.138: OSPF: rcv. v:2 t:1 l:84 rid:156.82.127.3 aid:0.0.0.0 chk:2D83 aut:0 auk: from Ethernet0
Feb 21 23:00:01.222: OSPF: rcv. v:2 t:1 l:68 rid:156.82.197.2 aid:0.0.0.0 chk:200 aut:0 auk: from Ethernet1
Feb 21 23:00:01.494: OSPF: rcv. v:2 t:1 l:68 rid:156.82.127.3 aid:0.0.0.0 chk:200 aut:0 auk: from Ethernet1
Feb 21 23:00:03.442: OSPF: rcv. v:2 t:1 l:84 rid:156.83.197.2 aid:0.0.0.0 chk:2D83 aut:0 auk: from Ethernet0
Feb 21 23:00:03.446: OSPF: rcv. v:2 t:1 l:68 rid:156.83.197.2 aid:0.0.0.0 chk:200 aut:0 auk: from Ethernet1
Feb 21 23:00:08.974: OSPF: rcv. v:2 t:1 l:84 rid:156.82.197.2 aid:0.0.0.0 chk:2D83 aut:0 auk: from Ethernet0
```

The example that follows shows sample *debug ip ospf packet* output when MD5 authentication is used.

```
OSPF_Router# debug ip ospf packet

OSPF: rcv. v:2 t:1 l:48 rid:200.0.0.116
      aid:0.0.0.0 chk:0 aut:2 keyid:1 seq:0x0
```

The following list offers descriptions of fields for the debug ip ospf packet command.

- **v:**. Indicates the OSPF version.

- **t:**. Indicates the OSPF packet type. Possible packet types include the following:
  - 1. Hello
  - 2. Data description
  - 3. Link-state request
  - 4. Link-state update
  - 5. Link-state acknowledgment
- **l:**. Indicates the OSPF packet length in bytes.

- **rid:**. Indicates the OSPF router ID.

- **aid:**. Indicates the OSPF area ID.

- **chk:**. Indicates the OSPF checksum.

- **aut:**. Indicates the OSPF authentication type. Possible authentication types are as follows:
  - 0. No authentication
  - 1. Simple password
  - 2. MD5
- **auk:**. Indicates the OSPF authentication key.

- **keyid:**. Indicates the MD5 key ID.

- **seq:**. Indicates the sequence number.

`debug ip ospf spf` Command

The `debug ip ospf spf` command enables you to view the actions and events being generated by OSPF's Shortest Path First (SPF) algorithm. The no form of this command disables debugging output. The basic syntax for this command is as follows:

```
[no] debug ip ospf spf
```

OSPF's full SPF contains three parts. First, the Dijkstra algorithm calculates the shortest path tree for the area to figure out all the intra-area routes. Then, all summary LSAs are scanned to calculate the inter-area routes. Finally, all external LSAs are scanned to calculate the external routes. If only `debug ip ospf spf` is done, all information on all three of these steps is shown. This information shows how OSPF decides to add a route from the LSAs and how its cost is calculated. Using the additional keywords displays only the step in which you are interested. Furthermore, for partial SPF, only summary or external LSAs are affected, in which case you would like to do either `debug ip ospf spf inter` or `debug ip ospf spf external` to monitor the partial SPF. You can specify an access to filter only calculation for LSA with specific LSA ID.

```
OSPF_Router# debug ip ospf spf ?
   external      OSPF spf external-route
   inter         OSPF spf inter-route
   intra         OSPF spf inter-route
```

This command provides a variety of useful information regarding SPF and the different options.

```
OSPF_Router# debug ip ospf spf external
OSPF spf external events debugging is on

OSPF_Router# debug ip ospf spf inter
OSPF spf inter events debugging is on

OSPF_Router# debug ip ospf spf intra
OSPF spf intra events debugging is on
```

`debug ip routing` Command

Use the `debug ip routing` EXEC command to display information about how the routing table is updated. All routing protocol can update the routing table so it is not OSPF-specific. The no form of this command disables debugging output. The basic syntax for this command is as follows:

```
[no] debug ip routing
```

The following example shows sample output generated by the debug ip routing command.

```
OSPF_Router# debug ip routing
RT: del 156.226.31.1156/30 via 156.20.18.26, ospf metric [110/4086]
RT: add 156.226.31.1156/30 via 156.20.18.22, ospf metric [110/2108]
RT: add 156.226.31.1156/30 via 156.20.18.26, ospf metric [110/2108]
RT: add 156.226.31.160/30 via 156.20.18.26, ospf metric [110/4086]
RT: del 156.226.31.160/30 via 156.20.18.26, ospf metric [110/4086]
RT: add 156.226.31.160/30 via 156.20.18.22, ospf metric [110/2108]
RT: add 156.226.31.160/30 via 156.20.18.26, ospf metric [110/2108]
RT: add 156.226.31.164/30 via 156.20.18.26, ospf metric [110/4086]
RT: del 156.226.31.164/30 via 156.20.18.26, ospf metric [110/4086]
RT: add 156.226.31.164/30 via 156.20.18.22, ospf metric [110/2108]
RT: add 156.226.31.164/30 via 156.20.18.26, ospf metric [110/2108]
RT: add 156.226.31.188/30 via 156.20.18.22, ospf metric [110/2108]
RT: add 156.226.31.188/30 via 156.20.18.26, ospf metric [110/2108]
RT: add 156.226.31.190/32 via 156.20.18.22, ospf metric [110/2108]
RT: add 156.226.31.190/32 via 156.20.18.26, ospf metric [110/2108]
RT: add 156.226.53.0/24 via 156.20.18.26, ospf metric [110/4086]
RT: add 156.226.54.0/24 via 156.20.18.26, ospf metric [110/4086]
RT: add 156.240.0.0/12 via 156.20.18.22, ospf metric [110/136]
RT: add 156.240.0.0/12 via 156.20.18.26, ospf metric [110/136]
RT: add 159.24.43.0/24 via 156.20.18.22, ospf metric [110/72]
RT: add 159.24.43.0/24 via 156.20.18.26, ospf metric [110/72]
RT: add 192.168.246.37/32 via 156.20.18.26, ospf metric [110/2108]
RT: add 192.168.246.38/32 via 156.20.18.22, ospf metric [110/2108]
RT: add 192.168.246.38/32 via 156.20.18.26, ospf metric [110/2108]
RT: add 192.168.246.39/32 via 156.20.18.22, ospf metric [110/2108]
RT: add 192.168.246.39/32 via 156.20.18.26, ospf metric [110/2108]
RT: add 192.168.246.40/32 via 156.20.18.22, ospf metric [110/2108]
RT: add 192.168.246.40/32 via 156.20.18.26, ospf metric [110/2108]
RT: add 192.168.246.41/32 via 156.20.18.22, ospf metric [110/2108]
RT: add 192.168.246.41/32 via 156.20.18.26, ospf metric [110/2108]
RT: add 192.168.246.42/32 via 156.20.18.22, ospf metric [110/2108]
RT: add 192.168.246.42/32 via 156.20.18.26, ospf metric [110/2108]
RT: add 192.168.246.46/32 via 156.20.18.22, ospf metric [110/2108]
RT: add 192.168.246.46/32 via 156.20.18.26, ospf metric [110/2108]
RT: add 192.168.246.48/32 via 156.20.18.22, ospf metric [110/2108]
RT: add 192.168.246.48/32 via 156.20.18.26, ospf metric [110/2108]
RT: add 192.168.247.0/24 via 156.20.18.26, ospf metric [110/4086]
RT: del 192.168.247.0/24 via 156.20.18.26, ospf metric [110/4086]
```

```
RT: add 192.168.247.0/24 via 156.20.18.22, ospf metric [110/2108]
RT: add 192.168.247.0/24 via 156.20.18.26, ospf metric [110/2108]
RT: network 192.168.247.0 is now variably masked
RT: add 192.168.247.2/32 via 156.20.18.22, ospf metric [110/2108]
RT: add 192.168.247.2/32 via 156.20.18.26, ospf metric [110/2108]
RT: add 192.168.247.3/32 via 156.20.18.22, ospf metric [110/2108]
RT: add 192.168.247.3/32 via 156.20.18.26, ospf metric [110/2108]
RT: add 192.168.247.4/32 via 156.20.18.22, ospf metric [110/2108]
```

The following list provides explanations for representative lines from the preceding output where a newly created entry has been added to the IP routing table.

- **metric change.** Indicates that this entry existed previously, but its metric changed and the change was reported by means of OSPF. The numbers inside the brackets report the administrative distance and the actual metric.

- **cache invalidation.** Indicates that the fast-switching cache was invalidated due to a routing table change.

- **new version.** Indicates the version number of the routing table. When the routing table changes, this number is incremented. The hexadecimal numbers are internal numbers that vary from version to version and software load to software load.

In the following output, the holddown and cache invalidation lines are displayed. Most of the distance vector routing protocols use holddown to avoid typical problems like counting to infinity and routing loops. If you look at the output *of show ip protocols*, you will see what the timer values are for holddown and cache invalidation.

cache invalidation corresponds to came out of holddown. delete route is triggered when a better path comes along. It gets rid of the old inferior route.

```
RT: delete route to 172.26.219.0 via 172.24.76.30, igrp metric [100/10816]
RT: no routes to 172.26.219.0, entering holddown
IP: cache invalidation from 0x115248 0x1378A, new version 5737
RT: 172.26.219.0 came out of holddown
```

Simple IP Troubleshooting Tools

Everyone is aware that networks break and must be repaired as quickly as possible. However, what no one is aware of is that you can isolate and correct a variety of network problems without expensive tools. This section discusses two of the more common features available to network engineers, ping and trace route. These two tools are used specifically for diagnosing IP connectivity within a network.

Pings and Extended Pings

Ping is a common network diagnostic tool found in UNIX stations, Windows NT, Windows 95, and your Cisco routers. It might help you uncover the cause for the various network difficulties. In an IP-based network (such as one running OSPF), the ping command is very useful. Ping sends a burst of data to the designated target and awaits a response.

What Is a Ping?

Ping is a network diagnostic tool that is included in all TCP/IP protocol stacks and is commonly used to verify connectivity to a particular system on a network. Ping sends an Internet Control Messaging Protocol or ICMP (type 8) "echo request" in the form of a data packet to a remote host and displays the results for each returned packet known as a (type 0) *echo reply.* The ping command also displays the time for a response to arrive in milliseconds (minimum/average/maximum).

When performing a ping, you are also verifying that IP is working and that you have connectivity to the site. This can help you determine protocol-related problems.

General Characteristics

The ping feature can be administratively disabled if needed. Disabling ping is typically done to preserve or enhance security within a network. The default ping packet size is 100 bytes within a Cisco router.

A *successful* ping will appear as follows:

```
OSPF_Router# ping 10.251.11.1

Type escape sequence to abort.
Sending 5, 100-byte ICMP Echoes to 10.251.11.1, timeout is 2 seconds:
!!!!!
Success rate is 100 percent (5/5), round-trip min/avg/max = 4/4/4 ms
```

An *unsuccessful* ping will appear as follows:

```
OSPF_Router# ping 10.251.10.1

Type escape sequence to abort.
Sending 5, 100-byte ICMP Echoes to 10.251.10.1, timeout is 2 seconds:
.....
Success rate is 0 percent (0/5)
```

Are Packets Being Dropped?

Ping inserts a sequence number in each packet it sends and notes which sequence number it receives back and in what order. This can be used to determine if packets are being dropped within your network or if they are being reordered. Both problems will require further investigation.

Is the Network Corrupting Your Packets?

The ping packet also contains the standard IP checksum. If the packet is corrupted or damaged, then the checksum will reflect it.

Round Trip Time (RTT)

Each packet also receives a timestamp when it is sent. This timestamp is then echoed back and it will be displayed for a response to arrive in milliseconds. There will be three values available to you: minimum, average, and maximum.

To verify your findings, determine what the expected round trip time should be. This can be calculated as follows:

One Way Trip: (packet size) * 8 / bandwidth in Kbps

For example, on a 56Kbps circuit with a 512 byte packet, you will calculate the round trip time as 512 * 8 / 56000 = .073 or 73 ms. If you want round trip, you will multiply 73 ms by 2 for a result of 146 ms as the average round trip time.

Please note that calculating the RTT can sometimes vary. This can occur on packet switched networks (Frame Relay), bandwidth changes, traffic congestion or utilization. A good rule of thumb is that if the RTT briefly increases or becomes sporadic, then do not be immediately concerned. Though steady increases over time would warrant further investigation.

TIPS

A router will typically place a `ping` in a lower priority than customer traffic, which can add 10ms to the round trip time.

Stress Testing

Ping will also allow you to perform a stress test. Obviously the normal packet size of 64 bytes will not suffice. In this case, you will want to use an extended ping, as described in the section that follows, to increase the packet size. You will first want to record the statistics on the interface you are stress testing. Then send a very large number of 1,500-byte packets (a minimum of 10,000 packets is the recommended standard).

You will also want to duplicate some of the possible test patterns if you are testing a serial line by using either an all 1s or all 0s test pattern. When this is complete, look at the interface statistics. If errors have increased, then the media is causing problems and you will want to have it investigated further. Another way to generate a large network load is to specify a timeout value of 0. This tells the router not to wait for the echo reply before sending the next ping packet. You can really hammer your network this way so be careful.

TIPS

During your testing of serial interfaces, if you see the total number of errors exceeds two percent of the total number packets on the circuit, then you might have a deeper problem and you should respond accordingly.

After you have run the extended ping tests, check if the input errors counter on the serial interface has increased as a result of the ping. If so, that means there is potentially a problem either in the WAN connection or the DSU.

If the input errors counter does not increase, that means the DSU, cable, router interface card, and applique are okay.

If this test was done as a result of high CRC and framing errors, then a clocking problem in the DSU might be the problem.

TIPS

On larger circuits, you might need to have more than one instance of `ping` running in order to stress it properly.

Executing an Extended Ping in a Cisco Router

Using an extended `ping` is very useful in determining the baseline operation of networks to determine what exactly is working and what is not.

TIPS

By selecting the extended command option with the display round trip time, you will be able to see any delays and the time interval between occurrences. It is a good idea to do a long extended `ping` sequence and plot the results in order to clearly see the change in round trip times.

To execute an extended `ping`, go into the router's Enable mode and enter the command *ping*. The options in brackets are default values.

```
OSPF_Router# ping
Protocol [ip]:
Target IP address: 156.12.254.1
Repeat count [5]:
Datagram size [100]:
Timeout in seconds [2]:
Extended commands [n]: yes
Source address:
Type of service [0]:
Set DF bit in IP header? [no]:
Validate reply data? [no]:
Data pattern [0xABCD]:
```

```
Loose, Strict, Record, Timestamp, Verbose[none]: record
Number of hops [ 9 ]:
Loose, Strict, Record, Timestamp, Verbose[RV]:
Sweep range of sizes [n]:
```

To fully utilize the configurable options of an extended `ping`, you need to understand what each option allows you to do. The following list describes the configurable options of an extended `ping`.

TIPS

When selecting the desired commands while performing an extended `ping`, remember the default setting is shown in brackets.

- **Protocol [ip]:**. You can also select various other protocols such as decnet, sna, and ipx. Some protocols can only be used when pinging from router to router.

- **Target IP address:**. This is the destination IP address of the device you are trying to ping.

- **Repeat count [5]:**. You select the number of pings packets you want to send here; the default is five.

- **Timeout in seconds [2]:**. How many seconds will the router wait for the echo reply before timing out and going onto the next packet.

- **Extended commands [n]:**. At this point, you can accept the characteristics of the ping up until this point or not.

- **Type of service [0]:**. You can select various services here as well such as tcp, tftp, telnet, ftp, http, etc., to help troubleshoot specific problems.

- **Validate reply data? [no]:**. Do you want the `ping` packet's checksum verified?

- **Data Pattern [0xABCD]:**. Other data patterns include 0xffff, 0x0000, 0x1010, or 0x0101. The last two data patterns can be used to duplicate a frame failure.

- **Number of hops [9]:**. How many hops should the `ping` travel to reach the desired destination?

TIPS

In complex networks you will sometimes find instances in which the outgoing interface of the router from which you are running the ping will not have a route or be prevented by an access list to the destination. In these cases, you should use the extended ping's source address field to set the ping's source address to another IP address that is permitted.

Understanding an Extended Ping with the Record Option

When using the record option, the <*> indicates that the route is complete.

```
Type escape sequence to abort.
Sending 5, 100-byte ICMP Echoes to 56.12.254.1, timeout is 2 seconds:
Packet has IP options: Total option bytes= 39, padded length=40
  Record route: <*> 0.0.0.0 0.0.0.0 0.0.0.0 0.0.0.0
              0.0.0.0 0.0.0.0 0.0.0.0 0.0.0.0 0.0.0.0

Reply to request 0 (72 ms). Received packet has options
  Total option bytes= 40, padded length=40
  Record route: 56.0.16.35 56.0.17.98 56.12.254.1 56.0.17.97
              56.0.16.39 56.0.16.35 <*> 0.0.0.0 0.0.0.0 0.0.0.0
  End of list
Reply to request 1 (76 ms). Received packet has options
  Total option bytes= 40, padded length=40
  Record route: 56.0.16.67 56.0.17.98 56.12.254.1 56.0.17.97
              56.0.16.39 56.0.16.35 <*> 0.0.0.0 0.0.0.0 0.0.0.0
  End of list
```

For additional information on using the ping and extended ping commands, refer to the *Cisco IOS Configuration Fundamentals Command Reference*.

trace *Command*

Trace is a common network diagnostic tool found on UNIX machines, Windows NT, Windows 95, and your Cisco router. Trace might help you uncover the cause of network difficulties.

What Is **trace**?

Trace is a network diagnostic tool that allows network engineers or users to trace and view the actual route an IP packet follows to the indicated host.

The *trace* command provides a method for determining which path packets traverse between two devices. Because the Trace utility reveals IP routing decisions, it is useful in discovering if the routers erroneously converged on a path that traverses a low-bandwidth link or a heavily congested router or segment.

How to Use **trace**

The trace command discovers the route a router's packets follow when traveling to their destinations. Network engineers could then use the results of the trace command to adjust routing protocol metrics to optimize the path between critical points.

Another use of trace will be for it to give indications if a link or segment has failed between two points.

In Cisco routers, if the trace command is executed in the router's privileged EXEC mode, it will prompt you for the supported IP header options to be specified, allowing the router to perform a more extensive range of test options.

trace Command Operation

The trace command generates an outgoing UDP message targeted to a destination device. The UDP packet header contains a PORT value that identifies the upper-layer application for which the packet is destined. Most trace implementations use a port value greater than 30000, a value unlikely to be used by the destination device. Cisco routers use a default port value of 33434.

TIPS

One unique characteristic of the **trace** command is that it only reports the path of the outgoing UDP packets. It is possible that the ICMP responses might take a different path than the outgoing UDP messages. There is no guarantee that your trace output reflects the path for both directions.

However, by exercising the loose source route option that is available in an extended **trace** command, you can create a **trace** from the source router to a remote router, then back to the source thereby testing both directions.

To discover each hop between the source and destination, trace probes each successive hop to the destination. By default, each hop is probed three times. This probing is done by modifying the IP Time-to-Live (TTL) value. The Time-To-Live (TTL) value is set in the IP header portion of the packet thereby ensuring that packets do not continuously traverse the network.

Step 1: trace Begins

The trace command works by using the error message generated by routers when a datagram exceeds its time-to-live (TTL) value. First, trace probe datagrams are sent out with its TTL value set to 1 (see Figure 8-4). This causes the first router it reaches to reduce the TTL by a factor of 1 to a value of 0. This causes the router (Router B) to discard the probe datagrams and send back a *"time exceeded"* ICMP error message.

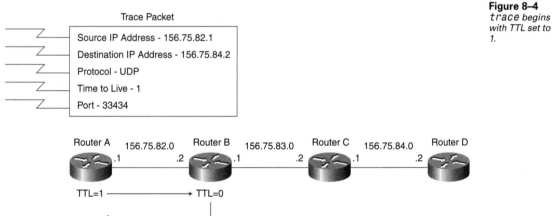

Figure 8–4
*trace begins
with TTL set to
1.*

Each outgoing trace packet can result in one of two ICMP error messages:

- A *"time exceeded"* error message indicates that an intermediate router has seen and discarded the probe because the TTL value has incremented to 0.

- A *"port unreachable"* error message indicates that the destination node has received the probe and discarded it because it could not deliver the packet to an application with the value indicated in port field of the packet.

TIPS

In a Cisco router, if the TTL timer (that is, the timeout in seconds value) goes off before one of the two possible ICMP responses come in, then `trace` prints an asterisk (*).

Step 2: Source Router Responds

Upon receipt of the ICMP error message, the source router (Router A) will then resend the UDP trace packet but this time it increments the TTL value by adding 1 to it. In the example shown in Figure 8-5, the TTL value will be increased to 2.

Figure 8–5
trace operation.

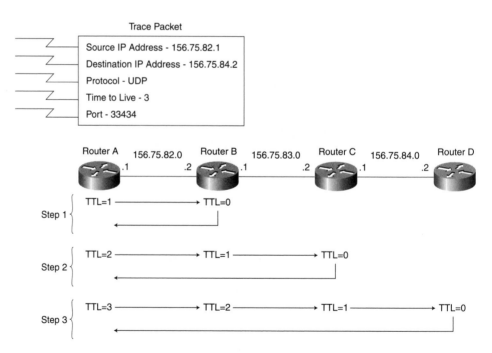

The UDP trace packet will reach the first router (Router B). This router will decrease the TTL value by one and then forward the packet to the next router (Router C) on the way to the destination device; this is determined by the routing table. Router C reduces the TTL to 0. This causes the router (Router C) to discard the probe datagrams and send back a *"time exceeded"* ICMP error message.

Step 3: **trace** Resent

The Trace utility will then resend the packet with the TTL set to a value of 3. This process will be repeated until the destination router is reached (Router D). At which point Router D receives the packet with a valid TTL. As the router examines the packet, it sees the port to which it is destined (hopefully, the port is unused since it can be a random value). Because the port is not found in the router, instead of issuing a *"time exceeded"* message, it returns the *"Port Unreachable"* ICMP error message. At which point the source router receives the packet back, deciphers it, and displays the final hop to the network engineer.

TIPS

The *trace* command terminates when the destination responds, when the maximum TTL is exceeded, or when the user interrupts the trace with the escape sequence, %%%%.

As with ping, it is a good idea to use the trace command when the network is functioning properly to see how the command works under normal conditions and so you have something to compare against when troubleshooting.

For more detailed information on using the trace and extended trace commands, please refer to the *Cisco IOS Configuration Fundamentals Command Reference*.

Executing the Extended **trace** Command in a Cisco Router

The following describes the fields that are unique to the extended trace sequence, as shown in the display:

```
OSPF_Router# trace
Protocol [ip]:
Target IP address: 156.12.254.41
Source address:
Numeric display [n]:
```

```
Timeout in seconds [3]:
Probe count [3]:
Minimum Time to Live [1]:
Maximum Time to Live [30]:
Port Number [33434]:
Loose, Strict, Record, Timestamp, Verbose [none]:
Type escape sequence to abort.
Tracing the route to 56.12.254.41

  1  156.0.16.71 56 msec
     156.0.16.39 52 msec
     156.0.16.71 52 msec
  2  156.0.17.97 56 msec 52 msec 56 msec
  3  156.12.254.41 [AS 65512] 76 msec * 56 msec
```

To fully utilize the configurable options of a trace you need to understand what each option allows you to do, as explained in the following list.

- **Target IP address:**. This option enables you to enter a host name or an IP address; there is no default.

- **Source address:**. This option indicates the IP address on the source router. As a default, the router will randomly determine the best.

- **Numeric display:**. The default for this option is to have both symbolic (names) and numeric displays of IP addresses.

- **Timeout in seconds:**. This option determines the number of seconds to wait for a response to a probe packet. The default is 3 seconds.

- **Probe count:**. This option sets the number of probes to be sent at each TTL level; the default is 3.

- **Minimum time to live [1]:**. This option sets the TTL value for the first probes; the default is 1, but it can be set to a higher value.

- **Maximum time to live [30]:**. This option sets the largest TTL value that can be used; the default is 30.

- **Port number:**. This option sets the destination port used by the UDP probe messages, default is 33434.

- **_Loose, Strict, Record, Timestamp, Verbose:_**. These are the various IP header options. You can specify any combination. The trace command issues prompts for the required fields. trace places the requested options in each probe, but there is no guarantee that all routers (or end nodes) will process the options you selected.

  - **_Loose_**. This option allows you to specify a list of nodes that must be traversed when going to the destination selected. Think of its operation like this: "You can take any path to the destination but it must include this specific set of routers."

TIPS

When you specify the routers for the **loose** option, be aware that the trace probe will follow the path as indicated in the sequence specified. If you specify a router on the other side of the network and then the one you are in, trace will send the probe out then come back your router and proceed along to the destination. This means you could make trace ping pong between two or more routers.

  - **_Strict_**. This option allows you to specify a list of nodes to traverse when going to the destination. Think of its operation like this: "this is the only path you can take to reach the destination." This strict path is based upon the node addresses you enter and their order. One final note, the nodes entered must also be sequentially adjacent (i.e. one hop apart from each other).

  - **_Record_**. This option allows you to specify the number of hops to leave room for, but the IP header will not support more than nine hops.

  - **_Timestamp_**. This option allows you to specify the number of timestamps to leave room for. You may specify up to nine timestamp slots. The time is recorded according to the remote router's clock. If you are concurrently using the record option, then no more than four hops will be recorded. (The IP option header space is shared by record route and timestamp.)

  - **_Verbose_**. If you select any option, the verbose mode is automatically selected and trace prints the contents of the option field in any incoming packets. You can prevent verbose mode by selecting verbose again, toggling its current setting.

TIPS

An interesting point of note is that the **verbose** option is Cisco-specific. The **trace** command will place the appropriate options in each packet; unfortunately, there is no guarantee that all routers will process the options.

CISCO TECHNICAL SUPPORT

When you have a problem that you cannot resolve, the resource of last resort is your Cisco Systems technical support representative. To analyze problem, your technical support representative will need certain information about the situation and the symptoms you are experiencing. To speed the problem isolation and resolution process, present the data discussed in the following sections when you contact your representative.

Gathering Network Information

Before gathering any specific data, compile a list of all symptoms that users have reported on the internetwork (such as connections dropping or slow host response).

The next step is to gather specific information. Typical information needed to troubleshoot internetworking problems falls into two general categories: information required for any situation and information specific to the topology, technology, protocol, or problem.

Information that is always required by technical support engineers includes the following:

- Configuration listing of all routers involved

- Complete specifications of all routers involved

- Version numbers of software (obtained with *show version* command) and firmware (obtained with the *show controllers* command) on all relevant routers

- Network topology map

- List of hosts and servers (host and server type, number on network, description of host operating systems implemented)

- List of network layer protocols, versions, and vendors

To assist you in gathering this required data, the *show tech-support* EXEC command has been added in Cisco IOS Release 11.1(4) and later. This command provides general information about the router that you can provide to your technical support representative when you are reporting a problem.

The *show tech-support* command outputs the equivalent of the show version, show running-config, show controllers, show stacks, show interfaces, show buffers, show process memory, and show process cpu EXEC commands. In addition, *show tech-support* also provides some platform-specific information that is not provided in the previous commands.

Specific requirements that vary depending on the situation include the following output from general and specific SHOW commands:

- show interfaces
- show controllers {serial ¦ token ¦ mci ¦ cbus ¦ fddi ¦ cxbus ¦ cybus}
- show processes {cpu ¦ mem}
- show buffer
- show mem summary
- Output from protocol-specific SHOW commands:
    - show *protocol* route
    - show *protocol* traffic
    - show *protocol* interfaces
    - show *protocol* arp

- Output from protocol-specific ping and trace diagnostic tests, as appropriate
- Output from relevant debug privileged EXEC commands, as appropriate
- Network analyzer traces, as appropriate
- Core dumps obtained by using the exception dump router configuration command, or by using the write core router configuration command if the system is operational, as appropriate.

Getting the Data from Your Router

You must tailor the way you obtain information from the router to the system you are using to retrieve the information. Following are some hints for different platforms:

- **PC or Macintosh.** Connect a PC or Macintosh to the console port of the router and log all output to a disk file (using a terminal emulation program). The exact procedure varies depending on the communication package used with the system.

- **Terminal Connected To Console Port Or Remote Terminal.** The only way to get information with a terminal connected to the console port or with a remote terminal is to attach a printer to the AUX port on the terminal (if one exists) and force all screen output to go to the printer. Using a terminal is undesirable because there is no way to capture the data to a file.

- **UNIX workstation.** At the UNIX prompt, enter the following command `script <filename>`, then Telnet to the router. The UNIX `script` command captures all screen output to the specified file name. To stop capturing output and close the file, enter the end-of-file character (typically ^D) for your UNIX system.

How Do I Get an Exception or Core Dump?

To obtain a core dump when a router crashes, use the `exception dump` ip-address router configuration command (where `ip-address` is the address of your TFTP server). To get a core dump, add this command to your configuration: `exception dump x.x.x.x`, where x.x.x.x is the address of your TFTP server. The core dump will be written to <hostname>-core where <hostname> is the name of the router as given with the hostname configuration command. This will cause the router to attempt to make a core dump if it crashes. This can fail if the router is sufficiently confused. The core dump file will be the size of memory available on the processor (for example, 4MB for a CSC/3). Depending on your TFTP server, you might also have to create these files before the router can write to them. You can test this by trying the TFTP put command from a workstation. You can also test crash dumps with the EXEC command `write core`. This will cause the router to generate a crash dump and is useful if the router is problematic, but has not crashed.

TIPS

TFTP has a problem with core dumps bigger than 16M, in which case it is recommended using rcp instead by configuring exception protocol rcp.

Cisco Connection Online (CCO)

Cisco Connection Online (CCO), formerly Cisco Information Online (CIO), is Cisco Systems' primary, real-time support channel. Maintenance customers and partners can self-register on CCO to obtain additional content and services.

Available 24 hours a day, 7 days a week, CCO provides a wealth of standard and value-added services to Cisco's customers and business partners. CCO services include product information, software updates, release notes, technical tips, the Bug Navigator, the Troubleshooting Engine, configuration notes, brochures, descriptions of service offerings, and download access to public and authorized files.

CCO serves a variety of users through two interfaces that are updated and enhanced simultaneously—a character-based version and a multimedia version that resides on the World Wide Web (WWW). The character-based CCO supports Zmodem, Kermit, Xmodem, FTP, Internet e-mail, and fax download options, and is excellent for quick access to information over lower bandwidths. The WWW version of CCO provides richly formatted documents with photographs, figures, graphics, and video, as well as hyperlinks to related information.

Accessing Cisco Connection Online (CCO)

You can access CCO in the following ways:

- **World Wide Web.** http://www.cisco.com
- **Telnet.** http://cco.cisco.com
- **Modem.** From North America, 408 526-8070; from Europe, 33 1 64 46 40 82. Use the following terminal settings: VT100 emulation; data bits: 8; stop bits: 1; parity: none; baud rate: up to 14.4Kbps.

For a copy of CCO's Frequently Asked Questions (FAQ), send e-mail to http://cco-help@cisco.com. For additional information, send e-mail to http://cco-team@cisco.com.

Technical Information Available on CCO

Following is a set of sample URLs intended to provide an example of the depth of information that is available on CCO. Much of this information is accessed via the "Service and Support" section, which is located at the following URL: `http://www.cisco.com/kobayashi/Support_root.shtml`. Some of the documentation you can expect to find on CCO is as follows:

- **Internetworking Primer.** This documentation provides a high-level overview of the Cisco IOS, LANs and WANs, desktop protocols, modems, and asynchronous protocols. The first three chapters are an excellent starting point for any new network engineers or managers unfamiliar with Cisco Equipment or internetworking. The URL for this documentation is: `http://www.cisco.com/univercd/data/doc/hardware/access/2500/ug/techovr.htm`.

- **Beginning IP for New Users.** This documentation gives you basic information you'll need to configure your router for routing IP, such as how addresses are broken down and how subnetting works. You will learn how to assign each interface on the router an IP address with a unique subnet. Do not worry; this document will show you many examples to help tie everything together. The URL for this documentation is: `http://www.cisco.com/warp/customer/701/3.html`.

- **Using BGP for Interdomain Routing.** This documentation provides a similarly detailed explanation/tutorial on the design and configuration of the BGP protocol. The URL for this documentation is: `http://www.cisco.com/univercd/data/doc/cintrnet/ics/icsbgp4.htm`.

Technical Assistance Available on CCO

Cisco Connection Online (CCO) is also a very important source for online technical assistance. The following are a few examples of the services a CCO user can access—without reliance on Cisco customer support staff.

- **Stack Decoder.** This tool lets you decode the output from the show stack command obtained after a Cisco router crashes. Additionally, it locates possible known bugs for your analysis. The URL for this tool is `http://cco.cisco.com/stack/stackdecoder.shtml`.

- **Bug Navigator II.** This tool lets you do your own research for known problems with Cisco hardware or software. In particular, the "IOS Software" section lets you search for bugs within a particular IOS version and release based on one or more software features. This is very useful if you are considering upgrading to a different version of IOS. By using it, you will be able to be aware of any software bugs before you implement the change. The URL for this tool is `http://cco.cisco.com/support/bugtools/bugtool.shtml`.

- **Search Cisco IOS Bugs by ID Number.** This can be used to obtain information on bugs that have been identified by Cisco staff. This is also a very good place to look during troubleshooting. The URL for this tool is `http://cco.cisco.com/kobayashi/bugs/bugs.html`.

- **Bug Watcher.** Enables you to create collections or bins of defects that you can use to monitor the status of specific defects. Watcher Bins are continuously updated by means of Bug Alert Agents. This is a very good proactive tool that is offered by Cisco. The URL for this tool is `http://cco.cisco.com/support/bugtools/homepage.shtml`.

- **Case Open Tool.** Open Cisco TAC cases directly from your Web Browser—no more waiting in the phone queue! Please note: This is only for cases that are priority 3 or 4. The URL for this tool is `http://cco.cisco.com/kobayashi/support/case_open.shtml`.

- **Case Query Tool.** Read the case notes for any TAC cases you have open. The URL for this tool is `http://cco.cisco.com/kobayashi/support/case_query.shtml`.

- **Case Update Tool.** Update the information in cases you have open with TAC online. The URL for this tool is `http://cco.cisco.com/kobayashi/support/case_updt.shtml`.

Online Documentation Available on CCO

Almost all Cisco published documentation can be accessed directly from CCO. All available online documentation is indexed at the following URL: `http://www.cisco.com/univercd/home/home.htm`. The list that follows provides information and URLs for some of the more useful documents.

- **Internetworking Technology Overview.** An introduction to Internetworking Technology, the URL for which is `http://www.cisco.com/univercd/data/doc/cintrnet/75818.htm`.

- **Internetwork Troubleshooting Guide.** Two manuals cover this and are located at the following URLs: `http://www.cisco.com/univercd/data/doc/cintrnet/itg_v1.htm` and `http://www.cisco.com/univercd/data/doc/cintrnet/75821.htm`.

- **Internetwork Design Guide.** Presents a set of general guidelines for planning internetworks and provides specific suggestions for several key internetworking implementations. The URL for this documentation is `http://www.cisco.com/univercd/data/doc/cintrnet/idg3/idgpref.htm`.

- **Internetworking Case Studies.** Case studies on a variety of internetworking technologies and applications. These make use of diagrams and configurations to illustrate the approach taken. The URL for this documentation is `http://www.cisco.com/univercd/data/doc/cintrnet/ics.htm`.

- **IOS Configuration Guides/Command References.** The Cisco IOS manual sets for each IOS version can be accessed online from this URL: `http://www.cco.cisco.com/univercd/data/doc/software.htm`.

- **Stratacom Online Documentation.** The Stratacom document set can be accessed online from the following URL: `http://www.cisco.com/univercd/data/doc/wanbu/8_2/82.htm`.

CHAPTER SUMMARY

This chapter discussed how to effectively monitor and troubleshoot your OSPF network. This information was presented in three sections: "Monitoring OSPF," "Troubleshooting OSPF," and "Cisco Technical Support." The "Monitoring OSPF" section discussed various methods of ensuring that OSPF is operating properly in your network. The "Troubleshooting OSPF" section examined ways to proactively prepare for the inevitable network problems. The "Cisco Technical Support" section discussed the resources available to you within Cisco, including several online troubleshooting tools.

CASE STUDY: IN THE TRENCHES WITH OSPF

This case study is intended to describe a "real world" case where this problem actually occurred and how it was identified and corrected. The case study then outlines some lessons to help prevent it from happening again in the future. The troubleshooting model introduced earlier in this chapter is used throughout this case study as a process to reference when performing network troubleshooting.

Recently, a large broadcast storm occurred in an OSPF Enterprise network, affecting a region of the network that consisted of approximately 50 geographically separate sites consisting of over 75 routers serving approximately 3,000 users. This condition brought all user WAN traffic in the impacted area to a standstill.

Through the course of our troubleshooting, we identified how and why "localized" broadcasts were erroneously being propagated across the WAN, resulting in a dramatic degradation in network performance. Additionally, several Cisco OSPF router configuration problems were identified and corrected during the course of troubleshooting.

Troubleshooting Methodology

When troubleshooting in any type of networking environment, a systematic troubleshooting methodology works best. The seven steps outlined throughout this section will help you to clearly define the specific symptoms associated with network problems, identify potential problems that could be causing the symptoms, and then systematically eliminate each potential problem (from most likely to least likely) until the symptoms disappear.

This process is not a rigid outline for troubleshooting an internetwork. Rather it is a foundation from which you can build a problem-solving process to suit your particular internetworking environment.

The following troubleshooting steps detail the problem-solving process:

1. Clearly define the problem.
2. Gather facts.
3. Consider possible problems.
4. Create an action plan.
5. Implement the action plan.
6. Gather results.
7. Reiterate the process, if needed, in steps 4–7.

Customer Reports a Network Slowdown

The customer has called the Network Operations Center (NOC) and reported a network slowdown at a number of critical sites. The situation is even more urgent, as the customer is preparing to run the end of inventory reconciliation report. The network must be available at this critical time or the customer will lose money.

Step 1: Define the Problem

The first step in any type of troubleshooting and repair scenario is to define the problem. What is actually happening is sometimes very different from what is reported; thus, the truth in this step is defining the *actual* problem. You need to do two things: identify the symptoms and perform an impact assessment.

Our customer called us and explained that the network response was extremely slow. This, of course, was a rather vague and broad description from a network operations standpoint. Due to the nature of the problem report (that is, it can sometimes be difficult to define "slow"), a clear understanding of the problem was required before we could proceed with developing an action plan. This was accomplished by gathering facts and asking several questions to the user reporting the problem. According to the users, the general symptoms included:

- Slow response (including a 30–40 percent packet loss) while connecting to any device on the WAN from the Downtown location (see Figure 8-6). We confirmed the slow response by executing a `ping` from ROUTER B to ROUTER C and we received an 800 millisecond round trip delay. A normal network round trip delay for other routers in our network had consistently been in the range of 100 to 150 milliseconds.

- Nearly 100 percent utilization was found on Router B's Frame Relay Permanent Virtual Circuit to Router C. This had been seen by our long distance carrier's Frame Relay network group, who had been monitoring Frame Relay switch statistics at our request.

- We were informed that impact on user productivity was so great that several users were sent home because they could not reliably access critical network resources.

- Other users reported that their ability to run inventory reports was being impaired and the deadline was quickly approaching.

Step 2: Gather Facts

After the problem is defined, it is then necessary to begin gathering the facts surrounding the problem. This step will provide the facts that were gained in this network case study.

Before starting to troubleshoot any type of networking problem, it is usually helpful to have a network diagram. Figure 8-6 shows the diagram we used.

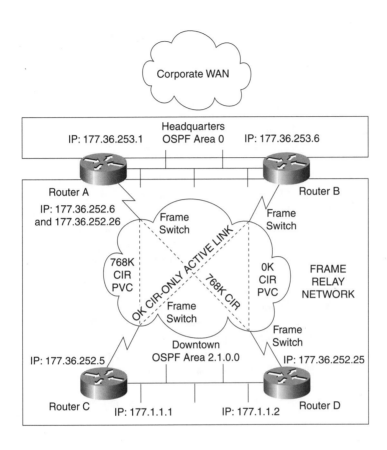

Figure 8–6
*Case study
WAN diagram.*

Following the previously mentioned troubleshooting methodology, we collected as many facts as possible and made some general observations by connecting to the routers in question. We gathered facts from several sources on the router, including the Cisco log buffer and by utilizing various Cisco SHOW commands. Our observations revealed the following facts and occurrences within the network.

Router B in Figure 8-6 reported high traffic input to the Ethernet segment at Headquarters. This caused the Ethernet connectivity to become so unstable that the links would become unavailable for brief periods. Consequently, OSPF adjacencies were being reformed repeatedly. The following is an excerpt from the SYSLOG on Router A:

```
Mar 1 00:08:17 UTC: %LINEPROTO-5-UPDOWN: Line protocol on Interface Ethernet0, changed state to down
Mar 1 00:08:29 UTC: %LINEPROTO-5-UPDOWN: Line protocol on Interface Ethernet0, changed state to up
Mar 1 00:08:35 UTC: %LINEPROTO-5-UPDOWN: Line protocol on Interface Ethernet0, changed state to down
Mar 1 00:08:39 UTC: %LINEPROTO-5-UPDOWN: Line protocol on Interface Ethernet0, changed state to up
```

As you can see by the SYSLOG entries, Ethernet connectivity was being lost for brief periods of time. The router was definitely showing us a contributing factor to the problems being reported by our customer.

Missing OSPF Adjacencies

No OSPF neighbors were formed between Routers A & C, A & D, or B & D. The only link that was actively carrying routed traffic was between Routers C & B. Unfortunately, this circuit was a 0K CIR Frame Relay link. This meant that all traffic between routers C & B was being marked as *discard eligible (DE)* by the Frame Relay switches in the Frame Relay cloud. (That is, all traffic between Router C& B was set at such a low priority for packet delivery and could be dropped at any time.) As is discussed later in this case study, the Cisco router commands to show this information are `show ip ospf neighbors` and `show frame pvc`. The output for `show frame pvc` follows. Note that the number of input packets and the number of in DE packets are the same.

```
ROUTER_C#Show frame pvc
PVC Statistics for interface Serial0/0:0.2 (Frame Relay DTE)
DLCI = 700, DLCI USAGE = LOCAL, PVC STATUS = ACTIVE, INTERFACE = Serial0/0:0.2
    input pkts 31341659    output pkts 12061107    in bytes 757769644
    out bytes 2564616415   dropped pkts 0          in FECN pkts 17
    in BECN pkts 0         out FECN pkts 0         out BECN pkts 0
    in DE pkts 31341659    out DE pkts 0
    out bcast pkts 2690375  out bcast bytes 250333218
    pvc create time 15w5d, last time pvc status changed 4w2d
```

Output Drops

A large number of output drops were noted on Router C's only active OSPF WAN interface (the one with the 0K CIR Frame Relay PVC). Output drops signify that the router is processing a very large number of outbound frames. In this case, the circuit could not accommodate the vast amount of data that the router was trying to output into it, so, as a result, the router was dropping frames. This observation is important because it directly affects the number of retransmits that the router sends and contributes to slow end-user throughput. This happens in a router when the circuit and router are overloaded with a large amount of input or output traffic. As discussed later in this case study, the Cisco command to see this happening is *show interface serial <interface number>*. The next section will specifically cover the numbers of input and output drops in the output of this useful IOS command.

Input Drops

Large numbers of input drops were observed on Router B's only active WAN interface (0K CIR Frame Relay PVC). Input drops signify that the router is processing a very large number of inbound frames. The router could not keep up with the data stream because there was so much inbound traffic. Consequently, the router was dropping many inbound frames resulting in large number of input drops being reported. This observation is important because it directly affects the number of retransmits that the router sends, contributing to slower end-user throughput. As discussed previously, the Cisco router command to do this is *show interface serial <interface number>*. The output of Router B's WAN interface follows:

```
ROUTER_B#show int s0/0:0
Serial0/0:0 is up, line protocol is up
  Hardware is DSX1
  Description: Frame Relay Circuit to Downtown
  MTU 1500 bytes, BW 1536 Kbit, DLY 20000 usec, rely 255/255, load 6/255
  Encapsulation FRAME-RELAY IETF, loopback not set, keepalive set (10 sec)
  LMI enq sent 11212, LMI stat recvd 11212, LMI upd recvd 0, DTE LMI up
  LMI enq recvd 0, LMI stat sent 0, LMI upd sent 0
  LMI DLCI 0 LMI type is ANSI Annex D frame relay DTE
  Broadcast queue 0/64, broadcasts sent/dropped 983815/57443, interface broadcasts 1035677
  Last input 00:00:00, output 00:00:00, output hang never
  Last clearing of "show interface" counters 1d22h
  Input queue: 0/75/421238 (size/max/drops); Total output drops: 32333
  Queueing strategy: weighted fair
  Output queue: 0/64/32333 (size/threshold/drops)
     Conversations 0/51 (active/max active)
     Reserved Conversations 0/0 (allocated/max allocated)
  5 minute input rate 50000 bits/sec, 19 packets/sec
  5 minute output rate 42000 bits/sec, 8 packets/sec
     1493015 packets input, 320768751 bytes, 0 no buffer
     Received 0 broadcasts, 2 runts, 0 giants, 0 throttles
     48 input errors, 35 CRC, 13 frame, 0 overrun, 0 ignored, 2 abort
     2335606 packets output, 845399484 bytes, 0 underruns
     0 output errors, 0 collisions, 1 interface resets
```

Gather More Facts

In an attempt to gather more facts to form an action plan, we needed to know if the problem was related to a hardware problem or a software problem. Through the use of Telnet, we determined that we could successfully connect to all routers, although the performance was slow. This ruled out the possibility of a complete hardware failure on any of the routers. We then began to shift our focus on the router configurations. Our initial examination of Router A's configuration showed that PVCs to C and D were defined, configured, and active (line up and line protocol up). The configuration that we observed follows:

```
ROUTER_A# show running-config
!
interface Serial1
 description Frame Relay PVCs Downtown to Router C
 no ip address
 encapsulation frame-relay IETF
 bandwidth 56
 no fair-queue
 frame-relay lmi-type ansi
!
interface Serial1.1 point-to-point
 description 768K CIR PVC to router C
 ip address 177.36.252.6 255.255.255.252
 frame-relay interface-dlci 700
!
interface Serial2
 description Frame Relay PVCs Downtown to Router D
 no ip address
 encapsulation frame-relay IETF
 bandwidth 56
 no fair-queue
 frame-relay lmi-type ansi
!
interface Serial2.1 point-to-point
 description 768K PVC to Router D
 ip address 177.36.252.26 255.255.255.252
 frame-relay interface-dlci 701
!
router ospf 204
 network 177.36.253.0 0.0.0.255 area 0
 network 177.36.252.2 0.0.0.0 area 2.1.0.0
 network 177.36.252.24 0.0.0.0 area 2.1.0.0
 area 2.1.0.0 authentication
 area 2.1.0.0 stub
```

Step 3: Consider Possible Problems

Very soon after our initial observations were made and the facts were gathered, we determined that hardware did not seem to be a problem. However, we recognized that there were actually two problems to confront:

- **Routing issues.** No OSPF adjacencies were being created on three of the four WAN links. Consequently, these links were not passing any routed customer information. Because we had previously ruled out hardware as an issue, we decided to it would be necessary confront this problem from a software configuration standpoint.

- **Performance issues.** A large number of output drops and input drops on the WAN link seemed to be directly related to user slowdowns. However, a circuit problem could not be fully ruled out at this time—if the circuits were truly being over utilized, they could potentially require an upgrade in speed. However, we determined that increasing the circuit speed might require more investigation after the routing issues were fully resolved.

Step 4: Create an Action Plan

Based on the previous troubleshooting methodology, we decided to use a "divide and conquer" approach by breaking up the problem into two pieces: routing issues and performance issues.

As part of our action plan, we decided we would correct the routing issues first, then proceed with the performance issues. We also decided that we would change only one variable at a time (that is, only make one router configuration change at a time), so that we could clearly understand the solution, after it is discovered.

Step 5: Implement the Action Plan

One of the best troubleshooting commands to use for dealing with OSPF routing issues is *show ip ospf neighbors*. The output of this command will display very useful information about OSPF adjacencies in any OSPF network; and as you know, OSPF routing is highly influenced by adjacencies.

The initial output of this command on ROUTER A and ROUTER B gave some very useful information, as shown in the following output.

```
ROUTER_A# show ip ospf neighbors
177.36.253.6      1    FULL/DR   00:00:32  177.4.255.32    Ethernet1
```

Our findings (from the show ip ospf neighbors output that follows) showed that Router A was adjacent with Router B and vice-versa. Router B was fully adjacent with C's backup link (0K CIR). These links were running at 0K CIR and all packets going into the network were being marked discard eligible. This helped us to understand why performance was so slow.

```
ROUTER_B# show ip ospf neighbors
177.36.253.1    1   FULL/BDR-    00:00:32   177.4.255.31   Ethernet1
177.36.252.5    1   FULL/ -      00:00:32   177.65.252.45  Serial2.1
```

Later, you will see that once the routing issues were corrected, the output of the same command on Router A will yield the following:

```
ROUTER_A# show ip ospf neighbors
177.36.252.1    1   2WAY/DROTHER   00:00:32   177.4.255.32   Ethernet1
177.36.252.5    1   FULL/ -        00:00:34   177.65.252.1   Serial1.1
        ***FULL T1 (768K CIR) Link to ROUTER C
177.65.252.25   1   FULL/ -        00:00:32   177.65.252.29  Serial2.1
        ***FULL T1 (768K CIR) Link to ROUTER D
```

Step 6: Gather Results

In this step, we begin to gather the results of the action plan that we had created to deal with the reported network problem.

Our first step in determining why the adjacencies were not being formed over the WAN links was to confirm that OSPF was enabled on them. By using the show ip ospf interfaces command, we quickly determined that indeed OSPF was NOT enabled on the WAN interfaces for Router A. Specifically, OSPF was not enabled for the WAN links to Routers C and D. As noted in the preceding command output, Ethernet0 on Router A had correctly formed an adjacency with Router B. The output of the show ip ospf interfaces command is as follows:

```
ROUTER_A# Show ip ospf interface
Ethernet0 is up, line protocol is up
   Internet Address 177.2.255.1/24, Area 0
   Process ID 202, Router ID 177.36.252.1 Network Type BROADCAST, Cost: 10
   Transmit Delay is 1 sec, State DROTHER, Priority 1
   Designated Router (ID) 177.2.255.4, Interface address 177.2.255.4
   Backup Designated router (ID) 177.32.252.6, Interface address 177.2.255.5
   Timer intervals configured, Hello 10, Dead 40, Wait 40, Retransmit 5
        Hello due in 00:00:02
```

```
    Neighbor Count is 1, Adjacent neighbor count is 1
        Adjacent with neighbor 177.36.253.6 (Designated Router)
Serial0 is up, line protocol is up
  OSPF not enabled on this interface
Serial0.1 is up, line protocol is up
  OSPF not enabled on this interface
Serial1 is up, line protocol is up
  OSPF not enabled on this interface
Serial1.2 is up, line protocol is up
  OSPF not enabled on this interface
```

This message "OSPF not enabled on this interface" explained why OSPF would not form an adjacency—*simply because it had not been enabled!*

Step 7: Reiterate the Process, if Needed, in Steps 4–7

Our action plan was successful, and we had identified errors in the router configurations that needed to be corrected. The question then became: "How do I turn on OSPF on the WAN interfaces s0.1 and s1.2 of router A?" A new solution was achieved in three steps:

1. Determine the networks that belong to s0.1 and s1.2. This was done by using the Cisco commands: *show ip int s0.1* and *show ip int s0.2*. The output from those commands will yield the IP address of each interface and the subnet mask that each is configured.

2. Add the network number(s) obtained in Step 1 to the OSPF process and area number to Router A's configuration.

3. Enable area authentication, because the design specification requires simple cleartext OSPF authentication.

At this point, it is necessary to reiterate the troubleshooting process and its steps to now begin making the changes to the router's configuration identified in the preceding three-step process.

Step 4: Create a New Action Plan

Remember that it is important to change only one variable at a time while executing an action plan. Additionally, it is considered good practice to log any changes that you are making to the router's configuration. Many terminal tools allow the terminal output to be redirected into an ASCII file. I highly recommend creating an audit trail for later retrieval and reference. This information is also good if you ever have to write an after action report or a case study!

The action plan was developed to implement steps described previously and will enable OSPF on the identified routers and observe the results after these actions had taken effect.

Step 5: Implement the New Action Plan

Identifying the steps needed to enable OSPF enabled us to formulate a new plan of action that consisted of taking the following actions to the router's configuration:

```
ROUTER_A#conf t
Enter configuration commands, one per line. End with CNTL/Z
ROUTER_A(config)#router ospf 202
ROUTER_A(config-router)#network 177.36.252.0 0.0.0.255 area 2.1.0.0
ROUTER_A(config-router)# area 2.1.0.0 authentication
```

After entering these commands, interfaces s0.1 and s1.2 began to "speak" OSPF and attempted to form an adjacency. The relevant new OSPF configuration in ROUTER A is as follows:

```
!
router ospf 202
  network 177.2.254.0 0.0.0.255 area 0
  network 177.36.252.0 0.0.0.255 area 2.1.0.0
  area 2.1.0.0 authentication
!
```

Step 6 Revisited: Gather Results

We then confirmed that the serial links were now "talking" OSPF by once again using the show ip ospf interfaces command. As we discovered, the routers were speaking OSPF, but were not forming adjacencies over the WAN link. This condition was confirmed by the neighbor and adjacency which counts were zero—as indicated by the output in bold that follows.

TIPS

Under a normal `show interface` command, the up status reported refers to the data link layer keepalive packet. The same is true when performing a `show ip ospf interface` command.

```
      ROUTER_A#Show ip ospf interface

Serial0.2 is up, line protocol is up
   Internet Address 177.36.252.6/30, Area 2.1.0.0
   Process ID 202, RouterID 177.36.252.26, Network Type POINT_TO_POINT, Cost:1
   Transmit Delay is 1 sec, State POINT_TO_POINT,
   Timer intervals configured, Hello 10, Dead 40, Wait 40, Retransmit 5
     Hello due in 00:00:03
   Neighbor Count is 0, Adjacent neighbor count is 0
     Adjacent with neighbor 177.3
Serial1.2 is up, line protocol is down
   Internet Address 177.36.252.26/30, Area 2.1.0.0
   Process ID 202, RouterID 177.36.252.26, Network Type POINT_TO_POINT, Cost:1
   Transmit Delay is 1 sec, State POINT_TO_POINT,
   Timer intervals configured, Hello 10, Dead 40, Wait 40, Retransmit 5
     Hello due in 00:00:08
   Neighbor Count is 0, Adjacent neighbor count is 0
```

Our past experiences in troubleshooting OSPF led us to believe that this was still some sort of configuration problem because hardware had been ruled out earlier in the troubleshooting process.

Step 7: Reiterate Steps 4-6

We then issued the command `show ip ospf neighbors` again to ensure the adjacencies had been properly formed.

```
ROUTER_A#show ip ospf neighbors

Neighbor ID      Pri  State     Dead Time  Address        Interface
177.32.252.6      1   FULL/DR   00:00:37   177.2.254.5    Ethernet0
177.36.254.5      1   INIT/ -   00:00:34   177.36.252.5   Serial0.2
177.36.254.25     1   INIT/ -   00:00:35   177.36.252.25  Serial1.2
```

However, over a period of minutes, we realized that the OSPF Neighbor State had not changed from INIT. This meant that each router has seen its neighbor's hello packets, but could not mutually agree on the parameters with which to form an adjacency. We certainly were getting closer to problem resolution, but still something else was wrong.

We decided that we needed more information to correct this problem, so we turned on OSPF event debugging. Executing the troubleshooting command debug IP OSPF events while in the Enable mode of a router does this. OSPF debugging allows us to uncover the inner workings of the OSPF process in an effort to determine why adjacencies were not properly formed, as demonstrated in the following output:

```
ROUTER_A# debug ip ospf events
OSPF events debugging is on
ROUTER_A# ter mon
```

NOTES

ter mon stands for "terminal monitor" and is a useful IOS command that allows the output from a debug session to be displayed on the current terminal that the user is working on. To disable ter mon, use the IOS command ter no mon.

Some more useful information now began to appear on the output from debug ip ospf events. The debug output informed us of an authentication key problem:

```
OSPF: Rcv pkt from 177.36.252.5, Serial0.2: Mismatch Authentication Key-Clear Text
OSPF: Rcv pkt from 177.36.252.25, Serial1.2: Mismatch Authentication Key-Clear Text
```

After speaking with our network design team, we received the correct OSPF authentication key and placed it on Serial0.2 and Serial1.2 on ROUTER A. Almost instantly, the OSPF adjacencies were formed and the states were FULL. The output that follows shows the relevant configuration modification and resulting OSPF events.

```
ROUTER_A#conf t
Enter configuration commands, one per line. End with CNTL/Z.
ROUTER_A(config)#int s0.2
ROUTER_A(config-subif)#ip ospf authentication-key secretkey
ROUTER_A(config-subif)#
OSPF: Receive dbd from 177.36.253.6 seq 0x2503
OSPF: 2 Way Communication to neighbor 177.36.254.5
OSPF: send DBD packet to 177.36.252.5 seq 0x22C3
OSPF: NBR Negotiation Done We are the SLAVE
OSPF: send DBD packet to 177.36.252.5 seq 0x2503
OSPF: Receive dbd from 177.36.254.5 seq 0x2504
OSPF: send DBD packet to 177.36.252.5 seq 0x2504
OSPF: Database request to 177.36.254.5
OSPF: sent LS REQ packet to 177.36.252.5, length 864
OSPF: Receive dbd from 177.36.254.5 seq 0x2505
OSPF: send DBD packet to 177.36.252.5 seq 0x2505
OSPF: Database request to 177.36.254.5
OSPF: sent LS REQ packet to 177.36.252.5, length 1080
OSPF: Receive dbd from 177.36.254.5 seq 0x2506
OSPF: Exchange Done with neighbor 177.36.254.5
OSPF: send DBD packet to 177.36.252.5 seq 0x2506
OSPF: Synchronized with neighbor 177.36.254.5, state:FULL


OSPF_ROUTER_A(config-subif)#
OSPF: Neighbor 177.36.254.25 is dead
OSPF: neighbor 177.36.254.25 is dead, state DOWN
OSPF: Tried to build Router LSA within MinLSInterval
OSPF: Rcv pkt from 177.36.252.25, Serial1.2 : Mismatch Authentication Key - Clear Textint
      s1.2

OSPF_ROUTER_A(config-subif)#ip ospf authentication-key secretkey
OSPF: Rcv pkt from 177.36.252.25, Serial1.2 : Mismatch Authentication Key - Clear Text

OSPF_ROUTER_A(config-subif)#
OSPF: 2 Way Communication to neighbor 177.36.254.25
OSPF: send DBD packet to 177.36.252.25 seq 0xCC5
OSPF: Receive dbd from 177.36.254.25 seq 0x794
OSPF: NBR Negotiation Done We are the SLAVE
OSPF: send DBD packet to 177.36.252.25 seq 0x794
OSPF: Receive dbd from 177.36.254.25 seq 0x795
OSPF: send DBD packet to 177.36.252.25 seq 0x795
OSPF: Receive dbd from 177.36.254.25 seq 0x796
OSPF: send DBD packet to 177.36.252.25 seq 0x796
OSPF: Receive dbd from 177.36.254.25 seq 0x797
OSPF: Exchange Done with neighbor 177.36.254.25
OSPF: Synchronized with neighbor 177.36.254.25, state:FULL
```

Step 6 Revisited Again: Gather Results

We then confirmed that the OSPF adjacency STATES were now correct because they both were FULL. This meant that the OSPF link-state databases for all routers were 100 percent synchronized with each other, and, most importantly, routing was now working correctly as shown in the following output.

```
ROUTER_A#show ip ospf neighbor

Neighbor ID    Pri  State     Dead Time   Address        Interface
177.32.253.6    1   FULL/DR   00:00:31    177.2.254.5    Ethernet0
177.36.254.5    1   FULL/ -   00:00:39    177.36.252.5   Serial0.2
177.36.254.25   1   FULL/ -   00:00:30    177.36.252.25  Serial1.2
```

By executing some trace routes, we confirmed that the primary links (768K Frame Links) were now routing traffic through the proper primary path, namely Router A. The final relevant OSPF router configuration for Router A was as follows:

```
!
router ospf 202
  network 177.2.254.0 0.0.0.255 area 0
  network 177.36.252.0 0.0.0.255 area 2.1.0.0
  area 2.1.0.0 authentication
  area 2.1.0.0 stub
!
```

This was certainly a solid fix relating to the originally reported routing problem. However, users were still complaining of a slowdown.

Problem #2: Performance Issues

In Step 3, we identified that there were, in fact, two problems being seen in the network. These two problems (routing and performance) were causing the customers' slow downs. At this point we have successfully resolved problem #1 and its routing issues. So we must now resolve the second problem: network performance.

Step 1: Define the Problem

At this point, the network was routing according to design, but there still was a high percentage of traffic coming into Router A from the LAN segment Downtown. Users Downtown were still complaining of a slowdown, so we had a clear problem definition. We used the troubleshooting model again to develop and implement an action plan.

Step 2: Gather Facts

We observed that there were still a significant amount of output drops on Router C and Router D. The following output is for Router C:

```
ROUTER_C#show int s0/0:0
Serial0/0:0 is up, line protocol is up
  Hardware is DSX1
  Description: Frame Relay Circuit to Headquarters
  MTU 1500 bytes, BW 1536 Kbit, DLY 20000 usec, rely 255/255, load 6/255
  Encapsulation FRAME-RELAY IETF, loopback not set, keepalive set (10 sec)
  LMI enq sent 16732, LMI stat recvd 16732, LMI upd recvd 0, DTE LMI up
  LMI enq recvd 0, LMI stat sent 0, LMI upd sent 0
  LMI DLCI 0 LMI type is ANSI Annex D frame relay DTE
  Broadcast queue 0/64, broadcasts sent/dropped 983815/57443, interface broadcasts 1035677
  Last input 00:00:00, output 00:00:00, output hang never
  Last clearing of "show interface" counters 1d22h
  Input queue: 0/75/48 (size/max/drops); Total output drops: 1500632
  Queueing strategy: weighted fair
  Output queue: 0/64/19 (size/threshold/drops)
     Conversations 0/51 (active/max active)
     Reserved Conversations 0/0 (allocated/max allocated)
  5 minute input rate 50000 bits/sec, 19 packets/sec
  5 minute output rate 42000 bits/sec, 8 packets/sec
     1493015 packets input, 320768751 bytes, 0 no buffer
     Received 0 broadcasts, 2 runts, 0 giants, 0 throttles
     48 input errors, 35 CRC, 13 frame, 0 overrun, 0 ignored, 2 abort
     2335606 packets output, 845399484 bytes, 0 underruns
     0 output errors, 0 collisions, 1 interface resets
```

This output is very useful in troubleshooting suspected utilization issues. The statistics that are presented here will show, for example, if the circuit is taking errors. Additionally, it will describe what kinds of errors the circuit is seeing. In this case, the output showed a large number of output drops.

The vast number of output drops was a signal that there was a lot of unnecessary traffic being routed across the WAN links. Essentially, a vicious cycle of repeated retransmits was formed, further aggravating the problem.

Step 4: Create an Action Plan

Troubleshooting WAN performance issues can be very difficult. As any good and honest network engineer will tell you, without the proper tools, solving these types of problems generally will be a "hit or miss" process. However, solid experience "in the trenches" of network troubleshooting can help isolate the problem and eventually resolve performance problems.

The action plan was to identify and correct why the router was dropping so many packets. From our past experiences and help from Cisco documentation, "drops" can be corrected by increasing the output queue on the WAN interface or if you turn off WFQ (Weighted Fair Queuing) by issuing the `no fair-queue` command.

NOTES

Weighted Fair Queuing is a packet prioritization technique that Cisco routers employ by default on all serial interfaces. It is a strategy that allows datastreams to be prioritized in a "fair" fashion.

For more information on Weighted Fair Queueing, check out the URL: `http://www.cisco.com/univercd/cc/td/doc/product/software/ios113ed/113ed_cr/fun_c/fcprt4/fcperfrm.htm#37357`.

Step 5: Implement the Action Plan

Hold Queues

In an effort to control the number of drops on Router C and Router D, the hold queues were increased to 300 on Router C and Router D. Our experiences with other routers in our network showed this to work well. The steps to do this were:

```
ROUTER_C#conf t
Enter configuration commands, one per line. End with CNTL/Z.
ROUTER_C(config-if)#hold-queue 300 out
ROUTER_C(config-if)#no fair-queue
```

In this particular situation, this change had negligible performance impact, and we found that at times performance actually got somewhat worse. It appeared that we now were dropping fewer frames and saturating an overloaded circuit with even more traffic as a result.

It soon became clear that we needed to better understand the traffic flow between Downtown and Headquarters. We reasoned that if we could determine the source and destination IP addresses being passed, we might be able to isolate the problem.

IP Accounting

Because we had no access to a "sniffer" or probe on these circuits, we enabled IP accounting on the serial interface of Router C to determine if there was a particular address that was generating the majority of the traffic. Router C was chosen because it was closest to the impacted users Downtown and we believed that it could provide us with the most relevant information for this problem. The steps to do this were as follows:

```
ROUTER_C# conf t
Enter configuration commands, one per line. End with CNTL/Z.
ROUTER_C(config)#int s0/0:0.1
ROUTER_C(config-if)#ip accounting
```

The results showed a tremendous amount (approximately 30 percent) of the utilization was coming from a system on the LAN segment. In particular, these packets were directed broadcasts from this device (destination 177.2.4.255). Directed broadcasts are a special type of broadcast, used often in the MS Windows WINS environment. Directed broadcasts can create a problem if there is an excessive number of them transgressing the WAN environment. By contrast, normal broadcasts (that is, destination 255.255.255.255) stay on the local LAN and do not impact WAN routing or performance. The relevant show ip accounting output is as follows:

```
ROUTER_C# show ip accounting
  Source           Destination        Packets        Bytes
  177.1.1.7        177.2.4.255        100322         53732122
```

TIPS

When examining network performance problems, it is critical to note that the subinterface command *ip accounting* should not be used arbitrarily because it imposes extra overhead (that is, CPU, memory) on the router. However, it is a very useful tool and can help to isolate performance issues quickly, especially if you do not have immediate access to a probe or "sniffer" device for packet analysis.

Step 6: Gather Results

Site documentation showed us that the Ethernet segments connected to the Downtown site were multi-netted (that is, they had multiple logical IP segments on the same physical wire). Figure 8-7 shows the Downtown LAN topology.

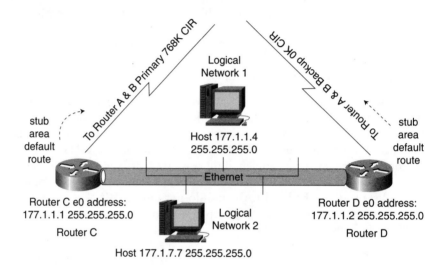

Figure 8–7
Downtown LAN topology.

Downtown LAN Topology: Two Logical
Networks on 1 Physical Segment:

*Problem: Routers C and D configured as
OSPF stub & only for Logical Network 1*

IP Accounting Data Analysis

Because Router C and Router D both had been configured as an OSPF stub area, they automatically forwarded any "unknown" packets through their default router (serial interface), namely to Router A.

The impact was an extremely high traffic load on Router C and Router D's WAN links to Router A. Previously, this was seen on the Ok CIR links to Router B.

This problem was resolved once secondary addresses were put on Router C & D, which correctly reflected the multi-netted configuration of Downtown location.

NOTES

Secondary IP addresses, although usable in a variety of situations, are generally used when there are not enough host addresses for a particular network segment. For example, the Downtown subnetting allows up to 254 hosts per logical subnet, but, in some cases, on one physical subnet there is a need to have 300-500 host addresses. Using secondary IP addresses on the router allows two logical subnets to use one physical subnet.

The commands to put the secondary IP addresses on Router C and Router D were as follows:

```
ROUTER_C#conf t
Enter configuration commands, one per line. End with CNTL/Z
ROUTER_C#int e0
ROUTER_C#ip address 177.1.7.1 255.255.255.0 secondary
```

When these secondary addresses were in place, Routers C and D "knew" to keep localized broadcast traffic local. *ip accounting* was again run on the Cisco routers which confirmed that directed broadcasts were no longer being propagated through the Cisco routers, since both Router C and D had correct IP addresses for all local "multi-netted" networks.

Performance greatly improved, as evidenced by the now stabilized number of drops and confirmed PVC utilization returning to normal levels. We made a phone call to the users who reported the initial problem, and the users confirmed that their performance was now working correctly.

Case Study Conclusion and Design Tips

An essential approach in troubleshooting and eventually correcting this problem was to follow a structured troubleshooting methodology. Using the seven steps to troubleshooting as a guide, we corrected these problems in an orderly fashion.

Through the course of troubleshooting this case study, we found the value of several key IOS commands to help resolve OSPF and performance-related problems:

- `show ip ospf neighbors`
- `show ip interfaces`
- `debug ip ospf events`
- `ip accounting` and `show IP accounting`

We discovered that OSPF stub area configurations have some dangers if there is a misconfigured network interface or router port on the local LAN that the router attaches to. In most cases, the benefit of having a smaller routing table generally outweighs the drawbacks of using stub area, but it is important to understand the implications that can be caused by OSPF stub area misconfigurations. We also found that it is also critical to have the correct authentication key in order to form an adjacency. For Cisco router performance problems, we examined why output drops were occurring and how to control them by raising output hold queues and turning off weighted fair queuing.

In conclusion, this case study demonstrates that if you follow a structured troubleshooting methodology with solid fundamentals, and dig deep into the trenches, you can divide and conquer any networking problem.

FREQUENTLY ASKED QUESTIONS

Q— *My routers are experiencing some performance problems and I can see that its interfaces are experiencing input and/or output drops. What is happening and how do I fix it?*

A— What are the causes of output queue drops? If the router interface is not able to clear up the queue as fast as the router is sending them, this will result in output drops.

How do you fix this problem? You can modify the output queue using the interface subcommand hold-queue *nn* out, where nn is a value. You should increment it by a value of 50 and monitor.

Q— *When doing a* debug ip ospf events *I get an error message that is telling me a bad checksum has occurred.*

A— Checksum messages indicate that the checksum within a packet did not compute properly which does happen sometime.

Q— *When doing a* debug ip ospf events *I get an error message that says the following:*
```
OSPF: Router/Net Link state Update timer in area 1
OSPF: No full nbrs to build net LSA
```

A— This error message indicates that the router is the OSPF Designated Router (DR) and there are no other routers on the segment to build an adjacency with. Therefore no network LSAs will be created.

Q— *How do I produce a stable OSPF network with serial links flapping?*

A— There is nothing you can do in the OSPF process to stabilize a network with flapping serials. You need to address the real problem and fix the flapping serial lines. If you want to "Band-Aid" the problem for a while, you could set the keepalives on the serial interfaces higher than 10 seconds, especially in point-to-point environments. Summarization is also an alternative to this problem.

Q— *What are the well-known class D IP addresses?*

A— Table 8-17 documents the well known class D IP addresses.

Table 8-17   *Well known class D IP addresses*

Class D IP Address	Purpose
224.0.0.1	All hosts on a subnet
224.0.0.2	All routers on a subnet
224.0.0.4	All DVMRP routers
224.0.0.6	All OSPF Designated Routers
224.0.0.9	RIP v2
224.0.1.1	Network Time Protocol (NTP)
224.0.1.2	SGI Dogfight
224.0.1.7	Audio news
224.0.1.11	IETF audio
224.0.1.12	IETF video

Q— *In Priority Queuing, are RIPs in the high queue? When we set up priority queuing, do IP RIP packets or OSPF LSA's automatically go into the high queue, or is there something that needs to be done to make this happen. I see that in Custom Queuing, the hello packets go into queue 0, but what about the update table packets?*

A— The four priority queues—high, medium, normal, and low—are listed in order from highest to lowest priority. Keepalives sourced by the network server are always assigned to the high-priority queue; all other management traffic (such as IGRP updates) must be configured. Packets that are not classified by the priority list mechanism are assigned to the normal queue.

To get IP RIP packets and OSPF LSA packets to go into the high queue, you need to specify the protocol or port number for the protocol. A list of protocol and port numbers can be found in RFC 1340 at: http://www.inter-nic.com/RFC/rfc1340.txt. RIP packets can be specified as high priority directly using a priority-list command:

```
router(config)#priority-list 1 protocol ip high udp rip,
```

OSPF as a protocol needs to be specified through an access list before it can be assigned to the priority-list:

```
router(config)#access-list 100 permit ospf any any
router(config)#access-list 100 permit udp any any eq rip /* for rip */
router(config)#priority-list 1 protocol ip high list 100
```

Q— *I have a Cisco 7010 router that is running OSPF and IGRP. OSPF is used to route within my network, and IGRP is used to my service provider. I redistribute between them. I also have two static routes. I have a requirement to advertise one of my static routes out all of my OSPF interfaces and my IGRP interface. The second static route needs to be advertised out all of my OSPF interfaces, but needs to be filtered from being advertised to my service provider via IGRP. I think I need to use the* distribute-list *and* access-list *commands in my IGRP process, but I am not sure how to do it.*

A— The best way is to use route-map. Here is an example:

```
!
router ospf 333
redistribute static subnets route-map ospf-static
network 128.30.0.0 0.0.255.255 area 0.0.0.0
!
router igrp 187
redistribute static subnets route-map igrp-static
network 128.99.0.0
!
ip route 128.30.20.0 255.255.255.0 128.30.28.21
ip route 128.30.26.0 255.255.255.0 128.30.28.22
ip route 128.101.0.0 255.255.0.0 128.99.15.2
!
access-list 7 permit 128.30.20.0 0.0.0.255
access-list 7 permit 128.30.26.0 0.0.0.255
access-list 7 deny any
access-list 8 permit 128.101.0.0 0.0.255.255
access-list 8 deny any
!
route-map ospf-static permit 10
match ip address 7
!
route-map igrp-static permit 10
match ip address 8
```

In the preceding example, there are three static routes defined. I want the first two static routes to be redistributed into my OSPF domain only, and the very last static route to be redistributed into my IGRP domain only.

Q— *When is a topology change from RIP, IGRP or EIGRP redistributed into OSPF? My router learns of a change of topology by its RIP, IGRP, or EIGRP process. It has another OSPF routing process running on another interface. The information from the first protocol is "redistributed" into OSPF. Does this redistribution occur every time a RIP, IGRP or EIGRP update is received? Or does OSPF compare the first routing DB with its own DB every dead interval?*

A— An OSPF update goes out every time a RIP, IGRP, or EIGRP update is received and the router notices a change in the routing information. Changes in the routing tables are caused by incoming routing updates or interface state changes.

Q— *Using OSPF, how do you generate a summary route? When I redistribute one OSPF process into another one (without the subnets parameter), a subnetted network is not redistributed and no summary route for that network is generated. I understand that OSPF is a classless protocol, but I expect OSPF to auto-summarize the subnets during the redistribution. The* area range *command didn't help either since summarization only takes place between areas only. What should I do?*

A— When OSPF redistributes routes from other protocols (including another OSPF process), you have to explicitly describe the summarization. In Cisco IOS 10.2 and later, they added the summary-address router subcommand to assist you.

Q— *What are the differences in memory and router performance requirements for OSPF and EIGRP? Which protocol (OSPF or EIGRP) requires less router CPU and memory to run? We are looking at implementing LS routing primarily with Cisco 2500 series routers with some Cisco 4000s mixed in. Also, we will be running DECNET and OSPF on routers running 10.0 and later code.*

A— There are no benchmarks, but I think EIGRP uses less memory than OSPF when the network is stable. Regarding CPU time, EIGRP will not use more than 50 percent of the CPU time when there are processes waiting for the

CPU. If no one else is competing for the resource, then it might use 100 percent if there is a need (this is good).

If you are using Cisco 2500s in a remote location situation, you can use default routes out so you don't need to burden these routers. Or you can try making the areas stub areas, etc. Use techniques such as these to eliminate too many LSAs going around. Do route summarizations too.

Q— *Do Cisco routers have any quick commands that can be executed from the keyboard?*

A— Yes. Appendix A provides a list of the keyboard commands that can be executed for Cisco routers.

Q— *Why does OSPF redistribute a static route, but not the default static route? What is the recommended way to get the default route redistributed in an OSPF-only network?*

A— You have to specify at least `default-info originate` and the router will announce the default into OSPF if it has one. The `default-info originate always` command announces the default into OSPF, even if the originator does not have a default route.

Q— *Does OSPF support load balancing among serial lines?*

A— Yes, load balancing works in OSPF with up to four equal-cost paths, serial or otherwise.

Q— *What does it mean that OSPF is in a "2-Way/drother" state?*

A— It means that you recognize that router as a neighbor, but because it isn't a DR or BDR, you didn't form an adjacency with it. Routers sharing a common segment, an Ethernet for example, that sends out hello packets and through this a designated and backup designated router are elected. The `show ip ospf interface` command will show the result of this election which can be DR (Designated Router), BDR (Backup Designated Router), or DROTHER (Designated Router Other).

Drother implies that on this segment a DR and BDR have already been elected. Therefore, all other routers on the segment will be in the state DROTHER. Two-way indicates that the router has seen itself in the hello packet but will not become a DR or BDR.

Q— *Will OSPF pick the default route based upon cost metrics? My OSPF network has connection to two different ISPs. I am generating the default route by using the* default-information originate *OSPF command on both of my ASBRs. Will my OSPF network routers pick the default route based on cost metrics? For example, will some of my OSPF network routers pick one of the ASBR as the default route and some the other ASBR based on the existing OSPF conditions at that given time? Please note that I am not using the "always" option in the* default-information originate *command because I want one of the ASBRs to be the default candidate when the ISPs link on one of the ASBRs goes down.*

A— Yes. Unless you are changing the default route to type 1 from type 2, the lower cost default route will be chosen by your entire OSPF domain over your higher cost default route.

Q— *I am having a problem using OSPF and subinterfaces over Frame Relay. I would like to use a multipoint subinterface over FR. Is it necessary to use fully-meshed topology?*

A— No, it is not necessary to fully mesh a FR multipoint to use OSPF. In a full mesh, OSPF can use the ip ospf network broadcast command to treat the FR cloud like a LAN (broadcast) media (9.21 and later). A partial mesh or hierarchical design can use the neighbor command to establish OSPF across non-broadcast media.

Q— *OSPF RFC 2178 was just released and it is not supported by Cisco yet. When will it be?*

A— According to Cisco, the only extensions that are not supported as in 11.2/11.3 are G.5, G.7, G.8, and G.9. They should all be supported by 12.0.

CHAPTER 9

Managing Your OSPF Network

"Change: If you are not riding the wave of change . . . You will find yourself beneath it!"—Successories

The management of your OSPF network is just as important as the design, implementation, and troubleshooting sections covered previously. In fact, a case could be made that proper network management is the most important aspect of networking. In many cases this a true statement; this is because organizations and users are now dependent upon the network to perform their daily activities. The success of a well-designed and seamlessly implemented OSPF network is lost in the user's cry of "My network is down and no one is doing anything about it."

This chapter, consisting of three major sections as outlined in the following list, addresses the techniques surrounding the proper management of any network.

- **Network Management.** This section discusses what network management is and why it is so important in today's complex networks. This section also covers the accepted model of network management as designed by the IETF through its publications of RFCs. In addition, you will see some examples of common network management systems and enhancements that make the basic function of managing a network easier to handle.

- **Simple Network Management Protocol (SNMP).** SNMP is truly the de facto standard of network management. This section discusses the components and operation of SNMPv1 with some references to SNMPv2 and SNMPv3 that are discussed in great depth in Chapter 12, "Future Network Considerations." This section also covers some of the particulars surrounding the hows and whys of Cisco's SNMP implementation within their network equipment.

- **Management Information Base (MIB).** MIBs are probably the least understood and yet the most powerful features available to network engineers and managers. This section discusses their overall operation under the SNMP umbrella of network management. This section also drills down specifically on the OSPF specific MIBs and briefly discusses the power they can bring if properly used.

NETWORK MANAGEMENT

As network deployment and use increases, network management is increasingly becoming the focus of many organizations. These organizations range from those using a network to support their core business, to those using networks as sales tools, to those outsourcing or selling network management solutions.

The true goal of everyone involved in network management is to *proactively* find and fix all network problems before users ever know a problem exists. There are many obstacles to tackle—ranging from the sheer scope of the project to many different possible management techniques—before you can achieve this goal. This chapter covers the more tested and accepted common techniques such as SNMP and MIBs. Chapter 12 discusses some of the techniques that are looming on the horizon such as RMON and SNMPv3.

In its simplest form, network management can be described as the monitoring and tracking of network equipment and the resources that link them together. The goal is to ensure the network is always available for use by everyone, all the time.

Network management, especially outsourced network management, brings to mind opportunities that allow today's network engineers and managers to reach towards a "bold new frontier." It used to be that corporate America had a dedicated staff of IS professionals responsible for every aspect of the corporate network which included:

- Designing the LANs and WANs
- Ordering the Equipment and Services
- Inventory Tracking
- Implementing the Required Equipment and Service

- Performance Analysis
- Security
- Change Management
- Configuration Management

- Contact Management
- Determining Standardization Requirements
- Documenting the Network
- Proactive and Reactive Monitoring

- Backup and Data Recovery
- Upgrading Licenses, Equipment and Services
- Analyze and Plan for Future Growth

All of these functions and responsibilities can be applied to both LANs and WANs. This is a daunting and exhaustive task for any organization, but it becomes even more so when it falls outside what a company would consider its "core" business. This is when the use of outsourced network management can become a real benefit to a company. Through outsourcing, a company can move many of these functions and responsibilities onto companies that have the capability to leverage the expertise needed to fulfill these needs. It is this author's opinion that companies should not completely remove their internal IS staffs, but rather increase their use of outsourcing. This will allow companies to focus on the business that made them successful in the first place.

Having your network properly managed should be your top priority, regardless of how you decide to staff this critical area. There are many other resources available that can help you decide which alternative is best for you. If you require further information, the following book and course should be helpful:

- *Network Planning, Procurement, & Management*, by Nathan J. Muller

- *Network Management* offered by American Research Group (ARG): `http://www.arg.com`

To summarize, network management is a mission critical aspect of any network. You can take one of two approaches to network management: you can be *pro*active or you can be *re*active—the former of which is more desirable. The differences in a customer's perception of the network can be profound. In a proactive environment, you can make sure everything is fixed before a network problem (with the potential of causing many negative repercussions) occurs. In a reactive environment, the negative repercussions have already occurred, and you must get the network up and running as soon as possible.

There is a variety of tools and technologies on the market that can assist you in managing your network. The remainder of this chapter will cover some of the tools and technologies available to your network.

Network Management Tools

There are literally hundreds of solutions, tools, and technologies on the market today to make the job of managing networks better, easier, and more efficient.

There are many different sources for information regarding Network Management Systems (NMSs), therefore you will not see coverage of specific systems, but rather details on some overall general characteristics that should be present in every Enterprise capable NMS.

Three tools from Cisco that have been developed to streamline network management are CiscoView, CiscoWorks, and ConfigMaker.

NOTES

There are many different tools available from Cisco to help you manage your network and even the ones listed here come in different varieties and have add-ons. They can be found at the following URLs:

http://www.cisco.com/public/Support_root.shtml

http://www.cisco.com/public/sw-center/sw-etmgmt.shtml

http://www.cisco.com/public/sw-center/sw-other.shtml

CiscoView

CiscoView is a GUI-based device management software application that provides dynamic status, statistics, and comprehensive configuration information for Cisco Systems' internetworking products (switches, routers, concentrators, and adapters). CiscoView graphically displays a real-time physical view of Cisco devices. Additionally, this SNMP-based network management tool provides monitoring functions and offers basic troubleshooting capabilities. Figure 9-1 shows a typical view of a router (4700) using CiscoView. When shown in color, you can easily see the interface status (that is, green is up and red is down, and so forth).

Using CiscoView, users can more easily understand the tremendous volume of management data available for internetworking devices. CiscoView organizes the data into graphical device representations presented in a clear, consistent format as shown in Figure 9-2, which shows a sample of the interface statistics from a 4700 series router.

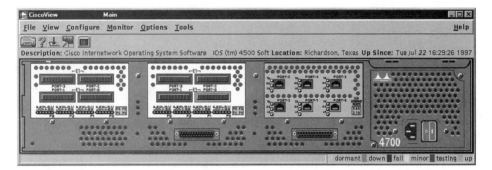

Figure 9–1
Viewing router status with CiscoView.

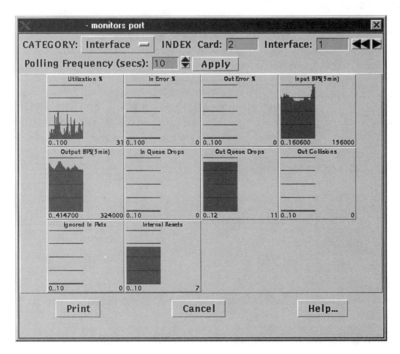

Figure 9–2
Viewing router interface statistics in CiscoView.

CiscoView software can be integrated with several of the leading SNMP-based network management platforms, providing a seamless, powerful network view. It is also included within CiscoWorks, CiscoWorks for Switched Internetworks, and CiscoWorks for Windows. CiscoView software can also be run on UNIX workstations as a fully functional, independent management application.

As previously mentioned, there are a variety of network management features incorporated within CiscoView, including the following:

- Graphical display of Cisco products from a centralized network management location, giving network managers a complete view of Cisco products without physically checking each device at remote sites

- An exception reporting design that enables network managers to quickly grasp essential inquiry information

- GUI interface that continuously shows an updated physical picture of routers, hubs, and switches or access servers

- Can be invoked several times in the same session to simultaneously support multiple switches, routers, hubs, or access servers

CiscoWorks

CiscoWorks network management software lets you monitor complex internetworks that use Cisco routing devices, and it helps you plan, troubleshoot, and analyze your network. CiscoWorks uses the Simple Network Management Protocol (SNMP) to monitor and control any SNMP device on the network.

CiscoWorks works directly with your SNMP network management platform, allowing CiscoWorks applications to be integrated with the features and applications of your platform. The following is a brief list of the features found in CiscoWorks:

- Configuration Management

- CiscoView

- Configuration Snap-In Manager

- Device Management

- Device Monitor

- Path Tool

- Security Manager

- Software Inventory Manager

- Software Library Manager

- Contact Management

- Show Commands

ConfigMaker

Cisco ConfigMaker is a freely available, easy-to-use Windows 95/NT 4.0 tool offering a GUI alternative to the existing Cisco command-line interface. ConfigMaker enables Cisco resellers or end users to configure one or a network of Cisco routers, Cisco access servers, Cisco Micro Hubs, Cisco Micro Switches, or Cisco Micro Webservers. You can find ConfigMaker at: `http://www.cisco.com/cgi-bin/tablebuild.pl/configmaker`.

The SNMP-based Internet Management Model

As specified in Internet RFCs and other documents, a network management system is comprised of the following items:

- **Managed Devices.** Sometimes called *network elements*, managed devices are hardware devices such as computers, routers, bridges, switches, and terminal servers that are connected to networks.

- **Agents.** Agents are software modules that reside in managed devices. They collect and store management information such as the number of error packets received by a network element.

- **Managed Object.** A managed object is a characteristic of something that can be managed. For example, a list of currently active TCP circuits in a particular host computer is a managed object. Managed objects differ from variables, which are particular object instances. Using our example, an object instance is a single active TCP circuit in a particular host computer. Managed objects can be scalar (defining a single object instance) or tabular (defining multiple, related instances).

- **Management Information Base (MIB).** A MIB is a collection of managed objects residing in a virtual information store. Collections of related managed objects are defined in specific MIB modules.

- **Syntax Notation.** A syntax notation is a language used to describe a MIB's managed objects in a machine-independent format. Consistent use of a syntax notation enables different types of computers to share information. Internet management systems use a subset of the International Organization for Standardization's (ISO's) *Open System Interconnection* (OSI) *Abstract Syntax Notation 1* (ASN.1) to define both the packets exchanged by the management protocol and the objects that are to be managed.

- **Structure of Management Information (SMI)**. The SMI defines the rules for describing management information. The SMI is defined using Abstract Syntax Notation 1 (ASN.1).

- **Network Management Stations (NMSs)**. Sometimes called *consoles*, these devices execute management applications that monitor and control network elements. Physically, NMSs are usually engineering workstation-caliber computers with fast CPUs, megapixel color displays, substantial memory, and abundant disk space. At least one NMS must be present in each managed environment.

- **Parties**. Newly defined in SNMPv2, a party is a logical SNMPv2 entity that can initiate or receive SNMPv2 communication. Each SNMPv2 party comprises a single, unique party identity, a logical network location, a single authentication protocol, and a single privacy protocol. SNMPv2 messages are communicated between two parties. An SNMPv2 entity can define multiple parties, each with different parameters. For example, different parties can use different authentication and/or privacy protocols and their associated restricted subset of operations.

- **Management Protocol**. A management protocol is used to convey management information between agents and NMSs. SNMP is the networking community's de facto standard management protocol.

Figure 9-3 graphically represents the most basic elements of the Internet management model.

The previous section covered the general network management model. In the following section, we will be more specific regarding the tools needed—SNMP.

SIMPLE NETWORK MANAGEMENT PROTOCOL (SNMP)

As TCP/IP developed through the US Department of Defense (DoD) Advanced Research Projects Agency (ARPA) in the late 1960s and early 1970s, it was accepted as a US DoD networking standard. The further development of ARPA, or rather the ARPA network (ARPANet), allowed for the continued development of a global set of networks based on the TCP/IP protocol. This global set of networks evolved into what is today referred to as the Internet.

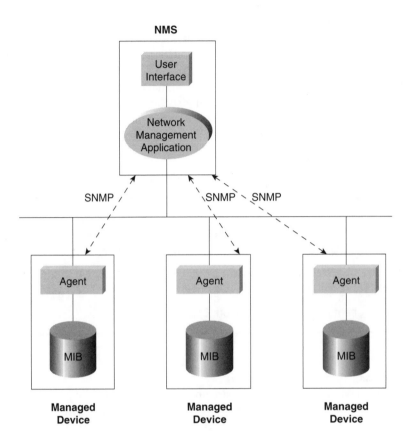

Figure 9–3
*A detailed
network
management
model.*

NOTES

In order to avoid confusion in this chapter, I will be referring to Simple Network Management Protocol Version 1 as SNMPv1, version two as SNMPv2, version 3 as SNMPv3, and general comments that cross versions as just SNMP. Although this may be a bit tedious, it will preserve the accuracy of the text.

Like the *Transmission Control Protocol* (TCP), SNMP is an *Internet* protocol. Internet protocols are created by the Internet community, a group of individuals and organizations that developed and/or regularly use a large, diverse international network called the Internet. The *Simple Network Management Protocol* (SNMP) is an application-layer protocol designed to facilitate the exchange of management information between network devices. By using SNMP-transported data (such as packets per second and network error rates), network engineers and managers can more easily manage network performance, find and solve network problems, and assist in planning for network growth.

TIPS

SNMP is part of a larger architecture called the Network Management Framework (NMF), which is defined in RFCs. The SNMPv1 NMF is defined in RFCs 1155, 1157, 1212, and 1902–1908. The SNMPv2 NMF is defined by RFCs 1441 through 1452. SNMPv3 has not achieved RFC status as of the publication of this book. We will be discussing SNMPv3 in greater detail in Chapter 12, "Future Network Considerations."

As the Internet developed, so did the desire and need to monitor the performance of the various network components that comprised the Internet. This desire manifested itself in the development of Simple Gateway Monitoring Protocol (SGMP). The Internet Activities Board (IAB)—renamed in 1992 to the Internet Architecture Board—was involved with the evolutionary changes to SGMP and recommended the development of an expanded Internet network management standard.

The IAB handed off this new project to the Internet Engineering Task Force (IETF) who began designing, testing, and implementing a new Internet management standard. Their efforts resulted in three new RFCs: 1065, 1066, and 1067. These three documents formed the basis of SNMPv1.

There are two versions of SNMP: version 1 and version 2. Most of the changes introduced in version 2 increase SNMP's security capabilities. Other changes increase interoperability by more rigorously defining the specifications for SNMP implementation. SNMP's creators believe that after a relatively brief period of coexistence, SNMP version 2 (SNMPv2) will largely replace SNMP version 1 (SNMPv1). SNMP is more commonly used within a TCP/IP environment, but RFCs have been written to enable operation over IPX and AppleTalk. This chapter focuses on the more common TCP/IP implementation.

Today, SNMP is the most popular protocol for managing diverse commercial internet-works, as well as those used in universities and research organizations. SNMP-related standardization activity continues even as vendors develop and release state-of-the-art, SNMP-based management applications. SNMP is a relatively simple protocol, yet its feature set is sufficiently powerful to handle the difficult problems presented when trying to manage today's heterogeneous networks.

Introduction to SNMP

Until the early-to-mid 1990s, the management method used for these two devices depended upon SNMP-compatible management platforms offered by the hardware vendors. They provided remote configuration of the devices, alarm capabilities for minor and major alarms, and network mapping. All provided benefits to network managers who no longer had to configure a device on site or look at the LEDs for alarms. Network management could now be controlled via a centrally located administration package compatible with industry-standard SNMP.

SNMP, in both agents and clients, is based on Management Information Bases (MIBs). MIBs (defined in detail in the section, "The Management Information Base") can be standards-based, complying with those written for particular applications to collect statistics or track information on a wide variety of networking activities. These MIBs are publicly available to any manufacturer to incorporate into its products.

Proprietary MIBs are those written by a particular manufacturer to track either specific network anomalies, such as bandwidth utilization, or to track particular device activity, such as packet discards.

These MIBs are the sole property of the manufacturer and might or might not be made available to other companies. MIBs are typically created to make a company's own devices or network management software product more valuable to the end users.

SNMP does have drawbacks, however. Most SNMP capability is embedded in network devices like hubs, routers, FRADs, DSU/CSUs, and switches. These devices primarily pass or route data. Although they can provide snapshots of the network at intervals ranging from five to thirty minutes via SNMP get request. commands issued by the network manager, they have neither the processing power nor the memory capacity to store real-time data for any length of time. This does not enable you to see what is going on in your network 100% of the time; instead, you have to piece together snapshots. If you want to see everything going on, you need to consider adding a device (that is, specialized server or poller) specifically designed to fulfill this requirement. Another way of achieving this it through your Network Management System (NMS), which is discussed in the next section.

Network Management System (NMS)

The Network Management System (also known as the manager) is software that has the capability of operating on one or more workstations. This software can be configured so it can be utilized to manage different portions of a network or multiple managers can manage the same network. The manager's requests are transmitted to one or more managed devices on the desired network. These requests are sent via TCP/IP. SNMP is not dependent upon TCP/IP for transport across a network. SNMP has the capability to be transported via numerous other transport mechanisms such as Novell's NetWare IPX and various other transport protocols. Though as previously mentioned, this book concentrates on the TCP/IP implementation. You can specifically define the NMS as follows:

- An NMS executes applications that monitor and control managed devices. They provide the bulk of the processing and memory resources required for network management. One or more NMSs must exist on any managed network.

- The network manager has a few commands at his/her fingertips to get information from a managed device. These commands are GETREQUEST, GETNEXTREQUEST, and SETREQUEST. Because SNMP is based on the utilization of the TCP/IP transport protocol, to issue any SNMP command the manager must have the IP address of the destination agent.

- The manager issues the GETREQUEST command to an agent (discussed in the next section). This command may be utilized in one of two ways; it can be used to view a single MIB variable, or a list of MIB variables from the destination agent.

- The GETNEXTREQUEST command is similar in nature to the GETREQUEST command. However, when the agent receives the particular request, it attempts to retrieve the next entry in the MIB for the identified managed object. To use an example, if the manager were to issue a sequence of the GETNEXTREQUEST commands to a managed object, the manager has the ability to "browse" through that managed object's MIB. Thus, a series of GETNEXTREQUEST commands can be used to read through a row with the incrementation of the values for the requested managed object and see how quickly the packets are processing, or perhaps keep on eye on critical failure marks.

- The final manager-based command is the SETREQUEST command. This command is similar to the previous two in one way; the network manager issues it to a defined agent. The SETREQUEST command requests the agent set the value of *an individual instance of a managed object*—these are variables stored at a device—or instances contained in the command. The SETREQUEST command is only successful if the network manager can write to the managed object. If the managed object is read-only, the command will fail since the value of the managed object instance could not be amended.

Agents

An agent is a network management software module that resides in a managed device. It has local knowledge of management information and translates that information into a form compatible with SNMP.

To be a managed device, each device must have firmware in the form of code. This firmware translates the requests from the SNMP manager and responds to these requests. The software, or firmware, not the device itself, is referred to as an agent. It is possible to manage a non-SNMP compatible device, but they must support a proprietary management protocol.

TIPS

In order to support a non-SNMP compatible device, you must first obtain a proxy agent. This proxy agent acts as an interpreter because it translates the SNMP requests into the proprietary protocol on the non-SNMP device.

SNMP agents have two commands, **GETRESPONSE** and **TRAP**, which function as follows:

- **GETRESPONSE**. This command flows from the agent to the NMS in response to any of the following manager-based commands: **GETREQUEST, GETNEXTREQUEST,** or **SETREQUEST**. It is returned as a **GETRESPONSE** PDU (Protocol Data Unit) that contains several fields. These fields help to note whether the received command was processed and, if successfully received and processed, it returns a listing of occurrences of the managed objects polled and the current values for each of those managed objects.

- **TRAP**. This command is not generated as a response to a manager-generated command. Rather, it is an unsolicited response. This command is an alarm condition established by the manager. When a particular predefined activity occurs or a specific threshold is breached (that is, a link or router failure) the agent generates a Trap PDU to the manager so the necessary corrective actions can take place.

Managed Devices

A managed device is a network node that contains an SNMP agent and resides on a managed network. Managed devices collect and store management information and make this information available to network management systems (NMSs) using SNMP.

Managed devices, sometimes called network elements, can be routers and access servers, switches and bridges, hubs, computer hosts, or printers. Figure 9-4 shows the relationship between an NMS, Agents, and MIBs.

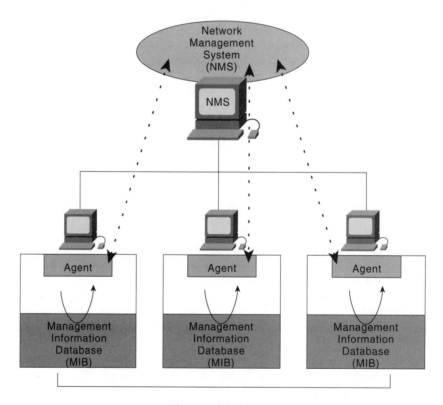

Managed Devices

The Management Information Base

The MIB is an established database of the hardware settings, variables, memory tables or records stored within files. These records are called data elements.

Data elements contain the information concerning the status, configuration, and statistical information base used to define the functionality and operational capacity of each managed device. This information is referred to as a MIB (Management Information Base). Each data element is referred to as a managed object. These managed objects are comprised of a name, one or more attributes, and a set of operations that can be performed on the managed object.

MIBs and Object Identifiers

A MIB can be depicted as an abstract tree with an unnamed root. Individual data items make up the leaves of the tree. *Object identifiers* (OIDs) uniquely identify or name MIB objects in the tree. Object IDs are like telephone numbers; they are organized hierarchically with specific digits assigned by different organizations.

The object ID structure of an SNMP MIB defines three main branches: Consultative Committee for International Telegraph and Telephone (CCITT), International Organization for Standardization (ISO), and joint ISO/CCITT. Much of the current MIB activity occurs in the portion of the ISO branch defined by object identifier 1.3.6.1 and dedicated to the Internet community.

The current Internet-standard MIB, MIB-II, is defined in RFC 1213 and contains 171 objects. These objects are grouped by protocol (including TCP, IP, *User Datagram Protocol* (UDP), SNMP, and others) and other categories, including "system" and "interfaces."

The MIB tree is extensible by virtue of experimental and private branches. Vendors can define their own private branches to include instances of their own products. For example, Cisco's private MIB is represented by the object identifier 1.3.6.1.4.1.9. It includes objects such as **HOSTCONFIGADDR**, which is identified, by object ID (OID) 1.3.6.1.4.1.9.2.2.1.51. The **HOSTCONFIGADDR** object specifies the address of the host that provided the host configuration file for a specific Cisco device.

The basic MIB structure, including MIB-II (object ID = 1.3.6.1.2.1) and the Cisco private MIB (object ID = 1.3.6.1.4.1.9), is shown in Figure 9-5. A more detailed version of Cisco's MIB is illustrated in Figure 9-6 later in the chapter.

Structure of Management Information (SMI) Definitions

The SMI specifies that all managed objects should have a name, a syntax, and an encoding. The *name* is the object ID, which was discussed in the preceding section. The *syntax* defines the object's data type (for example, "integer" or "string"). Subsets of ASN.1 definitions are used for the SMI syntax. The *encoding* describes how the information associated with the managed object is formatted as a series of data items for transmission on the network. Another ISO specification called the *Basic Encoding Rules* (BERs), details SMI encodings.

Figure 9–5
*Basic MIB
Structure.*

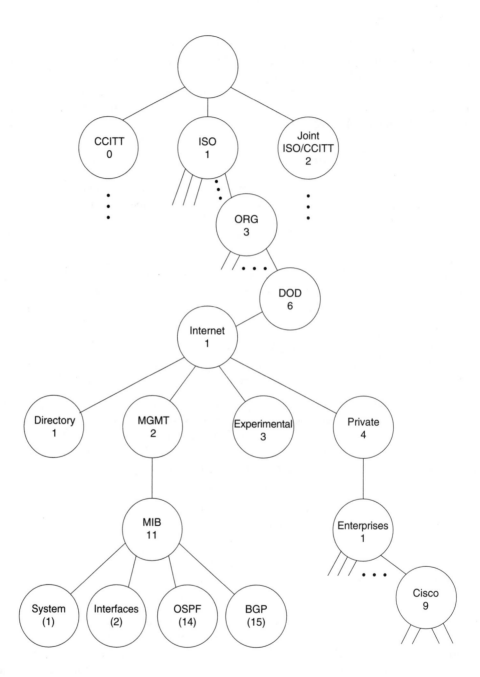

SMI data types are divided into three categories: *simple types, application-wide types*, and *simply constructed types*.

The SMI simple data types include four primitive ASN.1 types as follows:

- **Integers.** Unique values that are positive or negative whole numbers, including zero.

- **Octet strings.** Unique values that are an ordered sequence of zero or more octets.

- **Object IDs.** Unique values from the set of all object identifiers allocated according to the rules specified in ASN.1.

- **Bit strings.** New in SNMPv2, these comprise zero or more named bits that specify a value.

The application-wide data types refer to special data types defined by the SMI and are as follows:

- **Network addresses.** Represent an address from a particular protocol family.

- **Counters.** Non-negative integers that increment by positive one until they reach a maximum value, at which time they are reset to zero. The total number of bytes received on an interface is an example of a counter. In SNMPv1, counter size was not specified. In SNMPv2, 32-bit and 64-bit counters are defined.

- **Gauges.** Non-negative integers can increase or decrease, but latch at a maximum value. The length of an output packet queue (in packets) is an example of a gauge.

- **Time ticks.** Hundredths of a second since an event. The time since an interface entered its current state is an example of a tick.

- **Opaque.** Represents an arbitrary encoding. This data type is used to pass arbitrary information strings that do not conform to the strict data typing used by the SMI.

- **Integer.** Represents signed integer-valued information. This data type redefines the ASN.1 "integer" simple data type, which has arbitrary precision in ASN.1 but bounded precision in the SMI.

- **Unsigned integer.** Represents unsigned integer-valued information. It is useful when values are always non-negative. This data type redefines the ASN.1 "integer" simple data type, which has arbitrary precision in ASN.1 but bounded precision in the SMI.

The simply constructed types include two ASN.1 types that define multiple objects in tables and lists and are as follows:

- **Row.** References a row in a table. Each element of the row can be a simple type or an application-wide type.

- **Table.** References a table of zero or more rows. Each row has the same number of columns.

Additional Resources for Abstract Syntax Notation

ISO document 8825 (*Specification of Basic Encoding Rules for ASN.1*) defines ISO's BERs. The BERs enable dissimilar machines to exchange management information by specifying both the position of each bit within the transmitted octets and the structure of the bits. Bit structure is conveyed by describing the data type, length, and value.

The SMI for SNMPv2 includes two documents: RFCs 1443 and 1444. RFC 1443 (Textual Conventions) defines the data types used within the MIB modules. RFC 1444 (Conformance Statements) provides an implementation baseline. The SNMPv2 SMI also defines two new branches of the Internet MIB tree: security (1.3.6.1.5) and SNMPv2 (1.3.6.1.6).

SNMP Operation

SNMP itself is a simple request/response protocol. Network Management Systems can send multiple requests without receiving a response when using the UDP protocol, which is also connectionless.

The information previously discussed on Network Management Systems detailed how they used SNMP to accomplish their goals. This section will discuss in more detail actual SNMP commands, their purpose and functionality.

SNMP Operation Definitions

The six SNMP operations defined within SNMP are as follows:

- **GET.** This command allows the Network Management System to retrieve an individual non-tabled manageable object instance from the agent via SNMP. This operation is further defined in Figure 9-6.

- **GETNEXT.** This command allows the Network Management System to retrieve the next object instance from a table or list within an agent. In SNMPv1, when an NMS wants to retrieve all elements of a table from an agent, it initiates a **GET** operation, followed by a series of **GETNEXT** operations.

- **GETBULK.** This command is new for SNMPv2. The **GETBULK** operation was added to make it easier to acquire large amounts of related information without initiating repeated **GETNEXT** operations. **GETBULK** was designed to virtually eliminate the need for **GETNEXT** operations.

- **SET.** This command allows the Network Management System to set values in read-writable object instances within an agent.

- **TRAP.** This command is used by the agent to asynchronously inform the Network Management System of some event. The SNMPv2 trap message is designed to replace the SNMPv1 trap message.

- **INFORM.** This command is new for SNMPv2. The inform operation was added to allow one Network Management System to send trap information to another (that is, multiple Network Management Systems are monitoring and managing the same network).

Network Management System Operation

The flow chart presented in Figure 9-6 will enable you to better understand the sequence of events that happens when an NMS requests information through the use of SNMP. This flow of events is presented in a generic format from a high level perspective. As with any complex network operation, there are a great many events that also occur which allow the operation to take place. The sequence of events that occurs during an NMS request is as follows:

1. The network manager or engineer decides he needs information from a managed device. He will then select the information required within the Network Management System (NMS).

2. The Network Management System (NMS) reads the MIB database to select the correct Object Identifier (OID) that represents the information requested

3. The Network Management System (NMS) then selects the correct Protocol Data Unit (PDU) Format (that is, type of PDU) for the type of data being requested.

4. The Network Management System (NMS) then combines the selected MIB OID and local SNMP data (that is, version, community string) into the Protocol Data Unit (PDU).

5. The completed PDU is then compiled using Abstract Syntax Notation One (ASN.1) and the Basic Encoding Rules (BER). When completed, it is sent down the UDP/IP Protocol stack to the network layer and sent out onto the network for transmission to the managed device.

NOTES

You must know the IP address for the polled device for this process to succeed.

This is of course only the first part of the process (that is, the request for information); the second part of the process is where the managed device receives the request. The managed device then passes the request on to the SNMP Agent which then processes and replies to the request. This sequence of events is covered in the next section, "Agent Response to NMS Request."

Agent Response to NMS Request

The flow chart presented in Figure 9-7 describes the second part of the SNMP operation in which the SNMP request is received by the managed device, which passes it on to the agent who will process and answer the request. This flow of events is presented in a generic format from a high level perspective. As with any complex network operation, there are a great many events that also occur which allow the operation to take place. The sequence of events that occurs during an agent response to an NMS request is as follows:

1. The request arrives via the network and is given to the agent. The agent then uses Abstract Syntax Notation One (ASN.1) and the Basic Encoding Rules (BER) to translate them into a locally readable Protocol Data Unit (PDU).

2. The PDU is separated into MIB information and SNMP data. The SNMP data is then checked to ensure it is correct (that is, version and community string). If the SNMP data is correct, the agent proceeds to Step 3; if the SNMP data is not correct, the agent issues an authentication trap that the NMS will receive and process, letting the network manager know an authorized security breach has occurred.

3. The agent loads the Protocol Data Unit MIB information, then separates the PDU data field into individual MIB Object Identifier (OID) requests.

4. The agent processes each MIB OID by reading its database for the current value as determined by the OID.

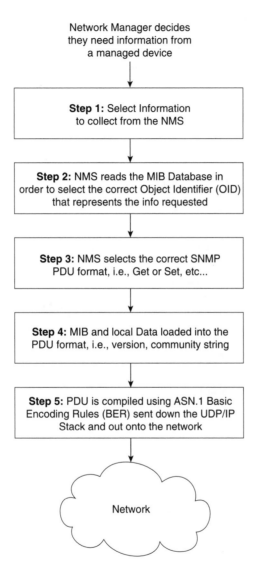

Network Manager decides
they need information from
a managed device

Step 1: Select Information
to collect from the NMS

Step 2: NMS reads the MIB Database in
order to select the correct Object Identifier (OID)
that represents the info requested

Step 3: NMS selects the correct SNMP
PDU format, i.e., Get or Set, etc...

Step 4: MIB and local Data loaded into the
PDU format, i.e., version, community string

Step 5: PDU is compiled using ASN.1 Basic
Encoding Rules (BER) sent down the UDP/IP
Stack and out onto the network

Network

Figure 9–6
*Network
Management
System
requests flow
chart.*

5. The agent builds a response similar to the process described in the previous
    section on NMS Operation (that is, this process in reverse). The response will
    be built with the values as requested by the NMS and SNMP data.

6. The entire transmission is also done in reverse. The agent compiles the PDU
    and sends it back down the UDP/IP protocol stack for transmission back out
    onto the network to be returned to the NMS.

Figure 9–7
*Agent
response flow
chart to NMS
request.*

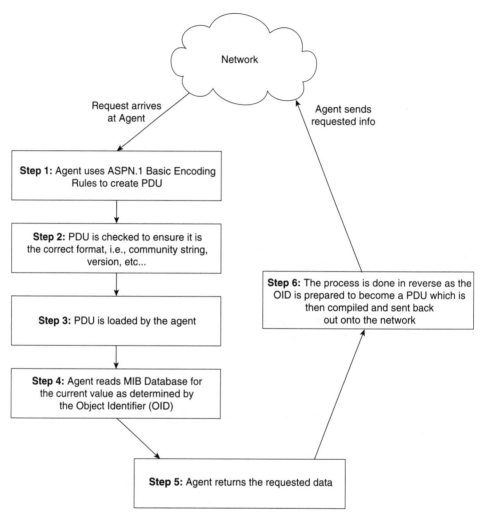

SNMP Messages

The TCP/IP protocol stack views SNMP as an application, which in many ways is true. However, it is more than just an application, it is a protocol as well. When data is requested of NMS, it passes the request onto SNMP. At that time, SNMP looks at the type of data requested and decides upon which message to send. The two types of SNMP messages—SNMPv1 and SNMPv2—are described in the following sections.

SNMPv1 Messages

SNMPv1 messages (packets) contain two parts. The first part contains a *version* and a *community name*. The second part contains the actual SNMP protocol data unit (PDU) specifying the operation to be performed (get, set, and so on) and the object instances involved in the operation. Figure 9-8 illustrates the SNMPv1 message format.

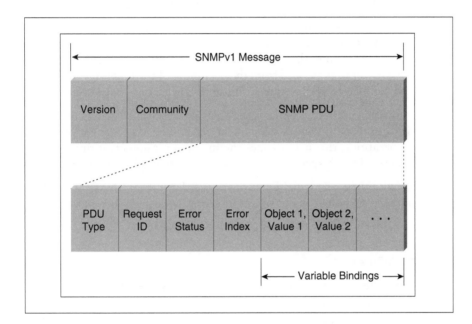

Figure 9-8
SNMPv1 message format.

TIPS

Trap messages have a slightly different format; for information on this format, consult the appropriate SNMP RFC.

The SNMP Version field is used to ensure that all network elements are running software based on the same SNMP version. The community name assigns an access environment for a set of NMSs using that community name. NMSs within the community can be said to exist within the same administrative domain. Because devices that do not know the proper community name are precluded from SNMP operations, network management personnel also have used the community name as a weak form of authentication.

The SNMP Protocol Data Unit (PDU) has the following fields:

- **PDU type.** This field specifies the type of PDU being transmitted.

- **Request-ID.** This field associates requests with responses.

- **Error-status.** This field indicates an error and an error type. In SNMPv2 GETBULK operations, this field becomes a NonRepeaters field. For these operations, this field defines the number of requested variables listed that should be retrieved no more than once from the beginning of the request. The field is used when some of the variables are scalar objects with only one variable.

- **Error-index.** This field associates the error with a particular object instance. In SNMPv2 GETBULK operations, this field becomes a Max Repetitions field. For these operations, this field defines the maximum number of times other variables, beyond those specified by the NonRepeaters field, should be retrieved.

- **Variable-bindings.** This field comprises the data of an SNMP PDU. Variable bindings associate particular object instances with their current values.

SNMPv2 Messages

Even though SNMPv2 will be formally presented in Chapter 12, it is more logical to include its message format here while covering SNMPv1.

Like SNMPv1 messages, SNMPv2 messages (shown in Figure 9-9) contain two parts. The first part of the SNMPv2 message (often referred to as a wrapper) contains the majority of the differences between SNMPv1 and SNMPv2. The second part of the SNMPv2 message (the PDU) is virtually identical to a SNMPv1 message (see the previous description of an SNMP PDU for differences).

The wrapper includes authentication and privacy information in the form of destination and source parties. As mentioned earlier, a party includes the specification of both an authentication and a privacy protocol. In addition to a destination and a source party, the wrapper includes a *context,* which specifies the managed objects visible to an operation.

The authentication protocol is designed to reliably identify the integrity of the originating SNMPv2 party. It consists of authentication information required to support the authentication protocol used. The privacy protocol is designed to protect information within the SNMPv2 message from disclosure. Only authenticated messages can be protected from disclosure. In other words, authentication is required for privacy. This is covered in greater detail in Chapter 12.

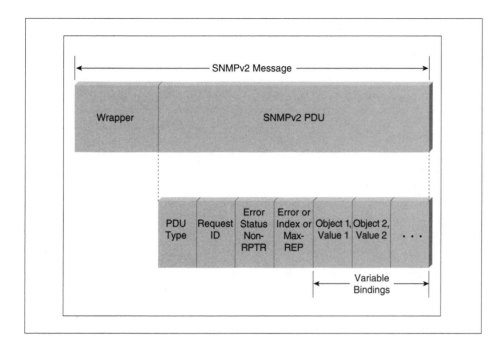

Figure 9–9
SNMPv2 message format.

Additional Resources for SNMP

Originally, SNMPv1 specified that SNMP should operate over the User Datagram Protocol (UDP) and IP. The SNMPv2 transport mapping document (RFC 1449) defines implementations of SNMP over other transport protocols, including OSI Connectionless Network Service (CLNS), AppleTalk's Datagram Delivery Protocol (DDP), and Novell's Internet Packet Exchange (IPX). RFC 1449 also includes instructions on how to provide an SNMPv1 proxy and use of the BER. TCP/IP is still SNMPv2's preferred transport mapping because UDP is compatible with SNMPv1 at both the transport and network layers.

Cisco's SNMP Implementation

Cisco Systems currently includes SNMP support in every router and communications server. Cisco SNMP agents communicate successfully with all SNMP-compliant NMSs, including those of Sun Microsystems (SunNet Manager), IBM (NetView/6000), and Hewlett-Packard (OpenView). The following section discusses how Cisco has implemented SNMP within its products.

SNMP Version Co-Existence

Cisco is a member of the Internet Engineering Task Force (IETF), and is active in defining the SNMPv2 and SNMPv3 standards. When the standards are final, Cisco will support the SNMPv2 and SNMPv3 agents in its access equipment operating systems. Until SNMPv3 becomes a standard, Cisco equipment will be "bilingual," supporting both SNMPv1 and SNMPv2.

Bilingual support of SNMP gives users flexibility by enabling them to migrate to SNMPv2 on their own timetables. During the period when SNMPv1 and SNMPv2 coexist, Cisco customers will not lose any management functionality. Cisco routers will be able to communicate with both SNMPv1 and SNMPv2 Network Management Systems (NMSs).

RFC 1452 defines a SNMPv1/v2 coexistence strategy. This strategy defines two basic techniques: a proxy agent and a bilingual Network Management System. The proxy agent translates information between SNMPv1 and SNMPv2 messages. The bilingual Network Management System (NMS) incorporates both SNMPv1 and SNMPv2 manager software, and, therefore, can communicate with both types of agents. When communication with an agent is required, the manager selects the appropriate protocol.

Cisco's bilingual agent support will work with both the proxy agent and the bilingual Network Management System (NMS) coexistence strategies, but neither will be a requirement. Because bilingual agents can communicate equally well with both SNMPv1 and SNMPv2 NMSs, users will not be forced to purchase additional SNMPv2 manager software or proxy agents. Depending upon the extent of changes within the forthcoming SNMPv3 standard, covered in Chapter 12, a similar strategy is anticipated that allows for the incorporation of SNMPv3 into network devices and Network Management Systems.

System Monitoring and Management Capabilities

Cisco routers provide many useful system monitoring and management capabilities to help administrators manage large Cisco router-based internetworks. System statistics can be tracked both by interface and by protocol. For example, administrators can query for, and receive, the number of *cyclic redundancy check* (CRC) errors on a particular interface or the number of AppleTalk packets sent to, or received from, an interface. This kind of information is an invaluable component of baselining your network performance.

NOTES

Network baselining enables you to establish a baseline traffic profile for your network. This will provide you with a good indicator going forward of how your network has responded to changes. Baselining should be done periodically so that you can take the measure of the network and its performance on a regular basis.

Cisco routers also can report a wide variety of information about their internal configuration and status. For example, engineers and managers can determine the following:

- The number of successful and unsuccessful attempts to allocate internal router buffers for information storage. These values tell administrators whether the router is in danger of losing packets because of lack of available queue space.

- The average CPU usage over five-second, one-minute, and five-minute periods. These values tell administrators whether the router is overused, underused, or correctly used.

- The temperature of air entering and leaving the router. This reading gives administrators information about the router's environmental situation. Specifically, the temperature of air entering the router can be too high if the router is installed in a room with insufficient ventilation. The temperature of air leaving the router can be too high if one or more of the router's air vents is covered.

- The voltage that exists on various electrical lines in the router. These values tell administrators about the router's electrical status. Specifically, the voltages on the +5 and +12V lines to the router's power supply can be discovered. Abnormal values can indicate power faults.

Cisco's MIB Extensions

With over 450 objects, Cisco's private MIB provides network managers with broad, powerful monitoring and control facilities. Cisco's private MIB supports DECnet (including DECnet routing and host tables), XNS, AppleTalk, Banyan VINES, Novell NetWare, and additional system variables that highlight such information as average CPU utilization over selectable intervals. Furthermore, Cisco developers can add private extensions to the MIB as required. This capability gives managers the flexibility to mold

Cisco's SNMP products to their own networks, optimizing management capabilities. Figure 9-10 illustrates Cisco's private MIB tree. This figure expands upon the lower right section of the diagram shown in Figure 9-5.

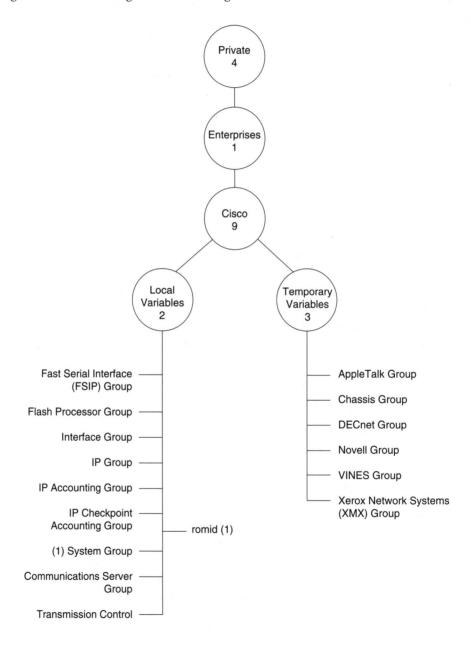

Figure 9–10
*Cisco's private
MIB structure.*

Cisco also supports other MIBs relevant to router operation. For example, support for some chassis MIB objects enables users to retrieve information about router chassis and installed cards. Card types, card serial numbers, the number of cards in a particular router, the ROM version of those cards, and many other useful variables can be retrieved. Support for the chassis MIB eases network administration. Those responsible for network maintenance can remotely query Cisco routers to quickly discover a router's hardware configuration, thereby saving time and money. This ability is provided through the use of Cisco's private MIB, as shown in Figure 9-11.

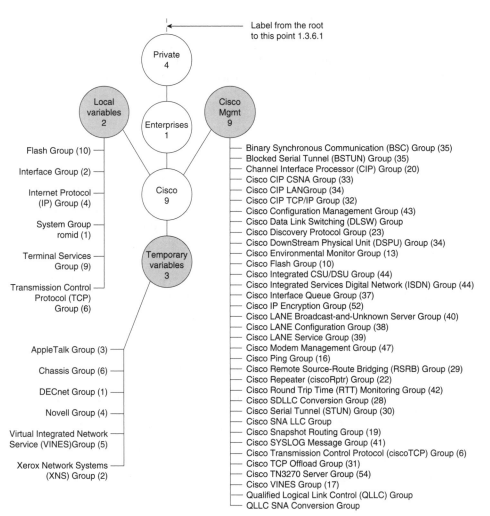

Figure 9–11
Detailed Cisco private MIB hierarchy.

Access Lists for SNMP

Access lists can be used to prevent SNMP messages from traversing certain router inter-faces, and therefore, from reaching certain network devices. For example, this feature can be used to prevent other NMSs from altering the configuration of a given router or router group. Access lists are extremely useful in complex internetworks and are imple-mented across the majority of Cisco's supported protocols.

Multiple Community Strings

For SNMPv1 operation, Cisco permits multiple community strings so that a router can belong to multiple communities. Further, community strings can be either read-only or read/write. This feature provides further security by restricting the capability to alter the configuration of Cisco devices to those that have the community string assigned the read/write capability.

Traps

Cisco's SNMP implementation allows trap messages to be directed to multiple manage-ment stations. This capability allows virtually instantaneous notification of network problems across the internetwork. If, for example, packet collisions are excessive in one area of the network, management stations throughout the internetwork can be notified immediately.

Cisco provides two extra traps useful in internetwork environments: `reload` and `tty connection-closed`. These traps serve to alert network administrators that routers are being reloaded (which, in turn, may indicate more serious problems) and that virtual terminal connections are closing.

Additional Resources on SNMP Operation

This section gave you a very brief overview of Network Management and SNMP. There are other areas concerning the operation of SNMP that you might need to understand or tasks you need to know how to perform with SNMP. That information is beyond the scope of this book although this section will provide you with some additional resources. There are also additional resources available in Chapter 12 and the bibliog-raphy at the end of the book.

SNMP Commands

The following URL is a link to the commands used to configure SNMP parameters, such as management station and traps.

```
http://www.cisco.com/univercd/cc/td/doc/product/access/acs_fix/750/
700cr/700crsnm.htm#xtocid109576
```

The following commands are covered in this section; reset SNMP trap host, set SNMP contact, set SNMP location, set SNMP trap, set SNMP trap host, and show SNMP.

Configuration Considerations for SNMP Inform Requests or Traps

The SNMP Inform Requests feature allows routers to send inform requests to SNMP managers. Routers can send notifications to SNMP managers when particular events occur. For example, an agent router might send a message to a manager when the agent router experiences an error condition.

SNMP notifications can be sent as traps or inform requests. Traps are unreliable because the receiver does not send any acknowledgment when it receives a trap. The sending device cannot determine if the trap was received. However, an SNMP manager that receives an **INFORMREQUEST** acknowledges the message with an SNMP response PDU. If the manager does not receive an **INFORMREQUEST**, it does not send a response. If the sender never receives a response, the **INFORMREQUEST** can be sent again. Thus, informs are more likely to reach their intended destination.

MANAGEMENT INFORMATION BASE (MIB)

From the perspective of a network manager, network management takes place between two major types of systems: those in control, called *managing systems*, and those observed and controlled, called *managed systems*. The most common managing system is called a *Network Management System* (NMS). Managed systems can include hosts, servers, or network components such as routers or intelligent repeaters.

To promote interoperability, cooperating systems must adhere to a common framework and a common language called a *protocol*. In the Network Management Framework, that protocol is the Simple Network Management Protocol (SNMP).

The exchange of information between managed network devices and a robust Network Management System (NMS) is essential for reliable performance of a managed network. Because some managed devices have a limited capability to run management software, most of the computer processing burden is assumed by the NMS. The NMS runs the network management applications, such as CiscoWorks or CiscoView, which present management information to network managers and other users.

In a managed device, specialized low-impact software modules, called *agents*, access information about the device and make it available to the NMS. Managed devices maintain values for a number of variables and report those, as required, to the NMS. For example, an agent might report such data as the number of bytes and packets in and out of the device, or the number of broadcast messages sent and received. In the Internet Network Management Framework, each of these variables is referred to as a *managed object*. A managed object is anything that can be managed, anything that an agent can access and report back to the NMS. All managed objects are contained in the *Management Information Base (MIB)*, a database of the managed objects.

An NMS can control a managed device by sending a message to an agent of that managed device requiring the device to change the value of one or more of its variables. The managed devices can respond to commands such as SET or GET commands, the former of which are used to control the device; the latter of which are used by the NMS to monitor the device.

Management Information Base (MIB) Components

A Management Information Base (MIB) is a collection of information that is organized hierarchically. MIBs are accessed using a network management protocol such as SNMP. MIBs are composed of managed objects and are identified by object identifiers. MIB data is organized into a *tree structure* as illustrated in Figures 9-5, 9-10, and 9-11. All the management for *Internet (1)* (that is, networking) devices fall under the branch labeled Internet. Within that branch are several other branches, which are as follows (refer to Figure 9-5):

- **Mgmt (2)**. This branch contains all the standardized management data. OSPF MIBs reside down this branch.

- **Experimental (3)**. This branch contains all the information for management data currently under development.

- **Private (4)**. This branch contains vendor-specific management data. Cisco's private MIBs reside down this branch.

As you can see, there are quite a few MIBs available. The good news is that they are all compiled using ASN.1, so they can be compiled and used by any NMS. The difference between managed objects and devices will be discussed in the next section.

Managed Objects

A managed object (sometimes called a MIB object, an object, or a MIB) is one of any number of specific characteristics of a managed device. Managed objects are composed of one or more object instances, which are essentially variables. There are two types of managed objects, which are defined as follows:

- **Scalar objects.** These objects define a single object instance.

- **Tabular objects.** These objects define multiple related object instances. These instances are grouped together in MIB tables.

An example of a managed object is **OSPFIFMETRICTABLE**, which is a scalar object. It contains a single object instance, in this case it is the metric associated with a router interface running OSPF.

Additional OSPF MIB information is provided later in this chapter in the section, "OSPF MIBS."

Object Identifiers

An object identifier (or object ID) uniquely identifies a managed object in the MIB hierarchy. The MIB hierarchy can be depicted as a tree, with a nameless root, the levels of which are assigned by different organizations. Figure 9-12 illustrates the MIB tree.

The top-level MIB object IDs belong to different standards organizations, and lower-level object IDs are allocated by associated organizations.

Vendors can define their own private branches that include managed objects for their own products. MIBs that have not been standardized are typically positioned in the experimental branch.

The managed object **OSPFIFMETRICTABLE** can be uniquely identified either by the object name:

```
iso.identified-organization.dod.internet.mgmt.MIB-2.OSPF.
ospfifmetrictable
```

or by the equivalent object identifier descriptor:

```
1.3.6.1.2.1.14.8
```

It is important to note that the textual name as shown is not used but rather the OID (that is, the string of numbers) is what is used to identify the data requested.

Figure 9–12
The MIB tree.

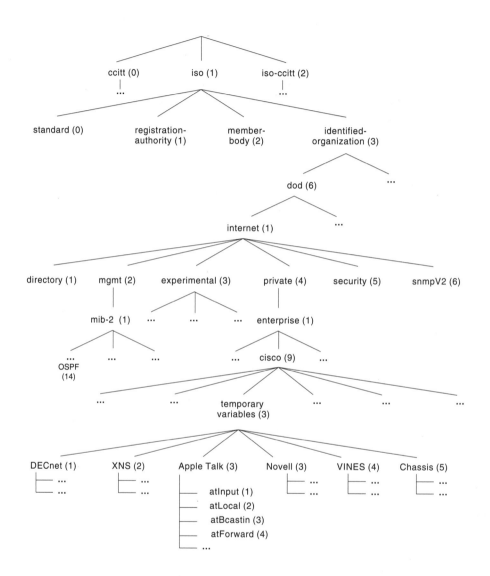

TIPS

Refer to Figure 9-12 to understand and see how each branch or segment of the MIB tree provides a number. When you reach the desired "leaf" MIB, the object descriptor has been derived as a series of numbers describing your path to that specific MIB.

MIBs and SNMP Interactions

MIB variables are accessible via the Simple Network Management Protocol (SNMP), which is an application-layer protocol designed to facilitate the exchange of management information between network devices. As previously described, the SNMP system consists of three parts: SNMP manager, SNMP agent, and MIB.

Instead of defining a large set of commands, SNMP places all operations in a **GETREQUST**, **GETNEXTREQUEST**, **GETBULKREQUEST**, and **SETREQUEST** format. For example, an SNMP manager can get a value from an SNMP agent or store a value in that SNMP agent. The SNMP manager can be part of a network management system (NMS), and the SNMP agent can reside on a networking device such as a router. You can compile a MIB with your network management software. If SNMP is configured on a router, the SNMP agent can respond to MIB-related queries being sent by the NMS. The SNMP agent gathers data from the MIB, which is the repository for information about device parameters and network data. The agent also can send traps, or notifications of certain events, to the manager. Table 9-1 describes the SNMP manager operations.

Table 9–1   *SNMP Manager Operations*

Operation	Description
GETREQUEST	Retrieves a value from a specific variable
GETNEXTREQUEST	Retrieves the value following the named variable. Often used to retrieve variables from within a table.
GETRESPONSE	The reply to a **GETREQUEST**, **GETNEXTREQUEST**, **GETBULKREQUEST**, and **SETREQUEST** sent by an NMS
GETBULKREQUEST	Similar to **GETNEXTREQUEST**, but fills the **GETRESPONSE** with up to **MAXREPETITION** number of **GETNEXT** interactions
SETREQUEST	Stores a value in a specific variable.
TRAP	An unsolicited message sent by an SNMP agent to an SNMP manager indicating that some event has occurred.

With the **GETNEXTREQUEST** operation, an SNMP manager does not need to know the exact variable name. A sequential search is performed to find the needed variable from within the MIB.

TIPS

The Cisco trap file, *mib.traps*, which documents the format of the Cisco traps, is available on the Cisco host *ftp.cisco.com/pub/mibs*. The SNMP manager uses information in the MIB to perform the operations described in Table 9-1.

Managing a Network with MIBs

This section introduces polling on Cisco routers. In addition to the specific router MIB variables that are recommended here, this information could also apply to other network devices (hubs, switches, hosts, end stations, and so forth). Just substitute MIBs that the devices support for the router MIB variables. There are three kinds of polling, which are described as follows:

- **Monitor Polling.** Determines the availability of devices.
- **Threshold Polling.** Detects error conditions.
- **Performance Polling.** Analyzes data for trends or performance measurements.

Monitor and threshold polling are functions of the management platform. Questions about configuring, debugging, and interpreting them should be directed to the platform vendor.

Monitor Polling

Monitor polling detects network changes and generates immediate alarms. These changes are "hard errors," like a device not responding or an interface status change. Any alarm generated by monitor polling should be acted on immediately. If your Network Management System is monitored around the clock, a monitor polling alarm should create a visible and audible alarm on the system, so the operator can take immediate action. If your Network Management System is not always monitored, a monitor polling alarm should send an alarm to the appropriate person, possibly via pager or e-mail.

Monitor polling applications are included with HP Openview and Netview 6000, and can be configured with Sun Net Manager. You can customize monitor polling with add-on products like NetLab's Nerve Center. The individual data points returned from monitor polling are not important. The monitor polling application analyzes the data points to generate alarms.

Threshold Polling

Many problems show up first as increased error conditions. They might eventually become hard errors, or they might be "phantom" problems that come and go. Threshold polling detects these escalating error conditions and acts before performance is severely impacted. To implement threshold polling, first decide for which MIB variables to poll, and then add other MIB variables as appropriate.

After you have decided on the threshold MIB variables, establish baseline values for these variables by starting a poll process on the MIB variables. After some period of time (for instance, one week), review this data to determine what values are "normal" for your router. Then, use these normal values to determine what the highest acceptable values, or thresholds, would be. A good rule of thumb is to set your thresholds 10–20 percent larger than the maximum values.

The threshold values for any particular MIB variable may be applied uniformly across all routers, or they could be customized for groups of routers that have similar characteristics (like core, distribution, and access).

You also need to decide on appropriate notification for threshold violations. These violations are not hard errors—immediate notification is unnecessary. Logging all threshold values and reviewing them daily usually works well. It is important to investigate repeated threshold violations, to determine if a problem has occurred that can be corrected or if your threshold values are too low.

Performance Polling

Performance polling gathers data over time that can be analyzed to determine trends and to aid in capacity planning. First, determine what MIB variables to poll for. One of the following sections, "Recommended MIBs for Data Collection," has some suggestions for variables that would be useful for Cisco routers.

For performance polling, individual data points are stored intermittently on the polling machine. Depending on the polling mechanism you are using, the data could be in either a raw format (the default for Openview and Netview 6000), or a relational database. CiscoWorks uses Sybase.

To keep the data manageable, aggregate the raw data periodically, and store it in another database or datafile for future reporting. Keep the raw data for a period of time for backups, but purge this data eventually and keep only the aggregate data. Use this aggregate data to produce reports that will be periodically reviewed to determine trends and patterns.

Performance Polling System Example

Individual MIB variables are grouped together in a series of polling groups. Each group is polled every five minutes and the data is stored in Sybase databases by poll group names. Every morning at 12:01 AM, the raw data in Sybase is aggregated into minimum, maximum, and averages for each hour and stored in another Sybase database (the user has written SQL programs to accomplish this).

Every Saturday morning at 1:00 AM the individual raw data points are purged from the database for the previous week. On the first day of each month, the hourly min/max/avg data is aggregated into daily min/max/avg data and stored in another database. A series of reports are generated from both the daily and hourly data for review at the Capacity Planning meeting on the first Tuesday of the month. After the reports are produced, the data from the hourly database is archived to tape.

The following section examines the MIBs Cisco recommends for use within your network.

Recommended MIBs for Data Collection

For overall router performance, the recommended MIB is as follows:

```
…mib.system.sysuptime
..cisco.local.lsystem.freeMem
..cisco.local.lsystem.avgBusy1
..cisco.local.lsystem.avgBusy5
..cisco.local.lsystem.avgBusyPer
..cisco.local.lsystem.bufferNoMem
..cisco.local.lsystem.bufferSmMiss
..cisco.local.lsystem.bufferMdMiss
..cisco.local.lsystem.bufferBgMiss
..cisco.local.lsystem.bufferLgMiss
..cisco.local.lsystem.bufferHgMiss
```

For all interfaces, the recommended MIB is as follows:

```
..cisco.local.lifTable.locIfInbitsSec
..cisco.local.lifTable.locIfOutbitsSec
..mib-2.interfaces.ifTable.ifInErrors
..mib-2.interfaces.ifTable.ifOutErrors
..cisco.local.lifTable.locIfInputQueueDrops
..cisco.local.lifTable.locIfOutputQueueDrops
..cisco.local.lifTable.locIfInIgnored
..cisco.local.lifTable.locIfresets
```

For serial interfaces, the recommended MIB is as follows:

```
.. cisco.local.lifTable.locIfCRC
.. cisco.local.lifTable.locIfAbort
.. cisco.local.lifTable.locIfFrame
.. cisco.local.lifTable.locIfCarTrans
.. cisco.local.lifTable.locIfOverrun
```

For Ethernet interfaces, the recommended MIB is as follows:

```
..cisco.local.lifTable.locIfCollisions
..cisco.local.lifTable.locIfRunts
..cisco.local.lifTable.locIfGiants
..cisco.local.lifTable.locIfFrame
```

For Token Ring interfaces, the recommended MIB is as follows (from RFC 1231):

```
dot5StatsLineErrors
dot5StatsBurstErrors
dot5StatsACErrors
dot5StatsAbortTransErrors
dot5StatsInternalErrors
dot5StatsFrameCopiedErrors
dot5StatsTokenErrors
dot5StatsSoftErrors
dot5StatsSignalLoss
dot5StatsFreqErrors
```

For FDDI interfaces, the recommended MIB is as follows (from RFC 1512):

```
snmpFddiMACLostCts
snmpFddiMACErrorCts
```

Accessing Cisco MIB Files

You can obtain the files that describe the MIBs supported by Cisco products using anonymous FTP or the World Wide Web to access Cisco Connection Online (CCO), formerly Cisco Information Online (CIO).

Via FTP, use the `ftp ftp.cisco.com` command. Log in with the username anonymous, and enter your e-mail name when prompted for the password. Use the `cd pub/mibs` command to go to the directory that contains the MIB files, and then issue the `get README` command to obtain the README file containing a description of the Cisco Systems public MIB area. To determine the MIBs supported for each Cisco product, go to the `supportlists` subdirectory where you will find directories for all Cisco products. Refer to the supportlist.txt file in each directory, as necessary, to determine the MIBs supported on that platform, by Cisco IOS release, and the location of the desired MIB file. Cisco IOS MIB files are in the *v1* and *v2* subdirectories. You can then use the FTP command `get mib-filename` to retrieve the MIB file.

A description of issues you might encounter when loading Cisco MIBs into your NMS is located at `ftp://www.cisco.com/pub/mibs/app_notes/mib-compilers`.

To access CCO via the WWW, use one of the following URLs:

```
http://www.cisco.com/public/mibs
ftp://www.cisco.com/pub/mibs
```

OSPF MIBs

As previously described in Chapter 4, "Introduction to OSPF," there are several RFCs that describe OSPF v2 MIBs (the most current of which is RFC 1850):

- RFC 1248

- RFC 1252

- RFC 1253

- RFC 1850

OSPF has a very large MIB, which provides you with a very powerful tool to monitor and configure the protocol. Figure 9-13 answers the question of where OSPF is located in the MIB tree.

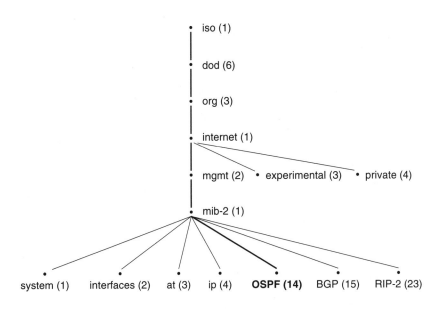

Figure 9–13
OSPF MIB tree location.

The OSPF MIB as described in RFC 1850 has an impressive list of characteristics:

- 12 Distinct Tables

- 110 Management Variables

- 65 of the Management Variables are read only OSPF values

- 45 configurable Management Variables

No doubt you are wondering how to keep track of the 110 management variables for OSPF and why you would want to? This is a valid question as the amount of information made available to you through MIBs is impressive. It is true that most implementations of OSPF will not be concerned with every management variable but somewhere someone had a need so it has been included. The more commonly used variables are provided in Figure 9-14.

Figure 9-14
*Detailed OSPF
MIB tree.*

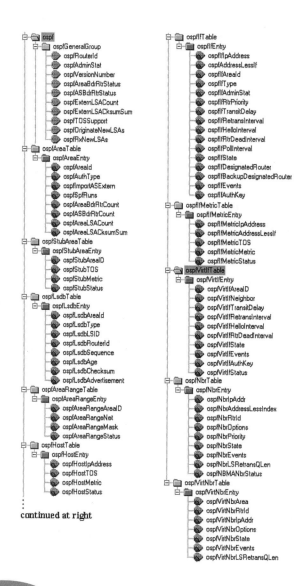

continued at right

NOTES

Figure 9-14 shows only the more commonly used OSPF MIB tables. The **OSPFGENER-ALGROUP, OSPFAREATABLE, OSPFSTUBAREATABLE, OSPFHOSTTABLE, OSPFIFTABLE, OSPFIFMET-RICTABLE, OSPFVIRTIFTABLE,** and **OSPFNBRTABLE** tables contain read/write entries. The **OSPFLSDBTABLE, OSPFAREARANGETABLE,** and **OSFPVIRTNBRTABLE** tables are read-only.

As Figure 9-14 shows, eleven tables are most commonly used in OSPF implementations or those that have not yet completed the migration to the newer RFCs. There are actually twelve tables possible, but Cisco does not yet support them all, so that information will be saved for the 2nd edition. Please refer to RFC 1850 for additional information regarding the other tables not commonly used in OSPF implementations. The following list briefly discusses some of the characteristics of each table's entries.

TIPS

For purposes of this section, remember that MIBs are a type of database so the terminology used reflects this, such as table and row.

- **OSPFGENERALGROUP.** This table is referred to as a group since it only has one row that contains global OSPF parameters within that router (that is, OSPF version number or OSPF router ID).

- **OSPFAREATABLE.** Within this table there is a separate row for each OSPF area that a router belongs to. Each area is identified by the unique OSPF area value.

- **OSPFSTUBAREATABLE.** Within this table there is a separate row for each OSPF *stub* area that a router belongs to. Other characteristics that are important to the operation of OSPF in a stub area are included in this table, i.e. metric and area ID.

- **OSPFLSDBTABLE.** This table provides information on OSPF's link state database. Each OSPF area is provided with a row for each LSA that is generated within that area. Needless to say this table can get very large as it also keeps track of the LSA sequence ID, type, age, checksum, etc.

- **OSPFAREARANGETABLE.** This table has become obsolete in the new RFC1850. Nevertheless, it is still commonly used. This table contains information regarding the IP address range of an OSPF area. Each area the router belongs to will have a row identified by the area ID.

- **OSPFHOSTTABLE.** This table identifies the hosts that are directly attached to the OSPF router. It provides information about these hosts such as IP address, metric and status.

- **OSPFIFTABLE.** This is another table that can get very large, as the MIB will create a row for each OSPF interface configured on a router. The OSPF authentication key is also stored here.

- **OSPFIFMETRICTABLE.** This table is very important as it contains the information regarding the OSPF cost of each interface. This information is then used to calculate the OSPF routing table.

- **OSPFVIRTIFTABLE.** This table contains all the virtual link information used within the router to include the area it will transit to and which other OSPF router it will connect to. It also holds the configurable OSPF information for a virtual link such as the OSPF timers, and authentication key.

- **OSPFNBRTABLE.** This table contains the OSPF neighbor information and each neighbor is uniquely identified by its IP address.

- **OSPFVIRTNBRTABLE.** This table is used by OSPF to monitor virtual link operation and events.

- **OSPFAREARANGETABLE.** This table is replaced in RFC 1850 by **OSPFAREAAGGRE-GATETABLE,** which creates a row for each range of IP addresses found within an OSPF area.

- **OSPFEXTLSDBTABLE.** A new table that has been added to the MIB, this table tracks all of the external LSAs that OSPF receives.

Configuring OSPF with MIBs

OSPF can be configured using the OSPF MIBs if desired, although it is not recommended unless you are very familiar with the OSPF MIB and both the SNMP and MIB operational characteristics. If not, then there is a very high chance you could cause severe problems in your network.

Because configuring OSPF through the router command line interface has been covered, this is by far the safest and most secure method. Therefore, it is not necessary to go into detail on how to duplicate this using the OSPF MIBs. Nevertheless, OSPF does come ready and willing to be configured in this manner. The MIBs are all set with some very accurate default values that, through minimal intervention on your behalf, can start the OSPF routing process.

NOTES

As a side note on this subject, I tried to configure a router to start the OSPF process, and the MIB was faster. But, when it came to configuring OSPF to my specific network environment (that is, when I needed to use loopback addresses or route summarization), the command line was faster. An interesting note is that when using the command line you have a variety of other features available that can enable you to double-check yourself and increase security.

The excerpt that follows is straight from RFC 1850 and details the procedure on how to configure a router for OSPF using the OSPF MIBs. This excerpt should provide you with what you need to know before you start and with the default OSPF values when it is started.

"OSPF is a powerful routing protocol, equipped with features to handle virtually any configuration requirement that might reasonably be found within an Autonomous System. With this power comes a fair degree of complexity, which the sheer number of objects in the MIB will attest to. Care has therefore been taken, in constructing this MIB, to define default values for virtually every object, to minimize the amount of parameterization required in the typical case. That default configuration is as follows:

Assuming the following conditions:

- IP has already been configured
- The ifTable has already been configured
- ifSpeed is estimated by the interface drivers
- The OSPF Process automatically discovers all IP
- Interfaces and creates corresponding OSPF Interfaces
- The TOS 0 metrics are autonomously derived from ifSpeed
- The OSPF Process automatically creates the Areas required for the Interfaces

The simplest configuration of an OSPF process requires that the OSPF process be enabled. This can be accomplished with a single SET: ospfAdminStat := enabled.

The configured system will have the following attributes:

- The RouterID will be one of the IP addresses of the device
- The device will be neither an area border router nor an autonomous system border router.
- Every IP Interface, with or without an address, will be an OSPF Interface.
- The AreaID of each interface will be 0.0.0.0, the backbone.
- Authentication will be disabled
- All broadcast and point-to-point interfaces will be operational. NBMA Interfaces require the configuration of at least one neighbor.
- Timers on all direct interfaces will be as follows:
  - Hello Interval: 10 seconds
  - Dead Timeout: 40 Seconds
  - Retransmission: 5 Seconds
  - Transit Delay: 1 Second
  - Poll Interval: 120 Seconds
- No direct links to hosts will be configured.
- No addresses will be summarized
- Metrics, being a measure of bit duration, are unambiguous and intelligent.
- No Virtual Links will be configured."

Additional Resources on OSPF MIBs

Finding additional resources that deal specifically with OSPF MIBs can be tricky because it is a very specific topic. However, there are a few resources that are very helpful, such as the following RFCs:

- RFC1850: OSPF v2 Management Information Base
- RFC2178: OSPF v2

The Entrance of Remote Monitoring (RMON) Technology

Even though SNMP and proprietary MIBs were a dramatic improvement over earlier management capabilities, more could be done to increase the information provided to the network managers while reducing impact to network bandwidth.

The next generation of network management began in 1992 with the development of remote monitoring (RMON) technology (RFC 1271) to proactively monitor Ethernet networks. RMON is now covered by RFC 1757, which combines 1271 with the RFC standard for Token Ring (RFC 1513). RMON2, continuing development of this technology, was introduced via RFC 2021 in February 1997, to provide more detailed information regarding protocol and application utilization. RMON will be covered in more depth in Chapter 12, "Future Network Considerations."

CHAPTER SUMMARY

This chapter discussed and proved the importance of consistent network management. We discussed the more commonly developed and deployed network management models. The first section briefly covered a few tools, some free of charge, that are available to assist you in managing your OSPF network.

The second section, "Simple Network Management Protocol," covered the use of SNMP and how it fits into today's complex networks as the de facto network management standard. This coverage included components found within an SNMP managed network such as the Network Management System (NMS), managed devices, and their SNMP agents. This section also covered SNMP's operation, commands, and the various messages used by SNMP to communicate with the devices in the network.

The third part of this chapter, "Management Information Bases (MIBs)" discussed the powerful tools known as MIBs and the role they play in network management. We were able to pull back the curtain a bit to see how MIBs are used by Network Management Systems to retrieve information from network devices. We also broke down the available OSPF MIBs and discussed how they can be used to find out important OSPF information on how and what it is doing within a router. We also discussed how the OSPF MIB has been designed with giving network managers the ability to quickly configure OSPF on routers. This information was provided directly from RFC 1850.

In conclusion, this chapter has covered how important proper network management is to any network. We have peeled back the onion in many places to understand how network management is actually being performed over the network through SNMP and its various features.

FREQUENTLY ASKED QUESTIONS (FAQs)

Q— *What version of SNMP is available on my Cisco IOS image?*

A— All software releases to date have included SNMPv1. In addition, releases prior to Cisco IOS 11.2F(6.0) (including all releases of 11.2 and 11.2P) supported the SNMPv2 Party-based protocol. Releases from Cisco IOS 11.2F(6.0) onwards have SNMPv2C support (SNMPv2, RFCs 1441-1452, was replaced by SNMPv2C, RFCs 1901-1908 in these releases).

Q— *Is the OSPF link-state database available to a MIB query?*

A— Yes, and so is the IP routing table (`IpRoutingTable`).

Q— *How can I obtain route redistribution parameters via SNMP requests for various protocols (RIP, OSPF, and so forth)?*

A— You cannot at this time. You can find a list of all presently supported at: `http://www.Cisco.com/public/mibs/v1`

Q— *Does Cisco implement 64-bit counters, especially for the IF-MIB? If not, when is 64-bit counter support expected?*

A— Cisco does not support 64-bit counters yet though when they exceed the 64-bit limit they will roll over. This is being worked on now.

Q— *What version of SNMP is required for 64-bit counter support?*

A— SNMPv2C is required for Counter64.

Q— *Does the Cisco IOS support subinterfaces in the* `IfTable`?

A— Generic support for sublayers in the `IfTable` has been present since Cisco IOS 11.1(1). For any given media type, it is up to the groups which support that media to determine the following:

- If sublayers are appropriate (with direction from IETF)

- How to support those sublayers

Q— *What is the minimum Cisco IOS version I should be running to see subinterfaces in SNMP tables?*

A— Cisco IOS 11.1.

Q— *Are the SNMP counters* `IfInOctets` *and* `IfOutOctets` *the same as the show interface in/out counters?*

A— Yes.

Q— *Do the* `ifInOctets` *and* `ifOutOctets` *counters include framing overhead (PPP, HDLC)?*

A— Yes.

Q— *On an ATM interface, do the counters include the cell header?*

A— ATM counters do not include ATM overhead (cell headers and AAL5 padding).

Q— *A customer has a Cisco 7507 running Cisco IOS 11.1.4.4. He tries to do snmpwalk on mib2, and all the interfaces return a value except the ATM interface; it does not return any value. He is also having problems with HP OpenView retrieving information for this interface. For example:*

```
ifDescr.1: ATM0/0
ifAdminStatus.1: up
ifOperStatus.1: up
ifInOctets.1: is not returned
ifInUcastPkts.1: is not returned
```

Is this a bug?

A— This has been fixed in Cisco IOS 11.1(5.0.2) via CSCdi63762. Keep in mind, in Cisco IOS 11.1 and later, sparse tables have been implemented, specifically in the `ifmib`, as well as other areas. Thus, there are valid situations where `ifInOctets`.1 would not be returned.

Q— *Some* `IfTable` *columns do not show up for certain interface types. Why? Is this a bug?*

A— This is not a bug. `IfTable` based on RFC 1573 is designed specifically so that some columns in a given row will not be instantiated based on `IfType`. Please read the RFC compliance statement for further clarification for which columns to expect for different media groups. An example of this would be ATM, which is a fixed length packet. As such, rows in the `IfTable` etc. would be based on `IfFixedLengthGroup`.

Q— *In which release is SNMPv2C support available?*

A— Cisco IOS 11.3 will be the first shipping release with SNMPv2C support.

Q— *P-SNMP CPU usage spikes to 90 percent (or higher). Is this a bug?*

A— No, this is not a bug. It is not unusual for IP-SNMP to take up 90 percent of the CPU on the router when the router is lightly loaded with other tasks. IP SNMP runs at a low priority and a CPU usage of 90 percent or higher means the router has the bandwidth to spend more time on SNMP. It might also mean that the router was responding to frequent polls from an NMS application, which could be a very bad thing.

Q— *Is there a way to tell the router to load a specific configuration file via TFTP from a specific host?*

A— Yes there is. Please refer to the following location for details:

`ftp://ftpeng.cisco.com/pub/mibs/app_notes/configset.`

Alternately, you may use the following UNIX SNMP script written by Matt Birkner, CCIE 3719, who is also a technical editor for this book. The seed file for this script needs to be in ASCII file format with one IP address per line and in the same directory as the script.

```
#!/bin/ksh
#
# Start of code
clear
print - " This code takes the seed file in the current directory
& will TFTP the config"
print - " Used by permission, Copyright 1998, Matt Birkner "
print - " Usage ./change_config <seed filename>"

for ROUTER in 'cat $1.seed'
do
(
print "Now connecting to router $ROUTER"
/tools/snmpset $ROUTER <SNMP Read/Write Community String>
.1.3.6.1.4.1.9.2.1.50.<TFTP Server IP address> s
<Config File Name>
sleep 2
```

```
/tools/snmpset $ROUTER <SNMP Read/Write Community String>
.1.3.6.1.4.1.9.2.1.54.0 i 1
)
print - " $ROUTER config written..Going to next."
done
```

<TFTP Server IP address> is the IP address of your TFTP server

<Config File Name> is the name of file that you will use to modify the Cisco router.

NOTES

The following sample configuration will shut off DNS in the router, set the routers time to follow GMT and cause the syslog to be time stamped. Alternately, this example could contain an entire router configuration or customized OSPF settings.

An example of the contents of <Config File Name> is as follows:

```
no ip domain-lookup
clock timezone GMT 0
clock summer-time GMT recurring
service timestamps log datetime localtime show-timezone
!
end
```

Q— *Is there an SNMP MIB to grab arp table information? We need both the IP and MAC address in the same table.*

A— Yes, **IPNETTOMEDIATABLE** in MIB-II (RFC 1213).

Q— *A customer activated Silicon Switching and now MIB values for interface statistics are only updated every 10 seconds. SNMP GETs for MIB values show no change if polled more often (in this case, 8 seconds). Is this is a bug?*

A— This is expected (not a bug). Part of the tradeoff for allowing the box to dedicate more resources to actually switching traffic is to poll less often for interface statistics. show interface should present the same behavior.

Q— *A customer is seeing two coldstart traps out of the router. Is this a bug?*

A— This behavior is not a bug. See bug report CSCdi54387. A coldstart trap is normally the first trap (and the first packet) to be sent to a trap destination. So the router needs to arp for the trap destination. Cisco devices drop the trap if an arp has to be sent out. Therefore, many customers were not seeing the coldstart trap before the fix, which was to send it twice. This is RFC compliant, as the network can also duplicate the coldstart traps.

Q— *What is the EXACT information contained in an SNMP trap, and where is it documented?*

A— For the list of objects on traps, check out: ftp://ftpeng.cisco.com/pub/mibs/traps. Note that the information at this site only specifies what should be contained within a trap. It does not mean that the trap has been implemented in the agent code yet.

Q— *Is there a tool for extracting MIBs from an RFC?*

A— Yes, try premosy <rfc> mib, where rfc is the text document from which mib is to be extracted.

Q— *I would like to capture SNMP traps on my workstation. What tool can I use for this?*

A— On SunOS machines, use /usr/local/bin/tcpdump. On Solaris, use /sw/current/solaris2bin/traprcv. On Windows, use MGSOFT MIB Master, located at http://www.mg-soft.com.

Q— *How are the MIB variables locIfInbitsSec and locIfOutbitsSec and calculated? Are the packet and frame header/trailer bytes included in the calculations?*

A— Those variables are an exponentially decayed five minute average of the amount of all traffic that comes in and goes out of the interface. "Exponentially decayed five minute average" means that the most recent sample is weighted more heavily than the oldest sample. The current sample period is 10 seconds.

Q— *Do the SNMP accounting tables contain addresses of access list violators?*

A— You can get the access list number violated by packets sourced from one address to another. See the IP accounting MIB in the MIB document found at: `ftp://ftp/pub/MIBs/v1/OLD-Cisco-IP-MIB.my`.

Q— *What is the minimum and maximum length of the* `snmp-server location` *and* `snmp-server contact` *fields?*

A— One (1) character is the minimum length and 233 characters is the maximum (limited by the length of a single command line in the parser).

Q— *Is there a way to get the serial number of a router using SNMP?*

A— The serial number of the router is not retrievable by default. You can retrieve only the serial number of the CPU (if it exists). You can, however, use the `snmp-server chassis-id` config command to set the SNMP MIB variable chassis ID. In this way, you could have the serial number of a remote router.

Q— *How can I get SNMP information on total collisions per-interface on a Catalyst 5000?*

A— Here is the MIB for the Workgroup products, including the 5000, `Cisco-STACK-MIB.my`, found on CCO. This MIB and RFC1213 (MIB-II) are the only MIBs supported on the Catalyst 5000. There is nothing that references collisions except for the MIB variable PORTADDITIONALSTATUS, which indicates that more than one collision has occurred on the interface when the variable has a value of two.

Q— *How can I tell if EIGRP is enabled on a interface via SNMP? Can I obtain EIGRP metrics through SNMP requests?*

A— You cannot at this time.

Q— *How can I obtain route redistribution parameters via SNMP requests for various protocols (RIP, OSPF, etc.)?*

A— You cannot at this time.

Q— *A network management workstation is attempting to perform SNMP network management functions on remote LAN concentrators. Their SNMP traffic must pass through one or more routers for which they do not* *have the community string. Can they manage the remote devices without having the SNMP community string?*

A— Yes. You only need the community string for the device that you are actually managing. You also need to make sure that the routers along the way are not filtering the SNMP port.

Q— *What is the impact of SNMP management traffic on router performance?*

A— All SNMP queries sent to a router are prioritized as either low or medium priority, depending on the version of code run by the route processor. This means that processes with a higher priority than the SNMP process will be serviced before SNMP. So, regardless of SNMP polling intensity, routing processes will generally be processed before SNMP requests because route processes are "high" priority.

You can view the priorities of each of the router's processes by doing a show process and looking in the Q column (L = Low, M = Medium, H = High). The router processes H before M, and M before L. Here is an example:

```
CPU utilization for five seconds: 6%/1%; one minute: 7%;
five minutes: 6%
PID Q T PC Runtime (ms) Invoked uSecs Stacks TTY Process
3 L E 50AE2 18124 41610 435 736/1000 0 ARP Input
6 H E 67864 959264 2167473 442 1602/2000 0 IP Input
43 M E 9DBB0 940300 141179 6660 528/1000 0 IP SNMP
```

Be cautious with the amount and frequency of polling. Often, network management platforms request more information than you think. Your routers can become processor-bound as a result of excessive information being polled, sometimes driving the route processor CPU utilization to 99 percent (despite the SNMP priority). The rule of thumb is that a minimum amount of information should be polled as infrequently as possible. You can use an analyzer to determine the amount and frequency of information being polled from a particular router. To avoid extensive polling, the SNMP priority should generally be set to "low." Do this with the hidden `snmp-server priority` command.

Q— *What's the difference between SNMP and SNMPv2 configuration in Cisco IOS? Which version of Cisco IOS supports SNMPv2?*

A— These are two different SNMP versions. The SNMP packet format is different in each, but there is no difference in configuring them in Cisco IOS. SNMPv2 provides more flexibility and is actually an enhancement to

SNMPv1. SNMPv2 is supported as of Cisco IOS 10.2. Cisco supports both versions of SNMP. Some NMS stations do not support SNMPv2 yet, so the SNMPv2 MIBs cause an error on the management platform (SNM, HPOV, NetView) when compiled.

Q— *What does Cisco's private MIB support?*

A— Cisco's private MIB supports DECnet (including DECnet routing and host tables), XNS, AppleTalk, VINES, NetWare, and additional system variables that highlight such information as average CPU utilization over selectable intervals. Cisco users can add private extensions to the MIB as required.

Q— *How can I find out where and how to access other vendor MIB variables that are supported by Cisco Systems.*

A— Other-vendor MIBs supported on Cisco products can be retrieved from CCO or via anonymous FTP. Cisco supports Novell's IPX (2.5), NLSP, and RIPSAP (22.0) MIBs, among others.

Q— *I can issue an SNMP ping directly to the router asking it to ping all DLCI partners, and it is successful. What does this indicate?*

A— This confirms that the protocol is configured and the protocol-to-DLCI mapping is correct at both ends.

Q— *Are there SNMP variables that will provide an accurate status on the DLCIs?*

A— Yes, RFC1315, and the Frame Relay DTR MIB.

The SNMP variable for a circuit's status is **FRCIRCUITSTATE**. Its ASN.1 OID form is 1.3.6.1.2.1.10.32.2.1.3. It resides in the **FRCIRCUITTABLE**; so to get the value (the actual status in this case), the index and the DLCI would be the first and second instance respectively. Through SNMP GET or GETNEXT requests, you should get the system internal circuit status. Valid values for it include the following:

- 1. invalid

- 2. active

- 3. inactive

For Cisco, you would see either 2 or 3.

PART 4

Network Security & Future Expansion

This section finishes up the book with the crucial topic of how to secure your OSPF network once it's in place. In addition, you'll also see the continuing developments in OSPF technology and what the future has in store for OSPF. This information is conveyed in the final three chapters of the book:

Chapter 10, **"Securing Your OSPF Network,"** covers network security and the various techniques that you can use to protect your OSPF network from outside attackers, including very basic security techniques, more advanced encryption, and filtering.

Chapter 11, **"The Continuing Evolution of OSPF,"** covers how to prepare your OSPF network for the future by tracking the IETF's working drafts. These documents are the true measure of how the OSPF Working Group, a section of the IETF, is keeping up with the increasing demands of the internetworking community.

Chapter 12, **"Future Network Considerations,"** covers some of the hot, new networking features that are making their presence felt in the industry, including SNMPv2 and v3, Remote Monitoring (RMON), and the dawning of the age of IPv6.

CHAPTER 10

Securing Your OSPF Network

"Pride: Pride Is A Personal Commitment. It Is An Attitude Which Separates Excellence From Mediocrity."—Successories

This chapter is the first in Part 4 and deals exclusively with network security and the various techniques that you can use to protect your OSPF network from outside attackers. It will cover a broad range of security topics from very basic security techniques to the more advanced forms of encryption and filtering. This chapter consists of four major parts:

- **Network Security.** This section introduces you to a variety of security threats and concerns that will demonstrate the need for a coordinated network security plan. Some of the more recent attacks against the Cisco IOS and how it has responded will be discussed. This section is not all doom and gloom, as it will also cover a variety of defensive techniques that have been developed to repel the attacks described.

- **Golden Rules of Designing a Secure Network.** This section covers the Golden Rules you must use to begin the development of a comprehensive network security plan. Many of the Golden Rules are common sense-oriented topics that network designers might forget in their rush to design the network. This chapter will also briefly discuss the need to include a comprehensive security plan in the initial stages of the network's design.

- **Securing Your OSPF Network.** This section contains the true meat of how to secure your network. This chapter will take a look at the entire range of security implementations you can use in your network—from simple configuration commands that should be deployed within your routers to how OSPF can protect the integrity of your routing structure.

- **Configuring Traffic Filters.** Do you have users travelling inside or outside your network? Is it possible that someone is trying to get into your network? Then this section is for you! This chapter will discuss the various types of filters—also known as access lists—and how to deploy them within your network to enable you to sleep better at night by getting very granular with their place with your security design.

NETWORK SECURITY

Network security must be an integral part of the design of every aspect of your network.

When most people talk about network security, they mean ensuring that users can only perform tasks they are authorized to do, can only obtain information they are authorized to have, and cannot cause damage to the data, applications, or operating environment of a system.

The word *security* connotes protection against malicious attack by outsiders. Security also involves controlling the effects of errors and equipment failures. Anything that can protect against a deliberate, intelligent, calculated attack will probably prevent random misfortune.

Network security has probably been one of the least considered aspects of network operation and design. As enterprise networks evolve, it has become an increasingly larger concern of many. Is this concern justified? A resounding yes—and the concerns are probably late in coming. Consider recent FBI statistics that estimate businesses in the United States alone lost an estimated $10 billion dollars from computer break-ins in 1997. That number is larger than the gross national product of many nations. When considered this way, you can easily see why people have dedicated their lives to computer theft. Are these security breaches occurring in the wide-area portion of your network as well? Although it might not be happening in your network yet, it is occurring elsewhere. Consider the excerpts in the following sections, which were taken from Cisco's home page (`http://www.cisco.com`) regarding their recent announcements in the security arena.

Network security is a broad topic that can be addressed at many different levels within the OSI model.

- **Data Link layer, or media level.** This is where packet sniffing and encryption problems can occur.

- **Network or Protocol layer.** The point at which Internet Protocol (IP) packets and routing updates are controlled.

- **Application layer.** This is where, for example, host-level bugs become issues.

Because network security is such a broad topic, this chapter will not delve too deeply into any one area. Everyone concerned with this subject must be aware of how this subject is stretched across every network.

It is important that you realize that *every* networking equipment manufacturer, network protocol, user, and service provider has security problems. Consider two examples. First, with today's technologies, a cyber thief could put a PC running some type of sniffer software with a cellular telephone and modem on a circuit. This is probably easier than you think if you consider the miles and miles of cabling stretching across the United States that is physically accessible. The second most obvious network protocol example is SNMP. If you had the SNMP community string, every SNMP manageable device would allow the cyber thief read/write access. I recommend dealing with a vendor, such as Cisco, that has an open disclosure policy of identified and corrected security breaches so you can react accordingly. The alternative is a vendor that does not share holes in their equipment and smiles while saying the system is completely protected. That is probably the biggest misconception of many, as you are only protected until a cyber thief decides he wants access.

The following security breach and defense technique examples are excerpts from Cisco's Web page. If you require more detailed information regarding them, you should read them from the source. The information is provided here to illustrate the point that every aspect of networking has to be aware of security and its impact on your network and organization.

Vulnerabilities in Cisco CHAP Authentication

Challenge Handshake Authentication Protocol (CHAP) is a security feature supported on lines using PPP encapsulation that prevents unauthorized access. CHAP does not itself prevent unauthorized access; it merely identifies the remote end. The router or access server then determines whether that user is allowed access.

A serious security vulnerability (bug ID CSCdi91594) exists in PPP CHAP authentication in all "classic" Cisco IOS software versions. The vulnerability permits attackers with appropriate skills and knowledge to completely circumvent CHAP authentication. Other PPP authentication methods are not affected.

Network Impact

A moderately sophisticated programmer with appropriate knowledge can set up an unauthorized PPP connection to any system that is running vulnerable software and that depends on CHAP for authentication. To gain this unauthorized access, an attacker must have the following:

- Knowledge of the details of this vulnerability.

- Access to modifiable code (generally meaning source code) for a PPP/CHAP implementation and sufficient programming skill to make simple changes to that code. Note that such source code is *widely* available on the Internet.

- A modest amount of information about the configuration of the network to be attacked, including such things as usernames and IP addresses.

This vulnerability cannot be exploited by an attacker using an unmodified, properly functioning PPP/CHAP implementation; the attacker must make modifications to his or her software to exploit this vulnerability.

Considering the three "minimum requirements" for this breach of security to succeed, you can easily see how after the attacker is in, an experienced hacker or cyber thief can cost your organization lots of money.

TCP Loopback DoS Attack (land.c) and Cisco Devices

Somebody has released a program, known as land.c, that can be used to launch denial of service attacks against various TCP implementations. The program sends a TCP SYN packet (a connection initiation), giving the target host's address as both source and destination and using the same port on the target host as both source and destination.

Network Impact

All Cisco IOS/700 software systems that can be reached via TCP from distrusted hosts are affected. Classic Cisco IOS software systems that are running vulnerable versions and that can be reached via TCP from distrusted hosts are affected.

This vulnerability enables attackers to deny service to legitimate users and to administrators. Recovery might require physically visiting the affected hardware. Appropriate firewalls and some configuration workarounds can block this attack. Cisco has classified the potential results of this attack by level of vulnerability.

- Highly vulnerable releases might hang indefinitely, requiring hardware resets, when attacked.

- Moderately vulnerable releases will not accept any new TCP connections for about 30 seconds after receiving an attack packet, permitting denial of service to administrators and possibly to users, but will recover and will continue to forward packets.

- Largely invulnerable releases will continue to operate normally with negligible performance impact.

"Smurfing" Denial of Service (DoS) Attacks

The "smurf" attack, named after its exploit program, is the most recent in the category of network-level attacks against hosts. A perpetrator sends a large amount of ICMP echo (ping) traffic at broadcast addresses, all of which has a spoofed source address of a victim. If the routing device delivering traffic to those broadcast addresses performs an IP broadcast to the layer 2 broadcast function, most hosts on that IP network will take the ICMP echo request and reply to it with one echo reply each, multiplying the traffic by the number of hosts responding. On a multi-access broadcast network, there could potentially be hundreds of machines replying to each packet.

Currently, the providers/machines most commonly hit are Internet Relay Chat (IRC) servers and their providers. There are two parties affected by this attack:

- The intermediary (broadcast) devices (referred to as "bounce sites" in this document)

- The spoofed address target (referred to as the "victim" in this document), in which the victim is the target of a large amount of traffic that the bounce sites generate

Assume a switched network consisting of 100 hosts, and that the attacker has access to T1 circuit. The attacker sends, for example, a 768 kbps stream of ICMP echo (ping) packets, with a spoofed source address of the victim, to the broadcast address of the bounce site.

These ping packets hit the bounce site's broadcast network of 100 hosts. Each takes the packet and responds to it, creating 100 ping replies outbound. By multiplying the bandwidth, you see that 76.8 Mbps is used outbound from the bounce site after the traffic is multiplied. This is then sent to the victim (the spoofed source of the originating packets).

TCP SYN Denial of Service Attacks & Defense Strategies

When a normal TCP connection starts, a destination host receives a SYN (synchronize/start) packet from a source host and sends back a SYN ACK (synchronize acknowledge). The destination host must then hear an ACK (acknowledge) of the SYN ACK before the connection is established. This is referred to as the "TCP three-way handshake."

While waiting for the ACK to the SYN ACK, a connection queue of finite size on the destination host keeps track of connections waiting to be completed. This queue typically empties quickly since the ACK is expected to arrive a few milliseconds after the SYN ACK.

The TCP SYN attack exploits this design by having an attacking source host generate TCP SYN packets with random source addresses toward a victim host. The victim destination host sends a SYN ACK back to the random source address and adds an entry to the connection queue. Because the SYN ACK is destined for an incorrect or non-existent host, the last part of the "three-way handshake" is never completed and the entry remains in the connection queue until a timer expires, typically for about one minute. By generating phony TCP SYN packets from random IP addresses at a rapid rate, it is possible to fill up the connection queue and deny TCP services (such as e-mail, file transfer, or WWW) to legitimate users.

There is no easy way to trace the originator of the attack because the IP address of the source is forged. The external manifestations of the problem include inability to get e-mail, inability to accept connections to WWW or FTP services, or a large number of TCP connections on your host in the state SYN_RCVD.

Attacks on Network Devices & Defense Strategies

This section will discuss some of the better known attacks that can be made against network devices and how to defend against them.

Devices Behind Firewalls

The TCP SYN attack is characterized by an influx of SYN packets from random source IP addresses. Any device behind a firewall that stops inbound SYN packets is already protected from this mode of attack, and no further action is needed. Examples of firewalls include a Cisco Private Internet Exchange (PIX) Firewall and a Cisco router configured with access lists.

For examples of how to set up access lists on a Cisco router, please refer to the document *Increasing Security on IP Networks* (also available from the Cisco Fax-on-Demand service at 415-596-4408, Doc ID# 116).

Protecting Devices Offering Publicly Available Services (Mail Servers, Public Web Servers)

Preventing SYN attacks on devices behind firewalls from random IP addresses is relatively simple because you can use access lists to explicitly limit inbound access to a select few IP addresses. However, in the case of a public Web server or mail server facing the Internet, there is no way to determine which incoming IP source addresses are friendly and which are unfriendly. Therefore, there is no clear-cut defense against an attack from a random IP address. Several options are available to hosts:

- Increase the size of the connection queue (SYN ACK queue).

- Decrease the time out waiting for the three-way handshake.

- Employ vendor software patches to detect and circumvent the problem (if available).

You should contact your host vendor to see if they have created specific patches to address the TCP SYN ACK attack.

TIPS

Filtering IP addresses at the server is ineffective because an attacker can vary his IP address, and the address might or might not be the same as that of a legitimate host.

UDP Diagnostic Port Denial of Service Attacks

What is a UDP diagnostic port attack? A sender transmits a volume of requests for UDP diagnostic services on the router, which causes all CPU resources to be consumed servicing the phony requests. There is a potential denial of service attack at Internet service providers (ISPs) that targets network devices.

Network Impact of the UDP Diagnostic Port Attack

By default, the Cisco router has a series of diagnostic ports enabled for certain UDP and TCP services including echo, chargen, and discard. When a host attaches to those ports, a small amount of CPU is consumed to service these requests.

If a single attacking device sends a large barrage of requests with different, random phony source IP addresses, it is possible that the Cisco router can become overwhelmed and slow down or fail.

The external manifestation of the problem includes a process table full error message (%SYS-3 NOPROC) or a very high CPU utilization. The exec command show process will show a lot of processes with the same name, for example, "UDP Echo."

Defending Against Attacks Directly to Network Devices

Any network device that has both the UDP and TCP diagnostic services available should be protected by a firewall or at least have the services disabled. For a Cisco router, this can be accomplished by using the following global configuration commands:

```
no service udp-small-servers
no service tcp-small-servers
```

Cisco IOS Password Encryption

A non-Cisco source has recently released a new program to decrypt user passwords (and other passwords) in Cisco configuration files. The program will not decrypt passwords set with the enable secret command.

The unexpected concern that this program has caused among Cisco customers indicates that many customers are relying on Cisco password encryption for more security than it was designed to provide. This document explains the security model behind Cisco password encryption and the security limitations of that encryption.

Network Impact: User Passwords (VTY & Enable)

User passwords and most other passwords (*not* enable secret-encrypted commands) in Cisco IOS configuration files are encrypted using a scheme that's very weak by modern cryptographic standards.

Although Cisco does not distribute a decryption program, at least two different decryption programs for Cisco IOS passwords are available to the public on the Internet; the first public release of such a program of which Cisco is aware was in early 1995. Any amateur cryptographer would be expected to be able to create a new program with no more than a few hours work.

The scheme used by Cisco IOS for user passwords was never intended to resist a determined, intelligent attack; it was designed to avoid casual "over-the-shoulder" password theft. The threat model was someone reading a password from an administrator's screen. The scheme was never supposed to protect against someone conducting a determined analysis of the configuration file.

Because of the weak encryption algorithm, it has always been Cisco's position that customers should treat any configuration file containing passwords as sensitive information, the same way they would treat a clear text list of passwords.

Enable Secret Passwords

enable secret-encrypted passwords are hashed using the MD5 algorithm. As far as anyone at Cisco knows, it is impossible to recover an enable secret password based on the contents of a configuration file (other than by obvious dictionary attacks).

This applies only to passwords set with enable secret, and *not* to passwords set with enable password. Indeed, the strength of the encryption used is the only significant difference between the two commands.

Other Passwords

Almost all passwords and other authentication strings in Cisco IOS configuration files are encrypted using the weak, reversible scheme used for user passwords. To determine which scheme has been used to encrypt a specific password, check the digit preceding the encrypted string in the configuration file. If that digit is a 7, the password has been encrypted using the weak algorithm. If the digit is a 5, the password has been hashed using the stronger MD5 algorithm. For example, in the configuration:

```
enable secret 5 $1$iUjJ$cDZ03KKGh7mHfX2RSbDqP
```

the `enable secret`-encrypted password has been hashed with MD5, whereas in the command:

```
username jbash password 7 7362E590E1B1C041B1E124C0A2F2E206832752E1A01134D
```

the password has been encrypted using the weak reversible algorithm.

Will the Algorithm Be Changed?

Cisco has no immediate plans to support a stronger encryption algorithm for Cisco IOS user passwords. If Cisco should decide to introduce such a feature in the future, that feature will definitely impose an additional ongoing administrative burden on users who choose to take advantage of it.

It is not, in the general case, possible to switch user passwords over to the MD5-based algorithm used for `enable secret`, because MD5 is a one-way hash, and the password can't be recovered from the encrypted data at all. In order to support certain authentication protocols (notably CHAP), the system needs access to the clear text of user passwords and, therefore, must store them using a reversible algorithm.

Key management issues would make it a nontrivial task to switch over to a stronger reversible algorithm, such as DES. Although it would be easy to modify Cisco IOS to use DES to encrypt passwords, there would be no security advantage in doing so if all Cisco IOS systems used the same DES key. If different keys were used by different systems, an administrative burden would be introduced for all Cisco IOS network administrators, and portability of configuration files between systems would be damaged. Customer demand for stronger reversible password encryption has been small.

Assessing the Need for Security

As more users access the Internet, and as companies expand their networks, the challenge to provide security for internal networks becomes increasingly difficult. Companies must determine which areas of their internal networks they must protect, learn how to restrict user access to these areas, and determine which types of network services they should filter to prevent potential security breaches.

It should now be obvious that security must be a consideration at all levels of your network. Complacency is also something you should try to avoid when considering security. The rapidly advancing sophistication of technology means that your security measures are limited in the length of time they will be effective.

GOLDEN RULES OF DESIGNING A SECURE NETWORK

Security measures keep people honest in the same way that locks do. Cyber thieves by their very nature go after the least defended part of a network. Consider this analogy. In a neighborhood where 25 percent of the homes have home security systems, thieves will target the least defended homes (those without security systems) first. This section provides specific actions you can take to improve the security of your network whether you already have network security in place or are designing a new network.

Document Your Security Plan

This does not mean write down all the network passwords under your keyboard! Instead, as you go through this process of identifying and designing your network security you need to document your findings and resulting security actions. Having a written "living" security document is vital to proper implementation of your overall network security strategy. It will also help those that come after you understand why the network security was implemented and designed in such a way, so it can also be a learning tool for future network engineers. This document should *not* be publicly accessible.

Know Your Enemy

This statement refers specifically to cyber thieves who are either *attackers* or *intruders*. Consider who might want to circumvent your security measures, and identify their motivations. Determine what they might want to do and the damage that they could cause to your network. For example, does your organization deal in money, electronic commerce, or sensitive data? Any of these can be of value to a thief.

Security measures can never make it impossible for a user to perform unauthorized tasks with a computer system. They can only make performing unauthorized tasks harder. The goal is to make sure the network security controls are beyond the attacker's ability or motivation.

Count the Cost

Security measures usually reduce convenience, especially for sophisticated users. Security can delay work and create expensive administrative and educational overhead. It can use significant computing resources and require dedicated hardware. Just as in anything in life, nothing that is worth having is free; you must work for the results you want to receive.

When you design your security measures, understand their costs and weigh those costs against the potential benefits. To do that, you must understand the costs of the measures themselves and the likelihood of security breaches. If you incur security costs out of proportion to the actual dangers, you have done yourself a disservice. For example, very few organizations can actually justify having the extreme security measures found within the Department of Defenses (DOD) network. Yes it is effective, but at what cost?

Identify Your Assumptions

Every security system has underlying assumptions. For example, you might assume that your network is not tapped, or that attackers know less than you do, or that they are using standard software, or that a locked room is safe. All of these assumptions are most likely incorrect and could cause holes in your security policy. Be sure to examine and justify your assumptions. Any hidden assumption is a potential security hole.

A nice rule of thumb here is to be painfully honest concerning your network security requirements and remember that when assumptions are incomplete or not duly considered, it can cause disastrous consequences. Sometimes when you are identifying your assumptions you might find an area of concern within your network that has nothing to do with security, so this is truly a double-edged sword.

Control & Limit Your Secrets

Most security is based on and required by secrets. Passwords and encryption keys—SNMP community strings, for example—are secrets. Too often, though, the secrets are not really all that secret. The most important part of keeping secrets is knowing the areas you need to protect. What knowledge would enable someone to circumvent your system? You should jealously guard that knowledge and assume that everything else is known to your adversaries. The more secrets you have, the harder it will be to keep all of them. Security systems should be designed so that only a limited number of secrets need to be kept.

Remember Human Factors

Many security procedures fail because their designers do not consider how users will react to them. For example, because they can be difficult to remember, automatically generated "nonsense" passwords are often found written on the undersides of keyboards. For convenience, a "secure" door that leads to the system's only tape drive is sometimes propped open. For expediency, unauthorized modems are often connected to a network to avoid onerous dial-in security measures.

If your security measures interfere too much with the essential use of the system or network, those measures will be resisted and perhaps circumvented by resourceful users. To get compliance, you must make sure that users can get their work done, and you must sell your security measures to users. Users must understand and accept the need for security. Communication with users is essential here because if users understand the business reasons behind your security measures, they will be more open to accepting them. No matter how hard you try, there will be users who will still try to *get around* your security.

Any user can compromise system security, at least to some degree. Passwords, for instance, can often be found simply by calling legitimate users on the telephone, claiming to be a system administrator, and asking for them. If your users understand security issues, and if they understand the reasons for your security measures, they are far less likely to make an intruder's job easier.

At a minimum, users should be taught never to release passwords or other secrets over unsecured telephone lines (especially cellular telephones) or electronic mail (e-mail). Users should be wary of questions asked by people who call them on the telephone. Some companies have implemented formalized network security training for their employees; that is, employees are not allowed access to the Internet until they have completed a formal training program. This is helpful in raising awareness in a user community, and it should be reinforced with a written security policy for your organization that is accessible to every user. One last point to make is that you should never violate your own security procedures, no matter how tempting it is to do so!

Know Your Weaknesses

Every security system has vulnerabilities, and identifying them is no place for egos but rather honesty and directness. It is sometimes very helpful to get another set of eyes to assist you in reviewing the network for weaknesses.

You should be able to understand your system's weak points and know how they could be exploited. You should also know the areas that present the largest danger and prevent access to them immediately. Understanding the weak points in your network is the first step toward turning them into secure areas.

Limit the Scope of Access

You should create appropriate barriers inside your network so that if intruders access one part of the network, they do not automatically have access to the rest of the network.

As with many things, the security of a network is only as good as the weakest security level of any single device in the system. Having a layered approach to security will certainly slow down an intruder and allow his or her detection. Having a nice big lock is good, but if that lock is your only line of defense, then you might want to consider adding motion sensors, a dog, outside lights, a home security system, and nosey neighbors! A rather simplistic analogy, but my point is that it is always harder to be a criminal when there are many barriers to overcome.

Understand Your Environment

Understanding how your system normally functions, knowing what is expected and what is unexpected, and being familiar with how devices are usually used, will help you to detect security problems. Noticing unusual events can help you to catch intruders before they can damage the system. Auditing tools can help you to detect those unusual events.

Auditing tools are very useful, though you will also want to ensure that there are methods for you to receive alarms when there is an attempt to violate or bypass the security measures in place. The thought here is that it is better to know it is happening *before* you lose something than to have to go back and audit the crime; it's an ounce of prevention!

Limit Your Trust

You should know exactly which software or hardware you rely on, and your security system should not have to rely upon the assumption that all software is bug-free. Learn from history by not reliving it, and remember to question everything!

Remember Physical Security

Physical access to a workstation, server, or router usually gives a sufficiently sophisticated user total control over that device. Physical access to a network link usually enables a person to tap that link, jam it, or inject traffic into it. It makes no sense to install complicated software security measures when access to the hardware is not controlled.

Security Is Persuasive

Almost any change you make in your system might have security effects. This is especially true when new services are created. Network engineers, system administrators, programmers, and users should consider the security implications of every change they make. Understanding the security implications of a change is something that takes practice. It requires lateral thinking and a willingness to explore every way in which a service could potentially be manipulated. Intelligent changes are good and can be judged accordingly; however, quick or ill-considered changes can often result in severe security problems.

Additional Resources on Network Security

Now that you know security should be a serious part of your network at all levels, and you know some of the Golden Rules of designing a secure network, you might need some additional information regarding the bane of "cyber thieves"—"cyber cops." An article entitled "cyber cops" in the March 10, 1997 issue of *Forbes Magazine* discussed how a Bill Gates-like college student decided the best way to stop cyber thieves was to show companies where their security holes were. A completely logical move, this resulted in a new company called Internet Security Systems (ISS) whose premise is to stage a break-in with their software and then help plug the holes. If you are interested in finding out more and using their evaluation software, you can check out their home page at `http://www.iss.net`, or you can reach them at 1 (800) 776-2362.

SECURING YOUR OSPF NETWORK

There are many ways to secure your network. The sections that follow discuss the easiest and most basic ways to do this. Controlling access to network equipment is the simplest. There are many levels of security, although understanding how to encrypt data and use OSPF authentication within your network should become familiar to you as well.

Controlling Access to Network Equipment

It is important to control access to all of your network equipment. Most equipment manufacturers now design their equipment with multiple levels of passwords, typically read and then read/write. This is probably the easiest and most basic step in securing your network.

This section will discuss some of the techniques and considerations you must take regarding Cisco router access and the operation of their passwords. You can control access to the router using the following methods:

- Console port access
- Telnet access (non-privileged & privileged)
- Terminal Access Controller Access Control System (TACACS)
- Simple Network Management Protocol (SNMP) access

- Controlling access to servers that contain configuration files

- Privilege level security

You can secure the first three of these methods by employing features within the router software. For each method, you can permit nonprivileged access and privileged access for a user (or group of users). Nonprivileged access allows users to monitor the router but not to configure the router. Privileged access enables the user to fully configure the router.

For console port and Telnet access, you can set up two types of passwords. The first type of password, the login password, allows the user nonprivileged access to the router. After accessing the router, the user can enter privileged mode by entering the `enable` command and the proper password. Privileged mode provides the user with full configuration capabilities.

SNMP access allows you to set up different SNMP community strings for both nonprivileged and privileged access. Nonprivileged access allows users on a host to send the router SNMP `get-request` and SNMP `get-next-request` messages. These messages are used for gathering statistics from the router. Privileged access allows users on a host to send the router SNMP `set-request` messages in order to make changes to the router's configurations and operational state.

Increasing SNMP Security

It is generally understood and agreed upon that in the networking arena, SNMP is not as secure as it can be. In networks where security is extremely important, you can also implement an access list on SNMP to limit who can access the device in question via SNMP. This can be accomplished as shown in the example that follows.

This example permits the host IP addresses of `10.1.3.5` and `10.5.2.53` to access SNMP on the device. You do this by adding the `access-list` number on the end of the `snmp-server` community command.

```
access-list 1 permit 10.1.3.5
access-list 1 permit 10.5.2.53
snmp-server community cisco5 1
```

Console Port Access

A console is a terminal (PC) attached directly to the router via the console port. Security is applied to the console by asking users to authenticate themselves via passwords. By default, there are no passwords associated with console access.

Telnet: Nonprivileged Mode Password (VTY)

Each Telnet port on the router is known as a *virtual terminal*. There is a maximum of five virtual terminal (VTY) ports on the router, allowing five concurrent Telnet sessions. (The communication server provides more VTY ports.) On the router, the virtual terminal ports are numbered 0 through 4. You can set up nonprivileged password for Telnet access via the virtual terminal ports with the following configuration commands. You configure a password for nonprivileged mode (also known as VTY) by entering the following commands in the router's configuration file. Remember passwords are case sensitive. In the following example, the password is ospf4U:

```
line console 0
login
password ospf4U
```

When you log in to the router, the router login prompt is provided:

```
User Access Verification
Password:
```

You must enter the password ospf4U to gain nonprivileged access to the router. The router response is as follows:

```
OSPF_Router>
```

Nonprivileged mode is signified on the router by the > prompt. At this point, you can enter a variety of commands to view statistics on the router, but you cannot change the configuration of the router.

NOTES

When considering what password format to use—all letters or numbers—it is best to make your passwords an alphanumeric combination with at least one capital letter. Remember that not all cyber thieves are outside your network, and this makes your passwords tougher to crack or guess. For example, the password ospf4U combines all of these suggestions!

Telnet: Privileged Mode Password (enable or exec)

Configure a password for privileged mode—enable or exec—by entering the following commands in the router's configuration file. In the following example, the password is MCI-good:

```
enable-password MCI-good
```

To access privileged mode, enter the following command:

```
OSPF_Router> enable
Password:
```

Enter the password MCI-good to gain privileged access to the router. The router responds as follows:

```
OSPF_Router#
```

Privileged mode is signified by the # prompt. In privileged mode (also known as enable mode), you can enter all commands to view statistics and configure the router.

Session Timeouts

Setting the login and enable passwords might not provide enough security in some cases. The timeout for an unattended console (by default 10 minutes) provides an additional security measure. If the console is left unattended in privileged mode, any user can modify the router's configuration. You can change the login timeout via the command exec-timeout *mm* *ss* where *mm* is minutes and *ss* is seconds. The following commands change the timeout to 1 minute and 30 seconds:

```
line console 0
exec-timeout 1 30
line vty 0 4
exec-timeout 1 30
line aux 0
exec-timeout 1 30
```

This command is useful not only from a security standpoint but from a network management standpoint as well. Let me explain. If a Telnet session is not closed properly, the router can still consider that session to be open although no activity is occurring. Large enterprise networks have this happen enough, and either the router will need to be rebooted or someone will have to gain access via the console port to break these "ghost" sessions. However, if you configure all ports (console, line vty, and aux) with this command, after 1 minute and 30 seconds (as specified in the preceding example), the router will disconnect the session for inactivity.

Password Encryption

Because protocol analyzers can examine packets (and read passwords), you can increase access security by configuring the Cisco IOS software to encrypt passwords. Encryption prevents the password from being readable in the configuration file.

All passwords on the router are visible via the write terminal and show configuration privileged mode commands. If you have access to privileged mode on the router, you can view all passwords in clear text by default. There is a way to hide clear text passwords. The command service password-encryption stores passwords in an encrypted manner, so that anyone performing a write terminal or show configuration will not be able to determine the clear text password. However, if you forget the password, regaining access to the router requires you to have physical access to the router.

TIPS

Although password encryption is helpful, it can be, and has been, compromised and thus should not be your only network security strategy.

The actual encryption process occurs when the current configuration is written or when a password is configured. Password encryption is applied to all passwords, including authentication key passwords, the privileged command password, console and virtual terminal line access passwords, and both OSPF and BGP neighbor passwords. The service password-encryption command is primarily used for keeping unauthorized individuals from viewing your password in your configuration file.

Restricting Telnet Access to Particular IP Addresses

If you want to allow only certain IP addresses to use Telnet to access the router, you must use the access-class command. The command access-class *nn* in defines an access list (from 1–99) that allows access to the virtual terminal lines on the router. The following configuration commands allow incoming Telnet access to the router only from hosts on network 192.85.55.0:

```
access-list 12 permit 192.85.55.0 0.0.0.255
line vty 0 4
access-class 12 in
```

Terminal Access Controller Access Control System (TACACS)

Nonprivileged (VTY) and privileged (enable) mode passwords are global and apply to every user accessing the router either from the console port or from a Telnet session. As an alternative, the Terminal Access Controller Access Control System (TACACS) provides a way to validate every user on an individual basis before he or she can gain access to the router or communication server.

TACACS was derived from the United States Department of Defense and is described in Request For Comments (RFC) 1492. TACACS is used to allow finer control over who can access the router in VTY and enable modes.

When TACACS is enabled in a router, the router will prompt the user for a username and a password. Then the router queries a TACACS server to see if the user provided the correct password. A TACACS server typically runs on a UNIX workstation. Public domain TACACS servers can be obtained via anonymous ftp to `ftp.cisco.com` in the `/pub` directory. Use the `/pub/README` file to find the file name. A fully supported TACACS server is bundled with CiscoWorks Version 3.

The configuration command `tacacs-server host` specifies which UNIX host running a TACACS server will validate requests sent by the router. You can enter the `tacacs-server host` command several times to specify multiple TACACS server hosts that a router can validate users against. This use of multiple servers is effective in case a single server fails. In that event, you could potentially be locked out of your network until the server is restored.

Nonprivileged Access

As previously discussed, if all servers are unavailable, you could be locked out of the router. In that event, the configuration command

```
tacacs-server last-resort [password ¦ succeed]
```

enables you to determine whether to allow a user to log in to the router with no password (succeed keyword) or to force the user to supply the standard login password (password keyword).

The following commands specify a TACACS server and allow a login to succeed if the server is down or unreachable:

```
tacacs-server host 129.140.1.1
tacacs-server last-resort succeed
```

To force users who access the router via Telnet to authenticate themselves using TACACS, enter the following configuration commands:

```
line vty 0 4
login tacacs
```

Privileged Access

This method of password checking can also be applied to the privileged mode password with the `enable use-tacacs` command. If all servers are unavailable, you could be locked out of the router. In that event, the configuration command `enable last-resort [succeed ¦ password]` enables you to determine whether to allow a user to log in to the router with no password (`succeed` keyword) or to force the user to supply the enable password (`password` keyword). There are significant risks to using the `succeed` keyword. If you use the `enable use-tacacs` command, you must also specify the `tacacs-server authenticate enable` command.

The `tacacs-server extended` command enables a Cisco device to run in extended TACACS mode. The UNIX system must be running the extended TACACS daemon, which can be obtained via anonymous ftp to `ftp.cisco.com`. The file name is `xtacacsd.shar`. This daemon enables communication servers and other equipment to talk to the UNIX system and update an audit trail with information on port usage, accounting data, or any other information the device can send.

The command `username <user> password [0 ¦ 7] <password>` enables you to store and maintain a list of users and their passwords on a Cisco device instead of on a TACACS server. The number 0 stores the password in clear text in the configuration file. The number 7 stores the password in an encrypted format. If you do not have a TACACS server and still want to authenticate users on an individual basis, you can set up users with the following configuration commands:

```
username rose password 7 rose-pass
username rebekah password 7 rebekah-pass
```

The two users, Rose and Rebekah, will be authenticated via passwords that are stored in encrypted format.

Simple Network Management Protocol (SNMP) Access

SNMP is another method you can use to access your network equipment. With SNMP, you can gather statistics or configure the router. In fact, you could even configure the router to start an OSPF routing process! SNMP is also very useful to help you gather statistics with **GETREQUEST** and **GETNEXTREQUEST** messages and configure routers with **SETREQUEST** messages. Each of these SNMP messages has a community string that is a clear text password sent in every packet between a management station and the router (which contains an SNMP agent). The SNMP community string is used to authenticate messages sent between the manager and agent. Only when the manager sends a message with the correct community string will the agent respond.

The SNMP agent on the router allows you to configure different community strings for nonprivileged and privileged access. You configure community strings on the router via the following configuration command:

```
snmp-server community <string> [RO | RW] [access-list]
```

Unfortunately, SNMP community strings are sent on the network in clear text ASCII. Thus, anyone who has the ability to capture a packet on the network can discover the community string. This might allow unauthorized users to query or modify routers via SNMP. For this reason, using the `no snmp-server trap-authentication` command might prevent intruders from using trap messages (sent between SNMP managers and agents) to discover community strings.

The Internet community, recognizing this problem, greatly enhanced the security of SNMP version 2 (SNMPv2) as described in RFC 1446. SNMPv2 uses the MD5 algorithm to authenticate communications between an SNMP server and agent. MD5 verifies the integrity of the communications, authenticates the origin, and checks for timeliness. Further, SNMPv2 can use the Data Encryption Standard (DES) for encrypting information.

Nonprivileged Mode (Read Only)

Use the RO keyword of the `snmp-server community` command to provide nonprivileged access to your routers via SNMP. The following configuration command sets the agent in the router to allow only SNMP **GETREQUEST** and **GETNEXTREQUEST** messages that are sent with the community string "public":

```
snmp-server community public RO 1
```

You can also specify a list of IP addresses that are allowed to send messages to the router using the `access-list` option with the `snmp-server community` command. In the following configuration example, only hosts 1.1.1.1 and 2.2.2.2 are allowed nonprivileged mode SNMP access to the router:

```
access-list 1 permit 1.1.1.1
access-list 1 permit 2.2.2.2
snmp-server community public RO 1
```

Privileged Mode (Read/Write)

Use the RW keyword of the `snmp-server community` command to provide privileged access to your routers via SNMP. The following configuration command sets the agent in the router to allow only SNMP **SETREQUEST** messages sent with the community string "private":

```
snmp-server community private RW 1
```

You can also specify a list of IP addresses that are allowed to send messages to the router by using the access-list option of the snmp-server community command. In the following configuration example, only hosts 5.5.5.5 and 6.6.6.6 are allowed privileged mode SNMP access to the router:

```
access-list 1 permit 5.5.5.5
access-list 1 permit 6.6.6.6
snmp-server community private RW 1
```

Backup Configuration Files

If a router regularly downloads configuration files from or to a Trivial File Transfer Protocol (TFTP) or Maintenance Operations Protocol (MOP) server, anyone who can access the server can modify the router configuration files stored on the server.

This can be a very serious security breach if this server is not also protected in your security plan. It is absolutely essential in today's Enterprise networks to at least backup your router configuration files. Therefore, because this function is so essential to the safe and continued operation of a network, it must also be protected.

Using Banners to Set Up Unauthorized Use Notifications

It is also wise to use the motd banner exec global configuration command to provide messages and unauthorized use notifications, which will be displayed on all new connections. For example, on any network equipment, you could enter the following message:

```
OSPF_Router (config)# motd banner
*********************************************************************
*               ! ! ! ! ! ! ! WARNING ! ! ! ! ! ! ! !              *
* THIS SYSTEM IS OWNED BY <company name>. UNAUTHORIZED ACCESS AND USE OF *
*    THIS SYSTEM IS NOT PERMITTED BY <company name> AND IS STRICTLY  *
*     PROHIBITED BY <company name> SECURITY POLICIES, REGULATIONS,   *
*                   STATE AND FEDERAL LAWS.                         *
*                                                                   *
*   UNAUTHORIZED USERS ARE SUBJECT TO CRIMINAL AND CIVIL PENALTIES  *
*       AS WELL AS COMPANY-INITIATED DISCIPLINARY PROCEEDINGS.      *
*********************************************************************
```

A message-of-the-day banner like this in your network equipment is effective. It pretty much covers all the possible consequences and goes so far as to state that there will be consequences based upon user's actions.

Privilege Level Security

This feature was introduced by Cisco in release 10.3 and allows for the establishment of 16 levels of access within the router. Default privilege levels are: 1=user and 15=privileged.

Privilege levels can be used a variety of ways within a router:

- They can be established for both commands and incoming terminal lines.
- Specialized enable passwords can be linked to privilege levels.
- They can be assigned to specialized exec and configure commands to control access.

Privilege Level Command Modes

There are a variety of different command modes that you can implement using privilege levels. All of them are global configuration commands except "exec".

configuration	line
controller	map-class
exec	map-list
hub	route-map
interface	router
ipx-router	

Privilege Level Configuration Example

To associate a privilege level with a specific command, you need to configure the router as shown here:

```
OSPF_Router(config)#privilege exec level 6 ping
OSPF_Router(config)#privilege exec level 6 clear
```

The preceding two commands, if applied to a router's VTY port (the ones you Telnet to), allow anyone accessing the router using just the vty command to perform extended pings and a variety of clear commands (that is counters, interface, router, and so forth).

To establish a specific enable password for a privilege level, you enter the following:

```
OSPF_Router(config)# enable password level <level #> <password>
```

To associate a privilege level with a terminal line, you enter the following:

```
OSPF_Router(config)# line vty 0 4
OSPF_Router(config-line)# privilege level <level #>
```

Network Data Encryption

To safeguard your network data, Cisco provides network data encryption and router authentication services. This section briefly discusses how this is done and how it can benefit your network. Further discussion on the proper techniques and process involved in deploying this feature in your network is beyond the scope of this book. At the end of this section, additional resources will be provided in case you need further reading on this subject.

Network data encryption is provided at the IP packet level. IP packet encryption prevents eavesdroppers from reading the data that is being transmitted. When IP packet encryption is used, IP packets can be seen during transmission, but the IP packet contents (payload) cannot be read. Specifically, the IP header and upper-layer protocol (TCP or UDP) headers are not encrypted, but all payload data within the TCP or UDP packet will be encrypted and therefore not readable during transmission.

The actual encryption and decryption of IP packets occurs only at routers that you configure for network data encryption with router authentication. Such routers are considered to be *peer encrypting routers* (or simply *peer routers*). Intermediate hops do not participate in encryption/decryption.

Typically, when an IP packet is initially generated at a host, it is unencrypted ("cleartext"). This occurs on a secured (internal) portion of your network. Then when the transmitted IP packet passes through an encrypting router, the router determines if the packet should be encrypted. If the packet is encrypted, the encrypted packet will travel through the unsecured network portion (usually an external network such as the Internet) until it reaches the remote peer encrypting router. At this point, the encrypted IP packet is decrypted and forwarded to the destination host as cleartext.

NOTES

It is important to remember that by requiring the routers to encrypt data, you are adding overhead to the routers' processing load. You will want to test this first to ensure that the routers in your network can handle the added load.

Router authentication enables peer encrypting routers to positively identify the source of incoming encrypted data. This means that attackers cannot forge transmitted data or tamper with transmitted data without detection. Router authentication occurs between peer routers each time a new *encrypted session* is established. An encrypted session is established each time an encrypting router receives an IP packet that should be encrypted (unless an encrypted session is already occurring at that time).

TIPS

The use of data encryption is applied to your data only after it leaves the router because that is the device applying the encryption. This is important to mention because the data will travel from the host to the router in an unsecured format.

To provide IP packet encryption with router authentication, Cisco implements the following standards: the Digital Signature Standard (DSS), the Diffie-Hellman (DH) public key algorithm, and the Data Encryption Standard (DES). DSS is used in router authentication. The DH algorithm and DES standard are used to initiate and conduct encrypted communication sessions between participating routers.

Additional Resources on Network Data Encryption

This section was provided to make you aware that it is possible to encrypt all the data flowing within your network. This is not to say that you should immediately deploy data encryption or that this is the best way to protect your data, only that it is possible.

The next section discusses how OSPF can encrypt routing updates, which does not encrypt the network's data. If you require further information on this subject, you should consult the *Cisco IOS Security* by Cisco Systems, Inc.

OSPF Neighbor Router Authentication

OSPF incorporates a minimal amount of security already within its design. That sounds contradictory, how can a protocol be designed with security, yet it be minimal? Simply put, when OSPF was designed, the necessary fields required for security were included in the design of OSPF's packets. Nevertheless, the security included within OSPF only protects its LSAs, thus protecting and maintaining the integrity of your networks routing tables. OSPF security is minimal because it does not protect the data flowing across the network but only how OSPF routers know to route it. This security was designed to protect only the integrity of the OSPF routing domain. You can prevent any OSPF router from receiving fraudulent route updates by configuring this type of security known as *neighbor router authentication.*

This section describes neighbor router authentication as part of a total security plan and explains what neighbor router authentication is, how it works, and why you should use it to increase your overall network security. There are several topics that are of importance regarding this issue:

- Benefits of neighbor authentication
- Conditions for deploying OSPF neighbor authentication
- How neighbor authentication works

There are several different ways that you can deploy this type of security within your OSPF network. The first way is by assigning the same OSPF key network-wide. The second is to assign a different key for every link within the network.

NOTES

This section refers to neighbor router authentication as "neighbor authentication." Neighbor router authentication is also sometimes called "route authentication."

Benefits of OSPF Neighbor Authentication

When configured, neighbor authentication occurs whenever routing updates are exchanged between neighboring OSPF routers. This authentication ensures that a router receives reliable routing information from a trusted source.

Without neighbor authentication, unauthorized or deliberately malicious routing updates could compromise the security of your network traffic. A security compromise could occur if an unfriendly party diverts or analyzes your network traffic.

For example, an unauthorized router could send a fictitious routing update to convince your router to send traffic to an incorrect destination. This diverted traffic could be analyzed to learn confidential information of your organization, or it could merely be used to disrupt your organization's ability to effectively communicate using the network. Neighbor authentication prevents any such fraudulent route updates from being received by your router.

Conditions for Deploying OSPF Neighbor Authentication

You should configure any router for OSPF neighbor authentication if that router meets any or all of these conditions:

- It is conceivable that the router might receive a false route update.
- If the router were to receive a false route update, your network might be compromised.
- You deem it necessary as part of your network security plan.

Remember that if you configure a router for neighbor authentication, you also need to configure the neighbor router for neighbor authentication.

How Neighbor Authentication Works

When neighbor authentication has been configured on a router, the router authenticates the source of each routing update packet that it receives. This is accomplished by the exchange of an authenticating key (sometimes referred to as a password) that is known to both the sending and the receiving router.

There are two types of neighbor authentication used: plaintext authentication and Message Digest Algorithm Version 5 (MD5) authentication. Both forms work in the same way, with the exception being that MD5 sends a "message digest" instead of the authenticating key itself. The message digest is created using the key and a message, but the key itself is not sent, preventing it from being read while it is being transmitted. Plaintext authentication sends the authenticating key itself over the wire.

NOTES

Note that plaintext authentication is not recommended for use as part of your security strategy. Its primary use is to avoid accidental changes to the routing infrastructure. Using MD5 authentication, however, is a recommended security practice.

TIPS

As with all keys, passwords, and other security secrets, it is imperative that you closely guard the authenticating keys used in neighbor authentication. The security benefits of this feature are reliant upon your keeping all authenticating keys confident. Also, when performing router management tasks via Simple Network Management Protocol (SNMP), do not ignore the risk associated with sending keys using non-encrypted SNMP.

Plaintext Authentication

Each participating neighbor router must share an authenticating key. This key is specified at each router during configuration. Multiple keys can be specified with OSPF; each key must then be identified by a key number. For example, you can have a different key for each WAN interface on a router running OSPF. The caveat is that the neighbor router off each interface must have a matching key configured on the receiving interface as shown in Figure 10-1.

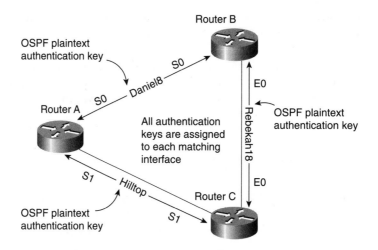

Figure 10–1
OSPF plaintext authentication.

In general, when a routing update is sent, the following authentication sequence occurs:

1. A router sends a routing update with an authentication key within an LSA.

2. The receiving (neighbor) router checks the received key against the same key stored in its own memory.

3. If the two keys match, the receiving router accepts the routing update packet. If the two keys do not match, the routing update packet is rejected.

MD5 Authentication

MD5 authentication works similarly to plaintext authentication, except that the key is never sent over the wire. Instead, the router uses the MD5 algorithm to produce a "message digest" of the key (also called a "hash"). The message digest is then sent instead of the key itself. This ensures that nobody can eavesdrop on the line and learn keys during transmission.

CONFIGURING TRAFFIC FILTERS

This section describes how to use traffic filters (also known as access lists) at your router to control network access. This is an important feature found within many routers. Filters will enable you to deploy an added layer of network security within your network and gain the benefits of a layered secure network.

Traffic filters enable you to control whether router traffic is forwarded or blocked at the router's interfaces. You should use traffic filters to provide a basic level of security for accessing your network. If you do not configure traffic filters on your router, all traffic passing through the router could be allowed onto all parts of your network.

By setting up traffic filters at your router, you can control which traffic enters or leaves your network. Traffic filters are commonly used in firewalls. Typically, a router configured for traffic filtering is positioned between your internal network and an external network such as the Internet. Using traffic filtering routers enables you to control what traffic is allowed onto your internal network. By combining the routers' filtering capabilities with that of a firewall, you can increase the security found in your network.

TIPS

If you are using filters in firewalls, then you should always have filters applied to your router as well. This decreases the likelihood that a cyber thief will gain access to your network.

Traffic filtering services on Cisco devices are provided by access lists (also called "filters"). Access lists must be defined on a per-protocol basis. In other words, you should define access lists for every protocol enabled on an interface if you want to control traffic flow for that protocol. This section will cover the following topics:

- Standard access lists
- Lock-and-key security (with dynamic access lists)

The first section describes standard static access lists, which are the most commonly used type of access lists. Static access lists should be used with each routed protocol that you have configured for router interfaces. Lock-and-key security, available only for IP traffic, provides additional security functions.

Access Lists

Access lists can be used for many purposes. For example, access lists can be used to:

- Control the transmission of packets on an interface
- Control virtual terminal line access
- Restrict contents of routing updates

Access lists can be used for these and other purposes. *However*, not all uses are recommended as specific security measures. Only the first listed use, controlling packet transmission, is recommended as a valid security measure. The following sections describe how to use access lists to control packet transmission.

Configuring Access Lists for Specific Protocols

To control packet transmission for a given protocol, you must configure an access list for that protocol. Table 10-1 identifies the protocols for which you can configure access lists.

TIPS

You should consider configuring access lists for each protocol that you have configured for an interface. Otherwise, the security is only partially applied to each interface within your network.

You must identify every access list by either a name or a number. You assign this name or number to each access list when you define the access list. Access lists of certain protocols must be identified by names, and access lists of other protocols must be identified by numbers. Some protocols can be identified by either names or numbers. When a number is used to identify an access list, the number must be within the specific range of numbers that is valid for the protocol.

Table 10-1 lists protocols that use access lists specified by numbers, and also includes the range of access list numbers that is valid for each protocol. Entries in *italics* indicate protocols for which you have the option of identifying access lists by names.

Table 10-1 *Protocols with access lists by range*

Protocol	Range
IP	*1–99*
Standard VINES	1–100
Extended IP	*100–199*
Extended VINES	101–200
Ethernet type code	200–299
Transparent bridging (protocol type)	200–299
Source-route bridging (protocol type)	*200–299*
Simple VINES	201–300
DECnet and extended DECnet	300–399
XNS	400–499
Extended XNS	500–599
AppleTalk	600–699
Ethernet address	700–799
Source-route bridging (vendor code)	700–799
Transparent bridging (vendor code)	700–799
IPX	*800–899*
Extended IPX	900–999
IPX SAP	1000–1099
Extended transparent bridging	1100–1199

Although each protocol has its own set of specific tasks and rules required for you to provide traffic filtering, in general, most protocols require at least two steps to be accomplished. The first step is to create an access list definition, and the second step is to apply the access list to an interface.

TIPS

Some protocols refer to access lists as "filters," and some protocols refer to the act of applying the access lists to interfaces as "filtering."

Creating Access Lists

Access list definitions provide a set of criteria that are applied to each packet that is processed by the router. The router decides whether to forward or block each packet based on whether or not the packet matches the access list criteria.

Typical criteria defined in access lists are packet source addresses, packet destination addresses, or upper-layer protocol of the packet. However, each protocol has its own specific set of criteria that can be defined.

For a given access list, you define each criteria in separate access list statements. These statements specify whether to block or forward packets that match the criteria listed. An access list, then, is the sum of individual statements that all share the same identifying name or number.

TIPS

Each additional access list statement that you enter is appended to the end of the access list statements. Also, you cannot delete individual statements after they have been created. You can only delete an entire access list.

The order of access list statements is important. When the router is deciding whether to forward or block a packet, the Cisco IOS software tests the packet against each criteria statement in the order the statements were created. After a match is found, no more criteria statements are checked.

If you create a criteria statement that explicitly permits all traffic, no statements added later will ever be checked. If you need additional statements, you must delete the access list and retype it with the new entries. When entering or modifying access lists, it is strongly suggested that you do not modify or alter them on-the-fly. You can design them on a TFTP server, in a word processor, or on paper. This author also recommends that you do not save the changes to the router until you are sure the desired security is adequately working. This will allow you a quick and easy back-out plan in case of errors.

At the end of every access list is an implied "deny all traffic" criteria statement. Therefore, if a packet does not match any of your criteria statements, the packet will be blocked.

Applying Access Lists to Interfaces

You can apply only one access list to an interface for a given protocol. With most protocols, you can apply access lists to interfaces as either inbound or outbound. If the access list is inbound, when the router receives a packet, the Cisco IOS software checks the access list's criteria statements for a match. If the packet is permitted, the software continues to process the packet. If the packet is denied, the software discards the packet.

If the access list is outbound, after receiving and routing a packet to the outbound interface, the software checks the access list's criteria statements for a match. If the packet is permitted, the software transmits the packet. If the packet is denied, the software discards the packet.

TIPS

For most protocols, if you define an inbound access list for traffic filtering, you should include explicit access list criteria statements to permit routing updates. If you do not, you might effectively lose communication from the interface when routing updates are blocked by the implicit "deny all traffic" statement at the end of the access list.

Additional Resources on Access Lists

The guidelines discussed previously apply, in general, to all protocols. However, the specific guidelines for creating access lists and applying them to interfaces vary from protocol to protocol. See the appropriate protocol-specific chapters in the Cisco IOS configuration guides and command references for detailed task information on each protocol-specific access list.

Lock-and-Key Security (Dynamic Access Lists)

To authorize remote access to local services, a common security solution is to create access lists as discussed previously. However, standard and static extended access lists have the following limitations:

- They can create the opportunity for break-ins by network hackers.

- They are difficult to manage in a large internetwork.

- They require the router to do excess processing, depending on entries in the access list.

- They do not offer a challenge mechanism to authenticate individual users.

An improved security solution is the lock-and-key access feature, which is available only with IP extended access lists. Lock-and-key access enables you to set up dynamic access lists that grant access per user to a specific source/destination host through a user authentication process. You can allow user access through a firewall dynamically, without compromising security restrictions.

TIPS

Caution: Enhancements to the `access-list` command are backward compatible; migrating from releases prior to Cisco IOS Release 11.1 converts your access lists automatically. However, releases prior to Cisco IOS Release 11.1 are not upwardly compatible with these enhancements. Therefore, if you save an access list with these images and then use software prior to Cisco IOS Release 11.1, the resulting access list will not be interpreted correctly. *This could cause severe security problems.* Save your old configuration files before booting these images.

In Cisco IOS Release 11.1 software, lock-and-key access is dependent on Telnet. Standard Telnet is the required application on the host platform that activates the authentication process.

Implementation Considerations of Lock-and-Key Access

Because lock-and-key access introduces a potential pathway through your network firewall, you need to evaluate the following serious considerations:

- *Primary consideration is dynamic access.* With dynamic access, there is the possibility that an unauthorized host, spoofing your authenticated address, can gain access behind the firewall. Lock-and-key access does not allow the address spoofing problem. The problem is identified here only as a concern to the user.

- *Performance is affected in the following two situations:*

  o Each dynamic access list forces an access-list rebuild on the silicon switching engine (SSE). This causes the SSE switching path to slow down momentarily.

  o Dynamic access lists require the idle timeout facility (even if the timeout is left to default) and, therefore, cannot be SSE switched. These entries must be handled in the protocol fast-switching path.

- *Pay close attention to the border router configurations.* Remote users create access list entries on the border router. The access list will grow and shrink dynamically. Entries are dynamically removed from the list after either the idle-timeout or max-timeout period expires. Large access lists degrade packet switching performance.

TIPS

Caution: Lock-and-key access allows an external event to create an opening in the firewall. After this opening exists, the router is susceptible to source address spoofing. To prevent this, you need to provide encryption support using IP encryption with authentication or encryption. This issue is discussed further in this section. Spoofing is a problem with all existing access lists. Lock-and-key access does not address this problem.

Here are two examples of when you might use lock-and-key access:

- When you want a remote host to be able to access a host in your internetwork via the Internet. Lock-and-key access limits access beyond your firewall on an individual host or net basis.

- When you want a subset of hosts on a network to access a host on a remote network protected by a firewall. With lock-and-key access, you can enable only a desired set of hosts to gain access by having them authenticate through a TACACS+ server.

The following process describes the lock-and-key access operation:

1. A user opens a Telnet session to a border router configured for lock-and-key access.

2. The Cisco IOS software receives the Telnet packet and performs a user authentication process. The user must pass authentication before access is allowed. The authentication process can be done by the router or a central access server such as a TACACS+ or a Radius server.

TIPS

It is highly recommended that you use the TACACS+ server for your authentication query process. TACACS+ provides authentication, authorization, and accounting services. It also provides protocol support, protocol specification, and a centralized security database.

3. When the user passes authentication, the software creates a temporary entry in the dynamic access list. The temporary entry inherits the attributes of the main dynamic access list. You can limit the range of networks to which the user is given temporary access.

4. The user exchanges data through the firewall and then logs out.

5. The software deletes the temporary access list entry when a configured timeout is reached or when the system administrator manually clears it. The timeout can either be an idle timeout or an absolute timeout.

TIPS

When the user terminates a session, the temporary access list entry remains until a configured timeout is reached or until it is cleared by the system administrator.

To configure lock-and-key access, perform the following steps beginning in global configuration mode:

1. Configure a dynamic access list, which serves as a template and placeholder for temporary access list entries. You configure the dynamic access list with the following command:
   ```
   access-list access-list-number [dynamic dynamic-name
   [timeout minutes]] {deny ¦ permit} protocol source
   source-wildcard destination destination-wildcard
   [precedence precedence] [tos tos] [established] [log]
   ```

2. Configure an interface. To do so, use the following command:
   ```
   interface type number
   ```

3. In interface configuration mode, apply the access list to the interface with the following command:
   ```
   ip access-group access-list-number
   ```

4. In global configuration mode, define one or more virtual terminal (VTY) ports. If you specify multiple VTY ports, they must all be configured identically because the software hunts for available VTY ports on a round-robin basis. If you do not want to configure all your VTY ports for lock-and-key access, you can specify only a particular group of VTY ports for lock-and-key support. You define virtual terminal (VTY) port(s) with the following command:
   ```
   line VTY line-number [ending-line-number]
   ```

5. Configure user authentication. Additional information on how you might design this type of authentication is discussed in the section that follows. To configure user authentication, use one of the following commands:
   ```
   login tacacs username name password secret
   password password  login local
   ```

6. Enable the creation of temporary access list entries. If the host argument is *not* specified, all hosts on the entire network are allowed to set up a temporary access list entry. The dynamic access list contains the network mask to enable the new network connection. To enable the creation of temporary access list entries, use the following command:

```
autocommand access-enable [host] [timeout minutes]
```

Configuring User Authentication

There are three possible methods for configuring an authentication query process (see Step 5 in the previous task list):

- Use a network access server such as a TACACS+ server. This method requires additional configuration steps on the TACACS+ server but allows for stricter authentication queries and more sophisticated tracking capabilities.
  `OSPF_Router(config)# login tacacs`.

- Use the username command. This method is more effective because authentication is determined on a user basis. The syntax for this command is:
  `OSPF_Router# username name password password`.

- Use the password and login commands. This method is less effective because the password is configured for the port, not for the user. Therefore, any user who knows the password can authenticate successfully. The syntax for these commands is as follows:
  `OSPF_Router# password password`
  `OSPF_Router# login local`

Dynamic Access List Golden Rules

Follow these guidelines when you configure dynamic access lists:

- Assign attributes to the dynamic access list in the same way you assign attributes for a static access list. The temporary access list entries inherit the attributes assigned to this list.

- Configure Telnet only, so that the user must use the authentication query process. Telnet access must be allowed to enable user authentication.

- Define either an idle timeout (with the `access-enable` command in the `auto-command` command) or an absolute timeout value (with the `timeout` keyword in the `access-list` command). Otherwise the temporary access list entry will remain even after the user has terminated his session.

- Configure the idle timeout value to be less than the absolute timeout value.

- Configure the idle timeout to be equal to the WAN idle timeout.

- Do NOT create more than one dynamic access list for any one access list. The software refers to only the first dynamic access list defined.

- Do NOT assign the same dynamic name on another access list. Doing so instructs the software to reuse the existing list. All named entries must be globally unique within the configuration.

- If the router executes the `autocommand` command, configure all virtual terminal (VTY) ports with the same `autocommand` command. Omitting an `autocommand` command on a VTY port allows a random host to gain EXEC mode access to the router and does not create a temporary access list entry in the dynamic access list.

When you create dynamic access lists, remember the following:

- The only value replaced in the temporary entry is the source or destination address, depending whether the access list was in the input access list or output access list. All other attributes, such as the port, are inherited from the main dynamic access list.

- Each addition to the dynamic list is always put at the beginning of the dynamic list. You cannot specify the order of temporary access list entries.

- Temporary access list entries are never written to NVRAM.

User authentication is successful when the following router events occur:

- The user connects via the virtual terminal port on the router.

- The router executes the configured `autocommand` command for the `access-enable` command.

- A temporary access list entry is created and the Telnet session is terminated, and the specified host has placed a temporary access list entry and has access inside the firewall.

You can verify that this operation is successful on the router either by asking the user to test the connection or by using the show-access-lists command to view dynamic access lists.

The following sample display illustrates what the end-user might see after successfully completing the authentication process. Notice that the connection was closed immediately after the password was entered and authenticated. The temporary access list entry has already been created, and the host that initiated the Telnet session has access inside the firewall:

```
OSPF_Router# telnet corporate
Trying 172.21.52.1 ...
Connected to corporate.abc.com.
Escape character is '^]'.
User Access Verification
Password:
Connection closed by foreign host.
```

Additional Resources on Lock-and-Key Security

This section introduced several new commands. If you need further information regarding their configuration and operation, see the following Cisco IOS publications:

- "IP Commands" chapter of the *Network Protocols Command Reference, Part 1*.

- "Interface Commands" chapter of the *Configuration Fundamentals Command Reference*.

- "IP Commands" chapter of the *Network Protocols Command Reference, Part 1*.

- "Terminal Lines and Modem Commands" chapter of the *Access Services Command Reference*.

Deleting a Dynamic Access List

If it becomes necessary to delete a dynamic access list, enter the following command (in privileged EXEC mode) for the process:

```
clear access-template [access-list-number ¦ name] [dynamic-name]
[source] [destination]
```

You can display temporary access list entries when they are in use. After a temporary access list entry is cleared by you or by the absolute or idle timeout parameter, it can no longer be displayed. The number of matches displayed indicates the number of times the access list entry was hit.

Display Dynamic & Temporary Access List Entries

It is always a good rule of thumb to check and verify the entries you have created *before* committing them to the router's memory. To view dynamic access lists and any temporary access list entries that are currently established, perform the following task in privileged EXEC mode:

```
show access-lists [access-list-number]
```

Lock-and-Key Access Example

The following example shows how to configure lock-and-key access. In this example, login is on the TACACS+ server, so no autocommand command appears in this configuration. Lock-and-key access is configured on the BRI0 interface. Four VTY ports are defined with the password "cisco."

```
aaa authentication login default tacacs+ enable
aaa accounting exec stop-only tacacs+
aaa accounting network stop-only tacacs+
enable password ciscotac
!
isdn switch-type basic-dms100
!
interface ethernet0
ip address 172.18.23.9 255.255.255.0
!!
interface BRI0
 ip address 172.18.21.1 255.255.255.0
 encapsulation ppp
 dialer idle-timeout 3600
 dialer wait-for-carrier-time 100
 dialer map ip 172.18.21.2 name diana
 dialer-group 1
 isdn spid1 2036333715291
 isdn spid2 2036339371566
 ppp authentication chap
 ip access-group 102 in
```

```
!
access-list 102 dynamic testlist timeout 5 permit ip any any
access-list 102 permit tcp any host 172.18.21.2 eq 23
!
ip route 172.18.250.0 255.255.255.0 172.18.21.2
priority-list 1 interface BRI0 high
tacacs-server host 172.18.23.21
tacacs-server host 172.18.23.14
tacacs-server key test1
tftp-server rom alias all
!
dialer-list 1 protocol ip permit
!
line con 0
 password cisco
line aux 0
line VTY 0 4
password cisco
!
```

CHAPTER SUMMARY

This chapter began with discussion of the various threats against your network in the network security section. Fortunately, you learned several defenses that were already available for your network. The section, "Golden Rules of Designing a Secure Network," covered a variety of questions that you should answer when considering how to design a comprehensive security policy for Enterprise networks. This section also discussed the many reasons that network security should be part of your network design from the beginning as opposed to an afterthought. The section, "Securing Your OSPF Network," covered many different techniques that can be used to increase the overall security of your network. That section also covered the neighbor authentication features that are found in OSPF and how to configure and deploy your routers to make use of this desirable OSPF feature. In the final section, "Configuring Traffic Filters," the various types of access lists were covered, along with a sample network that illustrated their deployment within a network router firewall design. The case study for this chapter will include the process of designing and setting up a router-based firewall structure for your network.

CASE STUDY: DESIGNING YOUR ROUTER FIREWALL ARCHITECTURE

This case study discusses the deployment of Cisco PIX Firewall within a network. A router firewall architecture is a network structure that exists between you and the outside world, the Internet for example, that is designed to protect your network from intruders (that is, cyber thieves). In most circumstances, intruders are represented by the global Internet and the thousands of remote networks it interconnects. Typically, a network firewall consists of several different machines, as shown in Figure 10-2.

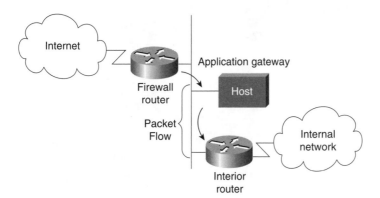

Figure 10–2
Typical firewall router deployment.

In this network architecture, the router that is connected to the Internet (exterior router) forces all incoming traffic to go to the application gateway. The router that is connected to the internal network (interior router) accepts packets only from the application gateway.

The application gateway institutes per-application and per-user policies. In effect, the gateway controls the delivery of network-based services both into and from the internal network. For example, only certain users might be allowed to communicate with the Internet, or only certain applications might be permitted to establish connections between an interior and exterior host.

The route and packet filters should be set up to reflect the same policies. If the only application that is permitted is electronic mail, then only electronic mail packets should be allowed through the interior router. This protects the application gateway and avoids overwhelming it with packets that it would otherwise discard.

Controlling Traffic Flow

This section uses the scenario illustrated in Figure 10-3 to describe the use of access lists to restrict traffic to and from a firewall router and a firewall communication server. You will notice the communications server that was added to the network architecture to service dial-in users.

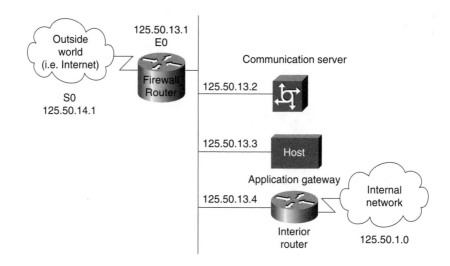

In this case study, the firewall router allows incoming new connections to one or more communication servers or hosts. Having a designated router act as a firewall is desirable because it clearly identifies the router's purpose as the external gateway and avoids encumbering other routers with this task. In the event that the internal network needs to isolate itself, the firewall router provides the point of isolation so that the rest of the internal network structure is not affected.

Connections to the hosts are restricted to incoming File Transfer Protocol (FTP) requests and e-mail services as described in the "Defining Access Lists" section later in this case study. The Telnet, or modem, connections coming into the communication server are screened by the communication server running TACACS username authentication, as described in the "Configuring the Firewall Communications Server" section later in this case study.

TIPS

Connections from one communication server modem line to another outgoing modem line (or to the outside world) should be disallowed to prevent unauthorized users from using your resources to launch an attack on the outside world. Because intruders have already passed the communication server TACACS authentication at this point, they are likely to have someone's password. It is an excellent idea to keep TACACS passwords and host passwords distinct from one another.

Configuring the Firewall Router

In the firewall router configuration that follows, subnet 152.50.13.0 of the Class B 152.50.0.0 network is the firewall subnet, and subnet 152.50.14.0 provides the connection to the worldwide Internet via a service provider:

```
interface ethernet 0
   ip address 125.50.13.1 255.255.255.0
interface serial 0
   ip address 125.50.14.1 255.255.255.0
router ospf 500
   network 125.50.0.0
```

This simple configuration provides *no security* and allows all traffic from the outside world onto all parts of your network. To provide security on the firewall router, use access lists and access groups as described in the next section.

Defining Firewall Access Lists

Access lists define the actual traffic that will be permitted or denied into the internal network, and an access group applies an access list definition to a specific router interface. Access lists can be used to do one of the following:

- Deny connections that are known to be a security risk and then permit all other connections.

- Permit those connections that are considered acceptable and deny all the rest.

For a router firewall implementation, the latter is the more secure method, and that will be how you will be using your access lists.

In this case study, incoming e-mail and news is permitted for a few hosts, but FTP, Telnet, and rlogin services are permitted only to hosts on the firewall subnet. IP *extended* access lists (range 100–199) and Transmission Control Protocol (TCP) or User Datagram Protocol (UDP) port numbers are used to filter traffic. When a connection is to be established for e-mail, Telnet, FTP, and so forth, the connection will attempt to open a service on a specified port number. Therefore, you can filter out selected types of connections by denying packets that are attempting to use that service.

Remember, an access list is invoked after a routing decision has been made but *before* the packet is sent out on an interface. The best place to define an access list is on a preferred host using your favorite text editor (such as Notepad). You can create a file that contains the `access-list` commands and then cut and paste directly into the router while in configuration mode.

It is advisable that you remove any instances of an old access list before loading a new or altered version. You can remove access lists with the following command while in configuration mode:

```
no access-list 101
```

The `access-list` command can now be used to permit any packets returning to machines from already established connections. With the `established` keyword, a match occurs if the TCP datagram has the acknowledgment (ACK) or reset (RST) bit set:

```
access-list 101 permit tcp 0.0.0.0 255.255.255.255 0.0.0.0
255.255.255.255 established
```

If any firewall routers share a common network with an outside provider, you might want to allow access from those hosts to your network. In this case study, the outside provider has a serial port that uses the firewall router Class B address (125.50.14.2) as a source address so your access-list statement to permit them access would be as follows:

```
access-list 101 permit ip 125.50.14.2 0.0.0.0 0.0.0.0 255.255.255.255
```

The following example illustrates how to deny traffic from a user attempting to spoof any of your internal addresses from the outside world:

```
access-list 101 deny ip 125.50.0.0 0.0.255.255 0.0.0.0 255.255.255.255
```

The following access list examples are designed based upon many of the well-known port numbers found within the TCP/IP protocol stack. For a list of some of the more common well-known port numbers, refer to Table 10-2, which appears later in the case study.

NOTES

Port 111 is only a directory service. If you can guess the ports on which the actual data services are provided, you can access them. Most RPC services do not have fixed port numbers. You should find the ports on which these services can be accessed and block them. Unfortunately, because ports can be bound anywhere, Cisco recommends blocking all UDP ports except DNS where practical.

Cisco recommends that you filter the finger TCP service at port 79 to prevent outsiders from learning about internal user directories and the names of hosts from which users log in.

The following two `access-list` commands will allow Domain Name System (DNS, port 53) and Network Time Protocol (NTP, port 123) requests and replies based upon their TCP/IP port addresses:

```
access-list 101 permit udp 0.0.0.0 255.255.255.255 0.0.0.0 255.255.255.255 eq 53
access-list 101 permit udp 0.0.0.0 255.255.255.255 0.0.0.0 255.255.255.255 eq 123
```

The following command denies the Network File Server (NFS) User Datagram Protocol (UDP, port 2049) port:

```
access-list 101 deny udp 0.0.0.0 255.255.255.255 0.0.0.0 255.255.255.255 eq 2049
```

The following commands deny OpenWindows on ports 2001 and 2002 and deny X11 on ports 6001 and 6002. This protects the first two screens on any host. If you have any machine that uses more than the first two screens, be sure to block the appropriate ports.

```
access-list 101 deny tcp 0.0.0.0 255.255.255.255 0.0.0.0 255.255.255.255 eq 6001
access-list 101 deny tcp 0.0.0.0 255.255.255.255 0.0.0.0 255.255.255.255 eq 6002
access-list 101 deny tcp 0.0.0.0 255.255.255.255 0.0.0.0 255.255.255.255 eq 2001
access-list 101 deny tcp 0.0.0.0 255.255.255.255 0.0.0.0 255.255.255.255 eq 2002
```

The following command permits Telnet access from anyone to the communication server (125.50.13.2):

```
access-list 101 permit tcp 0.0.0.0 255.255.255.255 125.50.13.2 0.0.0.0 eq 23
```

The following commands permit FTP access from anyone to the host 125.50.13.100 on subnet 125.50.13.0:

```
access-list 101 permit tcp 0.0.0.0 255.255.255.255 125.50.13.100 0.0.0.0 eq 21
access-list 101 permit tcp 0.0.0.0 255.255.255.255 125.50.13.100 0.0.0.0 eq 20
```

For the following examples, network 125.50.1.0 is on the internal network as shown in Figure 10-3.

The following access-list commands permit TCP and UDP connections for port numbers greater than 1023 to a very limited set of hosts. Make sure no communication servers or protocol translators are in this list.

```
access-list 101 permit tcp 0.0.0.0 255.255.255.255 125.50.13.100 0.0.0.0 gt 1023
access-list 101 permit tcp 0.0.0.0 255.255.255.255 125.50.1.100 0.0.0.0 gt 1023
access-list 101 permit tcp 0.0.0.0 255.255.255.255 125.50.1.101 0.0.0.0 gt 1023
access-list 101 permit udp 0.0.0.0 255.255.255.255 125.50.13.100 0.0.0.0 gt 1023
access-list 101 permit udp 0.0.0.0 255.255.255.255 125.50.1.100 0.0.0.0 gt 1023
access-list 101 permit udp 0.0.0.0 255.255.255.255 125.50.1.101 0.0.0.0 gt 1023
```

Standard FTP uses ports above 1023 for their data connections; therefore, for standard FTP operation, ports above 1023 must all be open. For more details, see the *File Transfer (FTP) Port Questions* later in the "Additional Firewall Security Considerations" section of this case study.

The following access-list commands permit DNS access to the DNS server(s) listed by the Network Information Center (NIC):

```
access-list 101 permit tcp 0.0.0.0 255.255.255.255 125.50.13.100 0.0.0.0 eq 53
access-list 101 permit tcp 0.0.0.0 255.255.255.255 125.50.1.100 0.0.0.0 eq 53
```

The following commands permit incoming Simple Mail Transfer Protocol (SMTP) e-mail to only a few machines:

```
access-list 101 permit tcp 0.0.0.0 255.255.255.255 125.50.13.100 0.0.0.0 eq 25
access-list 101 permit tcp 0.0.0.0 255.255.255.255 125.50.1.100 0.0.0.0 eq 25
```

The following commands allow internal Network News Transfer Protocol (NNTP) servers to receive NNTP connections from a list of authorized peers:

```
access-list 101 permit tcp 56.1.0.18 0.0.0.1 125.50.1.100 0.0.0.0 eq 119
access-list 101 permit tcp 182.12.18.32 0.0.0.0 125.50.1.100 0.0.0.0 eq 119
```

The following command permits Internet Control Message Protocol (ICMP) for error message feedback:

```
access-list 101 permit icmp 0.0.0.0 255.255.255.255 0.0.0.0 255.255.255.255
```

Every access list has an implicit deny all (that is, everything not mentioned in the access list) statement at the end of the list to ensure that attributes that are not *expressly permitted* will be denied. When put together without descriptions of each line's function, the completed access list will look like the following:

```
access-list 101 permit udp 0.0.0.0 255.255.255.255 0.0.0.0 255.255.255.255 eq 123
access-list 101 deny udp 0.0.0.0 255.255.255.255 0.0.0.0 255.255.255.255 eq 2049
access-list 101 deny tcp 0.0.0.0 255.255.255.255 0.0.0.0 255.255.255.255 eq 6001
access-list 101 deny tcp 0.0.0.0 255.255.255.255 0.0.0.0 255.255.255.255 eq 6002
access-list 101 deny tcp 0.0.0.0 255.255.255.255 0.0.0.0 255.255.255.255 eq 2001
access-list 101 deny tcp 0.0.0.0 255.255.255.255 0.0.0.0 255.255.255.255 eq 2002
access-list 101 permit tcp 0.0.0.0 255.255.255.255 125.50.13.2 0.0.0.0 eq 23
access-list 101 permit tcp 0.0.0.0 255.255.255.255 125.50.13.100 0.0.0.0 eq 21
access-list 101 permit tcp 0.0.0.0 255.255.255.255 125.50.13.100 0.0.0.0 eq 20
access-list 101 permit tcp 0.0.0.0 255.255.255.255 125.50.13.100 0.0.0.0 gt 1023
access-list 101 permit tcp 0.0.0.0 255.255.255.255 125.50.1.100 0.0.0.0 gt 1023
access-list 101 permit tcp 0.0.0.0 255.255.255.255 125.50.1.101 0.0.0.0 gt 1023
access-list 101 permit udp 0.0.0.0 255.255.255.255 125.50.13.100 0.0.0.0 gt 1023
access-list 101 permit udp 0.0.0.0 255.255.255.255 125.50.1.100 0.0.0.0 gt 1023
access-list 101 permit udp 0.0.0.0 255.255.255.255 125.50.1.101 0.0.0.0 gt 1023
access-list 101 permit tcp 0.0.0.0 255.255.255.255 125.50.13.100 0.0.0.0 eq 53
access-list 101 permit tcp 0.0.0.0 255.255.255.255 125.50.1.100 0.0.0.0 eq 53
access-list 101 permit tcp 0.0.0.0 255.255.255.255 125.50.13.100 0.0.0.0 eq 25
access-list 101 permit tcp 0.0.0.0 255.255.255.255 125.50.1.100 0.0.0.0 eq 25
access-list 101 permit tcp 56.1.0.18 0.0.0.1 125.50.1.100 0.0.0.0 eq 119
access-list 101 permit tcp 182.12.18.32 0.0.0.0 125.50.1.100 0.0.0.0 eq 119
access-list 101 permit icmp 0.0.0.0 255.255.255.255 0.0.0.0 255.255.255.255
```

Applying Access Lists to Interfaces

After this access list has been loaded onto the router and stored into nonvolatile random-access memory (NVRAM), assign it to the appropriate interface. In this case study, traffic coming from the outside world via the serial 0 interface of the firewall router is filtered (via access list 101) before it is placed on the subnet 125.50.13.0 (Ethernet 0). Therefore, the access-group command, which assigns an access list to filter incoming connections, must be assigned to Ethernet 0 as shown here:

```
interface ethernet 0
ip access-group 101 in
```

To control outgoing access to the Internet from the network, define an access list and apply it to the outgoing packets on serial 0 interface of the firewall router. To do this, returning packets from hosts using Telnet or FTP must be allowed to access the firewall subnetwork 125.50.13.0.

Configuring the Firewall Communication Server

In this case study, the firewall communication server has a single inbound modem on line 2:

```
interface Ethernet0
ip address 125.50.13.2 255.255.255.0
!
access-list 10 deny 125.50.14.0 0.0.0.255
access-list 10 permit 125.50.0.0 0.0.255.255
!
access-list 11 deny 125.50.13.2 0.0.0.0
access-list 11 permit 125.50.0.0 0.0.255.255
!
line 2
login tacacs
location FireWallCS#2
!
access-class 10 in
access-class 11 out
!
modem answer-timeout 60
modem InOut
telnet transparent
terminal-type dialup
flowcontrol hardware
stopbits 1
rxspeed 38400
txspeed 38400
!
tacacs-server host 125.50.1.100
tacacs-server host 125.50.1.101
tacacs-server extended
!
line vty 0 15
login tacacs
```

Defining the Communication Server's Access Lists

In this example, the network number is used to permit or deny access; therefore, standard IP access list numbers (range 1 through 99) are used. For incoming connections to modem lines, only packets from hosts on the internal Class B network and packets from those hosts on the firewall subnetwork are permitted:

```
access-list 10 deny 125.50.14.0 0.0.0.255
access-list 10 permit 125.50.0.0 0.0.255.255
```

Outgoing connections are allowed only to internal network hosts and to the communication server. This prevents a modem line in the outside world from calling out on a second modem line:

```
access-list 11 deny 125.50.13.2 0.0.0.0
access-list 11 permit 125.50.0.0 0.0.255.255
```

Applying Access Lists to Lines

Apply an access list to an asynchronous line with the access-class command. In this case study, the restrictions from access list 10 are applied to incoming connections on line 2. The restrictions from access list 11 are applied to outgoing connections on line 2:

```
access-class 10 in
access-class 11 out
```

Spoofing & In Bound Access Lists

In Software Release 9.21, Cisco introduced the ability to assign input access lists to an interface. This enables a network administrator to filter packets before they enter the router instead of as they leave the router. In most cases, input access lists and output access lists accomplish the same functionality. However, input access lists are considered more intuitive by some people and can be used to protect some types of IP address from "spoofing," whereas output access lists will not provide sufficient security.

Figure 10-4 illustrates a cyber thief host that is "spoofing," or illegally claiming to be an address that it is not. Someone in the outside world is claiming to originate traffic from network 125.50.13.0. Although the IP address is spoofed, the router interface to the outside world assumes that the packet is coming from 125.50.13.0. If the input access list on the router allows traffic coming from 125.50.13.0, it will accept the illegal packet.

Figure 10–4
*Spoofing
example.*

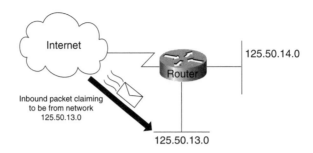

To avoid this spoofing situation, an input access list should be applied to the router interface to the outside world. This access list would not allow any packets with addresses that are from the internal networks of which the router is aware (13.0 and 14.0).

TIPS

If you have several internal networks connected to the firewall router and the router is using output filters, traffic between internal networks will see a reduction in performance created by the access list filters. If input filters are used only on the interface going from the router to the outside world, internal networks will not see any reduction in performance.

If an address uses source routing, it can send and receive traffic through the firewall router. For this reason, you should always disable source routing on the firewall router with the no ip source-route command.

Well-Known Port Assignments

Every application that intends to receive data from a TCP/IP network calls the TCP/IP service to acquire a *port*, a 16-bit number unique to that application on that particular host. Any well-formed incoming datagram with that port number in its TCP or UDP header is delivered to that application. Fragmented datagrams only contain port information in the first datagram fragment (fragment 0). By convention, any transmitting application also owns a port number on its host, and it supplies that port number in the destination port field of the datagrams it sends. The port numbers are divided into three ranges, as follows:

- Well-known ports range from 0–1023

- Registered ports range from 1024–49151

- Dynamic and/or private ports range from 49152–65535

Well-known ports are controlled and assigned by the IANA and on most systems can be used only by system (or root) processes or by programs executed by privileged users. Ports are used in the TCP [RFC793] to name the ends of logical connections that carry long term conversations. For providing services to unknown callers, a service contact port is defined. This list specifies the port used by the server process as its contact port. The contact port is sometimes called the "well-known port."

Table 10-2 *Port number assignments*

Port #	Port Type	Protocol	Keyword
0	TCP & UDP	Reserved	
1-4	TCP & UDP	Unassigned	
5	TCP & UDP	Remote Job Entry	RJE
7	TCP & UDP	Echo	ECHO
9	TCP & UDP	Discard	DISCARD
11	TCP & UDP	Active Users	USERS
13	TCP & UDP	Daytime	DAYTIME
15	TCP & UDP	Who is up or Netstat	NETSTAT
17	TCP & UDP	Quote of the Day	QUOTE
19	TCP & UDP	Character Generator	CHARGEN
20	TCP & UDP	File Transfer (Default Data)	FTP-DATA
21	TCP & UDP	File Transfer (Control)	FTP
23	TCP & UDP	Telnet	TELNET
25	TCP & UDP	Simple Mail Transfer Protocol (SMTP)	SMTP
37	TCP & UDP	Time	TIME
39	TCP & UDP	Resource Location Protocol	RLP
42	TCP & UDP	Host Name Server	NAMESERVER
43	TCP & UDP	Who Is	NICNAME

Table 10-2 *Port number assignments, continued*

Port #	Port Type	Protocol	Keyword
49	TCP & UDP	Terminal Access Controller Access Control System (TACACS)	TACACS
53	TCP & UDP	Domain Name Server	DOMAIN
67	TCP & UDP	Bootstrap Protocol Server	BOOTPS
68	TCP & UDP	Bootstrap Protocol Client	BOOTPC
69	TCP & UDP	Trivial File Transfer Protocol	TFTP
70	TCP & UDP	Gopher	GOPHER
75	TCP & UDP	Any private dial-out service	
77	TCP & UDP	Any private RJE service	
79	TCP & UDP	Finger	FINGER
80	TCP & UDP	Hypertext Transfer Protocol (HTTP)	WWW
87	TCP	Link—commonly used by intruders	
88	TCP & UDP	Kerberos	KERBEROS
89	TCP & UDP	Open Shortest Path First	OSPF
95	TCP	SUPDUP Protocol	SUPDUP
101	TCP	NIC Host Name Server	HOSTNAME
102	TCP	ISO-TSAP	ISO-TSAP
103	TCP	X400	X400
104	TCP	X400-SND	X400-SND
107	TCP & UDP	Remote Telnet Service	RTELNET
109	TCP	Post Office Protocol v2	POP2
110	TCP	Post Office Protocol v3	POP3
111	TCP & UDP	SUN Remote Procedure Call	SUNRPC
113	TCP & UDP	Authentication Service	AUTH
117	TCP & UDP	UUCP Path Service	UUCP-PATH
119	TCP & UDP	USENET Network News Transfer Protocol	NNTP
123	TCP & UDP	Network Time Protocol (NTP)	Well-Known
133-136	TCP & UDP	Unassigned	

Table 10-2 *Port number assignments, continued*

Port #	Port Type	Protocol	Keyword
137	UDP	NETBIOS Name Service	NETBIOS-NS
137	TCP	Unassigned	
138	UDP	NETBIOS Datagram Service	NETBIOS-DGM
138	TCP	Unassigned	
139	UDP	NETBIOS Session Service	NETBIOS-SSN
144	TCP	NeWS	Well-Known
161	TCP & UDP	Simple Network Mgmt. Protocol Q/R	SNMP
162	TCP & UDP	SNMP Event Traps	SNMP-TRAP
177	UDP	X Display Manager Control Protocol	xdmcp
179	TCP & UDP	Border Gateway Protocol (BGP)	Well-Known
194	TCP & UDP	Internet Relay Chat	IRC
195	UDP	DNSIX security protocol auditing	Dnsix
389	TCP & UDP	Lightweight Directory Access Protocol	LDAP
434	UDP	Mobile IP Registration	Mobile-ip
512	TCP	UNIX rexec (Control)	rexec
513	TCP & UDP	UNIX rlogin	rlogin
514	TCP & UDP	UNIX rsh and rcp, Remote Commands	rsh
514	TCP	System Logging	Syslog
515	TCP	UNIX Line Printer Remote Spooling	printer
517	TCP & UDP	Two User Interaction—talk	Well-Known
518	TCP & UDP	ntalk	Well-Known
520	UDP	Routing Information Protocol	RIP
525	UDP	Time Server	timed
540	TCP	UNIX-to-UNIX copy program daemon	uucpd
543	TCP	Kerberos login	klogin
544	TCP	Kerberos shell	kshell
1993	TCP	SNMP over TCP	

Table 10-2   *Port number assignments, continued*

Port #	Port Type	Protocol	Keyword
2000	TCP & UDP	Open Windows	Well-Known
2001		Auxiliary (AUX) port	
2049	UDP	Network File System (NFS)	Well-Known
4001		Auxiliary (AUX) port (stream)	
6000	TCP & UDP	X11 (X Windows)	Well-Known

NOTES

The following port numbers are also known by name: 53, 69, 87, 111, 512–515, 2000, 2049, and 6000.

Additional Firewall Security Considerations

This section addresses some specific topics regarding security and discusses some of the issues surrounding them.

File Transfer Protocol (FTP) Port

Many sites today choose to block incoming TCP sessions originated from the outside world while allowing outgoing connections. The trouble with this is that blocking incoming connections kills traditional FTP client programs because these programs use the PORT command to tell the server where to connect to send the file. The client opens a "control" connection to the server, but the server then opens a "data" connection to an effectively arbitrarily chosen port number (> 1023) on the client.

Fortunately, there is an alternative to this behavior that allows the client to open the "data" socket, which allows you to have the firewall and FTP, too. The client sends a PASV command to the server, receives back a port number for the data socket, opens the data socket to the indicated port, and finally sends the transfer.

In order to implement this, the standard FTP client program must be replaced with a modified one that supports the PASV command. Most recent implementations of the FTP server already support the PASV command. The only trouble with this idea is that it breaks down when the server site has also blocked arbitrary incoming connections.

Source files for a modified FTP program that works through a firewall are now available via anonymous FTP at `ftp.cisco.com`. The file is `/pub/passive-ftp.tar.Z`. This is a version of BSD 4.3 FTP with the PASV patches. It works through a firewall router that allows only incoming established connections.

TIPS

Caution: Care should be taken in providing anonymous FTP service on the host system. Anonymous FTP service allows anyone to access the hosts, without requiring an account on the host system. Many implementations of the FTP server have severe bugs in this area. Also, take care in the implementation and setup of the anonymous FTP service to prevent any obvious access violations. For most sites, anonymous FTP service is disabled.

Nonstandard Services

There are a number of nonstandard services available from the Internet that provide value-added services when connecting to the outside world. In the case of a connection to the Internet, these services can be very elaborate and complex. Examples of these services are World Wide Web (WWW), Wide Area Information Service (WAIS), Gopher, and Mosaic. Most of these systems are concerned with providing a wealth of information to the user in some organized fashion and allowing structured browsing and searching.

Most of these systems have their own defined protocol. Some, such as Mosaic, use several different protocols to obtain the information in question.

Use caution when designing access lists applicable to each of these services. In many cases, the access lists will become interrelated as these services become interrelated.

Specially Designed Firewalls

This chapter concentrated on security from a router-centric point of view. However, the truth is that in addition to router security, many organizations are deploying firewall security. Not only does a firewall provide you with a very tight degree of control, it has the added benefit of enabling the use of both Network Address Translation (NAT) and Demilitarized Zones (DMZs).

Network address translation will allow the use of unregistered address space on the inside of the firewall and registered space within the firewall. The Cisco PIX Firewall can operate with a mixture of both registered and unregistered IP addresses. In addition, it also supports port address translation (PAT) with port level multiplexing, which is a method to further conserve address space. Through the use of this feature, inside user local IP addresses are automatically converted to a single outside IP address and the PIX Firewall uses different port numbers to distinguish between hosts. Over 64,000 inside hosts can be served by a single outside IP address with PAT. For additional information on Cisco's PIX Firewall, please refer to the following Web site:

```
http://www.cisco.com/warp/public/751/pix/pie_ds.htm
```

FREQUENTLY ASKED QUESTIONS

Q— *I want to control which hosts can Telnet to or from the routers in my network. What is the easiest way to do that?*

A— Build a standard access list to define which IP addresses will be allowed, then apply the list to the console or VTY line. Doing this by using the `ip access-class #  in` command will limit inbound access to only those hosts allowed by your standard IP access list.

Q— *I want to control which hosts will be allowed to send data onto my wide-area network. What is the easiest way to do that?*

A— Build a standard access list that will define the hosts that are allowed to send data onto the network, and then apply the access list to the Ethernet interface. Do this by using the `ip access-group #  in` command, which will allow packets from only the hosts you defined to pass out onto the network.

Q— *What is the difference between the* `ip access-class` *command and the* `ip access-group` *command?*

A— When using the `ip access-class` command, you are controlling Telnet access. Use the `ip access-group` command to filter data packets.

Q— *How do I configure an OSPF private net for a firewall for Internet access? I currently have static routes for* `0.0.0.0` *via the firewall. I cannot redistribute this static route. This doesn't seem to work. I don't want to go to 100+ routers to add a static route. I have only one firewall now, but I might add a second one. The firewall does address translation; it masks our internal net numbers. How should I do this?*

A— On the firewall router running OSPF, enter this command:
```
default-information originate always
```

It will originate the default route to all your other OSPF routers in the domain. You don't need to configure default routes in all your OSPF routers in the domain.

Q— *How do you configure MD5 authentication on OSPF neighbor routing updates and exchanges? Is the MD5 authentication used for Hello protocol negotiations? Is the MD5 authentication used in all router protocol updates? Will you please provide a sample configuration?*

A— Here is a short description of MD5 authentication:

Message Digest Authentication is a cryptographic authentication. A key (password) and key identification are configured on each router. The router uses an algorithm based on the OSPF packet, the key, and the key-id to generate a message digest that is appended to the packet. Unlike the simple authentication, the key is not exchanged over the wire. A non-decreasing sequence number is also included in each OSPF packet to protect against replay attacks. This method also allows for uninterrupted transitions between keys. This is helpful for administrators who wish to change the OSPF password without disrupting communication. If an interface is configured with a new key, the router will send multiple copies of the same packet, each authenticated by different keys. The router will stop sending duplicate packets once it detects that all of its neighbors have adopted the new key. The following commands are used for message digest authentication.

- `ip ospf message-digest-key keyid md5 key` (used under the interface)

- `area area-id authentication message-digest` (used under router OSPF)

- `<process-id>`

For example:

```
interface Ethernet0 ip address 10.10.10.10 255.255.255.0
ip ospf message-digest-key 10 md5 mypassword
router ospf 10 network 10.10.0.0 0.0.255.255 area 0
area 0 authentication message-digest
```

Q— *I've heard that OSPF routing protocol exchanges are authenticated. What does this mean?*

A— This means that only trusted routers can participate in the autonomous system's routing. A single authentication scheme is used for each area. Each participating router can have a password.

Q— *Does using an extended IP access list prevent regular routing updates (such as OSPF)? I have to specify* `224.0.0.0` *(destination) in my access list before routing updates allow for OSPF's hello packets.*

A— Inbound access lists on an interface are applied to any IP traffic on that interface. Outbound access lists apply only to traffic switched through the router.

Q— *Can the* `distribute-list` `in¦out` *command be used with OSPF to filter routes?*

A— The `distribute-list` `in` command works on all OSPF routes. It is applied when OSPF routes are fed into the routing table. The `distribute-list` `out` command works only on the routes being redistributed from other processes into OSPF. It can be applied only to EXTERNAL_TYPE2 and EXTERNAL_TYPE1 routes and cannot be applied to INTRA and INTER routes.

Q— *Why would I want or need to consider adding a firewall or other "proxy" device to my network?*

A— If you want to increase the security and integrity of your network when connecting it to the Internet, you should consider adding a firewall. In addition, firewalls and proxy devices are able to translate private IP addresses into public IP addresses, thereby allowing your network to join the Internet.

Q— *For Internet access, I have a router with access lists in place to allow communications only with a TCP proxy server on the same segment. There is another router on this segment with filters in place also to allow communications only with the proxy server. Are there methods for implementing another filter(s) on both routers to allow SNMP management of the external router?*

A— You can use the `snmp-server` `access-list` command to restrict SNMP traffic. You will, however, have to allow SNMP (UDP) traffic through.

Q— *I have two devices: One device is* `164.72.98.45` *with a 9-bit mask, and the other device is* `192.186.14.97` *with a 12-bit mask. I want to allow only TCP connections on ports 5000 and 5020 between two devices through serial 0 of router A. One of the access list statements will be:*

```
access-list 110 permit tcp 192.168.14.97 <mask> 164.72.98.45
<mask> eq 5000
```

My question concerns the mask portion. For the `192.168.14.97`, *do I use a mask of* `0.0.0.240`, `0.0.0.15`, *or* `255.255.255.240`? *And for the* `164.72.98.45`, *do I use a mask of* `255.255.255.128`, `0.0.0.128`, *or* `0.0.0.127`?

A— If you want to permit only these two devices to talk to each other, use the mask `0.0.0.0` on both. The `0`'s in an access list mean that you do not want to deal with any portion of the address. The `255`'s mean that you don't care what is in a particular position in the address. The mask here is not used like the mask defined on the interface for the subnet mask portion.

Q— *I'm using the* `access-list nnn deny ip any any log` *command to track potential break-ins. This works fine in Cisco IOS 10.3, but it does not work in 10.2(11). Is there another way to do the same thing in Cisco IOS 10.2?*

A— No, not in 10.2. You need to upgrade your Cisco IOS.

Q— *Can access list wildcards be used both front and back (like *TOR*)? What level of Cisco IOS is required? I would like to filter all NetBIOS broadcasts except when the name contains a certain string, as in* `permit *TOR*`. *Is this possible?*

A— Yes. The following steps show you how to configure NetBIOS access filters using station names.

1. Assign the station access list name (note that there is an implicit deny all after the `permit` statement):

   ```
   netbios access-list host DEVICE permit *TOR*
                                           ^^^^^

        wildcard
   ```

2. Specify the direction of the message to be filtered on the interface:

   ```
   netbios input\output-access-filter host DEVICE
   ```

   Here is a configuration example:

   ```
   !
   hostname ROUTER
   !
   ```

```
netbios access-list host DEVICE permit *TOR*
!
interface TokenRing0
ip address 10.10.10.1 255.255.255.0
ring-speed 16
source-bridge 2 1 2000
source-bridge spanning
netbios input-access-filter host DEVICE
!
```

Q— *How can I build a firewall with my Cisco router?*

A— Complementing the Cisco PIX™ Firewall, the Cisco Internetwork Operating System (Cisco IOS™) software, too, can be configured as a potent firewall. You can combine extended IP access lists for packet filtering, several methods of user authentication, and Cisco's lock-and-key security solution to provide a strong, secure perimeter between "trusted" and "untrusted" networks.

The router can be configured to log security violations to a UNIX host's syslog facility. In Release 11.2 of Cisco IOS software, network managers can enable IP network-layer encryption and Network Address Translation (NAT) capability (a separately priced software option) in their router-based firewalls.

For more information on Cisco IOS security solutions, visit this Web site: `http://www.cisco.com/ warp/customer/732/Security/index.html`.

Q— *What other configuration options should I enable on the router to secure my network?*

A— Some additional options and the commands that will help protect the router from unauthorized access include the following:

- Disable proxy arp: `no ip proxy-arp`.

- Disable IP source routing: `no ip source-route`.

- Enable only required applications, such as the Domain Name Service (DNS), Simple Mail Transfer Protocol (SMTP), e-mail, outgoing Web client traffic, outgoing File Transfer Protocol (FTP)—for which passive (PASV) mode is most secure—and outgoing Telnet.

- Encrypt router passwords (`service password-encryption`) and encrypt the enable password with an MD5 hashing algorithm (`enable secret password`).

- Apply access lists and passwords to virtual terminal (VTY) ports.

- Enable route authentication in supported routing protocols.

Q— *Does Cisco support Kerberos?*

A— Cisco has announced plans to support Kerberos but has not announced specific products or time frames. Here is an excerpt from the Cisco IOS Security Architecture article:

> Kerberos is a secret-key network authentication system developed at Massachusetts Institute of Technology (MIT) that uses the Data Encryption Standard (DES) cryptographic algorithm for encryption and authentication. Kerberos was designed to authenticate requests for network resources. Kerberos, like other secret-key systems, requires trust in a third party; in this case, the Kerberos server. Cisco will integrate the client portion of Kerberos within the Cisco IOS in Cisco access servers.

Q— *Which IP address space is reserved for secure networks (full internal connectivity, but outside connections from corporate only through firewall proxy or router)?*

A— RFC 1597: Address Allocation for Private Internets (`http://ds.internic.net/rfc/rfc1597.txt`) covers this subject. An excerpt from this RFC follows.

> The Internet Assigned Numbers Authority (IANA) has reserved the following three blocks of the IP address space for private networks:

- `10.0.0.0–10.255.255.255`

- `172.16.0.0–172.31.255.255`

- `192.168.0.0–192.168.255.255`

> The first block is referred to as "24-bit block," the second as "20-bit block," and the third as "16-bit block." Note that the

first block is nothing but a single class A network number, the second block is a set of 16 contiguous class B network numbers, and third block is a set of 255 contiguous class C network numbers.

Q— *When setting up a router as a firewall (allowing only FTP traffic through), is there a way to log messages indicating failed attempts, what the server was connected to, and for how long?*

A— The best way to log connection attempts to the router is to use TACACS+. You can use access list violation logging in Cisco IOS 10.3(3) or higher to see the access list information.

Q— *Which version of Cisco IOS addresses the security issue of IP "spoofing?"*

A— All versions of Cisco IOS address the "spoofing" problem. For details, see the Details on CERT Advisory Dated 1/23/95 (`http://www.cisco.com/warp/customer/459/12.html`) and CERT Advisory 95:01 Response technical tips (`http://www.cisco.com/warp/customer/701/29.html`).

Q— *Is there a performance advantage when using the IP access list keyword* `established` *on an extended access list? Does using* `established` *make the access list more vulnerable? Do you have specific examples of the usage?*

A— There is no performance advantage per se. The `established` keyword simply means that packets with the ACK or RST bits set are allowed through. To better understand access lists in general, read Increasing Security on IP Networks (`http://www.cisco.com/warp/customer/701/31.html`). There are many examples there.

Q— *What TCP port numbers are required for FTP?*

A— FTP data is port 20, and FTP control is port 21. If you are trying to set up an access list, keep in mind that port 21 is the source port from the FTP server when it tries to establish the data connection back to the client. The destination port is a high-numbered port greater than 1023.

Q— *Can I apply IP filters (access list in Cisco IOS 10.3.4) so that multiple (adjacent) class C nets are covered in one command (similar to class B)? Or do I have to specify each class C individually?*

A— A mask can be specified to include multiple class C nets. For example:

```
access-list 1 permit 192.198.48.0 0.0.15.255
access-list 1 deny 0.0.0.0 255.255.255.255
```

This access list permits addresses from a range of class C nets that start with `192.198.48.0–192.198.63.0`.

Q— *How do you interpret the command* `access-list permit 130.10.8.0 0.0.7.255`?

A— First, you need to add a unique number between 1 and 99 after `access-list` and before `permit`. Then, when applied to something, the list will permit packets with a source address from `130.10.8.0–130.10.15.255` and deny all others.

Q— *My HTTPD program is set up to use port 80, and I want to limit accessing it from my network only. Will the following IP access list accomplish this without limiting other access, such as FTP, if I use it on my Internet serial connection:* `access-list 102 deny 80 0.0.0.0 255.255.255.255 0.0.0.0 255.255.255.255`?

A— There is an implicit deny all at the end of every access list. The access list is checked in the order of the statements, and if the first "true-condition" occurs, it is left in place. So you have to configure a permit of any-to-any at the end of your list. It would look something like this:

```
access-list 102 deny tcp 0.0.0.0 255.255.255.255 0.0.0.0
255.255.255.255 EQ 80
access-list 102 permit ip 0.0.0.0 255.255.255.255 0.0.0.0
255.255.255.255
```

Q— *How do I properly set the anti-spoofing filters in Cisco IOS 9.21(7)?*

A— See the information on CCO about the CERT Advisory Dated 1/23/95 (`http://www.cisco.com/warp/customer/69/12.html`). The defense is to set up your Internet firewall router to deny packets from outside your network that claim to have a source address inside your network. An example configuration follows:

```
access-list 101 deny 131.108.0.0 0.0.255.255 0.0.0.0
255.255.255.255
access-list 101 deny 198.92.93.0 0.0.0.255 0.0.0.0
255.255.255.255
```

Repeat the preceding commands, where `access-list 101` describes all possible source addresses on your network. The preceding example describes a network with internal source addresses of `131.108.x.x` and `198.92.93.x`. Then, for a router running 9.21 or later, continue with this command:

```
interface serial 0
description interface facing the Internet
ip access-group 101 in
```

If you do not have 9.21, an upgrade is not required if your Internet firewall is a two-port router (which it should be). Simply apply the `access-list 101` command (as previously demonstrated) to the LAN interface and not the serial interface, as shown in the following example:

```
interface ethernet 0
description LAN port on my internet router
ip access-group 101
```

The essence of this defense is that any packets coming from the Internet that claim to be from your network are thrown out, which prevents this type of attack.

Also, for good measure, all Internet firewalls should have the global command `no ip source-routing`. You can also see Increasing Security on IP Networks (`http://www.cisco.com/warp/customer/701/31.html`) for more information about firewalling your network.

Q— *How is CHAP security implemented with your products? When a user dials into a Cisco access server, does the access server make a call of some kind to a separate CHAP server, which then sends a random challenge to the remote users who must activate a software key or hand-held device to authenticate themselves?*

A— The CHAP password for each user must be configured on the Cisco 2511 using the `USERNAME` command (the password must be the same on both the 2511 and the remote device). When the user dials in, the 2511 challenges the user for the password. For a full description, see Configuring DDR (`http://www.cisco.com/univ-src/ccden/data/doc/software/11_0/ rpcg/cddr.htm`) in the Router Products Configuration Guide.

Q— *Does Cisco support encryption?*

A— Yes, refer to the following documents on CCO for more information.

- Cisco Network Encryption Services (`http://www.cisco.com/warp/public/732/Security/ncryp_tc.htm`)

- Cisco IOS Software (`http://www.cisco.com/univercd/data/ doc/cintrnet/prod_cat/79999.htm`)

- Cisco IOS Security Architecture (`http://www.cisco.com/warp/ public/732/Security/ossec_wp.htm`)

Q— *Cisco routers support the IP packet security types 130 and 133, which are for Basic and Extended IP security options (IPSO). However, if a router sees a packet with a different type number (assuming IPSO has not been configured), will the router forward the packet, or will it drop it and generate an ICMP error?*

A— If the router is not configured for IPSO, it forwards the packet. If the router is configured for IPSO, it drops the packet.

Q— *How can I provide ICMP packets to transmit and receive to a specific internal IP address via the Internet without compromising security to our internal network?*

A— You can set up an access list permitting only ICMP from that specific host through to your internal network.

Q— *I have a question regarding Novell IPX and routing via ISDN when using snapshot routing. I have one server and some workstations on one side, and a lot of servers on the other. When the one server has received its SAP update, it keeps the line up by sending Novell Security Packets to the other servers. Is there a way to keep it from doing this?*

A— You have to make sure that the security packets are not part of the interesting packets in the dialer list. Depending on what you want to do on the line, I would set up the dialer list on a permit basis. If, for example, you just enable NCP to do file copies or REMOTE CONSOLE and so on, you definitely have to exclude the security packets.

Q— *I need to know how to define an extended access list that will allow my users to access the Internet (using Netscape and Gopher) but keep intruders out. I am using Cisco 2513 with IOS v10.0(2).*

A— In general, you are asking about the `established` keyword, which can be defined within an access list to permit two-way communication with an Internet host if (and only if) the session was started on your side of the firewall. However, security and firewalling are big issues. Please look at Increasing Security on IP Networks (`http://www.cisco.com/warp/customer/590/3.html`) for more details on securing your firewall.

The Continuing Evolution of OSPF

Teamwork: "If everyone is moving forward together, then the success takes care of itself."—Successories

Network designers and engineers must continually strive to understand, and in many cases disseminate, new technologies. These new technologies can vary from the newest hardware, to changes in network management, to how routing protocols evolve in response to the changing face of internetworking. This chapter deals with the fundamental question; "What does the future hold for OSPF and *my* network?" This question can be best answered by tracking the Internet Engineering Task Force's (IETF) working drafts. These documents are the true measurement of how the OSPF Working Group, a section of the IETF, is keeping up with the increasing demands of the internetworking community. A prime example of its work is altering the operation of OSPF to meet the new IPv6 requirements.

The following sections cover what OSPF might be if these *Internet Drafts* become Request for Comments (RFCs). These drafts are working documents of the IETF, its areas, and its working groups and have the following characteristics:

- Documents are always subject to change

- Documents are valid for a maximum of six months

- Documents are subject to being replaced, updated, or made obsolete at any time

These drafts are always considered works in progress, but at this point, they are the best source of information by which to understand the direction in which OSPF is evolving.

To learn the current status of any Internet Draft, please check the `1id-abstracts.txt` listing contained in the Internet-Drafts Shadow Directories on `ftp.is.co.za` (Africa), `nic.nordu.net` (Europe), `munnari.oz.au` (Pacific Rim), `ds.internic.net` (U.S. East Coast), or `ftp.isi.edu` (U.S. West Coast).

NOTES

The `1id-abstracts.txt` document, which provides a status on Internet Drafts, only contains a brief summary of each draft. There are no statements within it that says how close it is to becoming an RFC or if it is being reviewed by a working group, and so forth.

The following sections cover each current Internet Draft dealing with OSPF. The basic facts regarding each draft include: date published, author(s), expiration date, and the file name in case further reading is required. Each Draft's abstract is included, and then a brief summary of the Draft's scope is provided. If further information on any of the previously listed items is required, then you should consult the Internet Draft.

OSPF STANDARDIZATION REPORT

Date Published: September 1998

Author: Moy

Expiration Date: March 1998

File Name: `draft-ietf-ospf-stdreport-04.txt`

In understanding the "core" evolution of OSPF, every network designer should refer to this document. This memo documents how the requirements have been met for advancing OSPF to a Full Standard (that is, an RFC), as set out in RFC 1264, Internet Routing Protocol Standardization Criteria. This document is also very useful if the reader is interested in tracing the modifications to OSPF since it held Internet Draft status.

OSPF FOR IPv6

Date Published: November 1997

Author: Coltun, Ferguson, Moy

Expiration Date: May 1998

File Name: `draft-ietf-OSPF-ospfv6-05.txt`

Abstract

This document describes the modifications to OSPF to support version 6 of the Internet Protocol (IPv6). The fundamental mechanisms of OSPF (flooding, DR election, area support, SPF calculations, etc.) remain unchanged. However, some changes have been necessary, either due to changes in protocol semantics between IPv4 and IPv6 or simply to handle the increased address size of IPv6.

Changes between OSPF for IPv4 and this document include addressing semantics that have been removed from OSPF packets and the basic LSAs. New LSAs have been created to carry IPv6 addresses and prefixes. OSPF now runs on a per-link basis, instead of on a per-IP-subnet basis. Flooding scope for LSAs has been generalized. Authentication has been removed from the OSPF protocol itself, instead relying on IPv6's Authentication Header and Encapsulating Security Payload.

Most packets in OSPF for IPv6 are almost as compact as those in OSPF for IPv4, even with the larger IPv6 addresses. Most field and packet size limitations present in OSPF for IPv4 have been relaxed.

In addition, option handling has been made more flexible. All of OSPF for IPv4's optional capabilities, including on-demand circuit support, NSSA areas, and the multicast extensions to OSPF (MOSPF) are also supported in OSPF for IPv6.

Draft Summary

This draft deals with the conversion of the existing OSPF standard to support the requirements for IPv6. The fundamental operation is essentially unchanged, but IPv6 has some specific requirements, such as increased address size, that must be taken into consideration.

This draft is divided up into two sections that cover all the new requirements. The first section describes the differences between OSPF for IPv4 and OSPF for IPv6. Some very interesting changes have taken place; these changes are detailed as follows:

- Protocol processing per-link, not per-subnet
- Removal of addressing semantics
- Addition of Flooding scope
- Explicit support for multiple instances per link
- Use of link-local addresses
- Authentication changes
- Packet format changes
- Link-state advertisements (LSA) format changes
- Handling unknown LSA types

The second section provides details on how OSPF should be implemented as a result of these changes. Some very interesting changes have taken place; these changes are detailed as follows:

- Protocol data structures
- Protocol Packet Processing
- The Routing table Structure
- LSAs
- Definition of self-originated LSAs
- Flooding
- Multiple interfaces to a single link

OSPF ADDRESS RESOLUTION ADVERTISEMENT OPTION

Date Published: March 1998

Author: Coltun & Heinanen

Expiration Date: May 1998

File Name: draft-ietf-ospf-ara-02.txt

Abstract

This document defines an optional extension to OSPF that enables routers to distribute IP to link-layer address resolution information. An OSPF Address Resolution Advertisement (ARA) may include media-specific information, such as a multipoint-to-point connection identifier along with the address resolution information to support media-specific functions. The ARA option can be used to support router-to-router inter-subnet shortcut architectures such as those described in the draft titled, "Intra-area IP unicast among routers over legacy ATM."

Draft Summary

This draft was written to enable OSPF to begin taking advantage of new characteristics of switching at the second layer of the OSI reference model. This type of switching is more commonly known as *switched Layer 2 technologies*.

The specific new characteristic this draft is concerned with is the new ability to provide inter-subnet shortcut data switching. This switching bypasses the Layer 3 forwarding intervention, which is where switching has traditionally been performed. For this Layer 2 switching to take place, the ingress device(s) must have the link-layer address of the egress device(s). This can either be accomplished through configuration or by dynamically resolving an IP address to a link-layer address.

This draft introduces a method for IP address to link-layer address resolution between routers and router-to-network inter-subnet shortcuts as previously discussed:

> "Address Resolution Advertisements (ARAs) are used to distribute the link-layer associations of routers (Router ARAs) and their directly connected networks (Network ARAs) within and between OSPF areas. Distribution of ARAs is performed using standard OSPF flooding mechanisms. ARA information is encapsulated in Opaque LSAs (as defined in the Opaque LSA Draft) and flooded using the mechanisms defined in in the Opaque LSA Draft)."

This draft does not define an ARA architecture, instead it is meant to be used with the architecture as described in the draft titled, "Intra-area IP unicast among routers over legacy ATM." The ARA option is designed to support the following types of operations:

- Shortcuts between core or access routers within ISP Backbones

- Shortcuts in enterprise networks between routers in the same OSPF autonomous system, between OSPF internal routers and autonomous system border routers (ASBR), or between routers and servers

- Distributed router architectures
- Interoperation with ION NHRP and ATMF MPOA
- Inter-subnet multicast shortcuts using LIJ or Point-to-MultiPoint procedures

OSPFv2 DOMAIN OF INTERPRETATION (DOI) FOR ISAKMP

Date Published: October 1997

Author: Atkinson

Expiration Date: May 1998

File Name: `draft-ietf-ospf-doi-00.txt`

Abstract

The Internet Security Association and Key Management Protocol (ISAKMP) defines a framework for security association management and cryptographic key establishment for the Internet. This framework consists of defined exchanges and processing guidelines that occur within a given Domain of Interpretation (DOI). This document details the OSPFv2 Domain of Interpretation, which is defined to cover the use of ISAKMP to negotiate Security Associations for the OSPFv2 routing protocol.

Draft Summary

This Internet Draft details the requirements necessary for using the cryptographic authentication method and operation to provide data authentication for OSPFv2. This Internet Draft is required because OSPF authentication is only on the routing information between participating routers; it does not protect data! If this draft becomes a standard, there will be a means of protecting the data OSPF carries that is very tightly coupled within OSPF.

OSPF NSSA OPTION

Date Published: December 1997

Author: Coltun, Fuller, & Murphy

Expiration Date: June 1998

File Name: `draft-ietf-ospf-nssa-update-03.txt`

Abstract

This Internet Draft documents an optional type of OSPF area, which is somewhat humorously referred to as a *not-so-stubby area* (NSSA). NSSAs are similar to the existing OSPF stub area configuration option but have the additional capability of importing AS external routes in a limited fashion.

The OSPF NSSA Option was originally defined in RFC 1587. All functional differences between this memo and RFC 1597, while expanding capability, are backward compatible in nature. Implementations of this memo and of RFC 1587 are interoperable.

Draft Summary

As previously discussed, NSSAs remove some of the topological limitations of regular stub areas by enabling the limited importing of external routes. This draft details some enhancements to NSSAs, with the most important change being an addition to the NSSA data structure and the operation of a OSPF router when configured as an NSSA Router. This data structure change is reflected by adding NSSATranslateState. This parameter enables you to control whether the NSSA Border Router performs translation of Type-7 LSAs into Type-5 LSAs and floods the translated Type-5 LSA. There are three settings possible:

- **Enabled.** Translation is always performed.

- **Elected.** Translation is performed because the router is the OSPF DR.

- **Disabled.** Translation is not currently being performed; this is the default setting.

This is not the only change being proposed, but it is the most fundamental. There are several other changes being performed as well, and they are as follows:

- Flooding of summary Type-3 LSAs into an NSSA will become optional

- External route calculations have been revised

- Multiple routers will be able to translate Type-7 LSAs into Type-5 LSAs

- When a new NSSA router begins translating LSAs, the previous translator, if elected by default, will cease translating

OSPF OPAQUE LSA

Date Published: February 1998

Author: Coltun

Expiration Date: August 1998

File name: `draft-ietf-ospf-opaque-04.txt`

Abstract

This memo defines enhancements to the OSPF protocol to support a new class of LSAs called Opaque LSAs. Opaque LSAs provide a generalized mechanism to allow for the future extensibility of OSPF. Opaque LSAs consist of a standard LSA header followed by application-specific information. The information field might be used directly by OSPF or by other applications. Standard OSPF link-state database flooding mechanisms are used to distribute Opaque LSAs to all or some limited portion of the OSPF topology.

Draft Summary

Opaque LSAs are very interesting in that they have not really been designed like the other OSPF LSAs. They are very forward looking by providing OSPF with a way to allow for future growth. This is also shown in the draft, as it not designed to address the exact operation of Opaque LSAs.

NOTES

The OSPF ARA Option is another Internet Draft for OSPF that has already been written that takes advantage of the proposed Opaque LSA.

An Opaque LSA has the standard LSA header followed by a 32-bit application-specific information field. The Opaque LSA will also use the link-state database (LSDB) as its distribution method for flooding within an OSPF network. This draft refers to this as the Flooding Scope.

There are three unique types of Opaque LSAs. Each has a different Flooding scope:

- **Type 9.** Link local scope and are not flooded beyond the local network.

- **Type 10.** Area local scope and are not flooded beyond their associated area.

- **Type 11.** Flooded throughout the OSPF Autonomous System and all transit areas but are not flooded into stub areas nor to routers not originating them and connected to a stub area.

OSPF OVER ATM AND PROXY PAR

Date Published: March 98

Author: Przygienda & Droz

Expiration Date: September 1998

File Name: `draft-ietf-OSPF-atm-01.txt`

Abstract

This draft specifies for OSPF implementers and users mechanisms describing how the protocol operates in ATM networks over PVC and SVC meshes with the presence of Proxy PAR.

These recommendations do not require any protocol changes and enable simpler, more efficient and cost- effective network designs. It is recommended that OSPF implementations should be able to support logical interfaces, each consisting of one or more virtual circuits and used as numbered logical point-to-point links (one VC) or logical NBMA networks (more than one VC) where a solution simulating broadcast interfaces is not appropriate. Proxy PAR can help to distribute configuration changes of such interfaces when OSPF capable routers are reconfigured on the ATM cloud.

Draft Summary

This Internet Draft details how OSPF, if it becomes a standard, will be able to operate effectively over ATM. Some of the more useful information as to why it is needed is detailed in the sections that follow.

Overview of PNNI Augmented Routing (PAR)

Private Network-Network Interface (PNNI) Augmented Routing is an extension to PNNI to allow the flooding of information in non-ATM devices. PAR uses a new PTSE type to carry this non-ATM-related information. The current version of PAR specifies IGs for the flooding of IPv4-related protocol information such as OSPF or BGP.

NOTES

Private Network-Network Interface (PNNI) is an ATM Forum specification that describes an ATM virtual circuit routing protocol, as well as a signaling protocol between ATM switches. It is used to enable ATM switches within a private network to interconnect. It is sometimes referred to as Private Network Node Interface.

Overview of Proxy PAR

Proxy PAR is a protocol that allows for different ATM-attached devices to interact with PAR-capable switches and obtain information about non-ATM services without having to run PAR. The main purpose of the protocol is to enable the automatic detection of devices over an ATM cloud in a distributed fashion, without relying on a broadcast facility.

The protocol does not specify how the distributed service registration and data delivered to the client are supposed to drive other protocols. For example, OSPF routers finding themselves through Proxy PAR could use this information to form a full mesh of point-to-point VCs and communicate using RFC 1483 (Multiprotocol Encapsulation over ATM Adaptation) encapsulation. In terms of the discovery of other devices such as IP routers, Proxy PAR is an alternative to LANE (LAN Emulation over ATM 1.0) or MARS (support for Multicast over UNI 3.0/3.1-based ATM Networks). It is expected that the guidelines defining how a certain protocol can make use of Proxy PAR and PAR should come from the group or standardization body that is responsible for the particular protocol.

TECHNIQUES IN OSPF-BASED NETWORK DEPLOYMENT

Date Published: March 1998

Author: Berkowitz

Expiration Date: September 1998

File Name: `draft-berkowitz-ospfdeploy-00.txt`

NOTES

This draft has not yet been formally accepted by the IETF, but it has been submitted to the OSPF Working Group for consideration.

Abstract

OSPF is the preferred interior routing protocol of the Internet. It is a complex protocol intended to deal with complex networks. Although it is a powerful mechanism, it does not handle all situations, and its appropriate use might not be obvious to beginners. Standards track documents deal with protocol design, but deployment of OSPF in many enterprise networks has been limited by a lack of information on the best current practice information for interior routing. Best Current Practices documents have focused on general exterior connectivity. This memorandum is intended to complement the protocol specification by describing the experience-based, vendor-independent techniques of OSPF and complementary technologies in representative networks. Better understanding of the use of OSPF features to help exterior connectivity will help reduce the demand for complex user BGP configuration.

Draft Summary

This working draft is one of the most impressive from a "how to" and "what if" standpoint when dealing with OSPF. It is not designed to change or expand OSPF, but rather, the author intends to provide information on different techniques for deploying OSPF. It has been written on the same premise as this text—theory is fine, but most people are more interested in practical application—an area of OSPF that is sorely lacking in documentation. This book and working draft will certainly go along way to filling this need.

The author cites five major topics within this draft, which are as follows:

- Barriers to Understanding OSPF Deployment
- Area Sizing and Numbering Strategies
- Increasing Backbone Reliability & Backbone of Backbones
- Transition and Network Consolidation
- Transition of Legacy Routing Protocol Domains to OSPF
- Traffic Management

Barriers to Understanding OSPF Deployment

This section of the Draft covers several of the more common misconceptions regarding the deployment of OSPF. It briefly discusses them, provides several good examples, and then provides suggestions on how to reduce the impact of these barriers. Some of the more interesting topics in this section concern virtual links. If you are seriously considering using virtual links, this entire draft should be consulted, as there are several places where they are discussed.

Area Sizing and Numbering Strategies

This section of the Draft covers some techniques and suggestions on how to deploy your use of IP addresses. It also briefly discusses some of the more common misconceptions surrounding OSPF and how it functions within an area that does not have a contiguous address range.

Increasing Backbone Reliability & Backbone of Backbones

These two sections cover the essential requirements and considerations that should be given to every OSPF area 0 and its future physical media. As previously discussed, the heart of every OSPF network is its backbone, in this OSPF area 0. By default, the OSPF network must be redundant to avoid being split in the event of a catastrophic failure.

This draft covers three useful and unique techniques you can use to achieve increased reliability.

- Virtual link solutions

- Adding additional circuits

- Use non-OSPF networks

Transition and Network Consolidation

This section concentrates on how to bring OSPF networks together so that there is single OSPF area 0. There are three solutions presented and very briefly discussed in this draft (if additional information on these subjects is required, this text covers transition and network consolidation in a bit more detail):

- Virtual link solutions

- Use external links

- Use two area 0s

Transition of Legacy Routing Protocol Domains to OSPF

This section of the Draft is very relevant to many network designers. If you have not encountered this particular problem, you will as more and more networks begin to conform to the IETF recommendations of OSPF as the IGP of choice. In this section, all of the examples deal with the acquired network and the belief that they are running RIP and need to be converted to OSPF. Many of the techniques in this section not only apply to RIP but to the overall process as presented in this section, including

- Problems of integrating a newly acquired enterprise; OSPF not used by new acquisition

- An OSPF and virtual link solution

- Run RIP in Company B area, with a link to Area 0 ASBR that learns RIP

- Run RIP in Company B area, with an ASBR in the transit nonzero area of Company A

- ASBR solution with NSSAs

Traffic Management

The last section in this draft deals with managing the various unique traffic needs that can be found in any network. Specifically, it deals with how to OSPF to meet these needs.

OSPF MULTIPLE AREA LINKS

Date Published: March 1998

Author: P. Murphy

Expiration Date: September 1998

File name: `draft-ietf-ospf-mlinks-01.txt`

Abstract

This memo describes an option to the OSPFv2 specification, which enables multiple areas to share the same link or one hop path. This option adds no additional link-state flooding over the link/path other than the normal LSDB exchange and update originating from the link/path's configured primary area. The option applies to standard areas, stub areas, and NSSAs. When it is properly done, it is easy to implement and configure. It eliminates the excess area 0 link-state baggage that accompanies the use of virtual links as currently practiced when configuring similar transits for standard OSPF areas. Routers with this option configured are backward compatible with routers running the standard OSPFv2 compliant implementation as defined in RFC 2178 and can be restricted to a subset of the OSPF routing domain. The application is applied only on OSPF border routers.

The implementation of OSPF multiple-area links requires a modification to the OSPF interface data structure, which enables an interface of an area border router to be connected to multiple areas. One area is always configured as the interface's primary area. Any additional areas that are configured for an interface are called the interface's secondary areas. Two adjacent border routers with mutually shared secondary areas might transit a secondary area's intra-area traffic over the adjacency. A typical application is a stub area or NSSA that is dual homed to the area 0 backbone and loosely joined internally by a slow speed connection.

If a high speed area 0 adjacency exists between the area's two border routers, this option enables the preferred path between the two parts to be the adjacent link. The current specification forces traffic to prefer the slow speed connection.

Another not so common application makes area 0 the secondary area over a local high speed LAN link with the primary area a local stub or NSSA.

Here, area 0 is not primary due to topological limitations, which restrict its applicability. For example, the local LAN link could be a campus backbone with dozens of routers on it, all part of the same NSSA, and splitting the NSSA would impact aggregation.

Draft Summary

This draft was developed to remove a flaw in the design of OSPF. The author does a good job of explaining why this is needed, so I will just summarize. You have two border routers connected via a DS3 link (area 0) and they are connected to two other routers making up NSSA 1. All paths are T1 speed except the area 0 link, and each has the same cost, as illustrated in Figure 11-1.

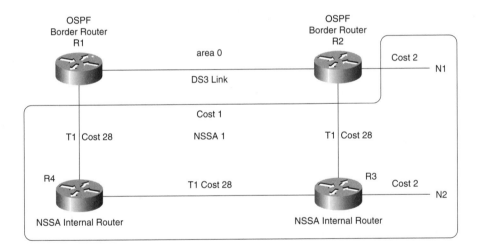

Figure 11–1
OSPF router path costs.

In the current OSPF specification, intra-area routes are *always* preferred over inter-area routes. When looking at Figure 11.1, you consider the path from R1 to N2 to be:

R1→R4→R3→N2 with a cost of 58

However, a more optimal path through the DS3 in area 0 exists. We can provide several more examples on how the DS3 link is never even seen as an option even though it is magnitudes larger than a T1. In the current specification, R4 does not even see the optimal path through the DS3 because it is an internal router to the NSSA. R1 will see it, but because there is an intra-area route to N1, it cannot take advantage of it. Therefore, a need is apparent that enables the link between R1 and R2 to be seen in area 0 and NSSA 1. You could create NSSA 1 into a regular area and add a virtual link that would add extra load to your routers.

The solution would be to allow the OSPF interface found in R1 and R2 that are the area 0 links to also belong to NSSA 1. Under the current specification, each routers' interface can only belong to one area. This draft creates a new parameter known as *secondary areas* with the original area becoming the primary area. Using Opaque LSAs, routing information is provided between participants.

This Internet Draft is highly recommended for additional reading as it has a lot of merit. Hopefully this Draft will be advanced to an RFC very soon.

OSPF Optimized Multipath (OSPF-OMP)

Date Published: March 1998

Author: Curtis Villamizar

Expiration Date: September 1998

File Name: `draft-ietf-ospf-omp-00.txt`

Abstract

OSPF may form multiple equal cost paths between points. This is true of any link-state protocol. In the absence of any explicit support to take advantage of this, a path may be chosen arbitrarily. Techniques have been utilized to divide traffic somewhat evenly among the available paths. These techniques have been referred to as Equal Cost Multipath (ECMP). An unequal division of traffic among the available paths is generally preferable. Routers generally have no knowledge of traffic loading on distant links and, therefore, have no basis to optimize the allocation of traffic.

Optimized Multipath is a compatible extension to OSPF, utilizing the Opaque LSA to distribute loading information, proposing a means to adjust forwarding, and providing an algorithm to make the adjustments gradually enough to ensure stability yet provide reasonably fast adjustment when needed.

Draft Summary

The author of this draft does an excellent good of explaining the need for this draft, and he goes through the various type of ECMP. He covers the three different techniques used in ECMP, as shown in the following list:

- Per packet round-robin forwarding.

- Dividing destination prefixes among available next hops in the forwarding entries.

- Dividing traffic according to a hash function applied to the source and destination pair.

Additional discussion then ensues on how and why they fall short in properly providing the required load-sensitive routing to demonstrate the need for the Internet Draft.

To expect any protocol to perform load-sensitive routing, it is necessary for the protocol to gain information on the different possible paths to the required destination. This Internet Draft proposes the use of Opaque LSAs that will flood the load information. After this information is received by OSPF, it can calculate the correct route. The Opaque LSA will be responsible for providing the correct route calculation. In addition, Opaques LSAs will provide the following information:

- Measure of link loading in each direction as a fraction of link capacity

- Measure of packets dropped due to queue overflow in each direction (if known) expressed as a fraction

- Link capacity in kilobits per second (or unity if less than 1,000 bits per second)

The information provided in the following list comes from sampling interface counter values that are available via SNMP:

- Bytes Out

- Bytes In

- Packets Out

- Packets In

- Output Queue Drops

- Input Queue Drops

CHAPTER SUMMARY

This chapter discussed IETF's Working Drafts, specifically those that apply to OSPF and its future. This information will enable you to be proactive in understanding how the upcoming changes to OSPF are going to affect your organization's network. It is important to note yet again that these drafts are considered works in progress and as such they can change at any time.

CASE STUDY: NETFLOW SWITCHING

NetFlow Switching is part of Cisco's new Internet of Quality Services initiative. It enables enterprise networks to meet and exceed many critical benefits by providing the following enhancements:

- Flexible and detailed accounting, billing, and charge back for network and application resource utilization, including dedicated line- and dial-access accounting.

- NetFlow provides both proactive network monitoring and trouble resolution. It allows for successful monitoring and profiling of customer network usage for use in the future.

- Responsive tactical network engineering and strategic network planning. The information collected by this tool can be used by NetSys.

- Excellent outbound marketing and customer service via intimate knowledge of customer network and application usage patterns. It allows detailed information based upon applications used by the customer to be examined in great detail.

What is NetFlow exactly? NetFlow is defined as a sequence of packets in one direction between given source and destination endpoints, which are identified by IP address. These flows can be extremely granular.

The difference between regular network switching and NetFlow Switching is that regular switching handles incoming packets with separate serial tasks for switching, services, and traffic measurements. The typical process involved with switching a packet is shown in Figure 11-2.

With NetFlow Switching, however, the process is applied to only the first packet of a flow. Information is extracted from the first packet and is used to build an entry in the NetFlow cache for this flow. Subsequent packets are handled via a single streamlined task, which handles switching, services, and data collection concurrently. Figure 11-3 illustrates the processes of NetFlow Switching.

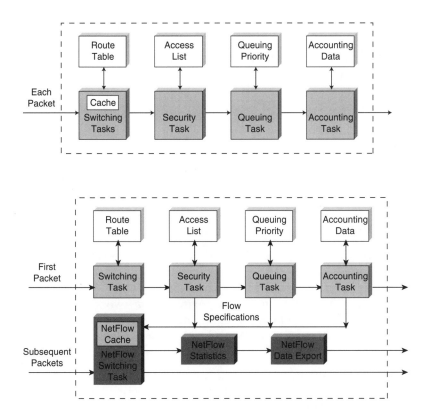

Figure 11–2
Regular network switching.

Figure 11–3
NetFlow Switching.

NetFlow Requirements and Deployment Strategy

NetFlow does not require the adoption of any new or proprietary protocols or new networking equipment. NetFlow may be deployed in an extremely flexible manner to include interface-by-interface deployment.

NetFlow does require a server upon which a software program referred to as Flow Collector is run. This software collects the data and stores it for use by network engineers. It has a variety of features to optimize the data collected based upon user requirements. This software also acts as a management platform of sorts for routers with the NetFlow capability. These Flow Collectors are designed to be deployed throughout the network and all will report to a central station referred to as the Central Flow Analyzer. It is this flow analyzer that enables the network engineers to manipulate the data and reports from the data collected by the flow collectors.

NetFlow operates in a very simple and effective manner by having a series of distributed collectors that receive information from the routers, and then send that consolidated information back to the Central Flow Analyzer. The following process flow describes how NetFlow operates:

1. Routers run NetFlow Switching.

2. NetFlow data is retrieved by Flow Collectors placed strategically throughout the network.

3. Central Flow Analyzer receives the data from Flow Collectors and has GUI Interface for network engineers.

NetFlow Operation

NetFlow is targeted to large Internet providers and enterprise networks. At this time, NetFlow is supported on the 7000 series routers and will soon be supported on the 4000s via the IOS. The improved NetFlow Switching capabilities over regular switching makes it highly desirable feature in any large enterprise network. The additional features via the Flow Collector and Central Flow Analyzer are useful in several ways, but foremost, the data can be used by NetSys, Cisco's network design and modeling software. NetFlow is a useful enhancement to NetSys that will benefit many networks.

NetFlow collects a variety of useful information from each flow, which it can manipulate and present so as to benefit network engineers. The actual NetFlow Central Flow Analyzer provides the following information:

- Target Router Specification

- Aggregation of Schemes

- Web Application

- Start and Stop Times

- Data Analysis

- Sorting Metrics

Another major benefit of NetFlow Switching is that it enhances the switching performance when packets have to go through a large number of policies. For example, in the presence of large number of access lists, only the first packet gets applied by those access lists and then a flow entry is created. All subsequent packets get switched without getting applied by the access lists.

Netflow is usually used on the edges of a network where there is a large number of access lists. This is usually where traffic analysis is required too.

NetFlow is a new offering, and as such, is going to have some inherent problems, but Cisco has stated that they are going to be making the router interfaces very open so their business partners can also develop value-added network management applications.

FREQUENTLY ASKED QUESTIONS

Q— *Where can I find out how to configure NetFlow?*

A— Refer to the following site: `http://www.cisco.com/univercd/cc/td/doc/product/software/ios113ed/113ed_cr/switch_c/xcnetflo.htm`

Q— *How can I find out what the NetFlow commands mean in a Cisco router?*

A— Refer to the following site: `http://www.cisco.com/warp/customer/732/netflow/nfsdi_tc.htm`.

Q— *What series of routers supports NetFlow Switching?*

A— NetFlow Switching is supported in current Cisco IOS software releases—beginning with Version 11.1(2)—for the Cisco 7500, the 7200 series, and the Cisco 7000 series systems with a Route/Switch Processor (RSP). On the Cisco 7500 series and Cisco 7000 series systems with an RSP, NetFlow Switching can operate on the RSP or on a distributed basis on individual Versatile Interface Processors (VIPs), although Cisco currently does not export NetFlow data from VIP cards. Currently, the recommendation is to use the 11.1CA base for the latest NetFlow features/stability.

Q— *How do you know when the NetFlow accounting cache has exceeded its allocated memory? Is there a message that identifies this?*

A— There is no systematic method or message. As normal IP accounting, this is a circular buffer that overflows when the finite cache is full. At this point, the accounting cache starts using the general IP accounting cache.

Q— *Can NetFlow accounting and IP detail accounting co-exist on the same router?*

A— Yes. They are independent and should be able to coexist.

Q— *Can I use NetFlow on IP encapsulated X.25 interfaces? Will NetFlow give me IP encapsulated X.25 packet advantages on serial interfaces?*

A— NetFlow is a switching mechanism. The cache is simply a piece of data necessary to implement the switching. Flow switching provides better performance over optimum switching if IP accounting or access lists are used. For X.25, you will get no advantage.

Q— *Are traffic statistics available with NetFlow Data Export? Are the variances of packet size and packet arrival rates available?*

A— No. NetFlow Switching is not for network management. NetFlow Switching is switching based on source and destination TCP/UDP port numbers out of various ports on the router. With this said, the NetFlow Data Export should be used only for looking at the performance of NetFlow Switching. It contains statistics about the various flows that are set up.

CHAPTER **12**

Future Network Considerations

"Possibilities: The sky is the limit when your heart is in it."—Successories

This final chapter discusses some of the hot new networking features that are making their presence felt on the networking scene. It might be that your network has already deployed these new features, but it is more likely that you are considering deploying or purchasing tools that make use of these advancements. This chapter is not meant to be the authority on what you can expect in networking. Rather, this chapter should be a logical conclusion to this book and a brief introduction to the possible future of networking. When possible, references have been provided for further research into areas that are outside the scope of this book. The areas that this chapter delves into are as follows:

- **Simple Network Management Protocol (SNMPv2 & v3).** Chapter 9 covered SNMPv1 in depth and briefly touched on SNMPv2. This chapter will begin to explore the features that make SNMPv2 unique, such as the new Alarm and Event groups that enable you to have quick and easy access to information concerning the state of your network. In addition, this chapter will also give a brief peek under the covers concerning the soon-to-be-released SNMPv3.

- **Remote Monitoring (RMON).** Remote monitoring is one of the fastest growing network management tools around. Its ability to monitor the performance of the entire network, as opposed to just the components, brings a new and powerful tool to both network engineers and managers. This section will cover both RMON1 and RMON2.

- **Internet Protocol Addressing Version 6 (IPv6).** IPv6, just the thought of it, brings a flood of emotions to everyone involved in networking. No matter what your thoughts on this next generation protocol, it is here, and it will be implemented. The mystery surrounding IPv6 is how and when it will be implemented. This section will examine its operation and the facts surrounding IPv6. This will give you an opportunity to explore some of the myths surrounding this protocol and its improvements over IPv4.

SIMPLE NETWORK MANAGEMENT PROTOCOL (SNMP): CONTINUING EVOLUTION

Although SNMPv1 was previously discussed in Chapter 9, it is important to conduct a brief review to ensure that the basic concepts are fresh in your mind as we discuss the new features of SNMPv2 and SNMPv3. You will briefly review SNMPv1, then move onto SNMPv2, after which a brief overview of SNMPv3 will be provided. Hopefully, this overview combined with the detailed description of the improvements that go along with SNMPv2 will give you some idea of the overall usefulness of SNMPv1 and the continued practical application of the evolutionary steps—SNMPv2 and SNMPv3.

There are two versions of SNMP: Version 1 and Version 2. Most of the changes introduced in Version 2 increase SNMP's security capabilities. Other changes increase interoperability by more rigorously defining the specifications for SNMP implementation. SNMP's creators believe that after a relatively brief period of coexistence, SNMP Version 2 (SNMPv2) will largely replace SNMP Version 1 (SNMPv1). SNMP is part of a larger architecture called the Network Management Framework (NMF), which is defined in *requests for comments* (RFCs). The SNMPv1 NMF is defined in RFCs 1155, 1157, and 1212, and the SNMPv2 NMF is defined in RFCs 1441 through 1452.

NOTES

It might seem that SNMP should not be in a chapter entitled "Future Network Considerations," but because many networks have not completed the move to SNMPv2 and because this chapter will cover SNMPv3, it seemed best to include SNMP within this chapter.

As the Internet developed, so did the desire and need to monitor the performance of the various network components that comprised the Internet. This desire manifested itself in the development of Simple Gateway Monitoring Protocol (SGMP). The Internet Activities Board (IAB) was renamed the Internet Architecture Board in 1992 (though still abbreviated IAB). The Internet Architecture Board was involved with the evolutionary changes to SGMP and recommended the development of an expanded Internet network management standard.

The IAB handed off this new project to the Internet Engineering Task Force (IETF) who began designing, testing, and implementing a new Internet management standard. The IETF's efforts resulted in three new RFCs: 1065, 1066, and 1067. These three documents formed the basis of SNMPv1.

Basic SNMP Architecture

SNMP is comprised of three essential ingredients: a network management system, an agent, and a Management Information Base (MIB). This organization of parts and information can be thought of as a client/server relationship.

The network management system acts as the server, and the MIB acts as the information being exchanged between the server and the client or agent. Figure 12-1 shows the relationship of all the primary SNMP components.

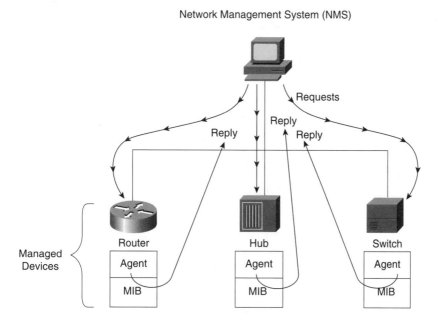

Figure 12–1
The relationship of primary SNMP components.

NOTES

To avoid confusion, in this chapter Simple Network Management Protocol version 1 is referred to as SNMPv1, version 2 is referred to as SNMPv2, version 3 is referred to as SNMPv3, and general comments that cross versions are referred to simply as SNMP. This method is a little tedious, but it helps preserve the accuracy of the text.

Network Management System (NMS)

The Network Management System (also known as *manager*) is software that has the capability of operating on one or more workstations. This software can be configured so it can be utilized to manage different portions of a network or so that multiple managers can manage the same network. An NMS executes applications that monitor and control managed devices. Applications provide the bulk of the processing and memory resources required for network management. One or more NMS must exist on any managed network. The manager's requests are transmitted to one or more managed devices on the desired network. These requests are sent via UDP. SNMP is not dependent upon TCP/IP for transport across a network, it has the capability to be transported via numerous other transport mechanisms such as Novell's NetWare IPX and various other transport protocols.

Managed Device

A managed device is a network node that contains an SNMP agent and resides on a managed network. Managed devices collect and store management information and make this information available to network management systems (NMSs) using SNMP. Managed devices, sometimes called network elements, can be routers and access servers, switches and bridges, hubs, computer hosts, or printers.

Agent

An agent is a network management software module that resides in a managed device. It has local knowledge of management information and translates that information into a form compatible with SNMP. To be a managed device, each device must have firmware in the form of code. This firmware translates the requests from the SNMP manager and responds to these requests. The software, or firmware, not the device itself, is referred to as an agent.

The Management Information Base

The MIB (Management Information Base) is an established database of the hardware settings, variables, memory tables, or records stored within files; these are called data elements. These data elements make up a configuration, status, and statistical information base used to define the functionality and operational capacity of each managed device. That information is referred to as a MIB. Each data element is referred to as a managed object. These managed objects are comprised of a name, one or more attributes, and a set of operations that can be performed on the managed object.

SNMPv2: A Brief Introduction

With the growth of networks and the Internet throughout the country and the world, the need to expand SNMP quickly became apparent. The result was SNMPv2, and as technology changes it is beginning to be revised so that soon we will have SNMPv3.

Problems arose in association with the SETREQUEST command in SNMPv1. SNMP Managers, either intentionally or unintentionally, were corrupting the configuration parameters of managed objects; this was seriously interfering with network operations. Seeing a need to fix this security problem, in the fall of 1992 the IETF established two working groups to define enhancements to SNMPv1.

The first group was to focus primarily on designing security functions, and the second group directed its combined efforts to defining enhancements to the SNMP protocol. What the two groups came up with was SNMPv2. This second version alleviated the security problems by adding encryption and authentication countermeasures. In addition to the security fixes, SNMPv2 incorporated a manager-to-manager capability and two new PDUs: **GETBULKREQUEST** and **INFORMREQUEST**.

The manager-to-manager capability enables SNMP to support distributed network management, where one network management system (NMS) can report management information to another network management system (NMS).

The additional two PDUs added in SNMPv2 are: **GETBULKREQUEST** and **INFORMREQUEST**. They supplement the five commands already in SNMPv1: **GETREQUEST, GETNEXTREQUEST,**

SETREQUEST, RESPONSE, and TRAP. Finally, to support manager-to-manager interaction SNMPv2 added Alarm and Event groups to the SNMPv2 MIB.

The Alarm group permits the managers to establish thresholds that, if breached, will trigger an alarm. The Event group specifies when a Trap should be issued based on one or more MIB values. These two groups also support the manager-to-manager capability that was introduced in version 2.

SNMPv2 Operational Enhancements

You might have thought that the GETBULKREQUEST is very similar to the GETNEXTREQUEST. This is true, but with one major exception. The GETBULKREQUEST tells the agent to return as much data as can fit into a response message starting with the next largest value than the requested managed object instance. The GETBULKREQUEST has two very important features:

- More efficient use of the transmission facility
- Reduction/elimination of certain error conditions that occur if a GETREQUEST command is used

The INFORMREQUEST supports the use of a hierarchical system of NMSs, and it also standardizes communication between NMSs. The enterprise network manager can establish the INFORMREQUEST command, so when certain criteria are met and thresholds are exceeded, an "event" is generated in which a transmission of an INFORMREQUEST command informs another NMS of the threshold violation. The Enterprise network manager can also program the various NMSs under his control to broadcast the INFORMREQUEST command to one or more NMSs. With the advent of this manager-to-manager communication and the use of alarms, one Enterprise Network Management Station (ENMS) can be monitored at all times while the others are programmed to report information to the ENMS only during those times when they are unattended.

Security Enhancements

The authentication protocol is designed to reliably identify the integrity of the originating SNMPv2 party. It consists of authentication information required to support the authentication protocol used. The privacy protocol is designed to protect information within the SNMPv2 message from disclosure. Only authenticated messages can be protected from disclosure. In other words, authentication is required for privacy.

The SNMPv2 specifications discuss two primary security protocols: one for authentication and one for privacy. These are the *Digest Authentication Protocol* and the *Symmetric Privacy Protocol.*

The Digest Authentication Protocol verifies that the message received is the same one that was sent. Data integrity is protected using a 128-bit *message digest* calculated according to the Message Digest 5 (MD5) algorithm. The digest is calculated at the sender and enclosed with the SNMPv2 message. The receiver verifies the digest. A secret value, known only to the sender and the receiver, is prefixed to the message. After the digest is used to verify message integrity, the secret value is used to verify the message's origin.

To help ensure message privacy, the Symmetric Privacy Protocol uses a secret encryption key known only to the sender and the receiver. Before the message is authenticated, this protocol uses the *Data Encryption Standard* (DES) algorithm to effect privacy. DES is a documented *National Institute of Standards and Technology (NIST)* and *American National Standards Institute (ANSI)* standard.

Additional SNMPv2 Resources

You can find general information about SNMPv2 at the following URL:
`http://www.ietf.org`.

You can find Cisco-specific SNMPv2 information at the following locations:

Cisco Network Management Toolkit:
`http://www.cisco.com/public/sw-center/netmgmt/cmtk/mibs.shtml`

Cisco MIBs: `http://www.cisco.com/public/mibs/`

Cisco Traps: `http://cio.cisco.com/public/mibs/traps/`

Guidelines for polling MIB variables:
`http://www.cisco.com/warp/public/701/38.html`

Router MIB Support Lists:
`http://www.cisco.com/public/mibs/supportlists/c7513/supportlist.html`

The SNMPv3 Effort

It is important to note that this information has not become any type of approved standard. This section will provide you with a proactive view of what is to come in the SNMPv3 arena. In addition, it will also provide you with the resources needed to research this project before it becomes a standard. Since it is not yet a standard, we will not spend very much time discussing it.

The SNMPv3 Working Group is chartered to prepare recommendations for the next generation of SNMP. The goal of the Working Group is to produce the necessary set of documents that provides a single standard for the next generation of core SNMP functions. If you require more information, this and other information can be found on their home page at the following URL:

```
http://www.ietf.org/html.charters/snmpv3-charter.html.
```

During the development of SNMPv3, the SNMPv3 Working Group has absorbed many of the outstanding documents from the SNMPv2 effort.

During the past several years, there have been a number of activities aimed at incorporating security and other improvements to SNMP. Unfortunately, strongly held differences on how to incorporate these improvements into SNMP prevented the SNMPv2 Working Group from coming to closure on a single approach. As a result, two different approaches (commonly called V2u and V2*) have emerged.

The Security and Administrative Framework Evolution for SNMP Advisory Team (the Advisory Team) was formed to provide a single recommended approach for SNMP evolution. The technical starting point for this Working Group will be the recommended approach provided by the Advisory Team.

This approach provides for the convergence of concepts and technical elements of V2u and V2*. The SNMPv3 Working Group is not starting new work and will use as many concepts, technical elements, and documentation as is practical from the V2u and V2* activities. Previous delays in providing a single standard for the next generation of SNMP core functions dictate that the Working Group move forward as quickly as possible to document and publish Internet Drafts and RFCs. To this end, the Working Group will make use of as much existing documentation as practical. Additionally, functional changes beyond those needed to provide a single approach will be strongly discouraged.

Timely completion of a single approach for SNMPv3 is crucial for the continued success of SNMP. Recognizing the need for prompt completion, the following objectives are provided to the Working Group:

- Accommodate the wide range of operational environments with differing management demands

- Facilitate the need to transition from previous, multiple protocols to SNMPv3

- Facilitate the ease of setup and maintenance activities

Goals and Milestones of the SNMPv3 Working Group

The following is the most current published list of the SNMPv3 Working Group's milestones in chronological order.

1. **Apr 97.** Working Group meeting at Memphis IETF to discuss SNMPv3 recommended approach, discuss Working Group Charter and the plan for completion

2. **Apr 97.** Post first SNMPv3 Internet-Draft, Modules, and Interface Definitions

3. **Jun 97.** Post revised SNMPv3 Modules and Interface Definitions Internet-Drafts

4. **Jul 97.** Post initial SNMPv3 Message Processing and Control Module Internet-Draft

5. **Jul 97.** Post initial SNMPv3 Security Model Module Internet-Draft

6. **Aug 97.** Finalize SNMPV3 Modules and Interface Definitions Internet-Draft and review other I-Ds at Munich IETF

7. **Sep 97.** Post revised SNMPv3 Message Processing and Control Module Internet-Draft

8. **Sep 97.** Post initial SNMPv3 Proxy Specification Internet-Draft

9. **Sep 97.** Post revised SNMPv3 Security Model Module Internet-Draft

10. **Sep 97.** Post revised SNMPv3 Local Processing Module Internet-Draft

11. **Sep 97.** Submit SNMPv3 Modules and Interface Definitions to IESG for consideration as a Proposed Standard

12. **Apr 98.** All SNMPv3 specifications submitted to IESG for consideration as Proposed Standards

---

NOTES

Additional SNMPv3 Resources
An Architecture for Describing SNMP Management Frameworks can be found at the following site:

```
ftp://ietf.org/internet-drafts/draft-ietf-snmpv3-next-gen-arch-07.txt
```

User-based Security Model (USM) for version 3 of the Simple Network Management Protocol (SNMPv3) can be found at the following site:

```
ftp://ietf.org/internet-drafts/draft-ietf-snmpv3-usm-04.txt
```

Message Processing and Dispatching for the Simple Network Management Protocol (SNMP) can be found at the following site:

```
ftp://ftp.ietf.org/internet-drafts/draft-ietf-snmpv3-v3mpc-model-07.txt
```

View-based Access Control Model (VACM) for the Simple Network Management Protocol (SNMP) can be found at the following site:

```
ftp://ietf.org/internet-drafts/draft-ietf-snmpv3-acm-05.txt
```

SNMPv3 Applications can be found at the following site:

```
ftp://ietf.org/internet-drafts/draft-ietf-snmpv3-appl-05.txt
```

REMOTE MONITORING (RMON)

The RMON standard was originally created for a distributed computing architecture, in which the agents and probes communicate using a central station, normally the manager, via the SNMP protocol. The RMON standard provides a powerful management tool for performing traffic analysis, troubleshooting, trend reporting, and proactive network management.

Some years ago there was a standard called Common Management Information Services and Protocols (CMIP). CMIP defined the format for exchanging data between network management systems and managed network devices or live facilities. It was supposed to be the end-all-be-all protocol for controlling Enterprise networks. Instead, a different standard became the preferred standard for network management. This standard has its origins back in 1988. It is called Simple Network Management Protocol (SNMP). Included in it is the Remote Monitoring (RMON) Management Information Base (MIB). Because SNMP has already been covered in detail in previous chapters, this section will focus on RMON1, and the newly developed RMON2, MIB.

RMON Overview

Remote Monitoring (RMON) standards provide distributed management architecture for performing traffic analysis, troubleshooting, trend reporting, and proactive network management. Normally, a RMON probe is attached to each segment; however, with the increasing high-performance of switched internetworks, a new standard needed to be developed to handle these technologies such as Virtual LANs (VLANs) and fast Ethernet inter-switch networks. RMON2 adds several key enhancements to the already manager-friendly RMON standard. The main feature is that it extends its reach to the third layer in the OSI reference model—the Network Layer. It provides network-layer host and matrix tables for monitoring layer three traffic by host, or by conversations for various network protocols. Furthermore, it provides this new layer connectivity without sacrificing the standard RMON attributes such as: bandwidth utilization, packet rate, and rate errors. Application Layer host and matrix tables are also included in this second version, for monitoring layer seven traffic, by host or conversation for various applications. Figure 12-2 shows the coverage provided by RMON.

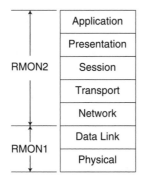

Figure 12–2
RMON coverage.

RMON also provides address mapping for aggregating the statistics by network address as well as MAC addresses for Ethernet and Token Ring networks.

It adds protocol directory and distribution groups for displaying selected protocols and their distribution for each LAN segment. Finally, it provides a user-defined history, which now extends beyond the Link-Layer statistics to include any RMON1&2, or MIB I or II statistics.

RMON1

The RMON standard was originally created for a distributed computing architecture, in which the agents and probes communicate using a central station, normally the manager, via the SNMP protocol. The RMON standard provides a powerful management tool for performing traffic analysis, troubleshooting, trend reporting, and proactive network management. An RMON probe, or agent, is generally attached to each network segment, thus providing visibility into all network activities. The main benefit when utilizing RMON technology is increased network availability for users and high productivity for network managers.

A basic RMON system can provide the following:

- Information enabling administrators to perform analysis of network utilization, including data and error statistics
- Historical information of network trends and statistical analysis
- Matrix information describing communications between systems and the quantity of data exchanged

RMON is an extension of the reach of the network manager's operation to other networks under his/her control. As probes, or RMON agents, monitor the flow of data on the remote network, they organize that information into a coherent format that the network manager can easily interpret and use to better manipulate the network. Figure 12-3 illustrates the function and routing of information from an RMON probe to the network manager's workstation.

Figure 12–3
Deployment of an RMON probe.

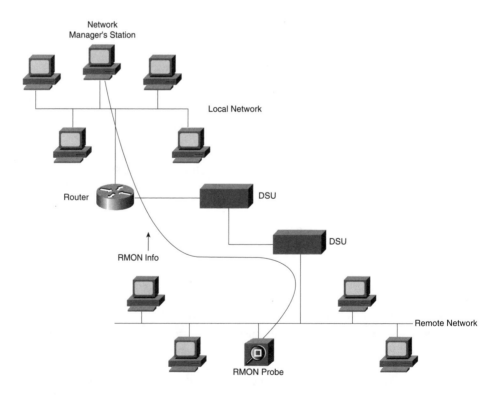

The RMON probe monitors and organizes data flow on the remote network, reducing the amount of bandwidth required to transmit the information to the manager's station. In doing so, this alleviates the problem associated with SNMP—the significant degradation of lower bandwidth when operating geographically separated networks. The WAN circuit used to connect the separate networks operates at a fraction of the operating rate of a LAN circuit—by reducing the potential of saturation on a WAN circuit, the overall network performance is increased.

Every RMON probe includes a MIB that defines each attribute of the object/device being monitored. RFC 1271, published in November 1991, was the first RMON MIB standard. It dealt strictly with Ethernet LANs. It provided network managers with comprehensive network fault tolerance, diagnosis, planning, and performance information. It delivered this information in nine groups of monitored elements. Each group provided specific data sets to meet common monitoring requirements. Following that, RFC 1513, published in September 1993, extended the RMON MIB to include Token Ring networks. Although RMON MIBs define the attributes of objects on the monitored networks, the value and usefulness of this information is dependent on the application the manager is using, and the extent he/she uses that information. The list that follows shows the various groups found within RMON and what they bring to your network.

- **Statistics.** Provides counters for packets, octets, broadcasts, errors, and offers, on segment or port

- **History.** Periodically samples and saves statistics group counters for later retrieval

- **Hosts.** Maintains statistics on each host device on the segment of port

- **Host Top N.** A user-defined subset report of the Hosts group, sorted by a statistical counter. By returning only the results, management traffic is minimized

- **Traffic Matrix.** Maintains conversation statistics between hosts and networks

- **Alarms.** A threshold that can be set on critical RMON variables for proactive network management

- **Events.** Generates SNMP traps when an Alarm group threshold is exceeded; also logs these events

- **Filters.** A filter engine that generates a packet stream from frames that match a specified pattern

- **Packet Capture.** Manages buffers for packets captured by the Filter group for uploading to the management console

- **Token Ring.** More specific information is as follows:
  - ○ **Ring station.** Provides detailed statistics on individual stations
  - ○ **Ring station order.** Provides an ordered list of stations currently on the ring
  - ○ **Ring station configuration.** Provides configuration and insertion/removal per station
  - ○ **Source routing.** Provides statistics on source routing, such as hop counts, and others

Although RMON has worked miracles with many enterprise networks, it still has several issues surrounding its operation that need to be worked out. With the advent of high-performance switched internetworks, new RMON instrumentation solutions were required to counter the dramatically increased number of segments, and the development of Virtual LANs (VLANs) plus fast Ethernet inter-switched links. The two main drawbacks to RMON are:

- It only specifies monitoring and diagnostics for network traffic at the MAC layer (Data Link).
- Because the RMON-based probes view the traffic on the local LAN segment, they are not able to identify network hosts and sources beyond the router connection. To do so, a probe must have the capability of identifying traffic at the network layer that would provide statistics for all hosts accessing that segment, regardless of the location or connectivity of the network.

NOTES

The downfall of RMON probes is that they need to be on each segment that you want to monitor. If, however, a device like a router is running RMON agent software, it too can be polled just like the probe.

This just goes to show that nothing answers 100% of the questions surrounding Enterprise networks.

RMON2

RMON2 overcomes these problems in several different ways. To begin with, by using RMON2-based probes, all RMON2 groups map into the major network-layer protocols such as IP, Novell's IPX, OSI, AppleTalk, Banyan VINES, and DECnet, giving a complete start-to-finish view of all network traffic. Also, RMON2 includes the specifications for monitoring application-layer traffic. This enables the network managers to monitor network applications such as Lotus Notes, Telnet, and Microsoft Mail. This newly developed capability, to monitor application-layer traffic, enables network managers to be proactive in troubleshooting key application-layer traffic within the network. The RMON alarms, statistics, history, and host/conversation groups in the RMON MIB can now be utilized for troubleshooting and maintaining network functionality based upon application-layer traffic.

RMON2 adds the following key enhancements:

- Network layer host and matrix tables for monitoring layer 3 traffic by host, by conversations for various protocols, and for the standard RMON attributes such as utilization, packet rate, errors, and others

- Application layer host and matrix tables for monitoring layer 7 traffic by host, by conversations for various applications, and for the standard RMON attributes such as utilization, packet rate, and errors

- Network address mapping for aggregating the statistics by network address as well as MAC address for Ethernet and Token Ring networks

- Protocol Directory and Distribution groups for displaying selected protocols and their distribution for each LAN segment

- User-definable history, which now extends beyond RMON1 link-layer statistics to include RMON1, RMON2, MIB-I, or MIB-II statistics

The list that follows shows the various MIB groups found within RMON2 and what each brings to your network.

- **Protocol Directory.** Provides a table of protocols for the agent that will monitor and maintain statistics

- **Protocol Distribution.** Provides a table of statistics for each protocol in the directory

- **Network Layer Host.** Statistics for each network layer address on segment, ring, or port

- **Network Layer Matrix.** Provides traffic statistics for pairs of network layer addresses

- **Application Layer Host.** Provides statistics by application layer protocol for each network address

- **Application Layer Matrix.** Provides traffic statistics by application layer protocol for pairs of network layer addresses

- **User Definable History.** Extends history beyond the RMON1 link-layer statistics to include RMON, RMON2, MIB-I, or MIB-II statistics

- **Address Mapping.** Provides a list of MAC-to-network address bindings

- **Configuration Group.** Provides a list of agent capabilities and configuration

RMON Configuration Example

This section provides a brief example of how to configure RMON using Cisco's IOS 11.1. It will detail the required IOS and provide a real life example for a 2500 series router.

Required Software

All IOS 11.1 or later software includes RMON alarms and events groups. In addition, full 9-group RMON support is available on the Ethernet port of 2500 series routers running the images detailed in Table 12-1.

Table 12-1   *Images and feature sets for RMON*

Image name	Feature set
igs-im-l	IP+RMON
igs-imn-l	IP+IPX+RMON
igs-imnr-l	IP+IPX+IBM+RMON
igs-imr-l	IP+IBM+RMON
igs-jlm-l	EN+CS+RMON
igs-jm-l	EN+RMON

Basic Configuration

To enable full RMON support on an Ethernet interface of a 2500 series router, enter the following:

```
interface Ethernet 0
rmon {native ¦ promiscuous}
snmp-server community <community> RW
snmp-server host <ip address> <community>
```

In native mode, RMON reports only on traffic through the router. In promiscuous mode, it reports on all traffic, including the traffic not destined for transmission through the router. Promiscuous mode is very CPU intensive. A performance hit of at least 20 percent per monitored Ethernet is not uncommon.

SNMP Read-Write access is necessary if you use an RMON console (such as Netscout).

The default size of the queue that holds the packets for analysis by RMON is 64 packets. To change the size of the RMON queue, type: `rmon queuesize <size>`

When you run in promiscuous mode, you will almost certainly have to increase the queuesize to prevent drops in the RMON input queue.

There is a hidden command to change the (default low) priority of the rmon process:
`rmon priority ( low ¦ normal ¦ high }`

Configuring Alarms and Events: New in 11.1(2)

In 11.1(1) you needed an RMON console (such as Netscout) to configure alarms and events. Starting in 11.1(2) you can do it on the command line. However, these commands are not documented in 11.1 manuals yet. These commands are available in *any* 11.1 image, not just the special 2500 RMON images. They enable you to set a threshold on any numeric MIB variable (not just RMON MIB variables) and generate an SNMP trap or other event when the threshold is crossed.

To configure alarms, you need to enter the following:

```
rmon alarm <alarm-number> <MIB object> <interval> { delta ¦absolute }
rising-threshold <rising-value> [<event-number>] falling-threshold
<falling-value> [<event-number>] [owner <owner>]
no rmon alarm <alarm-number>
```

To configure events, you need to enter the following:

```
rmon event <event-number> [log] [trap <community>]
[description <description>] [owner <owner>]
```

Assume, for example, that you need to configure RMON to generate a trap if CPU utilization reaches or exceeds 60 percent, and rearm the trap if utilization drops to 40 percent or less. The sampling interval is 20 seconds. You would need to enter the following:

```
rmon alarm 1 lsystem.56.0 20 absolute rising-threshold 60 1
falling-threshold 40 2 owner me
rmon event 1 log trap public description "cpu busy" owner me
rmon event 2 log description "cpu not too busy"
```

For another example, assume you need to configure a 2500 series router to send a trap and log an event when the alarm threshold, on monitoring its own ifInOctets (ifEntry.10.1), exceeds an absolute value of 90000. The monitoring is done every 60 seconds and the falling threshold is 85000. In this case, the Netview management station received a trap: router.rtp.cisco.com: A RMON Rising Alarm: Bytes received exceeded threshold 90000; value=483123 (sample type=1; alarm index=10). You would need to enter the following:

```
snmp-server host 171.68.118.100 public
snmp-server community public RO
rmon event 1 log trap public description "High ifInOctets" owner jdoe
rmon alarm 10 ifEntry.10.1 60 absolute rising-threshold 90000 1
falling-threshold 85000 owner jdoe
```

Keep in mind that you can enter the MIB to be a threshold as a full dotted-decimal value (such as, 1.3.6.1.2.1.2.2.1.10.1) in which case the box converts it (to ifEntry.10.1, in this case).

To get to the bottom line, the command-line syntax for adding events to a router is as follows:

```
rmon event <#> {<log><trap>} <community> <description<string>><owner>
rmon alarm <#> <mib-variable> <interval-seconds> { delta ¦ absolute }
rising-threshold <mib_value> <num_event_tofire> falling-threshold
<mib_value> <num_event_tofire> <owner>
```

For a final example, look at the following code:

```
rmon event 1 log trap public description "Rising Event for bufferFail"
owner admin
rmon event 2 log trap public description "Falling Event f/bufferFail"
owner admin
rmon alarm 1 lsystem.46.0 30 delta rising-threshold 5 1
falling-threshold 5 2 owner admin
```

SNMP VERSUS RMON

These days, corporate MIS departments typically get fewer resources while facing daunting challenges. Consequently, networking engineers have a difficult time staying current with new releases of products in their network and keeping up with new technologies. However, what are the best technologies available for your network?

That question can be answered in several different ways depending upon your thoughts. It is a basic truth of a healthy and well-performing network that network managers and engineers need better tools with a standards-based architecture.

One basic fact is that SNMP and RMON are both being used to determine network health and performance. This section will attempt to give an objective view of them both while comparing and contrasting each. This information will enable you, the network manager, to make the correct decisions for your network.

These observations ring true, but often go unheard. In order to prove these thoughts on what can be termed "a business," refer to International Data Corporation's June, 1997 report, "*Managing Data Overload*," which cites three industry trends driving network monitoring:

- The increased deployment of switched topologies

- The increased use of Web-based computing

- The enterprise's requirement to establish service-level contracts with their carriers

The report further contends, "The combination of RMON with network element management software products is integral to end-user network management strategies."

Regarding revenue potential, it continues, "Network element management software represent . . . a $250.4 million opportunity in 1997 and will grow to $482.6 million in 2001. Interlinked with this device-driven management market is RMON instrumentation and reporting, an $827.3 million market in 1997."

SNMP and RMON: Network Management Standards

The first standard for network management evolved into a specification that became known as Simple Network Management Protocol (SNMP), based upon the TCP/IP protocol stack, and was given RFC number 1098 by the Internet Engineering Task Force (IETF). By embedding SNMP within data communication devices, multivendor management systems can manage these devices from a central site and view information graphically. However, there are significant limitations to this important standard.

SNMP allows devices to be polled regularly, but it does not provide for extensive proactive monitoring of critical functions or the monitoring of network traffic on a LAN segment. SNMP-based devices will only identify traffic specifically addressed to itself and cannot provide statistics on "conversations" between devices, an important concept for network troubleshooting.

RMON1, developed by the IETF (Internet Engineering Task Force), became a standard in 1992 as RFC number 1271 (now RFC 1757). The RMON specification was developed to provide traffic statistics and analysis on many network parameters for comprehensive network fault diagnosis, planning, and performance tuning. RMON delivers seamless multivendor interoperability between SNMP management stations and monitoring agents. RMON provides a standard set of MIBs, which collect rich network statistical information not available from SNMP. Finally, RMON allows proactive network diagnostics via its powerful Alarm Group, which lets users set thresholds and receive automatic alarms for threshold violators.

RMON2 defines the specification for monitoring traffic for distributed applications such as Lotus Notes, Microsoft Mail, and Sybase by outlining how logical filters can be constructed for remote agents. With this capability, the network manager can proactively monitor and troubleshoot any essential application-layer traffic within an enterprise network. RMON Alarms, Statistics, History, and Host/conversation groups are used for troubleshooting and maintaining network availability based upon application layer traffic—the most critical traffic in the network.

What Is the Difference Between RMON and SNMP?

Although the Simple Network Management Protocol (SNMP) is useful for monitoring network resources, it is geared toward node management rather than network management. SNMP is used to monitor device-specific information by polling different resources (routers, etc.) on the network but it provides no consistent view of overall network operation and health.

SNMP also uses frequent polling as its foundation of operation. SNMP polling consumes valuable network bandwidth as well as network node resources such as router and server CPU cycles. On the other hand, if polling is done too infrequently, valuable information is lost. This is truly a catch 22 associated with managing an efficient network. Figure 12-4 shows the true extent of how SNMP consumes valuable bandwidth.

RMON addresses these problems by transparently monitoring network operation from a network agent. Various groups of information, defined in the RMON MIBs, allow an RMON agent to collect information on network statistics, hosts, and conversations. The RMON agent compiles this information by observing the traffic on the network.

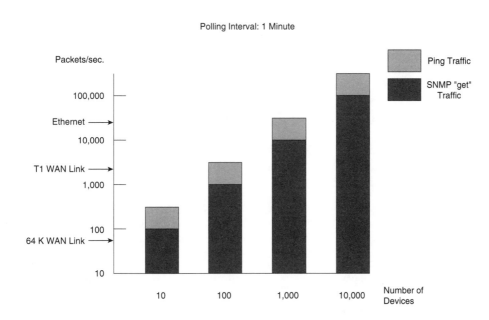

Polling Interval: 1 Minute

Packets/sec.

Ping Traffic

SNMP "get"
Traffic

100,000

Ethernet

10,000

T1 WAN Link

1,000

100

64 K WAN Link

10

10   100   1,000   10,000   Number of
                                        Devices

Figure 12–4
*Average SNMP
bandwidth
utilization.*

The polling that takes place between the management station and the probe is just to transfer statistics that have already been gathered by a RMON probe.

A history group enables an agent to collect historical information about network operation, further reducing the amount of polling required. Other RMON groups set thresholds for any RMON-defined operational parameter, enabling management by exception. Traps are generated when the thresholds are exceeded.

Conclusions on SNMP Versus RMON

Both SNMP and RMON are useful within a network. However, it is this author's opinion that the future is going to be found in primarily using RMON-based solutions. There is a chance that the upcoming SNMPv3 will address some of its predecessor's shortcomings. As with many things, only time will tell which becomes dominant—or maybe they both have a place.

INTERNET PROTOCOL ADDRESSING V6 (IPV6)

The Internet Protocol, Next Generation (also known as IPv6), was designed to combat the growing concerns of the quickly shrinking Internet address supply. IPv4 host implementations also lack essential features such as auto configuration and network layer security. IPv6 brings with it several advances in the field of Internet protocols. IPv6 is a set of specifications from the Internet Engineering Task Force (IETF) designed as a Darwin-like evolutionary step from IPv4—the current version. IPv6 provides expanded addressing, added security, and investment protection for those standing firm with IPv4. The following list covers several of the key advances included with the IPv6 proposed standard

- **Expanded Addressing Capabilities.** IPv6 supports more levels of addressing hierarchy and a greater number of addressable nodes by increasing the IP address size from 32-bit to 128 bits.

- **Simpler Header Format.** To provide more efficient packet handling and to reduce the bandwidth cost of IPv6 header, some of the old IPv4 header fields have been dropped or moved to optional extension headers.

- **Improved Support for Extensions and Options.** Adjustments to the IP header options and the way they're encoded allow for a more efficient forwarding, less restrictive limitations on the length of options, and more flexibility when introducing new options in the future.

- **Flow Labeling Capability.** This new capability was added to enable the labeling of packets belonging to particular traffic flows for which the sender requests special handling.

- **Authentication and Privacy Capabilities.** Extensions to support authentication, data integrity, and data confidentiality are specified for IPv6. You could expand upon these features even more.

The first questions you should be asking yourself is, "Why do we need another version?" The reasons for adding another version are numerous:

- Solves the Internet IP address scaling problem

- Provides a flexible transition mechanism for the current Internet

- Designed to comply with the needs of new markets such as nomadic personal computers, networked entertainment, and device control

- Integrates multimedia, security, and auto-configuration

IPv6 is designed to interoperate with IPv4. Specific mechanisms were embedded within IPv6 to support an easy transition and compatibility with IPv4. IPv6 also supports large hierarchical addresses, which will enable the Internet to continue to grow. The address structure of IPv6 is designed to support carrying addresses of other Internet protocol suites, such as IPX. IPv6 also provides a platform for new Internet compatibility, to include support for real-time flows, provider selections, host mobility, end-to-end security, and auto configuration and reconfiguration. Each of the key advances in IPv6, as listed previously, are detailed in the pages that follow.

There are many books and white papers available on IPv6, but none of them address the reluctance behind implementing it. Confusion and concern is to be expected regarding the massive change IPv6 represents to the networking arena as a whole. Nevertheless, some disturbing myths have surrounded IPv6. The following will address the myths surrounding IPv6.

Myth 1: We Need IPv6 Because We Are Running Out of Address Space!

There is a fact in this myth: yes, we will run out of address space in IPv4, but so will IPv6. The InterNIC is the authority that assigns IP addresses, and since 1991 the InterNIC has become more stringent about handing out IP addresses. However, most predictions for IPv4 address depletion state that will not happen until well into the next century. Fortunately, the creators of IPv6 have taken the 32-bit address of IPv4 and increased it to 128 bits in IPv6, which will provide us with: 340,282,366,920,938,463,463,374,607,431,768,211,456 addresses

You can figure out how to write that in words, but to me it is just a HUGE number of addresses. Estimates state that IPv6 will support thousands of unique addresses for each square meter on the surface of the earth.

Myth 2: We Can Patch IPv4 to Duplicate IPv6

It is understood that a migration from IPv4 to IPv6 will be a challenging process. Nevertheless, the idea that patching IPv4 will make everything all right is flawed. One example of an IPv4 patch is network address translation (NAT) that preserves IPv4 address space by intercepting traffic and converting private IP addresses into unique Internet addresses. Other examples include the various quality-of-service and security enhancements being proposed to IPv4.

These patches might prove to be valuable in certain limited and short-term scenarios, but they ultimately will limit connectivity, interoperability, and network performance. In general, IPv4 patches are no substitute for IPv6—a protocol suite that has been designed from the ground up with scalable addressing, advanced routing, security, quality-of-service, and related features from the beginning.

Future network requirements will require extremely high levels of connectivity both internally and externally to your network. We are seeing the future quickly emerging around us in the form of the World Wide Web, increased multimedia, transaction-oriented applications, and ever more interactive applications.

Myth 3: IPv6 Will Only Benefit Hierarchical Networks

The truth is that IPv6 will provide many benefits for hierarchical networks. However, there is a variety of features that it brings to the table that will benefit every level of network user. These benefits are outlined in the following list.

- Increased security and authentication that will benefit applications

- Automatic configuration features that will benefit mobile network users

- Quality of Service features already integrated into the stack will benefit interactive multimedia applications

Myth 4: Who Needs the Ability to Assign Addresses to a Large Number of Diverse Network Devices?

New and very diverse network devices are already here. Take a moment to consider what is already available for use within a business setting or home.

- Personal Data Assistants (PDAs)

- Cellular Phone/Pagers Combinations with Voice Mail

- Web Integrated Televisions

- Embedded network components within office equipment

- Embedded network components within home appliances

- Satellite links in your car

- Hand-Held Global Positioning systems

These devices are only a few steps away from being incorporated into every network; and make no mistake, the ability to log onto the Internet and check the status of your home appliances and security system is not far away. The possibilities are endless and mind-boggling.

As new devices make their way onto the Internet, they will strain the existing network fabric in ways the early IP protocol designers could hardly have imagined. IPv6 address space will enable businesses to take advantage of this yet untapped market.

IPv6 Design Goals

IPv6 has been designed to enable high-performance, scalable internetworks to remain viable well into the next century. A large part of this design process involved correcting the inadequacies of IPv4. It is only by delving into the full range of IPv6 improvements that the full benefits to enterprise networks can be evaluated.

With the advent of IPv6 comes more efficient Internet protocols with several features. The most common features appear in the following list.

- 128-bit network addresses instead of 32-bit
- More efficient IP header with extensions for applications and options
- Streamlined packet design to include no header checksum
- A flow label for quality-of-service requirements
- Prevention of intermediate fragmentation of datagrams
- Built in security for authentication and encryption

These enhancements will be detailed later in the chapter. Other qualities are less tangible and relate to the fresh start that IPv6 gives to those who build and administer networks.

Addressing and Routing

IPv6 will enable Internet backbone designers to create a highly flexible and open-ended global routing hierarchy. At the level of the Internet backbone where major enterprises and Internet Service Provider (ISP) networks come together, it is necessary to maintain a hierarchical addressing system, much like that of the national and international telephone systems.

For example, large central-office phone switches only need a three-digit national area code prefix to route a long-distance telephone call to the correct local exchange. Without an address hierarchy, backbone routers would be forced to store routing table information on the accessibility of every network in the world.

As discussed in previous chapters, given the current number of IP subnets in the world and the growth of the Internet, this is not feasible. However, if there was a hierarchical addressing structure, then backbone routers could use IP address prefixes to determine how traffic should be routed through the backbone.

Currently, IPv4 uses a technique called Classless InterDomain Routing (CIDR), which allows flexible use of variable-length network prefixes. The availability of CIDR routing does not guarantee an efficient and scalable hierarchy. In many cases, legacy IPv4 address assignments that originated before CIDR do not facilitate summarization. In fact, much of the IPv4 address space was formed before the current access provider hierarchy was developed. This lack of uniformity in the current hierarchical system, coupled with the rationing of IPv4 addresses, means that Internet addressing and routing is filled with complications at all levels.

Transitioning and Implementing IPv6

Few in the industry would argue with the principle that IPv6 represents a major leap forward for the Internet and the enterprises that rely on internetworking technology.

What is not agreed upon in the industry, however, is which shape and speed the transition from IPv4 to IPv6 will take:

- Wholesale rapid adoption of IPv6 in the very near future
- Wait until address-space exhaustion and other issues force conversion

But given the magnitude of a migration that affects so many millions of network devices, it is clear that there will be an extended period when IPv4 and IPv6 will coexist at many levels on the Internet.

Another assumption made by IPv6 transition designers is the likelihood that many upgraded hosts and routers will need to retain downward compatibility with IPv4 devices for an extended time period (possibly years or even indefinitely). It was also assumed that upgraded devices should have the option of retaining their IPv4 addressing. To accomplish these goals, IPv6 transition relies on several special functions that have been built into the IPv6 standards work, including dual-stack hosts and routers and tunneling IPv6 via IPv4.

There are many proposals being studied for implementing IPv6. The three most popular are as follows:

- TUBA (TCP and UDP with Bigger Addresses)
- CATNIP (Common Architecture for the Internet)
- SIPP (Simple Internet Protocol Plus)

Expanded Addressing Capabilities

IPv6 addresses are 128-bits long and are used as identifiers for individual interfaces and sets of interfaces. All types of IPv6 addresses are assigned to interfaces, not nodes. There are three types of IPv6 addresses: unicast—identify a single interface; anycast—identify a set of interfaces such that a packet sent to an anycast address will be delivered to one member of the set; and multicast—identify a group of interfaces so that a packet sent to a multicast address is delivered to all of the interfaces in the group. With the advent of the multicast address, the broadcast addresses of IPv4 became obsolete. The leading bits in the address indicate the specific type of IPv6 address. The variable length field comprising these leading bits is called the Format Prefix (FP). Table 12-2 describes the initial allocation of those prefixes.

Table 12-2 *Initial allocation of IPv6 prefixes*

Allocation	Prefix (Binary)	Fraction of Address Space
Reserved	0000 0000	1/256
Unassigned	0000 0001	1/256
Reserved for NSAP Allocation	0000 001	1/128
Reserved for IPX Allocation	0000 010	1/128
Unassigned	0000 011	1/128
Unassigned	0000 1	1/32
Unassigned	0001	1/16
Unassigned	001	1/8
Provider-Based Unicast Address	010	1/8
Unassigned	011	1/8
Neutral-Interconnect-Based Unicast Addresses	100	1/8
Unassigned	101	1/8
Unassigned	110	1/8
Unassigned	1110	1/16
Unassigned	1111 0	1/32
Unassigned	1111 10	1/64
Unassigned	1111 110	1/128
Unassigned	1111 1110 0	1/512
Link-Local Use Addresses	1111 1110 10	1/1024
Site-Local Use Addresses	1111 1110 11	1/1024
Multicast Addresses	1111 1111	1/256

This initial allocation supports the direct allocation of provider addresses, local use addresses, and multicast address. There is also a reserved space for NSAP and IPX addresses, and neutral-interconnect addresses. You will notice that anycast addresses are not allocated an IP. This is because the anycast addresses are allocated out of the unicast address space.

Unicast addresses identify exactly one interface. They are defined as aggregatable global unicast address formats. There are many forms of unicast address format assignments in IPv6. They are broken down into the following categories:

- Global Provider-Based Addresses
- Neutral-Interconnect Addresses
- NSAP Addresses
- IPX Hierarchical Addresses
- Site-Local-Use Addresses
- Link-Local-Use Addresses
- IPv4-Capable host Addresses

These categories organize addresses into a three-level architecture: public topology, site topology, and interface identifiers.

Public Topology

Public topology is a collection of providers and exchanges that provide public Internet transit services. It is divided into a set of Top Level Aggregators (TLA) and a possible hierarchy of Next Level Aggregators (NLA). 13 bits are assigned to specify the TLA and 32 bits for the NLA space.

Site Topology

Site topology is local to a specific site or organization that does not provide public services to nodes outside the site. Site topology is specified as a 16-bit field for Site Level Aggregators (SLA).

Interface Identifiers

The third level of this architecture is the Interface Identifiers. Simply put, Interface Identifiers identify interfaces on links. They must be 64 bits in length and constructed per Institute of Electrical and Electrical Engineers (IEEE) standards.

Provider-Based Unicast Addresses

Provider-based unicast addresses are used for global communications. Figure 12-5 shows the format for a provider-based unicast address.

3	n bits	m bits	o bits	p bits	o-p bits
010	Registry ID	Provider ID	Subscriber ID	Subnet ID	Interface ID

Figure 12–5
Provider-based unicast addressing.

The first three bits identify the address as a provider-based unicast address. The Registry ID identifies Internet address registry, which assigns provider identifier (Provider ID) to Internet Service Providers (ISPs). The ISP then assigns portions of the address space to their subscribers. The Subscriber ID distinguishes among multiple subscribers attached to the ISP identified in the Provider ID. The Subnet ID identifies a specific physical link—there can be many subnets on the same physical link. Finally, the Interface ID can identify a single interface among the group of interfaces identified by the Subnet prefix. This is similar in practice to using subnet masking to increase the size of your network. For instance, each person is given his or her address. When a mail message comes down the pike addressed to Joe Eastern, the message would first hit the ISP then "unwrap" itself to find Joe on the server.

Local-Use Addresses

A Local-Use address is a unicast address having only a local routability scope. This scope is within the subnet or within the subscriber network. These local addresses are intended to be used within a site for "plug and play" communication and for bootstrapping to the use of global addresses. The most beneficial aspect of the Local-Use address is that it enables organizations not connected to the global Internet to operate without the need to request an address prefix from the global Internet address space. Instead, the organization uses the combination of the Subnet ID and Interface ID to form a local-use address. Later, when the company or organization gets to the point where they need, or want, to connect to the global Internet, they can use their Subnet ID and Interface ID in conjunction with a global prefix (example Registry ID, and Provider ID and Subscriber ID) to create a global IP address.

There are two types of Local-Use unicast addresses: Link-Local and Site-Local. The former is used on a site link and the latter on a single site. Link-Local Use addresses have the format illustrated in Figure 12-6.

Figure 12–6
Link-Local Use
addresses.

10 bits	n bits	118-n bits
1111111010	0	Interface ID

They are designed to be used for addressing on a site link for purposes such as auto-address configuration. Figure 12-7 illustrates the format for Site-Local Use addresses.

Figure 12–7
Site-Local Use
addresses.

10 bits	n bits	m bits	118-n-m bits
1111111011	0	Subnet ID	Interface ID

IPv6 Addresses with Embedded IPv4 Addresses

Fortunately, IPv6 includes transition mechanisms for routers and hosts to dynamically tunnel IPv6 packets over an IPv4 routing infrastructure. The nodes that use this technique are assigned special IPv6 unicast addresses. These addresses carry an IPv4 address in the low-order 32-bits. These addresses are called *IPv4-compatible IPv6 addresses*. Figure 12-8 illustrates the format for IPv4-compatible IPv6 addresses.

80 bits	16	32 bits
0000...................0000	0000	IPv4 Address

Figure 12–8
*IPv4-compatible
IPv6 addresses.*

A second type of these embedded addresses is called an *IPv4-mapped IPv6 address.* This address is used to represent the addresses of nodes that use IPv4 addresses exclusively. Figure 12-9 illustrates the format for IPv4-mapped IPv6 addresses.

80 bits	16	32 bits
0000...................0000	FFFF	IPv4 Address

Figure 12–9
*IPv4-mapped
IPv6 addresses.*

Anycast Addresses

The anycast address is a 128-bit address that is assigned to more than one interface. The anycast addresses have a specific property that informs the packet sent to an anycast address to be routed to the "closest" interface having that address. This "closeness," of course, is determined by the routing protocol's measure of distance.

Anycast addresses have a function called *source selected policies.* This function permits a node to select which of several ISPs it wants to carry its traffic, when used as part of a route sequence. This function can be implemented by configuring anycast addresses to identify sets of routers belonging to ISPs. They can then be utilized as intermediate addresses in the new IPv6 routing header. Doing this would cause the packet to be delivered by a particular route. Anycast addresses can also be used to identify a set of routers attached to a single subnet, or perhaps even used to identify the set of routers providing entry to a routing domain. Figure 12-10 illustrates the operation of anycast addresses in a network.

Anycast addresses are allocated from the unicast address space, using any of the unicast address formats discussed earlier. For all practical purposes, anycast addresses are indistinguishable from unicast address. A unicast address assigned to more than one interface is turned into an anycast address; the nodes to which the anycast address is going must be explicitly configured to read and understand that the incoming packet has an anycast address.

Figure 12–10
*IPv6 anycast in
operation.*

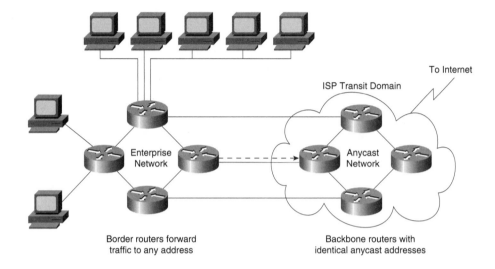

Multicast Addresses

IPv6 multicast addresses are an identifier for a group of interfaces. These interfaces may belong to any number of multicast groups. Figure 12-11 illustrates the format for multicast addresses.

Figure 12–11
*IPv6 multicast
addresses.*

8	4	4	112 bits
11111111	FLGS	SCOP	Group ID

The 8 bits at the beginning identify this address as a multicast address as referenced in Table 12-2. The 4 bits identified as FLGS is a set of four flags: |0|0|0|T|. The high-order three flags are reserved, and must be initialized to 0. The final flag has two options either T=0 or T=1. If T=0, this indicates a permanently assigned, or "well-known," multicast address, assigned by the global Internet numbering authority. T=1 is an indication of a non-permanently assigned, or "transient," multicast address.

The other 4-bit field is the SCOP (Scope) field. SCOP is a 4-bit multicast scope value used to limit the range of the multicast grouping. The scope value can have the following values:

0 Reserved	8 (Organization-local scope)
1 Node-local scope	9 (unassigned)
2 Link-local scope	A (unassigned)
3 (unassigned)	B (unassigned)
4 (unassigned)	C (unassigned)
5 Site-local scope	D (unassigned)
6 (unassigned)	E (unassigned)
7 (unassigned)	F (unassigned)

Finally, the Group ID identifies the multicast group within the given scope whether it is a permanent or transient address. These group IDs have taken the place of the IPv4 multicast address. This enables a group of hosts to be designated as group "accounting," for example. On the same segment is another group designated as "marketing," for example. Your packets enter this segment, and they are destined to the "accounting" group. Thus, the "marketing" group does not get them, which reduces network traffic and increases security. Figure 12-12 illustrates the operation of multicast addresses in a network.

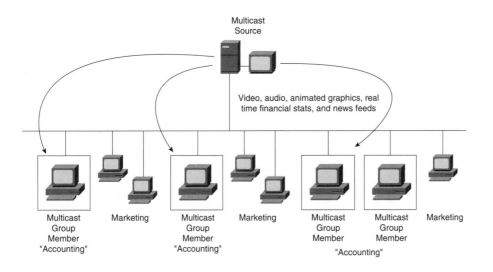

Figure 12–12
Multicast in operation.

IPv6 Headers

The changes to the IPv4 header provide support for the new 128-bit addresses and they remove obsolete and unneeded fields. Figure 12-13 illustrates the basic layout for the IPv6 header.

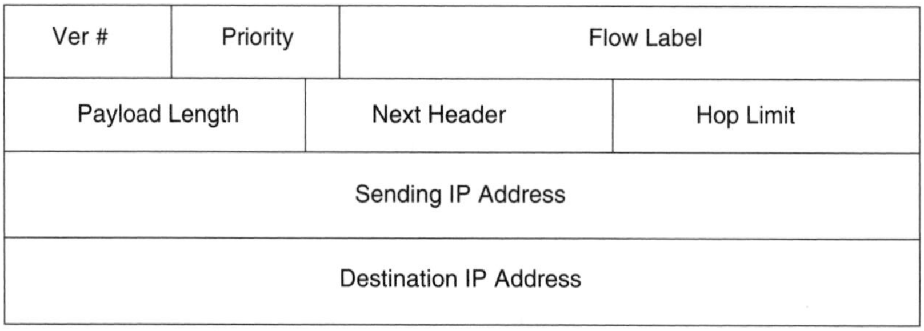

Figure 12–13
IPv6 packet header format.

The following list describes the IPv6 packet header format fields in greater detail.

- **Ver #.** The version number is a 4-bit field that holds the release number of the IP version—6 with IPv6.

- **Priority.** The Priority field is a 4-bit field, which holds a value indicating the priority of the datagram. This priority is used to determine the transmission order of datagrams in the line-up. I will go into further detail on the Priority field a bit later in the chapter.

- **Flow Label.** The Flow Label field is 24 bits long. Currently it is still under development. More than likely, it will be combined with the source address to provide flow identification on the network.

- **Payload Length.** The Payload Length field is 16 bits long and is used to specify the total length of the IP datagram, in bytes.

- **Next Header.** The Next Header field indicates which header follows the IP header when other applications want to "piggy-back" on the IP header itself. The Next Header field identifies the other applications by several different values as defined in Table 12-3.

Table 12-3   *Next Header field values*

Value	Description
0	Hop-by-Hop Options
4	IP
6	TCP
17	UDP
43	Routing
44	Fragment
45	Inter-Domain Routine
46	Resource Reservation
50	Encapsulating Security
51	Authentication
58	ICMP
59	No Next Header
60	Destination Options

- **Hop limit.** The Hop Limit field determines the number of hops the datagram can travel. As each datagram is forwarded, the number is decremented by 1. When the Hop Limit field is reduced to 0, the datagram is discarded.

- **Sending and Destination Address.** These fields are both 128-bit addresses that correspond to the machine the datagram is being sent from and its intended target.

Figure 12-14 shows the layout for IPv6 packets.

The Priority Classification Field

As mentioned earlier, the Priority Classification field is a 4-bit field that holds the value of the datagram, which ultimately determines the transmission order of that datagram. What is briefly explained here is the intricate workings of this tiny 4-bit field. The field divided the datagram into one of two classifications: Congestion Controlled or Non-Congestion Controlled. The latter are always routed as a priority over the former. If the datagram is Congestion Controlled it is sensitive to congestion on the network bandwidth. If congestion occurs while the datagram is on the network, it can be slowed down and held in temporary caches until the problem is resolved and the bandwidth clears. Furthermore, each of the classifications is broken down even further into sub-categories. The subcategories of non-congestion controlled datagrams have not been accepted as standard yet; however, the powers that be have accepted the sub categories classification of the congestion controlled datagrams as defined in Table 12-4.

4 bits	4 bits	24 bits
Version	Priority	Flow Label
36 bits	8 bits	8 bits
Payload Length	Next Header	Hop Limit
128 bits		
Source Address		
128 bits		
Destination Address		

Table 12-4   *Congestion controlled priorities*

Value	Description
0	No Priority Specified
1	Background (news)
2	Unattended Data Transfer (e-mail traffic)
3	Unassigned
4	Attended Bulk Transfer (FTP & Telnet)
5	Unassigned
6	Interactive Traffic (Telnet & Remote Session Traffic)
7	Controlled Traffic (Routing & Network Management Traffic)

Flow Labels

The Flow Label field is new to the IPv6 header. It can be used to help identify the sender and destination of many IP datagrams. It does this by establishing a specified value of the flow label for all datagrams in the transmission. The routers in the path to the server assemble entries in their routing caches, indicating which way to route the datagrams with an identical flow label.

There are some concerns you might have, such as large caches and repeated values. These potential problems have been fixed with IPv6. To prevent caches from growing too large or holding old information, IPv6 stipulates the cache maintained in a routing device cannot be kept for more than six seconds. If a new datagram with the same flow label is not received within that period, the data in the cache is dumped. To prevent repeated values from the sending machine, the sender must wait six seconds before using the same flow label value for another destination. IPv6 also allows flow labels to be used to reserve a route for time-critical applications. This is useful when using a real-time application that has to send several datagrams along the same route as it needs as rapid a transmission of those datagrams as possible. It establishes the route by sending datagrams ahead of time, all the while being careful not to exceed the time-out on the interim routers. This allows for the constant flow of data from sender to receiver without having to wait while the sending machine contacts the router every time it sends a packet.

IPv6 Header Extensions

IPv6 has the ability to allow additional headers to be tacked onto the original IP header. This might be needed when a simple routing to the destination is not possible, or when special services, such as authentication, are required for the datagram. With this in mind, IPv6 defines many types of Header extensions. These extensions are identified by a number placed in the next header field of the original IP header. Many extensions can be appended onto one IP header, with each extension's next header field indicating the next extensions.

Routing Headers

A routing header extension can be added to the IP header when the transmitting machine wants to control the routing of a particular datagram, instead of leaving it to the whim of the routers along the path. This extension can also be used to give route instructions to the destination machine. The routing extension includes fields for each IP address in the desired route.

Fragment Headers

As of this writing, when you send a particularly long datagram, your ISP might fragment it and send it as many smaller datagrams. With the fragment header of IPv6, you decide when to fragment your message and if so, where to do it, so that loss of data is minimized. The Fragment Header can be added to an IP header to enable a machine to fragment a large datagram into smaller parts. This was built into IPv6 to facilitate better use of fragmentation. If a particular datagram is very large, the fragmentation can be enabled to pass the datagram along the network quicker, they also allow for better use of WAN (Wide Area Network) bandwidth.

Hop-by-Hop Headers

Hop-by-Hop headers are used to instruct, via IP options, every machine the datagram passes through. There are three options included in the Hop-by-Hop header field. These all have a standard format of a Type Value, a Length, and a Value. To further confuse you, there are three types of Hop-by-Hop headers, including: Pad1, PadN, and Jumbo Payload

The Pad1 option is the simplest, by far. It is a single byte with a value of 0, no length, and no value. It is used primarily in the alteration of the order and position of other options in the header when necessary. This is usually determined by the application the user is using and is transparent. The PadN option is very similar. The only difference being that the PadN has N zeros placed in the Value field and a calculated value for the length. Finally, there is the Jumbo Payload extension option. This is used for datagrams that exceed 65,535 bytes. To handle these larger datagram lengths, the IP header's length field is set to 0. This will then redirect the routers to the extension to pick-up a correct length value. The Length field is defined in the extension header using 32-bits. This is in excess of 4 terabytes.

CHAPTER SUMMARY

This chapter explored the features that made SNMPv2 unique. These features include the new Alarm and Event groups that enable you have quick and easy access to information concerning the state of your network. When properly utilized, they can also provide the Network manager with a powerful tool. By utilizing SNMPv2, you, as the network manager, have a one-click access to all components on your network. If your network is geographically separated, the distributed manager has the capability to have the error messages sent directly to your NMS. The newly developed Alarm and Event Groups in the SNMP MIBII do this. Overall, this manager-friendly protocol will save both time and money. In addition, you were also given a brief peek under the covers concerning the soon to be released SNMPv3.

RMON is the fastest growing network management tool around. Its ability to monitor the performance of the entire network as opposed to just the components brings a new and powerful tool to both network engineers and managers. This section covered both

RMON1 and RMON2 so you gained an understanding of how when combined they cover every layer of the OSI model. This chapter discussed how RMON enables you, the manager, to monitor traffic at all layers of your network by providing host and matrix tables. In addition this chapter discussed how RMON allows you to monitor by host, or conversation, various network protocols.

This chapter then covered IPv6 and removed some of the myths and mystery surrounding it. This section allowed you to explore some of the new features surrounding this protocol and how it has improved over IPv4. IPv6 has a newly designed header format that allows for easier transmission across your network, and it also frees up the bandwidth by eliminating the need for all IP datagrams to be transmitted over the entire network.

CASE STUDY: IMPLEMENTING IPv6 IN YOUR NETWORK

This case study will briefly describe one way of slowly implementing IPv6 in your network if your network has a large number of users whose connectivity requirements focus primarily on access to local e-mail, database, and applications servers.

When considering how to implement IPv6, it might be best to initially upgrade only isolated workgroups and departments to IPv6, and implement backbone router upgrades at a slower rate. This is an excellent way for enterprise networks to gracefully transition to IPv6.

As enterprise routing protocols such as OSPF for IPv6 mature, the core backbone IPv6 connections can be deployed. After the first few IPv6 routers are in place, it might be desirable to connect the various IPv6 workgroups with router-to-router tunnels. In this case, one or more routers providing IPv6 connectivity would need to be configured as tunnel endpoints.

From a routing protocol standpoint, tunnels appear as a single IPv6 hop, even if the tunnel is comprised of many IPv4 hops across different types of media. IPv6 routers running OSPF can propagate link-state advertisements through tunnels, just as they would across conventional point-to-point links. In an IPv6 environment, OSPF will have the advantage of flexible metrics for tunnel routes, to ensure that each tunnel is given its proper weight within the topology. In general, routers make packet-forwarding decisions in a tunneling environment in the same way that they make decisions in the IPv6-only network. The underlying IPv4 connections are essentially transparent to IPv6 routing protocols.

FREQUENTLY ASKED QUESTIONS

Q— *From where did RMONv2 derive?*

A— The IETF (Internet Engineering Task Force) developed RMONv2 to provide Network Managers the ability to view data rates on their network and the network layer. The built-in feature set is going to enable network managers to more accurately see the complete picture of the network. Many manufactures are currently pursuing this.

Q— *Will I have to change all IP addresses on my network if my company adopts IPv6?*

A— No. The new standard defines how Ipv4 and IPv6 are interoperable.

Q— *When should I migrate from IPv4 to IPv6?*

A— First of all, relax. You should not have to worry about this for a while yet. In the meantime, Cisco Systems, in conjunction with other network vendors, have already incorporate many of the new and exciting features of IPv6. Things such as classless interdomain routing (CIDR) and Network Address Translation (NAT) provide the means to resolve the current limitations of IP address assignments.

Q— *Where can I find more information about SNMPv2?*

A— Refer to the following sites for more information:

```
www.snmp.cs.utwente.nl/int
www.simple-times.org/pub/simple-times/usec
www.snmp.com
www.aw.com/cp/stallings3.html
```

Q— *Where can I find more information on SNMPv3?*

A— The best, and most up to date source can be found at:
`http://www.snmp.com/v2status.html`

To join the SNMPv3 mailing list, send mail to: `snmpv3-request@tis.com` with "subscribe" in the mail message.

The mailing list archive can be found at
`ftp://ftp.tis.com/pub/ietf/snmpv3`

Q— *What do Cisco routers do for the following SNMP MIB variables:* `ifInNUcastPkts`, `ifInDiscards`, `ifInErrors`, `ifInUnknownProtos`, `ifOutOctets`, `ifOutUcastPkts`, `ifOutDiscards`, `ifOutErrors`, *and* `ifOutQLen`*?*

A— The following list provides details on these SNMP MIB variables.

- `ifInNUcastPkts`. Counts of inbound broadcast and multicast packets
- `ifInDiscards`. Counts as no buffers as reflected in `show int`
- `ifInErrors`. Counts of all input errors as reflected in `show int`
- `ifInUnknownProtos`. Counts as unclassified errors
- `ifOutOctets`. Counts of the number of bytes output by the interface as shown in `show int`
- `ifOutUcastPkts`. Counts of outbound broadcast and multicast packets
- `ifOutDiscards`. Counts as output drops as shown in `show int`
- `ifOutErrors`. Counts as output errors as shown in `show int`
- `ifOutQLen`. The number of packets allowed to be on the output queue as shown in `show int`

The variables previously listed that do not say they appear in `show int` are not available anywhere other than SNMP.

Q— *Explain the relationship between the show interface statements* `no buffers` *and* `input queue drops`*. Why do the* `inDiscards` *of SNMP give* `no buffers` *counts and not* `input queue drops`*, even though the* `outDiscards` *of SNMP do give output queue drops?*

A— The `locIfInputQueueDrops`/`ifInDiscards` work differently than `locIfOutputQueueDrops`/`ifOutDiscards`. The `ifInDiscards` counts the number of packets that were thrown away for lack of a system resource such as a buffer. This is generally a subset of the `locIfInputQueueDrops`. You will often see `locIfInputQueueDrops` = `ifInDiscards`. However, `locIfInputQueueDrops` also counts the number of packets dropped because of hitting the input queue limit. So more generally, you will see `locIfInputQueueDrops` > `ifInDiscards`.

To recap:

> `locIfInputQueueDrops` = Queue Limit Drops + No Buffer Drops
> `ifInDiscards` = No Buffer Drops (and is a subset of locIfInputQueue-Drops)

The `locIfOutputQueueDrops` and `ifOutDiscards` are always equal when they count the same events. (These events are hitting the output queue limit, and do not have a hardware `tx` buffer when a packet is fast-switched from one interface to another.)

Q— *Can I poll "no buffers" on a router?*

A— Yes. You can poll no buffers by polling for `ifInDiscards`. you can also use the `MIB OLD-CISCO-MEMORY-MIB.my` to get all of the buffer information on a router. You can use a short script to place these into a table that can be read through a browser or imported into a spreadsheet.

Q— *How do I poll "Queue Limit Drops" on a router?*

A— There is no way via SNMP or the show interface commands to break out the individual elements that go into the output drops. Here is some new information about what goes into the output drops counter:

```
Input drops ==
Queue limit drops +
Throttling drops +
SMT queue full drops +
RSRB drops +
no buffer drops
```

In addition, SNMP counters are never cleared, even if interfaces have been cleared.

Q— *How can you identify what interface number to use in the MIB name?*

A— Each row of the interfaces table has an associated number, called an `ifIndex`. You use the `ifIndex` number to get a specific instance of an interface group object. For example, `ifInNUcastPkts.1` would find the number of broadcast packets received on interface number one. You can then find the description of interface number one by looking at the object, which holds the interface description (from MIB-II) `ifDescr.1`.

Q— *Why would I need the* `snmp-server enable traps <trap-type> <trap-option>` *command?*

A— To enable all traps of a given type or types (that is, if the given trap type is generating noise in which you aren't interested).

Q— *Why does the* `snmp-server enable traps <trap-type> <trap-option>` *command only have a subset of the traps?*

A— Most of the trap types in the `snmp-server enable traps <trap-type> <trap-option>` command have associated MIB `notificationEnable` objects that map to this CLI command. No effort has been made as yet to provide this global enable option to traps that do not have this equivalent MIB control.

Q— *Would the above commands ever be used together?*

A— It is up to you. For example, you could enable all Frame Relay traps, and not want trap receiver *xxyy* to see them, but only trap receiver bumble.

Q— *Where can I get a better definition of the trap types listed under the* `snmp-server host <host> <com-string> <trap-type>` *command? (For example, the documentation explains "config" as: Send configuration traps.) I would like to know what events send a trap.*

A— Each of the trap type labels is supposed to reflect the name of the MIB in which the associated traps are defined. For instance, config would be from the `CISCO-CONFIG-MAN-MIB.my`, envmon would be from the `CISCO-ENVMON-MIB.my`, etc.

Q— *Does Cisco implement 64-bit counters, especially for the IF-MIB? If not, when is 64-bit counter support expected?*

A— Cisco does not support 64 bit counters yet. This is being worked on now.

Q— *What version of SNMP is required for 64-bit counter support?*

A— SNMPv2C is required for Counter64.

Q— *Does the Cisco IOS support sub-interfaces in the ifTable?*

A— Generic support for sublayers in the ifTable has been present since Cisco IOS 11.1(1). For any given media type, it is up to the groups that support that media to determine the following factors:

1. If sublayers are appropriate (with direction from IETF).

2. How to support those sublayers.

Q— *What is the minimum Cisco IOS version I should be running to see sub-interfaces in SNMP tables?*

A— Cisco IOS 11.1.

Q— *Are the SNMP counters* `ifInOctects` *and* `ifOutOctets` *the same as the* `show interface` *in/out counters?*

A— Yes.

Q— *Do the* `ifInOctets` *and* `ifOutOctets` *counters include framing overhead (PPP, HDLC)?*

A— Yes.

Q— *On an ATM interface, do the counters include the cell header?*

A— ATM counters do not include ATM overhead (cell headers and AAL5 padding).

Q— *Some ifTable columns do not show up for certain interface types. Why? Is this a bug?*

A— This is not a bug. ifTable based on RFC 1573 is designed specifically so that some columns in a given row will not be instantiated based on ifType. Please read the RFC compliance statement for further clarification for which columns to expect for different media groups. An example of this would be ATM, which is a fixed length packet. As such, rows in the ifTable, etc. would be based on `ifFixedLengthGroup`.

Q— *In which release is SNMPv2C support available?*

A— Cisco IOS 11.3 will be the first shipping release with SNMPv2C support.

Q— *Is there a way to tell the router to load a specific configuration file via TFTP from a specific host?*

A— Yes. `ftp://ftpeng.cisco.com/pub/mibs/app_notes/configset`

Q— *Is there an SNMP MIB to grab arp table information? We need both the IP and MAC address in the same table.*

A— Yes. `ipNetToMediaTable` in MIB-II (RFC 1213)

Q— *I activated Silicon Switching and now MIB values for interface statistics are only updated every 10 seconds. SNMP GETs for MIB values show no change if polled more often (in this case, 8 seconds). Is this is a bug?*

A— This is expected (it's not a bug). Part of the tradeoff for allowing the box to dedicate more resources to actually switching traffic is to poll less often for interface statistics. "Show interface" should present the same behavior.

Q— *Is there a tool for extracting MIBs from an RFC?*

A— Yes, try `premosy < rfc > mib`, where `rfc` is the text document from which `mib` is to be extracted.

Q— *I would like to capture SNMP traps on my workstation. What tool can I use for this?*

A— On SunOS machines, use `/usr/local/bin/tcpdump`.

On Solaris, use `/sw/current/solaris2bin/traprcv`.

On Windows, use: `http://www.mg-soft.com`.

Q— *Is there a way to automatically route IP accounting information to a host's SYSLOG file? What are some guidelines/performance issues related to setting the accounting threshold and transits?*

A— If you want the IP accounting info, you need to use SNMP to get the information. The router will not "send" the IP accounting info to a SYSLOG server. I don't think there are any set guidelines for setting the thresholds and transits in IP accounting. Performance is based on how often you use SNMP to get the IP accounting info and how much info you have to get. Be sure to set your SNMP packet-size to 8192 when getting this info.

Q— *What is the best way to block SNMP from coming in on a serial port of a Cisco 2501 that is attached to the Internet? I have an access list for other restrictions already.*

A— If you already have an extended access list, you only need to block UDP ports 161 and 162.

Q— *How do you reload a Cisco 2511 using the SNMP protocol?*

A— Use the MIB variable `tsMsgSend` with an instance of 0 and a value of 2. Then issue the SET. You also need to add the command `snmp-server system-shutdown` in the router, as well as have a RW community string.

Q— *What's the difference between SNMP and SNMP2 configuration in Cisco IOS? Which version of Cisco IOS supports SNMP2?*

A— These are two different SNMP versions. The SNMP packet format is different in each, but there is no difference in configuring them in Cisco IOS. SNMPv2 provides more flexibility and is actually an enhancement to SNMPv1. SNMPv2 is supported as of Cisco IOS 10.2. Cisco supports both. Some NMS stations do not support SNMPv2 yet, so the SNMPv2 MIBs cause an error on the management platform (SNM, HPOV, NetView) when compiled

Q— *Can SNMP give a non-privileged user access to a "privileged" command, such as* `clear counter`*?*

A— Yes, you can do a privileged command via SNMP sets. If you have an NMS, SNMP can be used to execute some privileged commands.

Q— *Can Cisco VLANs be configured via SNMP with Cisco IOS 11.0(3)?*

A— You are able to set up different bridge groups, but not via SNMP. You cannot configure a Cisco router at all via SNMP. There is nothing in the Cisco MIBs to enable you to configure via SNMP; you can only monitor. This might change in the future, however.

Cisco Keyboard Commands

Table A-1   *Keyboard commands executed for Cisco routers*

Keystroke	Effect
Arrow keys	Useful only with an ANSO/VT100 emulating terminal. Left and right arrows move the cursor left or right one character within the current line. Up and down arrows display the previous or next lines from the command history buffer.
Backspace	Delete character before cursor
Del	Delete character before cursor
Tab	Command completion
?	Help
Ctrl A	Move cursor to beginning of line
Ctrl B	Back cursor up one character
Ctrl D	Delete the character cursor is on
Ctrl E	Move cursor to end of line
Ctrl H	Delete character before cursor
Ctrl I	Command completion
Ctrl K	Delete characters to end of line (see also Ctrl Y)
Ctrl L	Redisplay line

Table A-1   *Keyboard commands executed for Cisco routers, continued*

Keystroke	Effect
Ctrl N	Bring up next line from the command history buffer
Ctrl P	Bring up previous line from the command history buffer
Ctrl R	Retype line (useful when debug output trashes the screen)
Ctrl T	Transpose characters
Ctrl U	Delete characters to beginning of line (characters go to cut buffer)
Ctrl V	Quoted insert (take the character literally instead of as editor command; used to insert control character)
Ctrl W	Delete previous word
Ctrl X	Delete characters to beginning of line (characters go to cut buffer)
Ctrl Y	Yank: restore cut characters from buffer after cursor
Esc	Show last line from command history buffer
Esc O	Escape prefix sent by BT100 terminal prior to code for arrow key
Esc Q	Quoted insert (take the next character literally instead of as editor command; used to insert control character)
Esc [	Escape prefix sent by BT100 terminal prior to code for arrow key
Esc b	Move cursor back one word
Esc c	Capitalize word after cursor
Esc d	Delete word (from cursor forward)
Esc f	Move cursor forward one word
Esc I	Tab
Esc l	Change word after cursor to lowercase
Esc q	Quoted insert (take the next character literally instead of as editor command; used to insert control character)
Esc u	Change word after cursor to uppercase
Esc y	Switch to previous cut buffer and (yank) it at cursor
Esc Del	Delete word before cursor

Bibliography

ARTICLES

Stallings, William and Benjamin Smith. "SNMP Version 2," *Byte, August 1994*

BOOKS

Abe, George. *Residential Broadband.* Indianapolis, IN: New Riders: Macmillan Technical Publishing, 1997.

Anonymous. *Maximum Security: A Hacker's Guide to Protecting Your Internet Site and Network.* Indianapolis, IN: Sams.net, 1997.

Black, Uyless. *Frame Relay Networks.* New York, NY: McGraw-Hill, 1996.

Cheswick, William R. and Steven M. Bellovin. *Firewalls and Internet Security: Repelling the Wily Hacker.* Reading, MA: Addison-Wesley, 1994.

Comer, Douglas. *Internetworking with TCP/IP, Volume 1.* Englewood Cliffs, NJ: Prentice-Hall International, 1991.

Derfler, Frank and Steve Rigney. *TCP/IP: A Survival Guide for Users.* New York, NY: MIS Press, 1998.

Ford, Merilee, with H. Kim Lew, Steve Spanier, and Tim Stevenson. *Internetworking Technologies Handbook.* Indianapolis, IN: New Riders Publishing, 1997.

Garms, Jason, et al. *Windows NT Server 4 Unleashed.* Indianapolis, IN: SAMS Publishing, 1996.

Halabi, Bassam. *Internet Routing Architectures.* Indianapolis, IN: New Riders Publishing, 1997.

Held, Gilbert. *LAN Management with SNMP and RMON.* New York, NY: John Wiley and Sons, Inc., 1996.

Huitema, Christian. *Routing in the Internet.* Englewood Cliffs, NJ: Prentice Hall PTR, 1995.

Lewis, Chris. *Cisco TCP/IP Routing Professional Reference.* New York, NY: McGraw Hill, 1998.

Miller, Mark. *Managing Internetworks with SNMP,* Second Edition. New York, NY: M&T Books, 1997.

Miller, Mark. *Troubleshooting TCP/IP,* Second Edition. New York, NY: M&T Books, 1996.

Muller, Nathan. *Network Planning, Procurement, & Management.* New York, NY: McGraw-Hill, 1996.

Moy, John. *OSPF Anatomy of an Internet Routing Protocol.* Reading, MA: Addison-Wesley/Longman, 1997.

Naugle, Mathew. *Network Protocol Handbook.* New York, NY: McGraw-Hill, 1994.

Parker, Timothy, Ph.D. *Teach Yourself TCP/IP in 14 Days,* Second Edition. Indianapolis, IN: SAMS Publishing, 1996.

Perlman, Radia. *Interconnections.* Reading, MA: Addison-Wesley, 1992.

CISCO SYSTEMS DOCUMENTATION AND RESOURCES

Cisco Systems. *Cisco Connection On-Line.* www.cisco.com (version current at 15 January 1998).

Cisco Training CD-ROM, Cisco Systems, San Jose, CA.

Cisco Systems. *Introduction to CISCO Router Configuration Guide.* IOS Release 11.1; 1996.

Cisco Systems. *Introduction to CISCO Router Configuration Guide.* IOS Release 11.2; 1997.

Cisco Systems. *Advanced CISCO Router Configuration Guide.* IOS Release 11.1; 1996.

Cisco Systems. *Advanced CISCO Router Configuration Guide.* IOS Release 11.2; 1997.

Cisco Systems. *CISCO IOS Release Command Summary 11.1.* 1996.

Cisco Systems. *CISCO IOS Release Command Summary 11.2.* 1997.

Cisco Systems. *CISCO IOS Release Command Summary 11.3.* 1998.

Cisco Systems. *Internetworking Case Studies.* `www.cisco.com/univercd/cc/td/doc/cisintwk/ics/icsospf.htm`

Cisco Systems. *Planning a Migration to IP Version 6. [15 January 1998]*

Cisco Systems. *Internet Protocol, Version 6 (IPV6). [10 December 1997]*

IPv6 STANDARDS (BAY NETWORKS)

Haskin, D., and E. Allen. *IP Version 6 over PPP, IETF RFC 2023.* November 1997.

International Data Corporation. *Managing Data Overload.* June 1997.

Malkin, G., and R. Minnear. *RIPng for IPv6, IETF RFC 2080.* January 1997.

RFCs

Baker, F., and R. Coltun. *OSPF Version 2 Management Information Base (RFC 1248).* July 1991.

Baker, F., and R. Coltun. *OSPF Version 2 Management Information Base (RFC 1252) [obsoletes 1248].* July 1991.

Baker, F., and R. Coltun. *OSPF Version 2 Management Information Base (RFC 1253) [obsoletes 1252].* August 1991.

Baker, F., and R. Coltun. *OSPF Version 2 Management Information Base (RFC 1850) [obsoletes 1253].* November 1995.

Chapin, L. (IAB). *Applicability Statement for OSPF (RFC 1370).* October 1992.

DeSouza, O., and M. Rodriguez. *Guidelines for Running OSPF Over Frame Relay Networks (RFC 1586).* March 1994.

Fuller, V., and R. Coltun. *The OSPF NSSA Option (RFC 1587).* March 1994.

Gross, P. (IESG). *Choosing a "Common IGP" for the IP Internet (RFC 1371)*. October 1992.

Moy, J. *Extending OSPF to Support Demand Circuits (RFC 1793)*. April 1995.

Moy, J. *MOSPF: Analysis and Experience (RFC 1585)*. March 1994.

Moy, J. *Multicast Extensions to OSPF (RFC 1584)*. March 1994.

Moy, J. *OSPF Database Overflow (RFC 1765)*. March 1995.

Moy, J. *OSPF Version 2 (RFC 1583)[obsoletes 1247]*. March 1994.

Moy, J. *OSPF Version 2 (RFC 2178) [obsoletes 1583]*. July 1997.

Moy, J. *Experience with the OSPF Protocol (RFC 1246)*. July 1991.

Moy, J. *OSPF Protocol Analysis (RFC 1245)*. July 1991.

Moy, J. *OSPF Specification Version 1 (RFC 1131)*. October 1989.

Moy, J. *OSPF Version 2 (RFC 1247) [obsoletes 1131]*. July 1991.

Varadhan, K. *BGP OSPF Interaction (RFC 1364) [obsoletes 1247 & 1267]*. September 1992.

Varadhan, K. *BGP OSPF Interaction (RFC 1403) [obsoletes 1364]*. January 1993.

Varadhan, K., with S. Hares and Y. Rekhter. *BGP4/IDRP for IP—OSPF Interaction (RFC 1745)*. December 1994.

PROJECTS

OSPF: Open Shortest Path First (final project for Dr. Debby Koren, Tel-Aviv University) by Beniluz daniel, Berkman omer and Ravid carmel. `http://www.uniinc.msk.ru/tech1/1995/ospf/ospf.htm`. (version current at 18 October 1997)

WEB SITE DOCUMENTATION

Cisco Documentation.

`www.cisco.com/univercd/data/doc/cintrnet/itg/itg_v1/itg_IP.htm`. (version current at 27 February 1998)

Cisco Systems. *OSPF Design Guide*. `www.cisco.com/warp/public/458/10.html`. (version current at 19 April 1998)

3COM Web Site. www.3com.com. (version current at 18 October 1997)

Bay Networks Home Page. www.baynetworks.com. (version current at 10 December 1997)

SEMINARS

Kahn, Atif, "Networkers: Designing OSPF Networks," PowerPoint Presentation for Cisco Systems. [November 1997]

Index